LATIN AMERICA
IN THE INTERNATIONAL
POLITICAL SYSTEM

■

Third Edition

LATIN AMERICA
IN THE INTERNATIONAL
POLITICAL SYSTEM

——————■——————

G. POPE ATKINS

WESTVIEW PRESS
Boulder • San Francisco • Oxford

Published in 1995 in the United States of America by Westview Press, Inc., 5500 Central Avenue, Boulder, Colorado 80301-2877, and in the United Kingdom by Westview Press, 12 Hid's Copse Road, Cumnor Hill, Oxford OX2 9JJ

First edition published in 1977 by The Free Press

Library of Congress Cataloging-in-Publication Data
Atkins, G. Pope, 1934–
 Latin America in the international political system / G. Pope
Atkins.—3rd ed.
  p. cm.
 Includes bibliographical references and index.
 ISBN 0-8133-8666-7. — ISBN 0-8133-8667-5 (pbk.)
 1. Latin America—Foreign Relations. I. Title.
JX1393.L3A88 1995
327'.098—dc20   94-29605
                                                                      CIP

Printed and bound in the United States of America

  The paper used in this publication meets the requirements
 of the American National Standard for Permanence of Paper
 for Printed Library Materials Z39.48-1984.

10   9   8   7   6   5   4   3   2   1

*To Taylor, Maggie, Ginny, Jeff, and Kristy,
and Carly and Tyler*

Contents

PART THREE
INTERNATIONAL INSTITUTIONS

Tables and Maps

Tables

Maps

Preface

Fundamental changes have taken place in Latin America's international relations since the publication of the second edition of this book in 1989. This third edition has been updated and revised especially in terms of post–cold war developments, which have had a dramatic impact on virtually every aspect of Latin America's international relations. East-West conflict is no longer relevant, requiring policy reorientations on the part of all actors and rethinking within international institutions. Yet other changes have been the result of trends evident long before the officially declared end of the cold war, especially critical political and economic developments within Latin America not necessarily related to superpower competition. In any event, a common set of issues (but with varying approaches about how to deal with them) has risen to the top of virtually every actor's agenda. Among them are trade and investment, democracy and human rights, immigrants and refugees, drug trafficking, and, to a lesser extent, the physical environment.

The first edition of this book was issued at the beginning of a heightened and sustained scholarly interest in Latin America's international relations. Intended to fill a gap in the scholarly literature, it was followed a dozen years later by a second edition. A large number of other studies have appeared that address general and specific aspects of Latin America in the international system. Nevertheless, the original purpose of this book still seems timely: to provide a topically complete and analytically integrated political science survey of Latin America's international relations. As in the past, it is further intended to serve as a classroom text at the upper undergraduate or beginning graduate level and as a general reference source for anyone seeking description and analysis of the subject.

The discussion remains organized around the idea of the Latin American region as a separate international subsystem within the global system, with special consideration given to both further subsystems within the region and to the increasing globalization of the entire region. I am still persuaded of the utility and validity of a systems perspective around which to organize an introduction to the analysis of such a complex subject. Hence, the emphasis is on the foreign policies of the states and other actors within and outside of the region, and the international interactions and institutions associated with their relations. This allows the specific Latin American focus and the attendant issues to be pursued in such a way that adds to general, rather than parochial, knowledge. But this is not a book on methodology. Rather, extant theories of international and comparative politics are applied to aid in the understanding of Latin America, and the need for concepts to refer to the world of experience is stressed. The concluding chapter is intended to draw the entire work together in theoretical terms. The result is admittedly a somewhat impatient critique of extant explanations of Latin America's international relations.

A fundamental assumption also remains: Latin America should be the subject and not the object of study. This essential point of reference is reflected in a determined effort to concentrate primarily on Latin America, with U.S.–Latin American relations, current issues, and other considerations subsumed under that overall objective.

In attempting to produce a study that delineates the Latin American regional subsystem, the treatment of some subjects is necessarily sketchy. Readers are alerted to the structures and processes relevant to the Latin American international subsystem, but with some sacrifice of detail in order to present a conceptually complete systemic overview without writing an overly long book.

I wish to extend my gratitude to colleagues in the United States, Latin America, and Europe who over the years have offered encouragement, advice, suggestions, comments, criticism, and information during the life of the first two editions and for this third edition. Special acknowledgment is made to Alan Adams, Allison Temple Bacon, Morris Blachman, Jack Child, Peter Cleaves, Isaac Cohen, Esperanza Duran, Wolf Grabendorff, Fred Halliday, Margaret Daly Hayes, Luis Esteben Julia, John Lovell, John Martz, Helen Purkitt, Roberto Russell, Lars Schoultz, Max Sherman, Larry Thompson, Debbie Warden, Howard Wiarda, Charles Wilson, Larman Wilson, and, posthumously, to the late Harold Blakemore, Harold Eugene Davis, and Thomas McGann. I also acknowledge my debt to the students who have come under my guidance during many years of teaching the subject. Finally, I pay special tribute to my wife, Joan, for her continuing professional and personal support. I am fully responsible for all that follows.

G. Pope Atkins
Austin, Texas

PART ONE

———————————— ■ ————————————

A Framework for Analysis

The first two chapters of this book establish the framework within which the entire study is cast. Chapter 1 discusses systems theory as an organizing device for analyzing international relations in general. Chapter 2 applies these abstract concepts to Latin America and identifies assumptions and problems in viewing Latin America as a regional subsystem of the global international system. Together these chapters provide a way to integrate the vast data concerning Latin America's international relations. Using this framework for analysis, the rest of the book provides a detailed examination of the various elements of Latin America's international relations.

1

CHAPTER ONE

———————— ■ ————————

The International System

POLITICAL SCIENTISTS CONSTRUCT organizing devices designed to assist in the understanding of political data by ordering seemingly disparate facts and events into some meaningful pattern that can be analyzed. An organizing device may be called an *approach*, a *paradigm*, a *quasi-theory*, a *conceptual framework*, or an *analytic framework*. All of these terms are roughly synonymous; regardless of which one is used, such devices have three specific purposes. First, an analytic framework (the term I prefer) provides a method of systematically determining which facts are pertinent and which should be ignored. Second, it enables one to present methodically the selected data in a coherent and logical manner. Finally, it facilitates the orderly comparison of related sets of phenomena. This chapter discusses international systems theory to the extent that it provides the analytic framework used in this book for selecting, organizing, and comparing data relating to Latin American international relations. The chapter begins with a discussion of how the approach applies to the study of international relations in general as well as Latin America's international relations in particular.

A SYSTEMS PERSPECTIVE

The Approach to This Study

A number of characteristics have evolved in the academic study of IR (as specialists tend to refer to the field of international relations). Whether specialists prefer IR to be considered an autonomous discipline or, more likely, as a field of political science, the core concepts they deal with are rooted in the study of politics. The decline of interest in diplomatic or international history on the part of historians, and economists' often restricted definition of politics, have further lodged the study of IR into the discipline of political science. Furthermore, within the political science emphasis, IR no longer constitutes a single field. It has generally evolved into three separate but related areas of study: the international system and its array of subfields; foreign policy analysis and comparative foreign policy; and international political economy.

This book seeks to provide a general survey of Latin American international relations. Thus it seems appropriate to begin with an overview of the concept of international systems and the constituent parts and processes. Within this primary focus, this book integrates some basic elements of foreign policy analysis, including comparative aspects. International political economy, which stresses the interrelationship of international political and economic systems and offers models of foreign economic policy, is referred to as a crucial consideration, but it, too, is subsumed under the primary paradigm. Likewise, historical and legal-institutional descriptions and interpretations and analyses of ideologies are pursued inasmuch as they reinforce the basic approach.

The study of any field of politics involves the problem of how an analyst handles values—not only as a detached observer but in making interpretations and defining policy preferences as well. At several points in the book my policy evaluations flow from the prior conceptualizations, descriptions, and analyses. Objectivity is an appropriate goal; however, "value-free" analysis is not only difficult to achieve but is also not necessarily desirable. The resolution of this problem depends on the position taken toward evidence and inference. I have attempted to identify issues and summarize competing arguments first, and to postpone normative conclusions and policy prescriptions until after analyzing a variety of political structures and processes.

Systems Theory as an Analytic Framework

Systems theory by its very nature emphasizes structures and processes in the study of politics. This is because a system by definition consists fundamentally of the interaction between two or more distinct units and the functions of that interaction. "Structure" means the system's form and configuration—the way in which its elements are organized and interrelated. The structure of a system is characterized by both differentiation (the presence and workings of separate units) and by integration (the overall organization of the system, perhaps including subsystems). "Process" is the series of specific, continuous, and interdependent operations of the system—in effect, the activities and interactions of the units and subsystems that have consequences, results, or outcomes. Process indicates that a system is dynamic. Structure and process both imply regularity of relations, mutual dependence, and some measure of coordination among the units and subsystems.

A systems approach offers distinct advantages for organizing, integrating, and analyzing the subject matter. It provides a broad overview of politics and facilitates the analysis of a range of relationships in the political process. Systems theory helps us to integrate political knowledge because we can apply its fundamental concepts to any level of activity, including substate and nonstate systems, state politics, various groupings of states and other actors (such as in a geographic region), and the entire global international system. Within each of these often interrelated system levels are found discrete structures and processes.

Analyzing international relations in terms of a systems framework is among the most important developments in the study of IR. Specialists apply systemic concepts to all of the fields of analysis identified earlier—the international system, foreign policy, and international political economy. The international system is a complex political, military, economic, and social structure of both power and interdependence. It is composed of state and nonstate actors interacting in cooperation and conflict, informal power relationships, and formal international institutions. Thus analysis of the international system includes the patterns of interaction among the units and the ways in which the system is regulated. Foreign policy analysis deals with the nature and actions, either singly or in comparison, of the nation-state as it functions in the international system. Inquiry is focused on the attributes of the states and the way decision makers form images, expectations, and perceptions, respond to motivations and aspirations, process information, formulate interests, analyze situations, select objectives, and decide upon and execute courses of action. In this conceptualization, the international system comprises the extrasocietal environment that gives rise to decisions and in which subsequent policy action takes place. Foreign policy becomes international relations, and analysis shifts back to the overall system level, when state action is taken and other states or nonstate entities react, thereby commencing interaction.

Scholars have increasingly directed attention to an assortment of non–nation-state actors that are units in the system—such as nongovernmental international organizations, multinational corporations, guerrilla groups, political parties, and others. Thus students of IR have had to adjust their notions of the international system and foreign policy analysis in order to account for the presence, characteristics, decisions, and activities of these other actors and the systemic interactions in which they are involved. They have also applied systems thinking to international political economy, which, as will be made clear in this book, is related (often to a high degree) to both the international system and foreign policy analysis as well as to certain nonstate actors.

A subsystemic area of inquiry, as implied in the preceding commentary, lies between the individual actor and the global system. International subsystems are defined as groupings of some of the total system's units (nation-states and other actors) that interact on a regular basis distinct from the entire process but not autonomous from it. Several different kinds of international subsystems may be identified—for example, the regularized interaction of two states, international organizations of all kinds, ideological or common-interest groupings, and geographic regions. Most of the elements of a system apply to subsystems; their analysis likewise involves the concepts of actors, interaction, regulation, and even further subsystems, as well as the elements of international political economy.

Thus regional international relations, such as those of Latin America, can be viewed as international subsystems. In fact, analysts of Latin American international relations today tend to follow the general study of IR, at the same time adopting certain specific adjustments as regional observers. Most of them have overtly or implicitly employed a systems perspective as an analytic framework to guide their inquiry. A regional perspective offers analytic advantages. For example, it avoids overemphasis on the roles of great powers and superpowers and their interrelations, which, understandably, has engaged most IR analysts. It recognizes that lesser powers also play serious international roles.

Nature of the International System

When applied to international politics, systems theory presents some methodological problems. Some critics argue that an international system does not exist and, therefore, that international politics are not susceptible to systems theorizing. This view assumes that IR should deal only with the flux of changing concrete situations that are not amenable to systemic generalization or theoretical explanation and that students in the field must be satisfied with describing particular past or current events. More specifically, it assumes that international relations are anarchic, since no centralized international decision-making authority exists and a system, by definition, requires regularity. This view is similar to the position taken by some historians who view history as a series of new and unique events and who deny the existence of behavioral patterns. A similar perspective is also expressed by some sociologists who find individual psychological patterns of behavior, but no social system as such.

One can hardly claim, in reply, that international events fall into immutable patterns, and one must acknowledge that the international system clearly differs in fundamental ways from domestic processes. The essential problem with a systems approach is that of regulation: The international arena, unlike the domestic realm, lacks higher authoritative decision-making agencies able to make and enforce rules and reconcile conflicting parties. Furthermore, virtually no feeling of loyalty or legitimacy exists above the level of the nation-state. The nation-state continues to be the central structural feature and decisional source in the system. Certain other actors also occupy important positions, which serves to further decentralize the system.

International relations, however, do not merely consist of anarchic competition. A degree of integration is found, although it is considerably less than in most domestic (state) systems. In reality, state independence is far from absolute, whether in the domestic or the international domain, and interdependence is a fact as well as a theory of international life. The distribution of power and influence among states and other actors has always had a primary structural influence; the "balance of power" has been recognized by strategists for centuries as an informal controlling device. Formal regulatory institutions are embodied in international law, organizations, and other interstate regimes; various forms of informal consensus also exist. Although any authoritative activity of such institutions is ultimately limited by the sovereign autonomy of the member states, many formal and informal rules are voluntarily accepted and followed. In addition, the variety of regularized and sustained patterns of interaction is significant and, in some instances, predictable.

In sum, regular (but not in the sense of unchanging) patterns of international activities are common enough to warrant the claim that an international system exists and that systems theory may be usefully applied to the analysis of international relations. Most thoughtful historians recognize that even unique events take place within some (probably changing) structure. If we view a system, at the very least, as a group of related units that interact with and affect each other, then interstate relations constitute a system. Today's international system may be characterized as primitive, undeveloped, rudimentary, and decentralized, but it is nevertheless a real system and a viable target for systems theory. A good argument is made that it is inefficient and dangerous, but whether it is good or bad depends on the analyst's point of view and has little to do with whether or not an international system exists.

THE UNITS (ACTORS)
IN INTERNATIONAL RELATIONS

Nation-States

The most important differentiated units in international politics today, as in the past three centuries, are sovereign nation-states. At present they number almost 200 and are located in all parts of the world. Although the nation-state has never been and is not now the only unit or actor in the international system, it is and will continue for the foreseeable future to be the most prominent one. As such, it is the central concept in world politics and provides the starting point for an understanding of the international system.

The modern state system evolved after the collapse of feudalism and the dual empire-papacy system in Europe at the end of the Middle Ages. The new system developed throughout the fifteenth and sixteenth centuries and was legally institutionalized by the Peace of Westphalia (1648), which settled the Thirty Years War among kings, pope, and emperor (supported by feudal lords). The peace arrangement recognized the independence of secular nation-states from the Holy Roman Empire and the papacy. This system subsequently spread from Europe to all parts of the world. The process was not completed in Europe until the late nineteenth century, when Italy and Germany each were finally consolidated. In the meantime, after their own emergence, the new European states began to expand their power around the globe through colonization and trade. This movement was led first by Portugal in the early fifteenth century and Spain beginning in the 1490s, followed by France, Holland, and Great Britain in the sixteenth century. Eventually, almost all European states adopted imperialist policies, and overseas empires were established in most of the non-European world.

Independent nation-states of the European type did not appear outside of Europe until the United States of America was established in 1776. Most of Latin America followed suit between 1804 and 1824 and Japan in the late nineteenth century (through a nonrevolutionary process of "opening" to the outside world). China did not effectively become a nation-state in the Western sense until after 1911, the year of Sun Yat Sen's revolution. The European empires in Asia, Africa, and the Caribbean largely broke up in the twentieth century. Most of the new states in those areas were born after World War II, including two of the most populous nations in the world, India and Indonesia. Thus, what originated as a European system became a global one through several kinds of change. The political values of the West, in the sense of organizing human affairs at a fundamental level into something called the nation-state, were extended virtually to the entire world.

The modern state is endowed with two unique characteristics that it shares with no other entity—the attribute of sovereignty and the relationship of nationalism to statehood. Sovereignty and nationalism are distinct concepts, but they are related in their complex evolution over the past three and a half centuries.

Introduced in sixteenth-century international law, sovereignty is traditionally defined as the state's supreme authority over its citizens, which is absolute and indivisible, making it the final arbiter in their lives. Whether sovereignty is, indeed, indivisible has long been a matter of debate. The idea was the product of the times that witnessed the rise of the nation-state under absolute monarchs. It replaced the medieval concept of limited sovereignty under natural (divine) law embodied in the contractual relationship of the feudal system. The concept of sovereignty stressed the superiority of the territorial state to both imperial universalism and feudal localism and reflected the need for central government authority, embodied in the monarch ("the sovereign"), in order to create domestic order and stability in a given territory.

States and nations have existed throughout recorded history, but only after the consolidation of feudal units into kingdoms in Western Europe were the two elements combined. Since then, a principal theme of system development has been the search by multicultural states for a single nationhood and by homogeneous nations for statehood. These processes involve the melding of distinct entities that are not necessarily coterminous—the state (a legal-political entity defined in terms of territory, population, and effective autonomous government) and the nation (a social-cultural entity defined in terms of people who, for whatever reasons, share a sense of sameness and uniqueness). From the rise of the modern state until the late eighteenth century, dynastic states worked to create nations of their domains, with the "sovereign" serving as the symbol of national identity among the people living within the state borders. With the American and French revolutions (1776/1789) and the subsequent development of republicanism, nationalism came to be identified with "the people." Thereafter, national groups sought to create states that conformed to national boundaries and the idea of "national self-determination" was born. Since then, a tension has existed over the nature and relationship of nations and states. Thus the term "nation-state" is, to a considerable degree, a misnomer.

A major change in the concept of sovereignty also occurred with the development of republicanism in the late eighteenth century. The locus of state sovereignty shifted from the tangible person of the monarch to the abstraction of "we the people." This transition required the doctrine of popular sovereignty to emerge, in which the voice of the people (*vox populi*) replaced the voice of God (*vox Dei*) as the ultimate base of authority.

The notion of popular sovereignty suggests this question: Can the state realistically be personified? That is, can a nonhuman abstraction act, or should one look instead to individual persons as the real actors in the system? Social psychologists have raised a parallel problem: Is there such a thing as group behavior, or is it merely the behavior of individuals in groups? Analysts have tended to attribute action to states as a convenient expression, but they recognize that human beings in fact make decisions and act on behalf of states and their societies. The personification of the state is both a legal and convenient way of referring to the behavior of an identifiable collection of human beings. We must, however, still inquire into the sources of "state behavior."

State Action

Foreign policy analysis focuses on how and why decision makers behave the way they do. Thus the identification of the intellectual, psychological, and institutional factors that affect the reasoning processes by which leaders arrive at decisions is the central analytic element. As in the general study of IR, most foreign policy analysts have overtly or implicitly employed a systems perspective as an analytic framework to guide their inquiry. Within this outlook, however, particular decision models place different emphases on the different ingredients of policymaking. While no satisfactory overarching theory of foreign policy has emerged to explain the behavior of decision makers, and in important ways the competing designs are mutually exclusive, the theoretical effort has nevertheless produced sets of models that, when taken together, alert us to the various factors that may influence decisional processes. They may be categorized as rational actor, perceptual, and bureaucratic-organizational process models.

The "rational actor" model of decision-making has been a primary point of departure for many IR analysts and practitioners. It assumes that foreign policy makers follow (or should follow) an architectonic plan of state purposes and goals and logical strategic and tactical procedures. According to this model, when faced with a problem that requires solution, rational individuals should follow a certain detached and sequential process: define the situation, solicit as much information as possible, specify the goal or goals to be achieved, rank priorities, consider possible alternative means for achieving the goals, calculate the cost and risk of each option, select the best (most rational) action to be pursued, take the necessary steps to implement the decision, and, after the fact, evaluate the consequences of actions so as to learn from experience.

Other foreign policy analysts, seeing the rational model as fundamentally flawed in assuming decisions to be the result of consistent monolithic state processes, constructed alternative theories emphasizing the centrality of fallible human beings. They argue that the human element in decision-making not only intrudes on but departs from rational processes.

One group of theorists focuses on the response of decision makers to perceptions and images that they hold of the world, their own societies, and themselves, and the way they form foreign policy motivations, aspirations, and expectations in response to stimuli from both intrasocietal and extrasocietal environments. Such analysts distinguish between the decision maker's objective environment (reality) and psychological environment (the perception or image of reality) and the difficulty of reconciling the two. They argue that a decision maker's failure to grasp a situation can have less to do with the information received ("intelligence failures") than with the manner in which the information is mentally processed. Theorists emphasize such phenomena as selective attention (seeing only what one wants to see) and rationalization (dismissing that which does not conform to one's images).

Other specialists—advocates of bureaucratic-organizational process models—contend that foreign policies most often are the result of group dynamics and institutional biases within competing bureaucracies and other organizations central to the policy process. These theorists argue that the activities of groups and organizations have their own group dynamics far different from a collective application of the rational policy process. In the case of bureaucratic politics, institutional biases may overtly or subconsciously shape the definition of the problem and the prescription for its solution. In organizational processes (in bureaucracies and elsewhere), pressures for group conformity may lead individual members to compromise or abandon their doubts or preferences. Critics of this approach say it aspires to explain too much from a narrow conceptual base, but that it does offer insights about the limitations of groups that make it a useful corollary to more comprehensive models.

A political process model that takes into account a wide range of factors in the overall decision-making system may provide a useful analytic framework for organizing foreign policy data. It assumes that politics consists of a wide range of factors and that foreign policy decisions are made within the broad context of the overall political system. It is, essentially, an operationalization of the systems perspective on the state level. The entire set of system activities tend to bear on decision-making. On one side, a variety of influences that arise in the intrasocietal and extrasocietal environments are filtered through the political system and brought to bear on decision makers. These influences are converted through a decision process (which includes rational, perceptual, and bureaucratic-organizational considerations) into policy. Decisions may be generally characterized as foreign policy orientations. In addition, certain influences and many decisions may also be depicted in terms of capability analysis.

"Orientations" are the actual substance of policies finally decided upon. They are the result of decision makers' evaluations of the state's place in the international system and their choice of methods for coping with the external world. Some analysts equate orientation with a state's tendencies regarding alignment. I, however, prefer to adopt a broader perspective and describe policy orientations in terms of four dimensions: ends and means, alignment, national roles, and status-quo or revisionist commitments.

Ends-means analysis inquires into a state's calculation of purposes, interests, and goals and the relations between the policy objectives and the policy instruments and techniques. It may also include reference to ethical and moral considerations. Ultimate state objectives are usually articulated as those identified with the concept of "national interest," often referred to as "vital interests." Vital interests are said to be self-preservation, security, and social and economic well-being. They are expressed in the most general and often symbolic or even mythical terms, which makes the idea of "national interest" highly ambiguous. This analytic interpretation runs the danger of ignoring or not recognizing dissent within the decisional unit based on differing particular interests, ideologies, or other values that may lead to different conclusions about what constitutes "national interest."

The choice of instruments and tactics can involve varying combinations of policies: multilateral, bilateral, or unilateral and active or passive. A multilateral orientation tends to seek joint action through international organizations, alliances, and coalitions, an approach that contrasts with bilateral (state to state) or unilateral ("go it alone") approaches. The more active a state, the more likely it is to initiate action rather than only respond to or resist the initiatives taken by others. An important aspect of activism is the degree of willingness to intervene in the affairs of other states through diplomatic, economic, or military means. Some states passively choose not to compete.

A second dimension of state orientation concerns tendencies regarding alignment. Does a state choose military alliance and economic or political coalition with other states? Or does it prefer some form of neutrality, nonalignment, or isolation? Neutrality may refer to the legal status chosen by a state during armed hostilities; such a choice entails defined rights and responsibilities that distinguish neutrals from belligerents. Another meaning of neutrality, also recognized in international law, has to do with states that are neutralized through the actions of others, usually through agreement among the great powers to impose and guarantee the neutrality. Neutrality may also mean nonalignment—a voluntary rejection of alliance, a refusal to align with the great powers or their blocs—without reference to legal status. An isolationist strategy is indicated by a low level of involvement in aspects of the international system, from attempts to seal off the country against external penetration to reducing diplomatic or commercial transactions.

The third dimension, called "national roles," refers to policymakers' views of what the nation-state should do in the world based on their perceptions of both the outside world and their own societies. Role conceptions define the kinds of actions appropriate to national values. They are associated only with states that are actively involved in global or regional affairs. For example, following the lead of K. J. Holsti (1992), some typical national roles that are suggestive of U.S. perceptions of its functions in the Caribbean Basin may be posited: the role of "regional defender/leader/policeman," protecting other states in a defined area; of "mediator," assisting in international conflict resolution; and of "protector of the faith," urging, in recent decades, anticommunism and democratic development.

Finally, foreign policy orientations may be understood in terms of a state's commitment to either the status quo or to revisionism. A state may pursue a policy of the status quo if it is satisfied with its lot in the international system, or at least is willing to accept it. A state with a revisionist commitment is dissatisfied with the status quo and desires to change the distribution of the rewards of the system in a way more to its advantage. A status quo state pursues policies aimed at keeping things the way they are and thus will usually be defensive in nature, oriented toward the preservation of peace and stability. Contrarily, the revisionist state is more likely to be on the offensive, less interested in peaceful and stable processes that it considers to work to its disadvantage.

Capability analysis, which is crucial to foreign policy formulation at several stages of the process, is partly an inventory of relative strengths and weaknesses as measured by a state's military, economic, political, and other resources. But analysis goes far beyond this essentially technical calculation to consider a broad range of "situational factors" that give rise to or help shape policy decisions. These factors arise in the real-world settings or conditions in the intrasocietal and international environments and in the political system itself. They impinge on the state actions, either limiting the freedom of or offering opportunities to the decision makers. Their structures and events may impose requirements on policymakers to the extent that, in some cases, they may find decisions largely determined for them. The analyst should be skeptical, however, of theories of environmental determinism.

Among the external environmental factors that influence decisions are the capabilities and the actual or anticipated actions of other states, real and imagined threats, and considerations of coping with moves made by other states by resisting, cooperating, or accommodating them. A state's geographic setting influences such variables as world position, the presence of more or less powerful neighbors, and whether climate, terrain, and natural resources are favorable or unfavorable. The social setting of other states must also be considered, not only in terms of their strength in potential conflict but also in terms of their ability to cooperate in mutual enterprises. From the intrasocietal environment come such influences as nationalism, ideology, religion, the state of the economy, and the nature of social stability. Inside the political system, interest groups, political parties, and elites may interact with decision makers, and public opinion, public relations activities, the communications media, and elections also influence policy decisions. Within government, association among and within the bureaucracies and interpersonal relationships among key decision makers affect decisional outcomes.

Other Actors

Although the modern nation-state is the prime actor in international politics, other entities have also played important roles and continue to do so. Any analysis focusing exclusively on the policies of nation-states ignores the important impact of other kinds of international actors. The state has never been the sole actor in the modern international political system, nor is politics only the result of state interaction. Many nonstate entities are capable of initiating cross-national interaction with other entities, and such nonstate actors can play important roles. The state-centric model of the international system, by focusing exclusively on the nation-state, precludes analysis of actors that affect politics in profound ways.

The basic state units have changed over time. Chinese states, Greek city-states, Egyptian and Indian civilizations, pre-Columbian American entities such as the Aztec and Inca empires and others, as well as European empires and feudal realms, all preceded the nation-state and, in some cases, paralleled for a time or even survived along with the nation-state's ultimate spread around the globe. During the more than three centuries of nation-state dominance, additional actors have also appeared in the system. The Roman Catholic Church is an example of an actor predating the nation-state and today formally recognized by many nation-states. At times individual persons who were not government officials or representatives of other groups have been international actors. A variety of subnational entities have been actors: tribal groupings, leaders of breakaway provinces, sides in a civil war, rebel and revolutionary forces, governments in exile, and political parties and labor unions that do not act exclusively within state boundaries. International governmental organizations (IGOs) may sometimes be considered actors (the United Nations, the European Community, the Organization of American States, and so on). Nongovernmental international organizations (NGOs), such as the International Red Cross, also act on their own in the system. Multinational corporations (MNCs) are also prominent actors, especially since their accelerated development as part of twentieth-century capitalist economies.

THE INTEGRATED INTERNATIONAL SYSTEM

The international system comprises, in sum, the international political-military-economic-social system of states and other actors and their policies and interactions, the distribution of power and patterns of interdependence, and systemic change. The international system has been integrated through the means of both power distribution and international institutions. The balance of power provides an informal mechanism for regulating international conflict. International law, organizations, and regimes represent formal attempts to control and accommodate power politics as well as to promote interstate cooperation. Competition and conflict seem to be inherent in the nation-state system, based as it is on the concept of sovereignty and characterized by nationalism and a heavy emphasis on the role of power. States assume that they must use their own resources to achieve their objectives or to prevent successful challenges by other states. Consequently, the regulation of conflict—its limitation and adjustment—is a major concern for most states. At the same time, regulation also involves the search for cooperative measures designed to resolve problems relating to military force, economic interdependence, national development, and the physical environment itself.

Distribution of Power and Influence

Balance-of-power theories imply equilibrium and stability within a system composed of several largely autonomous political forces. The equilibrium concept in systems theory, as well as the traditional view of the balance of power, assume that when stability or equilibrium is disturbed, either by an outside force or by internal change in one of the system components, the system itself exhibits a tendency either to reestablish the original equilibrium or to adopt a new one. According to this theory, the various states in the international system, each with a different level of capability, group themselves in such a way that no single state or group of states is strong enough to dominate the system; power is balanced by opposing power. If equilibrium is maintained, then aggression is deterred, peace assured, and the independence of small states guaranteed. Conversely, war indicates disequilibrium, or a breakdown of the balance of power (dysfunction of the balance mechanism).

The theory of power balance is not universally accepted by scholars. Some reject it outright as an artifice, whereas others note that it may be exploited by states to justify their pursuit of policies aimed not at equilibrium but at a power imbalance in their favor. Still others deny the assumption that equilibrium is the normal or natural state of a system and actually view balance as abnormal. Political leaders have often pursued balance-of-power policies, however, usually aimed at achieving a "favorable" balance; an international "pecking order" based on power considerations does seem to exist, whether power distribution is balanced or random. Thus, insofar as the balance of power is defined as "distribution of power" rather than "power equilibrium," I believe that the theory correctly, if roughly, describes patterns of state relationships. I further assume that an excessive shift in the balance of power tends to generate forceful reactions from those principal states adversely affected, whether or not that reaction is automatic.

The basic types of balance that have existed in the nation-state system are multiple balance and simple balance. In a multiple system, several nations balance each other on a global scale with further balances perhaps found in certain regional areas. Multiple balance was the controlling pattern of international politics from the birth of the nation-state until World War II. During that time between five and seven great powers dominated the scene, with widespread dispersal of power among them. Such a pattern may contain a "balancer," or one state that remains aloof from alliance until the balance seems to be shifting, whereupon the balancer intervenes in favor of the weaker side in order to reestablish it (said to be the role frequently played by Great Britain).

Simple balance involves the concentration of power around two poles of roughly equal strength. Such a bipolar system existed after World War II, with the United States and the Soviet Union leading two sides composed of large groups of states. Bipolarity began to break up, and power consequently became dispersed in the early 1960s with the rise of new centers of political and economic, if not military, power. Military bipolarity still existed, although the superpower-led alliances showed elements of internal fragmentation and were challenged by a large (although often inwardly divided) Nonaligned Movement. Politically and economically the world was increasingly multipolar.

A variety of techniques exist for balancing power. The classic methods, aimed at either increasing the power of one pole or diminishing that of another, include shifting alliances, increasing armaments, seizing territory, creating buffer zones, intervening in the affairs of others, and setting states against each other in accordance with the principle of divide and conquer. Power-balancing also involves creating spheres of influence or control, such as the Soviet Union's influence in Eastern Europe until the late 1980s, the United States's influence in the Circum-Caribbean throughout most of the twentieth century, and, potentially, the influence of Japan, China, and India in parts of Asia; Egypt and Israel in the Middle East; and Brazil in South America.

The "unipolar" or imperial model of power distribution is one in which dominant authority is held by a single entity. It is not a "balancing" system—indeed, a principal purpose of balance-of-power operations is to avoid such single-actor domination. Unipolar systems were created by conquest, such as that resulting in the Roman, Ottoman, and Russian empires. Napoleon attempted to conquer Europe, and Hitler had more global ambitions. System stability depended on the dominant center's ability to control those who had been subjugated—a difficult task, evidenced by the fact that all such systems or attempts to create them engendered violent resistance.

Conditions in the post–cold war world have challenged theories of power relationships. With the sharp decline and then dissolution of the Soviet Union, leaving the United States as the only superpower, bipolarity is clearly ended but multipolarity as traditionally conceived has not returned. Some analysts see the new situation creating a de facto unipolar world. More of them, however, sharply question the possibilities for a worldwide imperial system. They dismiss the notion of conquest and see too many limitations on U.S. power to lead to general economic or military domination. They also note a strong U.S. reluctance to play a global police role.

An aspect of balance-of-power theory particularly relevant to this study is the fundamental principle that proximate geographic areas are linked to a state's vital core interests. Thus, powerful states react to unfavorable events in proximate states or to actions of external states that may compete for influence in those adjacent areas. This principle accounts, for example, for U.S. opposition to other foreign influences in the Caribbean zone. Spheres of influence are essentially nonnegotiable for great powers. They are particularly important when the geographic interests of great powers overlap or when more remote powers challenge the primacy of another great power's sphere of influence.

International Institutions

A number of international institutions serve as formal regulatory instruments in the international system. Some regulation has been achieved by international law and organizations and by other specialized interstate regimes.

International law, a body of formal regulatory rules, dates from the very beginnings of the nation-state system and has been an integral part of its evolution. The concept of sovereignty is a central tenet of international law, but it also poses a central problem: If the state is the supreme authority within its territorial bounds, are there any international laws to which the state itself is subservient? This difficulty has forced international law to rely on consent, with states reserving to themselves legal interpretation and the nature and application of law. This decentralized legal system in the international sphere was effective when the great powers generally agreed to uphold certain rules of conduct. Such was the case for almost three centuries, until the outbreak of World War I, when European powers agreed upon and enforced the law. Since then, however, no such agreement has existed. Despite these problems, a huge amount of day-to-day international business is facilitated and guided by legal agreement.

Weaker states, including older small powers and newer developing nations, have had an ambivalent attitude toward international law. On the one hand they see the need for legal restraint of the larger powers, but on the other hand they recognize that law tends to reflect the interests of those powers. They often view it as the codification of the international power structure in which violators among the weaker states are punished by the stronger ones. At the same time, their own impact on law has been significant. Their interpretation of law differs in several respects from the traditional postulates, which they view as inimical to their own interests. They stress the development of law to reflect their concerns in such areas as nationalization of foreign enterprise, territorial sea limits, and nonintervention of one state in the affairs of another.

Intergovernmental organizations began to develop in the nineteenth century and expanded and accelerated in the twentieth. They are created and directed by governments on the general and regional levels as well as other functional levels. The leaders of most nations recognize a difficult dilemma: The nature of the system is conflictual but mutual interdependence requires cooperation. IGOs are creations of the nation-states themselves, developed by leaders in response to the practical necessities of international life and as attempts to make international relations function more smoothly. They are the result of state agreements to engage in regularized consultation, to follow mutually agreed upon rules of behavior, and to establish administrative machinery to implement joint decisions.

Regional organizations, as the name implies, regulate international politics within defined geographic areas. They date from the latter half of the nineteenth century, when European Public Unions and the Inter-American System were organized. Regional organizations may be classified according to their basic purposes. Some have been concerned essentially with mutual defense, such as the

North Atlantic Treaty Organization (NATO) and the Warsaw Pact during the cold war. These alliances represented formal organizational aspects of balance-of-power structures. Others have been primarily concerned with specific fields of cooperation, such as the economic and political integration schemes in Europe and Latin America. Multipurpose organizations have also been created, such as the Arab League and the Organization of African Unity.

General (global or universal) international organizations are a product of the twentieth century. Three of them have appeared: (1) The Hague System, initiated in 1899 and ending with the outbreak of World War I; (2) the League of Nations, founded in the wake of World War I and continuing until the end of World War II; and (3) the United Nations (UN), created during World War II and developing to the present day with considerable complexity. Membership in these organizations has included the vast majority of states in existence during their respective tenures. They have been fundamentally, though not exclusively, responses to the problems of war and have used a variety of approaches for promoting peace by attacking what their advocates have assumed to be the causes of war. The Hague System dealt especially with arbitration, disarmament, development of international law, and creation of permanent global international agencies. These elements were continued by the League of Nations and the United Nations, although the pursuit of collective security was their primary rationale.

Those who originated the concept of collective security thought of it as the integration of power as opposed to the balance of power, with most of the powers of the world coming together in a global organization to deter aggression. Collective security has been largely a failure, and attempts in the post–cold war era to resuscitate collective security has been a difficult and controversial enterprise. The League and the UN also sought to create a "grand debate" of the issues among their members, to promote economic and social development, to adopt common international legal standards, to bring about colonial adjustments, to facilitate pacific settlement of disputes, to control or reduce military armaments, and to improve international administration.

Another set of IGOs, of varying complexity but neither regional nor general, have performed a multiplicity of specialized international functions. They include such entities as commodities agreements (the Organization of Petroleum Exporting Countries, OPEC, is probably the best-known), the Commonwealth of Nations, the Nonaligned Movement, and others.

International regimes, often but not always associated with IGOs, are attempts at international governance and regulation of international systems. One of the principal roles of IGOs is to sponsor, facilitate, or serve as regimes, but they are not the exclusive source of such governance. Regimes may be organized outside of IGOs through special conferences, bilateral or multilateral treaties, and informal agreements and understandings. Regimes focus on the congeries of forces at work in selected issue-areas and attempt to resolve tensions between order and disorder. They ideally constitute mutually accepted norms, values, expectations, rules, procedures, and perceptions of legitimacy, allowing international actors to cooperate on a regularized basis and deal with shared problems of common concern in the absence of higher authority. Regime-building may occur on bilateral, regional, global, or other levels or on some combination of them. Many different kinds of international problems, including mutual security, terrorism, arms races, economic development, trade, financial relations, scarcity of resources, borders and waterways, and many other concerns, have given rise to regimes.

Some random examples illustrate the phenomenon. The combined UN financial institutions—the International Monetary Fund, World Bank, and General Agreement on Tariffs and Trade—form a global economic regime. The Third World has challenged that regime and offered its alternative New International Economic Order (NIEO). The corpus of arms control agreements and the law of the sea are important treaty-based functional regimes. The Antarctic Treaty creates a specific geographic regional mode of governance in the uninhabited continent. The Organization of American States includes (among other things) extensive provisions and organizations seeking to protect and promote human rights among the states of the western hemisphere. The Panama Canal Treaties between Panama and the United States illustrate an important bilateral regime.

International Interactions

Policy Instruments and Forms of Interaction. Once an actor has decided upon a course of action, it mobilizes its resources or its "instruments of policy." The kinds of policy instruments and techniques available to decision makers to pursue their objectives cover a gamut of options. Positive action is not necessarily a consequence of the decisional process, for a state may decide to do nothing. Beyond nonaction, instruments may be classified in such categories as diplomatic, political, psychological, cultural, economic, or military resources. Thus, interactions in the system are largely identical with policy instruments. For example, war and economic assistance are policy instruments as well as forms of interaction. When the instruments of state action, once selected through the foreign policy process, are implemented, they then constitute part of international political processes and result in patterns of interaction that give further structure to the system.

Capability analysis, a concept introduced earlier, is also essential to understanding international interactions. In fact, the most meaningful view of foreign policy capability theorizes a range of power relationships. Capability is relative with respect to other states; it cannot exist without having one party to assert claims and another to respond. Brazil is considerably more powerful than, say, Romania, but the lack of significant interaction between them renders such an observation meaningless. A state may be weak in general terms vis-à-vis one state and powerful toward another. This principle would apply to the relations of Mexico to the United States and to Guatemala, respectively. A state may have power over another in one area of activity, but the roles may be reversed in another area. For example, in military terms, the United States is infinitely more powerful than Venezuela, which, due to its huge petroleum resources, sometimes has great leverage with regard to the energy needs of the United States. Capability also depends on the problem or situation in which it is being exercised. In 1965 the United States was capable of invading the Dominican Republic, quelling domestic chaos there, and restoring public order, but afterward it was incapable of establishing the U.S. system of democracy for Dominicans.

Cooperation and Conflict. Although we often classify the large number of diverse instruments and interactions in political, economic, military, and other categories, it is also useful to cut across these categories and think of them as either cooperative or conflictual in character.

"Cooperation" (or "collaboration," which is synonymous) means willingly working with others for a common purpose in harmonious relationships. It involves the conscious behavior of all of the actors, or differentiated units, designed to produce results of value to all of them. Cooperative measures include diplomatic representation, cultural activities, technical assistance, capital investment, economic aid, trade, military grants and aid, arms transfers, personnel exchanges, armed service missions, and other transactions. Thus, cooperation is perceived by the various actors as enhancing their own ability to achieve goals while also being compatible with the interests of others. Interests need not be mutual in the sense of sameness, but cooperation requires that they be complementary and noncontradictory, even if different. Cooperation implies a symmetry of relations acceptable to all parties, even if full satisfaction is lacking or some resentment is present.

Conflict is the opposite of cooperation. It refers to instruments of policy and patterns of politics involving coercion, contention, hostility, tension, struggle, divisiveness, and discord of action—in general, a variance of principles and interests and asymmetry of relations. Conflict is present in war, intervention, blockade, clandestine actions, subversion, hostile propaganda, and covert intelligence activities; terrorism, guerrilla warfare, diplomatic nonrecognition of new governments, and rupture of relations; economic pressures such as embargoes, boycotts, frozen assets, blacklists, and denial of aid; and the nationalization and expropriation of foreign enterprise. International conflicts arise out of incompatible objectives between states, which often resort to threats and sometimes ultimately to the use of force. The regulation of conflict and search for cooperation through direct negotiation, third-party activities (by states or IGOs), or creation of international regimes are among the most constant, persistent, and even poignant themes of international politics.

Diplomacy and Violence. The cooperation-conflict dichotomy is not exact nor is either category fixed or static. Even in the most cooperative relationships some level of conflict may arise; cooperative relations may become conflictual, and conflict may be transformed to cooperation. As a policy matter, cooperative and coercive instruments are rarely applied singly or in isolation; usually they come in some sort of tactical "mix" of tools. This being so, interaction processes are probably best understood in terms of diplomacy and violence.

The concept of diplomacy has more than one meaning. In a narrow sense, "diplomacy" refers to the conduct of negotiations and other relations between nation-states, the practices and procedures whereby states exchange official representatives and communicate with each other. In its broader meaning, "diplomacy" is synonymous with "bargaining," which is the general process, either formal or informal, whereby parties reach agreements. These agreements may relate to obligations undertaken in cooperative transactions or to the resolution of conflict. Bargaining entails the politics of influence, the process by which states and other actors seek to achieve their ends by influencing others to behave in a desired fashion through the mobilization of appropriate resources. Bargaining may include promises and rewards ("carrots") as well as threats and punishments ("sticks"). It may go on between friends, neutrals, opponents, and enemies.

The relationship between diplomacy (bargaining) and violence (the threat or use of force) is a subject of debate. Some would define bargaining as the attempt to induce or persuade without resorting to direct physical coercion. In this view, diplomacy may require the "stick," but it falls short of the actual use of armed force or other forms of violence. That is, states resort to force only when diplomacy fails. Another school extends the meaning of diplomacy to include the selective use of force, or the "diplomacy of violence." They consider war as an instrument of policy in the tradition of Clausewitz's dictum that "war is the continuation of diplomacy by other means," a deliberate and rational part of bargaining. Some historians of war and strategy understand this position as a preference for what war should be—an instrument of policy—but deny that it accurately describes what war actually is.

A fine line separates the use of diplomacy and of force as bargaining vehicles, but it is a critical distinction because cost and risk tend to rise sharply once armed action is undertaken. Furthermore, the use of armed force may go far beyond the purposes of a bargaining tool. War may range from being a limited political instrument to a broad assertion of raw power; it may aim to influence, to compel, or to seize. It may be a rational bargaining exercise, or it may be irrational or accidental. Even if initially conducted rationally, war may get out of control, and its termination, under many circumstances, rational or otherwise, may be difficult.

System Change

An important area of inquiry has to do with systemic change or transformation. How does a system shift from one historical dividing line to another? That is, how does it move in time? How do we detect the transformation of a system from one with certain characteristics to a new era with changed or different features? Analysts measure systemic change by focusing on significant shifts in both the distribution of political-military power and the patterns of economic-social interdependence. Thus they note dramatic ideas, movements, development, and events that precipitate changes in the actors and their relationships. They point to such factors as major military victories or defeats and collapsed or reshuffled alliances, alterations in the capability levels of the units and in the instrumentalities they use, shifts in the issues stimulating interaction, and increased or decreased levels of state interdependence and of other organizations and peoples.

For example, in the global system, the Thirty Years War, the Napoleonic wars, and the two world wars ended prior system configurations, introduced new ones, and precipitated continuing fundamental changes in their aftermath. World War II elevated the United States and the Soviet Union to a new superpower level, thus altering the nature and stratification of the differentiated units. The introduction of nuclear weapons permanently changed the nature of warfare and power and nuclear proliferation further transformed the way the system was integrated. Then, with the recovery of traditional power centers, and with energy resources and industrialization thrusting previously weak states into important international roles, the bipolar configuration assumed a new multipolarity. The end of the cold war in the late 1980s and early 1990s ushered in yet another historic phase of the modern international system, again reordering the global system and elevating new issues to the top priority.

INTERNATIONAL SUBSYSTEMS

Kinds of Subsystems

Component subsystems of the global international system operate at a level between nation-states (and other actors) and the worldwide system. Most of the elements of a system apply equally to subsystems, which are marked by differentiation and integration. The analysis of subsystems involves the concepts of individual unit-actors, foreign policy, interaction, regulation, further subsystems, and systemic change. Although some modifications must be made in these conceptual categories to accommodate the study of regional international relations, the same analytic questions and criteria already posed in the context of foreign policy analysis and the global international system are directly relevant.

Subsystems may be identified by examining the differentiation and integration of various actors—states, interstate organizations and associations, nonstate actors, and mixes of all kinds. The regularized interaction of two states could be considered a subsystem, such as that between Mexico and the United States or between Argentina and Brazil. International organizations of all kinds, irrespective of geography, may also be considered subsystems. Ideological or common-interest groupings that form international subsystems have included the industrialized states, the Communist world, and the Third World. Of particular importance, and of primary interest to this study, is the concept of the geographic regional subsystem, such as Latin America, the Middle East, Europe, Asia, and so on.

International subsystems, although marked by differentiation and integration, are not considered independent systems. Today, one worldwide international system encompasses virtually all actors, subsystems, and their interactions. (The "boundary" of a system is defined as that limit within which all system components are contained and outside of which no system interaction takes place.) Regional groupings and other associations are considered to be subsystems even though they are marked by all of the elements of a system for several reasons: (1) their units interact significantly with other units and subsystems beyond their boundaries; (2) outside actors are subsystem relevant; (3) regional actors may also form parts of other subsystems; and (4) subsystem groupings remain functionally inseparable from the global system.

Regional Subsystems

Although regions are relatively new foci for systems theory as such, the concept of the region has long been evident in both the study and practice of international relations. The concept of regional politics is nothing new, especially if one considers older concerns with regionalism, political and economic integration, and the voluminous literature on European international relations. International political processes have been interpreted to include regional spheres of influence in the balance of power, regional organization, regional integration (economic and political), regional security, and regional policies of the great powers, as well as the notion of regional subsystems. An academic concern with regional topics appeared even before World War I, but such concerns were not widespread until after the failure of collective security under the League of Nations to prevent World War II and the sanction of "regional arrangements" by the United Nations Charter. Latin American studies were an exception, as inter-American organizations, beginning in 1889, were the object of historical and institutional-legal scholarship. If we consider inter-American relations in general, a literature had begun to develop even before 1889. By and large, however, strong scholarly interest in regional topics is a post–World War II enterprise.

The early postwar writings were caught up in the debate between regionalists and universalists about the best arrangements for creating world order. Regionalists were primarily concerned with security arrangements for keeping the peace in delineated geographic areas and with describing existing organizations in legal terms. The regionalism versus globalism debate centered on the regional commissions and activities of the United Nations and the activities of specialized regional organizations. In the mid-1950s, regionalist scholarly interest began to focus on economic and political integration; scholars searched for ways in which national political actors within defined geographic zones could shift at least part of their loyalties and decision-making to supranational regional institutions for their mutual benefit. Finally, with the impact of systems theory on the study of politics in general and international relations in particular, regional concerns became part of systems theory.

All of these approaches to the study of regions are linked by the common idea that geographic proximity defines one of the limits of inquiry. Consequently, the problem of defining what constitutes a region is common to all. The fundamental difference is that the peacekeeping, functional, and integration approaches include prescriptive doctrines and normative statements of preference (although scientific studies have attempted to determine their effectiveness), whereas systems theory is designed to order the objective study of reality (it is flexible enough to allow prescriptions and judgments to be considered, but not accepted as norms). Furthermore, the view of a given region as a subsystem is topically more inclusive than in the other regional approaches because it deals with the totality of regional policies and relations among actors. It includes and integrates consideration of structures, processes, and issues in other approaches and goes beyond them with an array of systemic elements.

BIBLIOGRAPHIC COMMENT

Hermann, Kegley, and Rosenau (1987) edited a collection on the comparative study of foreign policy. Some recent textbooks analyzing IR from a systems perspective are Deutsch (1988), Holsti (1992), Papp (1988), Pearson and Rochester (1992), and Schloming (1991). Kegley and Wittkopf (1988) emphasize international political economy. On world regions as foci for subsystem analysis see Boyd (1984), Cantori and Spiegel (1970), Falk and Mendlovitz (1973), Feld and Boyd (1980), Keohane and Nye (1977), and Yalem (1970).

CHAPTER TWO

■

The Latin American Regional Subsystem

THIS CHAPTER ATTEMPTS to define the Latin American international subsystem by identifying its principal structures and processes. Defining the subsystem and tracing its evolution provides an overview of the principal elements addressed in the rest of the book and also gives a sense of the subsystem's dynamism. The first part of the chapter delineates the Latin American subsystem in light of criteria applicable to any international regional subsystem. It posits a structure comprising the overall Latin American region, the important subsystems within Latin America where different conditions exist, and the external influences on Latin America and its various parts. The second part traces the subsystem's changing contours, from its beginning to the present. The third and final part makes some specific comments about Latin America's position in extraregional structures, especially the global system and some of its constituent elements. The primary factors in subsystem structure and change are power relationships, interdependence, and international institutions.

IDENTIFYING REGIONAL SUBSYSTEMS

Relevant Criteria

Scholars proposed differing definitions of regional subsystems, and their work on related issues is marked by conceptual disparity. A survey of the literature on regional subsystems by William Thompson (1973) is still especially helpful in establishing the criteria that should be applied in determining the validity of geographic regions as international subsystems. Thompson inventoried and evaluated twenty-one attributes that had been proposed by eighteen analysts to define a regional subsystem. He concluded that three criteria were necessary and sufficient: (1) that the regional actors be in geographic proximity (this condition is implied by the term "region," and it includes the identification of the differentiated units); (2) that there be both internal and external recognition of the region as a distinctive area; and (3) that the interaction among the actors and their patterns of relations exhibit a degree of regularity and intensity (this condition is implied by the concept of "subsystem" and is partly synonymous with the notion of integration). A regional subsystem, then, consists of a set of geographically proximate and regularly interacting states that share to some degree a sense of regional identity and are so perceived by external actors. These same criteria also identify further subsystems within the region.

Boundary and Actors

In studying a particular regional subsystem, one must first identify the boundary that delimits the region and sets it apart from other components of the larger international system. In an autonomous system, the boundary is defined as that limit containing all of the components and outside of which no system interaction takes place. Clearly, actors outside of a regional subsystem are significant because transboundary interaction takes place. Nevertheless, the boundary must set off the components of one subsystem from those of others, even if these distinctions may be less clearly defined than in an independent system.

The establishment of a typology of subsystem-relevant actors further helps to identify regional boundaries. The differentiated units include the regional states within the boundary, the external states that have regularized interaction with the regional actors, and several kinds of regional and external non–nation-state entities.

Geographic proximity within a physical boundary is a necessary characteristic of a regional subsystem, but it alone does not define the subsystem. Students of regional studies must guard against geographic determinism and beware of unwarranted assumptions about the character of relations within a given territory. The result may be a contrived region based merely on geographic convenience; if the proposed subsystem units have nothing more than their proximity in common, then the proposition is invalid. Therefore, after establishing the geographic limits of a region, the analyst must search for additional indications of subsystem qualities.

Perceptions

The second aspect of subsystem analysis is the extent of regional self-perception and the views of external actors about the region. Shared attributes among subsystem actors may help to delineate the region if they contribute to a regional self-consciousness. In systemic terms, however, common sociocultural, economic, and political traits are not topology requirements and there is no merit in putting such restrictions on regional designations. Proximate and interacting states may be rich or poor, culturally complex or simple, or politically and socially advanced or not (however defined) without violating the subsystem concept. The key consideration in subsystem analysis is the degree of mutual identity among the actors.

Interactions

The region, finally, is also defined by the regularity of relationships among the units, including the patterns and intensity of the various forms of interaction engaged in by the regional and external state and nonstate actors as well as the subsystem-related regulatory institutions and processes. What are the patterns and effects of such international contacts as diplomatic exchanges, communications, cultural relations, trade and investment, economic aid, and various kinds of military relations? Does an identifiable power configuration emerge among the regional actors or in regard to the region as part of the global structure? What is the degree of their economic and perhaps social interdependence? What is the role of regularized conflict, both within the region and with outside actors, in structuring the subsystem? What formal associations and organizations give further structure to regional politics?

Identifying the Latin American Subsystem

How valid is the view of Latin America as a regional subsystem? Do the thirty-three independent states in the region form a coherent entity for study? This question is the system theorist's version of the Latin Americanist's age-old query: To what extent can the area be regarded as a significant unit in the conduct of international affairs? In other words, do the independent states in the region form a coherent entity for study, or is Latin America only a convenient geographic description? These questions raise the larger problem of the appropriate "levels of analysis" in the study of IR. Many analysts are skeptical of regionwide conceptualizations, saying that the great differences and heterogeneity among the states within the region and their tremendous diversity in culture, size, and other aspects are so profound that generalizations are virtually impossible. Some even argue that Latin America no longer exists as a region susceptible to precise analysis; many of them prefer to concentrate on the individual countries and subregions within Latin America. Others advocate a larger regional level, the Inter-American System of all the states in the Western Hemisphere. In particular, they see inter-American cooperation as required for the resolution of the salient international issues and problems. Globalists say that the most important international structures and issues are essentially worldwide in scope. Consequently, rather than looking either at Latin America or the Western Hemisphere as a whole, or going inside Latin America to focus on individual countries and the subregions, analytic efforts should concentrate on the highest macro level, with a view to resolving current issues within global regimes.

In my view, an accurate definition of Latin America's international relations requires that we recognize a complex of Latin American regional, subregional, and individual country layers linked to the hemispheric and global levels of interaction. This is a demanding analytic task, but we cannot accept the idea that one or some levels of analysis offer the key to understanding at the exclusion or slighting of the others.

The following discussion argues that the entire Latin American region is a subsystem of the global international system and may indeed be regarded as a significant unit in the conduct of international affairs. Even as the international system has become more interdependent it has concurrently been defined more sharply by regions and subregions; Latin America has not been an exception in the simultaneous regionalization-subregionalization and globalization of the international system. Although a certain truth is evident in the argument that Latin America is so internally different and the world so interdependent that the region cannot be treated as a whole, it is exaggerated and misleading. The regional image is incomplete, however, with considerable and important limitations.

Thus the following discussion further asserts that recognition of several levels within the subsystem is crucial for our understanding of Latin America's international relations. A variety of such subsystems are possible, involving both subregions and the bilateral relations of individual Latin American states. The three most relevant ones are Mexico, the Circum-Caribbean, South America beyond the Caribbean (the Southern Cone and Brazil), and Brazil itself. We will also discuss further subordinate levels, such as Central America and the Commonwealth Caribbean Countries within the Circum-Caribbean, and the overlapping Andean and Amazonic subregions of South America.

THE LATIN AMERICAN REGIONAL LEVEL

Geographic Demarcation and Actor Typology

Identification of the regional line of demarcation begins with the notion of a geographic boundary delimiting the region and enclosing a set of physically proximate states. Latin America is thus defined as inclusive of that territory in the Western Hemisphere south of the United States. Measuring 7,000 miles from northern Mexico to Cape Horn at the far southern reaches of Chile and Argentina, Latin America comprises an area roughly two and a half times larger than the United States. It is populated by almost 450 million people and is occupied by thirty-three sovereign states, with a small remainder being British, Dutch, French, and U.S. dependencies. The northern part of the region—Mexico and the Caribbean region—is mostly south of the United States. Almost all of South America, however, lies east as well as south of North America; the Natal region (the "Brazilian Bulge") is only 1,900 miles from the closest point on the African continent.

The regional states located within the subsystem boundary form the central focus of the subsystem's international politics. These states may be subdivided into groupings that reflect their political culture and "age" as independent nation-states: *Ibero-America* refers to the nineteen nation-states of Spanish and Portuguese origin, all of them the "old" or "traditional" states in the context of Latin American studies. Eighteen of these form *Spanish America,* with widely varying stages of development and international capabilities. They are, in alphabetical order, Argentina, Bolivia, Chile, Colombia, Costa Rica, Cuba, Dominican Republic, Ecuador, El Salvador, Guatemala, Honduras, Mexico, Nicaragua, Panama, Paraguay, Peru, Uruguay, and Venezuela. They occupy some 57 percent of the total Latin American land area. Most of them achieved their independence from Spain between 1810 and 1824; Cuba did so in 1898 but was not technically sovereign until the end of U.S. military occupation in 1902, and Panama was a province of Colombia until it became formally independent in 1903. *Portuguese America,* or *Luso America,* refers to Brazil, which was under the colonial rule of Portugal until becoming independent in 1822. This giant of Latin America, the largest regional state in both population and territory and larger than the continental United States, covers about 40 percent of the Latin American terrain. The tiny island-nation of *Haiti* is the oldest regional state and also a "traditional" one

LATIN   AMERICA

for Latin Americanists. Haiti broke away from France in 1804, the first Latin American state to gain independence, in a successful black slaves' revolt. It has maintained its West African culture to the present day.

The remainder of the regional actors are thirteen "new" states, twelve of which are former British colonies that gained their independence between 1962 and 1984 and are known collectively as the *Commonwealth Caribbean Countries.* They are Antigua-Barbuda, Bahamas, Barbados, Belize, Dominica, Grenada, Guyana, Jamaica, St. Kitts–Nevis, St. Lucia, St. Vincent, and Trinidad-Tobago. Suriname, a former colony of the Netherlands, became independent in 1975.

The external sector is made up of those states outside the boundary that have significant relations with the regional actors. Political dependencies located within the regional boundary, numbering eleven administrative entities, represent the

THE CARIBBEAN AREA

continuing territorial presence by the controlling external states (the United Kingdom, France, the Netherlands, and the United States). Significant external states include not only those that possess regional territory but also those with any form of regularized interaction with the region in question, that participate in the regional distribution of power, have significant trade with or investment in the region, have membership or participate in regional organizations, have alliances or alignments with regional actors, or participate with some regularity with the region in other forms of international relations.

Historically the European states were among the most important components of the external sector, with Great Britain the single most important external actor during the nineteenth century. A number of them reasserted their Latin American interests, especially from the early 1970s. The United States, important in the northern portion of Latin America in the nineteenth century, has been the most significant (but not unchallenged) external actor for much of Latin America during most of the twentieth century. The Soviet Union expanded its activities beginning in about 1960 with its alignment with Cuba; after the dissolution of the Soviet Union, Russia and the other successor states were minor or nonexistent presences. Japan became a continuing economic force, also dating from the 1960s. An array of other external states have special bilateral or other particular relationships in the Latin American region.

Several kinds of nonstate entities also function as important actors in the Latin American subsystem. The oldest is the Holy See and the Roman Catholic Church organizational structure. Multinational corporations have also played important roles, as have international labor movements. Subnational insurgency groups have long been active in Latin America, especially since the late 1950s and continuing in some countries even today. Some country-specific "drug cartels" have also recently played significant subnational roles. In addition, the importance of transnational political parties, most prominently those originating in Europe, has been increasing.

Perceptions

The evidence supporting the existence of a regional awareness is varied. Fundamental differences and even uniqueness are obvious in Latin America. Diversity and exceptionality should not be overemphasized, however; the Latin American states have much in common, and in certain important ways mutual identification is prevalent. Although few generalizations would apply to all of the Latin American states, a degree of commonality exists among them, and certain generally, if not universally, applicable patterns and shared experiences and traits emerge out of the diversity. (The next chapter discusses this complexity, noting elements of both commonality and multiformity.)

Regional self-consciousness is difficult to measure, but evidence suggests a "push-pull" force working in Latin American relations, an ambivalent situation of mutual repulsion and attraction. The most obvious expressions of ambivalence are found in the relations between Brazil and Spanish America. Great diversity exists among the eighteen Spanish American states, but they also exhibit a certain cultural cohesion and mutual identity. At certain times within Spanish America, ambivalence has been reflected in the competition for leadership between Mexico and Argentina and sometimes between Colombia, Chile, Peru, and Venezuela. Mutual identity is also revealed by the sensitivity of political groups in one state to developments in others. Military establishments seem to communicate with their Latin American counterparts, as have certain political parties and, to a lesser extent, labor unions. Although different developmental models have been posed by Mexican, Cuban, Brazilian, Peruvian, and other experiences, it seems significant that regional debates tend to center upon which *Latin American* solutions to the problems of change are most viable, with minimal reference to nonregional models.

External states have tended to increase subsystem cohesion in Latin America by their very presence. No Latin American state has been a great power in the mainstream of global politics; all have operated from a position of weakness relative to the world powers, with some recent special exceptions. Although some have come close to breaking this mold at certain times, most of them have tended to band together against threats, real and imagined, from the outside world. For example, Spanish American unity, from the time of the wars for independence from Spain until the mid-1860s, insofar as it existed, was based largely on fear of foreigners and a desire to ally against them. Plans for economic integration since World War II have been motivated not only by hopes for mutual economic benefit but also by the possibility of escaping from economic dependence on external industrialized states. Furthermore, Latin Americans have tended to side with each other when outsiders have exerted pressure in the region, even when individual state interests have not been involved. For example, U.S. intervention in the Caribbean during the first third of the twentieth century evoked strong protests even from the remote Rio de la Plata region, which was largely unaffected by U.S. actions. By the mid-1970s, the Panama Canal issue was no longer simply a confrontation between Panama and the United States but had become a matter of concern for virtually all of Latin America, which supported Panamanian interests against the United States. In the 1980s conflict in Central America led to organization of the Contadora Group by Mexico, Colombia, Venezuela, and Panama, which was subsequently endorsed by a Contadora Support Group of South American states not directly affected by the Central American crisis. Another example of regional unity was the majority decision among Latin American states to express support for Argentina in its 1982 war with the United Kingdom over the Falkland/Malvinas Islands, despite their own unhappiness with Argentine aggression. The U.S. invasion of Panama in 1989 provoked a similar, if less intense, mutual condemnation.

Regularity of Interaction

Latin Americans have also formally organized among themselves, in rudimentary forms during the nineteenth century and intensely since World War II. A few examples, far from inclusive, illustrate the point. (Chapter 7 discusses this topic in detail.) The eleven-member Latin American Free Trade Association, established in 1961 and reorganized in 1980 as the Latin American Integration Association (LAIA), includes all of the large regional economies and so it represents an important transregional if not a total regional association. In 1975 the Latin American Economic System (SELA) was created and has near-universal regional membership. Latin American Groups (or GRULAS, from the Spanish name) have been created within or with reference to other international organizations, such as the United Nations, Third World associations, and the European Community, in order to caucus on a regional basis before confronting the outside world. The Latin American Parliament (with nineteen members), created in 1963, has been resuscitated in the 1990s. Most recently, the Rio Group has become preeminent as the leading Latin American organizational voice on the new agenda of issues; it represents at least 90 percent of the region's population and GDP. Statements emanating from these and other Latin American intergovernmental organizations indicate a renewed impetus for regional cooperation. In this organizational sense, in the post–cold war world the self-perception of a Latin American subsystem has actually increased in coherence. At the same time, Latin American governments and their regional IGOs have expressed strong concern with their common involvement in the global international system.

A significant portion of this book is concerned with organizational as well as other forms of interaction processes. Thus, where appropriate, the several criteria regarding subsystemic structures proposed in our definition of subsystem requirements are considered in the Latin American context. The general question to ask is whether a regularity of relations exists in these areas; if so, the concept of a Latin American subsystem would be further strengthened. The following chapters discuss interaction processes that provide considerable evidence for the regional subsystem theory. Nevertheless, viewing Latin America only in terms of a single unit is insufficient. We also need to highlight those subregions where different conditions exist.

FURTHER SUBSYSTEMS

Mexico

Mexico stands apart in Latin America because it is a large and important state that borders a superpower. It has a special structure of intense bilateral relations with the United States in addition to its inter-American and other international connections. Mexico is part of a North American continental subsystem shared with Canada and the United States, a great area outside of Latin America. Consequently, the Mexican international subsystem has been and is largely divorced from the broader inter-American arena. Many of the issues have been bilateral and "North American" in content because of territorial proximity, increasingly integrated economic and social structures, and close association with the domestic concerns in each country.

Mexico has almost always been of significant interest to one or another of the world's great powers, but the United States has long been the principal foreign presence in Mexico (the foreign menace, in the eyes of many Mexicans). In the nineteenth century Mexico suffered severe territorial losses to the United States as a result of Texas independence and the war of 1845–1848. European interventions also occurred, most notably Mexico's incorporation into the French empire from 1862–1865. Dictator Porfirio Díaz (1876–1910) allowed the United States and certain European states to dominate Mexico's economy. After the Mexican

Revolution of 1910, Mexico adopted highly protectionist economic policies and an essentially isolationist political orientation toward the outside world.

The evolution of the Mexican subsystem after World War II resulted in the basic reality of the special and complicated Mexican–U.S. bilateral association, in sharp contrast to the historical relationship, of a strong mutual dependency. Although the United States has clearly been the stronger partner, Mexico has had considerable say. Mexican nationalism has been strong, its foreign policy principles coherent, and its capability significant. This view of the relationship was sharply challenged by those who emphasized Mexico's relative weakness in most respects and said that the United States would dictate the relationship. But recent developments have confirmed the connection as symbiotic and unavoidably linked and that the United States cannot coerce Mexico without damaging itself. The most dramatic indication of the new interdependence is the North American Free Trade Agreement (NAFTA)—a trilateral pact between Mexico, the United States, and Canada—that went into effect on January 1, 1994.

The Circum-Caribbean

The Circum-Caribbean is a complex region. Its boundary as an international subsystem has been perceived by both local and external states to include the islands of the Caribbean Sea and those nearby in the Atlantic Ocean, the entire Central American isthmus and Yucatan Peninsula, and the north coast of South America, which extends to the Atlantic Ocean and beyond the Caribbean Sea as such. Thus, Colombia, Venezuela, Guyana, and Suriname are considered Caribbean states. Although Colombia is increasingly a part of the Caribbean region, it is also perceived as a Pacific Basin nation. Colombia and Venezuela are also involved in the Andean and Amazonic South American subsystems. U.S. policymakers have preferred the idea of a "Caribbean Basin" that conforms to the above definition. It is often viewed by Europeans as a U.S. invention, although in the nineteenth century Great Britain seemed to hold the same idea, as Venezuela and Mexico do today.

Caribbean states have been small, weak, and relatively noninstitutionalized, with the exceptions of Colombia and (more recently) Venezuela. Consequently, the region has continuously been the object of rivalry, pressure, intervention, and domination by greater powers. Nothing is new about great power conflict in the area; international relations have not changed for centuries, only the actors have shifted. During the colonial period Spain was dominant but it was challenged by France, Great Britain, the Netherlands, and even Denmark. In the nineteenth century Britain was preeminent but it, too, was challenged, by France and the United States—in both cases a major issue was control of a transisthmian canal. The United Kingdom and the United States neutralized each other on the issue, and France actually began construction of the present Panama Canal in 1881 but abandoned the project eight years later. Throughout the twentieth century Caribbean states have generally been in the U.S. sphere of influence. The Panama Canal, taken over and completed by the United States at the beginning of this century, has loomed large in U.S. calculations. It is still of concern, although the canal's strategic and commercial importance has declined. After 1959 the United States was primarily concerned with deterring the spread of communism and what it perceived as Soviet expansionism. The United States has been the international policeman in the area, more assertive and consequential there than in South America beyond the Caribbean. It intervened militarily as late as 1983 in Grenada and in Panama in 1989–1990. Most of the area is part of a U.S. bilateral trading system.

The U.S. presence in the Circum-Caribbean has been one of the clearest cases of hegemony in the international political system. That hegemony, however, has not been total, constant, or simple and has been subjected to numerous challenges. The territorial holdings of the United Kingdom, France, and the Netherlands have constituted a constant diversion from U.S. primacy. The Soviet Union aligned with Cuba after 1959 and supported Nicaragua after 1979. In the 1980s a number of local Latin American and nonhemispheric states and organizations disagreed with U.S. policies in Central America and pressed for changes. Furthermore, U.S. actions in the Caribbean over the years have often engendered strong domestic opposition in the United States. On balance, however, U.S. power and influence have been and continue to be the primary factors in Caribbean international politics. This has been confirmed in the post–cold war era, with the Soviet Union's virtual retirement from the region and then its dissolution and the Europeans' reluctance to be involved in an area where their interests are not primary.

The Circum-Caribbean may be further subdivided. Central America, the isthmian area between Mexico and Panama, displays systemic characteristics. Central American states have desired but failed to be politically united for more than a century and a half. They have banded together in political and economic unions but are sharply divided over a number of issues. The recent Central American crisis of civil war and international conflict provided another structural element that defines this area as a subsystem. The Commonwealth Caribbean Countries also make up a subsystem. They are located mostly in the eastern Caribbean zone except for Belize on the Central American isthmus. The Commonwealth states also exhibit an internal push-pull process; several of them failed to unite in the West Indies Federation and to become independent as a single state in 1962, but shortly thereafter they began their economic integration. They were further divided over the 1983 U.S. intervention of Grenada (a Commonwealth Caribbean Country), but they moved thereafter to repair the divisions.

The Southern Cone

The entire South American continent below Central America arguably forms an international subsystem. South America beyond the Caribbean, however, is a more coherent entity. In terms of international politics, this majority part of the continent is largely synonymous with what is often called the Southern Cone of South America. Actors in Southern Cone international relations are Argentina, Brazil, Chile, Uruguay, Paraguay, Bolivia, Peru, and sometimes Ecuador. Excluded are the northern tier states of Colombia, Venezuela, Guyana, and Suriname. Their concerns overlap those of the South American subsystem, especially on border questions, but the thrust of their international relations more often is oriented toward the Circum-Caribbean.

The Southern Cone thus defined forms a regional subsystem distinguished by a number of characteristics. A principal one has been the region's relative isolation from the mainstream of international politics, largely a function of its strikingly unique geographic situation. In addition, the leading Southern Cone states are relatively institutionalized. Their remote global location at great distances from Europe and the United States, combined with the relative strength of the key local states, has left the region free, for the most part, from inclusion in global balance-of-power rivalries and helped it resist outside influences in the handling of internal affairs. The region thus has not been part of a global balance-of-power system in which a great power plays the role of international policeman enforcing the peace. This relative foreign policy autonomy is dramatically different from the situation in northern Latin America.

Southern Cone states have a broad array of external relationships that add to their ability to balance outside influences. The subregion is a multilateralized trading area. Unlike Mexico and most of the Caribbean, which are largely confined to a bilateral economic network with the United States, the Southern Cone states have long-standing cultural as well as economic ties with Europe; Japan is also an important economic actor. The region's trade with Europe, notably, has included arms transfers. Brazil, especially, has diversified its economy and developed a broad set of bilateral relationships. The United States, by and large, has been one of several competitors in South America, never approaching a position of dominance as in the Circum-Caribbean or of primary importance as in Mexico. As a general matter, the United States, in its Latin American relationships, has had the least interest and influence in the Southern Cone, with the exception of Brazil, and its influence with Brazil declined dramatically after the mid-1960s. Of interest is the current role for European transnational actors—the political parties, labor unions, and churches.

Relative isolation from global power politics has allowed the major Southern Cone states to establish independent patterns of interaction involving their own set of subregional issues. The issues have involved local rivalry for leadership as well as national searches for security, power, well-being, prestige, and resources, depending on the relative capabilities of the states involved. Subregional international relations have brought strategic-geopolitical components to the foreign policies of the major Southern Cone states. They have developed such calculations primarily in regard to their own subregion, extended to include the South Atlantic and the Antarctic. Intraregional relations were long characterized by rather firm and persistent balances of power, in which the small states served as "buffers" in rivalries among the larger states. The adoption of geopolitical perspectives further distinguishes the Southern Cone subsystem from the more northerly parts of Latin America. Particularly ominous, and in further contradistinction to the rest of Latin America, nuclear questions were introduced into subregional international relations, with advanced capabilities on the part of Argentina and Brazil. This situation has been considerably ameliorated in recent years, but the technical knowledge remains. Finally, the Southern Cone links to the South Atlantic region and interests in the Antarctic are peculiar to the South American subregional states within Latin America.

The Southern Cone subsystem, like that of the Caribbean Basin, may be further subdivided. Three subgroupings in particular have emerged, marked by formal organizations as well as other characteristics, such as border disputes. The Platine countries—Brazil, Argentina, Uruguay, Paraguay, and Bolivia—have a self-identification, reflected, among other ways, in their organization of the Cuenca del Plata accord in 1969 for regional infrastructure development. In 1991, Argentina, Brazil, Paraguay, and Uruguay established the Southern Common Market (MERCOSUR). The Amazonic countries—Brazil, Suriname, Guyana, Venezuela, Colombia, Ecuador, Peru, and Bolivia—have a similar self-perception. They signed the Amazon Pact in 1978 for the controlled development of the Amazon Basin. In an Andean subsystem, part of the Southern Cone overlaps with the Circum-Caribbean. Extending beyond the Southern Cone, the Andean countries—Venezuela, Colombia, Ecuador, Peru, Bolivia, and Chile—have considered themselves an international unit in several ways. For example, integration was fostered in 1966 by the formation of the Andean Group, and these states (except for Venezuela) see themselves as part of an emerging Pacific Basin trading system. For some of them, territorial interests also extend to the Pacific Ocean; the Easter Islands belong to Chile and the Galapagos Islands to Ecuador.

Brazil

Brazil, as indicated above, is a key actor in the Southern Cone subsystem but is also separate from it. Brazil is the largest and strongest state in that subsystem as well as in Latin America at large, and in several respects its bilateral relationships should be viewed as a discrete subsystem. Brazil has long stood apart from the rest of Latin America because of its Portuguese cultural heritage, large size (territory, population, and economy), and ambition and potential to be an influential state in global politics. Long the "sleeping giant" of Latin America, and once the junior partner in a cooperative alignment with the United States, Brazil increased its self-confidence toward the United States and its overall ability to pursue an independent foreign policy without an assumption of mutual interests. It successfully expanded its bilateral relations and is not prepared to reemerge as subordinate in any future relationship. Among the Southern Cone states, Brazil in particular diversified its economy and developed a multilateral network of international trade and strong ties with its immediate neighbors, in Europe, the Middle East and Africa, and Japan, in addition to those with the United States. It engages in relations with the United States without an assumption of mutual interests, prefers to approach other nations of the world in terms of bilateral relations rather than in concert with the rest of Latin America, and is open to a further broadening of its external relationships. It is significant, moreover, that Brazil has developed the most highly multilateral network of international trade of the Latin American states. It must also be pointed out that Brazil has serious problems that limit its international freedom of action and diminish its ambitions as a regional and global actor. They include the world's largest external portfolio debt, failed economic policies, a highly class-conscious social system in which a large majority of citizens live in extreme poverty, and a fragmented and inefficient political system.

SUBSYSTEM CHANGE

Criteria

The criteria for identifying systemic change—detecting the transformation when a subsystem with certain characteristics becomes another kind of subsystem with different features—were identified in Chapter 1. Those few studies that have addressed subsystem change mostly deal with the European region, historically the center of the global system. But such studies are not necessarily conceptually relevant for the analysis of other regions. Asian and African subsystems have only recently been studied because they were largely colonial areas and therefore extensions of the European system. Most of Latin America was not such a colonial extension after the early nineteenth century, but neither was it in the mainstream of European-dominated international politics. It has had a unique evolution during the twentieth century, even as it becomes more globalized. Thus, Latin American subsystem change must be dealt with in its own terms.

After independence and through the mid-twentieth century, most of Latin America did not escape the pervasive influence of external states, first the nations of Europe and then the United States. Subsystem transformation depended not so much on intraregional changes as on changing external global systemic influences on the region as a whole and on the individual regional actors. After the mid-1960s, however, internal considerations became increasingly important. We may identify different eras in the development of Latin America in the global distribution of power and levels of interdependence. The Latin American subsystem and its subregional components have gone through distinct stages, with transitional periods signaling the end of one era and the initiation of another. However, the various subregions did not develop in exact parallel. Thus, most dates assigned in the following discussion should be considered approximate.

From Colonies to Nations

The Latin American subsystem evolved out of the colonial period, from the late fifteenth to the early nineteenth centuries, when colonialism bound the entire region to European powers. During that three-century era preceding Latin American independence, most of the region was part of the Spanish and Portuguese crowns. Their control of the New World's territory and riches was an important factor in the European-centered global balance-of-power structure. Portugal led the European actors in their expansion of power around the globe through colonization and trade. In the early fifteenth century Portugal expanded southward along the African coast and eastward to Asia. Spain followed, and after its discovery of the New World in 1492, the Americas became the object of contention for territorial control. Spain was the dominant world power throughout most of the sixteenth century, primarily because of its American empire, which eventually extended some 8,000 miles from San Francisco in North America to the Straits of Magellan. In 1530 Portugal finally began to settle Brazil and later pushed its frontier westward, but its American empire never rivaled that of Spain.

As Spain and Portugal became relatively weaker in international politics from the late sixteenth century onward, France, Britain, and the Netherlands challenged their Latin American primacy through pirate raids on shipping, some territorial acquisitions, and the establishment of trading relationships (legal and contraband). Nevertheless, Spain and Portugal were able to manipulate the European balance-of-power system sufficiently to maintain control over most of their American territory. By the end of the colonial period their empires were largely intact, with the relatively minor exceptions of the British, French, Dutch, and Danish West Indies.

Latin American independence, like that of the United States earlier, began largely as a sidelight of European international politics. That is, the European power system, badly shaken by the Napoleonic Wars, facilitated the Latin American revolutions. By 1800 Spain was bankrupt and poorly governed, having continuously lost to France and England in eighteenth-century dynastic struggles. Portugal had declined into poverty and was closely allied with and dependent on Great Britain. When French armies invaded the Iberian peninsula in 1807–1808, the Portuguese royal family fled to Brazil aboard a British naval vessel while the Spanish king and his heir were imprisoned. By the time Ferdinand VII returned to the throne in Madrid in 1814, most of Spanish America was in revolt against him. Disorder within Spain itself further reduced his ability to deal with rebellious colonists. The last of the viceroys in Spanish America was vanquished in 1824, with some British assistance, and the once vast Spanish American empire was reduced to Cuba and Puerto Rico.

The Portuguese royal family returned to Portugal in 1821. The following year Brazilians declared their independence. In contrast to the long and bitter struggle between Spain and its colonies, Portugal relinquished control with little opposition. Brazilians called upon the Portuguese prince (the heir to the throne), who had remained in Brazil as regent, to make the declaration of independence and rule as monarch of the new state.

European Dominance

The nineteenth century after the mid-1820s roughly marks the first era of the independent Latin American subsystem. Before this transition, the regional states had largely been pawns in the rivalries among the great European powers. The severance of the colonial ties that had bound the region to overseas powers for more than three centuries, and had almost entirely isolated it from the rest of the world outside Spain and Portugal, submitted the new Latin American states to the power vagaries of the international political system. In addition, the independence of the vast Latin American territory affected the global system by changing the distribution of power among European states and stimulating rivalry among them to gain regional influence or control. From the beginning of national independence throughout the nineteenth century, the Latin American states played passive roles in global politics. Securing independence from Spain and Portugal had thrust the new states into the mainstream of international power politics, but they were still subordinate to the outside world.

The major external actors were European and had a preponderance of economic, military, and technological capabilities as well as long experience in statecraft. The United States played an important role in areas contiguous to it, but it was otherwise weak in relation to the European states. Great Britain was the dominant (but not unchallenged) external actor and held the primary position in most of the region into the first years of the twentieth century. Britain's naval and merchant fleets dominated the Atlantic and discouraged other power excursions into the area until the turn of the century. It is true that Mexico lost half its territory to the United States between 1836 and 1848, that Mexico and the Dominican Republic were occupied by France and Spain, respectively, in the 1860s, and that other armed interventions were initiated in the area by France, Spain, the United States, Great Britain itself, and, later, Germany and Italy. Nevertheless, Britain shielded the Western Hemisphere from many other European designs, especially those of France and Spain, by largely controlling ocean communications between Europe and America. In the 1880s, a private French company began construction of the Panama Canal, but the project went bankrupt and was abandoned. Germany and Italy entered the scene with their respective national unifications in the 1870s. Germany became highly competitive, especially in commercial and military affairs.

At the beginning of the nineteenth century, the United States was a relatively weak external actor. It steadily rose in power during that century, expanding its territory almost three times over from 1802 to 1852 and, after the end of its Civil War in 1865, developing its industrial and military capabilities and increasing its population at rapid rates. The United States finally emerged as a great power at the turn of the century. In general, it was not a major factor in the nineteenth-century balance of power beyond North America, although some European leaders, particularly in Britain, recognized its power potential.

Despite the warning to Europe by President James Monroe in 1823 to keep "hands off" the Americas, the United States did not dominate affairs in the Western Hemisphere. This statement of the U.S. position was issued in the shadow of the British navy, for at that time the United States lacked the military power necessary to keep continental European forces out of the Americas while knowing that Great Britain could and would do so. The Monroe Doctrine (as it was later called) remained virtually forgotten in the United States for many years. Thus, Great Britain realized Monroe's purposes in the sense that it assured to some degree the independence of Latin American nations from the imperial designs of continental Europeans.

Until the mid-1890s, the United States displayed little interest in Latin American affairs beyond its own continental expansion, the possibility of an interoceanic canal in Central America, and unrealized proposals to annex Cuba, the Dominican Republic, and the Danish West Indies. The major exceptions to U.S. weakness in Latin America were its relations with its immediate neighbor, Mexico, and with Great Britain in Central America. The United States acquired about half of Mexico's national territory as the result of the annexation of Texas and the later war settlement in 1848. Britain was the chief U.S. rival in Central America, where the construction of a transisthmian canal was of continuing concern to both states and brought them into serious conflict. The two states signed the Clayton-Bulwer Treaty in 1850 that softened their intense rivalry by providing that neither would construct or exclusively control a canal or "exercise domain" over any part of Central America.

Distinctive subregional structures and self-consciousness in Latin America were not as clear in the postindependence period as they would later become. Nevertheless, the various subregional subsystems had begun to emerge, with some of their elements shaped during the colonial period. For example, Spanish control of the Caribbean, in contrast to its firm hold on other parts of the Spanish American empire, had been eroded by other European challengers who acquired territories there, and Brazil's separate identity was evident throughout the colonial period. Intra–Latin American distinctions became clearer as the century progressed. Important South American conflicts—between Argentina and Brazil on the Atlantic side and, on the Pacific coast, between Chile and the alliance of Peru and Bolivia—that developed in the early independence period became continuing elements of the Southern Cone subsystem. The Mexican identity was shaped by the aggressive policies of outsiders—first the disastrous war with the United States in the 1840s and then the occupation by France in the 1860s. The Caribbean Basin subsystem did not undergo major systemic change until the turn of the century, which saw the retirement of Great Britain and the emergence of the United States as the dominant power in the area. In contrast, during the 1860s the Southern Cone subsystem went through a transition period that solidified its identity and further set it off from northern Latin America. Southern Cone states developed more viable political systems. They strongly desired to modernize their nations in all respects and looked to foreigners for aid in doing so. Now secure from most threats of European intervention, they concentrated on internal problems and national development involving cooperative rather than conflictual relations with Europeans and the United States. The remoteness of these states played an important role in their development, as the external great powers concentrated on a new era of energetic imperialism in other parts of the world.

The Southern Cone balance-of-power system began with rivalry among the ABC states (Argentina, Brazil, and Chile), but it came to have implications for the entire subregion (Burr, 1967, is the primary source for this topic). Major developments in Southern Cone international relations during the nineteenth century included Chile's Policy of the Pacific aimed at domination of the west coast; Argentina's determination to be preeminent in the Rio de la Plata area and to restore the old viceregal boundaries (which had included Uruguay, Paraguay, and part of Bolivia) under its control; and Brazil's preoccupation with expanding and securing its own borders. Thus, Argentina contended with Chile for influence in Bolivia and Peru and with Brazil over Paraguay and Uruguay. In intraregional politics, the century witnessed a series of major South American wars or threats of war as well as other forms of power struggle.

The Southern Cone balance-of-power structure—in essence a microcosm, but not an imitation, of the European regional balance-of-power system—began to change in the 1860s. Argentina developed rapidly after its unification as a nation in 1861. Brazil extended its territory greatly, actually beginning in 1851 and continuing into the 1900s, by gaining territory from all eight of its neighboring states except for Peru. Brazil, however, was unable to match Argentina's spectacular economic growth. The Argentine-Brazilian competition was inconclusive for the remainder of the century.

A period of "condominium hegemony" extended from 1883 until 1924 (Bailey, 1967:58). Chile began to think in broader terms; it sought to preserve its power position by continuing to curry favor with Ecuador and Colombia against Peru and with Brazil and Paraguay against Argentina—out of fear that Argentina might cooperate with Bolivia and Peru to challenge its Policy of the Pacific. Chile and Argentina, after narrowly averting war in the 1890s, reached an accord in the Pactos de Mayo (1902). They explicitly recognized each other's sphere of influence, agreed to naval parity, and formalized the balance-of-power system between them. This agreement temporarily left Chile secure in the west, but the Atlantic rivalry between Argentina and Brazil continued. Largely confined to the Rio de la Plata region in the nineteenth century, the rivalry expanded in the twentieth century when both parties adopted policies asserting leadership of South America. The ABC concept effectively ended in the mid-1920s as Chile clearly was left behind, in terms of power, by both Argentina and Brazil, although Chile continued to maintain its power position as best it could. The Argentine-Brazilian competition remained indecisive for about four more decades.

The Rise of the United States
and the Decline of Europe

The second era of subsystem development dates roughly from the 1890s until the middle of World War II. During that time, the United States and Britain were the most significant external actors, but the former expanded its power while the latter declined in influence. The United States emerged as a great power, signaled by its victory in war with Spain in 1898. Thereafter, the United States assumed a new role of international police power in the Caribbean region and converted most of it into a bilateral trade area. It engaged in various forms of coercive unilateral intervention that impinged on the sovereignty of many of the Caribbean states. Interventions were designed to preempt European meddling, to enforce stability in the environs of the new Panama Canal, and to secure the Caribbean approaches to the isthmus, considered vital to U.S. strategic interests. That Britain largely retired from the Caribbean in the early 1900s, except for its territorial holdings, further relegated the region to the U.S. sphere of influence subject to a great deal of coercion. The principal exceptions to total U.S. hegemony were the territorial holdings of the United Kingdom, France, the Netherlands, and (until 1917) Denmark.

In the South American subsystem, however, the United States was only one of several competitors to the powerful British position. France and Germany were also important contenders. U.S. influence outside of the Caribbean area did not begin to rival that of Europe until World War I. After the war, Great Britain, which had been the major source of capital for South America, continued to play a major role but yielded first place to the United States.

The major Southern Cone states became active and more autonomous at the beginning of the twentieth century, even though their new roles coincided with the rise of U.S. power. With the opening of the Panama Canal under U.S. control, the U.S. domination of the Caribbean region, and the beginning of the Mexican Revolution in 1910, the Southern Cone subsystem was further set apart. Furthermore, far-reaching changes occurred in Southern Cone social, economic, and political systems during the first three decades of the twentieth century, as well as in power relationships among the states of the area and with outside powers. Brazil emerged from under the shadow of Great Britain and sought more autonomy in an "unwritten alliance" with the United States. Beginning with the Second Hague Peace Conference and continuing in the League of Nations and the evolving Inter-American System, Southern Cone states played an increasing role in global affairs. In intraregional relations, however, many of the same conflicts continued.

U.S. Hemispheric Hegemony

The third phase of change in the Latin American regional subsystem began during World War II and continued throughout the postwar period until the mid-1960s. It was given impetus with the advent of the cold war but shifted direction after 1959 following the Castro revolution in Cuba and its alignment with the Soviet Union.

Soon after World War II the international system was characterized by a loose bipolarity. U.S. officials tended to integrate the Latin American region as a unit in their global conceptualizations of East-West conflict, initially emphasizing its relative remoteness behind the front lines of the cold war. The United States had replaced all foreign powers throughout the hemisphere, except for a few of their small but burdensome colonies. The United States was the region's largest trading partner and capital investor, and it monopolized military relations. Between 1945 and 1948 the Inter-American System was formalized by the Inter-American Treaty of Reciprocal Assistance (Rio Treaty) and the Charter of the Organization of American States (OAS), which organized the weaker Latin American states into a bloc under the leadership of the more powerful United States. The Rio Treaty joined all twenty of the Latin American states with the United States in a formal inter-American mutual security alliance. The United States was subsequently able to convert the Inter-American System into an anti-Communist alliance. This move was accompanied by the largely successful U.S. effort to mold a mostly reliable Latin American voting bloc in the United Nations. Most Caribbean states were U.S. clients. The Southern Cone subsystem was less strictly under U.S. domination.

Outside powers offered little challenge to U.S. dominance because Latin America was not related to their primary concerns. West European states retreated from strong competition. They were first absorbed with their own recovery and reconstruction and then preoccupied with intra-European affairs, relations with the superpowers and their own security arrangements, and the dissolution of their empires in Asia and Africa. The Soviet Union indicated slight interest as well. It was fundamentally concerned with its own contiguous regions and the cold war with the United States and Western Europe. At the same time it regarded Latin America as inevitably a U.S. sphere of influence that precluded Communist advances. Infrequent perceived threats were dealt with individually by the United States. For example, the United States provided covert support for the overthrow of a leftist government in Guatemala in 1954. From the U.S. point of view, international communism posed little threat to Latin America, a calculation that, when coupled with the dominant U.S. power position, meant that the United States could devote minimal policy attention to the region.

After Cuba aligned with the Soviet bloc following the Castro revolution of 1959, U.S. policy calculations toward Latin America were dominated by fears of Soviet expansionism. At about the same time, the Latin American states increasingly resisted the U.S. effort to transform the entire Inter-American System into an anti-Communist alliance. By this time, the global structure was widely perceived as consisting of three "worlds": the First (industrialized and non-Communist) World, the Second (Communist) World, and the Third (developing and nonaligned) World. U.S. officials tended to view Latin America as part of the Third World, grouping the region with Asia and Africa especially in the developmental sense and ambiguously and reluctantly in terms of nonalignment.

The Soviet Union accepted the opportunity to erode the U.S. power position in the Caribbean. This development posed the first significant challenge to U.S. predominance in Latin America since World War II. The United States consequently assigned a prominent position to Latin America in its global policies and temporarily devoted more resources to its overall Latin American policy. These policies included both cooperative instruments through aid programs and coercive means through various forms of intervention. The new policy emphasis had special implications for the Circum-Caribbean.

U.S. and Latin American interests converged in what came to be called the Alliance for Progress. From 1959 to the mid-1960s, the United States temporarily defined the concept of security to include national development, which coincided with the Latin American states' primary economic interests. The United States also pursued coercive strategies, which included an exile invasion of Cuba in 1961 and multilateral agreements in the Inter-American System to impose sanctions on Cuba in 1962 and 1964. Once Cuba left the fold, the United States said it would not allow a similar occurrence again and forcibly returned the Dominican Republic to its sphere of influence through military intervention in 1965 in order to prevent "another Cuba." That intervention effectively ended the Alliance for Progress and the convergence of U.S. and Latin American interests.

In the meantime, a major series of cold war events occurred with the U.S.-Soviet confrontation in the Cuban missile crisis of October 1962, which was viewed by both antagonists in terms of global balances of power. The confrontation over the presence of Soviet missiles in Cuba was a major episode in the cold war, the significance of which went far beyond the Caribbean area and the rest of Latin America. It was a great world crisis in which both sides seemed to perceive a potential shift in the global power balance. A debate over whether Soviet missiles in Cuba in fact could have altered the strategic military balance ensued at the time and continued thereafter. At any rate, Fidel Castro was largely ignored in what was essentially a U.S.-Soviet confrontation. Interaction took place between the superpowers with little reference to the Cuban leader. An outcome of the confrontation was the Soviet agreement to remove its newly placed weapons in return for a U.S. pledge not to invade Cuba.

Regional Pluralism

The Latin American subsystem entered its fourth era beginning in the mid-1960s, when it became even more independent from outside actors, shaped more by the regional actors themselves than was traditionally the case. The period lasted until the late 1980s and the end of the cold war. Developing international relationships involved changes in U.S. policy in response to shifting calculations of "the Communist threat," the revival of activities by extrahemispheric states in Europe and Asia, and rising Latin American foreign policy assertiveness. The argument was heard that, given the intense application of U.S. power in the Circum-Caribbean after 1981, coupled with the severe economic crisis and heavy debt burden throughout Latin America from about the same date, the subsystem had entered a new era of dependency relationships. However, it is clear that the hemispheric position of the United States was increasingly challenged, resulting in a relative decline in U.S. influence, increased pluralism in the distribution of power, and elevated levels of economic and social interdependence.

For more than a decade beginning in the late 1960s, the United States chose policies that again placed a low priority on Latin America, even in the Circum-Caribbean. The Southern Cone recaptured its contours as an independent subsystem, eroded but still intact after the brief postwar period of U.S. predominance in the hemisphere. The Soviet-Cuban threat seemed to recede in the wake of the missile crisis. The United States abandoned developmentalist policies, so that levels of funding for foreign assistance programs, both economic and military, declined sharply, and direct arms sales were severely limited. The United States diminished its military presence beginning in the late 1960s. Certain bilateral relationships and specific issues were still important to the United States, such as negotiations with Panama over new canal treaties. Human rights policies pursued after 1976 further isolated the United States from those states subjected to U.S. sanctions.

The erosion of global bipolarity reflected Latin American positions and actions toward the United States; many of them resisted U.S. power—with some success. They clearly stated their lack of support for a united American front, which they viewed as a device to maintain their subordinate status under U.S. influence. This attitude was a culmination of trends gathering force after the mid-1960s, which included expropriating foreign enterprises and assuming control of national resources, broadening contacts with other world power centers, challenging the United States in the Inter-American System, and devoting more attention to organizing among themselves and excluding the United States. In general, Latin American states were prompted to cooperate and unite in order to bargain with the United States, but their cooperative efforts were limited and their bargaining power undermined by their own continuing rivalries and disputes. Latin Americans also increasingly joined with the Third World.

As U.S. influence waned in Latin America, external states initially showed little interest in taking advantage of those opportunities. Japan became an important economic force in the region; European governments and nonstate actors expanded their activities; and the Soviet Union increased its diplomatic, economic, and military presence. However, none of the external states, with the limited exception of the Soviet Union in Cuba, made major efforts to increase their strategic position through Latin American operations.

Economic debilities bearing on the Latin American states in the 1980s, including a large external debt owed to U.S. banks, clearly reduced their foreign policy capabilities. The regional states' ability to pursue independent foreign policies was eroded, but U.S. leverage as a creditor was far from absolute. The debt situations involved risks for all parties. This is not to argue that they placed equal constraints on creditors and debtors alike; indeed, Latin American governments were forced to adopt stabilization measures that caused domestic hardships and political tensions. Yet all of the major Latin American states, and even some of the smaller ones, maintained international orientations and policies in opposition to those of the United States. It is difficult to measure the extent to which debt rescheduling increased U.S. opportunities or how financial influence translated into political leverage.

Limitations on U.S. capabilities should not be overstated. The subsystem era saw the end of U.S. dominance, but those changes exhibited different contours in the various parts of Latin America. Subsystemic distinctions reflected different power realities.

Mexico was absorbed with its bilateral U.S. relations and issues involving trade, investment, capital flows, energy supplies, migration (both legal and illegal), boundary settlements, sharing of water resources, border communities, tourism, fishing rights, and so on. Of particular importance, the United States was Mexico's largest trading partner, and Mexico occupied third place in total U.S. trade. With regard to the dominant inter-American issues during most of the 1980s—Central American conflicts, intervention, Cuba, trade and investment, external debt, human rights, arms transfers, and the narcotics traffic—Mexico tended to differ with and oppose the United States on all of them. The United States was not in a position to bring about any fundamental reorientation of Mexican foreign policy, even with the severe debt problems beginning in 1982 (later accentuated by internal Mexican political and social problems). The United States continued as the much stronger nation, but Mexico was far from being its client.

Although the United States became increasingly isolated in the Circum-Caribbean during the 1980s, its power and influence continued to be the primary considerations in the subregion's international relations. U.S. relations with Cuba further deteriorated after 1975 because of its expanded African adventures in concert with the Soviet Union, and President Jimmy Carter accused the Soviet Union and Cuba of increased activities in Central America. The Reagan administration, inaugurated in 1981, was determined to increase the U.S. presence in the Caribbean and recapture its influence, beginning in Central America. From the U.S. point of view, the principal challenge to Caribbean security arose from Soviet policies and their relationship to Cuban and Nicaraguan actions. Although the Soviet Union and its partners showed a certain caution in their Caribbean activities, they did not retire in the face of strongly assertive U.S. actions. Furthermore, U.S. activities engendered strong domestic political opposition in the United States itself. Important challenges came from other sources as well, including the NATO allies.

One of the most striking new conditions of Circum-Caribbean international relations was the concerted rise to power and assertiveness of Latin American states.

Four of them—Mexico, Venezuela, Colombia, and Panama—organized the Contadora Group in 1983 to offer a formula for the negotiated settlement of Central American conflict. Four geographically removed South American states later joined in a Contadora Support Group. Mexico was particularly independent in its opposition to the United States. Even more stunning was the multilateral peace plan known as Esquipulus II, agreed to by the five Central American governments in August 1987. The result of an initiative by President Oscar Arias of Costa Rica, for which he was awarded the Nobel Peace Prize, Esquipulus II was opposed by the United States. Latin American dissatisfaction with U.S. hegemony was also reflected in the Inter-American System, where U.S. leadership continued to be resisted; it was no longer available to legitimize U.S. actions. In sum, U.S. hegemony was challenged by the regional states themselves, including the weakest among them in addition to those considered to be U.S. clients.

Numerous European actors also presented something of a challenge to U.S. domination of the Caribbean zone. They did not view Latin America in terms of primary security interests because of geographic, cultural, and political distance and higher priority concerns elsewhere. None of them attempted to increase their strategic power in the Circum-Caribbean, tending to defer to the United States on such matters. NATO members had only the contingency security concern that the Gulf of Mexico and Caribbean Sea be open for movements of military forces and supplies in the event of European war. After the Nicaraguan Revolution of 1979, Europeans took a political interest in the evolving Central American crisis and by and large dissented from the U.S. approach. Their concern had to do not so much with geopolitics, strategy, or balances of power as with the nature of commitments by the West to social change in the Third World in general. Europeans tended to agree that Soviet influence should be minimized and to be concerned about Nicaragua's authoritarian trends. They opposed unilateral coercion by the United States, however, and argued against military solutions. They applauded the Contadora initiative and the Esquipulus II plan.

But European opposition did not develop to the extent anticipated during the period immediately following the Nicaraguan Revolution when the situation was in flux. Europeans exercised little influence on Central American events or on restraining U.S. actions. Most of all, the 1983 U.S. military intervention in Grenada signaled a new and more serious phase. Without primary interests in the region, European governments drew back so as to avoid another alliance problem with the United States. At the same time, however, they warned the United States that the more coercive its actions in Central America, the more problems it would have with its European allies.

Certain continental and global trends converged to alter the nature of international relationships and foreign policy issues in the Southern Cone during this period. The U.S. presence in the Southern Cone and its relations with individual states—especially its economic relations—remained highly important. Nevertheless, a more open international environment and diffused external influences allowed local actors greater latitude in the conduct of their foreign relations and permitted extraregional states to institutionalize substantial involvement—with outsiders both building on traditional relationships and establishing new ones. By the mid-1980s almost all of the subregional states had moved away from military regimes to constitutional democracies. Intra-Southern Cone relationships underwent dramatic evolution, particularly with more cooperative Argentine-Brazilian and Argentine-Chilean relationships. A Brazilian-Argentine rapprochement began in 1979, survived the Anglo-Argentine war of 1982 and dramatic changes of government in both countries, and was extended thereafter. Argentina and Chile settled their contentious Beagle Channel dispute. These were both historic changes, given the traditions of Southern Cone rivalries. The Anglo-Argentine dispute over the Falklands/Malvinas continued, although the British and Argentines began to negotiate directly. On the extrahemispheric level, in addition to its long-standing ties to Europe, the Southern Cone established closer economic relations with Japan. Argentina after 1979 engaged the Soviet Union as its primary trading partner.

U.S. influence with Brazil declined dramatically after the mid-1960s. Brazil developed a multilateral network of international trade, became not only self-sufficient in military affairs but one of the world's major arms exporters, and reduced its dependence on imported oil. It developed strong ties with Europe, the Middle East and Africa, and Japan, in addition to those with the United States. Brazil's freedom of action was limited by its heavy external debt burden, yet it still maintained a high degree of independence. Although Brazil suffered serious debilities as the world's largest portfolio-debtor nation, it also had a well-diversified economy, which was rated as the eighth largest in the world. Under military governments in the 1960s and 1970s, Brazil sought great-power status. Although those ambitions receded, cooperative relations with Brazil for all external states stemmed from a convergence of interests rather than from an assertion of superior power.

Post–Cold War Era

After the mid-1980s, Latin America, along with the rest of the world, entered a new post–cold war era. The United States consequently abandoned its 180-year-old preoccupation with minimizing what it saw as hostile foreign intrusions in the Western Hemisphere. This allowed other issues to rise to the top of everyone's agenda, including international trade and investment, external debt, democracy, human rights, immigration, refugees, drug trafficking, and, to a lesser but increasing extent, the physical environment. Most Latin American states and the United States adopted a primarily (but not exclusively) economic foundation for inter-American relationships. The United States laid the foundations for negotiations for free-trade agreements by signing "framework agreements" with all of the regional states except Cuba and Haiti. Those states themselves sought to reform and strengthen their various subregional economic integration organizations.

A rapid reorientation of Mexican and U.S. policies toward one another took place. Beginning in the late 1980s, Mexico abandoned its protectionist trade and investment policies and pressed the United States for a free-trade agreement, the creation of which became the central goal of Mexican foreign policy. The United States responded positively, Canada joined the talks, and an agreement was signed and ratified by the three parties. The historic North American Free Trade Agreement went into effect on January 1, 1994.

Regional changes in the post–cold war era were extensive in the Circum-Caribbean, where East-West conflict had been most dramatically played out. The Soviet Union actually became a part of the Central American peace process when it ceased weapons transfers to Cuba and Nicaragua and pressured them to end arms deliveries to insurgents in El Salvador. In November 1989 the Soviet Union joined the United States in the UN Security Council to create a peacekeeping force for Central America. The February 1990 elections in Nicaragua that ejected the Sandinista government definitively ended the now reluctant Soviet role. With the decline of Soviet power, commitments to Cuba were sharply reduced. Cuba itself was internationally isolated and absorbed with internal problems. With the end of East-West conflict, the Central American peace process, though suffering delays, also enjoyed considerable success (see Chapter 11). The U.S. military intervention in Panama indicated that the United States was still willing to use physical force, although the Bush administration said Panama was a unique case. In addition to the U.S.–Circum-Caribbean framework agreements for the future negotiation of free trade, Mexico initiated negotiations with the five Central American states for the same purpose.

In the Southern Cone there surfaced positive domestic and international trends, with which the United States had little to do. Redemocratization and peaceful interstate relations, begun earlier in the 1980s, persisted. By the end of the cold war, all governments in the Southern Cone had moved away from military regimes to constitutional civilian rule. Nevertheless, democracy was under stress, and a number of countries were combatting guerrilla and drug-related violence. The subregion's traditional international rivalries were further muted in March 1991 when Brazil and Argentina were joined by Uruguay and Paraguay to form MERCOSUR. All of the subregional states favor free-trade agreements with the United States (some more enthusiastically than others), although they have also indicated a continuing interest in multilateralized international economic and other relationships.

Latin American governments and regional intergovernmental organizations indicate keen interest in participating in the global international system. They are sorting out what the post–cold war world will be and what roles they will play in it. Statements of Latin American governments and intergovernmental organizations reflect a changed general attitude toward the outside world. They indicate that Latin Americans are today generally less defensive toward and more willing to cooperate with the outside world, including the United States, than at any time since before the mid-1960s and that they are eager as a region to be an integral part of the emerging global order. The dominant military regimes during the 1970s and 1980s had reduced official Latin American participation in extraregional affairs, but the succeeding democratic governments sought to reintegrate. As a general matter, Latin Americans seek to maintain and expand their relations with extrahemispheric states and organizations, as part of their thrust to be active and important participants in whatever new global system finally emerges.

EXTRAREGIONAL SUBSYSTEMS

The post–cold war change, among other things, links the Latin American region and its subsystems to the global international system partly in terms of the simultaneous regionalization and globalization of international relations and its impact on the former. Thus further comment is necessary regarding Latin America's international participation beyond the region itself.

Over the years numerous extraregional international subsystems have included different combinations of Latin American states. Membership in these various international organizations (including those identified in Chapter 1) constitute extraregional subsystemic levels of analysis. In addition, certain subsystems have been perceived to constitute a special relationship or commitment beyond the requirements of formal membership. For example, since 1889, Latin Americans have almost universally been part of the Inter-American System, a Pan American subsystem involving a special organizational relationship with the United States and, more recently, with Canada. Some political leaders have floated different Pan Latin connections, usually of culture and trade (most frequently Pan Hispanism of Spanish America and Spain, but also Pan Iberian connections to include Brazil and Portugal). Beginning in 1961, Latin American states identified with the Third World; sixteen of them joined the Nonaligned Movement, and almost all of them became part of the NEIO. On the individual state level, Cuba under Castro was a member of the Communist world until the startling events of 1989–1990. The twelve English-speaking states in the Circum-Caribbean are, as former British colonies, members of the Commonwealth, where they make up one-fourth of the membership of forty-eight states. Some analysts perceive numerous Latin American states as part of an emerging Pacific Basin subsystem, predominately economic in nature.

Such alternatives to Latin American regionalism are discussed later (some are considered viable, others are not). The point is this: These still unsettled possibilities, though they may complicate the structure of the Latin American subsystem (as well as the global system), do not refute the regional-subregional concept. Actors can belong to several subsystems, which can overlap and are not always mutually exclusive. Analysts can choose from various levels for investigation, and Latin America itself can be set apart within the larger international system. The region, including its subsystems and extraregional participation, is both politically important and conceptually defensible.

BIBLIOGRAPHIC COMMENT

Thompson (1973) provides a critique of the literature defining regional subsystems. Yale H. Ferguson's chapter in Feld and Boyd (1980) is an excellent overview of Latin American IR from a subsystem perspective. Dent (1990, Part II) provides an analytic guide to the literature on Latin American IR. Since 1985, the Programa de Seguimiento de las Políticas Exteriores de Latinoamericana (PROSPEL), under the leadership of Chilean scholar Heraldo Muñoz, has published a substantial annual series titled *Anuario de Políticas Exteriores Latinoameri-*

canas. A large number of studies have detailed general Latin American international relations. Among the historical works over the years are Quesada (1918–1920), Rodríguez Larretta (1938), Rippy (1938), Davis, Finan, and Peck (1977), and Boersner (1990). Broad-gauged emphases on international politics are N. Bailey (1967), Tomassini (1981), and Jaguaribe (1985). International political economy is dealt with by Grunwald (1978) and Hartlyn and Morley (1986). Parkinson (1974) addresses the cold war period; Wesson (1982) considers declining U.S. influence; and Portales (1989), Tomassini (1991), Atkins (1992), and Lowenthal and Treverton (1994) deal with the post–cold war era. From the immense literature delineating the Circum-Caribbean, the following are a representative sampling: Atkins (1991), Adelman and Reiding (1984), Anderson (1984); Braveboy-Wagner (1989), Bryan and Serbín (1994), Child (1992), Cirincione (1985), Erisman (1992), Erisman and Martz (1982), Findling (1987), Griffith (1993), Heine and Manigat (1986), Ince (1979), LaFeber (1993), Langley (1976, 1989b), Leiken (1984), Leonard (1991), Millett and Will (1979); D. Perkins (1966), Ropp and Morris (1986), R. F. Smith (1981), Sutton (1991), and H.A. Watson (1993). Some books dealing with South America are Atkins (1990), S. Baily (1976), Barclay (1971), and Child (1985, 1988). On Latin America and the Pacific rim, see Braveboy-Wagner et al. (1993) and Winchester (1991).

PART TWO

■

The Actors

The next four chapters are concerned with the various actors in the Latin American subsystem. Chapters 3 through 5 explore the foreign policy processes of the regional and external states and Chapter 6 investigates the nature and interests of certain non–nation-state actors. The state-actor chapters concentrate on the policymakers' perceptions of their interests and situations, the basic foreign policy orientations they have adopted, their ends-means and capability calculations, the role of strategic-geopolitical thinking (for those states whose policies have been based on such considerations), and the various policy doctrines that have been adopted. Commentary is also devoted to Latin American decision-making structures and processes. The analysis is highly limited with respect to external states, however, as the subject goes beyond the purpose of this book, which is to portray the overall structure and processes of Latin America's system of international relations. Detailed discussions of specific policy decisions and the execution of policy through various instruments on the part of all actors are contained in Part Four.

CHAPTER THREE

———————— ■ ————————

The Latin American States

THE FOREIGN POLICIES of the Latin American states share certain basic elements. This chapter examines the motivations, strategies, and policy orientations of the regional decision makers from the perspective of the regional states themselves. The differences in their sizes and diversity in other respects makes comparative analysis difficult and any conclusions tentative. Nevertheless, such an analysis reveals a number of common traits as well as important distinctions. Three broad questions are considered: (1) What extrasocietal conditions shape Latin American foreign policies? (2) How is policy formulated? (3) What orientations have been adopted toward the outside world? In general, the realities of Latin American capabilities and the nature of nationalism, combined with the primacy of domestic political processes, form the most important influences bearing on the choice of foreign policy orientations.

CAPABILITY

Geographic Factors

A capability analysis of the Latin American states must pay special attention to political geography. The geographic positions of different parts of Latin America, combined with other capability factors, have fundamentally shaped perceptions and orientations toward the outside world and affected relations with outside states. The northern part of the region—Mexico and the Circum-Caribbean—has always been subjected to intense foreign pressures. Mexico's position on the U.S. border has influenced Mexican foreign policy in important ways. For many years Mexico experienced threat of or actual military intervention as well as economic dominance. That proximity has also facilitated, perhaps compelled, Mexico to engage in a broad range of interactions with the United States and with other nearby states. NAFTA, the historic free-trade agreement between Mexico, the United States, and Canada that went into effect on January 1, 1994, is a dramatic case in point. The Caribbean area was the scene of initial European rivalry and of U.S.-British rivalry in the nineteenth century; in the twentieth century it was drawn into a sphere of pervasive U.S. influence until that was challenged by the Soviet Union in Cuba and later Nicaragua. By 1990 the United States was again the dominant external influence. The United States intervened militarily and otherwise with varying intensity throughout this period, the latest military invasion occurring in Panama in 1989. The United States has also been the dominant external economic factor, with prospects for free-trade agreements with almost all of the local states. Thus, the intense interest of outside states in their affairs has been a primary policy-making factor for all states in northern Latin America.

Geography has influenced intraregional politics as well. The proximity of five small Central American states to relatively huge Mexico has influenced their foreign policies since the 1970s, and in the 1980s the Central American crisis, in turn, became of primary concern to Mexico. Mexico has been especially concerned with events in its immediate neighbor, Guatemala, involving competing territorial claims, immigrants and refugees, and guerrilla incursions. In January 1991, Mexico and the five Central American states (who in 1960 established their Central American Common Market) agreed to set up a free-trade area by the end of 1996. Venezuela's expansion of international influence in the 1970s, based on financial resources garnered from the sale of petroleum, extended to the rest of the Caribbean area. Even with the decline of those resources in the 1980s, Venezuela joined Colombia, Mexico, and Panama in the Contadora Group in a sustained effort to deal with the threat posed to them in proximate geographic areas. In 1987 the Central American states agreed to a complex long-term plan for peace and recovery in the region, which they continue to pursue in the mid-1990s.

The states in the Southern Cone subsystem have a strikingly unique geographic situation. The location of Brazil, Argentina, Uruguay, Paraguay, Bolivia, Chile, Peru, and Ecuador places them at great distances from both Europe and the United States, outside the mainstream of great-power global politics and beyond the immediate sphere of U.S. influence. Their isolation has not been total, however; the area has been subject to external coercion (less so in the twentieth century than in the nineteenth) and relies on the outside world to provide its major export markets. Most of the time, however, distance has given those states a measure of freedom in the international political system and the opportunity to pursue policies toward each other relatively free of outside considerations.

Their physical isolation has allowed the states in the Southern Cone subsystem to develop discrete perceptions, orientations, and actions within their subregion as well as toward the contiguous South Atlantic area and Antarctica. In intraregional international politics, the local great powers (Brazil and Argentina) often behave like great powers toward their neighbors; the middle powers (Chile and Peru) have acted accordingly; and the small powers (Uruguay, Paraguay, Bolivia, and Ecuador) have been as concerned with the stronger local states as with outsiders. The weak states in the Southern Cone, although isolated from the mainstream of world power politics, have been intimately caught up in rivalries among Argentina, Brazil, Chile, and Peru. Uruguay, Paraguay, and Bolivia are located between larger and more powerful states that compete for leadership in their locale. This "buffer status" has greatly influenced their domestic and foreign policy. They have also had serious conflicts with each other. In this regard, an important reality is that Brazil, the sometimes ambitious giant of South America, borders all states on the South American continent except for Chile and Ecuador, a fact not lost on decision makers in the rest of South America.

Brazil, Argentina, and Chile are the only states in Latin America to have developed significant geopolitical strategic schools of thought, and these concepts have been fundamental motivators in their foreign policies. These states have often acted on the basis of the geopolitical nature of the Southern Cone–South Atlantic–Antarctic region as well as in response to their individual national interests. The others have done so to a lesser extent or not at all. This policy-making consideration shows up in stark contrast to the situation in the northern half of Latin America, where the geopolitical interests of outsiders and their activities as local international policemen have precluded the local states from developing such policies.

A number of physical features have also affected the intraregional policies of several states. Mountains form the dominant characteristic of much of Latin America. They are found in many of the Caribbean islands, beginning almost at the Mexican border with the United States and continuing south through Central America, along South America's Caribbean coast and western continental reaches, and in Brazil. The Andes mountain chain (*cordillera*) extends from the Patagonian region of southern Chile and Argentina along the west coast of the continent near the Pacific shores, to the Caribbean coast, traversing Colombia and Venezuela. In width they vary from less than 100 miles in the south to about 400 miles in a plateau in Peru and Bolivia. They have provided a security barrier between Chile and Argentina, Chile and Bolivia, and Bolivia and Peru. The large Atacama desert between Chile and Peru has served the same function. The vast Amazon jungle basin, the heartland of South America that even today contains large undeveloped zones, has traditionally formed a barrier between Brazil and most of its neighbors. Few highways connect the Latin American nations, although South America contains several great river systems linking some of them. The Amazon River is the world's largest. It carries, by conservative estimate, 20 percent of the world's fresh water; 40 percent of the South American surface waters, found in the territories of eight nation-states, drains into it. Ocean ships are able to navigate some 900 miles upriver to Manaos, and smaller vessels can proceed 1,400 miles farther to Iquitos in Peru. Other important South American river systems are the Magdalena-Cauca in Colombia and the Orinoco in Venezuela, both of which rise in the interior and flow into the Caribbean Sea; both are navigable for considerable distances. The river complex of the Uruguay-Paraguay-Paraná-Pilcomayo, which empties into the Rio de la Plata estuary, is of great commercial and, in the minds of some local leaders, military significance. Navigable for 2,000 miles by oceangoing vessels, the system connects southern Brazil, Uruguay, Paraguay, and Argentina.

In South America, physical barriers have offered military protection to all states. At the same time, they have impeded international trade and other peaceful forms of intercourse. In the early 1960s Brazil began constructing a transcontinental highway and railroad network. This development, undertaken by a military regime for national security purposes, was met with mixed feelings by many South Americans. The opening of Brazil's interior simultaneously linked the entire continent, facilitating not only international trade but also the spread of Brazilian influence and, in the minds of the more fearful, aggression (a fear not borne out through time).

Territorial size is also a capability factor. With a total land area of about 8 million square miles, Latin America represents about one-sixth of the world's land area. The individual states, however, differ greatly in size. Brazil is the largest territorial state by a wide margin. Its 3.3 million square miles represent more than 40 percent of the entire surface area of Latin America. The smallest continental state, El Salvador, covers 8,083 square miles, and the smallest island nation, Grenada, 133 square miles. Other large states are Argentina, Mexico, Peru, Colombia, Bolivia, and Venezuela. Mexico and Bolivia at one time encompassed twice the territory they have today, but as the result of military defeats, each lost half its national domain to neighboring states.

Population Factors

Quantitative and qualitative aspects of Latin American populations are important sources of foreign policy strengths and weaknesses. Underpopulation was a primary concern in the region after national independence. The entire Latin American population in 1810 was probably only 20 million, and in 1900 little more than 60 million. In 1975 the total population was in excess of 300 million, growing faster than that of any other major region of the world. By the early 1990s it was well in excess of 400 million, forecast to reach about 600 million at the end of the twentieth century.

Population levels and density vary widely among the various states. Brazil's 150 million inhabitants make up about one-third of Latin America's total population. St. Kitts–Nevis is the least populous state, with some 40,000 inhabitants. Some Latin American nations are among the world's most densely populated, such as Barbados and El Salvador. Others are very lightly inhabited, such as Bolivia. Most of Latin America is urbanized, and urbanization continues apace throughout.

Latin America generally has much unoccupied territory, and several states could provide many more people with living space. Population variables, however, involve not only numbers of persons but qualitative considerations as well. For example, economic growth rates are not sufficient to dramatically decrease poverty levels, given the generally high population growth rates. Poverty, in turn, is correlated with socially undesirable traits, such as low literacy levels and lack of technical skills. Overall, poverty detracts from a nation's capability because productive human resources are undeveloped and large numbers of discontented sectors increase divisive social tensions.

Some Latin American states have much higher educational levels and standards of living than others. For example, estimated literacy in Argentina, Chile, Costa Rica, Cuba, Panama, and Uruguay ranges from 90 to 96 percent, and literacy rates in most of the Commonwealth Caribbean are impressive. Literacy is lowest in Haiti, and low literacy rates are also found in Guatemala, Bolivia, Nicaragua, Honduras, and El Salvador. Higher literacy rates are not an unmixed blessing, however. They can result in increased expectations that, if frustrated, may have a socially destabilizing impact.

Social Factors

Social tensions and lack of homogeneity detract from the strength of some states more than others. Racial and cultural variety in Latin America and complex intermixing have had different social impacts in the various states. Indigenous Indian peoples were the first Americans. By the time of European expansion into America after 1492, Indian groupings ranged from primitive nomadic tribes to the advanced and complex cultures and empires of the Aztecs and Incas (superior to those of parts of Europe at the time). The Spanish and Portuguese, coming first as conquerors and then as settlers, ruled, reduced most Indians to servile status, and further populated most of what is today called Latin America. Africans were later introduced in large numbers to certain less-populated parts of the region as slaves on sugar and cacao plantations and in gold, silver, and diamond mines. They were brought by the Spaniards and Portuguese as well as the British, French, and Dutch during the three-century colonial period. The British also brought East Indians (from South Asia) to their colonies as indentured immigrant labor from the 1830s until World War II. Chinese "coolies" were brought as "contract labor" to various parts of Latin America. Immigrants from virtually all parts of the globe migrated to the New World, mostly after Latin American states became independent. Thus, the Latin American states are culturally complex and dissimilar in many respects, combining indigenous, colonial Iberian, and imported cultural heritages to the extent that no "typical" Latin American state exists.

As a general rule skin color is correlated with class: The whitest persons are in the upper classes and, correspondingly, darker people are relegated to the lower social gradations. Strong class consciousness has created social tensions, alienated large social sectors, and weakened national unity. Even in the largely homogeneous black-populated new nations and in Haiti, the class system is rigidly structured, and little effort has been exerted by the upper classes to involve the masses more fully in national life. The few states with relatively small noncaucasian populations have not been divided by the problems of integrating minority races into national life, but class consciousness is still strong, based on such factors as family and economic status. Generally speaking, more class mobility exists in the cities than in rural areas.

Political Factors

Political instability is both a source and an expression of weakness, whereas stable political processes add to national strength. The politically unstable states in Latin America are less united on international issues and less able to deal with their own national development. Preoccupied with domestic problems or crises, they tend to consider foreign policy as relatively less important. In contrast, the Latin American states with the most effective foreign policies are also the most politically stable. They are more able to devote resources to international questions, and they have gained a certain amount of respect from other states.

During the early national period, few Latin American states were able to maintain internally stable political systems. Conflict and factionalism, including civil war and rebellion, as well as corrupt administrative practices, were common. This

TABLE 3.1 Some Capability Indicators (estimates for end of calendar year 1993)

State (capital city)	Area (square miles)	Total Population (thousands)	Growth Rate (% annual)	Literacy (%)	GDP ($bn)	External Debt ($bn)	Regular Armed Forces (number of personnel)			
							Army	Navy	Air Force	Total
Antigua-Barbuda (St. Johns)	171	64	0.5	89	0.4	0.2				
Argentina (Buenos Aires)	1,072,068	33,533	1.1	95	119.8	54.0	40,000	21,500	8,900	70,400
Bahamas (Nassau)	5,389	269	1.6	90	2.8	1.1	(defense force)			850
Barbados (Bridgetown)	166	255	0.2	99	1.7	0.7				
Belize (Belmopan)	8,867	204	2.4	91	0.5	0.1	600	50	15	665
Bolivia (La Paz)	424,163	7,544	2.3	78	6.8	3.7	25,000	4,500	4,000	33,500
Brazil (Brasilia)	3,286,473	156,664	1.4	81	366.6	123.3	196,000	50,000	50,700	296,700
Chile (Santiago)	286,400	13,740	1.5	93	38.3	16.9	54,000	25,000	12,800	91,800
Colombia (Bogotá)	439,513	34,943	1.8	87	52.7	17.0	120,000	13,000	7,000	140,000
Costa Rica (San José)	19,653	3,265	2.4	93	6.7	3.2	(security forces)			7,500
Cuba (Havana)	44,218	10,957	1.0	94	12.7	6.8	145,000	13,500	15,000	173,500
Dominica (Roseau)	305	87	1.3	94	0.8	a				
Dominican Republic (Santo Domingo)	18,703	7,684	1.9	83	8.8	4.7	15,000	4,000	4,200	23,200

(Continued)
TABLE 3.1   Some Capability Indicators (estimates for end of calendar year 1993)

State (capital city)	Area (square miles)	Total Population (thousands)	Growth Rate (% annual)	Literacy (%)	GDP ($bn)	External Debt ($bn)	Regular Armed Forces (number of personnel)			
							Army	Navy	Air Force	Total
Ecuador (Quito)	104,506	10,461	2.1	86	12.2	12.7	50,000	4,500	3,500	58,000
El Salvador (San Salvador)	8,083	5,637	2.0	73	6.2	2.6	28,000	620	2,000	30,620
Grenada (St. Georges)	133	94	0.2	98	0.2	0.1				
Guatemala (Guatemala)	42,040	10,466	2.6	55	13.1	2.5	42,000	1,200	700	43,900
Guyana (Georgetown)	82,978	735	−0.7	95	0.3	2.2	5,000	100	100	5,200
Haiti (Port-au-Prince)	10,714	6,385	1.7	53	2.0	1.0	7,000	250	150	7,400
Honduras (Tegucigalpa)	43,277	5,170	2.8	73	5.7	2.8	14,000	1,000	1,800	16,800
Jamaica (Kingston)	4,470	2,530	1.0	98	3.8	4.4	3,000	150	170	3,320
Mexico (Mexico, D.F.)	759,530	90,420	2.0	87	336.5	104.0	130,000	37,000	8,000	175,000
Nicaragua (Managua)	53,668	3,987	2.7	57	1.7	10.6	13,500	500	1,200	15,200
Panama (Panama)	29,208	2,579	2.0	88	6.5	5.2	11,000	400	400	11,800
Paraguay (Asunción)	157,047	5,071	2.8	90	7.4	1.2	12,500	3,000	1,000	16,500
Peru (Lima)	494,293	23,210	1.9	85	24.3	21.2	75,000	25,000	15,000	115,000

(Continued)
TABLE 3.1　Some Capability Indicators (estimates for end of calendar year 1993)

State (capital city)	Area (square miles)	Total Population (thousands)	Growth Rate (% annual)	Literacy (%)	GDP ($bn)	External Debt ($bn)	Regular Armed Forces (number of personnel)			
							Army	Navy	Air Force	Total
St. Kitts–Nevis (Basseterie)	150	40	0.1	98	0.2	a				
St. Lucia (Castries)	238	144	0.5	67	0.3	a				
St. Vincent–Grenadines (Kingston)	150	115	0.8	96	0.2	a				
Suriname (Paramaibo)	55,000	416	1.5	95	1.3	0.1	1,400	240	150	1,790
Trinidad-Tobago (Port of Spain)	1,864	1,314	1.1	95	5.3	2.4	2,000	500	50	2,550
Uruguay (Montevideo)	72,172	3,175	0.8	96	10.6	4.1	17,200	4,500	3,000	24,700
Venezuela (Caracas)	347,029	20,118	2.2	88	62.0	27.1	57,000[b]	11,000	7,000	75,000
Total	7,872,639	461,276			1,118.4	489.8	1,064,200	221,500	146,835	1,440,895

[a]Less than $100 million
[b]Includes 23,000 active national guard

Source: Central Intelligence Agency, *The World Factbook, 1993;* and International Institute of Strategic Studies, *The Military Balance, 1993–1994.* Projections and estimates by the author.

weakness frequently invited foreign intervention. The international effectiveness of the major states has depended largely on their internal stability. Brazil experienced little turmoil in the nineteenth century and was the major exception in this regard. The heir to the Portuguese crown gave up his claim and, as constitutional monarch, was the "moderating power" from 1822–1831; his son similarly reigned until 1889. Chile was the first Spanish American state to work its way out of chaos when, in the early 1830s, it entered a period of consolidating "oligarchical democracy." In the latter part of the century, Argentina began to move toward relatively stable systems, although a great deal of violence accompanied the process.

Mexico's political turmoil, beginning in 1910, for all practical purposes retired it from international politics for two decades. Mexico regained stability after the 1930s, however, and became an important actor in inter-American and, at times, world affairs, despite its geographic disadvantage in proximity to the United States. Brazil's stability since the mid-1960s, as in an earlier era, was fundamental to its uneven drive for world power. As Brazil's authoritarian government became fragmented in the late 1970s, its foreign policy followed suit. Brazil's main rival, Argentina, although loath to admit it, effectively dropped out of the Latin American leadership race, primarily because of problems directly related to political instability beginning in the late 1920s and accelerating after 1955. Argentina's return to popular civilian rule in 1983, replacing a military regime that had terrorized its own populace, instituted a policy of "reinsertion" into the international system. Chile's domestic political crisis beginning in 1970 caused severe foreign policy problems as well as weakness in dealing with them. A decade of civil war in Colombia beginning in 1948, and subsequent guerrilla insurgency and violence associated with narcotraffic, have kept Colombia from developing the international influence that should be possible, given its size and physical and human resources. In contrast, Venezuela's capability has been enhanced by a democratically legitimized political system and its vastly increased oil riches—especially in the 1970s—despite its small population and serious domestic social inequities. But as Venezuela's national income dropped with the decline in oil revenues in the 1980s, its domestic political consensus was reduced and led to several manifestations of political crisis.

Political stability is also of importance to the foreign policies of small states. Uruguay, for example, influenced inter-American relations for many years because of its prestige stemming from stable democratic development. It suffered a great loss in prestige, however, when its political stability and democratic government deteriorated along with its economic life in the decade after 1966. Costa Rica is another example of a small state respected for its democratic stability, developed after World War II. Conversely, small states can be particularly weakened by domestic political problems. For example, political instability in the Dominican Republic after 1961 led directly to the U.S. military intervention in 1965. Civil war and insurgency in Central America in the 1980s led, variously, to U.S., Cuban, Soviet, and other external involvement in local politics. Internecine strife in Grenada and in Panama was one reason for the U.S. military interventions in 1983 and 1989, respectively.

Military Factors

Although the military capability of Latin American states generally has not been significant in world politics, it has had substantial impact on inter-American relations. Throughout most of the nineteenth century and, in several instances, into the twentieth, Latin American armies were as a rule inadequately equipped, untrained militia led by officers lacking professional skills and knowledge. The armies tended to be bands of armed men loyal not to the nation or to any central government but to charismatic regional strongmen (*caudillos*). The Chilean army was the principal exception to this rule. The small navies were not much better, with the significant exception of Chile's and, to a degree, those of Argentina and Brazil. The major states of South America began modernizing efforts in the late nineteenth century, and eventually all Latin American military establishments undertook professionalization, all largely with foreign help.

Despite modernization, the Latin American armed forces have remained inferior to those of the world's great powers. Although some have reached relatively sophisticated levels, in worldwide terms they have remained unimportant. With some exceptions, the involvement of the states in extraregional politics has not relied on military capability. Those exceptions include a Brazilian army battalion that fought in Italy in World War II, a Mexican aircraft squadron stationed in the Philippines at the same time, a Colombian ground unit that participated in the UN force in Korea, another Colombian battalion that served with the UN Emergency Force in the Gaza Strip for two years after the Suez crisis of 1956, the Cuban army presence in Africa in concert with the Soviet Union beginning in late 1975, and an Argentine naval unit that joined in the Persian Gulf War in 1991. In regional terms, however, relative military capability has been of continuous significance since the wars for independence. Military units were mobilized in inter-American wars beginning in the early national period and as late as 1967. Relative military power has been a factor in the outcome of the many border and territorial disputes. An Inter-American Peace Force settled the Dominican civil war of 1965–1966 (under de facto U.S. leadership), and a similar organization was instrumental in bringing warfare between El Salvador and Honduras to an end in 1967. The Central American crisis in the 1980s actively involved the armed forces located in that subregion. In most Latin American states, military capability has been significant primarily in terms of internal problems—as a domestic political arbiter and as a defense against insurgency.

No nuclear weapons are possessed by Latin American states, but some developed the potential to manufacture them. Argentina became the most advanced in this regard, with Brazil close behind. Other Latin American states indicated interest in developing nuclear power programs and some of them began research to do so. In the 1980s, the prospects for nuclear weapons development in Argentina and Brazil were reduced by a combination of a return to democratic rule and financial crisis, which also deterred nuclear development in other Latin American programs.

Economic Factors

Economic problems trouble states, although examples of real economic strengths are also evident. A majority of the regional states remain characterized by economic monoculturism: National income depends heavily on the export of a few, perhaps only one or two, agricultural or mineral items, causing national economies to be strongly affected by the vagaries of world markets. Stagnation is averted as long as full export market demands exist, but economies tend to deteriorate when export products must compete in markets characterized by declining prices.

Weaknesses in the industrial sector are characteristics of economic monoculturism. Latin America traditionally relied on external industrialized states for manufactured goods as well as investment capital, for which it exchanged agricultural and mineral commodities. Industrialization has made some progress in most states and remarkable strides in a few, so that today industrial levels vary widely. Some economies are fairly well balanced industrially, including heavy industry. Brazil is especially notable, and Argentina, Chile, and Mexico have made advances in this regard. Others are in a "moderate" industrial development stage, such as Colombia, Peru, Trinidad-Tobago, and Venezuela. The remainder have only the beginnings of industrialization or are virtually nonindustrial. Latin America in general has certain natural disadvantages that detract from its industrial potential. For example, coal resources are small and generally of low quality, and power sources are deficient. Hydroelectric potential is great, but the best sites are remote from urban centers. Platine states in the Southern Cone, led by Brazil and Argentina, have cooperated to their mutual benefit in dam building projects to realize hydroelectric potential.

A continuing myth, dating from the European discovery of the New World, pictures the Latin American region as possessing immense mineral resources that need only investment capital and managerial skills to be developed. The region is not generally rich in minerals, although a minority of states are especially well endowed in certain resources. Some of them rank high in world levels of reserves and production, such as Bolivia in tin; Chile in nitrates and copper; Mexico in silver, lead, and zinc; Peru in vanadium and bismuth; and Venezuela and Mexico in oil. Even though these minerals are crucial necessities for the external industrialized nations, the Latin American states have only seldom derived serious bargaining leverage, with the important exception of oil in the 1970s. Nationalization of foreign-owned extractive industries in some nations eliminated many foreign economic elites, but the heavy reliance on mineral resources continued and the problems of monoculturism persisted.

Special mention should be made of oil resources. Ten Latin American nations produce oil, but it is significant as an export in only four—Venezuela, Mexico, Ecuador, and Colombia. Venezuela's petroleum industry began to grow especially in the 1920s, and thereafter it has consistently been among the world's major oil producers and exporters. Mexican reserves and production have also achieved a very high volume in world terms. With the energy crisis of the 1970s and dramatic increases in world market oil prices, Venezuela and Mexico profited enormously. Conversely, the decline of the price of oil in the 1980s was an important factor in their economic crises.

The huge external debt out of proportion to the size of Latin American economies was the most serious international economic problem throughout the 1980s. By the 1990s the debt continued to be a vital concern, but it became subsumed under broader questions of international trade and investment. External debt is closely linked not only to trade balances but also to more general international relations and questions of internal stability. Analysts should ask how dependent Latin Americans are on the international economic system and whether they are able to respond to outside pressures and consider the effect of domestic austerity programs, negotiated with the International Monetary Fund in concert with external government and commercial bank creditors, on domestic developmental demands. Latin American leaders generally argue that too much austerity bears too heavily on the poorest sectors of society, leading to social violence and ultimately to political chaos. Leaders of democratic polities, most of whom had succeeded military regimes that had presided over the increases in public debt, further argue that democracies are at stake.

NATIONALISM

The Analytic Problem

Nationalism is a fundamental force in Latin America's foreign policy. An analysis of this phenomenon is complicated, however, first by the lack of a precise and widely accepted definition and, second, because the Latin American variety of nationalism is highly complex. Despite definitional elusiveness and regional complexity, the importance of nationalism to Latin American foreign policy formulation cannot be denied.

Classic definitions characterize nationalism as a "group consciousness" in which individuals identify themselves with and give supreme loyalty to the abstraction of the nation, which reinforces the state as the ultimate source of authority and legitimacy. This definition should be modified with the caveat that particular nationalists may use nationalism to attempt to capture control of the state and its authority, claiming to speak for "the nation" in order to gain advantage over political competitors. Nationalism is also a structural and institutional phenomenon—it represents the lodging of social functions and their structural base in the nation-state.

Latin American nationalism involves several forms and different orientations. It assumes multiple ideologies and loyalties even within individual nations. Latin American nationalism, variously, stems from both internal and external sources, is based on indigenous social values, imitates the values of outsiders, or stands in opposition to external values or interference. The effects of nationalism have varied, ranging in style from militant, intolerant, xenophobic, aggressive, and divisive at the one extreme, to pacific, benign, internationally cooperative, and domestically unifying at the other extreme.

The diversity of nationalism has led to domestic political tensions and resulted in a variety of foreign policies. The following discussion will identify only those variants of nationalism that have relevance for Latin American foreign policy, ignoring those of essentially domestic consequence.

Early Nationalist Sentiments

The roots of Latin American nationalism are found in the colonial era, when some native elites developed a sense of separate identity from Spain and Portugal. Between 1810 and 1824, when most of Spanish America ended its colonial status and achieved national independence, the fighting intensified the anti-Spanish feeling that had been building for some time. This Spanish American aversion has been called "creole nationalism," a term that grew out of the bitterness of *criollos* (Spaniards born in the New World and their offspring) toward the privileged Spanish authorities in America (*peninsulares*). It survived throughout the nineteenth century, prodded on by Spanish hostility toward the lost colonies and by xenophobia among some Spanish Americans, to whom anything Spanish was anathema.

The nationalist outcome in Brazil was very different. The royal Braganza family had fled from Portugal to Brazil during the Napoleonic invasion of the Iberian peninsula in 1807 and 1808 (the Spanish king and the heir to the throne had been arrested by the French). The Portuguese royal family returned to Lisbon in 1820, leaving Prince Pedro in America as regent to rule Brazil. He came under the influence of Brazilian nationalists and led the successful independence movement in 1822 with little bloodshed. Anti-Portuguese feeling was to be found among native Brazilians, but it was modified by the wide acceptance of two members of the old royal family, who would have succeeded to the Portuguese throne, as sovereigns of Brazil until 1889.

A strong sense of "Americanism" and Spanish American solidarity existed among some leaders of the new Latin American states. Sometimes called "continental nationalists," such prominent patriots as Simón Bolívar and José de San Martín hoped for political unity in Spanish America and visualized some sort of league of states to be organized along the lines of the viceregal boundaries. These plans were frustrated, however, as the Spanish American empire broke up into sixteen (later eighteen) separate nations. A number of boundary conflicts among the new states, inter-American wars, and foreign interventions helped to develop individual nationalist sentiments and to erode continental nationalism. Loyalties were often local rather than national in scope, although international conflict promoted national unity in the face of foreign threats.

A great deal of nineteenth-century Latin American nationalism, largely restricted to the small elite power groups, was often a superficial imitation of European and North American strains. Independence was won just as modern nationalism was taking shape in these other areas of the globe, stimulated by the American and French Revolutions (1776/1789). These elites, however, were divided among themselves.

In Spanish America, competing groups were organized into primitive political parties, actually cliques, labeled Conservative and Liberal (a European borrowing), each with a different nationalist perspective. Conservatives generally wished to perpetuate the colonial system, but with themselves rather than the Spaniards as leaders; they looked to the past for national identity and unity—a past that included authoritarian central governments, Roman Catholicism, rigid social stratification, and other elements of the Hispanic colonial tradition. Liberals rejected the colonial past. They were anti-Spanish to varying degrees and to some extent opposed the political, social, and educational roles of the Church, adopted anticlerical positions, and sought to replace the authoritarian political system with progressive forms and principles copied, especially, from France, Britain, and the United States.

Modernization and Nationalism

Later forms of Latin American nationalism were rooted in the values and tensions associated with the processes of political, social, and economic modernization. They dated essentially from the late nineteenth century, when modernization, largely fostered by native elites in league with foreign interests, helped to create new, politically aware socioeconomic groups. The rise of new social classes stimulated nationalist sentiments among the mobilized groups as they attempted to establish a broad consensus that would better serve their interests as they challenged traditional elite power structures. The continuing process of economic development and social conflict was further shaped by the impact of two world wars, the repercussions of the interbellum worldwide depression, the cold war, and foreign military intervention, as well as investment and economic assistance. The following discussion identifies the main forms of nationalism stimulated by modernization (following the categories posited by Whitaker and Jordan, 1966).

Modernism refers to the pursuit of national unification and development by progressive elites, usually with foreign help. The drive to develop, beginning in the nineteenth century, was itself a nationalist urge, a nation-building process looking to Europe and the United States for inspiration and identified with political and economic liberalism and cultural cosmopolitanism. Modernist advocates asserted that the best way to strengthen the nation was to draw as fully as possible on foreign sources, including capital investments, managerial skills, and mass immigration. Modernism was especially vigorous in Brazil, Argentina, Chile, Uruguay, and Mexico, where foreign enterprise and European immigration (of less significance in Mexico than the others) assumed great importance in national development.

Nativism, a Spanish American concept, was a nationalist reaction to modernism. It opposed the influx of foreign immigrants and other influences. It was based on both *criollo* national values and opposition to the values of others. Nativists such as the Argentines José Hernández, writing in the late nineteenth century, and Ricardo Rojas, in the early twentieth, urged that tradition be protected and their nation ridded of European cultural hegemony. Nativists often viewed their national pasts nostalgically and romantically and saw the nation's history as a struggle between natives and immigrants.

Antiyankeeism was related to nativism during the first third of the twentieth century. Traces of anti-Americanism were found throughout the nineteenth century, but they were not sustained until many Latin Americans were outraged by U.S. military and economic intervention in the Caribbean area. The expansion of U.S. interests stimulated nationalism not only in politics and economics but in cultural matters as well. A number of literary expressions of *antiyanquismo* during that time declared disillusionment with the course the U.S. democratic experiment had taken and warned of the threat of North American materialism to Hispanic spiritualism. Such sentiments existed in Brazil, but they were less pronounced there than in Spanish America as Brazilian leaders encouraged friendship with the United States. Brazilians, to the present day, do not hold the same suspicions and hostility toward foreigners as Spanish Americans.

The United States was severely criticized for its interventions. Antiyankeeism increased gradually during the three decades after World War II and sharply in the 1980s, not only because of such events as the military invasion of the Dominican Republic in 1965, subversion in Chile in the 1970s, and coercive policies in the Circum-Caribbean in the 1980s, but also because of resentment over U.S. economic and trade policies. At the same time, Latin American governments themselves were under pressures stemming from economic dislocations and social change and the United States presents a tangible object for resentment.

Economic nationalism was first embraced by the new upper middle class, primarily the industrial and entrepreneurial sectors, that emerged from the modernization process. It was later adopted by representatives of the other middle sectors, organized labor, and the student movement. (The appearance of the student movement paralleled modernization in the early twentieth century.) In contrast to the foreign orientation of the earlier modernists, economic nationalists stood for a modified statism. Although economic nationalism allows for an important role for private enterprise, its basic tenets held that the nation owns the subsoil and natural resources and that the national good prevails over private property rights.

Economic nationalism intensified after World War II and again in the late 1960s. In both periods the major stimulus was provided by U.S. economic policies. A major rallying point was a program of economic nationalism formulated by the UN Economic Commission for Latin America under the leadership of, first, the Argentine Raúl Prebisch and then the Mexican Víctor Urquidi. They argued that Latin America should develop its own industry by establishing protective tariffs and creating common markets. They also advocated commodity agreements and better terms of trade with other states in the UN Conference on Trade and Development (UNCTAD). They did not reject the use of foreign capital but argued that foreign interests should not interfere with Latin American industrialization. More radical schools of economic nationalism advocated the expropriation and nationalization of existing foreign enterprises and exclusion of further foreign investment. Prebisch and Urquidi would allow such investment, but only under closely supervised conditions.

Military socialism was a variant of economic nationalism that was combined with calls for social justice and distinguished by the stress put on the dominant role of the armed forces. It involved reform-oriented military regimes that abandoned their traditional role as defenders of the status quo in alliance with the upper classes and were willing to nationalize foreign enterprise. In 1936 a notable revolutionary movement in Paraguay was led by military men advocating a socialist program. Military socialist governments in Bolivia were in power from 1936 to 1943. The linking of military-led social reform with economic nationalism and anti-Americanism was found in the late 1960s and early 1970s, most significantly in the case of Peru. There the armed forces came to power in 1968 and embarked on a major social reform and economic development program counter to traditional upper-class interests. They also nationalized a subsidiary of Standard Oil Company and seized lands belonging to U.S. firms for a land reform program.

The military government asserted national rights to the land and subsoil resources and stated that foreign companies would not be allowed to control the national wealth. A similar government took power briefly in Bolivia in 1969. It also moved against U.S. companies and succeeded in nationalizing a Gulf Oil Company subsidiary.

Revolutionary nationalism was used by the radical Left as they attempted to use popular nationalism to further their cause. In the 1930s and 1940s Soviet-oriented Marxist movements tried to capture nationalism for the proletariat, often working with popular fronts composed of other leftist and sometimes centrist parties. Although Communists supported populism, they never controlled it. Their greatest successes occurred in Chile, where a Popular Front of Communists, Socialists, and Radicals governed under a Radical president from 1938 to 1952 (the Communists separated in 1947). A coalition of leftist parties was again in power under President Salvador Allende from 1970 to 1973.

Revolutionary nationalism was vividly expressed by the Cuban Revolution of 1959. Fidel Castro's combination of Cuban nationalism (in the tradition of José Martí) and Marxism-Leninism during the 1960s forced Latin America as well as the United States to recognize the slowness of economic and social development in the region. The Castro revolution provided ideological inspiration for other groups that began to use violence aimed at overthrowing the existing order and to express hatred for the United States. The new radical left was hostile to the orthodox Communist parties and scornful of their tactic of peaceful coexistence. They abandoned traditional modernist social values, including constitutional processes, claiming to have lost faith in the ability of "bourgeois democracy" (*democracia burguesa*) to achieve social justice. Revolutionary nationalism was not successful in gaining power outside of Cuba until the Sandinista movement eventually gained control of the government in Nicaragua after the revolution of 1979.

Post–Cold War Nationalism

A salient characteristic of the post–cold war era is the emergence in Latin America of a new, more positive nationalism that contrasts with the prior prevailing defensive postures. The change actually began to occur in the 1980s before the end of the cold war, with the result that Latin Americans today are generally less defensive toward each other and the outside world than at any time since the mid-1960s. They are more willing to engage in international cooperation (including, significantly, with the United States) and are eager to be an integral part of the emerging global system. (The following discussion relies on Atkins, 1992; and Cohen, 1992, 1993.)

This is not to deny the continued existence of xenophobia, antiyankeeism, economic nationalism, and revolutionary nationalism, which have declined but not yet disappeared. Some nationalists still argue that Latin Americans must organize among themselves as a way to assert their independence against imperialism. Others voiced apprehension that the disappearance of the Soviet Union and the U.S. victory in the Persian Gulf War in 1991 would inspire the United States to assume the role of world policeman, especially imposing its will in Latin America. Others say that U.S. offers of hemispheric free trade are aimed at resurrecting and institutionalizing U.S. regional imperialism. However, much of the Latin American Left, which is marked by considerable diversity, has deserted, at least temporarily, these types of arguments. They say that anti-imperialism is not a viable basis for a united Latin American front toward the outside world. Likewise, much of the nationalism of the politically heterogeneous Right, a substantial portion of which had an inherent suspicion of the outside world, has been marginalized or undergone changes in its perceptions and prescriptions.

The new nationalism is an excellent measure of changes in Latin American foreign policies. Statements from a majority of Latin American governments and their multilateral organizations, backed by policy actions, demonstrate that they seek to (1) strengthen their democracy through economic and social development and regional cooperation and integration; (2) negotiate agreements with external creditors rather than form a collective moratorium or "debtors' cartel"; (3) create a free international trading system; (4) deal jointly with problems of clandestine arms trade, terrorism, drug trafficking, and environmental degradation; and (5) promote discussions with other states and IGOs in a climate of goodwill.

The ascension of the new nationalism is a consequence of the confluence of a number of factors: First, Latin Americans had dismal experiences with military regimes, especially their repression and economic failure, which led to disenchantment not only with the Right and the Left but the dominant defensive foreign policy models generally adopted after World War II. Second, in the midst of the most severe depression in a half-century, Latin Americans, having decreased the polarization of their domestic politics, searched for alternative developmental models for economic reactivation. Third, the return to democracy and civilian rule combined with the adoption of economic neoliberalism to bring an unprecedented degree of homogeneity to prevailing Latin American political systems and a consensus about foreign policies. Fourth, the end of East-West conflict elevated other issues of more importance to Latin Americans—especially economic development and democratic strengthening—to the top of a mutually agreed-upon inter-American agenda. Finally, despite certain apprehensions, Latin Americans perceived that the United States, free of its cold war obsessions, was less inclined to intervene, less concerned with placing itself on the side of the status quo, and more willing to cooperate on a partnership basis. A caveat is in order, however: The positive nature of this nationalism is not necessarily permanent. It could revert to xenophobia if improvements in living standards and other areas of social equity are not forthcoming.

The New States

Special mention should be made of the nationalist orientations of twelve of the "new states"—the former British dependencies in the Circum-Caribbean that gained their independence beginning in 1962. The former British colonies, never Latin and no longer British, have searched for an American identity. Many of them formed the West Indies Federation between 1958 and 1962, anticipating the emergence of a single independent state. It dissolved, however, and separate entities were created, with others remaining dependent on Great Britain. Only four years after the dissolution of the federation, the new states and dependencies began to establish Pan Caribbean ties, based on their common political and social heritage, through economic integration organizations. The independent Commonwealth Caribbean Countries also sought ties with other regional states. All of them eventually joined the Organization of American States to establish formal affiliations with the rest of the Americas. They also continued their Old World ties, as members of the Commonwealth and signatories of the Lomé Convention with the European Community, which gives them special trading benefits.

Cultural ties with the United Kingdom are elusive. A British cultural facade was superimposed, variously, on African, East Indian, Oriental, and other ethnicities. Barbados is the most "English" among these new nations, duplicating Old World ways to a remarkable degree. Trinidad-Tobago perceives itself as "American" more than the others but has not rejected the British tradition. All but Guyana are constitutional monarchies with a governor-general representing the British crown (but with no political power). Although they criticize British policies, especially regarding aid and trade, anti-British nationalism is minimal.

FOREIGN POLICY DECISION STRUCTURE

The Primacy of Domestic Politics

Many students of foreign policy emphasize the interplay between domestic politics and foreign policy. In the case of Latin America, the latter tends to be an extension or projection of the former, even though foreign policy decision-making by its nature differs somewhat from the domestic process. Foreign policy can also be an important mode for furthering domestic political goals, including in the hands of opportunistic politicians who lack popular support or wish to divert attention from domestic political crises by focusing on nationalist foreign policy causes. Political advantage has been sought, and often gained, by both government and opposition leaders by raising such issues as territorial disputes with neighboring states, intervention by external powers, imperialism by foreign entrepreneurs, nationalization of foreign enterprises, and so on.

The foreign policy formulation process differs from state to state in Latin America because of variations in capability factors, including proximity to greater powers, the degree and character of social complexity, political organization and style, specific experiences and issues, and so on. This diversity makes regional generalizations difficult. Nevertheless, assuming that commonalities do exist, and that the same social milieu gives rise to foreign policy decisions as to domestic ones, some tentative observations and conclusions may be set down.

A problem for the analysis of Latin American foreign policy formulation has been the erroneous assumption or impression, expressed especially by dependency theorists, that those processes are overwhelmingly dominated by foreign influences, especially from the United States. If, indeed, foreigners are dominant, we may easily dismiss questions of foreign policy formulation. Such has probably been the case, at least at times, for certain small states, as in the Caribbean area during the period of intense U.S. imperialism during the first third of this century and, to a lesser but still important extent, in the 1980s. The same was said for Cuba, which was characterized as a Soviet "puppet" until the end of the cold war, and for Nicaragua in its relationship with the Soviet Union under the Sandinista government. Even for the weakest and most externally dominated states, however, this generalization is not completely accurate even when foreign pressures are being applied. In the 1980s even El Salvador and Cuba, in their relations with the United States and the Soviet Union, respectively, exhibited a certain independence in their decision-making capacities. This view of foreign dominance ignores the political complexity and relative foreign policy autonomy of the major regional states, as well as the isolated international environment of some of the smaller ones. This is not to deny that external factors play crucial roles in Latin American policy formulation, but it is to assert that those factors are not ubiquitous or omnipotent and are part of a more complex political process. Nor should we forget that many regional situations and issues require decisions largely divorced from U.S. or other external pressures.

Domestic Input Channels

Crucial among foreign policy factors are the views of politically powerful interest groups. Economic organizations, such as coffee growers in Colombia and meat and wheat producers in Argentina, especially attempt to influence foreign policy decisions. However, organized interest groups outside of the economic arena are rarely concerned primarily with influencing foreign policy, so that their impact on international relations tends to be a "spin-off" of domestic politics.

Foreign policy traditionally was monopolized by elite social sectors and represented their values and interests, with little reference to the larger public. The landed aristocracy and wealthy commercial urbanites have been internationally oriented, frequently with a special interest in foreign trade policy. Therefore, they have seen their interests served by friendly relations with foreign investors and the maintenance and expansion of foreign markets. Powerful agrarian, commercial, and sometimes industrial societies have been organized in almost every Latin American state to represent elite sectors and to promote their economic, including international, interests.

Economic development created new classes, which have challenged the upper class elite sector (who, ironically, had sponsored the development) for a share of social and economic benefits. As Latin America developed economically, the middle class expanded significantly. Its size varies considerably from state to state, but it generally challenged the modernist assumptions of traditional elites and substituted economic nationalism as the dominant basis for foreign policy perspectives. Most of the middle class, however, took little interest in foreign policy and was more narrowly concerned with career and employment opportunities. However, as the middle class expanded, became more secure, and acquired more political power, it took increased interest in foreign policy issues, usually urging more independent national roles in international politics but generally avoiding xenophobia.

Altogether new groupings also appeared and expanded as a result of continuing modernization, most notably in urban and mining labor. The dominant foreign policy perspective was anticapitalist and anti–United States. Labor unions were important in the early 1990s in Argentina, Mexico, Bolivia, Venezuela, and Peru. Unions had been highly influential in some countries in the past, as in Brazil and Chile before the advent of military regimes in 1964 and 1973, respectively (they began to recapture somewhat their positions after those countries returned to elected civilian rule, in 1985 in Brazil and 1989 in Chile). Their influence is rising in other countries as economies recover and democracy becomes more institutionalized. In any event, the energies of labor unions are directed primarily at gaining more economic benefits for their members. However, when nationalization of important foreign corporations and government direction of internationally concerned local enterprises occurred, labor was drawn into the foreign policy arena, since the state became the manager toward whom labor must then direct its attention. Conversely, with the widespread adoption of what were termed neoliberal economic policies, privatization of state-run enterprises, and increased acceptance of foreign investment, labor relations will shift back to the private sector. This trend may foreshadow more conflictual relations with external business enterprises.

Peasants (*campesinos*), traditionally inert, have in some states demanded improvements in their socioeconomic conditions. Nowhere, however, are they organized to exert much leverage in foreign policy, nor do they show real interest in doing so. They have been of foreign policy significance, however, in states where rural guerrilla activities occurred or where drug trafficking depended on their coca production—both sometimes foreign-inspired and foreign-supported enterprises. Governments have been aware of the peasants' importance in the insurgents' strategies and the drug traffickers' operations and sometimes have been willing to exchange some agrarian reform for *campesino* support, which can translate into neutrality in guerrilla warfare or cooperation in attempts to stem the drug trade. Success in the latter effort especially has been difficult to achieve.

It is not easy to measure the degree to which public opinion influences foreign policy. States with high literacy levels, good educational systems, and competent newspapers and other forms of communications that enjoy relative freedom of expression generally also exhibit a high level of public awareness of foreign policy issues. This applies to Argentina, Uruguay, Costa Rica, Mexico, Venezuela, Chile, Colombia, and most of the Commonwealth Caribbean Countries. Even in these states, however, and certainly in the others, public debates over foreign policy are seldom carried on in a systematic way, and elections rarely hinge on foreign policy issues other than economic ones (although exceptions have existed). Consequently, political parties tend not to pursue strong or consistent positions on international issues in their campaigns and other public statements. Although they have used nationalist themes as campaign issues, efforts have been directed more at winning elections than at forming a basis for policy. The external debt question was a major issue in elections in the 1980s but was closely linked to domestic economic and social concerns.

The Roman Catholic Church has also sometimes influenced foreign policy decision-making. Church interests were traditionally associated with the small oligarchies and their politics of the status quo. The church's political power was seriously eroded over the years to the point where it no longer had such strong influence on decision-making. As its power declined, the church's policies, including those concerning international relations, changed from predictably supporting upper-class interests. Deep divisions exist within the church—in individual national organizations, Latin American regional meetings, and relations with the Holy See (see Chapter 6).

Decision-making Agents

The main feature of Latin American decision-making processes is the primary role of the chief executive and, conversely, the relative weakness of the legislative and judicial branches in policy formulation. Executive power is derived not only from constitutional provisions—the president normally is charged with responsibility and authority in the conduct of external affairs—but even more from the political culture that places high reliance on the executive power, whether or not it is operating under republican constitutional procedures.

The idea of republicanism with the presidential system was adopted by almost all the Latin American states when they became independent in the early nineteenth century. However, the widespread existence of the *caudillo* in Spanish America, or the *coroneis* in Brazil (a local strongman, boss; literally, a man on horseback), reflected a disposition for authoritarianism and personalism and an emphasis on individual personalities rather than public issues. *Caudillismo,* typical of the nineteenth century, declined as a governmental form in the twentieth century. Some caudillos were still found in the 1960s, but the last approximations disappeared during the 1980s.

In the meantime, beginning in the late nineteenth and early twentieth centuries, constitutional democracies were established for various periods of time in several states. Nevertheless, the executives, whether achieving office constitutionally through elections or arbitrarily through force, continued to be shaped by tradition. Personalism and even authoritarianism have been reflected in many democratic experiments. Elected presidents in most instances have dominated their legislatures and exercised extraordinary powers. Fidel Castro of Cuba exhibits traditional Latin American attributes despite the Marxist-Leninist ideology of his movement. Military rule was a common form of government, especially in the 1960s and 1970s. In contrast to caudillos, who erected dictatorships over the military and consolidated personal power, military rule involved leaders who held power as agents for the entire military establishment and superimposed the military structure over governmental organization. Military regimes, although authoritarian, are by definition not personalist.

Although political culture provides the most important source of Latin American executive power in foreign (and other) affairs, constitutional provisions are also important sources of power as well as restrictions on executive freedom. Formal constitutional authority is divided between executive and legislative branches. Latin American constitutions, like most of those around the world that structure presidential systems, give the chief executive primary responsibility and authority in foreign affairs, including national defense. The president is charged with such matters as negotiating treaties, with congressional approval; making diplomatic appointments, also usually requiring congressional approval; and acting as commander in chief of the armed forces, although presidents no longer take the field at the head of their forces. Congressional constitutional roles in foreign policy stem from their required consent to treaties prior to ratification and their power to confirm diplomatic and military appointments, to interrogate ministers (in some countries), and, most important, to appropriate funds.

Presidential-congressional conflict in Latin America has often been tense, especially in multiparty systems. Congresses have often blocked international agreements negotiated by the executive. Congresses have, from time to time, refused to approve appointments or appropriate monies to finance foreign policy projects or administration. They have sometimes exercised their power to deny a president's travel request. These constitutional powers, however, are insufficient to allow congresses to compete effectively with executive position, prestige, organization, and other resources in foreign affairs.

The foreign minister usually makes day-to-day policy decisions and acts as a spokesperson for the chief executive. The foreign minister normally (although certainly not always) is a distinguished and notable public person. Latin America has produced, over the years, a number of skillful, internationally renowned *cancilleres* (foreign ministers). In the less personalist and more institutionalized political systems, they are supported by permanent career foreign services, which have been increasingly professionalized with the intensification of Latin American involvement in international politics since World War II. The diplomatic services traditionally were recruited from and dominated by the small upper-class elite. This situation continues in a large number of countries despite important changes in class mobility in the societies at large. Thus, Latin American diplomats traditionally have tended to have upper-class attributes—to be sophisticated, cosmopolitan, well-educated, and conservative—and to share upper-class interests and goals in foreign policy matters. They remain so in those countries where tradition continues. This description does not apply to nations with large middle classes or those that have undergone revolutionary or other rapid social change.

Composed of pragmatic, professional diplomats, the foreign services tend to adjust and accommodate to changing administrations and policies. Foreign service academies have been established in the major Latin American countries, and the recruitment of diplomatic personnel according to merit is required by law in most states. Admission to the service in many states, however, is often the result of personal contacts or political influence. On occasion, ambassadors are well-known intellectuals or artists who carry a great deal of prestige with them to the nation where they are accredited. More often they are prominent political figures; sometimes they are appointed so as to remove them from competition for political power with the chief executive. Some career diplomats achieve ambassadorial rank, but they are usually not posted to major capitals.

Foreign ministries have been increasingly challenged by other bureaucracies in foreign policy administration. Ministries of the armed forces have had inherent interests and roles in foreign policy. These concerns stem from their role in national defense, their regularized contacts with their counterparts in the Americas, and their dependence on external states for arms and training. They have also been a force for industrialization, in order to build up their own countries' arms production, notably in Argentina, Chile, Mexico, and especially Brazil (which became virtually self-sufficient in military arms and equipment and one of the world's principal arms exporters). The military often controlled some or all intelligence services; for those services that were not formally part of the defense establishment, the armed forces supplied active or retired personnel to direct and staff them. Beginning in the 1980s, however, several civilian governments acted to "civilianize" the intelligence services because of their human rights abuses by the preceding military regimes. Finally, for two decades from the early 1960s, many military establishments viewed themselves as having crucial nation-building roles, whether they exercised power as direct rulers or as an interest group, and consequently they were caught up in broad economic and social development issues and concerned with foreign policy decisions related to developmental strategies. With the decline of military governments in the 1980s, and with the loss of prestige that generally accompanied their exit from power, their foreign policy roles were reduced, although they remained influential.

Other agencies have also been drawn into the foreign policy process. An interior ministry (usually called *gobernación*) generally controls the national policy forces and therefore often has paramilitary functions involving international concerns, especially as they have related to urban guerrilla warfare. The minister of interior is usually the ranking cabinet member according to law or practice and consequently often has a voice in general policy matters. Other bureaucracies, such as the finance or economics ministry, the central bank, and many autonomous or semiautonomous economic and development agencies established in recent years are involved in matters relating to their provinces. For example, the extensive economic content of Latin American foreign policies moved beyond traditional concerns with foreign trade, investment, and immigration, to newer ones involving international economic institutions, expropriation of foreign enterprises, regional integration, foreign economic aid, and "developmentalism" in general. These concerns most recently have been widely reoriented in terms of economic neoliberalism.

FOREIGN POLICY ORIENTATIONS

Ends and Means

Objectives and Tactics. Latin American states pursue national interests that are common to virtually all states as they attempt to ensure their survival, security, and well-being. In the Latin American context, these ultimate objectives translate into long-range goals that reflect the regional states' capability levels, national consciousnesses, and domestic politics. Their primary interests have traditionally been to maintain their sovereignty and independence from outside states, to strengthen their economies, and to achieve national prestige. Some states have sought to assert their leadership in inter-American affairs and, at times and on a more modest scale, in world affairs. In fact, in assessing policy, a basic distinction should be made between actions formulated for intraregional relations and those for relations with external actors.

The limitations of Latin American capability bear strongly on the choice of policy means as well as ends. In the global arena, the fact that Latin Americans have operated from a position of relative weakness has significantly affected their selection of policy instruments and strategies. Most Latin American states are weak in a global sense, ranking low in the order of world power stratification. In general, the range of techniques available to the Latin American states in global politics has been limited because they must rely on persuasions other than physical power, either military or economic. The regional states tend to exert influence as best they can with such tactics as: (1) playing active roles in international organizations and attempting to align among themselves in relations with the outside world; (2) promoting international law and supporting such principles and procedures as nonintervention and peaceful settlement of disputes; (3) appealing to humanitarian sentiments and moral principles; (4) exploiting the rivalries of greater powers while remaining as noncommittal as possible themselves; and (5) bargaining with nations that provide markets for their natural resources and other goods.

Intraregional politics are more complex, in that Latin America is a microcosm of the global system with a wide range of relative power positions and, consequently, of ends and means adopted by the regional states toward each other. Latin American great powers have played the game of power politics within the regions—most notably in the Southern Cone—including the pursuit of imperialist goals and the use of military force as well as other techniques. The other states are thus reduced to using small-state tactics in their relations with the larger Latin American states. They attempt to restrain the larger ones through international organization and law and by capitalizing on regional rivalries—a combination of persuasion and manipulation.

Latin Americans have also cooperated among themselves, within international organizations and through informal means of association. From the national beginnings to the present day, Latin American states have participated in organizations on all levels—among themselves within their own region, in the Inter-American System of multilateral cooperation with the United States and Canada, and in global, Third World, and specialized extrahemispheric institutions. In the extraregional institutions, Latin Americans tend to associate among themselves as a regional bloc. They have generally worked together, formally and informally, in order to realize mutual goals and to facilitate their common bargaining power with the outside world. In the latter instance, their reasoning is that cooperation among themselves and presentation of a united front to the outside world partially compensates for their individual weaknesses in international relations. Despite many failures, frustrations, and disappointments over the years, Latin Americans have persisted in the organizational-associational tactic.

Beginning in the 1980s and continuing into the post–cold war era, Latin Americans have engaged in a form of association called *concertación*—meaning "acting in concert" or intra–Latin American foreign policy collaboration and cooperation. It has been pursued in the revival of intergovernmental organizations dealing with virtually all of the multilateral issues. It was further reflected in a movement away from old diplomatic formality and protocol to intraregional consultation involving frequent personal contacts at all levels of authority (Frohman, 1990). For skeptical observers, the revived enthusiasm for concerted action represented nothing new and so was not especially significant—it was, they said, no more than a new version of the old rhetoric about Latin American unity. For others, however, concertación was not the mere extension of the long-established inclination to mutual association toward the outside world, but an important qualitative change involving shared Latin American policy orientations and increased assertiveness toward the United States and other outsiders (Karl, 1989). In this sense concertación also means "harmonization." They explain collaboration as the combination of a decline of U.S. hegemonic capabilities and Latin American democratic governments seeking collective self-protection. Some of the latter analysts say that the convergence of Latin American foreign policies has been profound but not total—that each government retains its own foreign policy framework and interests that reflect its traditions, objectives, conditions, and capabilities (Klaveren, 1990). The factors inspiring the "new nationalism" in Latin America, discussed above, were also behind the thrust for concertación.

Independence and Autonomy. The desire for an independent or autonomous role in international relations, not defined in an absolute sense but as "more freedom of action," is a reflection of Latin American national consciousness. The realization of independence in foreign policy, however, has been frustrated by capability deficiencies, and in important ways the regional states have been subordinate to or at times even subjugated by external states. Thus a corollary objective has been to reduce their political, military, and especially economic reliance on outside actors. Freedom of action is difficult for all relatively small states, and the notion of sovereign independence for them in a strict sense is fictional. Nevertheless, as many regional actors stand in a dependent relationship to external actors, others have achieved a modicum of autonomy, and independence is a serious aspiration with virtually all of them. The pursuit of autonomy in foreign policy is not only difficult for many states but often paradoxical. Latin American states want to achieve or maintain independence in their international actions, but to do so they must be strong in relation to the outside world; to become strong they must obtain some sort of assistance from the outside world toward which they wish to be independent, thus increasing the chances for a dependent relationship. Much of Latin America's continuing dilemma, then, is this: How are nations to improve their capability and modernize their societies while preventing inordinate influence in their economies and political systems?

The greatest dependence on others has been economic and financial, areas in which the Latin American states as a whole are the most vulnerable to external influences. Their reliance on public and private investment and loans has circumscribed their independence to varying degrees. Because export markets are crucial to their well-being, most Latin American states strive to maintain friendly relations with their best customers. They have long sought foreign investment capital and assumed it was necessary for economic growth. Increasingly, however, expropriation of foreign enterprise was demanded by certain nationalist groups and effected by some governments. Beginning in the 1930s and increasingly throughout the 1960s and 1970s, governments were forced to calculate the relative economic and political benefits and risks between maintaining their appeal to foreign investors and pursuing expropriation. The thrust for expropriation declined in the 1980s and then was replaced with a new effort to engage in free trade with outside states and to attract private foreign investment. The process reflects a sense of urgency and determination, and it is politically difficult, entailing dislocations and abrupt changes.

Latin Americans have often attempted to remain independent from external actors by playing them against each other. The exploitation of great-power rivalries has long been a favored technique. For example, Colombia played on the rivalries among Great Britain, the United States, and France throughout the nineteenth century and thereby maintained control of the isthmus of Panama; but when the rivalry faded after 1901 and the United States was left unchallenged, Colombia lost control of her useful province. In addition, Latin American states seek to "diversify" their dependence by accepting economic, military, and other aid from a variety of external states, hoping that no single one will have an overwhelming position of influence. On the inter-American scene, the small states have attempted to exploit local great-power rivalries. For example, both Uruguay and Paraguay, with varying success, have tried to balance Argentina and Brazil. During the cold war, Latin Americans were well aware of U.S. concern about the growth of communism in Latin America and were sometimes able to exploit it to their benefit by persuading the United States to commit relatively large amounts of aid.

A certain foreign policy autonomy of the Latin American states was evident before the end of the cold war (Atkins, 1992). After the mid-1960s most Latin American governments increasingly sought more freedom of action, with varying success. They generally had no more than a nominal commitment to U.S.-defined strategic denial and emphasized their own economic development. U.S. relations with Mexico were increasingly characterized by mutual dependence. Brazil and other key South American states did not simply follow the lead of the United States (or of anyone else) in international relations, despite such debilities as huge external debt. Even in Central America the United States did not get its way easily. Two peace initiatives, the Contadora process and the Esquipulus II accord, meant that U.S. primacy was challenged by the Latin American states themselves, including all of the most important ones and even several weak ones who were supposed to be U.S. clients. In the post–cold war period, the thrust for independence in foreign policy has become more pronounced. Latin Americans themselves have taken greater initiative in international relations, revealed in their determined regional and subregional organizational activities and regular interstate consultations and informal understandings from which the United States and other outsiders are excluded (John Martz in Atkins, 1992).

Leadership Aspirations. Latin American states' aspirations for playing important individual power roles have been modest. They have generally eschewed efforts to enhance their world power beyond ensuring their physical survival and garnering economic benefits. Some of them have had the potential and ambition to change this status upward, although they have not been taken seriously in power terms by the leaders of the international system, with the tentative exceptions of Argentina before World War I and Brazil for a time after the mid-1970s. Argentina, from the turn of this century until the late 1920s, seemed to be headed for great-power status but instead entered a long period of steady decline. Brazil in the late 1970s perhaps rivaled in power such important states as Indonesia and India, but severe internal political, economic, and social problems eroded its capabilities in the 1980s and 1990s. At times, several Latin American states have played key roles in inter-American affairs—Chile, Mexico, Venezuela, Colombia, and Peru, in addition to Brazil and Argentina. None, so far, has done so for a sustained period.

Economic Policies. International economic policy represents the clearest nexus between Latin American domestic and foreign policy. In virtually every Latin American state since independence, foreign policy has to some degree been an extension of domestic economic interests and concerns. Other objectives often are compromised for economic ones. For example, much of the increase in Latin American relations with Communist states from the late 1960s was explained in terms of economic needs with minimal reference to ideological positions. Even the most conservative and anti-Communist (including military) governments adopted pragmatic stances toward the Soviet Union and Eastern Europe when trade relations were offered, especially with the Soviet willingness to accept terms of trade skewed sharply in favor of Latin America.

The foreign trade of every regional state is crucial to its economic well-being. Exports are required to generate the foreign currency necessary to pay for essential imports and to help repay foreign debt. Export taxes and import duties provide a significant source of government revenue for various operations, including development programs. Therefore, Latin American foreign policies usually aim to maximize export opportunities, which includes both protecting and expanding markets. Latin American diplomats spend a great deal of their time aiding exporters. They play the traditional diplomatic game of projecting a favorable national image at least partly to promote the confidence of outsiders in their economic worthiness.

Alignment

Isolationism and Neutralism. Latin American states have generally come to accept their small-power roles. Concomitantly, they have assumed noncommittal positions in great-power conflicts as much as possible.

Upon becoming independent, most Spanish American states and Brazil were the first "new states" to understand and oppose imperialism by attempting isolationism and considering neutralism. Yet Latin Americans sought the support of European states to assist their national development and reconciled finally to the United States as chief guarantor of their sovereignty and security. During World War I, Latin America failed to respond to U.S. urging for hemispheric solidarity. The leading states of Argentina, Chile, Colombia, and Mexico were neutral. During World War II, however, only Argentina and Chile remained neutral until the latter months of the hostilities.

After World War II, Latin American states sought to remain aloof in the cold war, with varying degrees of success. Isolationist positions toward global rivalries were pursued in a political and military sense, but Latin Americans remained active in world economic relations. "Aloofness" and "isolationism" did not mean "neutralism" or "nonalignment," however, except in a few instances, and only a small minority of Latin American states adopted neutral positions in international politics. Then, in the late 1960s, a number of Latin American states began to adopt some form of the nonaligned orientation.

One of the earliest and most important neutralist postures was *justicialismo* in Argentina, a "third position" claiming to reconcile capitalism and communism adopted under President Juan Perón (1946–1955). Perón's strategy did not represent a link between Latin America and the incipient Afro-Asian bloc that developed into the Nonaligned Movement during the cold war. His concept was more akin to the "third way" advocated by President Charles de Gaulle of France. It was a Peronist version of Argentine traditions of neutralism, nonintervention, and policy independence, reflected in the rejection of alliances in the nineteenth century and later neutrality in the two world wars. Neutralist orientations were articulated by the administration of Jacobo Arbenz Guzmán in Guatemala (1950–1954) and the brief presidency of Jânio Quadros in Brazil (January–August 1961). Their neutralism paralleled the Nonaligned Movement's concept of "noncommitment," but neither of them became members (although Brazil sent observers to the Belgrade meeting in 1961).

Strong Latin American political forces worked against neutralism following World War II. The armed forces generally desired close relations with the United States, and the internationalist upper and middle classes recognized the importance of traditional trading relationships and the perils of radical change to their social and economic positions. In fact all Latin American states joined in formal military alliance with the United States in the Rio Treaty of 1947. Beginning in the early 1960s, however, and accelerating thereafter, a large number of Latin American states joined the Nonaligned Movement.

Nonalignment. Latin American nonalignment has been a multifaceted objective variously interpreted by Latin American governments. Interest in the Nonaligned Movement revealed mixed motives, with domestic imperatives helping to explain the degree of commitment or level of activity. Although most Latin American states remained formally allied with the United States through the Rio Treaty, some joined the Nonaligned Movement because they saw their interests as more congruent with those of Asia and Africa. Cuba withdrew from the treaty and aligned with the Soviet Union. Nicaragua also sought political-military unity with the Soviet Union. For most of the other states the Rio Treaty was moribund. Only one of the new states (Trinidad-Tobago) adhered to the treaty after becoming independent.

Nonalignment was also part of the overall Latin American strategy aimed at reducing dependence on the United States through developing diversified external bilateral and organizational relationships as alternatives to the status quo balance of power. The Nonaligned Movement had the practical advantage of placing participants in a position to bargain for assistance from both sides in the East-West competition. Other Latin American states did not participate in the movement, some because their U.S. alignment was more beneficial to them and others because they found little value in adopting a neutral posture.

Eventually sixteen Latin American states became full members of the Nonaligned Movement. They were Argentina, Belize, Bolivia, Chile, Colombia, Cuba, Ecuador, Grenada, Guyana, Jamaica, Nicaragua, Panama, Peru, St. Lucia, Suriname, and Trinidad-Tobago. Eight more had attended as observers: Barbados, Brazil, Costa Rica, Dominica, El Salvador, Mexico, Uruguay, and Venezuela. The nine Latin American states not participating in the Nonaligned Movement were Antigua-Barbuda, Bahamas, Dominican Republic, Guatemala, Haiti, Honduras, Paraguay, St. Kitts–Nevis, and St. Vincent. In addition, three Latin American regional organizations—the United Nations Economic Commission for Latin America and the Caribbean, the Latin American Economic System, and the Latin American Energy Organization—sent observers to nonaligned meetings over the years.

National Security and Geopolitics

Latin Americans have sometimes formulated policies in terms of the traditional national security concern about military threats to territorial integrity and physical safety posed by foreign incursions, whether the European great powers, the United States, or other Latin American states. From the earliest days of statehood, Latin Americans tended to band together when outsiders intervened or exerted other pressures. Since World War II, however, in most Latin American countries for most of the time, national security has been synonymous with national development, with emphasis on internal unity and economic well-being. External threat perceptions tended to be limited to contiguous border and territorial disputes and, in some cases, great-power intervention. As a general but not exclusive matter, whenever the subject of security entered the policy debate, the imperative to promote national socioeconomic well-being tended to supplant military defensive preparations.

Important exceptions to this trend were found in the geopolitical strategic visions in the Southern Cone states, dating from the nineteenth century. They were most notable in Brazil, Argentina, and Chile and particularly strong within the armed forces and their civilian allies, where geopolitical strategic outlooks influenced their foreign policies. Geopolitical schools of thought include general theories of IR, explanations of Southern Cone international politics, and specific prescriptions for state action (both domestic and foreign). These theories guided both domestic and foreign policies of Southern Cone military regimes from the early 1960s into the 1980s. Geopolitical bases for policy declined with the return to democratic civilian governments in the Southern Cone. In my view Southern Cone geopoliticians do not espouse serious theories of IR, but their conjectures must be taken seriously as guides to understanding aspects of their foreign policies.

Jack Child (1985) defines geopolitics (certainly as used by Southern Cone proponents) as the relationship of geography to power politics. He warns against equating "geopolitics" with "political geography," or the wide-ranging relationship of politics to geography. (An earlier section in this chapter indicates how some geographical factors have influenced foreign policies—an exercise in political geography.) Political geography, he says, fails to capture the aggressiveness and theoretical content of Southern Cone geopolitics. That thinking is based in the organic theory of the state, an approach in disrepute in Europe and the United States since its absorption by fascist theorists in the 1930s. It has nevertheless been carried on in Southern Cone writings and, from the 1960s into the 1980s, formed the basis for military government practice. Those writings draw heavily on the German *geopolitik-realpolitik* traditions, extreme versions of power politics viewing international relations as a Darwinian process in which the strongest and most ruthless states survive and dominate the weaker ones. States are living organisms competing and struggling in a world where might makes right. They drive to expand to their full capacity, both geographically and in terms of power, through the extension of "living frontiers."

According to Child, Brazil has produced the most significant geopolitical schools, whereas Argentine thinking largely rests on perceptions of Brazilian expansionism and encroachment into Argentina's natural sphere of influence. Argentine schools adopt a more maritime orientation than the Brazilian ones. Chilean geopolitics is the least developed of the three; it is also largely maritime in content. One major theme in Southern Cone geopolitics is the previously noted ABC rivalry for influence, extended to include security and ambitions in the South Atlantic and Antarctica. Brazil's security concerns further extend to West Africa and Chile's to the South Pacific; Brazil also relates geopolitics to its thrust to be a world power (*grandeza*). Nuclear considerations have entered Argentine and Brazilian calculations. During the periods of military regimes, the geopolitical theories provided models for authoritarian national security states in their different forms.

Geopolitical thinking justified domestic repression. The military regimes smothered the political opposition in the name of national security doctrines that were in part concerned with fears of "the enemy within." Those fears propelled "security forces" into "internal wars," which started as counterinsurgency movements but eventually led to the widespread killing of many civilians.

The geopolitical thinking that flourished in the Southern Cone in the 1960s and 1970s declined as bases for policy in the 1980s as military regimes gave way to constitutional governments. A simultaneous shift in geopolitical thinking began in about 1982, arising among reformist geopoliticians associated with the Peruvian army and spreading from there (Child, 1990). It advocated an end to chauvinism, argued that democracy was weakened by geopolitically based conflicts and competition with neighbors, and called for integrated interstate approaches to common problems. It was also critical of the United States and its domination of the Inter-American System to the detriment of Latin American interests. In my view, this current of thinking is not so much geopolitics (as defined above) as much as a rejection of it and the adoption of regionalism.

BIBLIOGRAPHIC COMMENT

Davis, Wilson, and others (1975) was the first comprehensive application of foreign policy analysis to the regional states, followed by Ferris and Lincoln (1981), Drekonja and Tokatlian (1983), Lincoln and Ferris (1984), Muñoz and Tulchin (1984), and Puig (1984); Braveboy-Wagner (1989), and Bryan and Serbín (1994) do so for the English-speaking states. Russell (1990) applies decision theory to the analysis of Latin American foreign policy making; Tomassini (1988) and Klaveren (1992) are articles in a similar theoretical vein; and Ebel, Taras, and Cochrane (1991) consider the effect of political culture in the Circum-Caribbean. Whitaker and Jordan (1966) is a thorough general work on Latin American nationalism, and Baily (1971) analyzes a collection of readings on the subject. Cohen (1992, 1993) lays out the elements of the "new nationalism" of the 1980s and 1990s. On the concept of *concertación* and related aspects, see Frohman (1990), Karl (1989), and Klaveren (1990). Child (1985, 1988, 1990) provide authoritative works on Latin American geopolitical thinking and Pittman (1981) is a thorough presentation of Latin American geopolitical writings.

CHAPTER FOUR

Nonhemispheric States and Canada

THE LATIN AMERICAN POLICIES of selected states outside the Western Hemisphere and of Canada are examined in this chapter. Much of the study of Latin America's international relations was traditionally preoccupied with the role of the United States. As the following discussion should indicate, however, other external states have been closely involved in the region, a matter now well recognized by analysts. European involvement reached its greatest height prior to World War I. It was revived in the 1970s and carried forward to the present day. The presence of the Soviet Union was notable after 1917 but not prominent until the connection with Cuba after 1959. Since the Soviet Union's dissolution in 1991, Russia and the other successor states have had little interest in the region. A broad array of other nonhemispheric states developed Latin American policies. Three of them are treated in this chapter: Japan, with overwhelmingly economic interests; Israel, with an essentially political approach toward Latin America and, until recently, an important military supplier; and the People's Republic of China, a highly significant global actor with vacillating Latin American policies. The position of Canada is also analyzed in recognition of its increasingly significant regional activity.

EUROPEAN PERSPECTIVES OF LATIN AMERICA

Origins of Policies

During the colonial period most of the Latin American region was ruled by Spain and Portugal, with the small Caribbean remainder belonging to other European masters. The region was of immense importance to the two primary imperial powers. For the challengers to the Iberian position in the Americas, actions in the region were a part of, and often a sidelight to, their competition with other European states on a sometimes global scale. Nevertheless, the foundations for Spanish, Portuguese, and other European views of Latin America as a weak and even inferior set of entities were established during the colonial era. Furthermore, cer-

81

tain Spanish, British, French, Dutch, and Danish colonies obtained during the active colonial presence, some as late as the first third of the nineteenth century, remained territorial intrusions in the Latin American subsystem, some of them to the present day. In the meantime, after the successful movements for independence, the emergence of new Latin American states between 1804 and 1824 and their subsequent search for nationhood stimulated rivalry among the external powers to gain regional influence or control.

The United Kingdom's interests in Latin America date from the colonial period (as England before 1707 and Great Britain after that date) when it gained territorial and commercial positions in the region. During an early stage of the Latin American movements for independence, while Spain was ruled by Napoleon, the British apparently intended to annex large portions of Spanish territory. However, after an unsuccessful military effort in the Plata River region in 1807 and 1808 and an aborted one in Mexico in 1808, Britain changed its approach. From 1808–1824 Britain covertly assisted the Spanish American patriots in order to prevent France from taking advantage of the situation, correctly assuming that Britain would be able to dominate the new states sufficiently to achieve its purposes without colonizing them. In 1825 Britain recognized the independent Latin American republics, even though it preferred they choose some kind of monarchy. Thereafter, Great Britain was the dominant external power in Latin America, with the important exception of Mexico.

British goals were first and foremost commercial in nature. Holding a primary position in most of the region, Britain was focused on extending its new industrial strength by consolidating and expanding its economic position in Latin America. Its merchant fleets and superior naval power dominated the Atlantic and served to support British commercial objectives, at the same time denying expansion by other external states. Great Britain became especially well entrenched in southern South America, holding preeminent commercial positions in Argentina, Brazil, and Uruguay. British interests were not entirely economic, however, at least not in the Caribbean area, where it had ambitions to build and control a Central American canal and to protect existing colonies. Great Britain felt obliged to prevent or impede French intrusion and U.S. expansion into the area. It initially attempted to act in concert with the United States to deter other European expansion. In 1823, Britain proposed a bilateral declaration asserting that neither party had territorial designs on the Spanish Empire and opposing any attempt by the Holy Alliance and Spain to recapture former Spanish colonies. U.S. President James Monroe refused to join in such a declaration and issued his own unilateral statement. Britain encountered strong U.S. opposition over the canal issue. In order to soften the intense rivalry, Britain agreed with the United States in the Clayton-Bulwer Treaty of 1850 that neither would unilaterally pursue a transisthmian canal project.

Acquisition of additional territory was not an important aspect of British policy by this time. The only land annexed during the Latin American national period was the remote Falkland Islands in the South Atlantic Ocean, acquired by force from Argentina in 1833 but based on an earlier claim. Between 1844 and 1860, Britain exercised a protectorate over the Central American Mosquito coast, roughly the Caribbean coast of Nicaragua today. Already existing colonies gave rise to a number of boundary disputes with Latin American states, some of which continue into the 1990s. These disputes have included conflict with Argentina over the Falklands (called the Islas Malvinas in Argentina), with Venezuela over British Guiana (now Guyana) boundary, and with Mexico and Guatemala over parts of British Honduras (now Belize).

Spain, the preeminent colonial power in Latin America, was reduced to marginal importance after Spanish American independence. Spain sought to recover its former colonies from time to time, but it was then a minor European power and did not figure prominently in regional affairs. After unsuccessfully opposing the independence of its American colonies, Spain was obsessed with the desire to regain the empire. When Ferdinand VII returned to the Spanish throne in 1815, he attempted to gain support for Spanish reconquest of the region. But British opposition restrained France and other European states sympathetic to Spain, and by 1824 reconquest was an unrealistic prospect. Nevertheless, even after most of Spanish America was safely independent, Spain refused to recognize its former colonies and intermittently plotted to recover them.

For most of the nineteenth century, beginning in 1820, Spain was deeply divided by revolution and civil war. Policies toward the Americas reflected the cleavages in Spanish politics. The Liberal government, which came to power after Ferdinand's death in 1833, temporarily abandoned plans for reconquest and pursued a conciliatory policy toward Latin America. Despite violent opposition from traditionalists, Spain began to recognize the sovereign independence of Latin American states, beginning with Mexico in 1836. It also began to negotiate for indemnification for damages sustained by Spanish nationals during the preceding years of violence and over the question of nationality status for Spaniards who had chosen to remain in America or who were then beginning to emigrate there. Questions of recognition, debt, and citizenship dominated relations until they had been substantially settled, with some exceptions, by the mid-1860s (Víctor Alba in Davis, Wilson, and others, 1975:Ch. 4).

In contrast to the bitterness that prevailed between Spain and Spanish America during the movements for independence and the early national period, Portugal relinquished control of Brazil in a relatively peaceful manner. Portugal had not exercised as strict control over Brazil as Spain had in its American empire, except during the Portuguese royal family residence in Brazil from 1808 to 1821 while the French occupied Portugal. When the Brazilians decided to declare their independence in 1822, they were led by the heir to the Portuguese throne, who was then regent in Brazil. He and his son ruled as emperors of Brazil until 1889. Portugal almost immediately reconciled itself to the loss of its American colony, recognizing the independent Brazilian state in 1825. This Portuguese policy was heavily influenced by Great Britain, which had maintained an alliance with Portugal since the early eighteenth century and continued to exercise influence throughout the nineteenth century and beyond. In 1810, Great Britain and Portugal, whose government was then in Brazil, had signed trade agreements giving the British a preeminent position in Brazilian markets. The British had been responsible two years earlier for the royal family's escape to Brazil aboard a British ship during the Napoleonic invasions. Subsequently, Britain had acted as the diplomatic intermediary between Portugal and Brazil during their negotiations for recognition. An independent Brazil was favorable to British interests, and Britain used its influence over the subservient Portuguese government. Portugal was also the weaker partner in the Portuguese-Brazilian relationship.

By the time of Latin American independence, France had lost much of its American empire, but it persisted more than any other external state in its designs on Latin American territory during the nineteenth century. The French imperialist thrust eventually ended in total frustration. The vast Louisiana Territory, which France had acquired from Spain by treaty in 1800, was sold to the United States in 1803. France's prize possession, the western part of the island of Saint Dominique (today's Haiti), obtained in 1713, gained its independence in 1804 after a long slave revolt. France refused to recognize Haitian independence until 1837. France attempted to use the Holy Alliance, a continental European antirepublican league formed after Napoleon's final defeat in 1815, to assist Spain in regaining its American empire, after which France expected to have dominant influence. Britain, by then in control of the seas, made its opposition clear, and France abandoned the scheme in 1823. France sent naval forces to blockade Vera Cruz and Buenos Aires in the 1830s to assert the claims of its citizens, but to no avail. France joined Britain in another blockade of Buenos Aires from 1845 to 1849 in support of Argentines and Uruguayans opposing Argentine dictator Juan Manuel de Rosas, but the intervention gained little.

The Latter Nineteenth Century to World War I

European involvement with the new Latin American states reached its height during the latter half of the nineteenth century and in the twentieth century to World War I. Britain's commercial interests and France's frustrated imperial ambitions continued as before. Germany and Italy entered the Latin American scene in the 1870s as their respective national unifications were taking place. Germany became highly competitive, and by the end of the century occupied third place in Latin American trade, behind Great Britain and the United States and well ahead of France. Italy sent large numbers of immigrants, especially to southern South America, and to Argentina in particular. Britain, France, the Netherlands, Spain (until 1898) and Denmark (until 1917) continued to maintain relatively small colonies, all in the Caribbean area except for the British Falkland Islands Colony. European armed intervention occurred from time to time, sometimes in concert. Increasingly, however, with the development of major South American states and the rise of U.S. power in the Circum-Caribbean, Europeans turned to more cooperative relationships. Their last military intervention was a combined British-German-Italian blockade of Venezuela in 1902–1903.

European objectives were mixed. Latin America was not an arena of European power politics and imperialism to the same extent as in other parts of the world. It was, however, the object of rivalry for economic, political, cultural, and military influence. The rapid industrialization of European states led to an increase in their need for food and raw materials and to a more intense search for markets for their manufactured goods, investment capital, technical and managerial skills, and surplus population. In addition, the international rules of the game dictated that if one great power aided in economic development, cultural exchange, or military modernization, the other great powers were obliged to follow suit. Various goals were interrelated: The exportation of military expertise and technology or of cultural benefits might bring increased exportation of economic goods and assist political expansion into a peripheral and neglected area at relatively low cost. For some political and military leaders in Germany and France, Latin America assumed some importance in their strategic calculations for then present and future contingencies. From 1885 until the outbreak of World War I, the European military missions in the Southern Cone, and the provisions for training Latin American officers in Europe, were aimed at strengthening military and political relations that might become important in the event of European war. They also served economic and prestige purposes. Of particular note were the activities of Germany in Chile, Argentina, and Bolivia and of France in Peru, Brazil, Uruguay, and Paraguay—whereby they extended to the Americas their worldwide competition to establish useful military relations.

British domination of the seas, aided by the possession of naval bases in Latin America, after the advent of steam shipping, was directed toward economic ends. Britain intervened at times to protect its citizens and investments and to collect debts, on occasion in concert with other European powers, but all in all it resorted to little military interference in Latin American affairs. Britain continued to be the major investor and trader. It was especially well entrenched in Argentina and had important investments in and trade with Brazil, Uruguay, Mexico, Venezuela, and Colombia. British emigration to Latin America was also important, but it did not approach the numbers of some other European countries. British settlers were largely, but not exclusively, connected with British capital enterprises.

Britain began to retire from the Caribbean at the turn of the century and to give the United States a largely free hand in the area. The Hay-Pauncefote Treaty of 1901 replaced the Clayton-Bulwer Treaty of 1850, allowing the United States to build and exclusively control an interoceanic canal. Britain maintained its Caribbean colonies and economic interests, but it became a secondary external influence in the area. It retained major interests in South America, however, especially in commercial and financial affairs, although to its chagrin its preeminence eroded after the turn of the century through the efforts of the United States and Germany. Nevertheless, Britain's investments and trade levels in Latin America reached their peak on the eve of World War I. The investments constituted about one-fourth of Britain's overseas total, with special concentrations in Argentina and Brazil.

Throughout the remainder of the nineteenth century, Spanish foreign policy was fundamentally European oriented and Spanish America was of slight and mostly emotional concern. Spain again took up efforts to recover at least part of the old empire after the end of the Carlist civil wars. In 1861, taking advantage of political chaos in Santo Domingo, Spain persuaded its former colony to petition for reannexation. Dominicans again rebelled in 1865 and regained independence. Also in 1861, Spain joined Britain and France in a military intervention against Mexico for payment of debts, but Spain and England retired when French desires to occupy Mexico became clear. In this case Spain did not intend to extend control over Mexico. In 1864 Spain sent a small naval squadron to attack Peru and Bolivia, which then bombarded Chile when the latter came to the aid of her neighbor. The adventure gained nothing for Spain.

Despite these events, Spanish American conservatives had a great deal of sympathy for Spain. Liberals, on the other hand, tended toward hispanophobia and yankeephilia. Spain ruined the remaining potential for Spanish American goodwill, however, by its harsh treatment of its remaining colony in Cuba (which included Puerto Rico). Latin American public opinion widely supported the Cuban patriot cause. After Spain relinquished its last American territory as a result of a brief war with the United States in 1898, however, sympathy with Spain was revived as hostility toward the United States increased.

In reaction to the war with the United States over Cuba, a number of well-known Spanish intellectuals promoted the idea of a common civilization or cultural community between Spain and Spanish America. The Spanish government expressed sympathy for what was called *hispanismo* but devoted minimal resources beyond financing some cultural exchange. The Spanish government saw cultural solidarity as a way to make Spain more competitive economically and to promote Spanish influence and prestige in Latin America, but Spain's economy was unable to compete in Latin American markets with the rest of Europe and the United States.

French interest in Latin America by the time of World War I had become essentially economic, in contrast to the earlier nineteenth-century imperialist thrust. In addition, the height of French cultural influence and the beginnings of its military cooperation in South America occurred at the turn of the century and up to World War I. These changes in emphasis came, however, after France had engaged in two more disastrous colonial adventures—its occupation of Mexico in the 1860s and its support for a private French company's Panama Canal enterprise.

Mexican civil war beginning in 1857 led to the repudiation of foreign debts and to a joint French-Spanish-British military intervention in 1861–1862 to force a debt agreement. After Great Britain and Spain withdrew, French troops took Mexico City. Prince Maximilian of Austria became emperor of Mexico in April 1864, supported by the French army. However, continued resistance of Mexican patriots under Benito Juárez, and U.S. opposition to the French occupation coming at the end of the U.S. Civil War, ended French imperial ambitions in Latin America with a humiliating departure from Mexico.

France soon took up a new American scheme—the linking of the Atlantic and Pacific oceans with a transisthmian canal. With British and U.S. power neutralized in Central America by their 1850 treaty, a private French company began construction of the Panama Canal. Mismanagement, unsound engineering, yellow fever, and corruption led to bankruptcy and abandonment of the project in 1888, with less than a quarter of the canal completed. The canal equity was eventually sold to the United States in 1902.

France had important economic interests in Latin America in the latter part of the century. During the 1890s and until the eve of World War I, it occupied fourth place in commercial trade with the region, behind Britain, the United States, and Germany. France was not really competitive with the three leading states, however, lagging far behind Germany. Moreover, France was already burdened at the time with heavy investments in Russia, Spain, North Africa, and the Middle East.

A German interest in Latin America can be traced to the colonial period when Spain allowed individual German families to make economic investments in Venezuela. After Latin American independence, Germans were prominent in the great European migrations to America, and the city-states of Hamburg and Bremen established important trading relations in Latin America. Following German unification and the establishment of the empire in 1871, Germany wove political, military, cultural, and economic relations into a complex series of policies toward Latin America. In particular, migrations of people and capital and trading relations increased.

Germans settled in considerable numbers in Argentina and Brazil, and significant numbers went to Chile, Peru, Bolivia, Mexico, Guatemala, and Venezuela. Germany's economic performance was especially impressive from about the turn of the century to the eve of World War I. By 1913 Germany was third in both exports to and imports from Latin America. Argentina was Germany's most important trading partner, with Brazil, Chile, and Bolivia also of significance. The extent of German trade and investment in Latin America is all the more remarkable in view of the fact that Germany suffered from an inadequate supply of foreign investment capital during that period, and that the focus of its investment and trade was in Central Europe, even while it recorded impressive gains in the United States, Great Britain, and the Middle East. The spread of German enterprise around the world created an urge to establish colonies and naval strength to promote and protect German overseas markets. Germany did not seek Latin American colonies, however, presumably deterred by the possibility of British and U.S. economic retaliation.

The Interbellum Period

European interest in Latin America sharply declined as a result of World War I but was rekindled throughout the 1920s and 1930s. European policies, however, remained relatively constant in concept if not in intensity during the interbellum period. All European states now pursued primarily commercial interests, with Britain retaining the largest share but strongly challenged by the United States, Germany, and France. Germany and France again played leading roles in the development of South American armies, with essentially the same partners as during the pre–World War I period. Because of a strong German presence in Latin America in the 1930s, supported by local political groups sympathetic to Nazi Germany and Fascist Italy, Europe temporarily and peripherally included the region in its strategic concerns.

British influence in Latin America, which had begun to wane at the turn of the century, declined considerably after World War I. A mild boom occurred in the 1920s, when the Prince of Wales, later King Edward VIII, traveled in 1925 to Chile, Argentina, and Brazil attempting to bolster British trade with them. Argentina continued to be the most important state in British economic calculations. In almost every year until 1946, at least 10 percent of total British capital invested abroad, and 30 percent of that in Latin America, was in Argentina. In 1947 the Perón government purchased the British-owned railway and tram lines, eliminating Britain's largest capital enterprise in Argentina.

Spain had little interest in Latin America between the wars. Its policy was restricted largely to an emotionalized form of cultural activity, although a modicum of economic, political, and even military cooperation took place. Before (but not during) World War II, Spain received small numbers of Latin American officers at its training centers.

The Spanish Civil War from 1936 to 1939 sharply divided Latin American public opinion. After its conclusion in 1939, General Francisco Franco adopted a new form of Pan Hispanism called *hispanidad* and made it the basis for Spanish policy toward Latin America. Hispanidad was an amalgam of some of the cultural tenets of *hispanismo* with *falangismo,* the Spanish variant of fascism. The overblown rhetoric of hispanidad notwithstanding, the reestablishment of the American empire was an unrealistic goal. Franco probably aimed for the development of a Spanish American bloc supportive of Spain in international politics. He was successful in only the most reactionary sectors.

World War I seriously interrupted German relations with Latin America. During the postwar Weimar period, Germany recovered its trading position somewhat, although it reached its prewar levels only in Argentina. German investments remained low. Germany was deeply affected by the world depression and its economic relations suffered drastically. Military relations with Latin America were revived in the 1920s along prewar lines—with Chile, Argentina, and Bolivia—which continued to World War II.

German National Socialist (Nazi) policy in Latin America beginning in 1933 succeeded in increasing trade, and by 1938 Germany had regained its prewar commercial position in the region. Germany's principal economic efforts were consistent with past interests, but the policies took on new strategic overtones consistent with Germany's desire to stockpile war-related raw materials as well as to encourage German export of manufactured goods for the sake of balance of payments. Hitler reorganized the German Chamber of Commerce to assist in collecting information regarding military and political conditions abroad as well as financial and commercial intelligence information. He also exerted pressure on German overseas firms to dismiss Jewish employees and to withhold advertising from newspapers unfriendly to the Third Reich (Heilman, 1973:83–94).

The Hitler regime introduced a new ideological factor in German foreign policy as it sought to mobilize German communities in Latin America in support of the Nazi Party in order to project a positive image of the New Germany and to further its economic goals there. Although the number of German communities existing in Latin America was small, the homeland considered them significant. Some cultural organizations had been established in years past, and Germany had always prevailed on German migrants to support the "mother culture." Hitler demanded political as well as cultural loyalty. The Nazi party had attempted to organize and control counterparts in Latin America as early as 1930, more than two years before coming to power in Germany, and it continued its efforts after 1933. The infusion of German overseas schools with Nazi ideology received special attention, along with other forms of propaganda and often clumsy fifth-column efforts. All of these attempts caused friction within the German communities and between Germany and virtually every Latin American government where they were attempted, including Argentina and Brazil, where otherwise sympathetic regimes were in power. World War II severed German contacts with Latin America.

Post–World War II and the Cold War

Following World War II, war-exhausted Europeans retreated from competition in Latin America. Initial postwar European policies in Latin America were subordinate to their preoccupations with essentially European affairs. They were absorbed with reconstruction and then maintenance of recovered prosperity, relations with the superpowers, organizing the North Atlantic Treaty Organization (NATO), and developing formal European integration associations that culminated with the establishment of the European Community (EC). Several of them were also faced with making new arrangements with their old colonial empires. Latin America had only a peripheral place in these concerns.

Eventually, European states revived their interests in Latin America and again assumed important roles there. Especially after the mid-1960s, they expanded existing relations and initiated new ones in the way of diplomatic contacts, cultural exchanges, economic assistance, private investment, and especially trade relations, including arms sales. Trade and investment were of paramount importance, supported by increased diplomatic contacts and some economic assistance. Even with the expanded relationships, Latin America generally was not as important to the European states as other world regions.

None of the European states viewed Latin America in security terms in the post–World War II period because of geographic and political distance and higher priority concerns elsewhere. They tended to defer to the United States on security issues. Their policies were not devoid of such content, however. NATO members had a contingency concern that the Gulf of Mexico and Caribbean Sea be open for movements of military forces and supplies in the event of European war. This concern was latent, however, and not an essential factor in policy calculations. With few exceptions they did not make significant efforts to extend their ideologies to the region.

In the 1980s Europeans emphasized three areas of concern regarding Latin America, largely in reaction to U.S. policies: (1) the question of debt, as both a political and financial issue; (2) the problems of Latin American democracy as the region moved away from military regimes; and (3) the phenomenon of Third World revolution, at least as manifested in Central America. European transnational parties—especially Social Democratic parties and the Socialist International, and Christian Democratic parties and the Christian Democratic World Union—began to pay more attention to their Latin American colleagues and emphasized these three sets of issues.

A number of political interests and activities in specific countries were particularly notable, sometimes including ideological elements. Spain, under General Franco, courted Latin America through the medium of a less aggressive version of hispanidad in an attempt to win votes for Spanish entry into the United Nations. The first UN General Assembly refused membership to Spain because of its non-democratic Fascist government, but finally, in 1956, Spain joined the world body, with the support of sixteen of nineteen Latin American votes. Thereafter, Spain attempted, with some success, to gain Latin American support in the UN for its otherwise quixotic quest to force Britain to return Gibraltar to Spain. But Spain turned more attention to Europe and otherwise paid scant attention to Latin America. The main issues for Spain in Latin America involved continuing Mexican hostility toward Franco and the question of Cuban indemnification for Spanish property seized by the Castro government in 1959. After Franco's death in 1974, Spanish officials suggested a new era of Latin American relationships. After joining NATO and the EC, Spain made overtures to serve as a cultural and political bridge between the two regions.

The postwar peace settlement restructured Germany, dividing it into east and west sectors, the latter constituting the Federal Republic of Germany (West Germany). This development ushered in a new foreign policy era for Germany. Some ideological concerns motivated aspects of German policy. Germany wanted to break with its National Socialist past, but publicity concerning Nazi personalities who had migrated to Latin America occasionally caused embarrassment. Of more importance were German attempts to prevent Latin American recognition of East Germany and to promote German reunification. The Hallstein Doctrine of 1955 stated that Germany considered the recognition of East Germany an unfriendly act. In general, Latin American governments supported Germany regarding Eastern Europe. *Ostpolitik,* led by Willy Brandt beginning in 1969 and culminating in 1972 with a treaty between the two German entities, defused the anti-Communist element of German policy to a considerable degree. In 1979, Chancellor Helmut Schmidt visited Latin America to signal increased trade and investment, but this eventuality was deterred by the region's severe debt crisis beginning in 1982.

The United Kingdom, France, and the Netherlands had Caribbean dependencies to accommodate. British policies also involved conflicts with Venezuela over Guyana, with Guatemala over Belize, and with Argentina over the Falkland Islands (the Anglo-Argentine war of 1982 and its aftermath was the most dramatic of these). Other states also looked for Latin American support on individual matters in the United Nations. For example, Portugal sought and usually received Brazil's supporting vote in the UN, even on colonial issues. Some countries based certain policies on the fact that they had large national populations resident in Latin American countries, such as Italy's policies toward Argentina and Portugal's toward Brazil.

Economic relations with Latin America superseded political interests for most of the European states. The postwar pattern of relations and degree of interest, however, varied greatly among the Europeans. Particularly notable was that British economic relations dropped sharply. The United Kingdom's first priority was to resupply its Commonwealth partners and to rebuild Britain itself, after which increasing attention was turned to relations with continental Europe. Otherwise, Europe's trade increased with Latin America, which in time also became the preferred region for private investment after Europe itself. Germany became the most aggressive European trader and investor, paying special attention to Brazil and Argentina. French trade levels in Latin America fluctuated widely and the pattern of trade also shifted. Prior to 1951 Argentina was France's largest regional buyer and seller; after that date, Brazil became its major trading partner in both imports and exports. Spain's economic relations with Latin America after World War II were limited but more than negligible. Spain increased its share of Latin American trade only slightly until the death of Franco in 1974, but renewed Spanish economic growth thereafter led to increased Latin American trade and investment. In contrast, Portuguese trade declined with Latin America; most of it remained with Brazil and on a lower level even there.

The EC was a new actor in Latin America. It played an expanding role as European states increasingly chose to pursue their economic interests mutually through the EC rather than bilaterally. In the early 1970s, the EC began to look beyond its own integration and to formulate policies toward the developing world. The EC established permanent consultation mechanisms with Latin America on the ambassadorial level in Brussels. Beginning in 1971, a regular series of multilateral diplomatic meetings were held semiannually to discuss interregional relations. The EC worked directly with the several Latin American economic organizations and, in time, with the Latin American Economic System (SELA). In October 1984, through the initiative of the Commission of the EC, the Institute for European–Latin American Relations/Instituto de Relaciones Europeo–Latinoamericanos (IRELA) was created, located in Madrid and directed by the German Latin Americanist Wolf Grabendorff. Among its several functions, IRELA organizes conferences and colloquia, collects and analyzes information on a range of specific subjects, and issues a number of publications.

In 1971 the EC established a Generalized System of Preference (GSP) giving concessional terms of trade for certain Third World exports, including those in Latin America. In 1974 the EC signed the Lomé Convention (the fourth extension went into effect in 1990) expanding special trade concessions and development aid to former European colonies, which in Latin America include the twelve Commonwealth Caribbean Countries, Suriname, and, as of 1990 as a special case, the Dominican Republic. But the majority of Latin Americans complained that their most important export items were not on the GSP list and that further disadvantages caused by the Lomé Convention worsened their terms of trade in relation to other developing economies. (See Chapter 10 for detailed discussion.)

EC concerns went beyond economics with their role in Latin American subsystem conflict. Specifically, the EC took positions in the Anglo-Argentine war of 1982—a move that created discord among member states. After Argentina invaded the United Kingdom's Falkland Islands Colony on April 2, 1982, the EC responded to a UK appeal for its support by deciding on April 16 to condemn Argentina for its aggression and to impose sanctions; it banned European arms sales to and embargoed imports from Argentina. Members made it clear, however, that the measures were designed to convince Argentina to abandon force and did not imply an endorsement of British counterforce. Support eroded especially after May 2, when a British submarine torpedoed and sank an Argentine cruiser, an act widely perceived to have violated Britain's own rules of engagement. The British engaged in intense diplomacy with their reluctant EC partners, and the majority decided to extend the sanctions indefinitely, although Ireland and Italy refused to vote in favor. The EC lifted its sanctions on June 20, 1982, after British armed forces had prevailed in the South Atlantic.

Post–Cold War Trends

New developments that paralleled the end of the cold war influenced European policies toward Latin America. Europe's priorities were the difficult tasks of continuing the evolution of the EC, redefining the meaning of the Western alliance, and deciding the nature of relations with the states in what had been known as Eastern Europe. Primary among them was the notion of "Europe 1992"—the plan laid out in the intra-EC Maastricht Treaty to create a Single European Market (SEM) by December 31, 1992. On that date the EC was also transformed into the European Union (EU). But the ratification process revealed sufficient public skepticism or hostility to force compromises in the depth and speed of increased integration. Movement toward the SEM continued but fell short of that originally planned. In addition, the dissolution of the Soviet bloc in Eastern Europe led the states there to seek some sort of EC membership.

With regard to Latin America, Europeans continued to emphasize the importance of trade and investment but were ambiguous in their calculations about the conditions in the region and how they affected European interests. EC–Latin American economic relations had been increasingly marginalized. From the mid-1960s to early 1990s, Latin America's portion of the EC's total trade declined by approximately half. Europeans applauded Latin America's redemocratized political systems and recovering economies but also expressed doubts about their sustainability. Yet economic relations were of more interest to the EC as the Latin American economies underwent internal reform and became more open to the outside world. Germany was most notable in this regard, having the largest volume of Latin American trade and investment of the EC members. Europeans see opportunities in the North American Free Trade Agreement (NAFTA) and its possible extension to the rest of the Americas under the U.S. Enterprise for the Americas Initiative (EAI), depending on what rules of origin are adopted. Europeans are also concerned about narcotics trafficking in Europe, much of which originates in and flows from Latin America. Certain cultural links remained strong: Spanish policy was most strongly influenced by this consideration, and it was also an important factor in Italian, Portuguese, and German calculations. European political parties and their foundations, churches, and trade unions continued to be active in the region.

A great deal of Latin American speculation on the future of their relations with Europe was distinctly pessimistic. Some writers (for example, Heine, 1991; and Berrocal, 1989) emphasized the disequilibrium created by strong political bonds and weak economic ties and were skeptical about both Europe's willingness and Latin America's capability to implement new economic strategies. They stressed Latin America's frustrated expectations about relations engendered by EC protectionism and passivity toward the external debt and Europe's lack of the political will to establish complementary relations with Latin America to halt further distancing of the two regions. Furthermore, Latin American exports to the EC were especially vulnerable if stricter EC regulations and preferences for Eastern European products became realities (Grabendorff, 1992). The prospect of a more intensely integrated EC, and its expansion to include the former Eastern European states, threatened indirect trade diversion from Latin America. (For the fourteen

Caribbean signatories of the Lomé Convention, the preferential arrangements set out will continue unchanged.)

RUSSIA, THE SOVIET UNION, AND THE COMMONWEALTH OF INDEPENDENT STATES

Latin America in Soviet Policy

Tsarist Russia paid little attention to geographically remote Latin America and had only sporadic contacts with the region during the colonial period and throughout the nineteenth century. The first formal relations with a Latin American state came not until 1885, when diplomatic and commercial ties were established with Argentina, which were soon followed by similar arrangements with Mexico in 1887 and Uruguay in 1890.

The Soviet Union, after its establishment in 1917 until its dissolution in 1991, went through several distinct periods in its Latin American policies. The Soviet Union initially showed little interest in Latin America. Its policy was preoccupied with Europe, Asia, and the Middle East. The Soviet view of Latin America and commitment of minimal resources there conformed with the earlier Imperial Russian lack of interest. Following the Russian Revolution of 1917, Soviet foreign policy espoused world revolution. Soviet leaders did not ignore Latin America— the Bolshevik government attempted to create and control Latin American Communist parties and sporadically established diplomatic relations with Latin American governments—but the region did not occupy a prominent place in their calculations. They openly stated that other areas were more urgent for Soviet policy. The Soviet Union attached more importance to the Latin American area after World War II, but its interest was still limited. The rigidity of Stalinist policy and the intransigence of local Communist parties at the height of the cold war all but made it impossible for the Soviets to collaborate with the Latin American states. Only after Stalin's death in 1953 was the Soviet Union to establish diplomatic, commercial, and cultural ties.

The Soviet presence in Latin America became especially significant after the Soviet involvement in the Castro revolution in Cuba in 1960. Even then, the acceptance of Marxism-Leninism by the Cuban revolutionary leadership apparently took Soviet leaders by surprise, offering them unsought and unexpected opportunities in the Caribbean. Nevertheless, a close relationship with Cuba provided the Soviet Union with its first high-priority interest in the region. Soviet activities increased around the rest of Latin America after 1964, especially in the form of expanded trade and diplomatic relations. The new attention was reflected in the establishment in 1961 of the Institute of Latin American Studies in the Academy of Sciences of the USSR at Moscow. Even with this heightened awareness of Latin America, the area remained of relatively low priority in Soviet calculations compared to that of other world regions.

Evolving Policy Calculations

After the Revolution of 1917, a difficult analytic question was posed: To what degree was Soviet policy rooted in Marxist-Leninist ideology and to what extent did it simply reflect the pursuit of national interest by a state in the international political system? The ultimate Soviet objective may have been to achieve political power in Latin America and to communize the area. The evidence suggests, however, that even in the long run this world revolutionary purpose was not a primary motivation for Soviet policy toward Latin America. Rather, Soviet goals seemed continuously to have been aimed at weakening U.S. influence in the region and to increasing Moscow's as much as possible. Soviet policymakers generally perceived limited opportunities in Latin America and their actions were cautious, the major exception being the reckless attempt to install missiles in Cuba in 1962. Soviet tactics, by and large, were prudent and opportunistic, taking advantage of existing conditions rather than attempting to create more favorable situations. The Soviet Union seemed to concentrate modestly on building its own influence and detracting from that of the United States, whether or not situations seemed to offer immediate prospects for Communist revolution. In sum, the Soviets assigned Latin America a low priority, sought limited objectives there, and applied generally cautious policies.

It may be argued that Soviet policies on Latin America resulted from the confluence of ideology and pragmatism. Pragmatic considerations restrained Soviet policy and discouraged imprudent "revolutionary" activities, and ideological justifications fitted power calculations of cost and risk.

For a half-century prior to the Cuban Revolution, Soviet policymakers took into account several practical considerations, which were summed up in their concept of "geographic fatalism." They viewed Latin America as an area in which the Soviet Union was placed at a great disadvantage because of geography, which meant that few opportunities to influence regional affairs would arise. The area was physically remote from the Soviet Union and far from its primary concerns; vigorous Soviet activity would require resources it did not have or could not profitably invest. The concept of geographic fatalism would seem to differ little from traditional geopolitical views. More important, Latin America was seen to be dominated by the United States, which would tolerate no revolutionary government there nor allow Soviet influence to gain a strong foothold. The main constraint, however, was that the Soviet Union was deeply absorbed in its own domestic problems and involved in international affairs of higher priority than those with Latin America.

Events seemed to confirm the persistence of geographic fate. After the Bolshevik Revolution through World War II, the Soviet Union worked primarily with Latin American Communist parties through the Latin American section of the Comintern. Direct diplomatic relations with other states were few and slow in coming, so that little opportunity was presented for interstate relations. From 1917 until 1933, most Latin American states followed the U.S. lead in refusing to recognize the Soviet Union. The Good Neighbor Policy after 1933 kept Latin America in line with U.S. desires even as the Soviet Union was recognized. After World War II during the cold war years, Soviet probes into Latin America brought strong responses from the United States. For example, the United States successfully supported an intervention in 1954 against a leftist regime in Guatemala that had been mildly aided by the Soviet Union. Soviet activities in the region during the first fifteen postwar years were few, as the United States seemed to have a controlling influence in the area.

Related to the notion of geographic fatalism was the Soviet willingness to compromise its Latin American activities when good U.S. relations were desired. Prior to 1933 Soviet objectives in the region were shaped by its desire to attain formal U.S. recognition. After recognition was granted in that year, its objective was to maintain good relations with the United States. Partly for these reasons, Soviet activities in Latin America in competition with the United States were subdued. Later, the Soviet policy of peaceful coexistence with the United States during the 1960s and détente in the 1970s had the same effect.

The Cuban Revolution of 1959 and the unexpected survival of the Castro regime at least temporarily changed this Soviet view of geographic fatalism. The Soviet Union initially watched the course of the Cuban Revolution with skepticism and surprise, assuming first that it was not a radical revolution and then, when it proved to be one, that the United States would not allow it to survive. Under these circumstances, there seemed to be no advantage in supporting Castro's struggle in the 1950s. The Soviets made the first tentative contacts in 1960, when the new regime had been in power for more than a year. Within Cuba the Communist party did not ally with Castro until his victory had been virtually assured. Only then did the Soviet Union seem to believe that Castro represented a genuine Latin American social revolution that could resist the United States. The Soviets first gave Castro verbal support, then later gave economic and finally military assistance. After 1961 it seemed for a time that the United States might no longer be able to dominate affairs in the Caribbean, that Castro was a precursor of regional change toward leftist regimes and, consequently, that the Soviet Union could influence at least part of Latin America. But Soviet policy received a major blow when the United States forced it to remove its offensive missiles so boldly placed in Cuba in 1962.

The Missile Crisis of 1962

Soviet intentions and power calculations leading to the superpower confrontation in 1962 are difficult to assess because of the secretiveness of the Soviet decision-making process. Nevertheless, strong opinions on the subject were put forward. For example, former Secretary of State Dean Acheson (1966) argued that the Soviet Union had three objectives: (1) to increase the Soviet nuclear first-strike capability against the United States by about half again; (2) to discredit U.S. influence in Latin America; and (3) to force the United States to pay so high a price for the removal of the missiles as to bring further discredit to the United States in Europe and Southeast Asia.

The first strategic motivation mentioned by Acheson was held plausible by most of the participating U.S. decision makers at the time and was accepted by a number of analysts, especially the Soviet attempt to enhance its first-strike missile capabilities. Acheson's second and third points were widely disputed, however. Adam Ulam's authoritative analysis found them highly questionable, concluding that such objectives were highly disproportionate to the means employed and the risks assumed.

Revised Policy Calculations

When the United States intervened in the Dominican Republic in 1965 to prevent a "second Cuba," it signaled the Soviet Union that it remained determined to dominate the Caribbean region. Nevertheless, the Castro revolution proved durable, and other governments hostile to the United States emerged in several parts of the hemisphere. Most important, Marxist Salvador Allende was elected president of Chile. Although these occurrences seemed to refute the notion of U.S. regional invincibility, other events were in the mold of past Soviet expectations. Cuban revolutionary hero Che Guevara died in 1967 while leading a guerrilla band against Bolivian military forces, and a reactionary military coup deposed Chilean President Allende in 1973. Both outcomes were linked to U.S. actions. The Soviet Union again tested the U.S. security position in 1970 by planning the construction of a submarine base in Cuba, but when the United States vigorously protested, it aborted the plan rather than risk another military crisis with the United States.

Other calculations seemed further to restrain Soviet policies in Latin America. Ironically, because of its "success" in Cuba, the Soviet Union became more aware of the financial and political costs and risks of policy and of its military limitations. The Cuban experience suggested three basic lessons for the Soviet Union. First, the financial costs of a Soviet commitment to an economically underdeveloped ally were high and tended to escalate. It was widely assumed that during the 1960s Cuba cost the Soviet Union the equivalent of between $350 and $400 million per year and that this cost rose to about $500 million annually in the 1970s and at least doubled to $1 billion in the 1980s. To support a comparable revolution in a larger Latin American nation presumably would cost proportionally more and would involve potentially staggering financial commitments.

Second, a close relationship with a Latin American state did not guarantee that the Soviet Union would have its way politically, or that political gains would be worth the economic costs. Cuba at times asserted its independence from Soviet leadership and publicly attacked Soviet policies toward the rest of Latin America. The Soviet Union, by its very presence, stirred nationalist resistance to its overtures. As in other parts of the world, communism proved to be compatible with nationalism rather than monolithic and was subject neither to overriding intellectual orthodoxy nor necessarily to Soviet direction. Soviet military strength was not present in America to enforce compliance as it was in Eastern Europe. Political, economic, and military support to a movement like that in Cuba could not easily be reduced or terminated. The collapse of a regime closely allied with the Soviet Union because of insufficient assistance would mean a great loss of prestige. (The above line of analysis, further reflected in the following section, generally concurs with that of Duncan, 1985; and Blasier, 1988.)

The Soviet Union and Central American Conflict

Soviet motivations for its Central American involvement after the late 1970s were sharply debated. The Reagan administration, reinforced by the Kissinger Commission report of January 1984, offered one explanation of Soviet policies. It contended that the principal thrust was Soviet expansionism, in particular Soviet-backed and Cuban-managed support for violent revolution in Central America, aimed at establishing Cuban-style Marxist-Leninist dictatorships allied with the Soviet Union. The U.S. administration also advanced the "domino theory"— that the Soviet Union, enjoying a permanent presence in the Caribbean through its Cuban surrogate, was acting to reinforce and expand this penetration into Nicaragua. Cuban assistance, the argument continued, sought to transform additional countries into Marxist states, beginning with El Salvador. From there communism would spread to the other small Central American countries and then threaten the major bordering states of Mexico to the north and Colombia and Venezuela to the south; Mexico was the "big domino." Certain implications evolved from this calculation of Soviet motives. In particular, Communist expansion, leading to a more extensive permanent presence, would offer the Soviet Union significant military advantages with the establishment of military bases in the region. Such bases, in addition to threatening the Panama Canal and lines of communication in the Caribbean, would allow the placement of hostile forces and weapons (conventional and nuclear) capable of striking deep within the United States and Latin American states. They would allow extended Soviet naval operations without the necessity of returning to the Soviet Union. Such a situation would force significant alterations in the U.S. forward deployment strategy, as a previously secure area would either require resources to be diverted from other areas or the creation of new ones.

U.S. assumptions about the expansionist purposes of the Soviet Union and its aligned partners may be challenged by plausible alternative explanations. The Reagan administration–Kissinger Commission analysis about the sources of Soviet behavior, with its exclusionary emphasis on ideology and expansionism, was incomplete. Those who held this view made assertions about Soviet motivations but did not ask the same questions about the Soviets that, we may assume, they asked of themselves. What goals were realistically attainable? What costs and risks were acceptable? If Soviet policy exhibited a certain ideological consistency, it also behaved as a state in the international system. Soviet perceptions of historical inevitability and their impact on Soviet behavior could not be ignored, but, in the meantime, the Soviet Union was required to make more proximate strategic and tactical decisions. It seemed likely that maximum Soviet objectives in Central America conformed to its traditional Latin American purposes—to weaken U.S. influence and increase its own as much as possible—but within the limits of modest political and financial cost and risk. That is, the Soviet Union probably saw Central America as a target of opportunity, not of deep strategic value, and as a vulnerable investment. Furthermore, viewing Cuba and Nicaragua simply as Soviet surrogates, proxies, or puppets erroneously assumed that Cuba and Nicaragua would simply follow the Soviet lead under any circumstances. Evidence suggested diverging as well as complementary interests among them.

Yet the Soviet Union did not respond to strong U.S. anti-Communist, antiexpansionist actions in Central America. This persistence defied the U.S. assumption that the Soviet Union would retreat in the face of strong counterpressures to its expansionist probing. The decline of U.S.-Soviet relations after 1979 under both President Carter and President Reagan helped explain the lack of Soviet response to forceful U.S. actions. From the Soviet view, meddling in

Central America was appropriate as long as "détente" and "peaceful coexistence" were already eroded. Conversely, better general relations with the United States, particularly regarding arms control, might lead the Soviets to reduce their Central American activities.

The motivations behind Soviet behavior, however, were more complex than the above analysis might imply. The world, including Central America, presented a highly complex picture; dialectically, it was dynamic and in constant flux. Soviet historicist ideology demanded the promotion of Communist influence, but only under favorable circumstances. The Nicaraguan Revolution of 1979 gave heightened possibilities for Soviet influence in Central America and shifted its thinking about opportunities in the U.S. sphere of influence. But the latter part of the ideological equation ("under favorable circumstances") led the Soviet Union to more pragmatic modes of ends-means and capability calculations. Although Soviet actions might respond to a "new détente," more important factors were at work—external problems involving Afghanistan, Poland, China, and the Middle East; internal economic and leadership concerns; and recognition of the high cost concomitant to the survival of a revolutionary regime.

The End of the Cold War and After

Remarkable Soviet foreign policy reorientations after 1985, and the subsequent end of the cold war and dissolution of the Soviet Union, had profound consequences for the Soviet and then Russian presence in Latin America. These eventualities were precipitated by the rise of Mikhail Gorbachev to premier of the Soviet Union in 1985 and his adoption of *glasnost, perestroika,* and New Thinking in foreign policy. In the late 1980s, Gorbachev replaced the officials controlling the Soviet Communist party with his reform-minded supporters. The Soviet leadership concluded that under socialism the Soviet economy was actually falling farther behind the major industrial states. Furthermore, Soviet officials no longer viewed the United States as a military threat or competitor, in view of U.S.-Soviet convergence on many issues. These realities called for pragmatism in foreign policy. In Latin America, New Thinking led to a retreat from involvement in Central America and reduced priorities in Cuban relations.

The Soviet Union dramatically changed its Central American actions. It stopped delivery of heavy weapons to Cuba and Nicaragua, and in October 1989, Soviet Foreign Minister Eduard Sheverdnadze visited those two countries and applied pressure to end shipments to the Farabundo Martí National Liberation Front (FMLN) in El Salvador. The Soviet Union worked with the United States in the UN Security Council, which in November 1989 unanimously passed a resolution creating a UN peacekeeping force in Central America. All of these moves supported the Central American peace process set in motion by the Esquipulus II initiative (see Chapter 11). The remarkable elections in Nicaragua in February 1990 ended Sandinista rule as well as the Soviet role there. According to Blasier (1993), Soviet advice to undertake free elections and abide by the results may have influenced the Sandinista's decision to do so. (Castro strongly disagreed with the advice because of the disturbing implications for Cuba.) Blasier also notes the muted Soviet reaction in December 1989 to the U.S. invasion of Panama.

The long-standing relationship with Cuba was profoundly altered after 1985. With the decline of the Soviet economy and political-military power, commitments and assistance to Cuba were drastically reduced, as Soviet officials saw various generous subsidies and aid to Cuba as a significant area in which to economize. They also concluded that the new Soviet political-strategic priorities were not enhanced by Cuban cooperation. In April 1989, Gorbachev visited Castro in Havana to alert him about reduced Soviet economic support. Castro, with a huge stake in the status quo, vehemently resisted the changing relationship. Nevertheless, in 1990 the Soviets discontinued subsidizing petroleum deliveries to Cuba and Cuban sugar exports to the Soviet Union, two especially heavy blows to the Cuban economy. In fact, the Soviets put all trade on a commercial basis at world market prices. In 1990–1991 they sharply cut Cuban grant and technical aid programs, including the number of technicians and advisers in Cuba.

Soviet decision-making regarding Cuba was a controversial matter within the changing Soviet political system. According to Cole Blasier (1991, 1993), after Gorbachev's visit to Cuba in 1989, "the USSR stood balanced between the old and new"—feeling a continued responsibility toward Cuba while fundamentally restructuring the relationship. The official policy was to remain helpful to Castro and to protect the long-term Soviet policy investment in Cuba to the extent that it could, even though it had become so costly for the Soviet economy and not politically important enough to justify support at the previous generous levels. This compromise approach was strongly opposed by two contending groups. On one side, "conservative" military and intelligence officers and Communist party traditionalists, placing value on Castro's ideological orthodoxy and his survival as a Soviet ally, favored continued generous economic support. On the other side, "reformists" urged reducing assistance to Cuba even more, not only because of the economic drain but the political cost of supporting the personalist and repressive Castro regime. The failed August 1991 coup against Gorbachev largely decided the issue in favor of the reformists, since the leaders of the pro-Castro conservative group had been among the elements of the unsuccessful coup makers. In September 1991 Gorbachev announced that many Soviet troops would be withdrawn from Cuba. The move, Blasier says, was more symbolic than of practical importance but may have been partly designed to avoid the possibility of the troops' involvement in Cuban civil strife.

The reformists had been increasingly impatient with Gorbachev before the coup and were by and large allied with Boris Yeltsin when he succeeded Gorbachev as premier. When the Soviet Union was dissolved and replaced by Russia and the other members of the Commonwealth of Independent States (CIS), Moscow undertook relations with Latin America. On June 15, 1993, the Soviet combat brigade departed as planned, ending the Russian military presence except for some 500–1000 Russian soldiers and technicians who remained at the electronic intelligence gathering facility in Lourdes, Cuba. In July 1993, Russia granted Cuba a $380 million credit for trade cooperation and to complete projects earlier initiated by the Soviet Union. It was only a fraction of the assistance issuing from Moscow in previous years (Blasier, 1993).

OTHER STATES

Japan

Japan historically had a modest interest in Latin America until after World War II. Its new and expanded role was impressive, restricted as it was to economic affairs and concern for overseas Japanese communities. After 1960 Japan greatly increased its activities to become a leading investor and trader, but with virtually no political dimension to its diplomacy. This approach was consciously and carefully pursued by Japanese decision makers. With the end of the cold war and Latin America's adoption of economic neoliberalism and democratization, Japan accelerated its regional activities and added certain political dimensions to its calculations. Nevertheless, its policy remains primarily oriented toward economic objectives. Japan is much less interested in trade and investment relations with Latin America than with the United States, Europe, and neighboring Asian states. But its global economic power makes its relations with Latin America among the latter's high foreign policy priorities.

Japan's self-imposed isolation from the early seventeenth until the middle of the nineteenth centuries precluded ties with Latin America. (The following commentary is based on Peter Wehner and Eric Fredell in Perry and Wehner, 1985:Ch. 7; Purcell and Immerman, 1992; and Stallings and Székely, 1993.) Toward the end of the nineteenth century and thereafter, Japan gradually increased relations through trade treaties and emigration. Even then, policies were fundamentally apolitical. Following World War II, Japan began to expand its regional involvement, with policies again revolving around economic relations and migration. Although Latin America did not rank high compared to most of Japan's other regional economic involvements, the development of relations with Latin America over the succeeding decades was particularly striking in view of Japan's past isolationism.

Japan undertook its postwar policies on Latin America in the context of its general foreign policy positions. Largely imposed after the war by the victorious United States, and reflected in Japan's new constitution, these positions also comported with the Japanese public's preferences. They focused energies almost exclusively on economic matters, allocating few resources toward defense and placing Japan under the protection of the U.S. security umbrella. In the mid-1970s Japan began to reappraise its defense doctrines, but this reappraisal had little impact on its Latin American outlook. Japan's alliance with the United States remained too important to be eroded by taking contrary positions on relatively peripheral political or security matters like the Central American crisis. Other benefits also derived from this apolitical diplomatic posture. Not only was it considered appropriate to Japan's purposes of economic expansion and protection of overseas Japanese, it allowed Japan to avoid involvement in local Latin American conflicts and to carry on its burgeoning trade with all regime types from right to left.

Latin America became Japan's principal postwar emigration outlet. About a million Japanese migrated to South America from the end of World War II to the early 1980s. The vast majority settled in Brazil, with about 80,000 in Peru, 30,000 in Argentina, and 10,000 in Bolivia. Trade relations, virtually nonexistent in the 1950s, increased from only $600,000 in 1960 to $15 billion in the early 1980s. It was supported by a substantial amount of investment and financial and technical assistance. Japanese communities in South America facilitated the trading relationships.

Japanese economic expansion in Latin America rested on a striking economic complementarity involving trade, investment, and technical and financial assistance. Japan was required to import raw materials and food, whereas certain Latin American economies needed to export them; Japan had to export large quantities of its manufactured goods, and Latin America provided markets. Japan aimed its investment, as well as financial and technical assistance, at developing Latin American raw materials and agricultural products for export to Japan; the exchange earned was then devoted to purchasing Japanese goods. In this closed process, Latin Americans received capital and technology.

After the mid-1980s, global and regional developments further influenced Japan's Latin American policies. Japan's interest in Latin America increased with the opening of the region's economies to increased external trade and investment. Nevertheless, Japanese officials are cautious, wary of Latin America's ability to sustain economic reform, maintain political stability, and avoid xenophobia, yet attracted to the region's natural resources and potentially large market. In 1991 Japan's exports to Latin America surpassed the level of 1981, the year preceding the onset of the debt crisis (Purcell and Immerman, 1992). At the behest of the United States as part of the Enterprise for the Americas initiative, Japan agreed to contribute $500 million over five years to a multilateral investment fund administered by the Inter-American Development Bank (IDB). Japan expressed support for Latin American democratization and respect for human rights in several ways. Given Japan's historic economic orientation in its Latin American policies, however, it seems that the new thrust for democracy and human rights, like its overseas development assistance and contributions to the IDB, are adjuncts to economic objectives—to support the further development of Latin American market economies with which Japan trades and invests. Nevertheless, Japan also has indicated interests in its aid policies to promote cooperation regarding environmental and narcotics issues. Japan also differentiates among the regional states. It has increased its investments especially in Mexico, Brazil, and Argentina (in that order).

Israel

Israel, in sharp contrast to Japan, approached Latin America in essentially political terms. Those political interests initially centered on gaining support for the creation of an independent Israeli state, later on combatting competing Arab influences, and always on protecting local Jewish communities. Policies also focused on protecting Israel's domestic arms industry, with Israel earning foreign exchange through large arms sales to Latin American states and supporting U.S. security interests in certain direct ways. Overall, Israel's objectives in Latin America may be described as active but of low priority. (The following commentary follows the analysis of Edy Kaufman, in Perry and Wehner, 1985:Ch. 8; Kaufman, Shapira, and Barromi, 1979; and essays in Fernández, 1990.)

Prior to the establishment of the Israeli state in 1948, and even before World War II, the Zionist movement sought and gained Latin American support for the legitimation of an Israeli state. As Latin American membership in the UN initially constituted more than a third of the total, Latin American voting power was crucial to Israel for decisions made following the withdrawal of the British Mandate from Palestine. The Latin American bloc overwhelmingly supported the Israeli cause. Israeli policies toward Latin America developed slowly thereafter, as Israel devoted its scarce resources to establishing a presence in Europe and the United States. Israeli aims in Latin America always sought to protect the well-being of Jewish communities, found in all parts of the region, and to keep their support.

Israel began to place more importance on Latin America in the early 1960s. Some issues were temporary, such as the diplomatic crisis with Argentina over the kidnapping of the former Nazi Adolf Eichmann. More lasting were those issues related to the Israeli perception, during the chronic Middle East conflict, that Latin American support for its independence was eroding. As Arab states and, later, the PLO increased their activities in Latin America, Israel redoubled its diplomatic efforts. By 1968 Israel had diplomatic relations with seventeen Latin American states, only excluding some small countries. Cuba severed ties in 1973 as part of Castro's drive for leadership of the Nonaligned Movement. Israel was shocked by the support of a number of Latin American delegations for the anti-Zionist resolution passed by the General Assembly in 1975. By that time, with the decline of Latin America's relative voting power and of Israel's position in the UN, Israel had shifted its instrumental emphasis in Latin America to bilateral diplomatic efforts.

Israel attempted to garner what economic gains it could in Latin America, but economic aims were of low priority and commercial transactions modest. Argentina, Chile, Brazil, Mexico, and Venezuela were its major regional trading partners. Part of the activity was in banking, which was tied to local Jewish communities, particularly in Brazil. Oil imports from Mexico were a security matter for Israel, representing part of its effort to diversify its sources. Israel became particularly active in the transference of armaments and related technical assistance as well as other forms of technology.

Israel saw arms transfers to Latin America as of commercial value as well as helpful to keeping Israeli arms factories in production during periods of relative peace. Military transfers were a post-1967 phenomenon; they began after the Six-Day War, when Israel decided to build its own heavy arms industry. When the domestic demand was low, exports kept the arms industry at a high level of readiness. In addition, with weaponry quickly becoming obsolete, the export sale of "older generation" products helped cover the high costs of defense. Arms export policies generally had broad party support in the Israeli Knesset, but some cleavages surfaced from time to time. Criticism was voiced by prominent political leaders, yet both major parties when in power made extensive arms sales to Latin America. Sales to Argentina when it was under military regime from 1977–1983 was a particularly sensitive issue because of the large number of Jews who were victims of repression there.

Israel saw Latin America as an arena where it could both further its own national interests and demonstrate its usefulness to its all-important ally, the United States. Consequently, Israeli diplomacy involved itself in Central American conflict after 1979 in Guatemala and El Salvador and with the *contra* movement in

Nicaragua, in order to supplement U.S. efforts in the region. Israel publicly expressed sympathy with the U.S. invasion of Grenada in 1983. Thus, part of Israel's Latin American policies stemmed from its perception of the region as a U.S. sphere of influence in which Israel might benefit its bilateral relations with the United States. With the end of the cold war, the military dimension of Israel's Latin American relations declined, to the relief of many Israeli analysts who found highly embarrassing the Central American military connection and the activities of certain Israeli agents.

The People's Republic of China

From the establishment of the People's Republic of China (PRC) in 1949 following Mao Tse Tung's revolution, until the Cuban Revolution of 1959, the PRC evidenced slight interest in Latin America. This was based on a combination of factors, including China's preoccupation with consolidating its own revolution, its concerns with strengthening its relations with the Soviet Union and the United States, Latin America's geographic remoteness, and the Chinese assumption that it was in the U.S. sphere of influence. Chinese policy, to the extent that it existed, rhetorically opposed U.S. imperialism and advocated armed guerrilla struggle to overthrow Latin American regimes. Latin America generally followed the U.S. lead in isolating the PRC in world politics, including opposition to its admission to the United Nations.

The PRC attempted to establish a close relationship with Cuba after the Castro revolution. It stressed the parallel nature of their revolutions and the compatibility of Maoist and Fidelista theories of rural guerrilla warfare. By then China and the Soviet Union had fallen out over a number of fundamental issues. Thus, in Latin America only Cuba had diplomatic ties with the PRC and was the only one to support China's admission to the UN. The two states also commenced a modest barter trade of sugar for rice. The relationship turned conflictual, however, and Cuba refused to align with the PRC against the Soviet Union. Castro accused the PRC of subversive activities in Cuba and complained of Chinese deceit in their trading relationship. The Soviet Union simultaneously outmaneuvered the PRC with economic and military assistance to Cuba.

The PRC developed only a few cooperative relations in Latin America. It began to trade with Mexico in 1963, then with Argentina and Brazil. The divisive Cultural Revolution (1966–1969) isolated the PRC in world politics and drastically reduced what contacts existed with Latin America. Its relations increased after 1970 and changed in style, but the PRC did not become an important regional actor. PRC leadership shifted away from dogmatic revolutionary ideology, and the PRC's friendlier relations with the United States in 1971 enhanced its acceptance among Latin Americans. A majority of Latin American governments voted for PRC entry into the UN in October 1971, and China reciprocated by supporting Latin American governments in the law of the sea negotiations, in which they claimed 200-mile territorial sea limits. PRC propaganda continued its anti-imperialist rhetoric against both the United States and the Soviet Union and in support of armed struggle. In practice, however, the PRC expressed a desire for diplomatic and trade relations with Latin American governments, both civilian and military. Extensive diplomatic exchanges were established after 1970 with

Chile, Peru, Argentina, Mexico, and Brazil, but international trade never developed beyond a small scale. Propaganda statements were softened in the 1980s.

Canada

Canada's serious interest in Latin America began relatively recently, essentially in the late 1960s. Until then, Canada's activity in Latin America was muted by a perception of the predominant U.S. regional role and the enormous importance of its bilateral relationship with the United States. It was further restricted by Canada's orientation toward Europe and membership in the British Commonwealth and, after World War II, in NATO.

In 1867 the United Kingdom formed the Dominion of Canada as a self-governing entity, but Canada conducted its international relations through the British diplomatic system. In 1931 Canada gained sovereign independence within the British Commonwealth and commenced to prosecute its own foreign policy. Yet, as Thomas C. Bruneau (in Perry and Wehner:Ch.6, 1985) points out, Canada sent its first diplomatic missions to Latin America in 1941 and in 1960 organized the Latin American Division in the Department of External Affairs. In the private sector, as Bruneau further notes, Canadian economic involvement dated at least from the late nineteenth century with the activities of Canadian banks, mining firms, and commercial enterprises. But Canada declined to join the Inter-American System, both when it was founded in 1889 and when it was organized around the Organization of American States (OAS) in 1948.

Canadian commercial banks undertook an important post–World War II role in the English-speaking Caribbean, becoming active in the British colonies and dominating their banking systems after they gained independence beginning in the early 1960s. Canadian banks expanded into other states in the Caribbean. It took independent action in Latin America in 1962 when Prime Minister John G. Diefenbaker's Conservative government decided to continue diplomatic and trade relations with Fidel Castro's Cuba after they had been ruptured by the United States and almost all of the Latin American states (Hebron, 1992).

Beginning in 1968, the Liberal government of Prime Minister Pierre Trudeau reoriented Canadian policies in Latin America. Canada's increased attention was reflected in its augmented diplomatic representation in the region. In 1972 Canada became a member of the Inter-American Development Bank (the first non-member of the OAS to do so) and a permanent observer to the OAS. Its primary regional interest continued to be commercial and economic, and its policies had little political-security content. In about 1976 Canadian officials adopted a "hemispheric middle power" concept that emphasized bilateral relations, especially trade, with certain Latin American states (Dosman, 1992). The priority partners were Brazil, Mexico, Chile, Colombia, and Venezuela, with whom Canada's trade expanded significantly. Canada not only counted on their expanding economies but also perceived them as becoming relatively independent of the United States and sharing common positions, not in congruence with those of the United States, on the law of the sea negotiations, conflict in Central America, and the issue of Cuba (Dosman, 1992). Development assistance was extended almost entirely to the Commonwealth Caribbean Countries, where Canada felt it had special interests and responsibilities.

The Latin American debt crisis, beginning in 1982, caused Canada to alter its positive view of the region's potential and its own role. The idea of hemispheric middle power partnerships was abandoned and replaced by a Third World perception. Canada paid more attention to Central America, sharing European views that conflict there was the result of internal social, political, and economic factors and not, as the United States said, a function of East-West conflict. It shifted economic relations to Asia and the Pacific Rim, although its presence in the Commonwealth Caribbean continued. The result was the neglect of the larger Latin American countries with whom Canada had recently established strong relationships.

Canada's Latin American policies entered a new, intense, and apparently long-term phase in 1989. In that year the Conservative government of Brian Mulroney adopted a new "Latin American Strategy" calling for higher priority in Latin American relations, including OAS membership and a number of related actions. Canadian officials responsible for the region found the existing unbalanced and neglectful approach worrisome, especially in view of the end of the cold war and the rapid evolution of global and inter-American developments. In 1989 Canada finally became a full member of the OAS. The inter-American agenda included a number of hemispheric problems of interest to Canada that it saw amenable to multilateral cooperation: democracy and human rights; immigrants and refugee flows; trade, investment, debt, and development assistance; narcotics trafficking; and environmental degradation. Canada also participated directly and substantially in the diplomacy and military organization of the first United Nations peace-keeping operation in the Americas—the UN Observer Group in Central America (ONUCA) (Child, 1992). In 1991 Canada joined the United States and Mexico in trilateral negotiations that resulted in the historic North American Free Trade Agreement. Canada revived its partnership with the major South American states, facilitated by their return to democracy and market economies.

By the mid-1990s, Canada had undertaken a significant role in inter-American relations. Its regional policy-making was consequently more complex, in consonance with the dynamism of the region itself and the multifarious agenda of the Inter-American System. Although Canada's newly adopted regional activism and partnership in NAFTA are in addition to its traditional globalism, both are consonant with other policy principles in place since World War II: self-perception as a "middle power"; commitment to multilateralism as the way to deal with pressing international problems in which it was particularly concerned, including active participation in global peacekeeping and (more recently) peacemaking; diplomatic role as third-party "honest broker"; the search for global and regional security based on international law; and the pursuit of Third World development through social and economic equity. The new orientation is not problem-free, however. There is strong domestic opposition to NAFTA from trade unions, certain business enterprises, and the public. Canada continues to disagree strongly with the United States over the latter's persistent isolation of Cuba. Peacekeeping and other multilateral actions are a costly burden to Canada's government budget. Nevertheless, Canada has chosen to play a high-profile role in the hemisphere and has already made long-term institutional commitments to do so.

BIBLIOGRAPHIC COMMENT

The first notable comparative analysis of the nonhemispheric states' policies toward Latin America is Goldhamer (1972). Perry and Wehner (1985) edited a useful collection of essays, with chapters on seven nonhemispheric states and Canada. Grabendorff and Roett (1985) edited an important book with reference to European policies, and Duran (1985) is an excellent treatment. Mower (1982) is a good study of European Community policies. Substantial articles on post–cold war European policy are Grabendorff (1992), and Freres, Klaveren, and Ruiz-Giménez (1992). The Soviet presence is studied by Blasier (1988), Duncan (1985), Miller (1989), Mujal-Leon (1988), and Varas (1987); and post–cold war developments by Blasier (1991, 1993), Duncan (1992), W.S. Smith (1992), and Adams (1993). On Japan's actions, see Purcell and Immerman (1992) and Stallings and Székely (1993). On Israel's policies, Kaufman, Shapira, and Barromi (1979) is the best treatment. Fernández (1990) analyzes the Middle East and Central America. C. Johnson (1970), and Connelly and Cornejo Bustamante (1992) treat China's general relations, and Li (1991) focuses on economic connections. On Canada, see Ogelsby (1976), Rochlin (1992), Haar and Dosman (1994), Dosman (1992), Hebron (1993), and Schuyler (1991).

CHAPTER FIVE

———————— ■ ————————

The United States

THE UNITED STATES is the most important external actor in Latin America. The purpose of this chapter is to present a broad overview of the Latin American policy of the United States, focusing on U.S. interests and orientations. The discussion begins with an analysis of Latin America's position in U.S. foreign policy calculations, addressing the fundamental calculations that U.S. decision makers have made about the position of Latin America in U.S. foreign policies. The evolution of policy objectives, strategic assessments, and accompanying doctrines are then traced in some detail.

THE LATIN AMERICAN POSITION IN U.S. POLICY

Policy Ends and Means

U.S. relations with Latin America seem to be characterized by abrupt changes in U.S. policy, especially in the twentieth century after the rise of the United States to great-power and then superpower status. The intensity of U.S. interest and the extent of its activities have varied over time and according to the subregions involved. However, from the beginning of U.S.–Latin American relations in the early nineteenth century to the late 1980s, at a fundamental level U.S. policy was consistent and continuous. Although purposes were often couched in moral rhetoric, they were almost always calculated in terms of national security. Specifically, the traditional goal of keeping hostile foreign influences out of the Western Hemisphere was the key to understanding U.S. policy behavior in Latin America until the end of the cold war. For 180 years, U.S. policymakers had a special way of thinking about the region that Lars Schoultz (1987) has labeled "strategic denial," until the post–cold war era when they discarded it as the guiding policy framework.

Strategic denial meant that U.S. policymakers were preoccupied with threats that great powers outside the hemisphere might pose to U.S. security through their operations in Latin America. They attempted to prevent, exclude, or minimize foreign (nonhemispheric) influence and control in Latin America. Such intrusions were viewed as inimical to U.S. military, political, and economic interests (as specifically defined at different times and places). The United States feared some part of the region might serve as a military base of operations against it, and it competed vigorously against the economic influence of other external industrial states. This outlook was relatively constant from as early as 1811 until the late 1980s, whether the extrahemispheric rival was Great Britain in 1811, France and Spain in the 1820s, Great Britain again in the 1850s, Germany at the turn of the century and again in the 1930s, or the Soviet Union after 1947. A related ideological element was present: The United States feared that threats might penetrate the region in such forms as monarchism in the nineteenth century, fascism in the 1930s, and communism during the cold war. Geographic distinctions and capability estimates were factored into the security calculations. Policymakers adopted differentiated views of the subregions within Latin America, and distinct capability considerations were applied to these separate policy arenas. Thus, the degree of U.S. concern with Latin America and the level of its activities there fluctuated with perceptions of foreign threats. Shifting U.S. policy approaches—whether interventionist, noninterventionist, developmentalist, or benign neglect—sprang initially from the objective of excluding foreign threats if they were perceived to exist.

Other objectives were sought but more often than not they were linked to the long-range purpose of strategic denial. Once the preliminary concern with Latin American security with respect to nonhemispheric actors was minimally satisfied, the United States felt free to pursue closer objectives, which were usually (but not always) justified by linking them to long-term concerns with "foreigners." The goal of promoting, encouraging, or developing political and economic stability in Latin America derived from the assumption by U.S. leaders that the overall interests of the United States, as a major, industrial, metropolitan, status quo state, were best served in a secure, peaceful, and stable world. When applied to Latin America, this general goal was often a corollary to that of excluding foreign influence, in that the maintenance of Latin American stability was presumed to be a prerequisite for reducing nonhemispheric threats in the region. Likewise, the consistent pursuit of commercial advantage and vacillating attempts to "democratize" Latin America were often considered to be useful "springboards" to realizing the superior objectives. Economic and democratic development were seen as paths to stability and as ways to preempt certain foreign overtures by offering economic and political alternatives. Military interventions, occasioned by the fear of intervention by other outsiders and designed to preempt them, also sought to bring stability to the object-state of the coercion.

This interpretation runs counter to arguments that the "strategic denial" framework is really a cover for commercial interests and economic domination, or, after World War II and especially in the 1980s, a pretense for simplistic anticommunism. The historical evidence suggests, however, that security against foreign threats transcended other considerations. That is, U.S. policy goals and orientations toward the other Americas were arrived at based on external threat perceptions or the lack of a sense of threat. The intensity of U.S. interest and activities paralleled the degree of external threat perception. As a general matter, over time, the United States was most active in Latin America when nonhemispheric states seemed most threatening. Conversely, during periods when such threats seemed to be low or nonexistent, policy became less connected with security problems. At those times, the United States was inclined to slight the region. This allowed private interests a free hand in their commercial activities, often supported in different ways by U.S. policy. The United States sometimes also pressed Latin America for procedural democracy, on occasion linking the issue to substantive human rights demands, a stance more often than not justified in terms of the quest for security through political stability. A lack of foreign threats muted even the concern with stability, with the United States sometimes choosing to do little if anything.

Strategic denial sometimes led to positive actions, such as inter-American cooperation in the 1930s and World War II and the Alliance for Progress in the 1960s. Some threats were truly provocative, as during the Cuban missile crisis in 1962 when the Soviet Union placed nuclear weapons in Cuba. But more often than not, in my view, strategic denial resulted in misguided policies—based on exaggerated perceptions of threat—to dysfunctional consequences, as during the Caribbean imperialist period of U.S. policy during the first third of the twentieth century, as well as Central American policies and those toward Panama during the 1980s (Atkins, 1992:3).

Analysts who have investigated the perceptions that U.S. decision makers have had of Latin Americans tend to be struck by the persistence of negative stereotypes and paternalistic attitudes. Since the strategic denial paradigm concentrated on what great-power rivals might do in Latin America to affect U.S. security, U.S. policymakers tended to view Latin Americans themselves as unimportant players on the international stage. And although strategic denial meant attempting to assure the independence and self-determination of Latin America with regard to the other external states, a strain of paternalism still colored U.S. policy. U.S. officials have often taken a paternal attitude toward Latin Americans, reluctant to relinquish predominance in the region (especially in the Caribbean area) and assuming that Latin Americans were incapable of handling their own affairs without U.S. supervision.

These paternalist attitudes were reinforced with a negative appraisal of Latin American political culture. U.S. disdain for the peoples and institutions of the region was evident in the earliest days of inter-American relations and carried forward thereafter. John J. Johnson (1990), in a study of the Spanish American struggle for independence while strategic denial was first articulated, analyzed the pronounced shift in the U.S. view, from a proinsurgent perspective prior to Latin American independence to one of limited interest and disdain for the peoples and institutions of the region by 1830. He concluded that in the complexity and confusion of recent U.S. policy, the early policy reveals "more than mere glimmerings of why a cloud of misunderstanding, apprehension, and distrust has overhung hemispheric relations for more than two centuries."

Policy Arenas and Strategic Perceptions

The United States further formulated its Latin American policies on the subregional levels. Geographic and other extrasocietal conditions affected U.S. strategic calculations, perceptions, and capabilities. Consequently, the United States had overlapping but distinct policies toward the overall Latin American region, Mexico, the Circum-Caribbean and sometimes its subdivisions, and the Southern

Cone of South America, with a special view of Brazil. It simultaneously pursued the entire range of bilateral relations. In other words, distinct U.S. policy arenas followed the lines of the various Latin American subregions identified in Chapter 2, and these separate areas of policy and the structures of the subregions themselves mutually influenced and reinforced one another.

The United States has always had a special and intense interest in Mexico. As discussed in Chapter 2, U.S. policy toward Mexico was always determined primarily by territorial proximity. Thus many of the considerations in this relationship were largely divorced from those at work in the larger inter-American arena. Issues tended to be "North American" in content and closely associated with U.S. domestic concerns. In the nineteenth century the United States gained immense territory from Mexico as a result of Texas independence and the war of 1845–1848. European interventions also occurred, most notably Mexico's incorporation into the French empire from 1862–1865 while the United States was occupied with its civil war. But during the dictatorship of Porfirio Díaz (1876–1910), U.S. entrepreneurs dominated certain aspects of the Mexican economy. After the Mexican Revolution of 1910, Mexico adopted highly protectionist economic policies and an essentially isolationist political orientation. U.S. policy after World War II confronted increasing U.S.–Mexican mutual economic and social dependency even as the United States continued to be the much more powerful partner. This was in sharp contrast to the historical relationship, shaped to a considerable extent by expanding economic and social linkages. Mexico fit awkwardly into U.S. cold war constructs.

U.S. officials always considered the Circum-Caribbean—which they preferred to call the Caribbean Basin—to be especially important to U.S. security and well-being. Actions there were more assertive and consequential than in South America beyond the Caribbean. During periods of intense interest based on perceived external threats, the United States attempted to dominate the Caribbean, whereas it was usually satisfied with a more restricted leadership role in the more southerly South American zones. The United States intervened militarily only in Mexico and the Caribbean; it never intervened with troops in the Southern Cone. The most recent U.S. military intervention in Mexico was in 1914; that in the Circum-Caribbean, Panama in 1989/1990. Furthermore, only in the Circum-Caribbean did the United States develop a continuing strategic view giving rise to an active policy. Similar elements in South America beyond the Caribbean were expressed from time to time, in special circumstances such as World War II, but were not sustained.

Brazil also occupied a special role in U.S. policy. The United States long cultivated amicable relations with the "sleeping giant" of Latin America, accelerating efforts in the mid-1970s as Brazil seemed on the verge of realizing its world power ambitions. U.S. policies toward Brazil, once the junior partner in a cooperative alignment with the United States, implied a regard for its increasing regional and even world importance; but that regard declined as Brazil's economic and political problems increased in the 1980s and into the 1990s.

The United States had relatively little interest in and influence with the other states in the Southern Cone. As a general matter, it assigned the subregion the lowest priority in its Latin American policies. The United States did exert leverage in the region (especially economic) and sometimes took coercive measures. But it only intermittently felt threatened by the activities of extrahemispheric interests there, as during the two world wars and episodically during the cold war. Thus U.S. officials, except perhaps for a period during World War II, did not consider the Southern Cone to be part of its sphere of influence.

Democracy and Human Rights

Historically, the most perplexing and chronically troublesome aspects of U.S. policy on Latin American were the proper official attitude to be taken toward Latin American governmental forms and behavior and the extension of U.S values to other states. The fundamental issue was whether to pursue republican forms of government (representative democracy) and the protection of human rights as goals of policy. The U.S. government and its articulate populace always sympathized with democratic elements in Latin America, and formal commitments to democratic processes were made through several inter-American conventions. The actual promotion of democracy, however, received shifting emphasis over the years.

U.S. attempts to extend the practices of representative democracy and protection of human rights were ambiguous and vacillating. When resources were committed to the goal of democratic development, it was usually viewed as an instrumental objective aimed at achieving stability and thus contributing to security against outside threats. Determining the relationship between democratic development in Latin America and the maintenance of political stability and prevention of foreign control was a long-standing problem in U.S. politics. On one side, analysts pointed out the inherent conflict between democratic development and political stability, as the concern for stability caused the United States to tolerate and even support certain dictators and military regimes. Because they cooperated with the United States, these regimes were said to achieve stability. For the most part, the United States accommodated itself to such dictatorships and military regimes and regarded them as conducive at least to temporary stability.

Another policy view maintained that ultimate stability could be achieved not by dictators and armed forces but only through open democratic societies and free elections in which all political groups shared equal opportunity. When dictators and military regimes were perceived as detrimental to achieving stability, U.S. policy shifted against some of them. The reason for supporting democratic development in Latin America in the image of U.S. values was the assumption that open societies and popular participation were the soundest paths to progress and therefore to political stability.

Especially after World War II, policy debates focused on whether instability was more the result of external subversion or of internal conditions. Related arguments concerned the relative merits of shoring up the status quo or encouraging reform (but not radical solutions, which were assumed by both sides to risk foreign orientation). The assumption that the departure of dictators created chaos leading to opportunities for local Communists linked to the Soviet Union had currency after the Cuban Revolution of 1959 and again with the Nicaraguan Revolution of 1979. The public debate revolving around the Reagan administration's Central American policies in the 1980s was but a recent manifestation of these old positions. In fact, policy actions eventually tended to involve some combination of both interventionist and cooperative means for dealing with instability. By the mid-1980s, a consensus had been reached within U.S. policy circles that democratic forms in Latin America best served U.S. interests and should be promoted. The debate continued, however, over how to go about this enterprise.

The Search for New Paradigms

As the international system entered a new post–cold war era in the late 1980s, the United States faced the fundamental problem of redefining its purposes in Latin America and reorienting its policies there. (The following discussion is based on Atkins, 1992.) Because the Soviet Union and Communist expansionism had been the focus of strategic denial for more than four decades, the declaration of an end to the cold war had a major impact on U.S. policy calculations toward Latin America. With the end of East-West conflict and the eventual collapse of the Soviet Union, and no other security threats (as traditionally conceived) on the horizon, the notion of strategic denial was rendered irrelevant as a foundation for Latin American policy and had to be discarded. The new set of issues that assumed top priority were not new but took on increased urgency: problems of international trade and investment, external debt, democracy, human rights, immigration, refugees, drug trafficking, and the physical environment. Strategic denial was an unrealistic basis for dealing with the most significant issues on the inter-American agenda. Critics of U.S. policy during the previous decade had argued that the doctrine had been outmoded long before the end of the cold war. The Bush administration accepted this reality and strategic denial gave way to the other issues. Thus the United States abandoned its 180-year-old preoccupation in the Latin American region with minimizing what it saw as hostile foreign intrusions in the Western Hemisphere.

With strategic denial now irrelevant, U.S. decision makers searched for a new general framework for processing the specific issues. One possibility was to retreat into a posture of "benign neglect," since the U.S. relationship with Latin America, although involving important concerns, was overshadowed by events elsewhere that created an intense competition for U.S. resources. The argument for this eventuality was that the past is the guide to the future—that the lack of a foreign threat had always led to U.S. disinterest and would continue to do so. Opponents to this approach warned of the shortsightedness of withdrawal, since the crucial problems in inter-American relations, which in any event would inevitably intrude onto the U.S. foreign policy agenda, needed to be confronted directly and dealt with effectively. President George Bush signaled the new foundation of U.S. policy by adopting an economic focus, with strong acknowledgment of the essentiality of Latin American democracy and respect for human rights. The Clinton administration continued the same emphases, making the two elements coequal.

EVOLUTION OF POLICY

The Nineteenth Century

Isolationism and the Western Hemisphere Idea. The U.S. foreign policy orientation, beginning with independence in the late eighteenth century and continuing throughout most of the nineteenth century, was characterized by isolationism. However, policy was never founded on a literally isolationist basis of absolute nonintercourse with the rest of the world. Isolationism was relevant primarily to Europe, and then in the special sense of political noninvolvement or "nonentanglement."

The principle of noninvolvement did not extend to U.S. relations with Latin America in the same sense that it was applied to European affairs. The initial U.S. orientation toward Latin America was contained in the Western Hemisphere Idea, also known as the Doctrine of the Two Spheres. This concept posited a special relationship between the United States and Latin America. It was based on the geographic separation of the Americas from Europe and on the notions of political, economic, and social separation of the morally superior New World from the evil, autocratic Old World. The essence of the idea was that the Western (American) Hemisphere was separate and distinct from Europe and had its own set of interests. In general, this notion served as the basis for both the isolation of the Americas from Europe and for ties among the Americas themselves.

The notion of strategic denial was established at the very beginning of inter-American relations in the first quarter of the nineteenth century, in consonance with the isolationist orientation and the Western Hemisphere Idea. The emergence of new Latin American states stimulated international rivalry to gain regional influence or control. The United States was weak in relation to the European powers, but it nevertheless enunciated principles that laid the foundations for the strategic denial approach. The first such statement was the U.S. Congress' No-Transfer Resolution of 1811. At the time, Great Britain was on the verge of war with the United States and threatened to seize Spanish Florida and use it as a military base. In response, the U.S. Congress adopted the resolution that asserted, among other things, that the United States "cannot without serious inquietude see any part of the said territory pass into the hands of any foreign Power." The United States was also worried that the British might take Cuba as well. The No-Transfer Resolution was also in accordance with the Western Hemisphere Idea in stating that although the United States had no objection to Spain's retention of its American possessions, the transfer of lands bordering the United States to a third party (meaning Great Britain) would be viewed unfavorably. U.S. fear of nonhemispheric influences, as well as the idea of hemispheric separateness, was further revealed in December 1823, when President James Monroe issued a warning to Europe against trying to recolonize the area, warning France and Spain in particular to keep "hands off" the Western Hemisphere. This broader expression of strategic denial was later called the Monroe Doctrine.

Initial contacts with Latin America itself were slow in developing. The United States began the recognition process in Latin America in 1822, partly out of sympathy with the Latin Americans, but more in the unfulfilled hope that they thereby would not be dependent on Great Britain or recolonized by France or

Spain. Despite recognition and Monroe's pronouncement (in the midst of the recognition process), the United States did not desire closer political relations. It turned down Latin American overtures to form an inter-American defense alliance against Europe. It was eager for expanded commercial contacts but was preempted by British economic power.

The main U.S. policies were related to ambition for continental expansion. Years of conflict with Mexico culminated in war between the two states (1846–1848), which resulted in huge territorial gains for the victorious United States. In addition, the United States felt that the destiny of the Caribbean region directly affected its security. Cuba was of special importance, with strong interest also shown in building a Central American isthmian canal. The U.S. public sympathized with Cuban insurgents revolting against Spanish authority between 1868 and 1878, but the United States remained neutral even though the Cubans requested its intervention in their favor. The United States also refused schemes to purchase the Danish West Indies and to annex Santo Domingo as well as Cuba. It did not engage in extensive interaction with the rest of Latin America beyond Mexico and the Caribbean.

The Monroe Doctrine. What came to be known as the Monroe Doctrine defined the U.S. attitude toward Europe's relationship with the Americas, and that of the United States toward Latin America. It reflected more than anything else the U.S. desire to limit foreign influence in the Americas. The essence of the policy, first enunciated in 1823 and later considered the "cornerstone" of overall U.S. foreign policy, was a desire for Europe to keep its "hands off" the Western Hemisphere. The policy had its genesis in President Monroe's "declaration" or "principles"; the term "doctrine" was not used until much later. In a sense the Monroe Doctrine had already been partially stated by the U.S. Congress in the 1811 No-Transfer Resolution.

Monroe's statement, included in his annual message to Congress on December 2, 1823, was inspired by the perception of two separate threats. The first was the fear of Russian colonization of the North American Pacific coast, which led to the general declaration "that the American continents, by the free and independent condition which they have assumed and maintain, are henceforth not to be considered as subjects for future colonization by any European power." The second part addressed the challenge represented by Spain's desire to retrieve its New World empire with the help of the French-led Holy Alliance. After noting that "the political system of the allied powers is essentially different ... from that of America," Monroe said:

> We owe it therefore to candor, and to the amicable relations existing between the United States and those powers, to declare that we should consider any attempt on their part to extend their system to any portions of this Hemisphere, as dangerous to our peace and safety. With the existing Colonies or dependencies of any European power, we have not interfered, and shall not interfere. But with the governments who have declared their independence, and have maintained it, and whose independence we have, on great consideration, and on just principles, acknowledged, we could not view any interposition for the purpose of oppressing them, or controlling them in any other manner, their destiny, by any European power, in any other light, than as the manifestation of an unfriendly disposition towards the United States.

Monroe also assured Europe of U.S. reciprocity: "Our policy in regard to Europe, which was adopted at an early state of the wars which have so long agitated that quarter of the globe, nevertheless remains the same, which is, not to interfere in the internal concerns of any of its powers."

Monroe's declaration was unilateral, fairly narrow in scope, and intended to be temporary. Its unilateral nature was made clear in two ways. First, the United States had turned down a British proposal that the two states issue a joint declaration. Second, immediately after making the pronouncement, the United States rebuffed Latin American suggestions for treaties of alliance. Monroe restricted his warning to future colonization and was tolerant toward existing colonies; he mentioned nothing of prohibiting other forms of European intervention or influence as later interpretations were to do. That the policy was intended to be temporary was indicated by the fact that, for most of the half-century following Monroe's pronouncement, it was largely ignored as a policy guide. Once the immediate danger had passed, and during the long period of U.S. military weakness and domestic preoccupations, Monroe's words were virtually forgotten. A number of European military interventions occurred in Latin America and the United States did nothing. Great Britain undertook responsibility for the protection of Latin America from the designs of other European powers.

Manifest Destiny. During the first half of the nineteenth century, the United States was preoccupied with continental expansion, expressed in the ideology of "manifest destiny." The idea that the United States was entitled to expand its control across the virgin continent from one ocean to the other was widespread. The process of continental expansion inevitably brought the United States into conflict with Mexico and eventually led to Caribbean imperialism.

In only fifty years, between 1803 and 1853, the territory of the United States expanded from the area occupied by the original thirteen colonies to essentially its present boundaries, with most of the added territory taken from what was originally Spanish America. The first and largest single acquisition was the purchase in 1803 of the Louisiana Territory from France, to whom Spain had ceded the area in 1800. Its addition more than doubled the U.S. territorial size. For fifteen years after the Louisiana Purchase, the United States negotiated with Spain for the "Floridas," actually seizing some territory in 1810 and 1813. In 1819, the two states signed the Adams-Onís Treaty (it went into effect in 1821), in which Spain ceded to the United States all of its Gulf Coast lands east of the Mississippi River.

The United States and Mexico clashed for decades over the Texas question. Texans won their independence in 1836 after a violent struggle, and finally, in 1845, Texas became a state in the union. Mexican objections to the annexation and continuing U.S. expansionist tendencies led to war (1846–1848). Under the Treaty of Guadalupe Hidalgo, signed in 1848, Mexico ceded half of its national territory to the United States, including what today constitutes much of the U.S. West and Southwest. In 1853, exactly fifty years after the Louisiana Purchase, the continental dimensions of the United States were completed, except for some later minor adjustments, with the Gadsden Purchase from Mexico. Although U.S. leaders from time to time considered pursuing territorial gains in the Caribbean region, no further Latin American territory was taken by the United States until after its war with Spain in 1898.

Democratic Policy and Pan Americanism. A U.S. policy tradition on the question of relations with nondemocratic regimes was established at the very start of inter-American relations. Throughout the nineteenth century and into the twentieth, Spanish-American political processes were characterized by dictatorship (Brazil was successfully governed under a constitutional monarch). The United States enunciated broad policy outlines in the spirit of its recognition of the revolutionary French government in 1793. On that occasion, Secretary of State Thomas Jefferson said: "We surely cannot deny to any nation that right whereon our own government is founded that everyone may govern itself under whatever form it pleases." Later, as president, Jefferson established a policy tradition when he applied this principle specifically to Latin America. With few exceptions, such as Secretary of State William H. Seward's opposition to monarchy in Mexico in 1865 (in fact, in opposition to French occupation), this Jeffersonian tradition guided policy until the presidency of Woodrow Wilson during World War I.

The United States inaugurated the Pan American movement in the 1880s, primarily for the purposes of promoting hemispheric trade and developing procedures for the peaceful settlement of disputes. It was not interested in security questions, the primary Latin American concern, and consistently strove to keep them off conference agendas. The First International Conference of American States, held in Washington in 1889–1990, initiated the Pan American policy of the United States. It reflected the interests of U.S. businesspeople who had recently discovered trade and investment opportunities in Latin America. Policy was also motivated by the potential of the Inter-American System as an instrument for promoting international stability through peaceful settlement procedures and for gathering Latin America together in a single organization under U.S. leadership, thus preempting other foreign influences.

The Latin American policy of the United States from the last decade of the nineteenth century through the first third of the twentieth was characterized by tension between the Monroe Doctrine and Pan Americanism; the latter began in earnest in 1889 but the former dominated until the 1930s. Both of these policy approaches flowed from the Western Hemisphere Idea positing a special relationship among the Americas. They were also contradictory, however, in that the Monroe Doctrine was a unilateral policy that came to justify U.S. intervention in the Caribbean area, while Pan Americanism was based on the idea of international equality and cooperation. Even though the inter-American conferences beginning in 1889 posited a policy of U.S. cooperation with Latin America, especially in matters of international trade, multilateral diplomacy was not a major aspect of U.S. policy until the 1930s. Meanwhile, unilateral imperialism superseded multilateral cooperation.

The Twentieth Century to World War II

U.S. Imperialism. During the last few years of the nineteenth century, the United States changed its policy orientation from traditional isolationism to a rudimentary internationalism. The nation passed through a period of policy transition that resulted in active participation in world affairs and elevation to the status of a great power. The new orientation revived U.S. interest in Latin America and ended its policy inaction, but it resulted in the beginnings of imperialism and coercive policies in the Caribbean area (as well as the far reaches of the Pacific Ocean). The United States demonstrated a new assertiveness in 1895, when it was willing to defy even Great Britain in the latter's dispute with Venezuela over the boundary with British Guiana. Richard Olney, secretary of state under President Grover Cleveland, asserted the Monroe Doctrine against Great Britain during the dispute. His note to the British foreign minister, which claimed U.S. hegemony in the Americas, was dubbed the Olney Corollary to the Monroe Doctrine.

A new wave of nationalism that swept the United States in the 1890s led to war with Spain and resulted in territorial acquisitions in the Caribbean area. A new interpretation of manifest destiny reaching beyond continental limits was typified by the "Expansionists of 1898" who molded U.S. public opinion; the Caribbean region loomed large in their strategic thinking. The most important of them was Captain (later Admiral) Alfred Thayer Mahan, who shaped official U.S. strategic thinking about the Caribbean area for many years to come. His converts and disciples included Senator Henry Cabot Lodge and President Theodore Roosevelt.

Mahan's thesis, developed from his study of naval history, revolved around his concern with the relationship of mercantilist imperialism and sea power to national security and progress ("destiny") (Mahan, 1918). In short, according to Mahan, national greatness depended on the three related factors of maritime strength, sea power, and imperialism; therefore, no great nation could be isolationist. U.S. policy action in the Caribbean area was crucial to Mahan and was one of the main subjects of his writing. He strongly advocated the construction of an isthmian canal because it would draw the Pacific, Atlantic, and Gulf Coasts of the North American continent closer together. Mahan also somberly warned of the "many latent and as yet unforeseen dangers to the peace of the Western Hemisphere, attendant upon the opening of the canal." He predicted that the then comparatively deserted Caribbean Sea would become, like the Red Sea, a great thoroughfare of shipping that would attract "the interest and ambition of maritime nations."

Mahan further warned that increased rivalry from Europe in the Caribbean as a result of "the piercing of the isthmus [would be] nothing but a disaster to the United States, in the present state of her military and naval preparation." With the enhanced commercial and military value of the Caribbean and the strategic importance of a canal, the "indifference of foreign nations" would pass away. It would be dangerous for the United States to build a canal without also constructing its own continental defenses, building a strong naval force for offensive power, controlling the entire Caribbean area through the acquisition of bases, and fortifying and exclusively controlling any canal.

Mexico as an object of policy occupied a position distinct from the Caribbean area and the rest of Latin America. According to Mahan, although Mexico's location on the southern boundary of the United States made it of considerably more interest than the Southern Cone, Mexico was of less strategic importance than most of the Caribbean. Partly because of the lack of potential Mexican naval facilities, Mahan considered it important for the United States to acquire bases in the Caribbean islands circling the eastern approaches to the isthmus.

The war with Spain in 1898 lasted only ten weeks, after which a peace treaty was concluded under terms dictated by the United States. As a result, the United

States annexed Puerto Rico, established a protectorate over Cuba, and occupied some smaller Caribbean islands. Furthermore, U.S. leaders became unequivocally determined to build and exclusively control a transisthmian canal, and concrete arrangements were so made. In 1917 the United States purchased the Danish West Indies (the U.S. Virgin Islands). With Spain now completely ejected from the hemisphere and Great Britain willing to retire from the Caribbean area, the new U.S. strategic position was supported by public opinion. The United States had overcome external challenges in those parts of Latin America where it had asserted its power.

In 1904 President Theodore Roosevelt enunciated the broadest extension of Monroe's principles by far. Known as the Roosevelt Corollary, the principle asserted that U.S. interventions in the Caribbean were justified. Two years before, Germany, Great Britain, and Italy had blockaded Venezuela to enforce their financial claims, but at the behest of the United States they agreed to submit the dispute to the Hague Court of Arbitration. The court's ruling, which upheld the argument of the European powers that they should receive preferential treatment in the payment of their claims, set a precedent for the use of force in the collection of public debts. In 1904 European creditor nations threatened force against the Dominican Republic to collect defaulted debts as they had in Venezuela. In response to the Dominican situation, Roosevelt included a statement in his annual message to Congress in 1904, which became his Corollary to the Monroe Doctrine and was also known as the "big stick policy":

> Chronic wrongdoing, or an impotence which results in a general loosening of the ties of civilized society, may in America ... ultimately require intervention by some civilized nation, and in the Western Hemisphere the adherence of the United States to the Monroe Doctrine may force the United States ... in flagrant cases of wrongdoing or impotence, to the exercise of an international police power.

The United States invoked the Roosevelt Corollary for the next quarter-century to justify its many interventions in a number of Caribbean states. Interventionist policies begun under President Roosevelt continued under Presidents William Howard Taft, Woodrow Wilson, and Calvin Coolidge. Several coercive instruments were employed, including the use or threat of armed invasion and military occupation, the imposition of treaties giving the United States the right to intervene, the establishment of customs receiverships and financial control, the recognition and nonrecognition of new governments used to influence their policies, and the supervision of elections.

Two long-range U.S. goals in Latin America—the exclusion of foreign influence and promotion of regional stability—were objectives of the active military, fiscal, and political interventions in the Caribbean. More specifically, interventions were used to secure and later protect the Panama Canal, to maintain law and order and protect the lives and property of citizens, to support North American investments and loans, and later, to encourage representative democracy. U.S. imperialism was aimed primarily at preventing other outside influences from dominating the area and at preempting European intervention. But after the U.S.

position against outside threats was secured and stability enforced, it vigorously pressed for further advantages.

Not all of these proximate goals were sought at once by all U.S. administrations, but all of them were considered to be concomitant with national security interests. For example, "dollar diplomacy," encouraged by the Taft administration, involved the manipulation of loans and investments by U.S. consortia in the Caribbean region (especially Nicaragua and Honduras). This practice was followed by military landings ("pecuniary intervention") to protect private U.S. commercial interests. Dollar diplomacy appeared simply to advance the interests of investors, but historians have since concluded that, from the point of view of the U.S. government if not that of the investors themselves, dollar diplomacy was also aimed at serving broader goals. U.S. investments, it was hoped, would keep out other foreign interests as well as support stability in small Caribbean states. Military intervention would protect and encourage U.S. investors at the same time that it, too, would enforce a degree of political stability in the Caribbean. In short, U.S. investors benefitted from coercive U.S. diplomacy, but they did so as a part of U.S. security policy.

When President Woodrow Wilson came to office in 1913, he altered the traditional U.S. view of Latin American regimes and revised U.S. democratic policies. The Wilson credo reconciled the president's liberal political principles with his policy of frequent intervention in the Caribbean by considering the following: Political instability in Caribbean countries was a threat to U.S. interests; instability was caused by political immaturity; maturity was measurable by the extent of progress toward constitutional democracy. As a policy matter Wilson assumed that democracy could be imposed by external pressure or force and that the United States, as the most politically mature (that is, democratic) and powerful nation in the Western Hemisphere, was responsible for taking an active role in the political development of Latin America.

The Good Neighbor Policy. U.S. policies from 1929 to 1945 contrasted sharply with those of 1895 to 1928. Basic U.S. goals, however, remained constant. The United States under the Good Neighbor Policy largely abandoned direct interventionary techniques, but the goals of foreign exclusion and Latin American stability remained, to be sought through cooperation rather than coercion. The reasons for the policy change lie in U.S. calculations of a changing strategic situation. After World War I European threats to hemispheric security were virtually nonexistent, and Latin American instability posed little direct threat to the United States. In addition, Latin American governments had made it clear that inter-American cooperation depended on the U.S. abandonment of interventionist practices. Intervention also aroused opposition in the United States. Consequently, coercion was greatly reduced.

The features of what became known as the Good Neighbor Policy were tentatively established during the administration of Herbert Hoover (1929–1933). Franklin D. Roosevelt, inaugurated in 1933, explicitly enunciated the policy and expanded it. President Hoover repudiated the Roosevelt Corollary to the Monroe Doctrine and significantly reduced Caribbean intervention. A memorandum written by Under Secretary of State J. Reuben Clark in 1928 and circulated to the Latin American governments in 1930 dissociated the Roosevelt Corollary from the doctrine, although it did not renounce the use of intervention as a policy instrument. Some U.S. troops were removed from the Caribbean area, and certain U.S. investors were told that they must seek local Latin American remedies for their problems.

President Roosevelt made the Good Neighbor Policy explicit, gave up intervention as a policy instrument (in both law and practice), and reinvigorated Pan American cooperation. In his inaugural address on March 4, 1933, he vowed that "in the field of foreign policy I would dedicate this nation to the policy of the good neighbor." The following month, he specifically applied the Good Neighbor Policy to Latin America in a Pan American Day speech, with these words: "The essential qualities of a true Pan Americanism must be the same as those which constitute a good neighbor, namely, mutual understanding, a sympathetic appreciation of the other's point of view. It is only in this manner that we can hope to build up a system of which confidence, friendship, and good will are the cornerstones."

A salient aspect of the Good Neighbor Policy, as directed by Secretary of State Cordell Hull and by Sumner Welles in his various official positions, was the Pan Americanization of the Monroe Doctrine. That is, direct intervention was renounced by the United States and regional organization was embraced as a major (but far from exclusive) policy instrument. In 1933 the United States accepted, with reservations, an inter-American treaty stipulating nonintervention by one American state in the affairs of another. Three years later it accepted another treaty without reservation agreeing to the principle of absolute nonintervention. Nonintervention was implemented with the U.S. abandonment of its five Caribbean protectorates—in Cuba, Haiti, the Dominican Republic, Nicaragua, and Panama—including the abrogation or revision of the treaties on which they were based. Situations that before would have occasioned intervention were dealt with through direct bilateral diplomatic negotiations, notably Mexico's expropriation of U.S. oil company properties.

Policies of nonintervention required a return to tradition with regard to U.S. efforts at democratization. Abandoning the nonrecognition of unconstitutional governments and adopting a policy of noninterference in the internal affairs of others meant dealing with dictatorships often on a partnership basis. As a result, nonintervention came under attack because it permitted the continued existence of dictators and allowed others to seize power. U.S. officials rejected the criticism, restated the commitment to nonintervention, and complained that those who deplored the effect of nonintervention were the very ones who had opposed prior intervention.

With the rise of the Fascist governments in Europe and their increased activities in Latin America, and especially with the threat of European war in the late 1930s, the United States was again concerned with foreign influences and Latin American stability. With intervention discredited, a cooperative hemispheric security system was constructed in the late 1930s and extended during World War II. Political, economic, and military collaboration took place during the war, on both bilateral and multilateral bases. Most Latin American states, with some important exceptions, cooperated with the United States during the war, and the domestic status quo was generally maintained.

The Truman and Eisenhower Administrations

The United States emerged from World War II as the most powerful state in the world with involvements on a global scale. Beginning in 1947, cold war criteria were fundamental to U.S. policy formulation. The connected themes of world-wide interests and cold war concerns shaped U.S. policy on Latin America. As a result, the degree to which Latin America received attention in U.S. policy priorities depended essentially on the extent of the Communist threat in the other Americas and the degree of U.S. involvement in other parts of the world. As an arena of cold war conflict, Latin America was only a minor theater until the advent of Castro's Cuba in 1959. By the mid-1960s the Cuban Revolution seemed an atypical case and Latin America again received little attention. The United States resumed direct interventionist techniques from time to time, especially in the Caribbean area.

The Western Hemisphere Idea of a "special relationship" among the Americas lost most of its meaning after World War II. With its acceptance of broad international roles and pursuit of intimate relations with Europe, the United States all but abandoned the idea of two separate and distinct world spheres. The idea lingered on, at least in U.S. rhetoric concerning its Latin American policy, but in reality no special inter-American relations existed in the sense of either exclusivity or high priority. The Alliance for Progress period in the early 1960s and Caribbean policies in the 1980s both placed high priority on Latin America, and each policy in its own way was pursued in the context of East-West conflict.

The United States had showed declining interest in Latin America during the latter part of World War II as Secretary Hull's ideas about globalism became dominant. "Good Neighbor" rhetoric was continued after the war, but U.S. interest in Latin America was superseded by problems related to the devastation of Europe, the "containment" of the Soviet Union, and later, by communism in Asia. The apparent lack of a serious foreign (that is, Communist) threat in Latin America did not allow the region to be easily fitted into global cold war policies. Soviet expansion in Latin America seemed as remote as the prospect of internal Communist subversion. President Harry S Truman and his secretaries of state, George C. Marshall and Dean Acheson, made clear to Latin America that U.S. leaders felt that world problems were more crucial elsewhere. They candidly stressed the remoteness of Latin America from cold war problems.

After President Dwight D. Eisenhower was inaugurated in 1953, he and Secretary of State John Foster Dulles indicated that bold Latin American policy departures were imminent. President Eisenhower appointed his brother, Dr. Milton Eisenhower, a scholar with Latin American interests, to visit and report on the region with a view to U.S. policy reform. Dr. Eisenhower's subsequent report, submitted on November 18, 1953, stressed the need for additional U.S. economic assistance to the area and for a general upgrading of Latin America in U.S. policy priorities. As it turned out, the Eisenhower policy contained little that was new for Latin America. The policy emphasis, until late in the administration, still focused on the cold war outside the hemisphere.

The only significant cold war events in Latin America prior to the Castro revolution in Cuba had to do with Communists in Guatemala gaining important positions in the leftist government of Jacobo Arbenz Guzmán (1951–1954). The United States obtained the adoption of a formal declaration against communism in the Americas at the Tenth Inter-American Conference at Caracas in 1954. Shortly thereafter the United States covertly sponsored a military coup that overthrew Arbenz. Except for the Guatemala case, the United States did not perceive a Communist threat in Latin America. Secretary Dulles, never complacent about communism, said at a press conference on November 5, 1957, that "we see no likelihood at the present time of communism getting into control of the political institutions of any of the American republics." Nevertheless, in its Pan American policies, the United States aimed primarily to convert the Inter-American System into an anti-Communist alliance.

U.S. policy changed during the last two years of the Eisenhower presidency, in orientation if not in purpose. The first catalyst for change was the treatment of Vice President Richard M. Nixon during his "goodwill" tour in 1958. Violent riots in Peru and Venezuela, at times threatening Nixon's physical safety, dramatized Latin American dissatisfaction with U.S. policy. The second and more important impetus for change was the Castro revolution in Cuba, coming to power on January 1, 1959. Castro's highly nationalist movement was strongly anti–United States in its ideological content; *antiyanquismo* eventually led to the embrace of Marxism-Leninism and alliance with the Soviet Union and its East European bloc. An important foreign intrusion was present in the Caribbean region, shaking the United States from its assumption of Latin American immunity from the cold war. The president proposed his "Eisenhower Plan" in 1960 for increased economic aid to Latin America, and corresponding funds were appropriated by Congress. Further plans were laid for forceful intervention against Castro. Both policy approaches—increased aid and intervention—were carried out by the succeeding Kennedy administration.

Policies toward the different types of Latin American regimes and democratization again vacillated in the postwar period. Toward the end of World War II, the Truman presidency briefly returned to the idea of intervention on behalf of democracy and in opposition to dictatorship. Political interventionist policies were pursued in Argentina in 1945 and 1946 as the United States actively opposed the presidential candidacy of Colonel Juan Perón, considered by U.S. officials to be Fascist-inclined. He subsequently won the presidency with ease; shortly thereafter, the United States ceased advocating intervention in the name of democracy.

After World War II, foreign aid programs, especially military, became caught up in policies and debates concerning Latin American dictators and democrats. Both the Truman and Eisenhower administrations signed mutual defense assistance pacts with several Latin American governments, including dictatorial and military regimes. Officials insisted that in each case the granting of aid was determined by its value in promoting mutual security rather than by the political form of its recipient.

The Kennedy and Johnson Administrations

During the abbreviated presidency of John F. Kennedy and the first part of Lyndon B. Johnson's administration, Latin America assumed a major position in

U.S. policy under the Alliance for Progress. In his inaugural address on January 20, 1961, Kennedy offered a "special pledge" to Latin America, promising to convert U.S. "good words into good deeds, in a new alliance for progress, to assist free men and free governments in casting off the chains of poverty." At a White House reception for Latin American diplomats on March 13, 1961, the president proposed a ten-year Alliance for Progress plan of inter-American cooperation for Latin American economic, social, and political development. In August, the Alliance for Progress was formally multilateralized at an inter-American conference, which enacted the "Charter of Punta del Este" detailing the goals and means of the effort.

President Kennedy, who had been highly critical of the Eisenhower administration's policies toward Latin American dictators and military regimes, stressed that economic development and social reform should take place within an emerging democratic framework with political freedom. The multilateral charter stated twelve goals for the Alliance, the first of which was "to improve and strengthen democratic institutions through application of the principle of self-determination by the people."

Thus, U.S. policy on Latin America assumed a position of high priority under the Kennedy administration. Nevertheless, policy continued to be formulated in a cold war context and in pursuit of traditional long-range goals. The United States feared that Communists would capture the revolutionary aspirations of a changing Latin America—that fidelismo would spread from Cuba to other parts of the region. Policy was directed at preventing foreign influence and maintaining political stability against communism through "developmentalism." It was hoped that social reform and economic growth would create political stability and deter Communist success. The purpose of economic assistance always had been to create the necessary economic conditions conducive to political stability. Now social conditions were also included in the stability formula. The efforts toward democratic development were also based on the premise that a counterideology to communism was needed. The purpose of military assistance was clearly stated to be a support for political stability, aimed especially at counterinsurgency and the maintenance of internal order considered necessary for economic and political development, with only modest attention paid to defense against offshore incursions. In addition, the United States attempted further to consolidate the Inter-American System into an anti-Communist alliance; it succeeded in gaining multilateral agreements to exclude Cuba from participation in the OAS in 1962 and in 1964 to impose diplomatic and economic sanctions on the Castro regime.

The anti-Communist, antimilitary, prodemocracy, and developmentalist goals of the Alliance for Progress suggested a belief that Latin America sorely needed to pursue material and social progress; if it did not come about within a democratic framework, Latin Americans would be tempted to embrace radical solutions of the Castro-Communist type. Much was made of the fact that Castro had succeeded dictator Fulgencio Batista, with whom the United States had enjoyed cordial relations. It was implied that the United States would not only promote democracy but would also oppose military coups and governments. This return to Wilsonian principles was motivated by the idea that dictators bequeathed a political vacuum to their successors that facilitated the Communist alternative. Therefore, the best way to oppose communism was to oppose repressive regimes, which make their nations vulnerable to political chaos and communism.

In addition to developmentalist strategies, the United States practiced military intervention. In April 1961 a U.S.-organized and U.S.-financed band of Cuban exiles invaded Cuba at the Bay of Pigs hoping to stimulate a popular uprising that would overthrow Castro. The intervention, planned under Eisenhower and carried out by Kennedy, was a total failure; the invaders were easily subdued by Cuban forces.

The Alliance for Progress immediately faced serious problems. From 1961 to 1963 military coups overthrew constitutionally elected governments in seven Latin American countries. The success of these coups challenged the ideological (democratic) commitment and assumptions of the Alliance. The United States generally refused to recognize the new governments, suspended diplomatic relations, and terminated economic and military assistance. Then, in 1963, the U.S. position regarding military aid and democracy shifted and remained unchanged until the mid-1970s. With some doubt about the effectiveness of antimilitary measures, the Kennedy policies took a pragmatic turn and accommodated military regimes. Latin American military establishments came to be viewed as important parts of the political-social structure that played valuable and necessary roles in the process of modernization and nation-building.

In the meantime, the Soviet Union had stationed its ballistic missiles on Cuban soil. The dramatic "missile crisis" of October 1962 was a confrontation between the United States and the Soviet Union over these weapons. Intense U.S. decision-making and action quickly followed the discovery of the missiles on October 14, 1962. President Kennedy organized his advisers as the Executive Committee of the National Security Council (Excom). His objectives were to compel the Soviet Union to remove its offensive nuclear weapons from Cuba while avoiding nuclear war. The costs and risks of several options were assessed by Excom and congressional and military leaders. The president finally decided to impose a blockade of Cuba, which was euphemistically referred to as a "quarantine." He had apparently decided that the presence of operational Soviet weapons in Cuba would constitute an adverse fundamental shift in the balance of world power and that therefore they must be removed, but he favored pressing for their removal rather than destroying them through direct military action. Those favoring air strikes or invasion contended that, as the missiles had already arrived in Cuba, a blockade would be futile. In addition, when the president announced the quarantine, he warned that any missile launched from Cuba on the United States would invite a U.S. retaliatory blow not on Cuba but on the Soviet Union.

The Cuban missile crisis came to an end in November 1962. The Soviet Union agreed to stop building bases in Cuba and to withdraw its nuclear weapons, bomber aircraft, and ground combat troops. In return, the United States lifted the blockade and pledged nonintervention in Cuba, subject to verification that Soviet weapons had been withdrawn. Thus, the United States was successful on the issue of ballistic missiles in Cuba; the Soviet Union did not, however, withdraw its combat unit as promised.

The Alliance for Progress was carried on by President Johnson after his inauguration in November 1963 following the assassination of President Kennedy. In

April 1965, Johnson initiated a massive U.S. intervention in the Dominican Republic in order to prevent "another Cuba." As the United States became more involved in the Vietnam conflict, however, its concern with Latin America receded. Furthermore, the Cuban case eventually proved to be atypical of Latin American politics. Cuba failed to export its revolution, and after 1967 it abandoned serious attempts to do so for more than a decade. The lack of a Communist threat to the hemisphere coincided with U.S. congressional disillusionment with foreign aid as a policy technique in the world at large and a general decline in available U.S. economic and military assistance funds. Latin Americans again complained that the United States was neglectful of their problems, despite U.S. protestations to the contrary.

The Johnson administration's approach to military governments continued to reflect a disagreement with the former policy and a belief in the need for "realism" as well as an optimistic attitude toward the military role in economic development and social reform. The United States also argued that it must work with existing military establishments even if they were corrupt or unprofessional in order to transform them through training over a period of time. The United States did not raise the issue of democracy in its relations with military governments coming to power from 1963 to 1968 in the Dominican Republic, Brazil, Peru, and Panama.

The Nixon and Ford Administrations

During the Nixon and Ford administrations (1969–1977), Latin America continued to be viewed as a low-priority area. President Nixon's regional policy was decidedly slow in appearing after his inauguration in January 1969, despite his insistence that Latin American problems would have the "highest priority." Then, in his first major address on Latin American relations before the OAS on April 14, 1969, the president indicated an abandonment of "developmentalism." He referred to the Alliance for Progress as a "great concept" but expressed disillusionment with the results of its programs. He then sent Governor Nelson Rockefeller of New York on a series of "study missions" to twenty Latin American states in May and June 1969. The governor's visits to three states were canceled because of rioting, and fourteen others experienced serious disorders upon his arrival. The Rockefeller Report was submitted on September 3, 1969, but few of its recommendations were implemented as policy.

President Nixon further outlined his policy in an address on October 31, 1969, adopting what came to be known as a "low-profile" approach. He called for a "new partnership" in inter-American affairs in which the United States "lectures less and listens more." He again rejected the social and economic developmental content of the Alliance for Progress, but he promised increases in economic aid and certain trade concessions. President Nixon showed no inclination to alter the pragmatic policies toward military governments already established.

U.S. policy under Nixon was said to be based on the principles of respect for diversity, mutual cooperation, and peaceful resolution of differences. Latin Americans were expected to take a larger leadership role in hemisphere affairs. In practice, the region was largely ignored, except for Castro in Cuba and the Marxist (but not Communist) government of Salvador Allende, which came to power in Chile in October 1970, and such specific issues as border questions with Mexico, nationalization of U.S. properties in Peru, and revision of the Panama Canal treaty. The U.S. Congress was unwilling to approve increased economic aid for Latin America, and the executive vacillated on trade concessions.

In October 1973, soon after becoming secretary of state, Henry Kissinger announced that Latin American policy was in the process of reformulation aimed at starting a New Dialogue with the other American states. The gist of Kissinger's policy statements, reinforced by remarks made by President Nixon and other U.S. officials, was to urge a new spirit of inter-American collaboration within the context of an interdependent world. The United States, the secretary said, recognized Latin American complaints that Washington had put aside its special commitments to the hemisphere, yet he asserted that it sought not dominance but community and a sharing of responsibilities with Latin America. He promised that the United States would not impose its political preferences on Latin American states and would seek a close and free association with them. The United States was prepared to consult with those nations and to adjust its positions on trade and monetary matters, rules regarding private investment and the roles of multinational corporations in underdeveloped nations, law of the sea, food and population programs, the transfer of technology, energy problems, development assistance, and restructuring of the OAS. Kissinger pointed out that the United States and Mexico had solved their long-standing Colorado River salinity dispute, that the United States and Panama had made significant progress toward a new canal treaty, and that the United States and Peru had settled their dispute concerning compensation for nationalized property.

Prospects for the New Dialogue declined beginning in mid-1974. President Nixon's attention was primarily directed toward defending himself against possible impeachment by the U.S. Congress, and Secretary Kissinger's energies were concentrated on problems in the Middle East. After Nixon's resignation in August 1974 and the succession of Gerald Ford to the presidency, U.S.–Latin American relations further deteriorated. President Ford contradicted the principles of the New Dialogue at a press conference in September 1974 by defending CIA activities in Chile preceding the fall of Allende, which he claimed were in the best interests of the Chilean people. The 1974 Trade Act excluded Venezuela and Ecuador from a generalized system of trade preferences because of their OPEC membership, even though they had not participated in the earlier OPEC-sponsored oil embargo. Consequently, Latin Americans insisted on postponing the meeting of foreign ministers that had been scheduled for March 1975 in Buenos Aires as the next step in the New Dialogue.

The United States then attempted to reconcile its difficulties with Latin America. President Ford asked Congress in April 1975 to grant him the authority to waive restrictions in the 1974 Trade Act, which he said had an unintended impact on Latin American relations. Secretary Kissinger offered, in a speech in Houston on March 1, 1975, "to continue the dialogue in a spirit of friendship and conciliation" despite some "temporary interruptions." The United States ceased opposing the Latin American majority that wished to end the isolation of Cuba, and in August 1975 the OAS essentially dropped the sanctions that had been imposed in 1964.

Balance-of-power thinking during the Nixon-Ford administrations, with foreign policy directed throughout by Henry Kissinger, helps to account for Latin America's continuing low priority in U.S. policy calculations. Détente between the superpowers indicated that the United States and the Soviet Union shared a mutual interest in maintaining the existing distribution of rewards and power in the international system. In this arrangement the United States assumed key responsibility for system maintenance in Latin America, sometimes as "policeman" and at least as power broker. Thus, with no strategic threat to the United States posed by either the regional states themselves or by an external state operating in the region, the United States was free to concentrate its efforts in other areas of the world.

The Carter Administration

President Jimmy Carter (1977–1981) stated at Notre Dame University in May 1977 that "we are now free of that inordinate fear of communism which once led us to embrace any dictator who joined us in that fear." After discounting the Soviet threat, Carter rested his global policies on three commitments: (1) to consider human rights as a fundamental tenet of U.S. foreign policy; (2) to reduce the danger of nuclear proliferation and the spread of conventional weapons; and (3) to rely on all forms of military cooperation as exceptional rather than normal instruments of policy. President Carter's policies on Latin America, based on these commitments, further isolated the United States from much of Latin America. U.S. relations with numerous states were strained over human rights, nonproliferation, and other issues. Furthermore, the Carter administration did not respond to Latin America's primary interests—namely, its economic demands, especially better access to U.S. capital and technology and more concessions for their commodity exports.

U.S. relations with Southern Cone states were reduced to low levels of activity. The United States banned Argentina, Chile, Paraguay, and Uruguay from receiving further arms transfers and certain forms of economic aid. Brazil, offended by the State Department's 1977 report on its human rights situation, refused to accept any more U.S. military assistance. President Carter further annoyed Brazil by opposing its acquisition of a nuclear reactor from West Germany, citing his commitment to nuclear nonproliferation. Brazil insisted that it was related to development of energy sources and had nothing to do with weapons.

In 1977 President Carter discussed placing a new emphasis on the long-neglected Caribbean region. High-level official visits were made around the area. At the same time, the president proposed restoration of U.S.-Cuban relations and tolerance for various ideologies in the region. However, his Caribbean policies met with several difficulties. U.S.-Cuban relations deteriorated after the Soviet Union and Cuba expanded their military activities in Africa. U.S. sanctions related to human rights abuses were applied to El Salvador, Guatemala, and Nicaragua. New canal treaties were signed with Panama and ratifications exchanged, but debate in the U.S. Senate and throughout the nation was vociferous, even though the treaties had been negotiated by four presidents from both political parties. Their conclusion reflected an official U.S. view, held since the mid-1960s, that the strategic and economic importance of the canal and the Caribbean had greatly decreased.

U.S.-Mexican relations were awkward despite the Carter administration's intent to improve them. The two governments strongly disagreed over several issues, especially those of Mexican migration to the United States and the price of Mexican natural gas exports.

The Carter administration's Latin American policy underwent important adjustments after 1979. By the end of 1979, the president publicly admitted that the Soviet Union was more threatening and less accommodating than he had anticipated. In the meantime, he revised his policies toward certain parts of the Caribbean because of increased Soviet-Cuban activity; his policies toward the rest of Latin America, however, remained essentially unchanged. After the overthrow of Somoza in Nicaragua, U.S. policy in time was antagonistic toward the Sandinista-dominated government on the grounds that it was providing Soviet arms to guerrillas in El Salvador. Fearing that events in El Salvador would parallel those in Nicaragua, Carter in January 1981 (only five days before the end of his term of office) lifted the ban on military assistance and resumed shipments to the military government despite the absence of any reforms. In the meantime, the United States also responded with hostility to a 1979 coup in Grenada led by the leftist New Jewel Movement, to which the Soviet Union and its East European bloc had extended aid (as had numerous non-Communist countries).

The Reagan Administration

When Ronald Reagan became president in 1981 he resolved to regain a dominant hemispheric role for the United States. He had sharply criticized President Carter's Latin American policies and set out to reverse them. President Reagan's worldview was based on the proposition that international disorder and terrorism resulted from the activities of the Soviet Union and its surrogates, of which Cuba was the most important. Opposition to Communist expansionism formed the basis for his global and regional policies. This approach necessitated reducing human rights concerns to a secondary position—not abandoning them but greatly reducing their emphasis. His anti-Communist policies also included a resuscitation of arms transfers and other military programs, which had been considerably diminished in prior years. Although the administration viewed all of Latin America in terms of East-West conflict, its most intense concern was with the Circum-Caribbean, particularly Central America. Consequently, with the exception of Mexico, U.S. efforts concentrated on small countries and paid relatively little attention to the major states in South America until events forced an extended range of concern.

Central America immediately became a front line in the new global cold war. The Reagan administration evolved a geopolitical strategic view of the Caribbean Basin with an emphasis on Central America. In July 1983 President Reagan appointed members to the National Bipartisan Commission on Central America, headed by former Secretary of State Henry Kissinger, to formulate and recommend U.S. strategy and tactics. The Kissinger Commission report, issued in January 1984, reinforced the administration's assumptions and policies but with qualifications and extensions.

The principal assumption was that the global balance of power could be shifted by the advance of Soviet power in Central America. The security of the Caribbean Basin was vital to the United States, whose interests were threatened by activities aimed at establishing Cuban-style Marxist-Leninist dictatorships allied with the Soviet Union. The "domino theory" was advanced. The Soviet Union, already enjoying a permanent presence in the Caribbean through its Cuban surrogate, was seen as acting to reinforce and expand this penetration into Nicaragua. At the same time, Cuban assistance to El Salvador threatened to convert that state to Marxism. From there, the argument continued, communism would spread to the other Central American countries and then threaten the major bordering states— Colombia and Venezuela to the south and, most ominously, Mexico to the north.

This calculation of U.S. interests and Soviet-Cuban motives led to a number of further assumptions: (1) vital Caribbean sea lanes and unimpeded passage through the Panama Canal, already threatened by Cuba's geographic position, would be more vulnerable with additional Soviet surrogates; (2) a more extensive permanent Soviet presence would offer the Soviet Union other significant military advantages by allowing the placement of hostile forces and weapons (conventional and nuclear) capable of striking deep within the United States and in Latin American states as well as extended Soviet naval operations; (3) all of these factors would force significant alterations in the U.S. forward deployment strategy, since a previously secure area would either require new resources to be created or existing ones to be diverted from other areas; (4) Communist takeovers would inevitably cause a vast increase in illegal immigration to the United States; and (5) U.S. worldwide credibility was at stake—in the words of the Kissinger report, "The triumph of hostile forces in what the Soviet Union calls the 'strategic rear' of the United States would be read as a sign of U.S. impotence." The conclusion was that the United States must act to prevent the transformation of its southern border into a hostile region.

The United States instituted a program of assistance to the anti-Sandinista Nicaraguan guerrillas (the *contras*), to the armed forces in El Salvador engaged in counterinsurgency efforts, and to Honduras for related services. U.S. actions were also directly interventionist; the most notable of these were the military invasion of Grenada in October 1983 and the mining of Nicaraguan harbors in March 1984. They were also developmental. The administration proposed the Caribbean Basin Initiative (CBI), which, at least in its initial form, insisted on the necessity for continued aggressive opposition to Soviet expansionism but also recognized poverty as a source of instability and outlined a program for trade preferences and economic aid to friendly Caribbean governments. The administration placed increasingly strong pressure on the Salvadoran government to follow a centrist course, effectively institute an agrarian reform program, hold free and fair elections, and curtail right-wing death squads. A similar course was urged on other Central American states.

In the meantime, other subregional and transregional problems intruded. Because U.S. policies in the Southern Cone had revolved around questions of human rights and military assistance during the Carter administration, President Reagan had to observe legislative controls and prohibition of arms transfers because of human rights violations in Argentina, Chile, Paraguay, and Uruguay.

Among several actions taken to reverse human rights policies toward the Southern Cone, the Reagan administration introduced legislation to repeal the ban on U.S. arms sales to Argentina and Chile. Congress agreed but required a presidential certification that both countries had made significant progress on human rights problems. These efforts came to an abrupt end, however, with the outbreak of the Anglo-Argentine military conflict in March 1982. After the return to democracy in Argentina in December 1983, the administration certified to Congress that Argentina had improved its human rights record and was eligible for military transfers that had been prohibited since 1977. With the return to democracy in other Southern Cone states (Uruguay, Brazil, and Bolivia joined Argentina; Peru had followed constitutional procedures since 1978), General Augusto Pinochet in Chile and Alfredo Stroessner in Paraguay stood alone as military heads of government. Prior U.S. prohibitions on arms transfers remained in effect for Chile and Paraguay; they were lifted elsewhere. Bolivia and Peru were central to U.S. efforts to control the international narcotics traffic, but bilateral programs designed to cut off the drug flow at its sources enjoyed little success. The debt question was a particularly difficult problem in U.S. policy toward all Southern Cone states.

Transregional problems of debt, narcotraffic, and migration became increasingly important during the Reagan administration. By 1988 some officials even said that these issues transcended the problem of Soviet expansionism. In April 1986 President Reagan issued a National Security Decision Directive declaring drug trafficking a threat to U.S. national security.

The Post–Cold War Era

The presidencies of George Bush (1989–1993) and Bill Clinton (inaugurated in 1993) coincide with the end of the cold war and the search for a new Latin American policy paradigm to replace the doctrine of strategic denial. President Bush was willing to compromise policy goals and make them less rigidly ideological. He and Secretary of State James Baker negotiated bipartisanship cooperation with Congress on Central American policy, in the process confirming the end of strategic denial. The agreement he reached with congressional leaders on March 24, 1989, in effect repudiated the basic tenets of the Reagan policies, in which Bush as vice president had played an active part. It agreed to support the Esquipulus II peace plan, to exclude the idea of overthrowing the Sandinistas, and to deny military support to the contras (although aid for humanitarian purposes was to be continued).

The Bush administration joined most Latin American states in adopting a primarily economic foundation for inter-American relationships, with agreement on the essentiality of continued democratic development. President Bush's surprise proposal in a speech on June 27, 1990, for a hemispheric free-trade area, one that was to go far beyond a North American agreement between the United States and Mexico, was a serious and historic initiative that was actively pursued. What began as a "primacy of Mexico" alignment for U.S. policy as part of an evolving North American Free Trade Agreement (which, as it turned out, also included Canada) became a "primacy of economics" orientation extended to all of the Americas. Earlier high-priority policies, notably the counternarcotics programs, were continued. They depended to a considerable extent on Latin American economic and democratic success and were closely linked to U.S. domestic concerns.

Another consideration was the possibility of seeking military or other coercive solutions. The U.S. military intervention in the Circum-Caribbean was a continuing reality in the post–cold war world—the action in Panama in December 1989 to overthrow and capture General Manuel Noriega was the first U.S. military intervention in the Caribbean area that had not been designed to preempt an external threat, the first since World War II that had not been explained in terms of Communist menace. The question thus arose if the United States would continue to be the local policeman in the Circum-Caribbean, to deal with the new priorities of narcotraffic and democracy, as well as the older ones of protecting American lives and the Panama Canal (although the old apprehension about hostile outsiders was no longer relevant). The Bush administration insisted that Panama was a unique case and did not set precedents for dealing with narcotraffic or dictatorship.

The Clinton administration was tentative in developing Latin American policies and appointing personnel to deal with the region. In the administration's first broad pronouncement on Latin American policy in May 1993, Secretary of State Warren Christopher said that the United States would make promotion of democracy, human rights and the rule of law, and the expansion of prosperity through economic development and trade the main elements of policy toward Latin America. President Clinton later undertook a major effort to gain congressional approval of NAFTA (which he had only tentatively supported during the election campaign). After a bitter political battle, Congress approved NAFTA, which went into effect on January 1, 1994. In the meantime, the president himself, along with other officials, sought to reassure Latin American leaders on trade issues and, in Central America, issues related to aid. The Clinton administration also reduced the emphasis on interdiction in narcotraffic after a National Security Council review concluded that U.S. military efforts had been of little consequence in reducing the flow of cocaine into the United States. The shift in policy was part of a new antidrug strategy that emphasized dealing with the demand for drugs within the United States through treatment and prevention programs.

BIBLIOGRAPHIC COMMENT

The first general survey of U.S. relations with Latin America was a diplomatic history by Latané (1900), later revised and retitled (1920). Stuart produced six editions beginning in 1922, the latest coauthored with Tigner (1975). Other histories are by Robertson (1923), Bemis (1943), Mecham (1965), Connell-Smith (1974), and Langley (1989a); Shavit (1992) is a useful historical dictionary. Political science surveys and thematic collections include Blasier (1985), Farer (1988), Hayes (1984), Kryzanek (1990, 1992), Lowenthal (1990), Martz (1988), Martz and Schoultz (1980), Molineau (1990), Poitras (1990), and Schoultz (1987). Wesson and Muñoz (1986) is a collection of Latin American views. Glinkin (1990) is an anti-imperialist interpretation by a prominent Soviet analyst. J. J. Johnson (1990) and Pike (1992) examine the foundations and development of negative U.S. perceptions of Latin Americans. Schoultz (1981) treats U.S. human rights policies, and Keogh (1985) edits a set of essays on U.S. human rights policies in Central America. Lowenthal and colleagues (1991) examine U.S. attempts to promote Latin American democracy, as does Carothers (1991) regarding the Reagan administration. Caribbean imperial policies are analyzed by Munro (1964, 1974), D. Perkins (1966), and R. F. Smith (1981). Mahan (1918) is one of his numerous works. Findling (1987) is a history of the United States in Central America from 1800 to the mid-1980s, Langley (1989b) traces U.S. actions in the Caribbean in the twentieth century, and Leonard (1991) analyzes Central American policies. Baily (1976) focuses on the United States and South America, and Pike (1977) does so regarding the Andean region. The major works on the Monroe Doctrine are by Alvarez (1924), May (1975), and, especially, D. Perkins (1927, 1933, 1937, 1963). Logan (1961) analyzes the "no transfer" principle; Whitaker (1954), the Western Hemisphere Idea; and Weinberg (1935), Manifest Destiny. Wood (1961, 1985) interprets the Good Neighbor Policy and its later dismantling. On the post–cold war era see Atkins (1992); Desch (1993); Hartlyn, Schoultz, and Varas (1992); Lowenthal and Treverton (1994); and Pastor (1992).

CHAPTER SIX

———————— ■ ————————

Transnational and Subnational Actors

INTERNATIONAL POLITICAL ANALYSIS focusing exclusively on the policies of nation-states ignores the important impact of other kinds of international entities. The nation-state has never been the sole actor in the modern international political system, nor politics the result of state interaction alone. Sovereign states remain the prime units, but the nonstate actors have shown a high degree of autonomy and have played central roles in politics. This chapter deals with five categories of nonstate entities, among the numerous existing groupings, that have been significant actors in the Latin American subsystem: the Roman Catholic Church, multinational business enterprise, international labor organizations, guerrilla insurgency groups, and transnational political parties.

THE ROMAN CATHOLIC CHURCH

The Church as Global Political Actor

Church policy and influence in Latin America, emanating from the papacy in Rome, is a complex subject for several reasons. First, the Roman Catholic Church is a special kind of international actor; the Holy See is not only a state presided over by the pope but is also the headquarters for a worldwide religious organization. Second, the church is a transnational unit but not as monolithic as its internal and global structures might imply. Nationalism, in Latin America and in other parts of the world, plays an important role in matters of religion and church politics as in other social arenas. Finally, deep divisions within the church over many issues, some of which have been evident since even before the Latin American national beginnings, have complicated the policies of the Holy See and its relations with Latin American churches and states, as well as inter–Latin American church relations.

The Holy See and the Vatican State. The nature of the Roman Catholic Church as an actor in the modern international political system is unique. References to the papacy as a nonstate actor are technically inaccurate since the Holy See and the Vatican in fact comprise a sovereign state, but the church predates the emergence of the modern nation-state by more than a millennium and has special characteristics. It is the oldest important actor in the current international political system and formally recognized by most of the nation-states. The church's independent attributes and sovereign status date from the Peace of Westphalia of 1648, with the Lateran Pacts signed with Italy in 1929 (revised in 1984) further confirming its status.

The Holy See constitutes the central government of the Roman Catholic Church. Its sovereignty is vested in a sacerdotal monarchy (the papacy) with governmental jurisdiction and temporal and spiritual authority as the capital of the global Roman Catholic Church. The Holy See has legal personality in international law, which allows it to enter into treaties as a juridically equal state and to engage in formal diplomatic relations. The Holy See has exchanged diplomatic missions since the fourth century and today engages in a broad scope of diplomatic activity. It is formally recognized by about 120 nation-states and carries on diplomatic relations with them, including most of the Latin American states. Participation in international organizations includes membership in a number of IGOs and NGOs and permanent observer status in the United Nations System, the Organization of American States, and the Council of Europe. The Holy See is signatory to many treaties, including the nuclear Non-Proliferation Treaty of 1971. The State of the Vatican City is the territorial base of the Holy See, superseding the former Papal States; the pope is head of state. Created in 1929 to administer the properties belonging to the Holy See, the Vatican also possesses personality under international law and enters into international agreements; it does not, however, exchange diplomatic representatives. (This definition draws on U.S. Department of State, 1987a.)

Until the latter part of the nineteenth century, the pope not only led the universal church but also headed a relatively large European state. The Italian peninsula was divided into a number of separate entities, significant among them the Papal States with Rome as the capital city. During the revolutions and wars attendant to the unification of Italy under a monarch, the papacy lost control over much of its territory. By 1861 the Papal States had been conquered by military force and annexed to the Kingdom of Italy; in 1870 Italian troops occupied Rome and the pope withdrew to the Vatican. Finally, the papacy and Italy signed the three Lateran treaties of 1929. Italy recognized the sovereignty of the Holy See and the creation of the State of the Vatican City, the pope dropped all claims to the former Papal States, and they both agreed on certain arrangements between church and state in Italy. Two additional pacts (concordats), signed by the Vatican and Italy in 1984 and put into effect the following year, revised parts of the Lateran treaties. These revisions changed certain aspects of the relationship between the Vatican and Italy but had no real consequence for the international activities of the Holy See.

Decisionmaking. Church divisiveness over current social issues is instructive with regard to its policy-making procedures and revealing of the decentralized nature of the church as a transnational actor. Thomas Sanders (1970) pointed out the gap between the ideal church decision-making model and the way in which policy is really formulated. According to the ideal model, broad policies are made by the pope at the top of the church structure and then move downward through the hierarchy for implementation by bishops around the world, finally being applied by priests and lay people. The emphasis throughout is on initiative and authority from above and obedience below. In fact, according to Sanders, official church teachings have tended to lag far behind social change, and the upper echelons of the hierarchy have been slow to absorb new social thought. The pope and most bishops have not been policy innovators; revision of papal policy usually has been in response to public pressures and to initiatives taken by church officials at lower levels of the hierarchy who eventually have been able to influence Vatican authorities. Church decisions and actions with regard to issues in Latin American international relations into the 1990s provide continuing evidence to support Sanders' thesis.

Perceptions of Latin America. A perception of Latin America as a distinct region has been revealed in church organizational structures. In 1858 the papacy established the Latin American Holy College (Colegio Pío Latinoamericano) in Rome, and in 1899 it sponsored the Latin American Plenary Council at the Vatican (Víctor Alba in Davis, Wilson, and others, 1975:106, 108). Much later, in 1953, Latin American bishops established a regional organization, the Conferencia Episcopal Latinoamericana (the Conference of Latin American Bishops, or CELAM). CELAM became an important inter–Latin American Catholic Church forum for debate and communication; the papacy has attempted to influence it in matters of papal policy. CELAM held its first conference in Rio de Janeiro in 1955, followed by assemblies in Bogotá (1968), Puebla (1979), and Santo Domingo (1992). CELAM searches for common positions among the bishops, takes into account papal teaching, issues policy statements, and offers guidance to national church officials. It has served the important function of regionally integrating the church in Latin America and eroding the old system of largely isolated national churches.

One Roman Catholic order that maintains extensive formal diplomatic relations with Latin America is the Sovereign Military Hospitaller Order of St. John of Jerusalem, of Rhodes, and of Malta (also known as the Knights of Malta, or the Knights of St. John, or the Knights Hospitallers). Founded in eleventh-century Jerusalem, this religious order later fought in the Crusades and eventually acquired great wealth and military power, including fortresses and fleets. Over the years it moved to Cyprus, to Rhodes, and to Malta, in the process becoming a powerful territorial state. French armed forces dislodged the order from Malta in 1798, after which its headquarters were located in Rome and dependent on the Holy See. Thus, by the time of Latin American independence, the Knights of Malta were no longer a military power and had lost their territorial base. Nevertheless, the order maintained its state status and supported diplomatic relations with the Holy See and with numerous nation-states around the world, today including nineteen states in Latin America. The order is, therefore, an actor in the Latin American subsystem. It still calls itself an order of chivalry of laymen and priests with mixed religious and military purposes, although in fact its activities in Latin America and elsewhere are concerned almost exclusively with various kinds of welfare work.

Mention should also be made of the important role played by foreign priests in the Latin American churches. After the nineteenth-century Latin American movements for independence, the church was subject to political attacks, often involving violence, by anticlerical liberal governments. As a result, the church was in a continuing state of crisis, unable to recruit sufficient clergy from local populations. Thus began the flow of clergy from Europe and subsequently from the United States. That movement has continued since World War II, and today the percentage of foreign clergy is as high as 80 percent in some countries and is significant in almost all others. Most of them come from France, Spain, and the United States.

Papal Relations with Latin America

The papal role in Latin America has never been as great as might be expected, given the hierarchical church structure that stresses obedience to higher authority and the fact that some 90 percent of all Latin Americans profess faith in Roman Catholicism. Rome's presence was minimal during the Latin American colonial period, despite Catholic Spain's aim to conquer and rule its part of America in the name of God and the Gospel as well as for Gold and Glory. The Spanish Crown jealously controlled religious as well as other affairs in the colonies, successfully resisting papal intrusion through the system of "royal patronage" (*patronato reál*) in which the crown made ecclesiastical appointments, controlled finances, and made basic policy decisions. Portuguese officials followed the Spanish lead and also insisted on independence regarding church governance in Brazil. The Holy See generally accepted Spanish and Portuguese sovereign power over the church in America, taking little action to assert itself there.

During the Spanish American wars for independence, the pope supported the Spanish king. In 1816 the pope issued an encyclical calling for Spanish American Catholics to be faithful to the king (Alba in Davis, Wilson, and others, 1975:104). The church in Spanish America was divided, however. Many of the lower clergy participated as patriots in the independence movements—the Mexican struggle, for example, was begun by two priests. The high clergy tended to be royalist until revolutionary success was evident, whereupon they generally supported the new nations against Spain.

During the Latin American national period, three forms of international relations involving the papacy have stood out: (1) the transition from conflict to diplomatic linkages in the nineteenth century; (2) papal third-party conflict resolution in the twentieth century; and (3) a series of papal visits to the region beginning in 1969, which were calculated efforts not only to address important human and theological issues but to ameliorate deep divisions over them within the church itself.

In the first stage, the early national period, papal relations with the Latin American states were largely conflictual. Papal influence was mixed but, by and large, not great. The Holy See continued its close ties with Spain and the Holy Roman Empire, which, in turn, were often hostile toward Latin America. The Holy See's relations with Brazil were much better than those with other Latin American states. Rome was closely tied to Portugal, but the Brazilian independence movement had been nearly bloodless, and independent Brazil was governed as a monarchy by the heirs to the Portuguese throne until 1889, so that Luso-Brazilian relations were relatively friendly. The Holy See and Brazil exchanged diplomatic representatives in 1830 and continuously maintained relations afterwards.

During this period, the Latin American churches were deeply divided over political issues and in sharp conflict with the temporal state. Church-state conflict existed virtually everywhere in the region to some degree; it was especially intense in Mexico and Colombia. The churches were caught up in the political struggles of their nations, largely fought out between opposing upper-class cliques organized into primitive political parties. Conservatives advocated traditionalism and authoritarianism, whereas liberals sought constitutional republicanism. One major issue stemmed from the nature of church-state relations inherited from the colonial period. During that time the church had enjoyed the legal status of an autonomous "estate," which included a number of special privileges such as maintaining its own judicial system. Liberals wanted to end the church's special status as part of their overall attempt to create societies in which all individuals were subject to common constitutional provisions and legal systems. Liberal anticlericalism was also directed against church wealth in several states.

The church hierarchy in Latin America responded to the liberal challenge by allying with conservatives and some of the most reactionary elements of society, thus gaining a reputation for opposing social change and perpetuating economic injustice. The Vatican further alienated its detractors by systematic attacks on such liberal tenets as rationalism, public education, economic progress, and materialism, and separation of church and state (as in the encyclical *Quanta Cura* in 1864), and by the doctrine of papal infallibility proclaimed in 1870, which made the pope's word final in matters of faith and doctrine.

The Latin American church-state conflict declined in the late nineteenth century, soon after the pope had suffered the loss of the Papal States in Italy and had become isolated in the Vatican. In this environment, the papacy pressed for expanded diplomatic relations, and by the beginning of the twentieth century it had established them with all Latin American states. These diplomatic channels were used to defend the church's property interests against liberal opposition. Anticlericalism remained strong among liberals, but an accommodation with the church was beginning to take place.

Two notable cases of successful papal mediation in serious Latin American conflicts, one involving Haiti and the Dominican Republic in the 1930s and the other Chile and Argentina in the 1970s and 1980s, illustrate papal activity in different parts of the region over time.

In October 1937, Dominican military forces attacked and killed large numbers of Haitian peasants near the border between the two countries. It was a bloody and tragic chapter in the long history of border disputes. A complex series of diplomatic maneuvering followed, and in time the dispute was taken up under two general inter-American treaties to which both countries were signatory. The agreement reached was widely acclaimed as a successful utilization of the Inter-American System's structure for peaceful settlement. In fact, as the U.S. minister in the Dominican Republic observed at the time, the actual instrument of the settlement was the diplomacy of the papal nuncio who was accredited to both countries. The church offered a common meeting ground in an otherwise distrustful and hostile situation. The convention finally signed in the context of inter-American treaties was in fact the protocol originally drafted and urged on the two states by the papal nuncio (Atkins and Wilson, 1972:56).

Argentina and Chile over the years contested the entire length of their mutual border. One issue involved a contentious and dangerous dispute over three islands in the Beagle Channel near Cape Horn. In 1971 they agreed to allow the British Crown to arbitrate the dispute, and six years later an award was handed down that largely favored the Chilean claims. The Argentine military government rejected the decision, and in late 1978 the two countries were on the verge of war. The Holy See's observer to the Organization of American States (OAS) urgently proposed papal mediation, which was readily accepted by both countries in January 1979. Almost two years later, in December 1980, the pope presented his peace proposal. Chile seemed ready to accept it, but Argentina stalled on responding. The effort was interrupted by the Anglo-Argentine war of 1982, but the papal role as third-party mediator was successfully revived. In January 1984, a month after the inauguration of civilian Argentine President Raúl Alfonsín, the two countries signed a declaration at public ceremonies in the Vatican pledging to solve the "southern question" in the framework of papal mediation. In November 1984 the two countries signed a treaty, again at the Vatican.

Over the years, papal nuncios had attempted to mediate in internal as well as other international conflicts. They did so when dictators fell in the 1940s and 1950s in Colombia, Costa Rica, and Venezuela, for example, and they attempted to avoid civil war in the Dominican Republic in 1965.

When Pope Paul VI arrived in Bogotá on August 22, 1968, he became the first pontiff to visit Latin America. He attended the World Eucharistic Congress and, afterward, addressed the meeting of CELAM at Medellín. Pope John Paul II, after becoming pope in October 1978, made an extensive series of visits over the years to all parts of Latin America. He traveled in the region on eleven occasions: in February 1979, to the Dominican Republic, Mexico, and the Bahamas; in July 1980, to Brazil; in 1983, to Central America; in January and February 1985, to fifteen cities in twelve days in Venezuela, Ecuador, and Peru, with a stopover in (Anglican) Trinidad-Tobago; in July 1986, to Colombia for a week; in April 1987, to ten cities in two weeks in Chile and Argentina; in May 1988, to Southern Cone nations; in 1990, again to Mexico; in October 1991, to Brazil for a second time, visiting ten cities in ten days; in October 1992, to Santo Domingo to commemorate Roman Catholicism's five hundred years in the Americas, and to attend the fourth assembly of CELAM; and in August 1993, to Jamaica and to Mexico for the third time. Almost one-fifth of Pope John Paul II's considerable overseas travel has been to Latin America.

This extensive papal attention is partly due to the fact that Latin America is on the verge of containing a majority of the world's Roman Catholics. Moreover, the Latin American church is severely divided over an array of fundamental social issues, giving rise to some of the most controversial movements within Roman Catholicism.

The Church and Social Change

After World War I, new issues began to transcend those previously associated with church-state conflict. New social and economic concerns increasingly divided the church and complicated papal–Latin American relations. Important religious changes entered in the Latin American political experience in the 1930s with the formation of Christian Democratic parties, Catholic Action groups, and Catholic labor unions. The upper clergy still tended to be conservative, but many local priests and laypeople became concerned with questions of the church's role in achieving social justice and economic development.

Beginning in the 1960s, social and economic change in Latin America accelerated dramatically. In response, church people included the entire spectrum: obedient conservatives, intransigent reactionaries, progressive reformers, and radical challengers seeking revolutionary transformations. In the 1960s the papacy finally addressed these questions directly, most notably in Pope John XXIII's encyclical *Mater et Magistra* (1961) and *Pacem in Terris* (1963), and Pope Paul VI's encyclical *Populorum Progreso* (1967). The worldwide ecclesiastical convention called Vatican II (1962–1965) dealt extensively with social and economic issues. Papal positions were also articulated during the numerous visits to Latin America. In general, papal policy moved away from supporting the political and social status quo, opting for some measure of reform and opposing both reaction and revolution. Despite papal statements for moderate change, however, the church was far from united. If anything, divisions intensified over social issues.

The lack of consensus within the church was clearly demonstrated during the visit of Pope Paul VI to Colombia in 1968 and those of Pope John Paul II after 1978. The debate from the beginning solidified opposing positions that continued over the years. Both popes reiterated their support for social progress but also maintained their theological conservatism and thus failed to appeal broadly to any faction. They chastised both conservatives and radicals, arguing that the church must lead in the fight against poverty and injustice and oppose the concentration of wealth and power in the hands of the few as well as abuses of political authority. They rejected as un-Christian and impractical the idea that violence was necessary to counter these injustices; but they also alienated many progressives who would otherwise agree with notions of orderly peaceful reform by reemphasizing the ban on artificial contraception contained in the encyclical *Humanae Vitae*. Church progressives and, increasingly, Latin American governments argued that without birth control and family planning programs, economic development would be impossible and, consequently, social injustice would persist.

Papal relations with the more radical movements within the Latin American church became increasingly important, and the related issues seemed to dominate the debate about the role of the church in social change. Some priests and laypeople argued the relevance of Marxism to Christian social change. Some expressed admiration for slain revolutionary hero Ernesto "Che" Guevara, and certain "Third World" priests joined guerrilla bands and engaged in violent acts. The young Colombian priest Camilo Torres Restrepo, for example, was killed by a Colombian army unit in 1966 while fighting as a member of a guerrilla group. In fact few priests joined guerrilla movements, and as military regimes disappeared and democratic governments ascended, what came to be known as liberation theology (and its related movements) came to be the more important drive for change.

Liberation theology generated a great deal of controversy within the church, with considerable disagreement among Latin American bishops and conflict with the Holy See. Liberation theology is, in sum, a "theology of the poor," which argues that the church should play a central political role in the struggles for human rights and social and economic justice for the popular masses. A Peruvian priest, Gustavo Gutiérrez, is considered the first theologian to write about the various tenets that had been developing since the late 1950s in Latin America in theological terms (he was the author of a 1971 book titled *A Theology of Liberation*). In time Gutiérrez was joined by a relatively small number of liberation theologians around the region, such as the Brazilian priest Leonardo Boff. However, priests and laypeople were much more numerous in taking action. In particular, liberation theologians and their activist colleagues helped spawn "base communities" (*comunidades eclesiales de base*—CEBs). In practice, most CEBs were composed of groups of poor people who emphasized lay leadership and stressed experience and biblical traditions as the sources of valid religious values.

Critics and opponents sharply challenged liberation theology. They charged that it was Marxism in Christian disguise, that it was an inappropriate challenge to church authority and politicization of religion, and that it represented a "theology of violence." The detractors said that the gospel and atheistic materialism were inherently contradictory. Matters coalesced in September 1984 when Cardinal Joseph Ratzinger, prefect since 1982 of the Vatican Congregation for the Doctrine of the Faith, issued *The Instruction on Certain Aspects of "Liberation Theology"* (Sigmund, 1990:Ch. 9). The document accused liberation theologians of using "concepts uncritically borrowed from Marxist ideology." Liberation theologians who did utilize Marxist concepts for analyzing society replied that they sought to recover the ancient Judeo-Christian tradition of biblical radicalism and that Marxist analysis was merely an analytic tool for understanding modern class conflict and poverty. Peter Hebblethwaite (1985) argued that Pope John XXIII's encyclical *Pacem en Terris* justified such thinking, in that it held that "good and commendable elements" could be found in systems of thought that also contained "falsity." Supporters also pointed out that the charge of politicization implied that Latin American religion in past ages was not political, clearly an insupportable proposition. What was new were the issues being addressed, not the church's political role. They argued that since the causes of poverty were part of social and economic structures, political action was necessary if those structures were to be changed. With regard to violence, some liberationists raised the question of whether it had theological significance but in fact did not dwell on this subject. According to Sigmund (1990:157), Gutiérrez proclaimed his adherence to Aquinas' just war doctrine and expressed reservations concerning European "theologies of revolution" that appeared to "baptize" violence.

Pope John Paul II remained unconvinced, however. He directly confronted liberation theology during his trips to Latin America. In September 1984 the Holy See published a paper pointing out its errors. The papacy issued warnings to the Peruvian hierarchy about the dangers of liberation theology, silenced Leonardo Boff in 1985–1986 (Boff left the ministry in 1992), and censured the two priests—Miguel D'Escoto and Ernesto Cardenal—who served in the Nicaraguan revolutionary Sandinista government. The pope's actions were based partly on opposition to political action by the clergy, saying they should restrict themselves to traditional pastoral concerns, and partly on the principle of obedience to papal authority. In several messages during his visits, the pope objected to those who he said distorted the evangelical message and put it at the service of ideological and political strategies in search of "illusory earthly liberation." The gap between wealth and poverty was evil, he said, but the church's spiritual mission must never be relegated to a secondary place behind social concerns.

The Challenge of Protestantism

Especially after World War II, Protestant fundamentalist, evangelical, and pentecostal groups grew steadily in the region. They eventually eroded to some degree the Roman Catholic domination in virtually all Latin American countries, and in some countries they claimed adherence by as much as 20 percent of the population. The Holy See and the church in Latin America viewed this expansion as a serious threat and responded with a sense of competition and conflict. Serbin (1993) points out that Roman Catholic enmity does not extend to the presence of "mainline" Protestant denominations (such as Anglicans, Presbyterians, and Lutherans) who have established ecumenical relationships with Roman Catholics.

Within Latin American Catholicism, considerable disagreement exists over how to respond to the threat. Some argue for a conservative approach that strengthens and preserves the existing church presence and activity. Others urge co-optation by way of a greater role for the laity. Pope John Paul II called for a "new evangelization" on the part of Roman Catholics, which was echoed by sympathetic elements at the fourth CELAM assembly at Santo Domingo in 1992. In his visit to Mexico in 1993, the pope's condemnation of the condition of Indians seemed at least partially inspired by the numbers who had converted to evangelical Protestantism, although he did not directly address the phenomenon. The CEBs find themselves particularly vulnerable to competition with Protestantism in attracting the poor.

BUSINESS ENTERPRISE

Corporations as System Actors

A multinational corporation is a group entity with a legal personality. Although corporate control remains centered within some sovereign state, the corporation exhibits a great deal of independence as an actor in the international political system. The prefix "multi" indicates that MNCs have business activities in a number of states and have extensive resources. Most major global corporations today are MNCs. They dominate the world industrial order but remain domiciled in industrial states.

Although private business enterprise has long been a part of the international scene, the MNC is a relatively new actor in world politics. International companies originally were creations and subjects of the state. For example, in colonial America the Dutch West Indies Company was chartered by the sovereign monarch and, while funded by private capital, it was subject to royal control and entitled to state protection. Over the years, however, the nature of overseas business enterprises underwent dramatic changes and, consequently, their roles as international actors changed accordingly. In the nineteenth century, business corporations began to develop in the capitalist economies in Great Britain, Europe, and the United States. They were not multinational in character, however, as their activities and power were restricted by the states granting corporate charters. International firms were generally limited to a specific economic activity, such as banking, mining, agriculture, or manufacturing, and their life spans and total assets were limited by law. By the time of World War I, however, according to Raymond Vernon (1971a:1–2), "corporations could be formed by practically anyone for practically any purpose without limit of time or size." Even more important, he said, "corporations by this time had acquired the extraordinary right to own other corporations." Consequently, separate companies could be created to perform different aspects of a total business activity, but all of the activities would be subject to centralized control, coordination, and support. Modern corporations acquired a distinct multinational character as they began to branch out into several different sovereign jurisdictions with various enterprises linked together by a single corporate structure.

The growth of MNCs was especially significant after World War II, the size of their overseas assets dwarfing those of the past. U.S., European, and Japanese companies increased their foreign assets at rapid rates in virtually all parts of the world. Later, MNCs evolved in newly industrializing parts of the world, including Latin America. Well over 4,000 MNCs now exist, accounting for about one-third of the gross world production of goods and services. But a great proportion of the activity is controlled by a small number of large corporations in a few industrial sectors. In the petroleum industry, the "Seven Sisters"—Exxon (Standard Oil of New Jersey), Standard Oil of California, The Royal Dutch Shell Group, Texaco, Gulf, Mobil, and British Petroleum—dominate the world's oil production, control more than half of the oil tanker tonnage, and retail about half of the petroleum products on world markets. Nine automotive producers—General Motors, Ford, Chrysler, Volkswagen, Fiat, British Motors, Nissan, Toyota, and Honda—dominate global automotive markets. The electronics industry, the third largest industrial sector, is composed essentially of the major U.S., Japanese, and European firms. A half-dozen mining companies account for three-fourths of the international trade in metals and other ores, and only a few companies control world chemical markets.

The main operational goal of both foreign and domestic corporate policy is assumed to be the maximization of profits. Business enterprises, like states, act in their own interests, which, ultimately, are survival, security, and well-being. Once the fundamental concerns of assuring survival and securing resources are provided for, policy success is measured in terms of monetary profit and corporate growth. Thus, foreign operations are rationalized in economic terms, principally the beneficial employment of capital resources. Modern technology has increasingly stimulated the growth of large companies requiring access to global markets, and the world economy encourages direct overseas investment. But international and multinational business relations, involving as they do corporate relations with both foreign and home governments, are inseparable from politics. Companies have used many of the same strategies in external relations as states have, including cooperative ones such as negotiation and persuasion as well as coercion and subversion. Consequently, MNCs have foreign departments or overseas divisions devoted to "foreign policy-making" and execution—these operations are complete with a foreign service and interact with sovereign states.

Corporate Actors in Latin America

International and multinational business enterprise in Latin America has been a controversial activity. Business entities have negotiated with sovereign states, but they have also engaged in espionage; they have pursued unsavory activities designed to influence foreign officials, such as bribery; and they have been involved in the subversion of governments. Spectacular examples of past business intervention include United Fruit Company activities in Central America from the early part of the twentieth century through the 1930s. Coercion through threats of violence to force small farmers to sell exclusively to United Fruit at company prices, bribery of public officials, and even the sponsoring of coups earned United Fruit the popular name of *el pulpo* (the octopus). Oil company ventures in Mexico and Peru often involved corrupt practices as well. In a more recent example, oil companies whose interests had been expropriated in Cuba by the Castro regime exerted pressure on the U.S. government in favor of the Bay of Pigs invasion. Later, International Telephone and Telegraph (ITT) took measures in Chile to disrupt the Marxist government of Salvador Allende in 1970–1973. Bribery of Latin American officials by U.S. companies, including United Brands in Honduras and Gulf Oil in Bolivia, was revealed in 1975.

Evidence also exists to support the view that U.S. companies cooperate with their Latin American hosts as good corporate citizens. For example, Stephen Rosenfield, writing in the *Washington Post* on January 28, 1972, reported on a series of discussions about relations between U.S. business firms and Latin American government officials, sponsored by the Council on Foreign Relations in 1971. He concluded that the proceedings revealed "not a calculated or malevolent or exploitation-minded conspiracy of the bureaucratic-investment complex"; rather, "there was evident an inclination to consider new forms of American economic participation on terms politically acceptable in the hemisphere, and a parallel inclination to avoid the kinds of political confrontation that would spoil the chances for future profit." In the latter 1980s and into the 1990s, the image of MNCs improved considerably, at least among those Latin American government officials and domestic sectors who embraced economic neoliberalism and sought increased foreign investment.

The Evolution of Business Activity in Latin America

The growth of business enterprise in Latin America has been an important aspect of the region's international relations. Latin America has been a major recipient of foreign investment and the scene of organized business activity throughout its national history.

British capital accounted for most of the foreign investment in Latin America from the early national period until the world depression of 1930. Toward the end of the nineteenth century, French, German, and U.S. capital became significant. By then, Latin America was receiving investments from virtually every nation in Europe and some from Japan. Most of the investment was portfolio in nature, financing projects through the purchase of Latin American government bonds and leaving operational administration to local management. However, important operations were also begun by foreign entrepreneurs through direct investment and management.

Toward the end of the nineteenth century, international business actors who were to enjoy many years of large-scale activity in Latin America began to appear. The most important sectors for foreign direct investments included extractive operations (petroleum production and tin, copper, and nitrate mining); forestry and agriculture (coffee, sugar, meats, and tropical fruits, including bananas); banking; and some specialized manufacturing areas. U.S. investors, unlike investors from other nations, were as interested in direct as in portfolio investments, and Latin American markets were seen to offer U.S. companies important opportunities. After 1930 portfolio investments greatly declined for a variety of reasons and direct investments increased. U.S. capital came to assume a dominant position. In the 1930s and 1940s no more than 300 U.S. companies dominated foreign business operations in Latin America, and by 1950 U.S. investments were twice as large as all others combined. European and Japanese investments were sharply reduced, especially by the impact of two world wars.

A few examples suffice to illustrate the growth of business actors in the Latin American region. Richard Van Alstyne (1955) offered the case of George Drabble of Manchester, who in the late 1840s went to Buenos Aires and in time "played a part in the formation of every important enterprise in that country during the next two decades"—including the first railway line built in Argentina, the Bank of London and the River Plate, the Buenos Aires Tramway Company, the Buenos Aires & Rosario Railway, and the River Plate Fresh Meat Company. Beginning in the late nineteenth century in Argentina, Armour and Company and Swift and Company competed with British concerns in meat processing and exporting. Both companies expanded to Uruguay and Paraguay, and through the 1960s those three countries were important suppliers for both companies' overall operations. In Chile and Peru, U.S. mining companies dominated copper and other mineral extraction from the late nineteenth century until the 1960s; the most important of these companies were Kennecott, Anaconda, and Cerro de Pasco. The Singer Company, founded in Boston in 1850, from the earliest days of its sewing machine business established foreign subsidiaries. By World War I, Singer was well established in all of Latin America. It remained so in the mid-1990s, with the Brazilian subsidiary being one of its largest branches.

In Peru in the 1870s a U.S. adventurer and railroad builder, Henry Meiggs, built lines across the Andes and created a financial empire. In Peru at about the same time, a young Irish immigrant, William Russell Grace, began a small business of servicing ships that transported guano fertilizer. He parlayed this modest beginning into the large and highly diversified W. R. Grace and Company headquartered in New York, a trading firm operating in all of Latin America. Known as Casa Grace in Latin America, its regional operations by the 1970s had dwindled to only a minority of its global business. During the latter part of the nineteenth century, Henry Meiggs's nephew, Minor Cooper Keith, established railways in Central America and then developed some banana plantations and shipping lines to U.S. ports. In 1899, after thirty years of intense rivalry with his competitors, Keith took over most of the other small banana companies and organized the United Fruit Company, thereafter a major political actor in Central America, with headquarters in New York. In 1970 the company acquired John Morrell and Company, adding meat packing to its Chiquita banana enterprise and changing its corporate name to United Brands. In 1984, Carl H. Lindner, a Cincinnati financier, gained controlling interest in United Brands. He broke up the United Brands conglomerate, selling off certain operations (but keeping the Morrell Co.). By 1990, when he renamed the company Chiquita Brands International, it was selling about one-third of the world's supply of bananas, most of which it grew in Central America. The company also applied the Chiquita name to other fruits and packaged goods and pushed for new markets.

The activities of oil companies have also been important in Latin America. The Standard Oil Company of New Jersey (created in 1873 by John D. Rockefeller as the Standard Oil Trust) and the binational Royal Dutch Shell Group (a merger in 1897 of the Royal Dutch Petroleum Company and the British-owned Shell Transport and Trading Company) established major operations in Mexico and Venezuela after the discovery of oil in both nations in the 1890s. The largest single petroleum operation in Latin America for many years was run in Venezuela by the Creole Oil Company, a subsidiary of Standard Oil. Both Standard and Shell had difficulties with Mexico beginning with the revolution in 1910 and were expropriated in 1938. In the 1930s Venezuela became the principal supplier for both companies, remaining so until their Middle East operations surpassed Venezuelan production in the 1960s. Venezuela nationalized the Standard and Shell operations in 1975. Gulf, Texaco, and other oil companies have also been active in a number of Latin American nations. They continued to operate in several countries, although they also were targets of Latin American nationalists and suffered expropriations, such as in Peru and Bolivia in the late 1960s.

European banks became well established in the region during the nineteenth century and remained so to the present day. Among the most important was the Bank of London and South America (BOLSA), a joint Canadian-British chartered enterprise. It was acquired by Lloyds Bank of London in 1971. French and German banks also gained important positions in the banking sector. The U.S. Federal Reserve Act became effective in June 1914, allowing U.S. banks to establish overseas branches. They were led by the National City Bank of New York (later First National City Bank, and then Citibank), which in 1914 opened its first overseas branch in Buenos Aires; considerable and continuous activity throughout the region ensued. Other U.S. banks followed suit, with the Chase Manhattan Bank, the Bank of Boston, and the Bank of America prominent among them. After World War II, Canada's giant chartered banks, such as the Royal Bank of Canada and Bank of Nova Scotia, expanded into the British Caribbean colonial islands and territories. They dominate the banking systems of the independent Commonwealth Caribbean Countries and are active in the remainder of the Circum-Caribbean (Hebron, 1993).

After World War II, U.S. and European companies placed a new emphasis on manufacturing, retailing, communications, and service industries in addition to the traditional concentration on extractive, agricultural, and trading concerns. ITT became a major and controversial actor in Latin America. Founded in 1920 by Virgin Islander Sosthenes Behn as a small telephone company in Puerto Rico, ITT became a worldwide telephone and cable communications firm operating extensively in Latin America. The Ford, Chrysler, General Motors, Volkswagen, Fiat, and Renault automotive companies placed assembly plants in Argentina, Brazil, and Mexico. Sears, Roebuck and Company founded a chain of stores in several parts of the region, selling goods produced mostly by local industries. The hotel industry expanded far beyond the long-popular tourist areas in Mexico and the Caribbean. Much of the business initially belonged to the Intercontinental Hotel Corporation, a subsidiary of Pan American World Airways. In the 1960s the Sheraton and Hilton chains expanded significantly into Latin America; Sheraton was acquired by ITT. Japanese corporations did not engage in overseas production facilities to the same extent as U.S. and European companies; rather, they sold products through large trading companies serving the industrial firms through overseas offices.

Important investment companies also appeared on the Latin American scene. Atlantic Community Development Group for Latin America (ADELA) was established in 1956 as a private multinational consortium sponsoring private foreign investment in Latin America. It is capitalized by contributions from U.S. and European firms to provide financial backing for new enterprises by Latin American businesspeople in a variety of fields. International Basic Economy Corporation (IBEC) was started by Nelson Rockefeller in 1947 to introduce new ventures to underdeveloped areas for both profit and local development. Significant Latin American ventures included the hybrid corn business in Brazil and the introduction of "supermarkets" to Venezuela, Peru, and Argentina.

Several multibusiness associations having a primary concern with Latin America have been organized. A nonprofit organization supported by member corporations, the United States Inter-American Council, was founded in New York in 1958. Its name was changed to Council for Latin America in 1965 and, in 1970, to Council of the Americas; it also opened a Washington office. The Council's stated purpose is "to further understanding and acceptance of the role of private enterprise as a positive force for the development of the Americas." The Inter-American Council for Commerce and Production (known by its Spanish acronym CICYP) was established in 1960 by U.S. and Latin American companies, individual businesspersons and economists, and developmental organizations. At its meetings in U.S. and Latin American cities, CICYP has stressed the role of private enterprise in Latin American economic integration, active business participation in the making of public economic policy, and the need to stimulate foreign private investments through such vehicles as ADELA.

The 1970s into the 1980s was a period characterized by difficult MNC–Latin American relations, in contrast to the expansion of direct foreign investment in the 1950s and 1960s. Certain Latin American governments engaged in nationalizations and many placed restrictions on the remittance of profits, discouraging MNC investments. Although commercial bank lending expanded significantly in the 1970s, the severe debt problems in the following decade further discouraged foreign private capital investment (Grosse, 1989). Existing ventures were scaled down or terminated and new ones were generally not forthcoming.

After the mid-1980s and into the 1990s, however, foreign investors renewed their interest in Latin America. Investment was sparked by developments in the region having to do with the end of the debt crisis and reduced inflation and with new neoliberal government policies that lowered barriers to trade and put foreign firms on a nondiscriminatory basis. From 1987 to 1993 U.S. companies significantly expanded their investments in Latin America as markets there were increasingly opened. According to the UN Economic Commission on Latin America and the Caribbean (*CEPAL News,* vol. XIII, no. 10, October 1993), during the first three years of the 1990s U.S. direct investment in the region increased by $12.6 billion, or 16.6 percent, to $88.9 billion. That amount represented 18.3 percent of total U.S. investment abroad ($486.7 billion). In Latin America it continued to be concentrated in finance (with a share of 46 percent) and manufacturing (30 percent), followed by banking (9 percent), petroleum (5 percent), trade (4 percent), and all other categories (7 percent). Bermuda was the largest beneficiary at $25.8 billion, an amount accounted for mostly by the financial sector and repayments of loans by finance affiliates; Panama ranked third, at $11.5 billion, largely for the same reason. Other leading recipients, with more balanced investment sectors, were Brazil ($16.1 billion) and Mexico ($13.3 billion). MNC operations in Chile, Argentina, and Venezuela were also notable.

These investors' positive expectations were also based on the freer trade throughout the hemisphere that was promised by the Enterprise for the Americas Initiative posed by the United States in June 1990. Most MNC executives looked favorably on the commencement of the NAFTA in January 1994. In this regard, Canadian banks and companies have become major players, with Canada's generally increased interest in the region in the post–cold war era and, more specifically, as a partner in the NAFTA.

LABOR ORGANIZATIONS

Labor Unions as International Actors

A number of regionally organized labor organizations, comprising national Latin American members and usually affiliated with some larger world movement, have been significant twentieth-century actors in the Latin American subsystem. International and multinational labor development has been slow and sporadic, however, and conflicts have often arisen between the different organizations. Latin American labor movements—stimulated by industrialization and the growth of the urban proletariat beginning in the late nineteenth century, but also including mineworkers as an important labor sector—have tended to be organized along national rather than international lines. Labor eventually became politically strong in some states, especially Mexico, Chile, Argentina, Bolivia, Venezuela, Colombia, and Peru and gained importance in Brazil, Uruguay, and Costa Rica. It has enjoyed less success in the rest of Latin America. The first regional organizations were founded soon after World War I, but their development was slowed by disputes among national members about goals, and they were characterized by clashes between contending workers with opposing ideologies.

The Pan American Federation of Labor (PAFL) was organized in 1918 largely on the combined initiative of the American Federation of Labor (AFL) and the Regional Confederation of Mexican Labor (CROM), which was founded in the same year. PAFL was effective only until the late 1920s, although it was not formally disbanded until after World War II. Its most active members, in addition to U.S. and Mexican unions, were largely those from Central America and the Caribbean islands. PAFL engaged primarily in extending financial assistance to its poorer members and in public protests about U.S. imperialism in Mexico and the Caribbean.

About the time that PAFL ceased to be effective in the late 1920s, two new and more radical regional labor confederations appeared. Both were established in 1929 and reflected the split within Latin American labor movements between anarcho-syndicalists and Communists. Those unions associated with the former ideology founded the Continental Association of American Workers (Asociación Continental Americana de Trabajadores—ACAT). By 1929 anarcho-syndicalists had lost control of much of the Latin American labor movement to Communists, and ACAT never had much political impact even though it continued to maintain a formal organization. Of more importance was its Communist-dominated rival, the Latin American Syndicalist Confederation (Confederación Sindical Latino Americana—CSLA), a product of the period of Communist history during which the Communist International instructed local Communist parties to establish separate labor union organizations under their control. Consequently, national affiliates of CSLA were established in those Latin American states where Communist parties existed. Some important national trade union organizations, insisting on autonomy of action, refused to join CSLA because it was directed from the Soviet Union. The most important example was the refusal of CROM of Mexico to join, even though it had declared itself both socialist and syndicalist. CSLA was dissolved in 1938 and superseded by a more broadly based labor organization.

The Confederation of Latin American Workers (Confederación de Trabajadores de América Latina—CTAL) represented the most ambitious and important effort to establish an all-inclusive regional trade union to date when its founding congress met in Mexico City in 1938. CTAL involved collaboration among most Communist, socialist, and liberal labor unions and paralleled popular front political party coalitions being formed at the same time. The guiding personality and long-term leader of CTAL was Vicente Lombardo Toledano, the radical Mexican intellectual, politician, and labor leader. Lombardo organized CTAL with the help of other Latin American trade union leaders, most prominently those from Cuba, Chile, and Colombia. Within a few years after its founding, CTAL's leadership became Communist-dominated and pro-Soviet. Lombardo's personal power declined after 1946 when his own union in Mexico, which he had founded in 1936, repudiated his leadership. Furthermore, with the onset of the cold war in 1947, collaboration ended between Communists and non-Communists in political parties and labor movements, and Communist labor influence declined drastically. CTAL lost the affiliation of several national unions that left in 1948 to found the Inter-American Federation of Labor. Until then CTAL had been the only labor confederation existing in Latin America. In 1950 it became the regional affiliate of the World Federation of Trade Unions (WFTU). Generally a Communist-dominated association with policy largely determined by the Soviet government, CTAL eventually was disbanded and replaced by the Single Central Association of Latin American Workers (Central Unica de Trabajadores de América Latina—CUTAL), but it lost a number of national member unions during the process of reorganization.

Most national Latin American trade unions belonged to the WFTU, a worldwide labor confederation, when it was founded in 1945. But in 1949 most of its non-Communist affiliates withdrew, and the WFTU became a leading Communist international front organization. In 1951 the WFTU was expelled from Paris, where it was founded, for "subversive activities." It moved its headquarters to Vienna but was ejected in 1956 for "endangering Austrian neutrality" and relocated in Prague, where it was lodged for almost 35 years. With the end of the cold war, Czechoslovakia ordered the WFTU to leave in 1991 on the grounds that no Czech trade union was any longer a WFTU member (United Kingdom, 1990). The collapse of communism in Central Europe and the Soviet Union, and the dissolution of the Soviet Union itself, greatly affected the WFTU and led numerous member unions to disaffiliate, although entities from about 150 countries remained as affiliates. Nevertheless, WFTU leadership acknowledged that the organization must fundamentally reevaluate its orientation in the post–cold war world and perhaps even become a democratic organization.

The Inter-American Federation of Labor (Confederación Interamericana de Trabajadores—CIT) was organized in 1948 by non-Communist former members of CTAL and other trade unions with the specific purpose of countering Communist influence in the Latin American labor movement. The efforts of the AFL of the United States and the Aprista party of Peru constituted the driving force behind the founding of CIT. CIT membership was inter-American in character, comprising twelve Latin American national labor confederations and the AFL of the United States and of Canada. CIT was superseded in 1951 with the founding in Mexico City of the Inter-American Regional Organization of Workers (Organización Regional Interamericana de Trabajadores—ORIT), which absorbed additional affiliates of CTAL at the time of its founding. ORIT was the American affiliate of the International Confederation of Free Trade Unions (ICFTU), founded in London in 1949 under U.S. and British labor leadership by those unions that withdrew from the Communist-controlled WFTU; its headquarters later moved to Brussels. ICFTU has worked closely with labor-oriented agencies in the United Nations system; it is especially interested in worker training and education. The AFL-CIO of the United States has ties with ORIT and has given it financial and technical aid.

A potentially powerful rival to both CTAL and ORIT appeared in 1952 with the formation of the Unionized Latin American Workers' Group (Agrupación de Trabajadores Latino Americanos Sindicalizados—ATLAS) by Argentine president Juan Perón. ATLAS, under the direction of the General Confederation of Labor of Argentina, was intended as an instrument of Peronista foreign policy to help extend Argentine influence in Spanish America. As an international labor organization, it organized and affiliated as members a number of national labor confederations outside of Argentina. ATLAS was only of temporary importance, however; it disbanded after Perón fell from power in 1955. CTAL had offered an alliance to ATLAS in 1953, but it was refused. After 1955 former ATLAS unions either joined ORIT or steered an independent course.

In 1954 an additional regional labor organization was founded, the Latin American Confederation of Christian Trade Unionists (Confederación Latino Americana de Sindicalistas Cristianos—CLASC). This organization is the Latin American regional affiliate of the International Federation of Christian Trade Unions founded in The Hague in 1920; its headquarters was later moved to Brussels. The parent world organization's program originally was based on the papal encyclical *Rerum Novarum* (1891), and later on the *Quadragerimo Anno* (1931), although its affiliates include Protestant as well as Roman Catholic federations. CLASC also has links to international associations of Christian Democratic political parties and trade unions. Its own national affiliates in Latin America include Christian trade unions and federations and a Catholic workers' association. CLASC, clearly leftist, is critical of the larger ORIT, which it considers to be dominated by the conservative U.S. labor movement. CLASC is also anti-Communist, however, and thus opposes the moribund CUTAL.

U.S. Labor and Latin America

The U.S. labor movement has exhibited alternating periods of concern with and indifference to Latin American regional organizations. After its involvement with PAFL from 1918 until the late 1920s, the AFL had few contacts with the Latin American labor movement until after World War II, when it was instrumental in organizing CIT and the successor ORIT. In 1946 the AFL sent Serafino Romualdi as its "labor ambassador" to Latin America. Romualdi negotiated with non-Communist trade unions and federations both in and out of the Communist-led CTAL, and within two years the rival CIT had been established. Romualdi had served briefly with the Latin American department of the International Ladies Garment Workers Union before going to Latin America. Upon his return in 1948 he became head of the inter-American affairs section of the AFL and held a similar position with the AFL-CIO after the U.S. labor merger in 1955. Romualdi also served as assistant secretary of ORIT and labor adviser to the Alliance for Progress; he retired in 1964. Romualdi died three years later in Mexico while on a lecture trip to the Cuernavaca Labor College run by ORIT.

In 1961 the AFL-CIO and a group of U.S. business corporations active in Latin America founded a U.S. Government-financed union-industry group called the American Institute for Free Labor Development (AIFLD). Romualdi was appointed its first director. The purpose of AIFLD in Latin America was to encourage the development of non-Communist trade unions, to the extent that a staff study by the U.S. Senate Foreign Relations Committee in 1968 criticized the AIFLD for being preoccupied with anticommunism in its Latin American operations. To the present day the AFL-CIO's foreign policies have continued to operate primarily through the AIFLD.

Changes in the foreign policies of U.S. labor in the late 1960s, extending into the 1990s, have had important implications for its Latin American relations—namely, a long period of reduced contacts. The AFL-CIO supported free trade as long as the balance of trade was favorable to the United States. The only qualifications were that agreements should be negotiated with states whose exports were harming specific U.S. industries and that the government should pay adjustment allowances for workers who were displaced because of foreign competition. But in the late 1960s, when the United States began to suffer large trade deficits, labor policy changed. The AFL-CIO began to champion protectionism in U.S. trade, favored a decrease rather than an increase in world economic interdependency, and drew back from its own commitments to international labor organizations.

In the early 1970s, U.S. labor leaders began to argue that protectionism was the only way for U.S. labor to guard against the effects of international competition. That position has continued into the mid-1990s. As trade balances turned against the United States, U.S. labor turned against free trade. Labor leaders complained that the tariff code and tax laws encouraged U.S.-based MNCs to manufacture in foreign settings at a lower cost and return finished products back to the United States. Consequently, they charged, U.S.-based MNCs were destroying jobs at home in their search for cheap labor abroad; in other words, by exporting jobs to their foreign subsidiaries and affiliates where lower labor costs prevailed, in order to produce goods that underpriced U.S.-made products, MNCs were quickly eliminating U.S. jobs. Arguing that labor was helpless in the changed international situation, U.S. labor leaders changed their trade policies away from supporting free-trade legislation.

In the post–cold war era the U.S. and neoliberal Latin American governments have emphasized free trade agreements. Thus U.S. labor has become vociferous in its opposition to arrangements for regional economic integration and free trade under the proposed U.S. Enterprise for the Americas Initiative. It also mounted serious but unsuccessful opposition to the approval by the U.S. Congress of the North American Free Trade Agreement, primarily out of fear that it would result in the migration of U.S. jobs to Mexico. Such concerns will likely constitute the most difficult issue for the AFL-CIO in any future debates over hemispheric free trade.

POLITICAL PARTIES

Political Parties as Independent Actors

Political parties are groups that seek to obtain public office and political power by presenting candidates to the electorate. Transnational political parties transcend national boundaries and seek international acceptance in an organized way. The affiliates to a transnational party share a philosophy and common goals to some degree, coordinate their interests and ideas, and offer mutual support. The national identities of transnational parties may be primary, but their connections across national boundaries are discernible.

A number of transnational parties have been active in Latin America. The most important ones originated outside the region and later established Latin American counterparts, including the Communist parties organized in the Comintern, the Social Democratic parties in the Socialist International, and the Christian Democratic parties in the Christian Democratic World Union. Political parties in the United States are only peripherally relevant to Latin America. The Democratic and Republican parties are essentially national parties and not internationalized. They have interests and sympathies abroad but have not established systematic transnational ties with kindred parties. Their Puerto Rican counterparts are active only in the context of U.S. national elections, in which Puerto Ricans vote.

The Comintern and the Socialist International both emerged from the nineteenth-century European socialist movement. The First International, originally called the Workers' International Association, was formed by Karl Marx in 1864 and dissolved in 1876. The Second International (the Labor International) held its first meeting in 1889 and continued until its collapse in 1914 with the outbreak of World War I. Neither the First nor Second International involved Latin America; except for small sections in the United States, both were European organizations.

Members of the internationals shared the goal of uniting the workers of the world and taking power from their class enemies, but tensions increased over the years between totalitarian and democratic strains of Marxism. They achieved separate identities after World War I and thereafter went their separate ideological and organizational ways as bitter rivals. The Third International, also called the Communist International and known as the Comintern, was founded by Lenin in 1919 following the successful Bolshevik Revolution of 1917 and the establishment of the Soviet Union. With the purpose of organizing revolutions through Communist parties in every country throughout the world, the Comintern developed extensive Latin American connections. It was dissolved in 1943.

Social Democrats opposing Bolshevist totalitarianism claimed to reconvene the Second International in 1920. In 1923 they called themselves the Socialist and Labor International and explicitly disassociated from the Comintern as a rival organization. The Socialist International remained an essentially European movement, with only a few small American elements. It was interrupted by World War II, but in 1945 it reorganized as the International Socialist Conference with headquarters in London. It took the name Socialist International in 1951 at the pivotal Frankfurt Conference, which adopted the "Principles and Tasks of Democratic Socialism." In time the Socialist International expanded to include Social Democratic and Labor parties in many countries, including those in Latin America.

In the meantime, another competing party emerged with yet another distinct orientation. Christian Democratic parties appeared around Europe in the 1890s espousing a sort of clerical Fabian socialism. More like interest groups than political parties, they defended Roman Catholic interests on the grassroots level. The European organizations broadened their bases and became real political parties in the 1920s. They were still Roman Catholic in outlook, but they sought to appeal to the interests of broader segments of the electorate. They also shifted from socialism to traditional liberalism. This fundamental change was in opposition to events within the socialist movement—both the adoption of bolshevism in the Communist International and the rise of trade union socialism in the Socialist International. The transnational Christian Democratic World Union was not formed until the late 1940s. By then its traditional liberal tenets (such as individualism, limited government roles, and laissez-faire economics) were identified with postwar conservatism. The transnational organization included Latin American counterparts.

Both the Social Democratic and Christian Democratic parties in Europe went through evolutionary stages of development that are relevant to understanding their Latin American connections. They gained governmental power in the 1920s and 1930s in Europe, but their general ineffectiveness convinced them of the need for broader electoral appeal. The religious base of the Christian Democrats precluded their appealing to anticlerical elements, and the trade unionist Social Democrats could make few inroads with propertied classes or industrial interests. After World War II, both of them reduced their ideological insistence in successful concerted efforts to broaden their political bases and consequently became the two major European parties. At the Frankfurt Conference in 1951, the Social Democrats acknowledged the utility of mixed private and public economic sectors, depending on individual national conditions, and in 1959 they formally disavowed Marxism and social revolution. Soon thereafter the Christian Democrats came to accept a degree of state intervention into economic and social affairs. Fundamental differences remained, however. In general, Christian Democrats may be characterized as moderate conservatives with a strong right wing, and the Social Democrats as moderate socialists with a strong left wing. Latin American counterparts did not necessarily follow the same process.

The Communist International and Latin America

In an earlier era international communism could have been called a major global transnational political party. After its founding in March 1919, the Comintern headquarters was in Moscow throughout its twenty-four-year existence. The Comintern included members in almost all countries, and they sent delegates to Moscow to plan the promotion of Communist revolutions outside of the Soviet Union. The Soviet government denied that the Comintern was an instrument of the Soviet state, although in fact it viewed the organization as a tool of Soviet policy.

The founding of local Communist parties and the Latin American section of the Comintern created opportunities for extending revolutionary activities in the region. Under Comintern guidance, the Mexican Communist party was more successful in fostering communism in Central America than in Mexico itself, as Mexicans preferred to make their own revolution without outside assistance. In South America the Argentine Communist party was the first to join the Comintern. A South American Comintern secretariat was set up in Buenos Aires in 1930 and assigned the task of strengthening Communist influence and supervising the flow of agents in the Southern Cone.

Between the two world wars, Soviet policy was aimed at creating loyal and disciplined local Communist parties, with some success. In Chile, the organization of a strong Communist party contributed to formation of a popular front coalition that brought the Radical party to power in 1938. Thus, Chile became the third country, after France and Spain, to be ruled by popular fronts. Otherwise, the Soviet strategy was a failure.

Communism faced the continuing dilemma of reconciling Soviet foreign policy interests, the narrow Comintern sectarian approach, and the needs of local Communist parties. In Latin America in the late 1920s and throughout the 1930s, Comintern tactics made little progress toward revolution, but they did provoke a rupture of Soviet diplomatic relations with Mexico and Argentina in 1930, Chile in 1932, and Brazil and Uruguay in 1936. Dogmatic Comintern directives to lo-

cal Communist parties and the Soviet preoccupation with domestic and proximate international problems did not enhance revolutionary chances. Furthermore,
radical Latin American nationalists initially were more inclined to opt for Italian
fascism than for Soviet communism.

In 1943 Moscow announced that the Comintern had been dissolved.
Throughout the 1920s and 1930s, the Soviet Union had remained the world's
only Communist country; obviously, the Comintern purpose of sparking revolution elsewhere had not succeeded. Thereafter, Communist parties continued to
work for the overthrow of established governments without the Comintern; in
Latin America they have succeeded nowhere. For a brief period during and immediately after World War II, from about 1941 to 1947, the Soviet Union and Latin
American Communist parties did enjoy influence in the region. The wartime alliance between the Soviet Union and the Western powers facilitated the expansion
of Soviet diplomatic contacts in the region, and Latin American Communist
parties achieved a certain level of prestige. Those parties were directed by Moscow
to support the Allied war effort and to use their influence to prevent strikes and
the disruption of war production. The onset of the cold war in 1947, however, reversed the trend. Soviet relations with Latin America became increasingly strained
as Stalin bitterly criticized Latin American governments for their close ties with
the United States and demanded that the local parties publicly declare their loyalty to the Soviet Union. Wartime goodwill toward the Soviet Union dissipated
and the newly intransigent Communist parties were outlawed. Better relations
were not possible until after Stalin's death in 1953, but the internecine strife
among various revolutionary groups after the Castro revolution of 1959 severely
detracted from the Communist parties' positions. The traditional Latin American
Communist parties remained loyal to the Communist party of the Soviet Union.
Thus the disappearance of the Soviet-led international Communist system with
the end of the cold war had drastic consequences not only for the organizational
and financial status of the Communist parties of Latin America but for their very
ideological identity. Their ingrained dogmatism has greatly limited their ability to
find answers to these problems.

The Socialist International and Latin America

Social democracy has a long history in Latin America. Some local parties, borrowing their social-democratic inspiration from Europe, date from the first decade of
the twentieth century. The importance to Latin America of the Socialist International (SI), however, is a much more recent phenomenon. In fact, its real impact
as an actor in Latin American international relations dates from about 1976 when
it began taking more interest in the Third World. After that date, the SI was more
active in Latin America than in any other region outside of Europe.

Despite the expressed desire at the Frankfurt Conference in 1951 to open to
the Third World and develop closer links with Latin American, Asian, and African
parties, the SI kept its essentially European character. In the 1970s some European leaders, notably Willy Brandt, Bruno Kreisky, and Olof Palme, strongly advocated expanding membership into Third World regions. They argued that social
democratic solidarity and mutual support would have a positive influence in furthering the struggle for social and economic equality on the part of popular move-

ments. Willy Brandt accepted the presidency of the SI at its general Geneva Conference in November 1976, partly on the condition that the SI would actively seek institutional cooperation with like-minded Third World parties and movements. Political parties and organizations from forty-two countries were represented at the Geneva Conference. By the mid-1980s, the SI global membership comprised sixty-four parties and affiliated groups from fifty countries, fifty-two observer parties and liberation fronts from thirty-seven countries, and ten international organizations as observers. Those from Europe were in a distinct minority.

Latin American membership in the SI grew rapidly. Two of the three heads of state present at the Geneva Conference in 1976 were from Latin America: President Carlos Andrés Pérez of Venezuela representing the Democratic Action party, and President Daniel Oduber of Costa Rica for the National Liberation party. The SI organized an ongoing Regional Conference on Latin America and the Caribbean, which held periodic meetings in different Latin American capitals. By 1983 Latin American parties and organizations who were members of the SI included: Dominican Revolutionary party, National Liberation party of Costa Rica, Radical party of Chile, Democratic Action party of Venezuela, Febrerista Revolutionary party of Paraguay, Ecuadorian Democratic Left, Popular Socialist party of Argentina, Jamaican People's National party, New Jewel Movement of Grenada, Progressive Labour party of St. Lucia, Working People's Alliance of Guyana, Independence party of Puerto Rico, APRA of Peru, Democratic Labor party of Brazil, Nicaraguan Sandinist Front, Panamanian Democratic Revolutionary party, Bolivian National Revolutionary Movement of the Left, and certain groups in El Salvador, Haiti, and Honduras.

The SI addressed a large number of issues concerning Latin America, both directly and indirectly. Among the first and continuing issues was the New International Economic Order (NIEO) and disarmament and arms control. At Geneva in 1976 the first great issue discussed was the new economic world order resolution asking for the reduction of inequalities, a commitment to economic solidarity, and satisfaction of the vital needs of all nations. The NIEO continued as a major topic at subsequent meetings, reflecting Brandt's views on the NIEO and the SI's new openness to the Third World. Calls were made for a new international financial and monetary system that would diminish the debts of the developing countries. Other resolutions emphasized disarmament, partly on the grounds that it would release resources for development. The Latin American nuclear-free zone treaty was viewed with great favor. The SI also backed the 1983 reports of the Brandt Commission and the Paline Commission on development and disarmament, respectively.

A second set of major issues with particular relevance for Latin America dealt with democracy, dictatorship, and human rights. Over the years a number of resolutions were passed on general subjects as well as on issues involving specifically named countries. Resolutions were passed, for example, expressing regret over the proliferation of military dictatorships institutionalizing the use of terror and torture; supporting the peoples' struggles for a democratic system that respects human rights and social development; and calling for an end to arbitrary detention, tortures, and killings and demanding the restoration of political freedom and the right of political parties and trade unions to work freely and openly. Other resolutions denounced disappearances, arbitrary detention, and persecution in Chile, Argentina, Uruguay, El Salvador, and Guatemala; expressed solidarity with democratic elements in Guyana, Suriname, Haiti, El Salvador, Bolivia, and Paraguay against dictatorial regimes; welcomed democratic elections in the Dominican Republic, Ecuador, Peru, Bolivia, Brazil, Argentina, and Uruguay; and hoped that the end of the Somoza dynasty would lead to the democratization of Nicaragua as well as of all of Central America. Other statements expressed support for the Sandinistas and denounced U.S. policy toward Nicaragua; supported the New Jewel Movement in Grenada; supported the Panamanian-U.S. treaties for the decolonization of the Panama Canal; declared solidarity with the Puerto Rican Independence party; and asked for humane treatment of illegal immigrants. An attempt by the Portuguese Socialist party to denounce the Cuban dictatorship was not carried, although the presence of Soviet, Cuban, and East German forces in Ethiopia was condemned. In August 1977 the SI organized a meeting with the Chilean Popular Union to elaborate an action program for the democratization of Chile. The Central American crisis beginning in the late 1970s occupied a great deal of SI attention, continuing into the late 1980s. Although the SI was able to make collective statements unfavorable to U.S. policy, deep divisions existed over attitudes toward the Sandinista government in Nicaragua.

GUERRILLA GROUPS

Guerrilla Insurgents as International Actors

Guerrilla groups have been a part of the Latin American scene since the early nineteenth-century wars for independence and of international significance since that time. They were most prominent, however, after the successful Cuban Revolution (1956–1959). The importance of guerrilla groups declined in the 1970s as counterinsurgency operations by governments (including especially repressive military regimes) proved effective. In certain states, however, they remained or reappeared as important actors. In Central America, the peace process begun in 1987 eventually led to the end of insurgencies in most states. In Colombia, the rise of narcotics traffickers' cartels and negotiations between the government and guerrilla groups led to a changed structure of internal violence; and in Peru, government operations finally had significant success in reducing insurgency activities in that country.

The nature and scope of the meaning of guerrilla insurgency should be clarified. John D. Martz (1970:143) defined guerrilla warfare as "armed protest against nationally constituted authority by an organized force other than the regular military establishment pursuing a set of broadly explicit objectives which extend beyond a mere change of governmental personnel and denial of legitimacy to the existing regime." In the same vein, Huntington (1974:3) said that insurgency, which challenges political systems at a fundamental level and employs violence to bring about the collapse of an incumbent regime, should be distinguished from other forms of violence aimed at reaping rewards from the political system (such as power, money, or recognition).

A further definitional problem is the indiscriminate way in which the terms "terrorist" and "terrorism" came to be used. These terms have emotional content that may disguise political preferences rather than reveal analytic precision. The result is a certain conceptual confusion surrounding the subject of subnational entities that engage in violence against the existing order.

The essential problem in the case of Latin America is to distinguish between terrorist and guerrilla groups and terrorism and insurgency. For terrorists, terrorism is the principal component of ideology and the use of terror an exclusive instrument. They engage in random or planned violence through such methods as assassination, kidnapping, bombing, and hijackings, against the general public (noncombatants) or against government officials for political purposes. Their intent is to induce terror—an intense, overmastering fear—in the minds of their targets. This concept of "terrorist" is too narrow to define the organized insurgent guerrilla groups, which are the more important actors in the Latin American context. Guerrillas do not necessarily employ the use of terror, and when they do, it is part of a larger set of instruments. Thus, guerrillas may avoid such use of violence and still be defined as guerrillas, whereas terrorists, by definition, engage essentially in terrorist acts. Although all guerrilla groups in Latin America have eventually used terror on some level (some more or less than others), few purely terrorist groups have existed. In the late 1960s, however, with the rise of urban guerrilla warfare, this distinction between insurgency and terrorism was blurred. The revival of guerrilla warfare in the late 1970s seemed once again to emphasize the distinction. Many terrorists have come from the radical right, such as the death squads that operated in Argentina, Brazil, Guatemala, and El Salvador. They usually had government connections and were devoted to preserving the status quo, not destroying it.

Guerrillas and terrorists have other distinguishing characteristics. Terrorists tend to aim at the general public and individual government officials but recognize that they are not equipped to confront security forces effectively and try to avoid them. Guerrillas engage the security forces as primary targets. Terrorist groups tend to be small, organized around isolated cells in order to escape detection. Guerrillas have more complex organizations and utilize a visible hierarchical military command structure.

The Cuban Model

The model for guerrilla groups in contemporary Latin America was provided by the successful Castro movement in Cuba. In December 1956 Fidel Castro and his band of eighty-two guerrillas landed on the northeastern coast of Cuba in the old yacht *Granma*, initiating a two-year insurgency against dictator Fulgencio Batista. The small group of only a dozen survivors, known as the 26th of July Movement, made their way into the mountainous eastern portion of the island called the Sierra Maestra. From there guerrilla activities increased and the Batista regime was overthrown. On January 1, 1959, Castro assumed power as the leader of the Cuban state.

Fidelista movements became widespread around Latin America, seeking to emulate the Cuban success and looking to Havana for leadership. Not until twenty years later in Nicaragua, however, did a second movement succeed in destroying an existing political system and gaining control of the state. While most Latin America guerrilla groups looked to Cuba for leadership and Castro exercised some influence over them, only a modicum of effort was made to organize these groups internationally. In December 1965 the Organization of Latin American Solidarity (OLAS) was organized under Cuban auspices as an agency to coordinate regional guerrilla activity. OLAS, a confederation of twenty-seven Latin American revolutionary movements, held its first conference in Havana in 1967.

Considerable differences in ideology and tactical preferences were found among Fidelista revolutionaries and between them and Soviet-supported Latin American Communist parties advocating orthodox Marxist-Leninist thought. Matters were complicated even more by China's positions on various issues and by its support for revolutionary activity in Latin America; by the survival of Maoism in Latin America after it had declined in the PRC itself; and by the influence of other ideologies, such as those of Trotsky, Bakunin, and certain Spanish theorists. In addition, an array of Latin American writers added their contributions to revolutionary literature. The most important Latin American theories, however, were the *foco* (rural cadre) concept of Fidelismo and ideas related to urban warfare.

The Castro experience served as the original principal source for guerrilla warfare doctrine. Che Guevara's statements provide a starting point for an analysis of insurgency doctrine. Guevara, who had been with Castro aboard the *Granma* and was a major figure in the subsequent insurgency movement and then in the revolutionary government, died in 1967 fighting in Bolivia (see discussion below). He was a hero to revolutionaries and had great influence on their activities through his writings on guerrilla strategy. Guevara reflected to a degree the theories of Mao Tse Tung and Ho Chi Minh, in that he sought to establish a rural peasant base for revolution. He differed from Soviet (Leninist) theory by insisting that it was unnecessary to wait until all of the objective conditions for revolution were present, as he believed that an insurrectional cadre or *foco* of thirty to fifty men could create the conditions to initiate the armed struggle. He also departed from Soviet doctrine by insisting that the guerrillas need not be tied to a political party. They were in "the vanguard," and after they gained power a revolutionary party could arise, as, he claimed, had been the case in the Cuban Revolution. The guerrilla *foco* would operate in the countryside (as in the Sierra Maestra) and create a peasant revolution. Unlike the theories of Mao and Ho, the *foco* would lead the revolution, not blend with the peasantry.

Regis Debray (1967) wrote a long pamphlet that also was viewed as a handbook on guerrilla warfare. Debray was the radical intellectual scion of a wealthy, conservative, aristocratic French family. He taught at the University of Havana after Castro came to power and later was with Guevara in Bolivia. He used the Castro experience as the model for further Latin American revolution, dismissing all other strategies, and drew heavily on Guevara's and Castro's writings and speeches. Debray argued, in sum: (1) that guerrilla struggle was the only effective means of achieving political and social change in Latin America; (2) that revolutionary power resided not with political parties but in guerrilla cadres and their military leadership; (3) that, since Castro was correct in his dictum that "cities are the graveyards of revolutionaries," war must be fought in the countryside; and (4) that mobile guerrilla *focos* would make the revolution, eventually gaining mass support. Debray said that Castro's contribution to Marxism-Leninism was his insistence that guerrillas must assume both political and military leadership of the revolution and defer the creation of a party.

Some writers argued that Fidelismo was more a matter of tactics than of ideology. They pointed out that Castro's guerrilla warfare was not in fact set in the theoretical mold that he and others later claimed. He pragmatically used ideology as it suited his needs, coming to power through the confluence of several factors that did not conform to subsequent theoretical explanations. Castro won not with peasant militia (or the proletariat) but with middle-class revolutionaries, and his *foco* did not create a revolutionary situation where none had existed— victory was due to nonguerrilla factors. Guerrilla determination was important, but so were the mistakes and incompetence of the enemy. The turning point in the Cuban Revolution came when Batista, responding to Castro, used repression in an attempt to control the major cities, turning the urban middle class against him and thereby losing his ability to rule. The regular armed forces were corrupt, undisciplined, and easily demoralized, and the Sierra Maestra provided a guerrilla sanctuary only because the army was unwilling to enter. Many significant revolutionary events occurred in the cities, initiated by urban guerrillas.

Urban warfare theory rose to prominence following Guevara's defeat in Bolivia. A widely read booklet that advocated the initiation and development of guerrilla forces in urban areas was the forty-one-page *Minimanual of the Urban Guerrilla*, written in 1970 by Carlos Marighella, a Brazilian. It received Cuban support with its publication in the official organ *Tricontinental* and was circulated abroad. Marighella, a dissident former member of the Brazilian Communist party and founder of an urban terrorist group in Brazil, was killed in a police ambush in São Paulo at the end of 1969. He had long opposed the rural guerrilla warfare thesis. Cuban support of his alternative strategy signified a fundamental change in Latin American insurgency thinking. Marighella summed up his strategy, in fact the fundamental statement about terrorism, thus: "It is necessary to turn political crisis into armed conflict by performing violent actions that will force those in power to transform the political situation of the country into a military situation. That will alienate the masses who, from then on, will revolt against the army and the police and thus blame them for this state of things."

This scenario for civil war—the strategy of militarization through urban terror that will invite repression and pave the way for popular revolt—proved to be utopian. Urban guerrillas discovered that the frequent popular response to indiscriminate terrorism was revulsion, and that if a government was sufficiently ruthless, effective repression was more likely to occur than popular uprising.

Latin American Guerrilla Movements

Significant guerrilla groups outside of Cuba first appeared in Peru. In October 1959 a group of young radicals committed to Fidelismo broke away from the reformist Aprista party. They called themselves APRA Rebelde for a brief time, until they reorganized as the Movement of the Revolutionary Left (MIR). After its leadership was killed in 1965 fighting the Peruvian army, MIR was relatively inactive even though it continued to exist into the 1970s. In 1962 a group of Peruvian Communist party members broke away and formed the National Liberation Army

(ELN); it, too, declined after 1965 but did not disappear. A Trotskyite peasant movement, the Revolutionary Leftist Front (FIR), was very active from 1962 to 1964, but its leaders were imprisoned and FIR dissolved.

In the meantime, another Peruvian insurgency developed and in the 1980s posed a serious threat to Peruvian governments. Following the Sino-Soviet split in 1964, the Peruvian Communist party divided into pro-Soviet and pro-Chinese groups. The Maoist factions in turn further divided and realigned, out of which emerged in 1970 the Sendero Luminoso (SL), meaning "Shining Path." The SL's principal leader from the beginning was Abimael Guzmán Reynoso (Comrade Gonzalo), a professor at the San Cristobal de Huamanga University in Ayacucho. The SL's ideology has often been referred to as Maoist (the theory of revolution beginning with rural peasant warfare eventually encircling the cities), but it first rooted in the radical thinking of José Carlos Mariátegui (1895–1930). Mariátegui was a noted Peruvian intellectual who had advocated combined Marxist and nationalist solutions to his country's problems. He was also founder of the party organization that ultimately led through a long and circuitous route to the organization of the SL. Indeed, the full original name of the movement was "The Revolutionary Student Front in the Shining Path of Mariátegui." Thus Maoism was blended with Mariátegui's concept of the Peruvian Indian's historical tradition of resistance to Spanish colonial rule and then to white and mestizo domination.

Guzmán built the SL organization in the countryside, and in May 1980 it began to engage in acts of sabotage and terror. The SL also had an urban structure from the beginning. The first guerrilla operations included urban warfare in Lima, although action was concentrated in the mountainous Ayacucho Department. The SL thereafter proved to be a disciplined, effective, and particularly ruthless guerrilla movement. In 1986 it expanded its activities to other parts of the country, both rural and urban. As the SL considered itself an indigenous nonaligned group and was openly contemptuous of other movements and their ideologies, it did not seek or receive outside assistance. The SL counted on support from *campesino* communities, which it recruited with a combination of rewards and severe punishment. In the mid-1980s, the SL forced a relationship with international drug traffickers in which the guerrillas attacked the army and the police in the prime coca-growing regions in exchange for money and weapons. In 1984 another terrorist group had emerged in Peru, the Castroite Movimiento Revolucionario Túpac Amaru (MRTA), in direct opposition to the SL. By 1993 some 20,000 Peruvians had been killed in the guerrilla struggle.

The Peruvian government had little success with counterinsurgency in the 1980s, although it was ruthlessly pursued. In 1992, however, the Peruvian government scored important victories over the insurgents. After the army captured the leader of the MRTA that movement began to disintegrate. Of more significance, Abimael Guzmán and other SL leaders were captured in Lima. The movement was not defeated, but its activity in Lima waned considerably, and the SL could no longer operate in rural areas with impunity.

Among other early groups were those organized in Venezuela, a major target of Castro's own international activities. In 1960 a group split from the ruling reformist Democratic Action party and formed the MIR. MIR engaged in joint operations with the guerrilla element of the Venezuelan Communist party, organized in 1962 and called the Armed Forces of National Liberation (FALN). By 1966 the two organizations had withdrawn from armed revolutionary tactics, and three years later they accepted President Rafael Caldera's offer of amnesty and formed their own political parties. Nevertheless, some small guerrilla remnants remained who in early 1973 merged to form the Revolutionary Integration Organization (OIR), but it had little success. A political party of former insurgents sometimes held the balance of power in the Venezuelan Congress, and, in 1989, it elected its candidate to a state governorship (Shugart, 1992:129–130).

One of the most effective groups operated in Uruguay. The National Liberation Front (FLN), popularly called the Tupamaros, was organized in 1963. Its operations increased in 1966 and it enjoyed considerable success for the next six years. In 1972, however, the Uruguayan army was given extraconstitutional powers and finally brought the Tupamaros under control.

Guerrilla activities in Colombia have been among the most persistent and longest lasting. The Fidelista ELN was formed in 1964. It was this group with whom the former Jesuit priest Camilo Torres, discussed earlier, was associated. After a number of its leaders were killed in 1972 and its commander defected in 1976, the ELN adopted an essentially defensive posture. The Armed Forces of Colombia (FARC) was organized in 1966, supported by Cuba. FARC became the most important guerrilla group in Colombia. The small Peking-oriented Popular Liberation Army (EPL) was formed in 1967, linked with the Revolutionary Workers party (PRT). The group suffered severe losses in the late 1960s and early 1970s and became a minor factor. Unusual in its origins was the 19th of April Movement (M-19). Organized in 1974, it took its name from the election of April 19, 1970, when former dictator Rojas Pinilla was defeated. Also of note was the Indian-based group, Quintine Lama.

In 1984 Colombian President Belisario Betancur (1982–1986) proposed a truce and an amnesty law, marking the beginning of negotiations with guerrilla groups, aimed at national reconciliation. The process was continued during the presidency of Virgilio Barco (1986–1990). In March 1990 the M-19 was finally persuaded to surrender its arms and join in electoral politics. Its presidential candidate in the May 1990 elections came in third with 13 percent of the vote. Shortly thereafter, in late 1990 and 1991, the EPL, PRT, and Quintine Lama also abandoned the armed struggle in agreements with President César Gaviria Trujillo, leaving only the ELN and FARC, by now involved in cocaine trafficking, in the field.

Insurgency in Brazil was fragmented, with competing groups organized along local rather than national lines. Two groups stood out among the many organizations that proliferated under frequently changing leadership—the National Liberation Action (ALN) and the Popular Revolutionary Vanguard (VPR). Both the ALN and the VPR were virtually eliminated by Brazilian forces in 1973, a date by which all Brazilian guerrilla forces had lost their effectiveness.

In Chile the most important of several guerrilla organizations was the MIR, formed in 1965 as a Fidelista group advocating armed struggle. It did not join Marxist President Allende's coalition government of 1970–1973 and, in fact, was highly critical of it. Most MIR leaders were arrested after the military coup in

1973. MIR continued to exist but disappeared in the late 1980s with Chile's return to constitutional government.

Insurgency organizations in Argentina were among the most active. Some were organized in the early 1960s, but they did not become prominent until late in the decade. The three most important groups were the Montoneros (MPM), the Peronist Armed Forces (FAP), and Revolutionary Armed Forces (FAR). The three closely linked groups claimed to be both Fidelista and Peronista, although they were as much as ejected from the Peronist party in 1973 and 1974. Large numbers of terrorist political murders in the 1970s inspired like retaliation by extremist right-wing groups. An intensive and bloody antiguerrilla campaign begun by the Peronist government in 1976 intensified after the military coup in 1977 in what was called the "dirty war." The guerrilla organizations were eliminated, but military actions went far beyond antiterrorism to deal brutally with many other people as well.

Insurgency in Bolivia was of special interest because of the direct connection with Cuban revolutionary leaders. Che Guevara in Cuba made plans for guerrilla action in Bolivia, hoping to stimulate a South American continentwide insurgency movement. He arrived in Bolivia in November 1966 and organized the ELN. It was initially composed of twenty Cubans (four of whom had been members of the Cuban Central Committee), twenty-nine Bolivians, and three Peruvians. After some initial successes in the Bolivian mountains, the ELN suffered increasing losses at the hands of the Bolivian army. In October 1967, Che and all but five guerrillas were killed by Bolivian military forces—an event that dealt a major blow to insurgency groups throughout Latin America.

When Bolivian troops seized Guevara they found a 30,000-word personal handwritten diary that detailed the eleven-month guerrilla campaign. Although Guevara repeated much of his earlier guerrilla doctrine in the diary, it also constituted a major source of evidence to argue the nonuniversality of the Cuban Revolution and its inapplicability to certain other situations. Guevara stressed the "continental magnitude of the task," writing that he wanted to create a series of "Vietnams" beginning in Bolivia and moving to neighboring nations. Yet his largely foreign band showed little understanding of Bolivian politics and culture; none of them spoke Quechua, the primary language of the Indians in their area of operations. Furthermore, the Bolivian government was able to capitalize on the fact that "foreigners" were attempting to capture the Bolivian nation, a situation that the guerrillas had not faced in Cuba. The regular Bolivian army units, unlike Batista's army in Cuba, were willing to encounter and able to defeat guerrillas in a mountainous environment. Most important, the diary bitterly described the Indian peasants' lack of support for the guerrillas and even their betrayal of the movement. (There were no Indians in Cuba, whereas they constituted a majority in Bolivia.) The guerrillas were unable to replenish their personnel losses with a single peasant recruit.

The ELN continued after Guevara's death, but in 1969 the new leadership was captured by government forces and the ELN was disarmed. The Bolivian MIR, formed in 1971, suffered heavy losses the following year. Jaime Paz Zamora, leader of the MIR, became Bolivia's vice-president in 1982 and was elected president in 1989.

The first important guerrilla groups in Central America operated in Guatemala beginning in 1961. Three major ones were organized: the FAR, the 13th of November Revolutionary Movement (MR-13), and the Organization of the Armed People. Guatemalan violence was extreme in the 1960s as right-wing groups responded in kind to guerrilla terrorism. The Guatemalan army conducted a brutal counterinsurgency campaign in the early 1960s, along with large-scale Indian population resettlements. The guerrillas were weakened yet managed to keep operating in remote areas, but in 1980 they were routed by another ruthless army campaign. Two years later the three guerrilla groups formed the Guatemalan National Revolutionary Union, which was able to engage in skirmishes and attacks on infrastructure targets but not capable of engaging the army in sustained operations. On October 2, 1987, the Guatemalan government, represented by army generals, and the guerrilla alliance announced a cease-fire and began talks seeking to end the twenty-six-year-old insurgency. The talks complied with the Central American peace agreement that had been signed by all Central American presidents in August 1987 (see Chapter 11 for more details on the Central American peace process and its relevance to ending insurgencies in most of the Central American states). The talks, in Madrid, Guatemala, and Mexico, took several years to complete, deadlocked over human rights issues and interrupted by sporadic insurgent action (the guerrillas reorganized as the Guatemalan United Revolutionary Front—URNG). In mid-1993, after the army leaders forced the president to resign, the new president, Ramiro de Leon Carpio, recommenced the peace negotiations.

In Nicaragua, a small Castroite organization was founded in 1961 called the Sandinist National Liberation Front (FSLN). It became inactive in 1970 but reactivated in 1972 as popular discontent with the ruling Somoza dictatorship increased. The Sandinistas and their allies finally overthrew General Somoza in 1979 (see Chapter 11).

As soon as the Sandinista guerrillas became governors they were opposed by counterrevolutionary guerrilla groups. Numerous organizations coalesced into three alliances. In time they were collectively known as the *contras* and supported by the Reagan administration as a key element in its anti-Sandinista policies, but they were loosely connected and had continuous internal disputes. The National Democratic Front (FDN) coalition, formed in 1981 by former National Guard officers, was the most important and militant; they recruited widely within Nicaragua and in time their ranks included many teenagers. The FDN was based in Honduras and operated in northern Nicaragua, seeking to overthrow the Sandinistas. A coalition of Indian groups—the Sandinista Unity of Miskitos, Sumos, and Ramas (MISURASATA), founded under another name in 1979 to oppose Somoza, was transformed in 1981 into an armed resistance against the Sandinista government. The government's resettlement of Indians as part of its counterinsurgency operations had led MISURASATA to join loosely with the FDN. The third principal contra element was the Democratic Revolutionary Alliance (ARDE), founded in late 1982. In stark contrast to the FDN, ARDE consisted of moderate political forces operating out of Costa Rica, which sought to return the Sandinista revolution to its original political pluralism. The two dominant forces within ARDE were the Sandinista Revolutionary Front, led by a disillusioned Sandinista hero in the fight against Somoza, and the Democratic Movement, whose members included prominent civilians who had opposed Somoza; some had been members of the Junta of Government after 1979 and some had been Sandinista supporters. They put together their revolutionary front in early 1982 and made clear their distance from the FDN because of its *somocista* background and different political objectives.

The FDN had begun operating with assistance from Argentine military intelligence officers and U.S. CIA agents. Most U.S. support went directly to the FDN, considered to be the best fighting force. In late 1984 the U.S. Congress prohibited direct CIA help. In July 1985 the United States persuaded the feuding contras to form the United Nicaraguan Opposition (UNO) to serve as an "umbrella" organization for the various rebel groups. Underlying the UNO effort was an attempt to enhance contra acceptability by a reluctant U.S. Congress. Various elements formed the three-man UNO Directorate but also acted independently. In 1986 Congress authorized an overt assistance program, but with restrictions. The Iran-contra affair in 1987, revealed in detail in congressional hearings, ended a covert operation, which was directed out of the National Security Council (NSC) staff organization and relied on private funding and logistical support designed to overcome the post–1984 congressional prohibitions. In 1989 the badly split contra leadership was reorganized under the Nicaraguan Resistance as the new "umbrella" unit, with a five-member directorate. The power struggle continued, however, given impetus by two factors: On February 3, 1988, the U.S. Congress rejected any further public aid to the contras, and on March 23 the contra leadership and the Sandinista government signed a temporary cease-fire and began negotiations to make it permanent. The contra alliance, which had been held together by a common enemy and U.S. support, was badly fractured.

The February 1990 elections, in which the UNO headed by presidential candidate Violeta Barrios de Chamorro defeated the Sandinista party and incumbent President Daniel Ortega, constituted a turning point in the Nicaraguan civil war. The contras did not transform itself into a political party for the elections nor become a part of the UNO coalition. Rather, they shared a mutual animosity with the UNO toward the Sandinista government and interest in voting it out of power (Shugart, 1992:137–139, 142, 145). On April 19, 1990, all parties (contras, Miskito Indian rebels then known as Yatama, Sandinistas, and the Chamorro government-elect), in concert with the UN Security Council with U.S. backing, reached agreements to end the civil war. Nevertheless, political distrust and armed violence persisted. Contra leaders were targets of assassinations and charged the Sandinistas with pursuing a systematic plan for their elimination. Hundreds of former contras, known as *recontras,* renewed guerrilla warfare to protest the failure of the government to deliver on its promises. Former Sandinista army officers organized armed groups of former Sandinista soldiers in response, resulting in outbreaks of fighting. By early 1994, however, the government had managed to disarm both sides, despite continuing political turmoil and sporadic terrorism.

In El Salvador, the Nicaraguan Revolution of July 1979 reinvigorated insurgent movements. The Farabundo Martí National Liberation Front (FMLN) had been formed in October 1980 to integrate five armed organizations. The Farabundo Martí Popular Forces of Liberation (FPL), founded in 1974, was the largest but suffered from violent internal disputes. A second FMLN guerrilla group was the Revolutionary Army of the People (ERP), and the Armed Forces of National Resistance (FARN) also joined. The Salvadoran Communist party decided to join the armed conflict in 1979 in alliance with the FMLN. The small Central American Workers' Revolutionary party (PRTC) adhered in late 1980.

The Democratic Revolutionary Front (FDR) was also established in 1980. It was a separate political wing attached to the FMLN that operated as a government-in-exile in Mexico, but without control over military decisions. The FDR was made up of democratic left organizations. Most important was the National Revolutionary Movement, a Social Democratic organization and member of the Socialist International. The Popular Socialist Christian Movement (MPSC), composed of former Christian Democrats who left the party in early 1980, was also part of the FDR. Much of the FDR membership had concluded that peaceful progress in El Salvador was no longer possible.

The FMLN initially followed a "total victory" strategy, which ended with the failure of the "final offensive" in January 1981 (just prior to the U.S. presidential inauguration). The insurgents then turned to sabotage of the country's infrastructure (the destruction of roads and bridges, communications facilities, electrical and water sources, and industrial plants). They refused government offers to participate in elections; they occasionally negotiated directly with the government, but the civil war continued unabated and stalemated.

In October 1987 intense negotiations occurred in compliance with the recently instituted Esquipulus II Central American peace accord (see Chapter 11). Following the government's defeat in legislative elections in March 1988, however, the FMLN decided to press for a full-scale insurrection. While periodic UN-mediated negotiations occurred in 1990 and 1991 the war continued at a standoff. Finally, on January 16, 1992, the government and the insurgents signed a comprehensive peace agreement in Mexico, and a UN-monitored cease-fire began on February 1. Under the pact the FMLN gave up the armed struggle, disarmed, and became a legally recognized political party; the Salvadoran army was also reduced by half, and certain paramilitary units known for human rights abuses were disbanded and a new integrated police force created. On March 20, 1994, in the culmination of the peace process that ended the civil war, national elections were held followed by a presidential runoff vote on April 23. The presidency was won by Armando Calderon Sol of the conservative Republican Nationalist Alliance (ARENA). Nevertheless, the second-place showing by Rubén Zamora, formerly a central figure of the FDR and presidential candidate of the Democratic Convergence leftist coalition (which included the FMLN), as well as FMLN success in mayoral races and those for the National Assembly, established the former insurgents as a significant political presence in the new El Salvador.

BIBLIOGRAPHIC COMMENT

Papal diplomacy in Latin America is addressed in a history by Manhattan (1946) and a provocative treatment by Víctor Alba in Davis, Wilson, and others (1975). Some works on the Latin American church that include transnational aspects are by D. H. Levine (1986), Lynch (1991), Sanders (1970), Schmitt (1972), Serbin

(1993), and Cleary and Stewart-Gambino (1992). The classic work on liberation theology is Gutiérrez (1973); Boff (1985) is of particular interest. On the debate over liberation theology, see Candelaria (1990), Hebblethwaite (1985), and Sigmund (1990). Martin (1990) and Stoll (1990) discuss the Protestant inroads. General treatments of business enterprise, with substantial reference to Latin America, are by Barnet and Muller (1975), Eells (1976), Sampson (1973, 1975), Vernon (1971a, 1971b), and Wilkins (1970, 1974). Studies of international businesses and MNCs in Latin America include Rippy (1958), Behrman (1972), Sigmund (1980), and Irish (1978). On international labor organizations and activities in Latin America, see Alba (1968), Alexander (1965), Levenstein (1971), Poblete Troncoso and Burnett (1960), Rens (1959), and Romualdi (1967). On recent developments see Grosse (1989) and Shugart (1992). United Kingdom (1990) gives details about the WFTU. Analyses of transnational political parties and Latin America are sparse. On the Comintern and Communist parties in Latin America, see Alexander (1963), Caballero (1986), Herman (1973), and Poppino (1964). Braunthal (1967–1980), Vellinga (1993), and Williams (1984) analyze the Socialist International. Some general works from the extensive literature on Latin American guerrilla groups are Gott (1970), Martz (1970), Mercier Vega (1969), R. H. Moss (1972), Radu and Tismanleanu (1986), Schump (1971), and Wickham-Crowley (1992). On the Cuban Revolution, see Bonachea and San Martín (1974), Bonachea and Valdes (1972), and Karol (1970); and the writings and speeches by Guevara (1961, 1973–1974), and those edited by Gerassi (1968). The editors of Guevara (1985) comment on his writings and add information on contemporary insurgencies. The most useful editions of Guevara's Bolivian diary in English are those edited by Scheer (1968), which contains an introduction by Fidel Castro, and James (1968), which includes "other captured documents" and a highly critical introduction by the editor; also of interest is an analytical document issued by the Pan American Union (1968). See also the writings of Debray (1967, 1970, 1976), and Marighella (1970, 1971). Castañeda (1993) analyzes the current state of the Latin American left.

PART THREE

———————— ■ ————————

International Institutions

The next three chapters deal with the large number of international governmental organizations (IGOs) relevant to Latin American international relations. IGOs sometimes behave as subsystem actors, and IGOs themselves often constitute international subsystems where regularized interaction takes place. They also serve as policy instruments by other actors and provide regulatory elements at various levels of international politics. Latin American states, since their national beginnings, have used international organizations as favored policy instruments. Thus, a large number of IGOs need to be analyzed as a category unto themselves.

This part of the book proceeds through a hierarchy of IGOs. Chapter 7 deals with the Latin American level, both regional and subregional, and analyzes attempts to form organizations aimed at political and economic integration and other interstate associations. Chapter 8 addresses the Inter-American System of organization and law, which reflects the Western Hemispheric regional search for security, peace, and national well-being. Chapter 9 is concerned with global organizations and some specific regimes, Third World structures, and other arrangements in the Western Hemisphere—both bilateral and multilateral—in which certain Latin American states have participated.

CHAPTER SEVEN

—————————— ■ ——————————

Latin American Integration and Association

LATIN AMERICAN STATE PARTICIPATION in international organizations at the Latin American regional and subregional levels is the subject of this chapter. Initiatives toward some sort of integration or association among some combination of Latin American states date from the movements for independence to the present day. The nineteenth-century Spanish American congresses for political-security union are discussed as well as regional conferences on international law. The complex subject of post–World War II projects aimed primarily at economic union is then taken up. The chapter next proceeds to a discussion of intra–Latin American organizations designed to promote both political and economic cooperation among the member states and to increase the region's bargaining power with the rest of the world. It ends with a treatment of the Latin American Nuclear Free Zone, a specialized regional international regime.

THE MOVEMENT FOR SPANISH AMERICAN UNION

Americanismo

Subregional integration was first attempted in Latin America during the nineteenth century when some Spanish American states attempted to form larger political entities and to join in mutual security alliances on a confederation basis. The first efforts began during the movements for independence and continued for about a half-century thereafter; they were largely abandoned after 1865. An ambivalent intra–Spanish American "love-hate" relationship was revealed that has survived to the present day. The early integration efforts were often referred to by Latin Americans as *Americanismo* or, sometimes, "continental nationalism." Some advocates of union were also found in Brazil. Usually, however, Americanismo was the idea of a kindred Spanish American spirit growing out of a common colonial heritage, revolutionary experience, and culture. It was a shared perception of Spanish American community that might form the basis of political unity. Americanismo also referred to patterns of unity among Spanish American states against outside powers.

Americanists variously wanted to form anywhere from one to four sovereign states out of the Spanish empire in America, but geographic realities, localism and regionalism, and interstate disputes led instead to the establishment of separate states that were often in conflict with one another. Simón Bolívar, the prestigious leader of independence in northern South America, was the chief advocate of Americanismo and the most active exponent of Spanish American solidarity. Other important leaders similarly were inspired to advocate permanent cooperation among the newly independent American states, but Bolívar more than they attempted to translate theory into practice. He first articulated the idea of the union of American states in his famous "Jamaica letter" of 1815. He envisaged three Spanish American federations, roughly composed of Mexico and Central America; the Spanish portions of northern South America, including Peru and Bolivia; and southern South America. In 1826 he proposed the total unification of Spanish America.

The four viceroyalties of the Spanish American empire soon divided into sixteen (later eighteen) separate states. Mexico and Central America formed a single empire in 1821, but Central America broke away and formed its own federation in 1823 and then split into five more states in 1838. In 1830 Gran Colombia divided into the three nations of Colombia, Venezuela, and Ecuador. The leaders of Buenos Aires attempted to mold a single independent state out of the Viceroyalty of La Plata, which they misnamed the United Provinces of La Plata, but it disintegrated into modern-day Argentina, Uruguay, Paraguay, and part of Bolivia. Chilean and Argentine leaders worked to frustrate attempts at union between Bolivia and Peru; after Peru gained independence in 1824, its province of Upper Peru separated to form the state of Bolivia.

Spanish American Alliance

Another effort at political union was aimed at forming some sort of federation or alliance among Spanish American states geared toward mutual security against external threats. As the separate nation-states were attempting to develop a self-conscious sense of their unique national identities and traditions, often impeded by strong intrastate regionalism, they also endeavored to associate on an international level. Four international Spanish American congresses were held between 1826 and 1865, with little in the way of substantive outcomes. Thus, not only did some of the state entities that initially emerged from the independence movements fragment, but attempts at alliance among the sovereign states were also frustrated and ended in disillusionment.

Participation in the four conferences held between 1826 and 1865 was primarily limited to the Spanish American states, and only a small minority actually attended. They signed agreements occasioned by fear of external threats, but once those threats subsided the proposals for union or alliance disintegrated into nationalism and particularism. Only one of the treaties, signed in 1848 (discussed below), actually went into effect. (Bailey, 1967:161–165; Mecham, 1965:85–92; and Inter-American Institute of Legal Studies, 1966:xv–xx provide numerous details for the following discussion of the four conferences.)

On December 7, 1824, the Colombian government, led by Bolívar, sent invitations to several states to attend a congress in Panama (a Colombian province), with the primary objective of establishing a Spanish American union. The possibility that Spain, with help from the Holy Alliance led by France, would attempt to reclaim its American empire by force was a special concern. Four states were represented—Gran Colombia (later Colombia, Ecuador, Panama, and Venezuela); the Central American Federation (later Costa Rica, Guatemala, Honduras, Nicaragua, and El Salvador); the United Mexican States; and Peru. Great Britain and the Netherlands, both enemies of Spain, sent unofficial observers at the invitation of conference organizers. Argentina declined to attend and stated that it intended to follow an independent course, apparently unwilling to accept Gran Colombia's regional leadership. Brazil and the United States received invitations, although Bolívar originally had opposed their attendance. He felt that Brazil had no common aversion to Spain and that the U.S. presence might offend Great Britain. The United States was invited because some Spanish American leaders believed that President Monroe's recent statement warning Europe to keep "hands off" the Americas might be used as the basis for an inter-American alliance. Brazil declined, little interested in helping to strengthen Spanish America. The United States hesitantly agreed to participate, apparently because of the possibility of increasing its trade with Latin America, but it made clear its lack of interest in making any mutual political or security commitments with the other American states. As it turned out, neither of the two U.S. delegates sent to Panama attended the congress. One died en route and the other arrived after the meeting had adjourned. Bolivia also appointed delegates but travel obstacles prevented them from reaching Panama in time to participate. Chile supported the Congress but did not appoint its delegates in time for them to attend.

The Congress of Panama met from June 22 to July 15, 1826. The major theme was Spanish America's unity and defense of its new sovereignty and territorial integrity. Four agreements were signed, the most important of which was the Treaty of Perpetual Union, League, and Confederation. It stated, in part: "The object of the perpetual compact will be to uphold in common, defensively and offensively, if necessary, the sovereignty and independence of all and every one of the confederated powers of America against all foreign domination." Even as the Panama Conference met, the threat from Spain and the Holy Alliance had subsided. Only Bolívar's Gran Colombia ratified the agreements, and his plan for a Spanish American political union ended in failure.

A second meeting was not held until almost two decades later. It was a conference in Lima, called the American Congress, from December 11, 1847, to March 1, 1848. Five South American states were represented—Bolivia, Chile, Ecuador, Colombia, and Peru. Mexico, preoccupied with its war with the United States, did not attend; Venezuela, Argentina, and Brazil declined their invitations. The United States received an unauthorized invitation from Colombia and an informal one from Peru but refused them. Indeed, the conference was partly motivated by fear of the United States because of its war with Mexico, and the organizers retracted the earlier invitations. The primary threat, however, was seen as Spain's brief attempt to reconquer the west coast of South America.

The American Congress drew up several treaties, the most important of which was a Treaty of Confederation. It provided that the contracting parties should aid one another with land and naval forces in the event of attack by a foreign power, that regular meetings should be held, and that disputes be peacefully settled according to a specified set of procedures. The other American governments, including the United States, were invited to subscribe to the several conventions, but the response was unanimously negative. A consular convention was the only one subsequently ratified by the signatories and the only one drafted by the several Spanish American congresses to enter into force.

The third conference, a one-day meeting, took place in Santiago, Chile on September 15, 1856. Only three states—Chile, Ecuador, and Peru—attended what was called the Continental Congress. Again, cooperation was inspired in part by fear of foreign aggression. This time the filibustering expeditions of William Walker and other U.S. adventurers in Central America and Mexico heightened apprehensions over U.S. territorial ambitions. The conference adopted yet another convention for alliance and confederation called the Continental Treaty. It established a permanent league of Latin American states with a congress and included mutual aid provisions and the pledge to prevent the organizing of hostile expeditions by political emigrés within any of the allied states. The other Spanish American states and Brazil were invited to join the union; the United States was not approached. None of the parties ratified the Continental Treaty.

The Second Lima Conference, the fourth and last Spanish American conference, was held from November 14, 1864, to March 13, 1865. It was attended by Bolivia, Chile, Colombia, Ecuador, El Salvador, Guatemala, Peru, and Venezuela. Argentina and Brazil still refused to consider plans of confederation. The threat of U.S. aggression had been halted by the Civil War, but a suggestion to invite the United States was turned down. Several European interventions urgently renewed the question of political union, including the French occupation of Mexico, the Spanish reoccupation of Santo Domingo, and the Spanish war with Peru and Chile. The Treaty of Union and Defensive Alliance was among the four conventions approved, which again agreed to confederation and pledged mutual defense against aggression. None of the treaties was ratified.

After the Second Lima Congress in 1865, the Spanish American states abandoned initiatives directed toward union and joined the rest of the region in placing their reliance on international law. International legal conferences included the Congress of Jurists at Lima (1877–1879), the Bolivarian Congress at Caracas in 1883, and the First South American Congress on Private International Law at Montevideo (1888–1889). They aimed to eliminate some of the causes of the civil strife and inter-American wars that continued to arise in Latin America and made difficult any efforts toward solidarity. In 1889, Latin Americans combined their emphasis on international law with regional organization by founding the Inter-American System in cooperation with the United States. Later, they participated in global international organizations, beginning with The Hague System at the turn of the century and then in the League of Nations and the United Nations System. In the late 1940s and early 1950s, Latin Americans undertook new initiatives toward unity that emphasized economic integration, without abandoning regional or global approaches to organization and law.

INTEGRATION MOVEMENTS

Initial Concepts

Latin American integration efforts after World War II expressed the idea that political union might ultimately grow out of economic integration, perhaps reflecting a continuing Latin American desire for political unity, but the basic drive was clearly for economic development. A linkage with the past was a continuing ambivalence in the constant clash between the desire for unity and national rivalries. The 1960s especially were years of great expectations for economic integration. Subsequent efforts, however, tended to be gradual and formalistic, even though the Latin American states' economic and social problems continued to grow and their desire for more independence from external powers remained unabated. Yet the fact of continued subregional integration efforts (as well as the organization of other related Latin American entities, discussed below) represented at least a partial commitment to cooperation for economic purposes. Furthermore, in the 1980s, Latin Americans undertook serious reform of their integration organizations that continued into the 1990s, with the further possibility of connecting them to free trade agreements with the United States.

Latin American economic integration organizations initially grew out of immediate post–World War II United Nations proposals, specifically those of the United Nations Economic Commission for Latin America (ECLA) (see Chapter 9). ECLA commissioned studies and sponsored conferences and negotiations. As a result, the Central American Common Market (CACM) and the Latin American Free Trade Association (LAFTA) were formed under its auspices.

The initial integration efforts included both economic and political considerations. From a purely economic standpoint, free-trade theory was embraced and applied to regional integration theory. Free trade was assumed to mean more trade, redounding to everyone's benefit. Proponents further assumed that successful integration required complementary economies among the member states, meaning that the national economies must produce different goods. With complementarity, "economies of scale" would develop, a modern version of the classic economic concept of "comparative advantage." In economies of scale, economic specialization exists in each national economy, with each member state exporting those products that it produces most efficiently and importing those that others produce most efficiently. Thus, the theory goes, various products originate at their most efficient and therefore least expensive source, which leads to lower prices. With costs and prices lowered to everyone's benefit, markets expand, giving incentive to increased investment and, consequently, to the expansion of existing industries and the creation of new ones. In sum, the theory of economies of scale within a regional integration context predicted that increased, sustained, and mutually beneficial economic growth would occur among member states.

The dangers of regional economic integration were also recognized. If economies of scale did not exist—that is, if "substitute" rather than complementary economies were the rule—the result of integration would be trade stagnation or trade diversion. Stagnation would occur because similar economies had little to trade. Trade diversion was the opposite of trade creation: instead of creating low-cost sources, trade is diverted from foreign sources to higher-cost regional sources, a scenario in which integration could worsen rather than better the economic situation. For example, before integration, a South American state imported automobiles from Europe, where particular models were produced most efficiently. Integration revised the common tariff structure, making the European source more expensive, and the state then imported similar automobiles from a regional state. However, the automobiles were produced less efficiently and more expensively than at the prior preintegration European source, resulting in higher costs and, perhaps, lower quality.

Early Planning Efforts

ECLA proposed at its first meeting in 1948 that the Latin American states consider arranging themselves into a series of subregional customs unions. The rationale for subregional groupings was that their markets would be more cohesive and viable than a single larger regional one and that, after subregional markets became operational, they could be melded into a larger entity. ECLA later urged that the subregional approach be abandoned in favor of integrating the entire Latin American region. The shift in emphasis, occurring in about 1958, was based as much on political as on economic concerns—ECLA theorists envisioned Latin American integration as a counterpoise to U.S. regional hegemony. They argued that the integration of all the Latin American states, and increased regional economic power, would result in more collective economic leverage. In fact, ECLA influence on economic integration in Latin America should not be overstated. ECLA gave impetus to the initial stages of integration and especially to the CACM, but it had little guiding influence on LAFTA's subsequent development and decreasingly on CACM's policies. By the early 1970s, ECLA's theories were widely discredited in Latin America.

The Inter-American System also gave impetus to and supported economic integration in Latin America. Official multilateral statements favored regionwide integration over subregional markets. Economic integration was officially adopted by the Inter-American System as part of the multilateralization of the Alliance for Progress in the 1960s. A major statement issued from a meeting of American presidents at Punta del Este in 1967. They agreed to the establishment of an organization linking the CACM and LAFTA and making it fully operative by 1985. The Inter-American Development Bank (IDB) actively supported economic integration. It lent funds to the CACM for integration projects and underwrote multinational programs in South America aimed at physical infrastructure development tying the nations together. The IDB founded the Institute for the Integration of Latin America (INTAL) in Buenos Aires in 1966. INTAL served as an economic integration research institute, training center, and technical assistance source, issuing policy studies and training (as well as attempting to persuade) Latin American government, business, and labor officials.

Latin American integration involved both regional and subregional approaches, with actual practice favoring the latter. Planning for the integration of five Central American states was well under way by the time ECLA shifted its position away from subregional integration, and those states were unwilling to give up their own common market (established in 1959) and join a larger enterprise. LAFTA, composed of eleven members, was founded in 1960. It did not truly form a Latin

American regional economy because all of the regional states were not members; nevertheless, it included all of the large states and most of the region's population and resources. Efforts continued to create an all-inclusive market, but without success.

Further subregional integration took place. The Andean Group was organized in 1966 within LAFTA, at about the same time that the Caribbean Free Trade Association (CARIFTA) was being organized. CARIFTA integrated more intensely to become the Caribbean Community. In 1980 LAFTA was superseded by the Latin American Integration Association (ALADI). Leaders of the various markets debated the merits of widening their membership or linking with other markets, but no important movement in this direction occurred. In fact, the formation of the Andean Group and ALADI signaled a move away from institutional convergence and indicated the problems besetting LAFTA that led to new ways of thinking about economic integration.

Problems of Economic Integration

Economic integration proceeded unevenly and, to its advocates, disappointingly. By the end of the 1960s, economic integration had slowed considerably. Among the problems were deeply ambivalent attitudes toward integration in both Latin America and the United States (Grunwald, Wionzcek, and Carnoy, 1972). At first the integration concept conflicted with U.S. policy traditions of bilateral relations and support of private economic enterprise and free trade. Under the Alliance for Progress, the United States generally endorsed and subsidized integration efforts because they promised to aid in Latin American economic development and, presumably, political stability. From the late 1960s onward, however, U.S. material assistance and policy commitments in fact did not support integration. U.S. preoccupation first with the Vietnam War and then with domestic problems, as well as decreasing foreign aid expenditures, precluded Latin American policy commitments in general, including support of economic integration.

Economic integration had wide appeal in Latin America, both as an "independence movement" against external (especially U.S.) economic domination and as a means to Latin American development. Important political and economic groups whose cooperation was necessary for successful integration, however, did not accept or were ambivalent toward integration policies. Military and business establishments were divided over integration issues. Certain industrialists and exporters formed interest groups that urged continuation of trade barriers. They were never won over by economists promoting integration. A general Latin American opinion developed that integrated markets would be especially vulnerable to U.S. economic penetration. The change in U.S. policy after about 1967 fueled these misgivings.

A number of other problems also worked against the development of a Latin American regional market and reduced the effectiveness of existing subregional organizations. The chief problems were the wide disparities in size, diversity, level of development, and rate of growth of the different economies; and nationalism, national rivalries, and competing ideologies. Central American conflict was particularly disruptive of the CACM. At the same time, certain successes also were evident, and efforts toward economic integration continued among most Latin American states outside of the Central American region.

Changing Concepts

Changing concepts of economic integration sought to alleviate some of the existing problems. The Andean Group approach conformed to positions worked out by theorists who challenged the free-trade model of regional integration on the grounds that the economically more advanced members of an integrated market tended to benefit more than the less developed members. For example, with reference to the poor lands of the world, Gunnar Myrdal (1957) had asserted that in general, the free play of market forces would "work more powerfully to create regional inequalities and to widen those which already exist." According to Philippe Schmitter (1972), economic integration of developing states based on free markets actually increased the chances for foreign penetration, especially by multinational corporations, rather than strengthen the member states relative to the rest of the world thereby allowing them increased independence in their collective policy-making. They and other critics of free trade recommended controlled markets to some degree, in order to include various forms of preferences or compensation for weaker states and conditions for external capital investment. The Andean Group was organized in consonance with this school of thought. Andean Group leaders favored cooperative regional development aimed at freedom from external actors through central planning and "directed economies" (*dirigisme*) rather than through laissez-faire free markets and private enterprise. Traditional concepts were further changed with the formation in 1980 of the Latin American Integration Association (LAIA) to supersede LAFTA. Whereas LAFTA allowed only multilateral integration agreements, LAIA encouraged extensive bilateral arrangements among member states to parallel multilateral agreements.

By the 1980s, with the decline of the integration efforts and lack of interest on the part of military regimes, the question was whether or not Latin American integration could succeed in stimulating increased international economic independence, domestic social progress, and regional political cohesion. Beginning in the mid-1980s and continuing into the 1990s, Latin American governments and IGOs (the Economic Commission for Latin America and the Caribbean—the renamed ECLA—prominently among them) revived the integration efforts. They reevaluated how they should organize among themselves within the rapidly changing international economic system and reoriented their integration purposes and strategies. As East-West conflict faded and trade and investment assumed primacy in the international system, they supported the new liberalism in international trade. The new approach was also a function of redemocratization, the emergence of a more positive nationalism, and the widespread adoption of economic neoliberalism in Latin America. According to Issac Cohen (1992, 1993), Latin Americans concluded that the prior purposes of economic integration—to enhance import substitution behind high import barriers against the outside world as much as to expand free trade among themselves—was no longer appropriate. The U.S. Enterprise of the Americas Initiative (EAI), which in June 1990 offered hemispheric free trade, further stimulated Latin American integration reform activity as Latin American governments anticipated free trade with the U.S. market. It also made the United States a potentially important actor in the integration process. An important institutional development in 1991 was the formation, within ALADI, of the four-member Common Market of the South (MERCOSUR). Certain Latin American states also undertook a new series of bilateral and multilateral agreements, specifying formal free-trade linkages but not creating new organizations. While the integration reform movement encountered difficulties, it reflected a sense of urgency and determination.

CENTRAL AMERICAN INTEGRATION

Early Central American Organizations

Attempts to integrate Central America into a single nation-state date from the earliest days of independence. The colonial Spanish captaincy general of Guatemala (that is, Central America) declared independence from Spain in 1821. It briefly joined the Mexican empire, but two years later opted for separate nationhood as the Federation of Central America, composed of five provinces. Foreign incursions from Mexico, Colombia, and Great Britain resulted in territorial losses in various parts of the region. Union based on fear of foreigners, however, was superseded by the disintegrative impetus of internal conflict. The violence of party politics (Liberals against Conservatives), coupled with localism and emerging nationalism, resulted in popular uprisings and civil wars, leading in 1838 to the dissolution of the Federation. Five separate states were established (Guatemala, El Salvador, Honduras, Nicaragua, and Costa Rica).

The idea of Central American union continued after the Federation was dissolved. Several agreements to unify the five states were negotiated during the nineteenth century, but none involved all of the states and none endured. An early twentieth-century expression of unity was the establishment of the Central American Court of Justice. Created in 1907 by all of the Central American states at the Washington Conference, the Court was to be a supranational instrument for the peaceful settlement of international disputes in Central America. The Court successfully averted some armed conflicts, but certain justices exhibited considerable national partisanship. In 1917 the Court ruled that the Bryan-Chamorro canal treaty between Nicaragua and the United States injured Costa Rica and El Salvador. Nicaragua then withdrew from the Court, and it ceased to exist in 1918.

The Organization of Central American States

The Organization of Central American States (ODECA) was founded in 1951 to promote Central American political and economic integration. ODECA had its headquarters in San Salvador and was composed of the traditional five Central American states. The ODECA Charter of San Salvador was signed on October 14, 1951, but did not go into effect until 1955. A revised charter of the same name signed on December 12, 1962, in Panama City became effective in 1965. Article 1 states that the five member states "are an economic-political community, which aspires to the integration of Central America," for which purpose ODECA was established. A complex structure of eight principal organs involving high-level national officials was established to achieve ODECA's purposes. They were the Meeting of Heads of State, the Conference of Ministers of Foreign Affairs, the permanent Executive Council, the Legislative Council, the Central American Court of Justice (reviving the early twentieth-century regional court idea), the Central American Economic Council, the Cultural and Educational Council, and the Central American Defense Council. In addition, the General Secretariat, known as the Central American Bureau, was later created to coordinate the work of the various ODECA organs. Their combined purposes were to promote uniform legislation; decide legal conflicts; plan and coordinate economic integration; promote educational, scientific, and cultural interchange; achieve uniformity in the educational systems; and advise on regional defense and mutual security.

ODECA never proved effective in realizing its purposes. It was of some importance in assisting economic unity, but its companion organization, the Central American Common Market, took the lead when it was founded. ODECA was confronted with a variety of disputes after its inception and had little success in settling them. For example, in December 1967 the foreign ministers met in Managua and sought, without success, to settle a border dispute between Honduras and El Salvador; the conflict was in fact resolved by the Inter-American System. The accelerating Central American international crisis and sharp intraregional conflicts after 1979 ended ODECA's functioning.

The Central American Common Market

The idea for Central American economic integration developed during the June 1951 meetings of ECLA in Mexico City. In 1952 ECLA established the Central American Economic Cooperation Committee (CCE), composed of the five Central American ministers of economy. The committee's studies led to the creation in 1954 of the Central American Advanced School of Public Administration (ESAPAC), located in San José, Costa Rica, and in 1956 to the establishment of the Central American Institute of Industrial Research (ICAITI) in Guatemala City.

A series of treaties signed from 1958 through 1960 led to the creation of the Central American Common Market. The process culminated in 1960 with the signing of two agreements: the General Treaty of Central American Economic Integration and the Convention Chartering the Central American Bank for Economic Integration. Together they consolidated, extended, and superseded the prior integration agreements. The General Treaty provided for the gradual realization of a Central American customs union, envisioning the eventual elimination of all trade barriers among its members and the establishment of a common external tariff for the rest of the world. It also projected a common customs administration, a unified fiscal policy, a regional industrial policy, and coordinated policies in public health, labor, education, transportation, and agriculture. It became effective for Guatemala, El Salvador, and Nicaragua on June 4, 1961; for Honduras on May 6, 1962; and for Costa Rica on September 9, 1963.

The CACM institutional structure consisted of the Economic Council, the Executive Council, and the Permanent Secretariat (located in Guatemala City). The Central American Bank for Economic Integration (located in Tegucigalpa) and the Central American Clearing House, both established in 1961, were recognized by the General Treaty. The two training schools (ESAPAC and ICAITI) came under CACM sponsorship. Mexico participated in the CACM by joining the clearing house, providing funds to the banks, and lending technical advisers to various bodies. Panama became a member of CCE in 1958; both Panama and the Dominican Republic expressed interest in joining CACM, but this eventuality was postponed because of increasing intraregional conflict in Central America after 1979.

CACM was successful in certain ways during its early years. Elimination of most tariff barriers between member countries during the first nine years (1961–1970) brought about a 700 percent increase in interregional trade and a 10 percent increase in trade with countries outside the market. The spectacular increase in trade stimulated the utilization of previously idle industries and promoted technical efficiency, particularly in textiles. It also created a favorable investment climate; as a result, many small industries were established, such as tire factories and food-processing plants. CACM was almost wholly responsible for increased foreign investment in the area and was an important factor in the GNP increases in the Central American region. Economic benefit went mostly to the industrial sector, which accounted for only about 16 percent of the region's GNP. Agriculture, the greatest contributor to the GNPs of individual countries, involved few economies of scale, was not emphasized in CACM policy, and was little affected by the common market.

The CACM faced economic and political disagreements that created serious conflict among its members. Economic gains, in terms of increased trade and industrial growth, were not shared equally by member states, and the CACM was unable to equalize the benefits. Honduras and Nicaragua, the two least developed members, benefited only slightly, whereas Guatemala and El Salvador, the most developed members, improved their trade considerably. Costa Rica held a middle position in both development and benefits. Nicaragua and Honduras had large trade imbalances with their colleagues. They also suffered from trade substitution, importing products from other CACM members that were more expensive and of lesser quality than similar products formerly imported from the United States and Europe. The market agreements had envisioned the planned distribution of industries among member states through an integrated industries scheme that assigned plants and production rights, but the CACM was unsuccessful in encouraging industries to locate in the less developed countries. El Salvador and Honduras went to war in 1969, further complicating the economic tensions and seriously disrupting the CACM. Trade disputes were difficult to resolve and led to various forms of penalties and retaliation that seriously disrupted the flow of trade. The economic difficulties were superseded by political and military conflicts after 1979 that as much as ended the common market.

In the mid-1980s, Central American leaders undertook initiatives as part of a regional peace process (see Chapter 11) to resuscitate economic and political integration. In May 1986, at a meeting in Esquipulas, Guatemala, the presidents of Guatemala, Honduras, Costa Rica, El Salvador, and Nicaragua agreed in principle to set up a Central American Parliament. In 1987 the five presidents signed a treaty creating the parliament, stipulating that elections in the various countries for its representatives would be direct and simultaneous. The treaty has been ratified by all parties except Costa Rica. Central American economic integration was revived. In June 1990, about a week prior to President Bush's speech proposing the EAI, the Central American presidents issued the Declaration of Antigua proposing to reconstruct their economies and the CACM with more open approaches to trade, investment, and external debt. Intragroup summit meetings were held and bilateral agreements signed as the complex efforts proceeded. Central American integration has been accelerated, and Mexico and the CACM have agreed to set up a free-trade zone by December 31, 1996.

CARIBBEAN INTEGRATION

Early Caribbean Integration

The United States and Great Britain cooperated in 1942 to establish the Anglo-American Caribbean Commission (AACC). (This section relies on Corkran, 1972.) The bipartite commission was designed to deal with certain wartime emergencies in the U.S. and British Caribbean dependencies. It developed measures to relieve the lack of ocean shipping and disruption of world markets and devised plans to defend them from attack. In 1940 the United States had leased British West Indian areas for use as military and naval bases, giving it a direct interest in the conditions in those areas governed by Great Britain (at the time threatened by German invasion) as well as its own Puerto Rico and Virgin Islands. The AACC largely succeeded in dealing with immediate economic and military emergencies, and it began long-term economic projects and stimulated inter-Caribbean cooperation.

In 1946 the AACC was reconstituted as the Caribbean Commission and broadened to include the participation of France and the Netherlands acting on behalf of their Caribbean dependencies, as well as the participation of delegates from the nonsovereign Caribbean entities themselves. More formal than the AACC, the four-power Caribbean Commission held the regularly scheduled West Indian Conference. Its Caribbean Research Council and the General Secretariat were located in Trinidad and headed by a secretary general. During its fifteen-year life, the Caribbean Commission undertook projects in agriculture, trade, fisheries, education, health, and other "functional" areas.

The four metropolitan powers agreed in 1959 to end the Caribbean Commission, and it was succeeded by the Caribbean Council in 1961. The members of the new council included the Caribbean entities themselves, except for France participating as a member "on behalf of" its American overseas departments. The Caribbean Council survived for three years. Among the problems leading to its dissolution (on June 30, 1965) were the breakup of the West Indies Federation in 1962, one of its largest members; the awkward position of France; and the impatience of Puerto Rico over what it perceived as the council's ineffectiveness in dealing with Caribbean problems.

Another organization promoting cooperation among nonsovereign Caribbean entities was created under Puerto Rican leadership but was an agency of the Puerto Rican government rather than an international organization. The Caribbean Economic Development Corporation (CODECA), a public corporation chartered in Puerto Rico with the "approval" of other West Indian entities, was established on July 1, 1965. CODECA's purpose was to enter into agreements with counterpart agencies in other territories for regional projects in an effort to bridge the differing levels of self-government in each. A new Puerto Rican government elected in 1968 was unenthusiastic about the idea and brought an end to CODECA.

The West Indies Federation

After World War II, British arrangements for its American colonies became its prime concern in the region. After the political eclipse of Winston Churchill, both major British political parties agreed that the colonial territories around the world should be guided toward independence within the Commonwealth through economic, social, and political development. They admitted that some were deficient in population or resources to the point that self-government should not go beyond internal affairs. By 1955 the British territories in Latin America were grouped together in ten Crown Colonies. The British Caribbean Territories, also known as the British West Indies, included nine Crown Colonies; the Falkland Islands, far removed from the Caribbean area, were a separate Crown Colony within a grouping called the Atlantic Ocean Dependencies (which also included the Crown Colonies of St. Helena and Ascension). A closer association of the British Caribbean Territories, including the idea of an independent federal state composed of some of them, had been discussed for many years. Planning to this end had been undertaken in 1945 by the British Colonial Office in cooperation with the local governments involved. They agreed to create a Caribbean federation, a goal that was finally accomplished in 1958 when the West Indies Federation was established.

The West Indies Federation was composed of ten entities—Antigua, Dominica, Montserrat, St. Christopher–Nevis–Anguilla, St. Lucia, St. Vincent, Barbados, Grenada, Jamaica, and Trinidad-Tobago. It was to be internally self-governing for a four-year transition period, with Great Britain responsible for foreign affairs and defense. After this transitional period the federation was to be given complete independence as a single, sovereign federal state. In 1962 the most important entities, Jamaica and Trinidad-Tobago, decided to secede in favor of separate independence, and the federation was dissolved.

After the collapse of the West Indies Federation, Britain was forced to develop new constitutional arrangements. In 1966 the British and dependency governments agreed to end the latters' colonial status and to make them "States in Association with Great Britain." Each was internally self-governing, but the United Kingdom was responsible for defense and foreign affairs. Most of them subsequently opted for sovereign independence. By 1983, all of the members of the defunct federation had become independent, except for Montserrat and Anguilla.

The Caribbean Free Trade Association

The agreement establishing the Caribbean Free Trade Association (CARIFTA) was signed in Antigua on December 15, 1965, by Antigua, Barbados, and British Guiana. Two years later, when additional entities agreed to join the association, the agreement was revised. CARIFTA came into being on May 1, 1968, and eventually its membership included four independent states, seven States in Association with Great Britain ("semi-independent" in the sense that, though not sovereign, they were internally self-governing), and one British colony. They all were located in the Circum-Caribbean and were members of the Commonwealth.

The CARIFTA charter established a free-trade area. Members opted for the free-market approach and pledged to eliminate tariffs and quota systems on each other's products on May 1, 1968. The inclusion of lists of "reserved commodities," on which trade barriers were to be gradually reduced until eliminated, allowed for exceptions based on the assumption that varying levels of economic development among the members required additional time for adjustments in certain areas. Member states were divided into two categories, the More Developed Countries (MDCs), made up of the independent states, and the Less Developed Countries (LDCs), composed of the nonsovereign entities. LDCs were given preferred treatment in the lifting of trade barriers.

CARIFTA's governing body was the Council of Ministers, made up of representatives from each member entity and responsible for broad policies aimed at furthering the process of regional economic integration. Administration was lodged with the Commonwealth Caribbean Regional Secretariat, located in Georgetown, Guyana. In 1969 CARIFTA established the Caribbean Bank (CARIBANK), with headquarters in Bridgetown, Barbados. The members contributed to the general fund, as did Canada and Great Britain. The bank also established a Special Development Fund and an Agricultural Development Fund for soft-currency loans, to which various members and the United States contributed funds. CARIBANK directed much of its efforts toward the LDCs, assisting in the formation of development plans, providing financial and technical aid, and fostering public and private investment.

The Caribbean Community

CARIFTA's founders had envisioned the association as a first step in Caribbean Commonwealth economic integration. In April 1972 the heads of government of CARIFTA member states met in Guyana and drew up the Georgetown Treaty establishing the Caribbean Common Market (CARICOM). Four states (Barbados, Guyana, Jamaica, and Trinidad-Tobago) adhered on July 4, 1973; most of the remaining CARIFTA members ratified the treaty on May 1, 1974. The thirteen members (all but one a sovereign state) were Antigua-Barbuda, the Bahamas, Barbados, Belize, Dominica, Grenada, Guyana, Jamaica, non-sovereign Montserrat, St. Christopher–Nevis, St. Lucia, St. Vincent, and Trinidad-Tobago. Three local non-Commonwealth Caribbean states were given permanent observer status: the Dominican Republic, Haiti, and Suriname. CARICOM eventually replaced CARIFTA.

CARICOM's objective, as set forth in its charter, was the economic integration of the member states through the establishment of a common market. CARICOM hoped to bring about accelerated and balanced development, greater economic independence from the outside world, and increased effectiveness "in dealing with states, groups of states and entities of whatever description." In addition to the removal of tariffs among the members, CARICOM also established a common external tariff; some articles were excepted, but they were to be "progressively eliminated." A Common Protective Policy was adopted to "operate by way of imposing quantitative restrictions for promoting industrial and agricultural development." The LDCs, apprehensive about the distribution of benefits, were again given special opportunities and preferred status.

CARICOM's governing board was the Conference of Heads of Government. It was assisted by the Common Market Council, composed of a minister from each participating member state. On August 1, 1973, the Commonwealth Caribbean Secretariat was renamed the Caribbean Community Secretariat. Seven additional institutions were mentioned in the charter, including four standing committees of ministers in the fields of agriculture, finance, labor, and mines, and three "associate institutions"—CARIBANK, the Caribbean Investment Corporation (created on June 1, 1973, to support investment programs in LDCs), and the Regional Shipping Council. CARIBANK resources were expanded. In addition to its eligibility to borrow from the World Bank and ongoing contributions from the United Kingdom, Canada, and the United States, it received contributions from Colombia, the Federal Republic of Germany, France, Italy, Mexico, the Netherlands, Sweden, and Venezuela.

CARICOM leaders considered their political objectives to be important. The charter established a Standing Committee of Ministers of Foreign Affairs, "to the end that Member States aim at the fullest possible coordination of their foreign policies within their respective competencies and seek to adopt as far as possible common positions in major international issues." This standing committee, made up of representatives from only the sovereign members, made advisory recommendations to CARICOM. Noneconomic functional relations were also provided for. The charter created a Conference of Ministers of Health and other associate institutions for education and meteorology.

CARICOM, like other regional integration organizations in the 1990s, undertook organizational reform. In July 1991 the annual meeting of heads of government agreed to move toward a single market and economy. In the same month, CARICOM and the United States signed a framework agreement establishing the intent to negotiate free trade. The CARICOM summit meeting in June 1992 adopted plans to establish a CARICOM investment fund and to implement a Common External Tariff (CET), a key element in creating a single market. Progress was slow, however, and tensions arose over specific aspects of increased integration. CARICOM continued to hold in abeyance the question of membership for its observers—the Dominican Republic, Haiti, and Suriname—saying it would deepen integration before widening membership.

The Organization of Eastern Caribbean States

In July 1981, seven of the smaller Commonwealth Caribbean island-states formed the Organization of Eastern Caribbean States (OECS) within CARICOM. The members are Antigua-Barbuda, Dominica, Grenada, Montserrat, St. Christopher–Nevis, St. Lucia, and St. Vincent. Their primary original purpose was to pool economic resources. A peripheral goal, and a voluntary one at that, was to coordinate foreign affairs and defense arrangements. The OECS was noteworthy for its role in the U.S. invasion of member Grenada in October 1983, only two years after OECS formation. Ignoring provisions of the Rio Treaty and the OAS

Charter, the United States chose a minor provision of the OECS Charter (of which it was not a signatory) as legal justification for the intervention. The United States persuaded OECS to request its military assistance. The subsequent U.S. invasion of Grenada involved participation by certain OECS members. Not all members supported the action, and the Grenada intervention deeply divided OECS as well as CARICOM. In the early 1990s, the OECS considered establishing its own single market and economy.

TRANSREGIONAL INTEGRATION

The Latin American Free Trade Association

In February 1960 seven Latin American states signed the Treaty of Montevideo establishing the Latin American Free Trade Association (LAFTA; or Asociación Latinoamericana de Libre Comercio—ALALC). The seven charter members when the treaty went into effect on June 1, 1961, were Argentina, Brazil, Chile, Peru, Paraguay, Mexico, and Uruguay. Four more states then joined—Colombia and Ecuador later in 1961, Venezuela in 1966, and Bolivia in 1967—bringing the total number of members to eleven. Thus, the market area included most of South America plus Mexico.

LAFTA, with headquarters in Montevideo, was administered by an annual conference where members negotiated trade liberalization and established programs. The Permanent Executive Committee of ambassadorial representatives, assisted by a secretariat, implemented the conference decisions. In 1965 LAFTA created a series of ministerial councils (foreign ministers, heads of central banks, transportation and communications ministers, and agriculture ministers) in an attempt to stimulate integration beyond the level of free-trade area.

LAFTA's goals, expressed in the Treaty of Montevideo, were "to establish, gradually and progressively, a Latin American common market," and for the members "to pool their efforts to achieve the progressive complementarity and integration of their economy on the basis of an effective reciprocity of benefits." LAFTA did not undertake to unify tariffs toward the outside world. Rather, it sought to establish only a free-trade area in which the members eliminated tariffs and other restrictions on "substantially all" of their trade with one another. The elimination of internal trade barriers was to be achieved incrementally over a twelve-year period and completed by 1973.

After the treaty went into effect, certain tariff reductions were resisted by some members. Difficulties stemmed from the diversity in the levels of economic development among the eleven member states. The less developed ones were unwilling to drop their import trade barriers irrevocably without parallel controlled allocation of industrial growth from which they would benefit. They felt that the "Big Three" economies—Mexico, Brazil, and Argentina—were benefiting disproportionately from intramarket trade and should make concessions to the weaker states. The Treaty of Montevideo had recognized Ecuador and Paraguay as "least developed" members that required certain special treatment, but the other members (Chile, Colombia, Peru, and Uruguay) insisted that, relative to the Big Three, they, too, were disadvantaged. Consequently, in 1963 the idea of allowing free-market forces to determine economic growth was essentially discarded and middle-level economies were classified as "insufficient markets." Inducements included complementation agreements whereby members participated in some aspect of a particular industrial enterprise, some preferential tariff treatment, escape clauses in certain trade concessions, and limited financial and technical assistance.

The 1963 compromises were insufficient to realize a regional mutuality of interest, and LAFTA's progress during the 1960s was unimpressive. By 1968 intramarket trade amounted to an average of 10 percent of each member's total trade as compared to about 7 percent in 1960; that average had ranged from 8 to 9 percent from 1950 to 1952 (Grunwald, Wionczek, and Carnoy, 1972:51). Trade barriers were not lowered on schedule, and industry was not stimulated to the extent hoped for. By 1968 LAFTA had virtually ceased to function, deadlocked over the free-trade versus regional-planning issue. In 1969 LAFTA members signed the Protocol of Caracas, which extended the deadline for establishing a free-trade area from 1973 to 1980, but Colombia and Uruguay refused to ratify. Few complementation agreements were signed. The failure to agree upon a program of joint development was the principal factor slowing the tariff-cutting process among LAFTA members. This situation led to its moribund state and then to the creation of the Andean Group.

The Andean Group

The Andean Common Market, usually referred to as the Andean Group (AG), was formed by LAFTA members who were dissatisfied with the course of integration but unwilling to resign from LAFTA or to abrogate the Treaty of Montevideo. The governments of Chile, Colombia, Venezuela, Ecuador, and Peru joined in the Declaration of Bogotá on August 17, 1966, announcing their intention to form a common market aimed at accommodating the differing levels of development of their economies. The declaration stated the signatories' dissatisfaction with LAFTA but emphasized their desire to integrate on a subregional basis within the LAFTA structure. They hoped to revitalize LAFTA and move toward a common market through planned industrialization rather than relying on free-market forces. Two treaties were subsequently drafted, one creating the Andean Development Corporation to help finance development projects and the other establishing the Andean subregional common market itself. The charter of the Andean Development Corporation was signed on February 7, 1968, and the Andean Pact (the Agreement of Cartagena) was signed on May 26, 1969, and entered into force on October 16, 1969. The charter Members of the AG were Bolivia (which had joined the negotiations in 1967), Chile, Colombia, Ecuador, and Peru. Venezuela delayed joining because of domestic pressure from industrialists who opposed ending protection of their high-cost industries but eventually dropped its demand for special status and became a member on February 13, 1973.

The Andean Pact contained four objectives: (1) to create a common market with virtually no trade barriers among its members and a common policy toward the outside world; (2) to establish an internal market for industrial production, with new industries assigned exclusively to different members; (3) to limit the power of multinational corporations in their dealings with the AG; and (4) to accommodate the less developed members (Bolivia and Ecuador) with special concessions. The pact established organizational machinery, with headquarters in Lima. It included the following bodies: (1) the Mixed Commission of ambassadorial representatives as supreme organ; (2) a council charged with presenting technical proposals to the commission; (3) an advisory consulting committee of integration experts; and (4) an economic and social council representing the interests of business and labor groups. A separate convention later established the Andean Development Corporation to serve as a regional development bank.

The Andean Pact called for a free-trade area to be created by eliminating tariffs among members in progressive, automatic, irrevocable steps over a ten-year period until 1982. Tariffs were eliminated on schedule. A common external tariff was instituted by 1976 to encourage the manufacture of certain goods within the market. Industrial development was to be stimulated further by an investment program and complementation agreements.

The AG gave special attention to the role of private foreign investment in the integrated market, a reflection of growing Latin American economic nationalism and recognition of the economic power of MNCs. AG leaders said that MNCs had been the major beneficiaries of other integrated economy arrangements, claiming that MNCs used their large resources and mobility to establish industries within the region and to produce for protected and expanded markets. Those leaders, however, also acknowledged their need for foreign capital and proposed to control rather than exclude it.

The Andean Pact Statute on Foreign Capital ("Decision 24"), adopted on January 1, 1971, and later modified, represented the only multilateral Latin American attempt to control investment in the region. The statute was a comprehensive industrialization policy and foreign investment code. It provided for step-by-step reductions of foreign-controlled investment, regulation of the international transfer of technology, planned distribution of industries throughout the Andean zone, conversion of foreign manufacturing firms to at least 51 percent local ownership, and restrictions on existing foreign banks.

The AG was faced with a number of economic and political difficulties, especially from 1972 to 1976. A major problem emerged with regard to Decision 24. Waivers and exceptions were granted extensively by Bolivia, Chile, and Peru; Chile was particularly adamant that the regulations be severely modified. After the 1973 coup in Chile, the military regime adopted free-market economic policies directly opposed to the AG strategy; in 1976 Chile withdrew from the agreement. A more general problem was the fact that most members had insufficient markets to support the development of industries that would be large and efficient enough to compete effectively with external industries in terms of cost and price. Longstanding intraregional boundary and territorial disputes, as well as changing governments with opposing political philosophies, further complicated economic cooperation.

After 1976 AG members substantially modified the Cartagena agreement with a series of protocols and formal decisions. Decision 24 was so modified that it was virtually abrogated. Deadlines for internal free trade and common external tariffs were extended. Industrial programs were delayed and state roles in them reduced. The organizational structure was also extended, with the creation in 1979 of the Andean Tribunal of Justice, the Andean Parliament, and the Council of Ministers of Foreign Affairs. With the formation of the foreign ministers council, the AG became overtly political and active. For example, a resolution was passed by the Andean foreign ministers on June 16, 1979, recognizing the popular forces in Nicaragua (the Sandinistas) as a belligerent in their fight with the Somoza dictatorship, thus legitimizing them with legal personality and opposing the U.S. view of the matter.

The AG went through another crisis in 1980 and 1981 owing to a coup in Bolivia and border fighting between Ecuador and Peru. The members formally declared a "relaunching" of the integration movement in September 1981. Afterwards progress was slow and the original *dirigisme* all but forgotten.

The AG was no exception to the general revival of Latin American interest in subregional integration. On December 5, 1991, an AG presidential summit agreed to consolidate a free-trade zone by the end of the month as a crucial step in establishing a common market with the implementation of common external tariffs within five years. But the Andean commerce ministers could not reach agreement at a follow-up meeting, and the free-trade agreement did not go into effect as scheduled. Consequently, on January 29, 1992, the presidents of Colombia and Venezuela signed an agreement on a common customs tariff for products from third countries, saying they anticipated it would serve as a basis for negotiating with other AG members.

The Latin American Integration Association

In the late 1970s the full LAFTA membership decided to reform extensively their integration arrangement. A new Treaty of Montevideo was signed on August 12, 1980, and adhered to by all LAFTA members. It instituted the Latin American Integration Association (LAIA, or Asociación Latinoamericana de Integración— ALADI) establishing a new juridical order for economic integration. The treaty entered into effect with full ratification in March 1981, superseding the 1960 treaty and replacing the LAFTA structure. Further development of LAIA took place during a transition period in which a number of measures were applied and further negotiations took place.

In certain ways LAIA is a continuation of LAFTA. (The following description is based on ALADI, 1980.) The members of LAIA consider integration to be the appropriate means for promoting regional development and cooperation. They posit the long-range goal to be the establishment of a regionwide Latin American common market. Moreover, specific aspects of the old scheme have been incorporated into the new one.

Notwithstanding these continuities, the 1980 treaty introduced fundamental changes in both the concept and operation of economic integration. First, LAIA provides for multiple levels of negotiation and cooperation. In fact, Argentina and Brazil had been the prime movers behind LAIA so that they could make bilateral agreements between themselves and Mexico. LAIA also allows for multilateral agreements not involving the full membership (LAFTA had sanctioned only multilateral agreements of a full-market scope). Second, LAIA expands LAFTA's basic commercial character by specifying three additional basic functions: the promotion and regulation of reciprocal trade, the creation of economic complementation, and the development of enlarged markets. Third, whereas LAFTA had recognized a special status for the relatively less developed economies, the new scheme incorporates more extensive provisions in their favor. It also defines the category of intermediate economic development to include countries that also receive special treatment. Finally, LAIA provides for limited participation by certain nonmember countries and private entities.

In sum, LAIA was designed to have greater negotiation and operational flexibility than LAFTA, to recognize the different levels of economic development among member countries, and to provide for a wider range of agreements. The following types of agreements were fashioned and reflected the overall new design.

1. *Regional tariff preference,* which would vary with different economic sectors and member countries, would be allowed to exclude a certain number of products. The most developed countries (Argentina, Brazil, and Mexico) would be allowed the fewest exceptions; intermediate countries (Chile, Colombia, Peru, and Uruguay) would be allowed more exceptions; and the least developed (Bolivia, Ecuador, and Paraguay) would enjoy the most exceptions. The regional tariff preference is a mechanism of a full multilateral character that applies preferences to the prevailing economic level of the various members and with reference to particular products.

2. *Agreements of regional scope* are those in which all member countries participate. They cover extensive activities, including economic complementation, agriculture, promotion of commerce, financial accords (such as for payments and credits), scientific and technological cooperation, promotion of tourism, and more. The first agreements were those "inherited" from LAFTA. A large number of new ones were instituted under LAIA.

3. *Agreements of partial scope* constitute a distinctive element in the new treaty and immediately became the most dynamic factor. These measures specify a limited restriction to the principle of multilaterality. All agreements between pairs or among groups of countries must be open to multilateralization through negotiation and be automatically open to the least developed members on a most-favored-nation basis. Although only member countries may initiate them, the adhesion of nonmembers is possible. This category is intended to overcome the disparity of economic development that plagued LAFTA in the past because not all the agreements were appropriate for all members.

With regard to both regional and partial agreements, all old LAFTA accords were renegotiated after 1980. The process was not completed until early 1988. New treaties, mostly bilateral, under both categories were completed at about the same time. Particularly notable were a voluminous series of treaties between Argentina and Brazil. LAIA added a parliamentary assembly to the institutional structure.

The Common Market of the South

The latest subregional integration organization is the Common Market of the South (Mercado Común del Sur—MERCOSUR), created in 1991 within LAIA but operating independently, as does the AG. MERCOSUR is rooted in the Brazil-Argentina Program for Integration and Cooperation agreement signed on July 29, 1986, which called not only for economic cooperation but cooperation in the diplomatic and nuclear arenas as well and was linked to the reestablishment of democracy in both states. The agreement was then offered to neighboring states, and on March 26, 1991, Argentina, Brazil, Paraguay, and Uruguay signed the Asunción Treaty agreeing to set up MERCOSUR. Bolivia considered applying for membership. The agreement envisaged an operational common market by December 31, 1994, with free movement of capital and goods, a common external tariff, and significant policy coordination. On December 17, 1991, the first meeting of the Council of Presidents took place in Brasilia. Regular meetings at ministerial and technical levels were also held on a regular basis. Brazil and Argentina, Latin America's first and third largest economies, are the core of MERCOSUR and account for its potential as an integration organization.

Other Developments

A growing number of bilateral and multilateral transregional accords have been signed on the assumption that wider and deeper Latin American integration will make regional markets more interesting for traders in the United States, the European Community, and Japan. Of particular interest was the possible merging and expansion of CACM and CARICOM, which would conceivably create a market of about 48 million people. On January 30–31, 1992, representatives of the two organizations held a joint conference in Honduras to consider a merger. Delegations were present from twenty-three countries, including nonmembers of either group—Panama, the Dominican Republic, Aruba, Curaçao, Suriname, and Puerto Rico (the last four are nonsovereign entities). Haiti and Cuba were not invited, Haiti because of the recent overthrow of a democratically elected government there and Cuba because certain anti-Castro Central Americans objected. The conference established general guidelines for future integration, created a biregional consultation forum, and authorized a joint mission to undertake a study of the implications of a CACM/CARICOM free-trade agreement and the measures required to make it operable. Central American representatives seemed to be more enthusiastic about intraregional integration, with CARICOM members interested in the idea but more cautious.

Additional multilateral and bilateral agreements were signed in the wake of the Bush administration's EAI proposal. In late 1990, Mexico, Colombia, and Venezuela formed the Group of 3 to coordinate their energy policies; in July 1991 they commenced negotiations looking to conclude a free-trade agreement by 1995. Chile and Venezuela negotiated an agreement to abolish tariffs on their trade by 1994. Mexico and Bolivia agreed to joint ventures and, through the Andean Development Corporation, of which Mexico is a member, for Mexican financing of Bolivian exports into Mexico. In January 1991 the presidents of Mexico and the five member states of CACM met and agreed to set up a free-trade area by December 31, 1996. On September 15, 1991, Mexico and Chile signed a free-trade agreement planning for tariffs on almost all of their bilateral trade to fall to zero by 1996. In late 1991, Venezuela announced a trade initiative to give immediate duty-free access to the products of Central America and the Caribbean, with the expectation that those countries would eventually reciprocate; negotiations with potential partners, including CARICOM, were soon forthcoming.

OTHER SOUTH AMERICAN ARRANGEMENTS

The Cuenca del Plata Accord

On April 23, 1969, five South American states (Argentina, Bolivia, Brazil, Paraguay, and Uruguay), all part of the complex Rio de la Plata system, signed a treaty for the development of the river basin (*cuenca*). An example of the integration of physical infrastructure resources, the Cuenca del Plata accord called for the multilateral development of international communications and water resources, especially hydroelectric power potential. The accord provided for a standing intergovernmental committee and annual meetings on the ministerial level. A consortium of international financial institutions, led by the Inter-American Development Bank, agreed to cooperate, and a foreign ministers' meeting of members in June 1974 established a development fund.

The Cuenca del Plata group achieved successes but revealed serious debilities as well. Some highway and hydroelectric projects were completed, but no development funds were expended. The most serious problem was essentially political, involving rivalry between Argentina and Brazil over strategic concerns and competition for influence with the buffer states in the Southern Cone. Mutual suspicions resulted in several uncoordinated bilateral river project agreements.

The Cuenca del Plata's fortunes improved in the 1980s. The solidification of an Argentine-Brazilian rapprochement after 1979 facilitated cooperation in basin projects. Construction of the Itaipú dam on the Paraná River—a project that created the world's largest source of hydroelectric power—was finally completed after years of delay due to Argentine-Brazilian bickering and paved the way for the creation of MERCOSUR.

Amazon Pact

Representatives of eight Amazon region states signed the Amazon Cooperation Treaty in Brasilia on July 3, 1978. They were the foreign ministers of Bolivia, Brazil, Colombia, Ecuador, Guyana, Peru, and Venezuela, and the prime minister of Suriname. The treaty committed the signatories to coordinated development of the Amazon Basin's communications and transport systems and natural resources and protection of the region's fragile ecology. It also gave Latin American enterprises the first opportunity to develop the region. In sum, the treaty called for Amazonic regional cooperation that would enable member nations to benefit from the basin's resources and spelled out the projects to be accomplished. The organizational structure was simple: Meetings of ministers were to convene annually in a different member country each year. On February 10, 1992, the presidents of the Amazon Accord member states met in Manaus to study proposals for the United Nations Conference on Environment and Development, held in Rio de Janeiro later that year.

REGIONWIDE AND TRANSREGIONAL ASSOCIATIONS

Beginning in the mid-1960s, multipurpose associations were organized among different sets of Latin American states. Their organization was largely based on the assumption that Latin American states would be more influential in the international system if they adopted common positions and regional unity toward the rest of the world.

The Special Latin American Coordinating Committee

The first transregional endeavor came in 1964 when the Latin American states joined informally in the Special Latin American Coordinating Committee (Comité Especial para la Coordinación Latinoamericana—CECLA). It was a caucusing group designed to increase regional unity for economic bargaining power with external states and international organizations. Foreign ministers from all Latin American states except for Cuba attended CECLA's first meeting in February 1964. They gathered at Alta Grácia (near Córdoba), Argentina, to establish regional policy positions for the imminent UNCTAD I (United Nations Conference on Trade and Development). Although no formal agreement was signed and no organizational apparatus was established, CECLA became a continuing conference that could be reconvened as its participants desired. The ministers held a series of meetings after 1964 to plan regional bloc positions for UNCTAD II (1967) and III (1971) and worked together within other international fora such as the General Agreement on Tariffs and Trade (GATT), the International Monetary Fund (IMF), and the World Bank (IBRD). CECLA operated as a caucusing group within the Organization of American States, especially in the work of the Inter-American Economic and Social Council. It provided a medium for joint Latin American negotiations with the United States and the European Economic Community (EEC).

CECLA enjoyed some success but also confronted difficulties in achieving Latin American unity. One of the most significant CECLA statements was the Consensus of Viña del Mar, formulated at a meeting in June 1969 at the Chilean resort town of the same name. This set of common Latin American positions on trade and economic development issues was sent directly to President Nixon. The following year CECLA used the same tactics toward Europe. Meeting in Buenos Aires in July 1970, Latin American foreign ministers issued a joint statement calling for more favorable terms of trade with and increased economic assistance from the EEC. CECLA reacted again in 1971 in response to the Nixon administration's general 10 percent trade surcharge: It issued the Manifesto of Latin America, pointing out that Latin America had a net deficit trade relationship with the United States and therefore was not responsible for the unfavorable U.S. trade balance. It asked the United States to exempt Latin America from the surcharge and, further, that it develop a system of general trade preferences for the region.

CECLA achievements were limited. Latin Americans generally were disappointed with the outcomes of the UNCTAD meetings. President Nixon responded favorably to the Consensus of Viña del Mar, dropping some U.S. trade and aid restrictions, but the U.S. Congress was unwilling to give in to other Latin American demands. In 1970 the EEC agreed to explore ways to improve its trade relationships with Latin America, but on a nonpreferential basis. The United States exempted Latin America from the 1971 trade surcharge. CECLA meetings resulted in a high degree of Latin American unity and coordinated positions on a number of economic issues, but intraregional disagreements similar to those within the economic integration organizations also arose. The economically more advanced nations, especially Mexico, Brazil, and Argentina, tended to differ from the rest over economic policy positions. In addition, rivalry among the larger states for leadership of CECLA, a reflection of their general regional rivalry, reduced CECLA's unity.

Latin American Economic System

The establishment of the Latin American Economic System (Sistema Económico Latinoamericano—SELA) was almost entirely the result of initiatives taken by Mexican President Luís Echevarría. At a meeting in Caracas in November 1974, Echevarría persuaded President Pérez of Venezuela to establish a joint permanent consultation arrangement in order to arrive at common economic and social policies, especially those regarding Latin American natural resources. The bilateral agreement was opened up to the adherence of all other Latin American states, without exception. Meeting in Panama on October 12, 1975, twenty-three Latin American states signed a formal constituent act, virtually identical to the earlier Mexican-Venezuelan declaration, establishing SELA. Additional new Caribbean states later signed the charter, bringing SELA's membership to all thirty-three states making up the Latin American regional subsystem.

According to the SELA Charter, it is "an organization for consultation, coordination, and joint economic and social promotion." The agreement proposed to pool the resources of member states in order to form agencies for the production and sale of Latin American raw materials, thus opening the possibility of forming multilateral state-owned transnational companies to develop and sell those commodities (such as bauxite, nickel, chrome, sugar, and cotton). In addition, SELA serves as an international bargaining tool based on the assumption that regional unity increases the strength of individual members toward the rest of the world, and in this sense it is a political arrangement. Because SELA proposed to formulate common regional positions prior to attending other international meetings, it replaced the informal CECLA as the regional caucus. SELA is not an economic integration scheme and did not propose to replace or unify the existing integration arrangements. However, it has the declared purpose of supporting regional integration.

SELA's principal organ is the Latin American Council, composed of ministers meeting at least once yearly. The initial council meeting was held in Caracas in January 1976 in order to agree on unified regional positions prior to the meeting of the developing nations' Group of 77 in Manila (March 1976) and a session of UNCTAD IV in Nairobi (May 1976). Council decisions, usually adopted by a two-thirds majority, are nonbinding; members are committed only to multilateral consultation. The Council is authorized to appoint a series of ad hoc Action Committees to supervise approved projects. A Permanent Secretariat, located in Caracas, provides operational support; it is headed by a secretary general serving a four-year term. Budget contributions are assigned to members in amounts decided by their relative ability to pay.

Rio Group

The Central American crisis of the 1980s combined with the earlier decline of the Inter-American System to inspire creation of Latin American organizational initiatives to resolve them. Out of these efforts grew the Rio Group, the informal name of a new and important multipurpose transregional association.

In January 1983, four states—Mexico, Venezuela, Colombia, and Panama—organized the Contadora Group and offered a plan for the negotiated settlement of Central American conflict. In July 1985, Argentina, Brazil, Peru, and Uruguay organized the Contadora Support Group. Joint meetings of the eight foreign ministers were held over the next eighteen months, but the Contadora process stalled nevertheless. In December 1986, the foreign ministers of the eight Contadora Group and Support Group states met in Rio de Janeiro and adopted a declaration creating the Permanent Mechanism of Consultation and Political Coordination, known as the Rio Group. (It was widely referred to at the time as the Group of 8, but as membership expanded the numerical designation became awkward, and "Rio Group" was generally settled on as the informal name.) The declaration said that, based on their experience of joint action in the Contadora process, the signatories had decided to systematize their political coordination through regular consultation on topics of common interest and in the context of growing Latin American unity. The Rio Group extended its agenda beyond Central American conflict to include a large number of international issues.

The declaration provided for regular meetings of foreign ministers. In addition, annual summit meetings of heads of state were begun in November 1987, and regular conferences of finance ministers were instituted beginning in December 1988. In June 1988, representatives from SELA, LAIA, ECLAC, and IDB were invited to participate directly in foreign ministers' meetings. The gathering of foreign ministers in February 1988 excluded Panama after the fall of its civilian president and rise of a de facto military dictatorship on the grounds that membership was inextricably linked to democratic government. Panama's suspension did not affect its membership in the Contadora Group, as the two organizations were formally kept apart.

The Rio declaration and the various meetings of ministers and presidents made clear the organization's purposes. In sum, they are to: (1) strengthen Latin American democracy through sustained economic and social development and regional cooperation and integration; (2) discuss all aspects of the Central American crisis and to reiterate support for the Central American peace process; (3) prefer negotiated agreements with external creditors over a collective moratorium or "debtors' cartel" and to suggest specific measures; (4) call attention to the problem of an unstable international financial system and the need to create a free and fair international trading system; (5) work toward a Latin American common market, with full awareness of the limitations of existing integration schemes; (6) cooperate for disarmament and scientific, technical, cultural, and educational interchange, and deal jointly with problems of clandestine arms trade, terrorism, drug trafficking, and environmental degradation; and (7) promote discussions with other states and IGOs in a climate of goodwill.

The Latin American Parliament

The Latin American Parliament was created in 1964. In 1987, a "treaty of institutionalization" gave it a stronger legal position as an IGO. Nineteen states are members. Their delegations must proportionately represent the political parties represented in the state legislatures. The Parliament's decisions are not binding on governments or political parties. It was intended to promote regionwide economic integration and development and to advocate political coordination among state congresses for community cooperation, but these purposes remain vague and stated in highly general terms. It nevertheless serves as a focal point for the discussion of economic integration and even political confederation.

THE LATIN AMERICAN NUCLEAR-FREE ZONE

In the early 1960s Brazil proposed that Latin America be made a nuclear-free zone. It noted that no nuclear weapons were present in the region and said that their introduction would have a destabilizing effect on Latin America's international politics. Brazil feared that any regional nuclear weapons acquisitions would stimulate an expensive and dangerous arms race. In 1961 Brazil formally proposed that the Latin American region be made a nuclear-free zone in a draft resolution to the UN General Assembly. Cuba supported the idea but insisted that Puerto Rico and the Panama Canal Zone be included and that foreign military bases (such as the U.S. naval station at Guantánamo Bay) be removed. The General Assembly did not vote on the resolution.

The Cuban missile crisis of 1962 supported fears that nuclear weapons would serve as a destabilizing element in Latin America and gave great impetus to the idea of a Latin American nuclear-free zone. Following the initiative of President João Goulart of Brazil, the presidents of Bolivia, Brazil, Chile, Ecuador, and Mexico signed the Five Presidents Declaration expressing readiness to sign an enabling treaty. The UN General Assembly formally supported the declaration on November 27, 1963. Mexico then assumed the initiative, led by Ambassador Alfonso García Robles, Mexican deputy foreign minister (and later recipient of the Nobel Peace Prize). A Latin American conference held in Mexico City in November 1965 created a commission to prepare a draft treaty, and in due course a draft was presented to the Latin American states for their adherence. The Treaty for the Prohibition of Nuclear Weapons in Latin America was signed on February 14, 1967, in Tlatelolco, the section of Mexico City where the Foreign Ministry is located, and is therefore known as the Treaty of Tlatelolco. The UN General Assembly endorsed the treaty on December 5, 1967; it entered into force April 22, 1968.

The Tlatelolco treaty is the first seeking to establish a nuclear-free zone in a populated world region. In fact, the fundamental concept of the treaty is to prevent the introduction of nuclear weapons into a geographic region already free of them. Article 1 unambiguously states the obligations of the Latin American signatories: They "undertake to use exclusively for peaceful purposes the nuclear material and facilities which are under their jurisdiction," and they agree to prohibit "the testing, use, manufacture, production, or acquisition" of any nuclear weapons, as well as their "receipt, storage, installation, deployment, and any form of possession of any nuclear weapons, directly or indirectly." Article 13 places all peaceful nuclear activities in Latin America under the safeguards system of the International Atomic Energy Agency (IAEA), a UN-sponsored organization with headquarters in Vienna. In 1969 the Organization for the Prohibition of Nuclear Weapons in Latin America (OPANAL) was established as a further control mechanism.

The idea of a nuclear-free zone has been accepted by an overwhelming majority of Latin American states. By 1985, twenty-six regional states had signed the treaty, leaving only five that have not signed. Cuba justifies its nonadherence by the strained U.S.-Cuban relations and the U.S. presence at Guantánamo. Dominica, St. Christopher–Nevis, St. Lucia, and St. Vincent and the Grenadines are still considering the measure. Two others—Belize and Guyana—have not been invited to subscribe to the treaty. They have been prevented from doing so by Guatemala and Venezuela, respectively, asserting Article 25 excluding states with territories subject to litigation or claims by other Latin American states. Argentina has signed but not ratified the treaty; Brazil and Chile have ratified but with the reservation that the treaty would not enter into force for them until all other eligible states had ratified it (that is, Argentina).

The basic treaty is restricted to the Latin American states themselves, but it was supplemented by two protocols designed to further ensure the region's nuclear-free condition. Protocol I commits external states with dependent territories inside the zone to place those territories under the same restrictions. Among the states responsible for territories within the geographical treaty limits, the Netherlands, the United Kingdom, and the United States have signed and ratified the protocol. The United States, whose territories include Puerto Rico and the Virgin Islands (and, for treaty purposes, the naval base at Guantánamo), delayed ratification until 1981. France signed but did not ratify the protocol; thus French Guiana, Martinique, and Guadeloupe are not militarily denuclearized. France says those Caribbean entities are integral parts of the metropole so that it has the prerogative to make nuclear policies as it wishes.

Under Protocol II, nonregional nuclear weapons states agree to respect the nonnuclear status of Latin America, not to contribute to violations of the treaty by states in the zone, and not to use or threaten to use nuclear weapons against them. Five nuclear powers—the United States, United Kingdom, France, the People's Republic of China, and the Soviet Union—have ratified Protocol II. The United States ratified it in 1971. French and Chinese adherence to Protocol II represents their first participation in any post–World War II arms control agreements.

BIBLIOGRAPHIC COMMENT

Cuevas Cancino (1955) and Lockey (1920) detail the nineteenth-century attempts at Spanish American union. The general subject of post–World War II integration efforts is analyzed by Gauhar (1985), Grunwald (1978), Grunwald, Wionczek, and Carnoy (1972), Herrera (1986), Krause and Mathis (1970), Maritano (1970), Nuñez del Arco, Margaín, and Cherol (1984), and P. H. Smith (1993); Cohen (1992, 1993) and Atkins (1992) provide analysis of current changing Latin American outlooks. The following works deal with particular

Latin American IGOs: in Central America—Cochrane (1969), Cohen Orantes (1972), Holbrik and Swan (1972), Karnes (1961), McClelland (1972), Schmitter (1972), and Shaw (1979); Anglo-American Caribbean Commission and its successor agencies—Corkran (1972); West Indies Federation—D. Lowenthal (1961), Mordecai (1968), and Springer (1962); Commonwealth Caribbean—Axline (1979) and Segal (1968); LAFTA—Cale (1969) and Milenky (1973); LAIA—see ALADI (1980); MERCOSUR—Institute for European–Latin American Relations (1991) and Manzetti (1992); Cuenca del Plata—Greño Velasco (1972) and Levin (1972); Amazon Basin Treaty—Franco Filho (1979) and Ware (1980); CECLA—United Nations (1972) and M.J.R. Martz (1979); Rio Group—Institute for European–Latin American Relations (1989) and Yopo (1991); and Tlatelolco Treaty—García Robles (1967, 1979).

CHAPTER EIGHT

■

The Inter-American System

WESTERN HEMISPHERIC ORGANIZATIONS for law, peace, security, and national development collectively form the Inter-American System (IAS) of institutionalized multilateral cooperation among the American states. Since 1948 the IAS has been largely (but not exclusively) institutionalized in the Organization of American States (OAS), the Inter-American Treaty of Reciprocal Assistance (Rio Treaty) regime, and the Inter-American Development Bank (IDB), with the OAS the preeminent institution. The IAS traces its genesis to 1889 through a direct lineage of international American conferences and other institutional paraphernalia. Today its membership includes all of the states in the Latin American region, Canada, and the United States, as well as certain extrahemispheric states (in the IDB). The institutions of the IAS have helped to regulate hemispheric relations by simultaneously offering opportunities for and imposing limitations on the policies of the member states. The system's level of effectiveness has had a complex history. It suffered a general decline for more than two decades beginning in the mid-1960s, but since then has had something of a revival.

REGIONAL ORGANIZATION AND LAW

The Pan American Idea

The Inter-American System is the political expression of Pan Americanism, a movement whose principles predate formal inter-American organization. According to Joseph B. Lockey (1920), the term "Pan American" came into use in the 1880s in connection with proposals that resulted in arrangements for the first inter-American conference. The underlying concept, however, was an earlier outgrowth of the Western Hemisphere Idea. This notion of a "special relationship" among the Americas because of their separation from Europe had provided the point of departure for the Monroe Doctrine as a unilateral policy of the United States toward Europe and the rest of the Americas; it also represented the ideological underpinnings for inter-American cooperation and organization. Some U.S. leaders supported the idea of an inter-American regional system early in the nineteenth century, but they were in a distinct minority. Some Latin American leaders were interested in an alliance based on Monroe's principles, but the United States rebuffed them. The Monroe Doctrine and Pan Americanism were incompatible despite the fact that they both stemmed from the Western Hemisphere Idea, for one was strictly unilateral in scope and the other was inherently multilateral. Eventually the United States and Latin America concurred that the Americas had common interests that should be promoted by institutionalized multilateral cooperation, although the tensions between unilateralism and multilateralism have persisted throughout the history of Pan Americanism to the present day.

Alejandro Alvarez (1868–1960), an eminent Chilean jurist, was an early advocate of juridical Pan Americanism. Alvarez developed important concepts of public international law, including the separation of inter-American from general international law. He considered inter-American law the legal extension of the Western Hemisphere Idea and Pan Americanism. Beginning in 1905 Alvarez advanced the idea that "because of geographical, ethnological, historical, social, political, economic, moral, and spiritual reasons the states of the New World were developing an American international law which supplemented existing international law and would eventually lead the way in molding the future of nations" (Bemis, 1943:238–239).

At the inter-American conference in 1910 the Chilean delegation, led by Alvarez, proposed a separate codification of American international law to be presented to the Third Hague Conference (which was never held). As head of the Rio Commission of Jurists, established in 1912, Alvarez supervised the project of drafting a separate code of inter-American law. He submitted a report on this project at the Fifth International Conference of American States in 1923. Alvarez continued his work on the Rio Commission after it was reestablished in 1923, and served for many years as a judge on the World Court. James Brown Scott of the United States, also a longtime member of the Rio Commission, strongly supported Alvarez's views in his own work and writings. The U.S. Government, however, did not. It had taken exception to the idea of the separation of international law proposed at the inter-American conference in 1890, negated the recommendation for the Third Hague Conference, opposed Alvarez's designs for many years, and thereafter preferred global international law.

Regional Organization as a Policy Instrument

The historical evidence suggests that the IAS has worked best, in the sense of maximum cooperation for complementary objectives and minimal conflict among the member states, when mutuality of interests has been present. Convergence of interests has been difficult to achieve, however, since Latin American and U.S. foreign policy instruments have usually reflected diverging long-range fundamental goals.

For its part, the United States, until the end of the cold war, sought primarily to exclude other foreign influences in Latin America and, as a corollary, to support political stability in the region. To these ends the United States attempted to unify Latin America in a formal organization characterized by friendly relations but under primary U.S. leadership (Larman C. Wilson in Davis, Wilson, and Others, 1975:Ch. 3). In fact, the United States pursued many of its regionwide Latin American policies through the multilateral institutions of the IAS, seeing the system as a way to organize all of Latin America under its leadership and preempt nonhemispheric influences. Since the end of the cold war the United States has been forced to reevaluate its purposes in Latin America. With external states posing no traditional security threat to the hemisphere, the United States has indicated willingness to deal with the major issues regarding inter-American relations within the framework of the IAS in addition to other institutions and processes.

Most Latin American states have sought to achieve as much autonomy as possible in world affairs, but their capability deficiencies have made them dependent to some degree on outsiders for protection and assistance. Given this state of affairs, they have attempted to limit the coercive actions of external states while gaining assistance from them through international organization. Through the IAS, the Latin Americans have worked for international economic cooperation, development funds, and trade preferences and rules more compatible with their interests. The organization also provides machinery for the peaceful settlement of disputes and mutual security—concepts compatible with the interests of militarily weak states. In addition, the rule of law, under which might does not necessarily make right, may be sought through international organization. Inter-American law, developed largely through the efforts of Latin American proponents, stresses the corollary of nonintervention and urges all states to pledge noninterference in the affairs of others.

Latin American attitudes toward regional organization tactics vary from state to state. For example, Argentina traditionally had an aversion to American regionalism, which it saw as dominated by the United States, in favor of universalism. This attitude was shared by Cuba from 1962, when it was denied participation in the OAS under U.S. pressure, and by Panama in pursuing its conflict with the United States over the canal in the United Nations. Brazil, after the late 1960s, reduced its use of international organization as a foreign policy instrument; with its self-perception as a relatively powerful state, it placed more emphasis on widening bilateral relationships. Until the late 1980s, many Latin American members were dissatisfied with U.S. policies and backed away from full participation in the IAS. They renewed their activity in the post–cold war period. In general, however, most Latin American states most of the time have viewed the IAS as serving their interests, even if they disagreed among themselves on specific tactics to be followed.

Systemic Considerations

The systemic patterns at work in the IAS reflect the structure of the Latin American regional subsystem. The behavior and alignments of states within the IAS are based on the Latin Americans' regional consciousness. Inter-American politics tend to divide member states into distinguishable camps with ambivalent views toward one another. The basic division places the United States on one side and all of Latin America on the other, in constant dialogue, and simultaneously attracted, repulsed, and mutually dependent. Within Latin America the eighteen Spanish American states tend to identify with each other, at the same time quarreling among themselves, with Brazil involved but standing apart. Haiti and the new states tend to operate on the periphery, although some of the latter, such as Trinidad-Tobago, have assumed active roles. The United States has created unity among some of the disunited states of Latin America, both intentionally and unintentionally. Latin American unity was fostered partly by the attraction-repulsion syndrome between Latin America and the United States and partly by overt U.S. attempts to unify the region under its leadership. U.S. coercion and economic power led to Latin American unity for its mutual protection and for bargaining for developmental resources.

ORGANIZATIONAL STRUCTURES

Institutional Development

The institutional history of the IAS began with the First International Conference of American States, a six-month gathering centered in Washington in 1889–1890. The conference did not adopt a U.S. proposal for a Pan American customs union, but it established a rudimentary regional structure by creating the International Union of American States and a supporting agency called the Commercial Bureau of the American Republics. The IAS developed in an ad hoc manner over the next fifty-five years. Seven more regular International Conferences of American States and three special conferences were held between 1901 and 1945 in different Latin American capital cities. Various organs and procedures were established at these meetings. The official name of the overall system was changed at the Buenos Aires Conference in 1910 to the Union of American Republics and in 1928 at the Havana Conference to the Union of American States. (See Table 8.1 for full titles of inter-American meetings, referred to in the text in a "shorthand" manner.)

The Commercial Bureau was located in Washington within the Department of State and charged with collecting and disseminating commercial information. It was reorganized at the Mexico meeting (1901–1902) as the International Bureau of the American Republics. A resolution at the Buenos Aires Conference in 1910 created the Pan American Union as the organization's secretariat, replacing the International Bureau as the agency overseeing day-to-day operations. It was administered by a director general with control vested in a Governing Board, with essentially economic functions that were dominated by the United States. Members agreed on certain reforms of the Pan American Union at the meetings held in 1923 and 1928. They gave member states freedom to choose their own representatives to the Governing Board. Latin Americans attempted without success to replace the U.S. secretary of state as chair and to rotate the director general's office, and U.S. dominance of the Pan American Union prevailed. Latin Americans often pointed out that the location of the Pan American Union building in Washington (constructed with funds donated by Andrew Carnegie and completed in 1910) between the State Department and the White House symbolized U.S. control of the IAS.

A number of specialized agencies were created between 1902 and the end of World War II. The Pan American Health Organization was established in 1902, the Inter-American Children's Institute in 1927, the Inter-American Commission of Women and the Pan American Institute of Geography and History in 1928, the Inter-American Indian Institute in 1940, the Inter-American Institute of Agricultural Sciences and the Inter-American Defense Board in 1942, and the Inter-American Statistical Institute in 1945. In addition, institutional developments

TABLE 8.1   Principal Inter-American Conferences, 1889–1994

International Conferences of American States

First (Washington, 1889–1890)	Seventh (Montevideo, 1933)
Second (Mexico, 1901–1902)	Eighth (Lima, 1938)
Third (Rio de Janeiro, 1906)	Ninth (Bogota, 1948)
Fourth (Buenos Aires, 1910)	Tenth (Caracas, 1954)—name
Fifth (Santiago, 1923)	changed to Inter-American
Sixth (Havana, 1928)	Conference

Special Conferences

International Conference of American States on Conciliation and Arbitration (Washington, 1928–1929)

Inter-American Conference for the Maintenance of Peace (Buenos Aires, 1936)

Inter-American Conference on Problems of War and Peace (Mexico, 1945)

Inter-American Conference for Maintenance of Continental Peace and Security (Rio de Janeiro, 1947)

First Meeting of American Presidents (Panama, 1956)

First Special Inter-American Conference (Washington, 1964)

Second Special Inter-American Conference (Rio de Janeiro, 1965)

Third Special Inter-American Conference (Buenos Aires, 1967)

Second Meeting of American Presidents (Punta del Este, 1967)

Meetings of Consultation of Ministers of Foreign Affairs

First (Panama, 1939)	Twelfth (Washington, 1967)
Second (Havana, 1940)	Thirteenth (Washington, 1969)
Third (Rio de Janeiro, 1945)	Fourteenth (Washington, 1971)
Fourth (Washington, 1951)	Fifteenth (Quito, 1974)
Fifth (Santiago, 1959)	Sixteenth (San José, 1975)
Sixth (San José, 1960)	Seventeenth (Washington, 1978)
Seventh (San José, 1960)	Eighteenth (Washington, 1979)
Eighth (Punta del Este, 1962)	Nineteenth (Washington, 1981)
Ninth (Washington, 1964)	Twentieth (Washington, 1982)
Tenth (Washington, 1965–1966)	Twenty-First (Washington, 1989–1990)
Eleventh (Washington, Buenos Aires, Punta del Este, 1967)	

Regular General Assembly Sessions

First (Washington, 1971)	Thirteenth (Washington, 1983)
Second (Washington, 1972)	Fourteenth (Brasilia, 1984)
Third (Washington, 1973)	Fifteenth (Bogotá, 1985)
Fourth (Atlanta, 1974)	Sixteenth (Guatemala, 1986)
Fifth (Washington, 1975)	Seventeenth (Washington, 1987)
Sixth (Santiago, 1976)	Eighteenth (San Salvador, 1988)
Seventh (St. Georges, 1977)	Nineteenth (Washington, 1989)
Eighth (Washington, 1978)	Twentieth (Asunción, 1990)
Ninth (La Paz, 1979)	Twenty-First (Santiago, 1991)
Tenth (Washington, 1980)	Twenty-Second (Nassau, 1992)
Eleventh (Castries, 1981)	Twenty-Third (Managua, 1993)
Twelfth (Washington, 1982)	Twenty-Fourth (Belém, 1994)

beginning in 1938 provided the first political-security organs. The Lima Conference in that year created the Meeting of Consultation of Ministers of Foreign Affairs to consider emergency security matters, at that time in the context of impending European war. The conference considered giving the consultative function to the Pan American Union, but decided against allowing the Governing Board any such political role.

Integrated Constitutional Bases

From 1945 to 1948 the institutions of the IAS were formally codified and expanded. Most important, the Rio Treaty was agreed upon and the OAS was established. The IDB was founded in 1959. The IAS subsequently underwent some restructuring, with the result that the principal institutions—the OAS, IDB, and Rio Treaty regime—operated under coordinated but individual conventions with overlapping but distinct membership.

Five conferences held between 1945 and 1985 produced documents that, if taken together, form the constitutional bases for the present IAS. At the first of these meetings, a special conference held in Mexico City in 1945 (the Chapultepec Conference), the codification and consolidation of the regional arrangements that had developed over the previous five and a half decades were envisioned. Latin Americans, fearful that the IAS was in danger of being downgraded or even dissolved because of U.S. enthusiasm for the global United Nations then being organized, wanted to give the regional organization a permanent juridical basis. To this end, the Chapultepec Conference authorized the drafting of three basic integrated documents: (1) a treaty of reciprocal assistance; (2) a basic constitution for regional organization; and (3) a treaty to coordinate and consolidate agreements on the pacific settlements of disputes.

The triad of inter-American documents was soon forthcoming. The special Rio de Janeiro Conference in 1947 resulted in the Inter-American Treaty of Reciprocal Assistance, commonly referred to as the Rio Treaty or Rio Pact. It went into effect on December 3, 1948, after ratification by the required two-thirds of the member states. In the meantime, the Bogotá Conference in 1948 issued several major documents. One was the Charter of the Organization of American States (Charter of Bogotá), to serve as the basic constitution for the American regional organization. The charter went into effect on December 13, 1951, although in practice its provisions were adhered to soon after the Bogotá meeting. The conference also issued the Inter-American Treaty on Pacific Settlement (Pact of Bogotá) outlining procedures for the peaceful resolution of inter-American disputes. Unlike the Rio Treaty and the charter, the Pact of Bogotá entered into force only with respect to those states ratifying it. It has been ratified and is still in force among thirteen states. For others, previous treaties that they have ratified are still in effect. The conference also approved a third document, the American Declaration on the Rights and Duties of Man, apparently considered less important than the others.

The Special Buenos Aires Conference in 1967 approved the Protocol of Amendment to the Charter of the OAS. This Protocol of Buenos Aires, which amended the original OAS organization and functions, entered into force in February 1970. The amendments strengthened economic and social functions relative to political ones, reflecting a shift in organizational emphasis away from the political-security interests of the United States toward the economic-social interests of the Latin American members.

Only three years after the Protocol of Buenos Aires charter amendments went into effect and brought about important institutional changes, another movement to restructure the OAS Charter as well as the Rio Treaty was underway. In 1973 the General Assembly of the OAS created the Special Committee to Study the Inter-American System and to Propose Measures for Restructuring It (CEESI, an acronym after the Spanish title). CEESI's deliberations, from June 1973 through February 1975, resulted in four proposals. The Protocol of Amendment to the Inter-American Treaty of Reciprocal Assistance was submitted to and approved by a Conference of Plenipotentiaries in July 1975 and sent to member states for ratification. It failed to receive enough ratifications to become effective. The Draft Amendments to the Charter of the OAS were taken over by the Permanent Council of the OAS in April 1976 for further consideration and languished thereafter. The Draft Convention on Cooperation for Development, with wording similar to that of the draft charter amendments calling for a comprehensive approach to economic development, became a dead issue. Consideration of the Draft Convention on Collective Economic Security for Development, which expressed concepts already included in the proposed amendments to both the Rio Treaty and the charter, was postponed indefinitely.

In time the OAS Charter was further amended. In 1985, after considerable negotiation and compromise, a special conference approved the Protocol of Cartagena de Indias. It became operative in November 1988. The principal effect was to emphasize further Latin American economic concerns and to strengthen the policy role of the Secretary General.

OAS Structure

The 1948 charter provided for four principal organs to govern the OAS. The Inter-American Conference (the new name for the International Conference of American States), a general decisional body to establish and reassess broad policy guidelines, was established as the supreme OAS organ. It was to meet every five years at least, but the last time delegates assembled was at Caracas in 1954. The next conference, scheduled for Quito in 1959, was indefinitely postponed because of an unfriendly atmosphere generated first by conflict between Peru and Ecuador and then between the United States and Cuba. An ad hoc conference was held in its place and major OAS business then came to be conducted by the foreign ministers' meeting.

The Meeting of Ministers of Foreign Affairs was also made one of the principal organs. The charter provided for the foreign ministers of each of the member states to meet in order to consult on matters dealing with threats to hemispheric peace, settling inter-American disputes, and resisting external attacks on the Americas. The ministers were advised by the Advisory Defense Committee, composed of high-ranking military officers from the states represented at foreign ministers' meetings.

The third major organ was the Council of the Organization of American States (COAS), composed of one permanent ambassadorial representative from each member state. The COAS handled matters referred to it by the Foreign Ministers' meeting and the Inter-American Conference. It supervised the Pan American Union and coordinated the activities of the Specialized Conferences. The Rio Treaty authorized the COAS to act provisionally as the Organ of Consultation when hemispheric security or peace was threatened. The charter created three organs subordinate to the COAS. The most important, as it turned out, was the Inter-American Economic and Social Council (IAECOSOC), which in 1962 established subordinate entities with special responsibilities in the administration of Alliance for Progress programs. A second COAS subsidiary was the Inter-American Council of Jurists, served by the Inter-American Juridical Committee. The third was the Inter-American Cultural Council, with a subagency called the Committee for Cultural Action.

The Specialized Conferences (not to be confused with the Special Conferences mentioned above) consisted of twelve organizations, institutes, agencies, committees, boards, and commissions created to deal with technical matters or specialized inter-American activities covering a wide range of endeavors. They operated either autonomously within the OAS or under "working agreements" with other OAS bodies. Eight of these organizations had been created prior to the adoption of the OAS Charter in 1948. Three additional ones were later established: the Inter-American Committee on Human Rights in 1959, the Special Consultative Committee on Security in 1962, and the Inter-American Nuclear Energy Commission in 1964. The Inter-American Peace Committee had been established by resolution in 1940, but it did not hold its first meeting until 1948. In addition, the Inter-American Defense College, a dependency of the Inter-American Defense Board, opened in Washington on October 9, 1962.

The Fifth Foreign Ministers Meeting (1959) created the Inter-American Commission on Human Rights as an OAS advisory group within the category of Specialized Conferences. Headquartered in Washington, D.C., the commission began to function in 1960 with limited powers to promote the observance and protection of human rights in the Americas.

The 1967 Protocol of Buenos Aires amended the 1948 charter and made some basic organizational changes. It abolished the moribund Inter-American Conference and created the General Assembly as the new supreme organ of the OAS. It directed the General Assembly to meet at least annually to decide on general policy guidelines, discuss any matter of interest to the members, and coordinate the work of other organs. The General Assembly assumed some functions of the old COAS, such as approving the OAS program budget, electing the secretary general and assistant secretary general, approving the admission of new members, and establishing working standards for the General Secretariat.

The General Assembly had two subordinate bodies. The Inter-American Juridical Committee was a merging of the old Inter-American Council of Jurists and its subordinate Inter-American Juridical Committee. The new committee, composed of eleven jurists from different states, was elected by the General Assembly for four-year terms on a staggered replacement basis. It was to advise the OAS on juridical matters and promote the further development and codification of international law, including that related to regional economic integration. The charter amendments also raised the status of the Inter-American Commission on Human

Rights from that of a Specialized Conference to an organ supervised by the General Assembly, charged with promoting the observance and protection of human rights in the Americas and investigating complaints of their violation.

The amendments did not change the composition or functions of the Meeting of Consultation of Ministers of Foreign Affairs, but its relative importance in the OAS was reduced with the elevation of two other organs to equal status. The Inter-American Economic and Social Council was raised from a subordinate position to full council level and charged with increased responsibilities. It was charged with coordinating OAS-sponsored economic and social development programs, evaluating the progress of those states receiving development assistance, and promoting Latin American economic integration. The other major organ, the Inter-American Council for Education, Science, and Culture, was an expanded and updated form of the old Inter-American Cultural Council. Its primary purpose was to promote educational, scientific, and cultural cooperation and exchange among the American states. Both councils were to meet at least annually.

The Permanent Council (PCOAS) succeeded the COAS but did not hold the central position formerly occupied by the latter. The level of authority was on a par with the foreign ministers' meetings and the two new councils. Its basic role was that of a peacekeeping mediator handling matters referred to it by the General Assembly or the Meeting of Ministers of Foreign Affairs. The PCOAS also served as the preparatory committee for the General Assembly, to prepare draft agendas, review the various matters to be considered by the latter, and recommend measures to the General Assembly regarding standards and functions of the General Secretariat. The PCOAS might act as the Provisional Organ of Consultation when emergency situations arose until a meeting of foreign ministers might be convened. The Inter-American Committee on Peaceful Settlement was established as a subsidiary body assisting the PCOAS with its peacekeeping responsibilities, replacing the Inter-American Peace Committee, which had been one of the Specialized Conferences.

The Specialized Conferences were reorganized into ten entities, including six Specialized Organizations and four Other Entities. All of the extant Specialized Conferences had been organized prior to the 1967 amendments, which made no important changes in their functions.

The General Secretariat (formerly the Pan American Union, but still known informally by its traditional name) occupied a key position in the revised organization. It was to serve the entire organization and its member governments in some capacity. The amendments increased the secretariat's duties and established a more flexible relationship between it and the other OAS organs. The secretary general was responsible to the General Assembly and was a nonvoting participant in all OAS meetings. The assistant secretary general, among other duties, served as secretary to the PCOAS. Both officials were elected by the General Assembly for a five-year term. They could be reelected once and their successors might not be of the same nationality.

The Inter-American Commission on Human Rights had a special institutional development. The Inter-American Specialized Conference on Human Rights, held in Costa Rica in 1969, produced the American Convention on Human

Rights (Pact of San José). The convention, which finally went into effect in 1978, incorporated and extended the 1948 American Declaration on the Rights and Duties of Man and related subsequent acts. It "recreated" the Inter-American Commission on Human Rights, composed of seven jurists selected by the Permanent Council to four-year terms, and further defined its procedures. It created the Inter-American Court of Human Rights, located in Costa Rica, with jurisdiction limited to cases voluntarily brought by signatory states.

After the Mexico City conference in 1945, the Pan American Union was headed by a secretary general, serving for a ten-year elected term. In practice, the secretary general was always a Latin American (that is, not a U.S. citizen). The first under the new system was Alberto Lleras Camargo, who served for eight years from 1946 to 1954, when he resigned in frustration. Lleras returned to his native Colombia to help end civil strife there and to serve as president of the nation, thereafter becoming publisher of the news magazine *Visión*. The second secretary general was Carlos Dávila, a Chilean political leader, journalist, and diplomat. Dávila served for a brief period from 1954 until his death on October 19, 1955. In January 1956 the COAS elected the former Uruguayan Foreign Minister José A. Mora as interim secretary general for two years and then to a full ten-year term, which expired in May 1968. When Mora completed his twelve years in the post in May 1968, he was succeeded by Galo Plaza Lasso, a former president of Ecuador and United Nations official, in a hotly contested election. Plaza was succeeded in July 1975 by Alejandro Orfila, who had been serving as the Argentine ambassador to the United States. Orfila resigned his post in 1984, a year before his second five-year term ended, and was replaced by João Clemente Baena Soares, a professional Brazilian diplomat who had spent most of his career in international organization posts.

Membership

Pan Americanism, based on the idea of a special relationship among the peoples of the Western Hemisphere, implies the desirability of universal membership in the IAS on the part of the sovereign American states. A near-universal majority of them belonged to the IAS from its beginnings until the early 1960s. In 1889–1890, at the First International Conference of American States, seventeen of the eighteen existing Latin American states (all except the Dominican Republic) plus the United States were present as contracting parties. The Dominican Republic joined subsequent conferences, as did Cuba and Panama after their independence in 1902. Thereafter until the 1960s all of the Latin American states and the United States were participants, but Canada declined to take part. Membership was at twenty-one in the 1960s when former British Caribbean dependencies began to achieve independence and sought to join the system. Decisions were made that allowed the new states to join the OAS without being required also to adhere to the Rio Treaty—or, by implication, the IDB or other elements operating under their own charter. Consequently, the various components of the IAS developed different memberships. The OAS included even nonregional entities as observers and the IDB sought them as members. In 1991 the OAS achieved universal membership of the thirty-five American states, the only IAS entity to do so.

In 1948 the charter members of the OAS were the United States and the then-twenty Latin American states. Cuba under the Castro government technically remained a member, although in 1962 its participation in the OAS was suspended, a sanction remaining in effect in 1994. Beginning in the latter 1960s, the newly independent former British Caribbean dependencies began to join the OAS. Belize and Guyana were not allowed to enlist because of unsettled boundary disputes with member-states Guatemala and Venezuela, respectively (as provided for in Article 8 of the OAS Charter), although Guyana was granted permanent observer status. The 1985 charter amendments, in effect in 1988, dropped the membership-denial provision, and Belize and Guyana both became full members in 1991. Suriname, a former colony of the Netherlands, adhered in 1975, the year it became independent. Canada, which had been a permanent observer, took full membership in 1989. Thus, in 1991, the OAS achieved universal membership of the thirty-five sovereign American states. The OAS also invited representatives from nonhemispheric states, the Holy See, and the United Nations to attend its meetings as permanent observers. Twenty-three entities presently have observer status. They are: Algeria, Austria, Belgium, Cyprus, Egypt, Equatorial Guinea, Finland, France, Germany, Greece, the Holy See, Israel, Italy, Japan, Morocco, Netherlands, Pakistan, Portugal, Saudi Arabia, South Korea, Spain, Switzerland, and the United Nations. The United Kingdom declined participation because of its continuing disputes with Argentina, Guatemala, and Venezuela.

The Rio Treaty also began with twenty-one signatories—the United States and the then-twenty Latin American states. Cuba unilaterally abrogated the treaty in 1962. When OAS membership began to expand in the 1960s, it was determined that also joining the Rio Treaty regime was not required, and Trinidad-Tobago became the only new participant. Thus membership remained at twenty-one signatory states. The Rio Treaty did not contemplate admitting extrahemispheric members or observers.

The IDB has forty-four members. They include twenty-six of the thirty-three sovereign states in the Latin American region plus the United States, Canada, and sixteen nonregional states. Participation was expanded to include American states not members of the OAS when Canada joined on May 3, 1972, having already contributed funds for a number of years (a special amendment to the bank's charter named Canada specifically as a member). Guyana was subsequently also allowed to adhere. When the United States began reducing its funding support to the bank in the early 1970s, the IDB sought capital resources from nonregional states and, since 1976, seventeen of them have joined. They are Belgium, Denmark, Germany, Israel, Japan, Spain, Switzerland, United Kingdom, Austria, Finland, France, Italy, Netherlands, Portugal, Sweden, and the Holy See. Yugoslavia had been a member from 1976 until civil war in the 1990s fragmented it into several entities. The seven OAS members not belonging to the bank are Antigua-Barbuda, Cuba, Dominica, Grenada, St. Christopher–Nevis, St. Lucia, and St. Vincent.

A seemingly common misunderstanding about the multilateral sanctions imposed on Cuba in 1962 should be clarified. Cuban membership in the IAS was not revoked. The OAS charter and other instruments make no provision for expulsion of a member. Rather, the Castro government was denied participation in the OAS and other agencies and conferences of the IAS, a provision that remained in effect even after other sanctions were effectively dropped in 1975. Thus, Cuba's activity was temporarily suspended but it technically remains a member of the OAS. Cuba is not a member of the IDB and it unilaterally abrogated the Rio Treaty.

INTER-AMERICAN POLICIES

Competing Purposes

The various constitutional bases for the IAS created the machinery described above in order to implement a number of Pan American principles that are reiterated in the constitutional instruments. The many principles developed since 1889 guiding inter-American policies and activities may be grouped under five main categories: (1) nonintervention and sovereign equality; (2) mutual security; (3) representative democracy and human rights; (4) peaceful settlement of disputes; and (5) economic cooperation and development. None of the policies appeared full-blown at the start; they were introduced at different times and evolved thereafter. They have been assigned different priorities and levels of commitment by the various member states—revealing the competing and often conflicting purposes at work in the system.

The Pan American movement has gone through several historical phases of shifting cleavages among the member states, usually between Latin America and the United States. The first phase spanned the years from 1889, when the First International Conference of American States was held, to 1928, when the Sixth Conference revealed such bitter Latin American hostility toward the United States that the survival of the movement was in jeopardy. During that time the United States was primarily interested in expanding commercial relations with Latin America. It secondarily sought to establish procedures for the peaceful settlement of Latin American disputes, which would promote regional political stability, facilitate international trade, and preempt nonhemispheric influences. The United States was not interested in a regional mutual security arrangement, preferring to pursue security unilaterally. The Latin American states shared U.S. interests in trade expansion and pacific settlement but viewed the IAS primarily as a way to achieve security against outside intervention, first from Europe and then from the United States itself. After enunciation of the Roosevelt Corollary in 1904 and extensive U.S. intervention in the Caribbean region thereafter, Latin American dismay with the regional organization increased. Restrained hostility toward the United States in the early 1900s developed into bitter public denunciations by the late 1920s. Latin Americans were unwilling to risk abandonment of the IAS despite their disappointment in its course.

The second era of Pan Americanism, beginning in the late 1920s and continuing through World War II, was marked by a general harmony of interests. The principal developments involved the progressive acceptance of nonintervention by the United States, followed by the building of regional security arrangements. Most members saw mutual advantages and concurring interests in regional organization, and the period represented the most harmonious in the history of the movement.

The third phase, from the end of World War II to the late 1950s, was again marked by diverging goals and conflicting relations. During this time the United States and Latin America completely reversed their respective views of inter-American organization from those initially held between 1889 and 1928. The United States pursued primarily mutual security goals in the context of a global cold war, whereas Latin America sought essentially to promote its economic interests. A brief period of converging interests, during what came to be known as the Alliance for Progress, extended roughly from 1959 to 1965. During this period, the United States broadened its notion of security to include economic and social concerns. As a result, a temporary convergence of U.S. and Latin American interests occurred even though they rested on different motivations.

The fourth phase began in the mid-1960s. From 1965 to 1979 the United States did not perceive a serious threat in Latin America, so its interest in the region's economic development declined. Latin American states were unified by their general consensus that U.S. trade and aid restrictions were a major source of their economic problems, and they sought through the IAS to gain more favorable arrangements. After 1979, when the Nicaraguan Revolution gave renewed strength to the U.S. perception of security threats in the Caribbean Basin, the importance of the IAS declined for most parties. On the one hand, the Latin American states refused to respond to hesitant U.S. steps to reinvigorate the mutual security procedures of the system. With no encouragement from Latin America, the United States pursued its security policies without the IAS. At the same time, it was unwilling to commit significant resources to the system's developmental programs.

The current phase, beginning in the late 1980s, parallels the emergence of a global post–cold war era. Interest has been revived on the part of most of the members of the IAS in resuscitating formal inter-American cooperation. As inter-American relations evolve in the post–cold war world, security issues involving threats from nonhemispheric entities have been nonexistent, although a number of intraregional situations remain problematical. Consequently, other issues have surfaced in the new common inter-American agenda, including international trade and investment, external debt, democracy, human rights, immigration, refugees, drug trafficking, and the physical environment. Most Latin American states, Canada, and the United States have adopted a primarily (but not exclusively) economic foundation for inter-American relationships, concentrating on free-trade agreements and international investment. The movement for an effective IAS was temporarily set back by the U.S. invasion of Panama in 1989, but the issue of unilateral intervention was soon transcended by the need to deal with the current set of pressing inter-American problems. Most members, some of them perhaps tentatively, have indicated a willingness to emphasize compatible interests and accommodate differences. The possibilities for a sustained revival of the IAS are enhanced by the diminished propensity of the United States to dictate unilaterally and the more positive Latin American nationalism.

In the following sections, each of the five categories of principles, policies, and activities identified above will be analyzed on its own terms.

Nonintervention

The principle of nonintervention, flowing from the corollaries of state sovereignty and juridical equality, became the cornerstone on which the IAS was built. The Latin American desire for nonintervention as a doctrine of international law predated the First Inter-American Conference in 1889. Afterward the Latin American states were vitally interested in the idea as a fundamental organizational principle. They finally succeeded in the 1930s in having nonintervention adopted as a concept of American international law and installed as the primary principle of Pan Americanism.

A doctrine enunciated by the Argentine jurist Carlos Calvo, in his book published in 1868, became the rallying point for early Latin American desires to establish nonintervention as a rule of international conduct. The Calvo Doctrine challenged the European legal position that foreign residents had rights to "just" treatment by their host states, especially with regard to pecuniary claims based upon injuries during civil war, acts of violence, and breaches of contract, whether or not the same standards were accorded national citizens. Calvo asserted that intervention by foreign governments to enforce the claims of their own citizens residing abroad was illegal, no matter what sort of treatment had been given them, because it violated the host state's sovereign independence. In sum, Calvo stressed the absolute equality of states and the inviolability of sovereignty, concluding that intervention to enforce pecuniary claims under any circumstances was invalid.

A resolution incorporating the essence of the Calvo Doctrine was proposed at the Washington Conference in 1889. It declared that states were under no obligation to favor foreigners with more protection than was afforded to native citizens and that the former had only the same legal rights as the latter. The United States voted against the resolution and was the only state to do so.

The Calvo Doctrine was modified in 1902, when three European states threatened Venezuela with intervention in order to collect public debts. The Argentine Foreign Minister Luís M. Drago proclaimed the illegality of armed intervention to force payment of foreign governmental debts, but with reference to public rather than private debt. The Drago Doctrine, like that of Calvo, stressed absolute sovereignty and territorial inviolability as superior to pecuniary claims. This position received wide support in Latin America and became the new point of departure for their demands within the IAS.

The Drago Doctrine was initially advanced in response to European intervention, but it was soon directed toward the United States when the interventionist features of the Monroe Doctrine became clear. The Roosevelt Corollary, enunciated in 1904, and the subsequent U.S. interventions in the Caribbean area based on it, definitively shifted Latin American fears from Europe to the United States.

For some three decades, Pan Americanism revolved around Latin American resistance to U.S. interventions in the Caribbean area. The first two inter-American conferences (1889/1890 and 1902) had been held prior to sustained U.S. intervention in the Caribbean, but at the next four conferences, convened between 1906 and 1928, the United States attempted to keep the conference agendas devoid of the intervention issue. The Latin American states, however, succeeded in using the meetings to attack U.S. intervention as both unjust and illegal. They protested U.S. interference in their domestic affairs as violations of their sovereignty and attempted to persuade the United States to accept the principle of nonintervention as the legal corollary of sovereignty. The ensuing debate reflected conflicting views as to what kinds of acts constituted intervention. The Latin American definition of intervention was a broad one including diplomatic, economic, and military actions. The United States had a narrow view limiting intervention to military activities justified as necessary for the security of all the Americas.

By the time of the Havana Conference of 1928, an impasse had been reached over the intervention issue. Latin Americans made it clear that future cooperation was contingent on the United States dropping its resistance to nonintervention. This open hostility threatened to destroy the IAS. Because of the urgency of the problem, and because of the lack of European threats to the hemisphere, the United States abandoned the Roosevelt Corollary and accepted nonintervention as a part of American international law. The United States had indicated a changed attitude as early as 1928 (see Chapter 5), and by 1933 it was willing to proceed along multilateral lines.

At the Montevideo Conference in 1933, the United States accepted a nonintervention treaty, although with reservations. The conference adopted the Convention on the Rights and Duties of States, embodying the Calvo and Drago doctrines as well as broader nonintervention principles long championed by Latin Americans. The key clause in Article VIII flatly stated that "no state has the right to intervene in the internal or external affairs of another." The United States signed and ratified the convention, but with the ambiguous reservation of its rights "by the law of nations as generally recognized," casting doubt on the U.S. commitment. Three years later, however, the United States accepted nonintervention as an unqualified legal principle. All of the American states adhered to a convention signed at the Buenos Aires Conference in 1936 entitled Additional Protocol Relative to Non-Intervention. This document, reaffirming the principles adopted in 1933, emphatically declared as inadmissable any intervention "directly or indirectly, and for whatever reason, in the internal or external affairs of the parties."

After 1936 nonintervention was reaffirmed at various conferences and incorporated into other treaties, most notably in the OAS Charter (especially Articles 18–22—Articles 15–20 in the 1948 charter). The charter provides, "No State or group of States has the right to intervene, directly or indirectly, for any reason whatsoever in the internal or external affairs of any other State." This principle prohibits not only armed force but "any other form of interference or attempted threat against the personality of the State or against its political, economic, and cultural elements." In addition, "No State may use or encourage the use of coercive measures of an economic or political character in order to force the sovereign will of another State and obtain from it advantages of any kind." The charter also establishes the inviolability of state territory, which may not be the object of even temporary military occupation "or of other measures of force taken by another State, directly or indirectly, on any grounds whatever." The signatories of the charter pledged "not to have recourse to the use of force, except in the case of self-defense in accordance with existing treaties." Finally, with reference to possible multilateral sanctions against a member state, the charter said, "Measures adopted for the maintenance of peace and security in accordance with existing treaties" did not violate the above principles.

Distinguishing between legally permissible and impermissible acts of intervention is difficult, with so little agreement on the exact meaning of the concept. The members of the IAS, after many years of debating the subject and using the concept in a variety of treaty provisions, have not devised a listing of the specific acts constituting intervention or agreed on a general working definition of the phenomenon. General agreement prevails that the use or threat of military force is interventionist, but intervention has been further conceived to indicate a wide range of actions in economic, diplomatic, legal, moral, and political contexts. It may refer to almost every form of international influence. To be useful as an analytic or operational concept, intervention needs to be defined more precisely than merely as a synonym for influence or, in effect, equated with almost all international politics.

The inter-American law of nonintervention has not deterred the United States from intervening in Latin America—nor has it deterred Latin Americans from interfering in each other's affairs. The United States has departed from the nonintervention principle on eight important occasions, all of which qualify as interventionist even according to a minimal definition: in Argentina in 1945–1946, Guatemala in 1954, Cuba in 1961, the Dominican Republic in 1965, Chile in 1970–1973, Grenada in 1983, Nicaragua in 1984, and Panama in 1989. Latin Americans also have been guilty of intervention, especially in a series of acts in the Caribbean region beginning in the late 1940s and continuing, off and on, into the 1980s. In my judgment, however, the Latin American consensus succeeded in deterring the United States from committing more extensive acts of intervention, at least prior to the decline of the IAS after the mid-1960s.

Mutual Security

Mutual security—the idea of "one for all and all for one" in combatting aggression—eventually developed into one of the main purposes of the IAS. The prohibition of intervention required the fashioning of multilateral security arrangements. They were first incorporated into the American regional system in 1938, refined during World War II and then stated in the OAS Charter and, most prominently, in the Rio Treaty. Some inter-American security concepts were aimed at preparing for defense against aggression from outside the hemisphere, but most of it involved disputes and interventions among the American states themselves.

The initial development of mutual security principles closely paralleled the resolution of the nonintervention issue—specifically, the changing nature of the Monroe Doctrine. From the time of Monroe's enunciation of these principles in 1823 until the threat of world war in the late 1930s, the United States considered the Monroe Doctrine to be a unilateral security concept. During World War I the United States desired a united American front against the Central Powers, but Latin America failed to comply. Of the eight Latin American states declaring war,

Brazil was the only major one, and the only one from South America. The other leading states—Argentina, Chile, Colombia, and Mexico—remained neutral. U.S. intervention in the Caribbean was prevalent, and hemispheric solidarity clearly was lacking.

From time to time a Latin American state would suggest that the Monroe Doctrine be multilaterally defined and enforced. One of the most important of those proposals was made in April 1920 by President Baltasar Brum of Uruguay. The Brum Doctrine, as it came to be known, called for the multilateralization of the Monroe Doctrine and the establishment of an American League of Nations. This proposal was submitted to the Santiago Conference in 1923, but neither the other Latin American states nor the United States offered encouragement. The former were intent on attacking the latter for its intervention in the name of the Monroe Doctrine, whereas the United States insisted on pursuing unilateral security policies.

In the 1930s the Monroe Doctrine was finally transformed from a prime principle of U.S. unilateral policy to a basis for multilateral mutual security agreement. This transformation has been referred to as the multilateralization, Pan Americanization, or continentalization of the Monroe Doctrine. It occurred in two stages, the first of which was the abandonment of the Roosevelt Corollary. The second phase, more directly related to the principle of mutual security, involved the acceptance of the idea of multilateral hemispheric defense. Inter-American machinery was then created to implement the newly accepted principles.

The first tentative step toward the defense of the entire hemisphere, which simultaneously applied the Monroe Doctrine to the principle of a multilateral defense, was taken at the Buenos Aires Conference in 1936. There, the United States urged some sort of hemispheric defense plan, thus revealing a willingness to change its unilateral security policies. The conference adopted only a rudimentary form of the "one for all and all for one" principle in the Convention for the Maintenance, Preservation, and Re-establishment of Peace. It provided that, "in the event that the peace of the American Republics is menaced," the members of the Inter-American System should "consult together for the purpose of finding and adopting methods of peaceful cooperation."

More measures were adopted at the Lima Conference in 1938. After considerable debate, the conferees adopted a statement of hemispheric solidarity known as the Declaration of Lima. It stated, in part, that all American states "affirmed the intention of the American Republics to help one another in case of a foreign attack, either direct or indirect, on any one of them." It represented a significant step toward multilateralizing the Monroe Doctrine, and later formed the basis for wartime inter-American security collaboration.

The first three Meetings of Consultation of Ministers of Foreign Affairs were held, under the authority of the Lima Declaration, during the World War II period—in 1939, 1940, and 1942. Soon after the German invasion of Poland on September 1, 1939, the First Meeting of Consultation of Ministers of Foreign Affairs was held in Panama. They agreed on the General Declaration of Neutrality, which affirmed and defined inter-American neutrality in the European war and established a neutrality zone around the Americas. The American states agreed to consult further as necessary and created the Inter-American Neutrality Committee, composed of seven international lawyers and located in Rio de Janeiro.

The second foreign ministers' meeting convened in Havana in July 1940, shortly after the fall of France. It adopted, among other things, the Declaration of Reciprocal Assistance and Cooperation for the Defense of the Americas, which further multilateralized the Monroe Doctrine in precise terms. It stated that an attack by a non-American state would be considered an attack on all the Americas, and cooperative defense measures would be taken after consultation.

After the Japanese attack on Pearl Harbor (December 7, 1941), the third foreign ministers' consultation was held in Rio de Janeiro in January 1942 in pursuance of the Havana declaration. The United States desired a resolution requiring the severance of diplomatic relations by all the American states with Japan, Germany, and Italy, and most Latin American states were willing to accept such a measure. Opposition by Argentina and Chile, however, resulted in a resolution that recommended only the rupture of relations. Another resolution created the Inter-American Defense Board, composed of military and naval advisers from all member states charged with studying the problems of hemispheric defense and recommending solutions. In addition, the Foreign Ministers agreed to establish the Emergency Advisory Committee for Political Defense, a seven-member body located in Montevideo, to investigate and coordinate measures to counter Axis subversive activities. The Inter-American Neutrality Committee was renamed the Inter-American Juridical Committee and its focus shifted to the legal problems of war.

Prior to the Rio meeting, twelve Latin American states had severed diplomatic relations with the Axis and nine of those had declared war. After the meeting, all other regional states except Argentina and Chile broke relations, and four more of them declared war. Chile and Argentina eventually ruptured relations and declared war in 1944 and 1945, respectively. Most of Latin America's armed forces did not have a major position in hemispheric defense and generally were assigned to supporting roles. There were important exceptions, however. Brazil sent an expeditionary force into combat in Italy, and the Brazilian navy assisted that of the United States in antisubmarine patrols off the Atlantic coast of South America; Mexico dispatched an aircraft squadron to the Philippine Islands. Most Latin American states cooperated in breaking Axis espionage networks and granted U.S. requests for base rights.

The Mexico City Conference in 1945 issued the Act of Chapultepec, which broadened the scope of aggression covered under mutual security arrangements to include attack by any state, meaning American as well as non-American ones. Inter-American security principles and consultation procedures had been fully defined by 1945 but had lapsed at the conclusion of the war. Therefore, at the Mexico City Conference, the drafting of a permanent treaty of reciprocal assistance was authorized to be one of the first postwar actions taken by the IAS. The Rio de Janeiro Conference of 1947 produced the Inter-American Treaty of Reciprocal Assistance (Rio Treaty), reaffirming the various wartime principles on a continuing basis. It was the first permanent collective defense treaty entered into by the United States and served as an initial guide for other arrangements during the cold war.

The Rio Treaty is the primary source of mutual security principles and procedures. These principles are repeated in summary form in the OAS Charter. The Rio Treaty distinguishes between armed attack and other forms of aggression and between aggression occurring within and outside of a designated geographic zone and specifies the collective responses called for under the various circumstances. It states that "an armed attack by any State against an American State shall be considered as an attack against all the American States" and that the contracting parties agree "to assist in meeting the attack." Procedurally, "the Organ of Consultation shall meet without delay for the purpose of examining those measures and agreeing upon the measures of a collective character that should be taken." These provisions applied in case of an armed attack within a precisely designated geographic region, which ranged from pole to pole and included all of the continental territory of the American states (including Alaska) and the adjacent islands but not the Hawaiian Islands. Canada and Greenland were covered by the treaty even though they were not signatories.

When an armed attack took place outside the zone, presumably against the overseas possessions or other national territory or against the military forces of an American state, or when other forms of aggression occurred inside or outside the zone (the treaty does not define specific acts), Article 6 provided that the Organ of Consultation would meet immediately in order to agree on the measures which should be taken.

Article 8 listed the measures that could be applied to aggressors, singly or in combination. They were "recall of chiefs of diplomatic missions; breaking of diplomatic relations; breaking of consular relations; partial or complete interruption of economic relations or of rail, sea, air, postal, telegraphic, telephonic, and radiotelephonic or radiotelegraphic communications; and use of armed force." Articles 17 and 18 provided that decisions by the Organ of Consultation be taken by a two-thirds majority vote, but in the case of inter-American disputes the directly interested parties were excluded from voting. Article 20 stipulated that decisions would be binding on all member states "with the sole exception that no State shall be required to use armed force without its consent."

Regional security procedures have been applied under the Rio Treaty, and the OAS Charter has been brought to bear on certain occasions. Between 1951 and 1990, the fourth through the twenty-first meetings of Consultation of Ministers of Foreign Affairs were held [to deal with perceived threats to hemispheric peace], eight of them under the Rio Treaty and ten in accordance with the OAS Charter. The foreign ministers also met informally on several occasions. Most of the cases involved inter-American disputes, and all but one of them dealt with the Caribbean area. Sanctions were applied three times: against the Dominican Republic in 1960 and against Cuba in 1962 and 1964.

A series of eleven cases involved long-standing and evolving Caribbean tensions and rivalries. They were: (1) conflict between Costa Rica and Nicaragua, 1948–1949; (2) conflict between the Dominican Republic and Haiti, 1949–1950; (3) conflict involving the Dominican Republic against Haiti, Cuba, and Guatemala, 1950; (4) conflict between Costa Rica and Nicaragua, 1955–1956; (5) conflict between Honduras and Nicaragua, 1957; (6) conflict between Panama and Cuba, 1959; (7) conflict among Nicaragua, Costa Rica, and Honduras, 1959; (8) conflict between Venezuela and the Dominican Republic, 1960–1962 (sanctions imposed on the Dominican Republic were the first levied under the Rio Treaty); (9) conflict between the Dominican Republic and Haiti, 1963–1965; (10) civil war in the Dominican Republic, 1965 (the foreign ministers met under the OAS Charter); and (11) war between El Salvador and Honduras, 1969. The IAS generally was able to halt hostilities among the disputants, if not to resolve the underlying causes of the conflict.

The situation between Panama and the United States in 1964 was a special case and represented the first involvement of a non–Latin American party in an application of the security procedures. Panama accused the United States of acts of aggression against its sovereignty during clashes between Panamanians and U.S. residents of the Canal Zone. The OAS Council met under the Rio Treaty, and at its urging the disputants agreed to reestablish diplomatic relations and begin friendly high-level negotiations to resolve their differences. From 1988–1990 situations in Panama again gave rise to security procedures. The Twenty First Meeting of Ministers of Foreign Affairs held three sessions, to consider, respectively: (1) political violence in Panama and the role of General Manuel Noriega (the ministers created a commission to negotiate a "national accord" in Panama to facilitate a democratic transfer of political power); (2) the U.S. military invasion of Panama (a majority of twenty ministers voted to declare the United States to be in violation of international law and to condemn the invasion); and (3) the violation by U.S. troops of the Nicaraguan embassy in Panama City (a majority of nineteen ministers again condemned the United States for violating international law).

Further applications of mutual security procedures in the Caribbean were closely linked to U.S. efforts to make the IAS an "anti-Communist alliance" and its subsequent decline. One case involved Guatemala in 1954. The Cuban missile crisis in 1962, and problems related to the Cuban situation from 1962 to 1975, also involved applications of these procedures. Finally, consultation took place in 1979 in the midst of the Nicaraguan Revolution. In only two instances were cases outside the Circum-Caribbean undertaken. The Nineteenth Meeting of Ministers of Foreign Affairs was called under the OAS Charter at the request of Ecuador in January 1981 to consider armed conflict between Ecuador and Peru; the disputants consequently agreed to a cease-fire. The Twentieth Meeting of Ministers considered the Anglo-Argentine South Atlantic war in 1982 (see below).

The Anti-Communist Alliance. The evolution of an anti-Communist ideological orthodoxy began with the Tenth Inter-American Conference in Caracas (1954). The conference reflected the tension between the U.S. concern over Communist subversion and the Latin American desire for economic assistance. The United States prevailed in obtaining a declaration of inter-American commitment to collective intervention against international communism. This declaration was tacitly directed against Guatemala, which the United States presumed to be the victim of international communism, and foreshadowed the intervention in Guatemala later that year. After vigorous debate, a U.S.-sponsored resolution was adopted that said, in part:

> The domination or control of the political institution of any American State by the international communist movement extending to this Hemisphere the political system of an

extracontinental power, would constitute a threat to the sovereignty and political independence of the American states, endangering the peace of America, and would call for a Meeting of Consultation to consider the adoption of appropriate action in accordance with existing treaties.

In June 1954 ten member states, at the behest of the United States, asked for the convocation of the Organ of Consultation. They cited their concern with "the demonstrated intervention of the international communist movement in the republic of Guatemala and the danger which this involves for the peace and security of the Continent." The OAS Council met provisionally as the Organ of Consultation and called for a foreign ministers' meeting, but after the leftist Guatemalan government was replaced by a rightist military regime the meeting was canceled. The Guatemalan situation had been resolved not by the IAS but by the United States unilaterally and covertly supporting a coup d'etat.

Sanctions were applied against Cuba at the Eighth Meeting of Consultation of Ministers of Foreign Affairs in Punta del Este (January 1962). The convocation was requested by Colombia and strongly supported by the United States. A resolution entitled "Exclusion of the Present Government of Cuba from Participation in the Inter-American System" was adopted. It declared "that as a consequence of repeated acts, the present Government of Cuba had voluntarily placed itself outside the Inter-American System" and its adherence to Marxism-Leninism was incompatible with the principles and objectives of the IAS, an incompatibility that excluded the Cuban government from participation in the IAS.

The resolution instructed the OAS Council "and the other organs and organizations of the Inter-American System [to] adopt without delay the measures necessary to comply with the resolution." Additional limited economic sanctions were imposed by another resolution—specifically, "to suspend immediately trade with Cuba in arms and implements of war of every kind."

A few months later, during the Cuban missile crisis in October 1962, the OAS followed President Kennedy's "quarantine of Cuba" with a meeting of the OAS Council. A resolution insisted on "the immediate dismantling and withdrawal from Cuba of all missiles and other weapons with any offensive capability" and urged members to "take all measures, individually and collectively, including the use of armed force."

Multilateral sanctions against Cuba were expanded at the ninth foreign ministers' meeting in July 1964. This time Cuba was found guilty of aggression against Venezuela. A resolution increased the limited sanctions of 1962: all members were called upon to end their diplomatic and consular relations with Cuba; to suspend all trade except for food, medicine, and medical equipment; to suspend all sea transportation with Cuba except for that related to humanitarian purposes; and to warn Cuba that any continued acts of aggression could invite armed force against it. In 1967, Venezuela, strongly backed by the United States, charged Cuba with further aggression. The twelfth meeting of foreign ministers in that year condemned Cuba anew, but not as strongly as Venezuela and the United States had desired, and the resolutions in reality lacked force.

Eventually a clear sentiment in favor of reconsidering the Cuban case developed, leading in 1975 to a major modification in the sanctions. Despite the changing Latin American views, the United States resisted any relaxation of Cuban isolation and for a time persuaded Latin American states not to ease the sanctions. At the fifteenth meeting of foreign ministers in November 1974, twelve Latin American states voted to end the sanctions—a majority of those who had imposed them earlier but two votes short of the necessary two-thirds majority. However, at the sixteenth meeting in July 1975, the foreign ministers enacted a "Freedom of Action Resolution" that released states from their obligation to enforce the 1964 sanctions. Sixteen states voted in favor of the resolution, including the United States, three opposed it, and two abstained. The denial of Cuba participation in the IAS was not addressed and continued to stand.

The Anglo-Argentine War. Continuing Latin American dissatisfaction with the state of mutual security processes was further revealed during the Anglo-Argentine War. On April 2, 1982, Argentina invaded the United Kingdom's Falkland Islands Colony in the South Atlantic Ocean, asserting that it was enforcing its rightful sovereignty over the territory. The United Kingdom dispatched a naval force to the South Atlantic and appealed to the United Nations and the European Community for support. The Argentine invasion and British counterforce created a bizarre situation for the IAS. Argentina had, in the view of most American states, committed aggression against a non-American state, but British counterforce required them to take up the conflict at the behest of Argentina. The United States was in a particularly uncomfortable position, not wanting a situation that, in effect, pitted its own alliances in Europe and the Americas against each other.

At Argentina's request, a meeting of the PCOAS under provisions of the OAS Charter was held in Washington, D.C. from April 5 to 13, 1982. Argentina was disappointed with the restrained response when, with all twenty-nine participating members OAS voting, the council passed a "resolution of concern." Less than a week later, Argentina called for another inter-American meeting, this time invoking the Rio Treaty. The Twentieth Meeting of Consultation of Ministers of Foreign Affairs was called as the Organ of Consultation under the Rio Treaty procedures. Only the twenty-one signatories of the Rio Treaty were eligible to participate, thus excluding eight of the nine English-speaking Caribbean states, seven of whom were strongly pro-British. By now British forces had penetrated the hemispheric security zone as defined by the Rio Treaty. The foreign ministers adopted a resolution supporting Argentine claims to sovereignty over the Malvinas (the name used by Argentines) but refused to invoke sanctions against the United Kingdom as requested by Argentina.

The twentieth meeting was reconvened May 27–29. In the meantime, the United States had abandoned neutrality, sided with the United Kingdom, and strongly opposed Argentina. British forces had landed on the islands and were advancing. The final resolution condemned "most vigorously" the United Kingdom's "unjustified and disproportionate attack" against Argentina and called on the United States to stop assisting Britain and end its sanctions against Argentina. But the foreign ministers again refused Argentina's request for sanctions. Resolutions were passed by the same votes at both sessions of the twentieth meeting: seventeen in favor, none opposed, and four abstentions (Chile, Colombia, Trinidad-Tobago, and the United States). The majority felt compelled to demonstrate solidarity on the issue of sovereignty but had reservations about Argentina's use of force to assert its claims. The military campaign came to an end on June 14 with a British victory and inter-American mutual security procedures were no longer appealed to in this issue.

Peaceful Settlement

Concern for the peaceful settlement of disputes dates from the very beginning of the Inter-American System. An important proposal for compulsory arbitration of inter-American disputes was on the agenda at the Washington Conference in 1889. Because of Chilean objections—it was unwilling to jeopardize its recent territorial gains in the War of the Pacific—a compromise was adopted. Arbitration was accepted as a principle of American international law, obligatory except for those cases in which a state determined that its independence would be compromised. Eleven states signed the treaty; but fifteen ratifications were required to place it in force, and none were forthcoming. Despite the initial impasse, inter-American provisions for the peaceful settlement of disputes were subsequently established. Consequently, pacific settlement principles and procedures, some of them contradictory, are contained in several treaties, and the current regime presents an uncoordinated system.

Between 1902 and 1935, eleven conventions, treaties, and protocols were signed and subsequently went into force. Taken together, they comprised the pre–World War II inter-American pacific settlement regime. They are still in force for those states that have not ratified the American Treaty on Pacific Settlement of 1948 (see below).

A compulsory arbitration treaty was signed at the Mexico City Conference in 1902. However, so many reservations were entered that the original compulsory intent was badly eroded; only six states subsequently ratified the treaty. The Santiago Conference of 1923 established further peacekeeping procedures with the adoption of the Treaty to Avoid or Prevent Conflicts Between the American States. Sponsored by Dr. Manuel Gondra, then foreign minister of Paraguay, it is known as the Gondra Treaty. It was ratified by twenty member states. It provides that all disputes that threaten to lead to armed conflict and cannot be settled through direct diplomatic negotiation be submitted to one of two commissions of inquiry, one in Montevideo and the other in Washington, D.C. The signatories agree to make no preparations for war from the time the commission is convened until six months after its report is issued, up to a total time span of eighteen months. The Gondra Treaty is designed primarily to establish a "cooling off" period for inter-American disputes.

The special Washington Conference (1928–1929) added two more conventions and a protocol to the corpus of pacific settlement instruments. The General Treaty of Inter-American Arbitration, ratified by sixteen states, mandates that contracting parties submit to arbitration any international dispute arising from a claim of right that could be decided by an application of legal principles. The Protocol of Progressive Arbitration, a protocol to the General Treaty of Inter-American Arbitration, was ratified by ten states; it establishes a procedure by which the exceptions or reservations attached to the General Treaty may from time to time be abandoned, thus "progressively" extending the field of arbitration. The General Convention of Inter-American Conciliation, ratified by eighteen member states, was intended as a supplement to the Gondra Treaty. It adds conciliatory functions to the duties of the commissions of inquiry and provides for states to resort to the commissions on a voluntary basis. Four years later, the Montevideo Conference (1933) adopted the Additional Protocol to the General Convention of Inter-American Conciliation; it was ratified by twelve states.

The Montevideo Conference also agreed to the Anti-War Treaty of Non-Aggression and Conciliation, eventually adhered to by twenty member states; it was sponsored by Argentine Foreign Minister Carlos Saavedra Lamas (for which he received the Nobel Peace Prize). At the special Buenos Aires Conference in 1935, the signing of the Inter-American Treaty of Good Offices and Mediation, later ratified by fifteen states, completed the pre–World War II pacific settlement regime.

In 1936 the Special Buenos Aires Conference added four instruments, completing the pre–World War II pacific settlement regime. They were: the Convention for the Maintenance, Preservation and Reestablishment of Peace, ratified by 17 states; the Treaty on the Prevention of Controversies, ratified by fourteen states; the Inter-American Treaty on Good Offices and Mediation, ratified by fifteen states; and the Convention to Coordinate, Extend and Assure the Fulfillment of the Existing Treaties Between the American States, ratified by 14 states.

Those attending the Mexico City Conference (1945) perceived a need for a single treaty to coordinate the various measures providing for the peaceful settlement of disputes. It ordered a draft treaty that was presented at the Bogotá Conference (1948). The Inter-American Treaty of Pacific Settlement called for obligatory settlement by the signatories. It sanctioned all the standard peaceful techniques as satisfactory alternatives, including good offices, mediation, investigation, conciliation, and arbitration, both by regional bodies and before the World Court. The debate over the treaty's adoption reflected a long-standing division, with some states contending that all states should be obligated to submit all their disputes for some sort of third-party settlement, and others favoring the availability of voluntary standing settlement procedures. The treaty entered into effect only for those states ratifying it and superseded all prior agreements to which they were party. Thirteen states have ratified the pact: Brazil, Colombia, Costa Rica, the Dominican Republic, El Salvador, Haiti, Honduras, Mexico, Nicaragua, Panama, Paraguay, Peru, and Uruguay. Earlier instruments remain in force for the remaining states.

Democracy and Human Rights

Several early Latin American doctrines attempting to resolve the tension in Pan Americanism caused by the conflicting demands of democracy and nonintervention preceded the formalization of the two principles in treaties. Three major Latin American exponents of democracy and human rights were especially notable: the Chilean Pedro Felix Vicuña, the Argentine Juan Bautista Alberdi, and the Ecuadorian Carlos R. Tobar. (This section relies on Wilson, 1964:85–88, and Bemis, 1943:412, n.40.)

Vicuña was perhaps the earliest American advocate of collective action to promote democracy. His plan, set forth in a pamphlet published in 1837, called for a "Great American Congress" to support democratic governments and popular revolutions and to oppose tyrannies. The regional organization would intervene on the side of constitutional governments, thus combining physical power with moral force. In 1844, Alberdi, the principal architect of the Argentine Constitution of 1853, supported Vicuña's idea of an American Congress. He further proposed an American Court with the right to intervene against any state violating its decisions. This court would be supported by the Latin American states and certain European states, but not the United States. Alberdi believed in national sovereignty and nonintervention, but he argued that ultimate sovereignty and rights of collective intervention resided with the international community to protect humanity and oppose tyranny. In 1907, Tobar, a retired Ecuadoran diplomat, proposed a policy of collective nonrecognition of governments coming to power by other than democratic means. The Tobar Doctrine argued that the American republics "should intervene, at least mediately and indirectly, in the internal dissensions of the republics of the continent. This intervention might be, at least, by denying recognition to governments *de facto* born of revolutions against the constitutional order."

Other Latin American propositions were interventionist and thus challenged the above doctrines. Principal among them was the Estrada Doctrine, advanced by Mexican Foreign Minister Genaro Estrada in 1930, which challenged the Tobar Doctrine. Estrada asserted the principle of continuous diplomacy and said that new governments should be automatically recognized—an act, he said, that did not indicate approval of a regime but rather acknowledged its existence and its political control of a state.

A dilemma between democracy and nonintervention has long existed for the IAS. The American states have committed themselves to the promotion of representative democracy and the protection of human rights (that is, to democracy in both its procedural aspects and its substantive or ethical content) at the same time that they have posited nonintervention as a basic principle. Consequently, they have been faced with this question: How can representative democracy be promoted and human rights enforced, including opposition to nondemocratic regimes, without violating the principle of nonintervention? Most Latin American states have adopted a preferential position toward nonintervention. From time to time, others have taken a more complex view and have been willing to allow some sort of collective action in certain instances.

In late 1945 and early 1946 the American states considered a proposal by Uruguayan Foreign Minister Eduardo Rodríguez Larreta appealing for collective intervention to oppose dictators and promote democracy and human rights. Rodríguez's plan (often erroneously referred to in English as the "Larreta" doctrine) was implicitly directed against Argentina, small Uruguay's then Fascist-inclined and more powerful neighbor. However, it had broad implications for general inter-American relations. Rodríguez argued that peace was safe only where democratic principles of government prevailed and that the inter-American obligation to promote democracy and human rights should transcend the principle of nonintervention. He proposed that in the case of the violation of the basic rights of man in any American state, "the community of nations should take collective multilateral action to restore full democracy there" (U.S. Department of State, *Bulletin*, November 25, 1945:864–866).

The United States fully endorsed the plan, and it was supported with some reservations by six Latin American governments. The remainder of the Latin American states, however, rejected the proposal outright or made such serious qualifications as to be tantamount to rejection. The Latin American view prevailed that no modification of the nonintervention principle was permissible, despite the awareness that absolute nonintervention tended to insulate oppressive governments from community action.

Principles of democracy and human rights were strongly reaffirmed in both the Rio Treaty and the OAS Charter. The Rio Treaty preamble stated that "peace is founded ... on the effectiveness of democracy for the international realization of justice and security." The preamble of the OAS Charter declared: "The true significance of American solidarity and good neighborliness can only mean the consolidation on this continent, within the framework of democratic institutions of a system of individual liberty and social justice based on respect for the essential rights of man." Chapter II of the amended charter, devoted to "Principles," included the statements that "the solidarity of the American States and the high aims which are sought through it require the political organization of those states on the basis of the effective exercise of representative democracy," and that "social justice and social security are bases of lasting peace." The same document, however, also posited nonintervention as a fundamental principle. At the Bogotá Conference in 1948, the United States advocated a return to the principle of continuous diplomacy advocated in the Estrada Doctrine. A resolution was adopted declaring that "continuity of diplomatic relations among the American States is desirable," and that "the establishment or maintenance of diplomatic relations with a government does not imply any judgment upon the domestic policy of that government."

The OAS Charter provides for collective action under certain circumstances, offering a possible solution to the dilemma. Most of the Latin American states, however, have been unwilling to invoke it or to compromise the rule of nonintervention in any manner. For them, nonintervention transcends even democratic development. The majority view nonintervention as an absolute legal obligation and the commitment to democracy as a relative moral obligation. This Latin American consensus has been made clear in several debates and decisions.

Shortly after the Rodríguez plan was rejected, inter-American judicial procedures began to be applied to Caribbean conflicts. They largely resulted from ideological differences between closely proximate dictatorial and (more or less) democratic states. The problem for the IAS was that two fundamental principles—the doctrines of nonintervention and democratic development—had been pitted against one another. The principle of nonintervention received higher priority. The OAS Council, at its meeting on April 8, 1950, resolved the following:

> [Considering] that both the principle of representative democracy and that of nonintervention are established in many inter-American pronouncements, and that both are basic principles of harmonious relations among the countries of America; and that there exists some confusion of ideas as to the means of harmonizing the effective execution and application of the basic principle of nonintervention and that of the exercise of

democracy; [be it resolved] to reaffirm the principles of representative democracy [but] to declare that the aforementioned principles do not in any way and under any concept authorize any governments to violate inter-American commitments relative to the principles of nonintervention.

The IAS appeared in one case to serve as an "antidictatorial alliance," but this case, too, exhibited its commitment to the nonintervention principle (Slater, 1967:Ch. 6). The sixth foreign ministers' meeting in August 1960 condemned the Trujillo dictatorship in the Dominican Republic for its assassination attempt against Romulo Betancourt, the democratically elected president of Venezuela. The foreign ministers voted to impose sanctions on the Trujillo regime, including the breaking of diplomatic relations and imposing an arms embargo. The debate did not revolve around a preoccupation with nonintervention, and the Trujillo dictatorship was almost universally detested. However, the Dominican government itself had violated the nonintervention principle and was guilty of aggression as well as the violation of human rights. The reason for the sanctions was not primarily to promote democracy and human rights but rather to punish Trujillo for intervening in Venezuelan affairs. Since the end of the Trujillo regime in 1961, no other "antidictatorial alliances" were found until the Nicaraguan case in 1978–1979.

The OAS became involved in the Nicaraguan civil war, but the United States had only limited influence in the process. The Seventeenth Meeting of Consultation of Ministers of Foreign Affairs convened in Washington on September 21, 1978, in response to the request by Venezuela to consider the worsening conflict in Nicaragua. The Somoza government in Nicaragua favored the convocation so that it could "demonstrate to the world how foreign interventions are trying to implant Marxist-Leninist ideals" in Nicaragua. The Human Rights Commission visited Nicaragua, and its report in October 1978 was highly critical of human rights violations by the Somoza government. The OAS attempted to mediate the situation, but the Somoza government rejected as interventionist the plan that called for an OAS-supervised referendum and Somoza's resignation. Thereafter, the revolutionary National Liberation Sandinist Front (FSLN) gained strength against the Somoza regime, and border disputes between Costa Rica and Nicaragua increased in number. In mid-October, at their seventeenth meeting, the foreign ministers censured Nicaragua for its air attacks near the Costa Rican border in which weapons were used against Costa Rican civilians.

In June 1979 the seventeenth meeting again reconvened, at U.S. request, to consider the "critical situation" in Nicaragua. After referring to mounting evidence of involvement by Cuba in the internal affairs of Nicaragua, U.S. Secretary of State Cyrus Vance submitted a resolution calling for the establishment of a government of national reconciliation and providing for the presence of an inter-American force for the maintenance of peace in Nicaragua. The proposal was rejected; the idea of a peace force again raised fears of intervention. The final resolution, adopted on June 23, referred to the inhumane conduct of the Somoza regime and called for its immediate replacement by a pluralist representative government, for the guarantee of respect for human rights for all Nicaraguans, and for the holding of free elections as soon as possible. It also resolved that OAS member states scrupulously respect the principle of nonintervention. The resolution was unprecedented. For the first time the IAS had called for the replacement of a head of state. Somoza and other dissenting military governments argued that the resolution was interventionist, but to no avail.

The IAS also pursued certain human rights cases. Included in the provisions of the American Convention of Human Rights are the right to life, liberty, personal security, habeas corpus, due process, equality before the law, fair trials, freedom from arbitrary arrest, and freedom of speech, assembly, association, political participation, and religion. The Inter-American Commission on Human Rights was established in 1960 as an OAS advisory group. Its power was limited to moral suasion and it was required to work in concert with an accused government. Cuba refused to allow the commission to investigate its situation in the early 1960s, and later Guatemala was unwilling to receive it in an investigatory role. The commission then played an active role in the Dominican crisis of 1965–1966 under an expanded mandate from the inter-American conference at Rio de Janeiro in 1965. It followed with investigations in Honduras, El Salvador, and Haiti; its factual findings were accepted, but no further actions were taken. In 1970 the commission was made an official body of the OAS, empowered to "keep vigilance over the observance of human rights." Its membership is composed of seven jurists elected by the council to four-year terms.

The reluctance of OAS members in the 1970s and 1980s to apply multilateral sanctions in cases of human rights violations was reflected in a series of cases. In 1970, in response to complaints filed against Brazil, the Human Rights Commission was refused permission from the Brazilian government to conduct an on-the-scene investigation. It continued to investigate from outside the country for four years, however, and presented its report to the OAS General Assembly at its 1974 meeting in Atlanta. The detailed account, containing considerable evidence gathered despite Brazil's opposition, concluded with a presumption of grave human rights violations, including torture and murder of political prisoners. The General Assembly voted unanimously to take note of the report with thanks to the commission for its work, but not to discuss it, and to table the study and its unprecedented charges.

The Human Rights Commission received complaints against the military government in Chile after the Allende government was overthrown in September 1973. The commission made a two-week visit to Chile in July–August 1974. Its investigations resulted in a 175-page report that found "extremely serious violations," citing summary executions, torture, mass detention, and various deprivations of legal and political rights. Chile strongly objected to the charges. Two years later, in March 1976, three of the seven commission members—jurists from Uruguay, Argentina, and the United States—announced that they would not seek reelection, and in April the executive secretary from Bolivia, who had served for sixteen years, resigned the post. All of them cited the lack of OAS action on their report on Chile as a major reason for their resignation. They questioned whether OAS members sincerely desired to further the cause of human rights.

The OAS General Assembly meeting in Santiago in June 1976 further revealed serious divisions over these basic questions. Three agenda items concerned human rights: the Human Rights Commission's annual report, its special report on

Chile and the latter's reply, and a proposal by Chile to limit the commission's mandate. The Human Rights Commission's annual report found flagrant human rights violations by sixteen member states, including the United States, and documented large numbers of abuses. The chief target was Chile, the subject of a special report charging that most human rights abuses continued. Chile issued a denial. The General Assembly again voted to "take note" of the commission's findings and to continue monitoring human rights in the hemisphere with special attention to Chile. Chile and Brazil abstained in the voting; the United States strongly supported the commission and its charges against Chile.

At the General Assembly meeting in 1977, U.S. Secretary of State Cyrus Vance introduced a resolution stating, in part, that "there are no circumstances which justify torture, summary executions or prolonged detention without trial contrary to law." The resolution passed by a vote of 14–0, with 8 abstentions and 3 absences. At the General Assembly meeting in 1981, however, President Reagan's Secretary of State Alexander Haig emphasized the Communist threat in Central America and dismissed the human rights issues. The Human Rights Commission had submitted reports on violations in Argentina, Bolivia, El Salvador, Guatemala, and Nicaragua. The assembly simply acknowledged their receipt.

In 1991, when almost all Latin American states had constitutional governments, the OAS strengthened the proposition that it should take direct action to defend representative democracy and human rights against internal infringements. As indicated above, in 1979 the OAS had established a new precedent when it called for the replacement of the ruling Somoza regime. At its annual meeting in June 1991, the OAS General Assembly mandated such actions when it adopted the Declaration of Santiago. The declaration instructed the Secretary General to call an immediate meeting of the OAS Permanent Council following any "sudden or irregular interruption" of democratic government in any of the member states, which in turn would "examine the situation, decide on and convene (within ten days) an ad hoc meeting of the Ministers of Foreign Affairs or a special session of the General Assembly. The purpose of the foreign ministers meeting or of the General Assembly "shall be to look into the events collectively and adopt any decisions deemed appropriate, in accordance with the Charter and international law." The declaration had earlier reiterated that one of the basic OAS purposes "is to promote and consolidate democracy with due respect for the principle of nonintervention." A year later the General Assembly created the OAS Unit for Democracy as a supporting agency. OAS members acted in the framework of the Declaration of Santiago when constitutional rule was abrogated in Haiti in September 1991 and in Peru in April 1992, directing multilateral responses in both cases without the approval of the respective governments in power. The sanctions that may be applied have not been specified; most member states continue to refuse even to contemplate coercive multilateral military sanctions.

Economic Cooperation

During the initial stages of the Inter-American System in the late nineteenth century, the United States was primarily interested in expanding its commercial relations, whereas Latin Americans were attracted for political and legal reasons, especially the need for security from outside incursions and promotion of the non-intervention principle. The U.S. proposal at the Washington Conference in 1889–1890 for an American customs union received almost no Latin American support. During the period of U.S. interventionism during the first third of the twentieth century, Latin Americans were suspicious of U.S. economic overtures and remained more interested in political and security issues rather than economic matters.

Important developments in inter-American economic cooperation occurred during the period surrounding World War II. The First Meeting of Consultation of Ministers of Foreign Affairs (1939) created the Inter-American Financial and Advisory Committee (FEAC), consisting of an economic expert from each member state, to anticipate economic problems consequent to war. The Second Meeting of Consultation in 1940 expanded FEAC's functions and endorsed a number of its projects. These included programs for marketing surplus products, concluding of commodity agreements, and establishing the Inter-American Development Commission (in June 1940) to aid in Latin American economic diversification. The Third Meeting of Consultation, held in 1942 soon after the Japanese attack on Pearl Harbor, gave FEAC the additional tasks of developing programs for the production of strategic materials, obtaining capital investments, improving transportation facilities, and breaking economic relations with Axis states. FEAC was one of the most active wartime inter-American agencies (Mecham, 1965:133–135, 142–145, 150).

During the initial post–World War II years, the United States was primarily interested in persuading the IAS to organize itself against communism in the Americas, whereas the Latin Americans emphasized multilateral technical assistance and economic development programs. Concomitant to the establishment of U.S. technical assistance programs on a worldwide scale after 1949, the OAS conducted relatively small but effective programs. The United States clearly was unwilling to establish large multilateral economic development programs.

When Latin American pressure mounted in the late 1950s, U.S. positions began to change. In September 1958 President Juscelino Kubitschek of Brazil proposed an "Operation Pan America" to an informal meeting of American foreign ministers in Washington. This economic development program was designed primarily to raise Latin American social and economic living standards. The foreign ministers recommended two important measures: (1) establishment of an inter-American financial institution for economic development; and (2) creation of a committee to recommend additional measures for economic cooperation.

Action soon followed. The Inter-American Development Bank was established on December 31, 1959. In 1960 the United States formally proposed an economic development program to be administered by the IDB; this Eisenhower Plan received inter-American support in the Act of Bogotá of 1960. The Alliance for Progress, articulated by President Kennedy in 1961, was multilateralized by the Charter of Punta del Este, enacted on August 17, 1961. The charter listed twelve goals toward which the American states agreed to work during the decade of the 1960s. In sum, they committed themselves to policies that would achieve substantial and sustained growth, more equitable distribution of income, economic diversification and industrialization, increased agricultural productivity, agrarian reform, educational advances, improved public health, increased availability of low-cost housing and public services, stable price levels, strengthened international economic integration, and stabilized earnings from primary product exports.

The IDB was the world's first regional multilateral bank, a lending agency designed to promote the economic and social development of its Latin American members. The first president was the eminent Chilean economist Felipe Herrera. He served two five-year terms, from the bank's inception until October 1970. Herrera was succeeded by Antonio Ortiz Mena in November 1970. Ortiz Mena, a former Mexican finance minister, was IDB president for seventeen years; he resigned in February 1988 during his fourth term. Uruguayan Foreign Minister Enrique Iglesias assumed the IDB presidency in April 1988. A prestigious economist and diplomat, he had been executive secretary of the UN Economic Commission on Latin America (ECLA) for thirteen years (1972–1985) prior to being named foreign minister.

IDB operations have been financed largely by member contributions as well as by special funds donated by individual states and the sale of bank bonds. When the bank was first organized an ordinary capital account was established for "hard loans" of an orthodox nature, and the Social Progress Trust Fund was created to finance social development projects with longer terms and lower interest rates than the ordinary loans. By 1965 the trust fund had been almost entirely disbursed; its remaining resources were transferred to the new and further capitalized Fund for Special Operations (FSO) to continue "soft loans." Total IDB capital resources had risen from $1.4 billion in 1960, to $11.5 billion in 1975, and to $44 billion in 1988.

The United States has been the largest subscriber to the IDB from the beginning. It reduced its support in the early 1970s, leading the bank to search for additional capital resources from other states. Canada, new Caribbean states, and then nonhemispheric state members pledged additional capital shares. Expanded membership broadened the IDB's financial base, with Latin Americans hoping that it would erode U.S. domination.

The issue of U.S. predominance in IDB lending decisions—voting power is weighted according to the relative size of a member's contribution in proportion to the total—has been debated throughout the life of the bank. The Board of Directors approves loans from the ordinary capital account by simple majority. FSO loans, however, require a two-thirds majority. Until 1976 the United States had about 40 percent of the FSO weighted voting; with new member contributions after that date, the U.S. voting proportion dropped to 34.5 percent in 1988. Latin American members then collectively controlled 54 percent, and the remaining nineteen members 11.5 percent.

From its inception, both advocates and critics of the bank's operations have viewed the institution as a "borrowers' bank," as voting power was as much in the hands of loan recipients as in those of the principal contributors. The United States argued that it should have an even greater share of the weighted voting. The U.S. Treasury, the primary voice in U.S. international financial matters, from the late 1960s resisted the vision of development elaborated by Felipe Herrera. For example, the IDB was a pioneer in agrarian reform lending, a practice the

United States considered outside the realm of sound development standards. The United States also expressed displeasure from time to time (especially during the Reagan administration) at the lack of a free-enterprise approach in Latin America and at the notion of the state as the primary force for development. In 1985 the United States clashed with the bank over expansion of its capital resources. The Reagan administration formally proposed to make an additional $9 billion contribution over four years contingent on an increased share of the weighted voting, an offer the Board of Directors rejected.

Latin Americans fear that ceding more control to the United States would allow it to impose its preferred development model on the entire region. U.S. standards, they said, did not apply to their developmental needs. Although Latin Americans were willing to accept the U.S. approach to the debt crisis after 1982, they resisted its ideas about economic development in the private sector. Latin Americans further claimed that at times the United States had, in effect, a veto power. They pointed out that the United States had blocked new developmental assistance to Peru in the late 1960s, Chile in the early 1970s, and Nicaragua in the 1980s when it was having bilateral political conflicts with those states. Moreover, they argued that development loan decisions must be restricted to economic criteria and must not be based on political and ideological debates.

The IDB has taken on a role in the investment element of an evolving hemispheric free-trade system, as envisioned in Enterprise for the Americas Initiative (EAI) articulated by President George Bush in June 1990. The EAI called for a special Multilateral Investment Fund (MIF), to be administered by the IDB and aimed at the promotion of regional private investment. The fund was established on February 11, 1992 with an initial capital of about $1.3 billion. The United States and Japan pledged $500 million each, and other members—Canada, France, Portugal, and Spain—combined for $257 million. The fund is designed to provide financial support and technical help to privatization initiatives. In addition, within the OAS, the Special Negotiating and Consulting Commission (CECON), a subordinate body of the Inter-American Economic and Social Council, undertook consideration of the role of the IAS in any hemispheric free-trade system. It sponsored studies and conferences, organized a meeting of ministers of foreign trade, and in general provided the principal OAS forum for informal multilateral discussions of the possibilities. A modicum of hemispheric administration of the EAI has been elaborated in the IDB, and some other inter-American agencies have displayed concern over some of its components. Thus the question remains of where the OAS and IDB will fit into the future administration of a hemispheric free-trade system. One possible institutional outcome is a hemispheric system regulated and maintained by an inter-American agency or agencies. That eventuality, even if realized, is a long way away.

BIBLIOGRAPHIC COMMENT

Some dated but still useful general studies of the IAS are by Connell-Smith (1966), Fenwick (1963), Fernández-Shaw (1963), Mecham (1961), Sepúlveda (1973), and Thomas and Thomas (1963); Stoetzer (1993) provides a comprehensive up-to-date treatment of the OAS; Martz and Schoultz (1980) edit a set of analytic essays; Scheman (1988) assesses the IAS and proposals for its reform; and Bryan (1986) discusses Commonwealth Caribbean perspectives of the OAS. Among the documentary collections and legal studies are Carnegie Endowment for International Peace (1931, 1940, 1943), Inter-American Institute for International Legal Studies (1966), and U.S. Senate, Committee on Foreign Relations and U.S. House of Representatives, Committee on Foreign Affairs (1988). Latin American views and other analyses of inter-American law are presented by Alvarez (1922), Caicedo Castilla (1970), Jacobini (1954), Rodley and Ronning (1974), Sepúlveda (1975), and Taylor (1963). On Pan American principles and practices, see Díaz Albonico (1977) on a wide range of activities; Wilson (1986) on Central American conflict in terms of nonintervention; Child (1980) on the inter-American military system and Gómez Robledo (1959) on general security arrangements; Corominas (1954), Jameson (1950), and U.S. Department of State (1962) on Caribbean conflict; Buergenthal, Norris, and Shelton (1983), Sandifer and Scheman (1966), and Wilson (1964) on democracy and human; Inter-American Development Bank (1966, 1974, 1985), Dell (1972), Herrera (1970), and Tussie (1994) on economic relations and the IDB.

CHAPTER NINE

—■—

Global, Extraregional, and Other Hemispheric Arrangements

THIS CHAPTER DEALS WITH the many international institutions beyond the Latin American region and the Inter-American System that are important to Latin America's international relations. With slight exception they are twentieth-century creations. They include the Hague Peace Conferences, the League of Nations, and the United Nations System; arms control agreements, the Antarctic Treaty, and law of the sea; the Nonaligned Movement, the New International Economic Order, and certain commodities agreements; and regimes in the Western Hemisphere involving the Panama Canal, the U.S.-Mexican border, and United States–centered free-trade agreements.

GLOBAL ORGANIZATIONS

The Hague System

Two great currents of international politics, arbitration and disarmament, played conspicuous roles in the international system at the beginning of the twentieth century. The first attempts to devise multilateral approaches to the problems of war and peace took place at two peace conferences at The Hague in 1899 and 1907. The Permanent Court of Arbitration (the Hague Court) was established in 1899 and revised in 1907, and declarations in both years placed limited prohibition on certain instruments of war. Plans for holding a third conference were dropped because of the increasing conflicts among nations immediately preceding World War I.

Planners of the First Peace Conference at The Hague (1899) largely ignored the Latin American states. Only Brazil and Mexico were invited, and only the latter attended. However, all twenty Latin American states were invited to the Second Peace Conference (1907) at the behest of the United States. Eighteen of them participated, with only Costa Rica and Honduras passing up the forty-four-state gathering. Prestigious Latin American representatives played active roles at the conference, especially Ruy Barbosa of Brazil, Luis M. Drago of Argentina, and Santiago Pérez Triana of Colombia. U.S. Professor Leo S. Rowe, later director general of the Pan American Union, said at the 1907 meeting of the American Political Science Association that Latin American participation "was but the formal recognition of an accomplished fact—the establishment of a group of sovereign and independent states in the southern hemisphere, whose political importance can no longer be ignored." In fact, their participation brought the Latin American region into international prominence for the first time.

Once they were offered the Hague Conference as a forum, the Latin American states mounted a concerted effort to have nonintervention accepted as a principle of international law. This effort paralleled their attempts to do the same in inter-American law. A resolution had been approved at the International Conference of American States at Rio de Janeiro in 1906 recommending that the forthcoming Hague Peace Conference discuss the Drago Doctrine regarding the legal prohibition of force for the collection of public pecuniary claims. With U.S. support, the Latin American delegates succeeded in having a version of the Drago Doctrine adopted as a principle of general international law, but they were greatly disappointed over the extent to which it was modified. The conference adopted the Porter Doctrine (submitted by U.S. delegate General Horace Porter), which prohibited the use of force in the collection of public debts unless the debtor state refused to submit the claim to arbitration or, having gone to arbitration, failed to comply with the decision. The Drago Doctrine itself tolerated no intervention whatsoever. No South American government ratified the convention, and the four Latin American states that did made reservations restoring the treaty to absolute nonintervention (Wilson, 1964:36–38 and Mecham, 1965:99). Despite their failure to have their version of the law adopted, Latin Americans had made it clear that another community existed championing international legal rules differing profoundly from those generally accepted in Europe and the United States.

Because of the relative military insignificance of Latin American armed forces in 1907, they received little consideration in disarmament questions. Yet one South American arrangement was of some importance. During discussions on the limitation of armed forces, the arms control agreements between Argentina and Chile (the "Pacts of May" of 1902) were given serious consideration by the European representatives, who viewed the agreements, providing for the arbitration of all differences between the two states and the limitation of their naval forces, as among the most modern of arms control arrangements.

The League of Nations

The Latin American states that had declared war on or severed relations with Germany during World War I participated in the subsequent Versailles Peace Conference. They strongly supported President Woodrow Wilson's project for a League of Nations. Ten of them signed the Versailles Treaty, which included the Covenant of the League of Nations, and thereby became charter members of the organization. Eventually, all twenty Latin American states joined the League for at least a limited time. Latin American participation in the League was intermittent, however, and never were all of them members at the same time. Fifteen Latin American states were members when the first League Assembly met in 1920. By 1923 all of them except the Dominican Republic, Ecuador, and Mexico were members. In 1934 only Brazil and Costa Rica, both of which had withdrawn in 1926, did not belong.

A regional consciousness was reflected both in Latin American behavior in the League and in the attitudes of the other members toward Latin America. An informal Latin American bloc was formed, primarily in order to assure the election of Latin American representatives to the Assembly and the Council and to obtain positions for their nationals in the Secretariat. Other states, anxious to keep Latin Americans as members in pursuit of the ideal of universality, established a special Liaison Bureau for the region and dispatched the Secretariat on a visit to Latin America (Bailey, 1967:146 and Rippy, 1958:519).

Latin American delegates in Geneva used every opportunity to lecture about their contributions to world peace. They also expressed basic principles that anticipated their later actions under the UN System. For example, in 1927 Chile proposed a system of regional Latin American agreements designed to prevent any competitive armaments. Security requirements in the region, the delegates said, were unique and European standards therefore should not apply. Furthermore, security should be achieved by means of a system of arbitration and conciliation. Indeed, most Latin American states opposed arms control through global arrangements, emphasizing that the region was appreciably different from the rest of the world. In 1928 Argentina declared arbitration to be "an essentially American principle" and a sufficient guarantee of security.

The Latin American states were attracted to the League for several reasons, including the prestige that membership might bring, the League's adherence to such principles as arbitration and judicial settlement, and its potential as a counterpoise to U.S. intervention. The League offered little opportunity for Latin America to press for economic advantages in the way of aid or trade preferences, as such activities were of peripheral importance to the organization. The Latin American states succeeded in accumulating a certain amount of prestige from their League activities and participation; they gained nonpermanent seats on the League Council and representation on the World Court and elected presidents of the Assembly. On the other hand, the League paid little attention to Latin American disputes and played almost no role in limiting U.S. power in Latin America.

The first major disappointment for Latin Americans occurred at the Versailles Conference when the League Covenant was adopted. Article X of the Covenant seemed to fulfill the Latin American desire for an international law of nonintervention. It read: "The Members of the League undertake to respect and preserve as against external aggression the territorial integrity and existing political independence of all Members of the League." However, Article XXI, included despite Latin American protests that it contradicted Article X, stated: "Nothing in this Covenant shall be deemed to affect the validity of international engagements, such as treaties of arbitration or regional understandings like the Monroe Doctrine, for securing the maintenance of peace." Article XXI was designed to make the Covenant more acceptable to the U.S. Senate; it prompted two Latin American delegations to withdraw from the conference. The Covenant made no other mention of regional arrangements.

Later events further eroded the League's utility as a counterweight to U.S. power in Latin America. The United States refused to join the League, freeing it from the limitations that could have been imposed by membership. Furthermore, the League largely refrained from dealing with inter-American problems. It ignored the Tacna-Arica dispute involving Chile versus Peru and Bolivia, as well as a dispute between Panama and Costa Rica, largely because of U.S. protests in both instances. The League attempted to settle two inter-American disputes—the Chaco War between Bolivia and Paraguay, and the Leticia conflict between Peru and Colombia—but both times it deferred to U.S. actions.

Intermittent clashes in the Chaco area between Bolivia and Paraguay beginning in 1927 led to full-scale war between them from 1932 to 1936. In September 1932, two months after the war broke out, the League Council established a commission to offer alternative plans to settle the war, but none was accepted. An inter-American committee, established at about the same time for the same purpose, deferred to the League Commission in 1933, but the effort still failed. In 1935 the League labeled Paraguay as the aggressor, making it the first state to be the object of League sanctions. Paraguay promptly withdrew from the League. In 1936, with the disputants exhausted by the bloody conflict and prepared to accept third-party assistance in its settlement, another inter-American commission was organized, in which the United States played an important role. The Inter-American System, not the League of Nations, finally arranged a settlement that Paraguay and Bolivia both accepted in 1938.

On the surface the League action in the Leticia affair might appear to have been successful, but in fact the United States played the leading role in its settlement. In 1933 Colombia appealed to the League Council to settle its decade-old argument with Peru over the ownership of the small Amazon River town of Leticia and the surrounding area. The international body established a special Administrative Commission for the Territory of Leticia, consisting of representatives from Spain, Brazil, and the United States. The commission administered the Leticia area for about a year in 1933–1934—the first police action in the history of general international organization—while mediation between the disputants was carried on. In 1934 sovereignty was awarded to Colombia. Neither the United States nor Brazil was a member of the League at the time. Brazil was closely aligned with the United States, and Spain was unassertive in the matter. Consequently, the United States controlled the commission of an international body to which it did not belong. Furthermore, the League was ignored in the protocol terminating the conflict, in which Colombia and Peru referred to their "historical, social, and sentimental ties" as members of the "American community" (Bailey, 1967:147–148).

The United Nations System

Latin American Participation. Regional participation in the United Nations has been universal and continuous, in contrast to the intermittent nature of Latin American membership in the League of Nations. Consequently, the Latin American states have always formed a significant proportion of the UN membership, although their relative voting strength declined as UN membership increased. The number of Latin American members remained constant at twenty from 1945, when the first General Assembly convened, until 1962. At that time, new states within the Latin American region began to join the UN and regional membership eventually grew in number to thirty-three. At the same time, total UN membership increased from fifty-one original members in 1945 to 162 as of 1987 (after which applications for membership increased as a result of post–cold war developments, with 181 members as of March 1994), reducing the Latin American proportion from about 39 percent to about 20 percent. Prior to 1955, reaching a decision in the General Assembly over united Latin American opposition was a difficult proposition. The reduction in relative Latin American strength after the mid-1950s was offset somewhat by a degree of voting solidarity among the regional states. Their influence has been greatest on "substantive" questions in the General Assembly requiring a two-thirds majority for adoption.

The relatively high degree of consistency with which the Latin American states have voted together in the world body indicates a measure of regional cohesion, although they have not voted en bloc. Prior to 1960 the regional states generally supported the United States on cold war issues, but their twenty votes were never automatically assured. On "anticolonial" (dependent area) questions, they tended to favor increased colonial self-government and independence, including UN supervision of the independence process. Latin American states joined the other developing country members in calling for maximum funding of technical assistance and economic development projects. They successfully urged the creation of an Economic Commission for Latin America within the Economic and Social Council.

Latin Americans were less amenable to U.S. leadership in the 1960s and began to divide on cold war issues. Cuba joined the Soviet bloc after 1960; others increasingly adopted independent stances. They also began to divide on colonial issues, although they were virtually unanimous in condemning racism in South Africa. Most Latin American members continued to vote consistently to extend economic and technical programs and voted with considerable unity on humanitarian and social cooperation and administrative matters. They also tended to vote as a bloc in UN elections.

Latin America's regional self-perception has been enhanced by their membership in the UN System. They formed a bloc at the San Francisco Conference in 1945. Thereafter, they met as a regional caucusing group during annual General Assembly meetings so as to ensure that Latin American interests were represented and maximum voting strength assured. The caucuses were informal in nature until the Ninth General Assembly convened in 1953 when the procedures were formalized. Thereafter, the self-named Latin American Caucusing Group held regular biweekly meetings chaired by the Latin American delegate who had been elected a vice-president of the General Assembly. When the OAS in 1964 imposed sanctions on Cuba isolating it diplomatically, the Latin American Caucusing Group reverted to informal meetings to which Cuba was not invited (with one exception in March 1973). Cuba was finally readmitted on January 29, 1975, when the caucus chairman convened a formal meeting with Cuba attending and no other Latin American state objected. The formal Latin American Caucusing Group was reinstituted with all regional states participating.

The Latin American caucus is the longest-standing regional grouping in the UN. Although its decisions are not binding on members, it has succeeded in defining regional positions on issues before the UN, gained general agreement on tactics to be pursued, and negotiated the election of Latin Americans to fill offices in various UN bodies.

UN Relationship to the Inter-American System. Some early proponents and founders of the global UN organization argued that the global institution was incompatible with regional organizations. More of them, including U.S. Secretary of State Cordell Hull, accepted the existence of regional organizations but insisted that they be superseded by the UN in authority. Enough pressure was brought to bear at the organizing conference at San Francisco in 1945, particularly by the Latin American states acting as a bloc, to have the UN Charter sanction regional organization. The effort was led by Alberto Lleras Camargo of Colombia (who became secretary general of the Pan American Union in 1946). The charter subjects regional arrangements to considerable direction by the UN, but in practice, the Inter-American System enjoyed significant autonomy until it began to erode in the early 1970s.

Article 51 of the UN Charter recognized regional arrangements as being compatible with global organization and especially appropriate to the settlement of regional disputes. The provision gave the Security Council the right to intervene in those settlements and allowed individual states the right to appeal directly to the global body. In practice, however, the UN deferred to the Inter-American System. Although some regional disputes were taken directly to the UN, and some OAS decisions were appealed there, the Inter-American System for the most part was the only forum for issues relating to American peace and security, with little UN action forthcoming.

A few examples suffice to illustrate the UN relationship with the Inter-American System. In June 1954 Guatemala appealed to the Security Council in accusing Honduras and Nicaragua of aggression. (Guatemala was not then a party to the Rio Treaty or the OAS Charter.) The Latin American members of the Security Council, supported by the United States, wanted to refer the matter to the OAS, but a resolution to that effect was vetoed by the Soviet Union. A French resolution calling for a cease-fire was then adopted. The Security Council considered a subsequent Guatemalan request for another review of the issue but then declined to place the issue on its agenda.

The OAS decision to apply sanctions against the Trujillo regime in the Dominican Republic for its assassination attempt against the president of Venezuela was appealed to the UN in 1960. The Soviet Union initiated a move in the Security Council to authorize the sanctions under Article 53 of the UN Charter, appearing to support U.S. policy. In fact, adoption of the resolution would have established the Security Council's authority over regional enforcement actions, providing a future opportunity for the Soviet Union to cast a veto in the eventuality of regional sanctions against Cuba. The Soviet proposal was voted down.

After the Bay of Pigs invasion in 1961, Cuba charged the United States and certain other Caribbean states with aggression and appealed to the Security Council for support. The council took no action. In settling the Cuban missile crisis in 1962, the United States and the Soviet Union agreed to have UN observers in Cuba monitor the removal of Soviet missiles, but Castro refused to receive a UN team and it was never sent. In 1967, at the Twelfth Meeting of Consultation of Ministers of Foreign Affairs of the OAS, the ministers expanded OAS sanctions against Cuba and reemphasized the practice of only reporting regional actions to the UN rather than gaining UN approval. They recommended that acts by Cuba that violated UN resolutions condemning armed intervention and subversion be brought to the attention of the UN by each OAS state. Also in 1967 the OAS established a permanent observer at the UN to act as liaison between the two organizations. In 1973 the attention of the Security Council was directed to disputes between the United States and Panama and between Britain and Guatemala over Belize. No actions were taken.

Direct UN activities in hemispheric conflict occurred during the Anglo-Argentine War of 1982 and in the Central American conflict. The Security Council, secretary general, and General Assembly were all involved in the South Atlantic conflict. On April 3, the day after Argentina invaded and took control of the British Falkland Islands Colony, the Security Council adopted Resolution 502, which demanded an immediate cessation of hostilities and withdrawal of Argentine forces and called on both governments to seek a diplomatic solution. The resolution became the foundation for British diplomacy throughout most of the crisis and the point of departure for other third-party efforts.

UN Secretary General Javier Pérez de Cuellar, a Peruvian diplomat who had assumed his position less than four months before the Argentine invasion, at first deferred to U.S. diplomacy; but after its failure the mediation efforts shifted to the secretary general. The disputants could not agree on the critical issue of sovereignty and the mediation effort collapsed.

The military campaign came to an end on June 14 when Argentine units in the islands surrendered to British forces. In the aftermath of the crisis, nineteen other Latin American states joined Argentina in introducing a resolution in the General Assembly calling for British-Argentine negotiations. The resolution was passed on November 4 by a vote of 90–12, with 52 abstentions. Ironically, the resolution was based on Security Council Resolution 502 of April 3, which had chastised Argentina and served British diplomacy. The United States voted for the resolution in a conciliatory gesture toward both Argentina and the rest of Latin America. British Prime Minister Margaret Thatcher referred to the nonbinding nature of the resolution and said that the United Kingdom was confident of its title to sovereignty and had no intention of negotiating with Argentina.

In another case before the UN, Nicaragua appealed in 1984 concerning its conflict with the United States. In March the United States had mined Nicaraguan ports as part of a series of actions against the revolutionary government in Managua. On March 29 Nicaragua asked the UN Security Council to consider this "escalation of acts of aggression." In the subsequent debate, all fourteen members of the Security Council other than the United States condemned the mining. On April 4 a resolution was proposed condemning the mining as a violation of international law, affirming the right of free navigation, and supporting the work of the Contadora Group. Thirteen votes were in favor, one member abstained, and the United States cast a veto.

The issue then went to the International Court of Justice (ICJ). Nicaragua instituted proceedings on April 9, 1984, charging the United States with using military force in violation of international law. Three days before, the United States had informed the UN secretary general that it was temporarily modifying its acceptance of compulsory jurisdiction by ruling out cases involving Central America for the next two years. After the Nicaraguan application, the United States argued that the ICJ did not have jurisdiction in the case. The court asserted its competence in the case, rejected the U.S. request that it not be heard, issued an injunction against further U.S. action against Nicaraguan ports, and called on the United States not to violate Nicaraguan sovereignty with other illegal military or paramilitary activities. The vote was 14–1, with only the U.S. judge dissenting.

The case then went to trial in November 1984. The court first addressed was the matter of ICJ jurisdiction and ruled 15–1, with the U.S. judge again dissenting, that it had authority to hear the case. The majority argued that Article 36 of the court's statute would be meaningless if compulsory jurisdiction could simply be rejected when disputes actually arose. The United States continued to maintain that the court had no jurisdiction and announced that it would participate no further. Nicaragua insisted that the case proceed and the court agreed.

The United States, on October 7, 1985, terminated its general acceptance of the ICJ's compulsory jurisdiction. It argued that whereas the United States had agreed to limited jurisdiction over particular cases, Nicaragua had never validly accepted the court's compulsory jurisdiction and therefore had no right to sue. In addition, Nicaragua's claims concerned collective security and self-defense matters that the UN Charter assigned to political bodies for resolution. The United States also argued that Nicaragua's evidence in the case was faulty. Nicaragua alleged that U.S. support for the Nicaraguan resistance was illegal because Nicaragua had not intervened against its neighbors. The United States argued, however, that Nicaragua's deep involvement in support of the Salvadoran insurgency gave the United States the right to act against Nicaragua as a matter of collective self-defense. On January 18, 1985, the United States withdrew from further participation in the case.

The ICJ handed down its decision on June 27, 1986, ruling on sixteen separate counts. The court rejected U.S. justifications of collective self-security for its interventions, held that the United States had violated international law in mining Nicaraguan harbors, and ruled that it should make reparations. The key issues were decided by votes of 12–3; the dissenting judges were from the United States, Japan, and the United Kingdom. However, the court unexpectedly rejected Nicaragua's argument that actions taken by the U.S.-supported contra guerrillas could be imputed to the United States. The majority acknowledged U.S. collaboration but saw insufficient evidence that the United States exercised such control that the contras were operating on its behalf. On July 31 the Security Council took up a Nicaraguan resolution calling for full compliance with the ICJ decision and cessation of support for the contras, which the United States vetoed. Neither the court nor the council had the capacity to enforce U.S. compliance.

Central American conflict in the 1980s and the lack of authoritative action by the Inter-American System led to the first direct UN involvement in western hemispheric conflict resolution. Specifically, the UN became closely involved in the 1987 Central American agreement (Esquipulus II) that detailed a comprehensive subregional peace plan. UN Secretary-General Pérez de Cuéllar was an active participant in the negotiations that in 1989 resulted in the Security Council's approval to organize the UN Observer Group in Central America

(ONUCA). ONUCA engaged in extensive peacekeeping and election monitoring operations in Central America (see Chapter 11).

This important new UN role in the Americas was part of the organization's post–cold war revitalization. It was generally well received in Central America and by other Latin Americans and opened the possibility of greater UN involvement in hemispheric conflict resolution, which until recently had been the de facto domain of the Inter-American System (Child, 1992).

Developmental Organizations. With the establishment of the United Nations System, Latin American states immediately turned to various UN agencies as alternatives both to bilateral U.S. assistance and, increasingly, to OAS agencies, which they viewed as dominated by the United States. Their first major accomplishment was the creation in 1948 of the Economic Commission for Latin America (ECLA; Comisión Economica para América Latina—CEPAL) as a subagency of the UN Economic and Social Council (ECOSOC) and headquartered in Santiago, Chile. In 1984 it was retitled the Economic Commission for Latin America and the Caribbean—ECLAC—to recognize the involvement of the newly independent Caribbean entities. Its general purpose was to formulate Latin American economic theory concerning development, trade, and regional integration and to coordinate policies designed to promote these enterprises. In 1962 ECLAC founded the Latin American Institute for Economic and Social Planning (ILPES), also located in Santiago, to provide training, information, and advice to regional developmental agencies.

ECLA membership was opened to UN members in the Americas and to states that had dependencies in the area. ECLAC has forty full members: the thirty-three Latin American states, Canada, United States, France, Netherlands, and United Kingdom, plus Portugal and Spain who were also invited to adhere. In addition, four entities were admitted as "associate members": Monserrat, British Virgin Islands, U.S. Virgin Islands, and Netherlands Antilles. ECLAC usually meets every two years, its sessions also attended by representatives of the UN and certain of its specialized agencies and of other IGOs as well as NGOs. Between 1948 and 1994, ECLAC held twenty-five regular sessions.

ECLAC's executive secretaries, all well-known Latin American economists, have combined political economic theory with diplomatic activism. The post was first filled by the Argentine Raúl Prebisch (1948–1963). He was succeeded by the Mexican Víctor Urquidi (1963–1972). The position was held by the Uruguayan Enrique Iglesias (1972–1985), who was followed by Gert Rosenthal. Their personal influence on institutional activities has been significant.

ECLA initially served as a major advocate of unorthodox development theory and policy. Acting as a promoter and political pressure group, ECLA influenced Latin American economists and government officials to a considerable but then declining degree. Prebisch, once the director of the Central Bank of Argentina, was Latin America's best-known economist and, in time, a leading voice for the world's developing nations. ECLA became a proving ground and proponent for his structuralist theory (see Chapter 13), which basically said that underdevelopment is caused by a combination of domestic and international economic structural realities. He elaborated his thesis into a comprehensive Latin American economic development theory and then extended it to the entire developing world. Prebisch left ECLA in 1963, but his influence continued as he became head of the United Nations Conference on Trade and Development, where he remained until 1968.

Víctor Urquidi followed the structuralist approach as successor to Prebisch at ECLA, but he also placed his own philosophy on ECLA activities. An economist of international repute, his writings and speeches revealed an optimistic view of Latin American development and a perception of Latin America as a unique, regional whole. He appealed to Latin Americans to think of themselves as part of "*a* Latin America and *a* Latin American economy," where he found more positive than negative factors.

Enrique Iglesias was also one of Latin America's leading economists and diplomats. He headed ECLAC for thirteen years and incrementally shifted his own thinking and the organization's approach. He moved the institutional position from one that vigorously promoted state intervention for economic development and import-substitution industrialization to a reliance on developing a combination of internal and external markets and recognizing an important role for private enterprise in Latin American development. Iglesias resigned in 1985 to become foreign minister of Uruguay as that country returned to elected civilian government. In 1987 he was appointed president of the Inter-American Development Bank.

Gert Rosenthal has presided over a difficult period for ECLAC beginning in the mid-1980s. Structuralism was generally abandoned around Latin America and monetarism and neoliberalism ascended to dominant positions as regional economic doctrines. ECLAC statements acknowledge that the old ideas of structural dependency are "no longer appropriate" and embrace the tenets of neoliberalism. ECLAC has vigorously supported the revival of Latin American subregional economic integration, but accompanied by privatization of domestic enterprises and more openness to integration organization partners as well as to the outside world—prominently with the United States (see discussion below).

The United Nations Conference on Trade and Development (UNCTAD) was organized as an institution attuned to the interests of underdeveloped nations. Latin Americans had important influences in UNCTAD through their own concerted bloc action and by virtue of the fact that it was headed by Prebisch from 1963–1968. A sequence of global meetings were held, attended by representatives of both the developing and the developed worlds. UNCTAD convened in plenary session about every four years: UNCTAD I (Geneva, 1964); UNCTAD II (New Delhi, 1968); UNCTAD III (Santiago, 1972); UNCTAD IV (Nairobi, 1976); UNCTAD V (Manila, 1979), UNCTAD VI (Belgrade, 1983), UNCTAD VII (Geneva, 1987), and UNCTAD VIII (Cartagena, 1992).

Latin American states caucused as a regional bloc prior to each UNCTAD session, first in the Special Latin American Coordinating Committee (CECLA) before UNCTAD I, II, and III, and then in the Latin American Economic System (SELA). They adopted common regional developmental strategies that became dominant themes during the global meetings. The largely unproductive effort to improve terms of trade for developing nations was a great disappointment to them. It was apparently a source of frustration for Prebisch and perhaps led to his resignation as secretary general of UNCTAD after the 1968 conference. He was succeeded by the Venezuelan Manuel Pérez-Guerrero.

UNCTAD from the beginning was the centerpiece of the Third World effort to create a New International Economic Order (NIEO). This international regime, centered in UNCTAD but involving numerous other organizations and activities, is discussed below.

Financial Institutions. The International Bank for Reconstruction and Development (IBRD or World Bank) had some activities in Latin America after it started operations in 1946. The UN Development Program (UNDP) instituted programs in Latin America from its beginning in 1953. Two IBRD affiliates, the International Finance Corporation (IFC) and the International Development Agency (IDA), were established (in 1956 and 1960, respectively) in response to the demands of developing nations for increased loans on more flexible terms than those originally offered by the IBRD.

The World Bank became caught up in the Latin American debt crisis in the 1980s. Former U.S. congressman Barber B. Conable became bank president in March 1986, stating that he wanted it involved more deeply into the efforts dealing with the debt. Conable strongly endorsed the role of the bank envisaged by U.S. Treasury Secretary James A. Baker in his "initiative" regarding the debt (see Chapter 10). As a congressman Conable had criticized the Reagan administration's initial suspicion of and hostility toward the World Bank. In 1991 Conable was succeeded by Lewis T. Preston as president of the World Bank.

The International Monetary Fund (IMF), also established in 1946, was designed to encourage trade by contributing to the maintenance of stable currencies and rates of exchange. It lent from funds contributed by member states to ease inflationary pressures and to cover trade deficits. Interest rates were nominal, but when negotiating "standby arrangements" for "drawing rights" with a potential recipient, the IMF usually insisted on conditions for domestic economic reforms. Those reforms were based on orthodox monetarist policies in opposition to the ECLA structuralist approach, creating tension between the two agencies. The IMF called for various austerity programs that it expected to bring economic stability, but ECLA claimed that they would retard economic growth. Latin American governments allied with ECLA whereas the United States supported the IMF. Latin Americans tended to view the IMF as an instrument of creditor states, especially the United States, and it became a frequent target of nationalist enmity.

After becoming IMF director in 1962, Pierre-Paul Schweitzer of France was able to improve the IMF reputation somewhat in Latin America. In 1972 U.S. efforts to have him replaced were strongly opposed by most Latin American states. Schweitzer was more willing than his predecessors had been to recognize that some IMF conditions were politically unacceptable to Latin Americans, and he was more sympathetic to their needs. For example, he assisted them in negotiations with creditors when they fell behind in payments, including in the instances of Chile, Argentina, and Brazil in the early 1970s. The next two IMF managing directors were also from France: Jacques de Larosiere, who served from 1978 to January 1987 (resigning about a year and a half before his second five-year term expired); and Michael Camdessus, formerly governor of the French central bank.

Tensions between the IMF and Latin American governments returned, however, with the onset of the Latin American debt crisis in 1981. Faced with the mounting inability to make payments due in late 1982, Latin American governments sought agreements with the IMF and the principal creditors. The IMF, at the very center of Latin American debt negotiations, remained committed to orthodox economics stressing debtor austerity in order to reduce inflation, lower imports, and increase exports—all measures aimed at enhancing the ability to service debt and invest internally for sustained development. Creditor banks and governments generally required debtors to come to an agreement with the IMF as a prerequisite to renegotiating lending arrangements. When agreed-upon austerity and credit targets were not met, the IMF did not hesitate to withhold portions of loans and private creditors to interrupt loan disbursements. IMF policies toward the Latin American debt crisis are discussed in more detail in Chapter 10.

SOME GLOBAL REGIMES

Arms Control

Various Latin American states have adhered to a wide range of arms control agreements since the late 1950s. The regime governing arms control in Latin America is diffuse, including several treaties negotiated in different forums. The Antarctic Treaty of 1959 was the earliest of the post–World War II arms control treaties involving Latin American states. Because it goes beyond arms control as such and involves other issues it is discussed separately below. The Latin American Nuclear-Free Zone is taken up in Chapter 7. (Background information in this section is based on U.S. Arms Control and Disarmament Agency, 1975.)

UN-Sponsored Treaties. The Charter of the United Nations, unlike the Covenant of the League of Nations, gave disarmament and arms control no particular priority. Eventually, however, the UN Disarmament Commission was established in 1952. At first the preserve of the major world powers, the commission was broadened to allow membership of smaller states and reconstituted in 1961 as the Eighteen Nation Disarmament Committee (ENDC). In 1969 membership was increased from eighteen to twenty-six and the body was reorganized as the Conference of the Committee on Disarmament (CCD). The ENDC included Brazil and Mexico; Argentina was added when the CCD was organized. Several multinational agreements to which Latin American states are a party emerged from these two committees.

A series of international arms control agreements were negotiated in the 1960s and 1970s under the auspices of the United Nations. The Limited (or Partial) Test Ban Treaty (Treaty Banning Nuclear Weapon Tests in the Atmosphere, in Outer Space, and Under Water, signed August 5, 1963, and entered into force October 10, 1963) prohibits nuclear weapons tests as indicated in its formal title. Although it is of primary relevance to the nuclear powers, the treaty was open to all states. Eventually 103 states signed it. The Outer Space Treaty (Treaty on Principles Governing the Activities of States in the Exploration and Use of Outer Space, Including the Moon and Other Celestial Bodies, signed January 26, 1967, and entered into force October 10, 1967) is based on the concept of some of the provisions of the Antarctic Treaty. It seeks to prohibit military competition in outer space before it begins. The Seabed Arms Control Treaty (Treaty on the Prohibition of the Emplacement of Nuclear Weapons and Other Weapons of Mass Destruction on the Seabed and the Ocean Floor and in the Subsoil Thereof, signed February 11, 1971, and entered into force May 18, 1972) also sought to prevent the introduction of international conflict and nuclear weapons into locations that had been free of them. The Biological Weapons Convention (Convention on the Prohibition of the Development, Production, and Stockpiling of Bacteriological and Toxin Weapons and on Their Destruction, signed April 10, 1972, and entered into force in 1975) prohibits the development, production, stockpiling, or acquisition of biological agents or toxins "of types and in quantities that have no justification for the prophylactic, protective, or other peaceful use," as well as weapons and means of delivery.

Another anti–biological warfare treaty, originally negotiated in 1925, was revived by the United Nations in 1969. The Geneva Protocol (Protocol for the Prohibition of the Use in War of Asphyxiating, Poisonous, or Other Gases, and of Bacteriological Methods of Warfare, signed June 17, 1925, and entered into force February 28, 1928) had been adhered to only by Chile, Mexico, and Venezuela among the Latin American states. The protocol restated certain provisions of the earlier peace treaties concluding World War I. It prohibited the use of gases and bacteriological weapons of war. Problems of treaty interpretation prevented the adherence of many states until 1969, when the CCD supported UN Secretary General U Thant's plea that the 1925 protocol be widely adopted with the simple acknowledgment that it prohibited the use of all chemical and biological weapons of war. Numerous states, including nine in Latin America, then adopted the 1925 protocol.

The Nonproliferation Treaty. The United States had a monopoly on nuclear weapons until 1949, when the Soviet Union achieved nuclear capability. By 1964 the United Kingdom, France, and the People's Republic of China had joined the "nuclear club." The Partial Test Ban Treaty of 1963, written by the United States, Soviet Union, and United Kingdom, reflected a general concern about the spread of nuclear weapons and was intended to inhibit their proliferation. Virtually all states except France and China approved of the nonproliferation concept contained in the 1963 treaty. In 1967 a draft nonproliferation treaty was developed through the initiative of both nuclear and nonnuclear states. The following year, the Conference of Non-Nuclear Nations opened for signature the Treaty on the Non-Proliferation of Nuclear Weapons, usually referred to as the Non-Proliferation Treaty (NPT). It was signed July 1, 1968, and entered into force March 5, 1970.

The major thrust of the NPT is to prohibit those states possessing nuclear weapons from transferring them to nonnuclear states and to prohibit the latter from building or acquiring them. Negotiations of the draft treaty revealed deep suspicions on the part of many nonnuclear states. As a result, important modifications representing concessions by the nuclear powers were included in the final NPT. The nonnuclear states argued that, since they were giving up the choice of "going nuclear," the nuclear states should accept safeguards ensuring they were not violating treaty agreements. The NPT provides for safeguards to be administered by the IAEA, and for a Review Conference to be held every five years. The nuclear states also committed themselves to negotiations aimed at ending the strategic stalemate and seeking general and complete disarmament, as well as to make peaceful nuclear technology available to the nonnuclear states on a nondiscriminatory basis.

The NPT was opened for signature in 1968 and in 1992 it was in force for 140 states (including the Holy See), a record number of adherents for an arms control agreement. A review conference is scheduled to take place in 1995 when the pact expires and must decide whether the pact will be extended (and if so whether indefinitely or with another expiration date), or if it should be renegotiated.

Two nuclear powers—China and France—have not joined the NPT and at least six states with significant nuclear activities (including Argentina and Brazil) remain outside the treaty. Twenty-seven of the thirty-three Latin American regional states are party to the NPT—all but Argentina, Brazil, Chile, Cuba, Guyana, and St. Kitts–Nevis.

Brazil earlier had been a leader of the disarmament movement. By 1968, however, Brazil had been ruled for four years by an ambitious military government and was a potential nuclear power reluctant to adhere to the NPT. Argentina, also governed by a military regime, apparently felt it must have the same options as Brazil, its longtime rival. With rapprochement between the two states dating from 1979, and the return to constitutional civilian governments in both countries in the early 1980s, the possibility for their adherence was enhanced. In November 1990 and July 1991, respectively, the presidents of Argentina and Brazil signed two bilateral accords, one renouncing the manufacture of nuclear weapons and pledging to open negotiations with the IAEA to set up an inspection system, another establishing a joint agency to monitor the safeguards agreement. In December 1992 they signed an agreement with the IAEA to carry out inspections in both countries. They have not indicated intent to join the NPT, even though their agreement with the IAEA provides safeguards as rigorous as the NPT regime.

The Antarctic Treaty

By the 1950s seven states around the globe had claimed sovereignty over some part of the Antarctic continent. Eight more states had explored the region but made no territorial claims and rejected those of other states. The larger Southern Cone states had extended their geopolitical concerns to Antarctica. Other issues, such as the Falklands/Malvinas dispute, the Beagle Channel settlement, and Argentine-Brazilian rivalry, were linked to territorial claims and competition for resources in Antarctica. Although relations in the Antarctic among the interested parties had been relatively peaceful, the potential for conflict existed.

The Antarctic Treaty of 1959 established a multinational collaborative regime for the region. It was signed in Washington on December 1, 1959, and entered into force on June 23, 1961, after ratification by the twelve signatory nations. Among them were the seven states who had claimed sovereignty over some part of the Antarctic continent (Argentina, Australia, Chile, France, New Zealand, Norway, and the United Kingdom; the claims made by Argentina, Chile, and the United Kingdom overlapped). The other five signatories—Belgium, Japan, South Africa, the United States, and the Soviet Union—had explored the region but made no territorial claims. These twelve countries, as "consultative members," formed the Council of Claimant States, whose authority was restricted to making recommendations by unanimous vote. Four additional states later became consultative members—Poland in 1977, West Germany in 1981, and Brazil and India in 1983—raising the total number to sixteen. The treaty was also open to accession by other states, and twelve states became "acceding members." Uruguay became an acceding member in 1980 and in 1984 reaffirmed its possible rights over Antarctic territory. Other Southern Cone states have not participated—Peru has little interest in Antarctica and Paraguay and Bolivia have ignored it.

The Antarctic Treaty made significant accomplishments after its inception. It succeeded in preventing conflict in the Antarctic, as it was designed to do. The signatory states agreed to set aside (but not renounce) their demands during the life of the treaty. The council also succeeded in its goals of internationalizing and demilitarizing Antarctica, prohibiting nuclear testing and radioactive waste disposal on the continent, and ensuring that the region was used for peaceful purposes (including, most prominently, cooperative exploration and scientific investigations). Signatory states were accorded free access to the entire region with mutual rights of inspection of all national installations. The treaty prohibits "any measures of a military nature, such as the establishment of military bases and fortifications, the carrying out of military maneuvers as well as the testing of any types of weapons." It allows military personnel and equipment to be used only for scientific and other peaceful purposes. No treaty violations have been reported.

Increasing pressures were exerted for changes in the Antarctic regime. At the first seven consultative meetings held under the treaty, the topic of resources was kept off the agenda (it had purposely not been addressed in the treaty), but in the 1970s concern was expressed about the future utility and continuing existence of the treaty if petroleum or natural gas should be discovered in the Antarctic or under the surrounding continental shelf. Consequently, in 1981, the consultative members agreed to establish principles for dealing with the issue of mineral resources. Events had caught up with Antarctic governance—especially the increased price of petroleum and improved technology for extracting resources in conditions of extreme cold. Marine resources, especially an abundant high-protein crustacean called krill, had also attracted attention. Japan, Poland, and the Soviet Union were the major harvesters, but other states indicated interest in having a share.

The status of the Antarctic Treaty was further complicated in the United Nations. Third World nations not a part of the Antarctic Treaty regime argued for globalization of the region's governance and distribution of its resources. On November 30, 1983, the UN General Assembly adopted a resolution calling for a thorough study of the issue. In response, the treaty nations tried to demonstrate the strength of the existing system. The Polar Research Board of the U.S. National Academy of Sciences held a workshop on the future of the Antarctic in January 1985 at Beardmore Station, a remote research camp near the South Pole. Twenty-five countries sent fifty-seven scientists, diplomats, international lawyers, environmentalists, and others to attend the workshop. The debate over whether Antarctica should be regulated by the Antarctic Treaty or by the United Nations apparently has become a dead issue.

Law of the Sea

The Inter-American Dispute. What began as a territorial sea issue between the United States and certain South American west coast states developed into a global concern in which all Latin American states became involved to some degree. The problem first centered upon the claims of Chile, Peru, and Ecuador to a 200-mile offshore territorial limit and the consequent political and legal conflict with the United States.

In 1947, presidential declarations emanating from Chile and Peru claimed sovereignty over the seas adjacent to their coasts extending to a distance of 200 nautical miles. In 1952 they were joined by Ecuador at the First Conference on the Exploitation and Conservation of the Maritime Resources of the South Pacific in Santiago. They signed a joint declaration establishing a 200-mile maritime zone, including both the sea and the underlying land area, over which they claimed "sole sovereignty and jurisdiction." Their rationale was that the offshore food and economic materials were essential national resources and that they had the right and duty to protect and regulate them against outside exploitation. They argued that the 200-mile boundary included the outer limits of the food-rich Humboldt Current, which formed a "natural" and specific maritime unit. The three states convened a second conference at Lima in December 1954, where they signed six supplementary agreements for joint defense in the event of outside violations of their sovereignty in the maritime zone. They created a standing committee, the South Pacific Commission, to hold annual consultative meetings.

Beginning in 1955, the United States sought, with no success, to negotiate its differences with the three South American states. The United States, along with other large maritime powers, adhered to the traditional 3-mile limit in territorial seas and a contiguous 12-mile zone reserved for exclusive fishing rights. The United States protested the South American claims as unilateral declarations at variance with the generally accepted limits of territorial waters. An attempt to negotiate the dispute was made at the Santiago Negotiations on Fishery Conservation Problems (September 14–October 5, 1955) attended by Chile, Peru, Ecuador, and the United States, but the fundamental disagreement remained. In February 1967 the United States proposed that the dispute be submitted to the International Court of Justice or that another conference be held. The South American states refused both proposals.

In September 1951 Ecuador seized and fined U.S.-owned tuna boats, accusing them of illegally fishing in Ecuadorian waters. Peru made its first such seizure in February 1955 and Chile in December 1957. The U.S. Congress had promulgated the Fishermen's Protective Act of 1954 providing that, in any case where a U.S. vessel was seized by a foreign country under territorial waters claims not recognized by the United States, the secretary of state should take action "to attend to the welfare of such vessel and its crew while it is held by such country and to secure the release of such vessel and crew" and to collect costs from the foreign country, and that the secretary of the treasury should reimburse the vessel's owners for any fines paid. A 1968 amendment broadened the scope of reimbursement and, more important, provided that if the foreign country did not reimburse the United States within 120 days of a claim, the secretary of state should withhold an amount equal to the claim from U.S. assistance funds programmed for the country. The Foreign Assistance Act of 1961 provided that, in determining a country's eligibility for assistance, consideration should be given to excluding those countries that had seized U.S. vessels. The Foreign Military Sales Act of 1963 provided that "no defense article or defense service shall be sold by the United States Government ... to any country which ... seizes or takes into custody or fines an American fishing vessel engaged in fishing more than twelve miles from the coast of that country" (Hagen, 1969). By this time, the question of law of the sea had evolved into a global issue.

The Global Concern. By the mid-1950s, a number of nations throughout the world, including others in Latin America, began to assert claims to an extension of the territorial seas or contiguous areas. Several factors caused the increased pressures for a change in the international law of the sea, including a growth in the economic uses of the oceans, dramatic advances in the technology for exploiting ocean resources, an increased awareness of environmental problems, and a general desire of small states forming the global majority to have a voice in the shaping of international law. The scope of the issue was formidable. The oceans cover about 70 percent of the earth's surface, over which some 95 percent of world trade moves, and contain huge petroleum and other mineral reserves. Virtually all states had some interest in the rules governing the oceans.

The United Nations first attempted to resolve some of the problems in 1958 at the First United Nations Conference on the Law of the Sea at Geneva. The conference partially codified the international law of the sea by adopting four conventions. The Second UN Law of the Sea Conference was held in 1960 to resolve more issues, but without success. In 1967 Malta placed its "Pardo Plan" on the UN General Assembly agenda. It addressed "the question of the reservation exclusively for peaceful purposes of the seabed and the ocean floor, and the subsoil thereof, underlying the high seas beyond the limits of national jurisdiction and the use of their resources in the interests of mankind." In response, the General Assembly created a thirty-two-nation Special Committee, which, after two years of study, produced a statement of principles but left many problems unresolved.

In December 1970 the General Assembly called for a Third UN Law of the Sea Conference to deal not only with the questions remaining from the previous two conferences but also with a number of new ones that had subsequently arisen. The Special Committee was enlarged to ninety-one nations and reconstituted as the UN Committee on the Peaceful Uses of the Seabed and the Ocean Floor Beyond the Limits of National Jurisdiction (Seabed Committee). It engaged in almost three years of preparatory work for a comprehensive conference. The Third United Nations Conference on the Law of the Sea (UNCLOS III) convened in December 1973. After nine years of intense negotiations among various nations of the world, it produced in 1982 a comprehensive treaty for a global law of the sea regime. Some 156 states participated, about 120 of which were coastal states.

Latin American Positions. During the years of negotiations for a modern and comprehensive law of the sea, different approaches developed to several of the related issues. Some coastal states viewed the decision to extend their national jurisdiction seaward as a sovereign right, considering contiguous oceans as vital national resources subject to territorial state sovereignty. Chile, Peru, and Ecuador were joined by Brazil in claiming a 200-mile territorial sea.

Most Caribbean states held a different view, expressed in the Declaration of Santo Domingo, formulated at the Specialized Conference of Caribbean Countries Concerning the Problems of the Sea, attended by fifteen states in 1972. The declaration was signed by Colombia, Costa Rica, the Dominican Republic, Guatemala, Haiti, Honduras, Mexico, Nicaragua, Trinidad-Tobago, and Venezuela. Five delegations declined to sign: Barbados, El Salvador, Guyana, Jamaica, and Panama. The declaration favored state sovereignty extending only to a limit of twelve nautical miles seaward, with ships afforded innocent (nonbelligerent) passage through the territorial sea on a nondiscriminatory basis. The Santo Domingo Declaration also proposed the concept of the "patrimonial sea," an area, including the territorial sea, not to exceed 200 nautical miles, within which a state exercised rights over resources but not sovereignty. Thus a state could not regulate navigation through the area, but it could manage the living and nonliving resources of the ocean, seabed, and subsoil. The concept was used during UNCLOS III to bring about a compromise among positions regarding sovereignty and resource allocation.

The negotiations also proceeded in a North-South context. The Pardo Plan had first formulated the idea of the "common heritage of mankind"; it quickly became a Third World rallying point. (As discussed earlier, the Third World would apply it to the Antarctic Treaty.) On April 30, 1982, the bulk of the Latin American states, like nearly all Third World states, voted in favor of the UN Convention on the Law of the Sea. The United States voted against it, and a number of developed states abstained. The vote was 130 states for the treaty, four opposed (United States, Israel, Turkey, and Venezuela), and seventeen abstentions (mostly the Soviet bloc, except for Romania, and the European states). The chief Third World negotiator was Alvaro de Soto of Peru.

The Law of the Sea Convention. The Law of the Sea Convention was opened for signature in December 1982 and entered into force a year after the sixtieth ratification. It sets a twelve-mile territorial waters limit, establishes a 200-mile exclusive "economic zone" for coastal nations (with a definition of oil-drilling rights), regulates shipping lanes and provides for rights of passage for civilian and military ships through narrow straits, guarantees free navigation for naval forces, regulates scientific exploration and fisheries, requires environmental protection and pollution controls, controls mining under the deep sea, and establishes a system of international courts to arbitrate disputes at sea. Most of the provisions had become the de facto source of the international law of the sea for both signatories and nonsignatories as soon as it was signed.

From the start of the negotiations, provisions regulating the mining of the profuse mineral nodules that lie in the seabed were the focus of differences that finally could not be resolved. A compromise was struck with the establishment of a dual authority, one that would mine on behalf of the less developed countries and another that would license private enterprise to have access to mining sites. But the Reagan administration, while acknowledging that the United States strongly desired almost all other treaty provisions, decided that Article 11 did not adequately protect the U.S. firms that were exploring and developing technology to mine the seabed.

THIRD WORLD ORGANIZATIONS

Latin America in the Third World

The membership of Latin American states in the Third World, which transcends regional boundaries, has constituted a loose global subsystem. Latin Americans sought alternatives to traditional power politics and the redistribution of political and economic power and rewards by aligning with other like-minded states in other parts of the globe. At the same time, Latin America's regional consciousness was reinforced in that it behaved as a regional bloc within the Third World. Latin America was, simultaneously, a regional unit with subregional distinctions and at least loosely part of the Third World, which in certain ways it led.

The term "Third World" entered the popular vocabulary after World War II. It came to refer to the countries of Asia, Africa, and Latin America, thus containing the majority of the world's populations, as distinguished from the First World (the United States and its partners) and the Second World (the Soviet Union and its Communist-state allies). The Third World was viewed as mostly nonaligned in international politics and composed of poor developing countries economically dependent on the rich nations. Third World nations were said to have a sense of community based on their common conditions of poverty, colonial history, and economic dependency and consequently to share the foreign policy orientations of nonalignment and developmentalism.

Some problems arise with this seemingly widely held view. In attempting to make precise definitions and identify common characteristics among Third World members, we discover important exceptions that challenge the rules. Furthermore, Third World unity and sense of community is illusory. The Latin American region certainly defies easy or general categorization. Yet the concrete movements and organizations that have evolved reflected real concerns and aspirations. Thus, the complexities of this subsystem must be confronted. The Third World requires a more discriminating definition, and the associated structures and processes more precise analysis, than those in the popular view.

The Third World evolved out of two separate but closely related associations, the Nonaligned Movement and the New International Economic Order. Thus, two parallel Third World conceptions of the international system emerged, one in reaction to the cold war and its aftermath and the other in response to the gap between rich and poor nations. The distinctions blurred as each movement extended its agenda and grew in size. Both sought Third World unity through a series of international conferences focusing on a wide range of economic, political, and security issues. Concerted action was difficult to achieve, however, given the large number of states involved, the diversity of their interests, and the divisiveness of regional and other issues. Nonalignment and development were multifaceted objectives variously interpreted by Third World governments. The divergences and regional issues generated tremendous strains in both movements.

Latin America's identification with the Third World, in the sense of both non-alignment and developmentalism, was loose and often inexact. By and large, the Latin American states identified first with their own regional developmental problems, perceiving a unique development tradition and tending to coalesce among themselves when confronting the international aspects of development. In fact, a clear Latin American bloc emerged within the Third World, in both the Non-aligned Movement and the NIEO, pressing regional positions on numerous issues.

The end of the cold war challenged the identity of both the Nonaligned Movement and the NIEO and, consequently, Latin American interest in both movements declined. The end of the cold war made irrelevant the simplistic perception of the international structure as one of the First, Second, and Third Worlds. Alignment became a nonissue. In fact, the Nonaligned Movement had already been increasingly concerned with the same developmental issues as the NIEO. But the demise of the Soviet Union reduced the leverage of the NIEO, since it no longer was able to exploit the rivalries of the two superpowers while remaining noncommittal itself.

The Nonaligned Movement

The Third World was first synonymous with the Nonaligned Movement, which traces its beginnings to the onset of the post–World War II cold war between East and West. Certain states in Asia and Africa, most of them former European colonies that had recently gained their independence, were the first participants. They sought to avoid political and military entanglements in the cold war by forming a Third World in the bipolar structure between the First and Second Worlds dominated by the United States and the Soviet Union. Membership in the Nonaligned Movement began at a series of informal conferences beginning in 1947. The first major meeting was at Bandung, Indonesia, in April 1955, where leaders of twenty-nine Asian and African states, including the People's Republic of China, attended the landmark event and proclaimed themselves to be a third force in world affairs. They called for nonalignment in the cold war and condemned colonialism as an evil. No Latin American state attended.

The Belgrade Conference of 1961 was a significant gathering. It was the first nonaligned summit meeting (the twenty-five delegates were heads of state) and it expanded Third World membership beyond Africa and Asia with the presence of Yugoslavia and Cuba. Third World leaders had considered inviting several Latin American states to attend, but states that were approached showed no interest because they had not been consulted beforehand about the invitation extended to Cuba (although three states sent observers).

By agreement reached in Belgrade in 1961, summit Conferences of Non-aligned Nations (to be attended by heads of state) would be held approximately every three years. Nine additional nonaligned summits have convened since: Cairo (1964), Lusaka (1970), Algiers (1973), Colombo (1976), Havana (1979), New Delhi (1983), Harare (1986), Belgrade (1989), and Jakarta (1992). Numerous other meetings have also convened over the years. Membership expanded to include an increasing number of Latin American states after 1961. Eventually sixteen of them became full members of the movement and an additional eight attended nonaligned conferences as observers. The remaining nine regional states have not participated. Three Latin American regional organizations also sent observers: the Economic Commission for Latin America and the Caribbean, Latin American Economic System, and Latin American Energy Organization.

Cuba, under the revolutionary leadership of Castro, became Latin America's most active and prominent member. Castro was a leading figure at the Algiers summit in 1973 and became president of the movement in 1979 for a four-year term. With Castro presiding at the sixth summit meeting in Havana in 1979, the members almost splintered over his proposal to recognize the Soviet Union as the "natural ally" of the Nonaligned Movement in the struggle against imperialism and to adopt the Soviet position in the policies of nonaligned states. President Tito of Yugoslavia and other delegates to the conference strongly opposed Castro, maintaining that imperialism and colonialism in whatever form should be condemned. Little support for the Cuban view was forthcoming, and the opposition led by Tito won an overwhelming victory in expunging references to the natural-allies thesis from the documents finally adopted. In addition, the annual Ministerial Meeting of the Coordinating Bureau (the executive committee of the movement) was abolished, depriving Castro of an important medium to express his views.

The Cuban chairmanship ran into further trouble in the immediate aftermath of the summit meeting. The annual meeting of nonaligned foreign ministers and delegation leaders in New York at the opening of the UN General Assembly session in 1979 failed for the first time to produce any substantive statement or serious discussion of priorities for handling the UN debates. At the same session of the General Assembly, Cuba stood for election as a nonpermanent member of the Security Council. It should have been assured an easy victory, with a potential of eighty-eight votes from the nonaligned UN members, plus twelve from the Soviet bloc. However, Colombia challenged as a candidate against Cuba and a total of 154 ballots produced a deadlock with neither side obtaining the necessary two-thirds majority. The Soviet Union's invasion of Afghanistan doused Cuba's chances. Both candidates stood down in favor of Mexico, which was not a member of the Nonaligned Movement.

After January 1981 President Reagan instituted a number of U.S. foreign policy changes on development issues, law of the sea, the Middle East, Southern Africa, Central America, and military expenditures. Much of the Third World saw these changes as an unwelcome return to the cold war. The result within the Nonaligned Movement was a substantial shift in Cuba's favor against U.S. policy. With the end of the cold war a few years later, however, the old issues faded and the Nonaligned Movement lost much of its reason for being. Fidel Castro did not attend the 1992 summit conference.

The New International Economic Order

A second Third World association came to be known as the New International Economic Order (NIEO). Almost all Latin American states joined this association. The origins of the NIEO may be traced to the First United Nations Conference on Trade and Development (UNCTAD I) held in Geneva in 1961. UNCTAD began as an ad hoc body, but, guided by its first secretary general, Raúl Prebisch of Argentina, the General Assembly converted it to a permanent organ in the United Nations System in December 1964. At UNCTAD I, Third World states formed the Group of 77, a coalition to unify and articulate their objections to the global trade, aid, and development practices of the mid-1960s. It then expanded in number but kept its original name. The Group of 77, led by Algeria, used its numerical majority to convene the Sixth Special Session of the General Assembly in 1974 and adopt a Declaration on the Establishment of a New International Economic Order. It also approved the Charter of Economic Rights and Duties of States sponsored by Mexican President Luís Echeverría. Thus, the formal establishment of the NIEO occurred in 1974, but it had grown out of earlier precedents and concerns. The NIEO created a North-South global confrontation between rich and poor nations on the idea that, by and large, the wealthy nations of the world were in the Northern Hemisphere and the poorer nations in the Southern Hemisphere. Consequently, the meaning of Third World was extended to be synonymous with the South in economic and developmental terms. The NIEO was pursued primarily through various United Nations organs. The Group of 77 met before sessions of the General Assembly and other gatherings to try to decide on a common course of action.

The Group of 77 had some success. It was instrumental in the creation of the Special United Nations Fund for Economic Development (SUNFED), the United Nations Capital Development Fund (UNCDF), and the International Development Association (IDA) as an affiliate of the World Bank. The Group of 77 organized a series of special UN conferences to address a wide range of other issues that they consider crucial to their interests: the environment, population, food, law of the sea, disarmament, women, industrialization, desertification, technology transfer, rural development, and the role of science and technology in development. These conferences, however, have rarely produced concrete results. The Group of 77 represents a majority of the UN membership and can pass any action that it chooses in the General Assembly—if it maintains its cohesiveness. It has not, however, been able to persuade or compel the North to accept its tenets or adopt its prescriptions.

For most of Latin America most of the time, the "Third World" has been synonymous with the "developing world." The regional actors, including members of the Nonaligned Movement, seem to have concluded that they share special economic problems with other developing nations, particularly in their relations with the developed world. In fact, the Latin American region took the lead in addressing a wide range of issues beginning in the early 1960s. The important issues, from their points of view, involved development and the world economy, especially world trade, public assistance, and private investment. At the same time, Latin America approached the NIEO as a regional bloc. Latin Americans placed as much reliance on their own regional integration and caucusing organizations as on the NIEO in approaching their problems. With the end of the cold war and the NIEO's significantly reduced leverage, Latin Americans placed even less reliance on the organization as a policy vehicle.

Commodity Agreements

Latin American states joined, and sometimes led, "commodity agreements," a process also referred to as "resources diplomacy." Both expressions are euphemisms for "cartel." States that produce primary materials, often having monocultural economies, were attracted to commodity agreements as a way to control markets for their export products. They sought to raise and then stabilize prices in world markets and sustain export earnings over a long period. In general, commodity agreements represented further efforts on the part of Latin American (and other) states to gain economic strength in relation to the more industrialized and richer states.

One of the earliest and clearly the most successful commodity agreements was the Organization of Petroleum Exporting Countries (OPEC). Five relatively obscure underdeveloped states banded together in 1960 to form OPEC. It eventually comprised thirteen members, with its headquarters located in Vienna. Venezuela was a charter member and Ecuador joined in 1973. A Venezuelan oil expert and government official, Juan Pablo Pérez Alfonso, played a prominent role in establishing OPEC. The stimulus occurred in 1959 when the major global oil companies acted in concert to reduce the price they paid for oil to the producing nations. The original five OPEC members met in Baghdad the following year in order, according to their charter, "to create an organization for regular consultation and for the coordination of oil policies." OPEC came into prominence with the energy crises in the 1970s. By mid-1973, thirteen years after its modest beginnings, OPEC was powerful enough to quadruple the price of petroleum on world markets and bring about a major redistribution of international income in favor of its member states. With the subsequent oil glut and serious disagreements among the members states, however, OPEC lost much of its leverage and its prominence as an effective commodity agreement. In 1990 Ecuador withdrew from the organization and Venezuela considered doing so.

A commodity agreement predating OPEC also enjoyed some success. An International Coffee Agreement signed in 1962 was the culmination of earlier efforts. Brazil had attempted from 1940 to 1945 to regulate production and achieve price stability in the global coffee market. The 1962 agreement, renewed for five years in 1968, was subscribed to by Brazil and Colombia (the world's largest coffee producers at the time), Ecuador, the Central American states, and a number of African producers. Consumer states also joined in agreeing to stabilize coffee prices. In 1962, when U.S. policy toward Latin America was cast in the context of the Alliance for Progress, any price increases resulting from the coffee agreement were viewed as a form of aid for development. Despite a great deal of internal dispute, especially between the Latin American and African groups, world coffee prices were brought under a modicum of control.

The coffee-producing states allowed the agreement to expire in 1973. They apparently felt that a formal agreement with the consumer states was no longer needed. Nevertheless, they were faced with the financial inability to limit coffee sales in order to keep prices at a desirable level. To this end, Venezuela in November 1974 announced that it would lend some of its profits from petroleum sales to Central America so that Central America could withhold part of their coffee production from international markets. Brazil and Colombia said they would finance their own stockpiling.

OPEC's success catalyzed efforts to regulate other commodities through associations of producer nations, and cartels with Latin American participants were created. An organization of copper producers, the Intergovernmental Council of Copper Exporting Countries (CIPIC), was established in 1967 and included Chile, Peru, Zambia, Zaire, and, later, Indonesia. The Organization of Iron Ore Exporting Countries (IOEC) was composed of Venezuela (a major leader), Chile, Peru, Brazil, Algeria, India, Australia, Canada, Sweden, Liberia, and Mauritania. Bolivia belongs to the International Tin Agreement. Jamaica is the chief producer and leader of the International Bauxite Association. Latin American banana producers organized the International Organization of Banana Exporters (IPEB).

Serious doubts exist about the long-term viability of the cartels, including OPEC. A successful cartel requires that producers be willing and able to withhold enough of their products to affect prices and that consumer demand remain relatively constant despite increased prices. These conditions are hard to satisfy, because producers often are unable to finance stockpiling or reduced production and consumers often turn to substitutes or are willing to do without. Petroleum seemed to be the exception, because producers had the financial ability to control the volume of supply and consumers had little choice other than to buy the crucial commodity at current world market prices. However, even OPEC ran into serious problems of supply, demand, and member cohesion. Furthermore, high prices stimulated the major consumers to increase oil conservation efforts, seek alternative energy sources, and, for those able to do so, increase their own oil production.

OTHER HEMISPHERIC ARRANGEMENTS

The Panama Canal

The idea of a canal across the Central America isthmus dates from the Spanish conquest in America. Columbus had made his voyages in search of a shorter sea route from Europe to Asia, and Cortés proposed that a canal be constructed along one of the routes that even today are considered to be the most practicable. Although Spanish kings were interested in such a project, they never actually began construction (Stuart and Tigner, 1975:184). After Latin American independence and through the remainder of the nineteenth century, the idea was taken up by the external states, particularly Great Britain, the United States, and France. The issue created a great deal of conflict between them as well as between Europe and certain local states.

The United States took the first important step to secure control of a Central American route. On December 12, 1846, the United States and New Grenada signed a treaty that, among other things, guaranteed the right of passage across the Colombian province of Panama to the United States. In the meantime, Great Britain had secured an important position in Central America. It had established sovereignty over British Honduras and the Bay Islands and, in 1844, proclaimed a protectorate over the "Mosquito Kingdom," which consisted roughly of today's

Caribbean coast of Nicaragua. In 1849 the United States signed treaties with Nicaragua to obtain a concession for a canal, contravening British claims in the area, and a treaty with Honduras granting U.S. control of Tigre Island in the Gulf of Fonseca. Britain promptly sent a naval force that took possession of the island. A compromise was achieved in the Clayton-Bulwer Treaty of 1850, in which both the United States and Great Britain, in essence, promised not to claim exclusive control over any canal in Central America and to guard the safety and neutrality of any canal that should be built.

With U.S. and British canal interests mutually neutralized, the French position became dominant. A private French company, organized by Ferdinand de Lesseps, the Suez Canal engineer, purchased a Colombian concession in 1879 to construct a canal across Panama. Construction began in February 1881, but eight years later the enterprise ended in bankruptcy and scandal with only about one-third of the canal completed.

With the emergence of the United States as a great power after the war with Spain in 1898, its desire to build and control a canal increased. By then Great Britain was more amenable to compromise. The U.S. secretary of state, John Hay, and the British ambassador to Washington, Lord Pauncefote, negotiated treaties intended to settle their Central American differences. After one treaty was rejected by the U.S. Senate, a second was ratified by both parties. The Hay-Pauncefote Treaty of 1901 expressly abrogated the Clayton-Bulwer Treaty, giving the United States the freedom to build and exclusively control a canal. It provided that the canal should be equally open to commercial and war vessels of all states with no discriminatory charges. Since the treaty contained no prohibition to the contrary, the United States also had the right to fortify and defend the canal. With U.S.-British conflict over a transisthmian canal settled, the canal issues shifted to disagreements between the United States and Colombia and, later, between the United States and Panama.

The United States undertook to choose a canal route. The Walker Commission had been charged by Congress in 1899 to study all possible routes, and it issued a voluminous report on November 1, 1901. The commission had narrowed the possibilities to a choice between two routes, one through Panama and the other through Nicaragua. When the French project failed in 1889, a new Panama Canal Company had taken over the property and attempted to sell its interest to the U.S. Congress. The Walker Commission calculated the total value of the Panama Canal Company's rights and property to be $40 million, as opposed to the company's demand for more than $109 million. The commission favored the Panama route from an engineering standpoint, but it recommended the Nicaraguan site because of the high Panamanian price. The U.S. House of Representatives, in accordance with the Walker Commission's recommendations, passed the Hepburn Bill in January 1902 authorizing the construction of a canal across Nicaragua. The French company responded in panic by offering to sell its interest to the United States for $40 million. Consequently, the Spooner Amendment to the Hepburn Bill authorized the Panama route as an alternative to the one across Nicaragua.

The United States negotiated an agreement with Colombia, which then governed Panama. The Hay-Herrán Treaty of 1903 granted the United States exclusive rights to construct and operate the Panama Canal and authorized the French

Panama Canal Company to transfer its concession. The U.S. Senate promptly consented to ratification, but the Colombian Senate decided to press for more advantages and unanimously rejected the treaty. French creditors were dismayed by the jeopardy in which their interests were placed, as the United States still had the Nicaraguan option. Consequently, agents of the French company organized a rebellion in Panama against Colombia, taking advantage of deep provincial resentment against the central government. Panamanian leaders long had felt neglected, and now, considering the canal as a great potential benefit to them, they saw their local interests threatened.

The Panamanian revolt began on November 2, 1902. A U.S. warship prevented Colombian troops from interfering by blockading their only route over water to Panama. Four days later, on November 6, the United States recognized Panama's sovereign independence. A Panamanian employee of the French canal company became the first president of the Republic of Panama, and the former chief engineer, Philippe Bunau-Varilla, who also had engineered the revolution, was appointed Panama's minister to the United States. He negotiated a canal treaty that was signed on November 18, 1903, only two weeks after the revolt had begun.

The Hay-Bunau-Varilla Treaty provided for U.S. use, occupation, and control, "in perpetuity," of a ten-mile strip of territory extending across Panama (the Canal Zone). The United States gained the use and occupation of other lands and waters outside the zone necessary to the canal's construction, operation, or protection. Panama agreed to U.S. treaty rights to intervene in Panamanian domestic affairs if necessary to maintain order and ensure Panamanian independence so as to protect the future canal. (The Panamanian Constitution of 1904 included Article VII of the 1903 treaty, which permitted U.S. military intervention "in case the Republic of Panama should not be, in the judgment of the United States, able to maintain … order.") In return, the United States agreed to pay Panama $10 million plus an annual subsidy of $250,000 beginning nine years after ratification of the treaty.

With the Panamanian route secured, the United States purchased the French company's assets. Construction began in 1906 and the Panama Canal opened to traffic in 1914.

The U.S. Good Neighbor Policy coincided with the rise of Panamanian nationalism, which centered on protests about the canal. The agitation culminated in the Hull-Alfaro Treaty in 1936 to amend the original 1903 treaty. The United States renounced its right to intervene in Panamanian affairs. In case of aggression endangering Panama or the canal, the two governments were to consult about mutual defense. The annual U.S. rental subsidy was raised to $430,000, and the United States accepted stricter limitations on the conduct of business and rights of residence in the Canal Zone. During World War II, after a series of difficult negotiations Panama gave the United States temporary permission to use certain existing military facilities and to construct new ones in Panama outside of the Canal Zone. In 1947 the two states signed a treaty providing for U.S. retention of fourteen military bases, but the Panamanian National Assembly refused to ratify in the face of a strong negative public reaction. The United States evacuated the bases. Panamanian dissatisfaction over the treaty arrangements led to further changes.

Negotiations begun in late 1953 resulted in a 1955 treaty further amending the original one. The Eisenhower-Remón Treaty increased the U.S. annuity to $1.93 million and transferred certain U.S. rights and properties to Panama.

The 1936 and 1955 amendments represented concessions on the part of the United States, but Panamanians considered the changes inadequate and felt that they did not address their most fundamental interests. They continued to agitate against the arrangement, sometimes in a violent manner. Riots and clashes between Zonians and Panamanians occurred on several occasions. Especially serious was a confrontation in 1964 in which four U.S. citizens and twenty-two Panamanians were killed. As a result, treaty revision talks were resumed, introducing a new era in the long, complex, and conflictual U.S.-Panamanian relationship.

Beginning in 1964, Panama specifically asserted a number of its long-standing resentments. It complained that during the 1903 negotiations its dependence on the United States for national survival forced it to accede to U.S. demands, and that Bunau-Varilla, the principal negotiator for Panama, had primarily represented the interests of the French canal company rather than those of the Panamanian nation. Panama also charged that all along it had been inadequately compensated for its concessions to the United States and expressed resentment over the affluence of people who lived in the Canal Zone. Most objectionable of all were treaty provisions giving a foreign power virtual sovereignty over a portion of Panama that physically divided the nation.

Following discussions of the canal issue in the Organization of American States and the United Nations, Panama and the United States agreed in 1964 to pursue bilateral negotiations for a new treaty. Basic U.S. objectives were that the canal should continue to be available to all commercial vessels on a nondiscriminatory basis at relatively low toll costs, that it should be operated and defended by the United States for an extended but specific time period, and that the United States should have the right to expand the canal capacity. Agreements were reached in 1967 on three draft treaties that provided for canal operation by a joint U.S.-Panamanian authority and for U.S. defense responsibilities. But a nationalist military government came to power in 1968 in Panama and formally rejected the treaties. In the meantime, considerable opposition was voiced in the U.S. Congress. Negotiations, resumed in 1971, were intense but inconclusive.

Panama, to the chagrin of the United States, brought up the issue before the UN Security Council during the meeting in Panama City in March 1973. Panama criticized the U.S. posture on the canal question and introduced a resolution calling for a treaty giving Panama "effective sovereignty" over the Canal Zone. The United States blocked the resolution by casting a veto, but it agreed to adjust its differences with Panama. U.S. Ambassador at Large Ellsworth Bunker, a highly experienced and prestigious diplomat, visited Panama in late 1973 and early 1974 to discuss the bases for a new treaty. The result was a Statement of Principles signed on February 7, 1974, by U.S. Secretary of State Henry Kissinger and Panamanian Foreign Minister Juan Tack. Designed to serve as guidelines for further treaty negotiations, the principles emphasized general areas of agreement but left some major issues open for later discussion.

Considerable opposition in the U.S. Senate, which had to advise and consent to ratification by a two-thirds majority, delayed the treaty-making process. The opposition's basic argument was simply that the Canal Zone was U.S. territory, legally agreed to by Panama, and that under the principles decided upon in 1974 the United States unnecessarily gave away an important possession. Their battle cry was "we bought it, we paid for it, it is ours." In 1976, then California Governor Ronald Reagan made the canal a potent issue during the presidential primary campaigns.

The final negotiation and signing of new treaties was left to President Jimmy Carter. On September 7, 1977, President Carter and the President of Panama, General Omar Torrijos, signed two Panama Canal Treaties. At the same time, a protocol to the neutrality treaty was signed by most other Latin American nations, thereby showing their strong approval. The bilateral treaties were sent to the U.S. Senate, where a particularly bitter and acrimonious process took place. The mobilization of the opposition was impressive. Supporters of the treaty, who finally but narrowly prevailed, led a public defense of the new arrangements. They argued that the new treaties would remove a major source of friction not only in U.S.-Panamanian relations but in inter-American affairs in general that would signal a new era of hemispheric cooperation. They pointed out that both the economic and military security importance of the canal, although still significant, had declined considerably. Treaty proponents said further that under the proposed new relationship the United States would have operational and defense rights for a time sufficient to work out future contingencies. They also raised the possibility of sabotage if agreement was not reached, noting that the canal was particularly vulnerable.

The new treaties and certain supporting documents finally went into effect. They were approved by national plebiscite in Panama. The Senate advised and consented to the neutrality treaty on March 17, 1978, and to the canal treaty on April 18, by votes of 68–32 (one more than necessary). Prior to Senate approval, the two governments had signed a clarifying Statement of Understanding in response to certain demands of a number of U.S. senators, an exercise that was necessary to secure sufficient senatorial votes. The two treaties were then ratified by both heads of state and entered into force on October 1, 1979.

The two treaties establish the new Panama Canal regime. The basic Panama Canal Treaty arranges for the canal's operation, maintenance, and defense through December 31, 1999. Its salient articles provide for: (1) assigning to Panama the normal local government functions in the former Canal Zone; (2) joint United States–Panamanian management and defense of the canal until the end of the century; (3) increasing Panamanian participation at every level of operations leading to its eventual unilateral management; (4) continuing control by the United States of all land and water areas necessary for the operation and defense of the canal; and (5) increasing the annuity paid to Panama with money derived from tolls and other canal revenues. The United States will continue to operate the canal, with Panamanian participation, until the year 2000, when Panama will assume control. Until that time, a nine-person board of directors will operate the canal, with five members from the United States and four from Panama. The canal was expected to be self-supporting, with income shared by the two countries.

The other treaty document, the Treaty Concerning the Permanent Neutrality and Operation of the Panama Canal, has no termination date and makes provisions for the canal after the year 1999 when Panama will be in charge of its operation. It guarantees that the canal will be kept permanently neutral in times of both peace and war, and that nondiscriminatory access and tolls will be provided for the vessels of all countries. The United States is permitted to act militarily to defend the canal's neutrality and to keep it open.

The additional Statement of Understanding clarifies U.S. rights under the neutrality treaty. It confirms that the United States has a permanent right to protect and defend the canal against any armed attack or threat to its security or to the free passage of ships of all nations. U.S. warships have the permanent right to transit the canal expeditiously and without conditions and, in case of need or emergency, to go to the head of the line of vessels (when the United States deems it necessary). The same obligations apply with regard to any other canal constructed in Panama. Although the former U.S.-administered Canal Zone ceased to exist when the treaties went into force, the United States retains the right to use areas and facilities necessary to the operation and defense of the canal. The United States may take the military action necessary to make sure the canal remains open and safe, but it does not have the right to intervene against Panamanian territorial integrity or political independence.

To comply with the basic bilateral framework established by the new treaties, the U.S. Congress passed the Panama Canal Act of 1979. (The treaties and U.S. obligations under them would have gone into effect whether or not the implementing legislation had been adopted.) The salient provisions of the act accomplished the following: (1) established a new U.S. government agency, the Panama Canal Commission, to manage and operate the canal until the end of the century; (2) specified the basis for setting tolls; (3) provided for U.S. participation in various binational bodies established by the treaties, including a Joint Commission on the Environment; (4) authorized an employment system covering Panama Canal Commission employees, including special retirement conditions and other provisions; (5) phased out the previous Canal Zone court system and established arrangements to cover the initial thirty-month transition period; (6) provided for the immigration to the United States of long-term local employees of the canal; and (7) directed the president to report annually to Congress on the implementation of the treaties.

Three parallel transition processes were provided for, all dating from October 1, 1979. The first was a thirty-month transition, which ended March 31, 1982, when Panama assumed total responsibility for local government and the U.S. community became subject to Panamanian authority. The U.S. judicial and police functions were phased out and, when the period ended, transferred to Panama. The United States continued to play a dominant role in the administration, operation, and defense of the canal itself. The transfer of full canal control to Panama entailed two more transitional phases. One ended as scheduled on December 31, 1989, when the U.S. administrator of the Panama Canal Commission was replaced by a Panamanian. The final phase will close at midnight on December 31, 1999, when Panama will assume full responsibility.

U.S. military forces of the Southern Command continued to operate from bases in Panama, as provided for in the treaties. On October 1, 1984, the Reagan administration complied with the provisions of the treaties and turned over Fort Gulick, the home of the U.S. Army School of the Americas, to Panama.

Mexican-U.S. Riverine Agreements

A U.S.-Mexican treaty in 1884 created the mixed International Boundary Commission to decide frontier questions. Some problems were settled by the commission, but not the important Chamizal dispute. The Rio Grande had continuously shifted its course southward, especially rapidly in the 1860s, transferring about 630 acres known as the Chamizal to the Texas side of the river. The Boundary Commission was unable to resolve conflicting claims and referred the problem to an international arbitral commission, which in 1911 gave the Chamizal to Mexico. The United States refused to accept the award and the dispute dragged on for another half-century. Finally, in 1962, the United States agreed to abide by the 1911 decision. In the Chamizal convention of 1963 the United States acknowledged Mexican sovereignty over the region and Mexico ceded the northern half of Córdova Island, lying in the Rio Grande, to the United States. The agreement also provided for the construction of a channel to divert the river so as to place the Chamizal on the Mexican side and for the building of three highways and two railway bridges across the river. Costs of these projects were to be shared equally by the two states.

The dispute concerning the Colorado River—which flows in a southerly direction from the state of Colorado, through Utah, along the Arizona-California border into the Mexican state of Sonora, and finally into the Gulf of California—arose from the fact that, in an apparent treaty violation, the United States was not delivering water of adequate quantity or quality to Mexico. In 1944 the United States agreed to deliver a minimum amount of water to Mexico from the Colorado River, received from the Morelos International Dam on the Mexico-Arizona border. In 1961 the U.S. Wellton-Mohawk Reclamation District began rinsing soil with methods that involved pumping highly saline waters into the Gila River near its confluence with the Colorado. Contaminated water began to kill the cotton crops in the Mexicali Valley of Mexico. After a decade of dispute, an agreement was put into effect in 1973. Under it the United States agreed to cleanse the water to a certain degree before sending it to Mexico.

Free-Trade Agreements

Enterprise for the Americas Initiative. In a surprise speech on June 27, 1990, President George Bush announced the Enterprise for the Americas Initiative (EAI), which contemplated a western hemispheric free-trade area (FTA). (This and the following two sections are based on Atkins, 1993). Only two weeks earlier, the President of Mexico had publicly proposed negotiations for a free-trade agreement with the United States. Other Latin American states, already actively reforming their own economic integration organizations, indicated they did not want to be left out of the North American market. Bush responded by launching his EAI, which proposed liberalized trade (its most important element), promotion of investment, and debt relief linked to environmental protection. He advocated expanding trade on both the global and regional levels. The former involved continuing the Uruguay Round of the General Agreement on Tariffs and Trade (GATT) (which was eventually completed and the agreement sent to the signatory states for ratification). On the regional level, Bush anticipated an agreement with Mexico as the first step, to be followed by negotiations with other states with the ultimate goal being a free-trade system throughout the Americas. The ensuing processes are discussed below.

As a general matter, these historic hemispheric developments reflected the fact that all parties had decided on an export-led strategy for economic recovery or development. The generally enthusiastic reception in Latin America stemmed from a perception that the United States, no longer burdened with cold war security calculations, was less paternalistic toward the region and more willing to proceed on a partnership basis in a search for mutual benefits. The Latin American nationalist trend, away from xenophobia and economic nationalism and toward a less defensive and more positive attitude toward the outside world, including the United States, also facilitated these developments (Cohen, 1992).

The North American Free Trade Agreement. Beginning in 1985, Mexico, in a fundamental international reorientation, began to reform its protectionist investment and trade policies and to press the United States for a U.S.-Mexican FTA. Mexico joined GATT in 1986, something the United States had long been urging, and in 1987 signed a framework agreement with the United States as the basis for further bargaining. On January 2, 1988, the Canada–United States Free Trade Agreement went into effect after two years of difficult negotiations. After Mexico and the United States agreed to commence free-trade negotiations, Canada, seeking to protect its agreement with the United States, indicated its interest in taking part, and trilateral talks commenced in June 1991. The U.S. Congress required that the negotiations include bilateral U.S.-Mexican discussions on labor and environmental issues. Congress also made progress on the NAFTA talks a prerequisite to extending accords elsewhere in the hemisphere.

After arduous negotiations, NAFTA was signed and eventually ratified by the three states in November/December 1993. The ratification process went smoothly in Mexico but was politically bitter in the United States and Canada, where organized labor groups were highly concerned with low-wage competition from Mexico. Environmental groups also raised issues about environmental protection, but in time became evenly divided for and against the pact. In Canada the process was complicated by antagonism toward the United States among certain members of Parliament. Consequently, President Bill Clinton, who had taken office on January 20, 1993, negotiated "side agreements" with Mexico to make NAFTA acceptable to certain members of Congress and met with the Canadian prime minister to informally resolve Canadian concerns. The Canada–United States FTA was largely superseded by NAFTA. After ratifications NAFTA went into effect on January 1, 1994.

NAFTA unites Canada, Mexico, and the United States in the world's largest free-trade zone, a market of more than 360 million people. The United States and Canada are each the other's largest trading partner and comprise the world's largest bilateral trade. The United States is by far Mexico's largest trading partner, and Mexico is the United States' third largest. Consistent with GATT rules, NAFTA will phase out barriers to trade in North America in goods and services, eliminating some immediately and others over different periods of up to fifteen years. Industries included, among others, are the automotive industry, land transportation and port services, textiles, banking, finance, insurance, telecommunications, textiles and apparel, and agriculture. Common North American rules of origin protect auto and textile industries in all three countries from extraregional competition. Florida frozen citrus juice producers are given special protection. NAFTA eliminates barriers to investment and strengthens the protection of intellectual property rights, such as high technology, publishing, and entertainment, which rely for protection on patents and copyrights. NAFTA also includes specific safeguards and escape clauses. It allows suspension of trade on some items in order to protect domestic industry, contains a dispute mechanism to solve trade conflicts, and grants each party the right to withdraw from NAFTA by giving six months' notice.

NAFTA provisions go beyond the conventional free-trade level. It is the first trade agreement to which the United States is a signatory that contains standards and measures concerning environmental problems and labor issues. The United States and Mexico had already signed a five-year Memorandum of Understanding regarding occupational health and safety standards, child labor, workers rights, and labor-management relations. One of the NAFTA side agreements established a mechanism for Mexico and the United States to address problems in each state's laws affecting minimum wages, child labor, and worker safety, but not regarding the right to organize or collective bargaining. A U.S.-Mexican Integrated Border Plan had gone into effect in February 1992 to address air, soil, water, and hazardous-waste problems along the border. NAFTA added a tripartite council to settle disputes over each country's enforcement of environmental laws, including sanctions for violations. The United States and Mexico will establish an $8 billion pollution cleanup program along their border, financed by a new North American Development Bank and loans from international agencies.

Hemispheric Free Trade. The United States negotiated framework agreements on trade and investment with Latin American states and groups of states that wished to free trade in the hemisphere. By mid-January 1992, with a broad positive response around the region beyond North America, the United States had signed separate framework agreements with two multilateral organizations and fourteen individual states, in addition to Canada and Mexico. The United States concluded agreements with the four-member Common Market of the South (MERCOSUR), made up of Argentina, Brazil, Paraguay, and Uruguay; and with the thirteen-member English-speaking Caribbean Community and Common Market (CARICOM), which includes twelve independent states plus nonsovereign Montserrat. The other fourteen bilateral framework agreements, in the order of signing, are as follows: Bolivia (in May 1990, just prior to the formal EAI proposal), Colombia, Ecuador, Chile, Honduras, Costa Rica, Venezuela, El Salvador, Peru, Nicaragua, Panama, Guatemala, Dominican Republic, and Suriname (in January 1992). Thus, with the NAFTA talks with Canada and Mexico and framework agreements extended to the rest of the Latin American region, the United States had negotiated or anticipated negotiating free trade with thirty-two of the other thirty-four American states (plus Montserrat), excluding only Cuba and Haiti.

The U.S.-Mexican framework agreement signed in 1987 served as the model for the sixteen additional ones. They constitute understandings about the process intended to lead to wider negotiations for commerce and investment. They do not include final concessions about substantive matters but set forth free-trade and free-market principles and identify key issues without specifying details. The agreements create councils in each instance to serve as consultation mechanisms. They also imply the understanding that modification of national economic policies is necessary before FTAs with the United States can be forthcoming. An implication of NAFTA for the rest of Latin America is the possibility of trade diversion, a major incentive for them to seek FTAs with the United States or NAFTA.

Three institutional outcomes seem possible: (1) a U.S.-centered hub-and-spoke system, in which the United States is the only American state with hemispheric free trade; (2) a set of integrated subregional free-trade agreements, envisioned in the EAI as the ideal model; or (3) a hemispheric system regulated and maintained by an inter-American agency or agencies. (Certain organizational arrangements were made for the elements of debt, investment, and the environment in the Inter-American Development Bank and the U.S. Treasury Department.) In any event, given the complexity of negotiating hemispheric free trade and the various problems to be overcome, its realization is a long time away.

BIBLIOGRAPHIC COMMENT

Scott (1909) provides a general work on the Hague Conferences with references to Latin American participation. Edwards (1937) and Kelchner (1929) analyze Latin America in the League of Nations. On the relationship of the UN to the OAS, see Bibliographic Commentary following Chapter 8. On arms control, see U.S. Arms Control and Disarmament Agency (1975), and Leventhal and Tanzer (1992). Child (1988) is the best single source on the international politics of the Antarctic. Morris (1990) addresses great power relations in Antarctica. Vargas Silva (1979) is a law of the sea handbook with a particular interest in Latin America; for a variety of particulars concerning Latin America, see Alvarado Garaicoa (1968), Hagen (1969), Orrego Vicuña (1976), Pontecorvo (1986), and Smetherman and Smetherman (1974). Ffrench-Davis and Tironi (1981), Navarette et al. (1980), and Tomassini (1982) discuss the NIEO with reference to Latin America. Levine (1992) considers the end of "Third Worldism" in Latin America. Araim (1990) discusses commodities agreements. General studies regarding the Panama Canal are provided by Ealy (1971) and Liss (1969). Hearings on the revised canal treaties are in U.S. Senate, Committee on Foreign Relations (1977/1978); U.S. Library of Congress (1977) presents a compendium of documents. On Mexican-U.S. riverine questions, see Eaton (1987), Enríquez Coyro (1975–1976), Hundley (1966), Liss (1965), and México (1975). On various aspects of hemispheric free trade, see Atkins (1993), Cohen (1993), Grinspun and Cameron (1993), Saborio et al. (1992), SELA (1991), Moss (1994), and Weintraub (1991, 1993).

PART FOUR

■

Instruments and Interaction

The policy instruments selected by the various actors in the Latin American subsystem and the resulting patterns and processes of interaction are addressed in this part of the book. Chapter 10 deals with diplomacy and Chapter 11 with violence and accommodation. Both chapters identify policy considerations behind the choice of political, economic, military, and other instruments; the patterns of relationships resulting from their interaction; the functions of the distribution of power; and of interdependence reflected in the activities of international institutions. Diplomacy, violence, and accommodation are not discrete categories but overlapping dynamic processes. The classifications are intended to indicate an analytic continuum: diplomacy may involve both cooperative and coercive measures; and violence, comprising hostility and compulsion and its possible resolution, involves some level of diplomacy that may lead to cooperation. These processes and outcomes are not inevitable but provide a logical framework for discussion of foreign policy instruments and international interactions.

CHAPTER TEN

—————— ■ ——————

Diplomacy

THE BARGAINING USES of political, economic, military, and cultural foreign policy instruments chosen by Latin American subsystem actors, and the international patterns they create, are examined in this chapter. Although these instruments and interactions are essentially cooperative in nature, they also have a coercive element as actors attempt to sway one another. External actors have attempted to accrue what is essentially political influence in the region through, among other things, their involvement with Latin American economies and military establishments. Latin American actors have been the purveyors as well as the receivers of influence, in both intraregional relations and toward the outside world.

ECONOMIC RELATIONS

Patterns of Commercial Relations

Once Latin American barriers to investment and trade were dropped along with their dependence on Spain and Portugal in the early nineteenth century, Britain immediately dominated Latin American commerce and maintained an advantage over other industrial states. In the late nineteenth century British preeminence eroded, especially through the efforts of the United States and Germany. The Latin American states mainly had colonial plantation economies. The economically more powerful external states sought export markets for their manufactured goods, investment capital, technical skills, and surplus populations and cultivated Latin American sources of food and raw materials. The most efficient Latin American industries were often foreign owned and managed and produced for foreign rather than domestic markets.

Foreign capital was more attracted to portfolio than to direct investments. Beginning with Argentina in 1824, most Latin American government bonds were sold in the London money market, with the remainder primarily in France and the United States. By 1827 every bond sale had been defaulted, a situation postponing further flotations for three to four decades (except for Brazil). British capital again financed large bond issues by fifteen Latin American governments in the 1860s and 1870s; by 1877 more than two-thirds of the total value was again in default. In the 1880s Latin American debt servicing improved. But French investors who purchased bonds in the 1860s and 1870s in Haiti, Mexico, Honduras, Peru, and Argentina suffered heavy losses when they were defaulted (Rippy, 1958:331–333).

Direct investment was also important. Britain was especially well entrenched in Argentina, with holdings there representing between 40 and 50 percent of Britain's total Latin American investment. Britain also had substantial levels of investment in Brazil, Mexico, Venezuela, and Colombia. Some private U.S. capital migrated to Latin America before 1830; by 1870 virtually every Latin American state had received some such investments, with the preponderance in Mexico, Cuba, and Chile. U.S. capital flows increased dramatically after the Civil War. At the turn of the century about two-thirds of the U.S. investment in Latin America was concentrated in Mexico (Bernstein, 1966). The main recipients of French capital were Brazil, Chile, and Mexico. Rippy (1958:334) says that by the turn of the century, foreigners owned all or almost all of Latin America's railroads, tramways, river shipping businesses, port facilities, and major mining companies, as well as a large number of ranches and farms, manufacturing and processing plants, forestry operations, commercial banks and other enterprises, as well as all of the ocean shipping lines operating in the region.

As Latin American populations grew rapidly after 1900, demands for consumer goods increased. These goods were not available from domestic industries, however, and the region's international trade expanded dramatically. Total Latin American trade increased threefold from 1885 to 1913 on the eve of World War I (Rippy, 1958:390). Britain remained the principal trader and investor, but the United States registered the greatest increases in trade and investment and ranked second in both areas. German and French trade and investment also remained significant.

World War I cut off much of Europe's trade with Latin America, but it recovered soon after the war. U.S. investments more than tripled during the postwar period until 1930, with almost every Latin American state receiving some U.S. capital. British investments remained relatively stable until they began to decline after 1928, never to recover to their pre-1928 levels. German and French holdings declined in the 1920s. Regional trade and foreign investment declined severely during the world depression beginning in 1930 until 1939. The lack of capital and the shrinkage of purchasing power in markets around the globe were exacerbated by protectionist policies adopted by most trading partners. In addition to adopting economic controls, some Latin American states expropriated foreign enterprises, notably oil company subsidiaries in Mexico and Bolivia in 1938.

World War II stimulated Latin American international trade, especially with the Allies, who purchased the region's raw materials in large amounts for their war effort. However, new investment capital did not flow into the region until after the conflict was settled in 1945. During the postwar period, foreign corporations in Latin America still produced food and raw materials for export to industrial states, and the Latin American states continued to import capital machinery and manufactured goods. A number of them also imported significant amounts of agricultural products. Foreign exchange reserves accumulated during the war were partly used to retire bonds at a rapid pace in order to reduce levels of portfolio investments. Some states repatriated a number of foreign enterprises. Argentina took over British railways and other transportation facilities, and several governments purchased public utilities from their foreign owners. However, total direct investments increased, with the United States the main source of capital. The levels of portfolio investment increased only slightly.

Trade and investment figures illustrate U.S. economic dominance during the postwar era. For most Latin American states, at least one-third (often much more) of their total trade was with the United States. Through the 1960s U.S. investments accounted for about 40 percent of the total invested in Brazil, about half of that in Colombia and Peru, and almost 75 percent in Chile, with the largest single U.S. investment in Latin America in Venezuelan petroleum. Other nations were also active. Germany and Japan were the strongest competitors to the dominant U.S. position. British investments and trade fell off sharply after World War II. France also had a low level of trade, except with Brazil. The United States and other investors suffered large losses with the nationalization and expropriation of foreign enterprise in Cuba after 1959, in Chile and Peru in the late 1960s and early 1970s, and especially in Venezuela in the mid-1970s. The Soviet Union and China mounted drives in the 1960s and 1970s to increase their trade with Latin America but they held only a minor share, except for the Soviet Union with Cuba.

The 1980s Debt Situation

Latin American international economic relations were dominated after the early 1980s by problems of external debt. Although they were part of a global phenomenon, debt problems had special relevance for Latin America. The regional situation was distinguished from previous ones by its sheer magnitude. All Latin American countries had accumulated high levels of debt in relation to the size of their economies and had encountered serious problems with servicing them. Almost two-thirds of all bank loans to developing countries beginning in the early 1970s went to Latin America. Activities related to the resolution of debt issues continued to dominate U.S., European, and Japanese economic relations with the individual Latin American states and affected a wider range of political and military interactions.

The problem began in the late 1960s when Latin American governments and private enterprises decided to accelerate domestic development by borrowing abroad from international lending institutions and private commercial banks. The arrangements included two types of creditors: private suppliers, such as commercial banks, which provided direct loans and markets for the flotation of bonds; and public sources, including bilateral government agencies and the multilateral (general and regional) financial institutions. Borrowers included Latin American governments, government agencies, and private sector entities. The doubling of oil prices in 1973 spurred further borrowing to pay for higher-priced oil imports, and a reduction in interest rates after 1976 accelerated borrowing even further.

Debt-service capacity remained satisfactory, except for occasional problems, until the end of the 1970s. Commercial banks competed vigorously to place loans in the profitable market. They operated on the theory that governments, by definition, were not vulnerable to bankruptcy as private corporations were, and on the assumption that the IMF would rescue governments that encountered liquidity problems. Latin American governments, for their part, saw no need to adjust monetary or fiscal policies or engage in domestic austerity programs, and fiscal deficits increased. In a number of important cases, a significant portion of borrowed funds was diverted from developmental purposes to budgetary support, military expenditures, and capital flight. High-level corruption was sometimes a serious problem as well.

Not only did the size of public debt increase dramatically, but its structure also changed significantly. The greatest change was the increase in medium-term loans granted by private banks. Latin Americans gained unprecedented access to international bank syndicates and the Euromarket, and by 1980 the level of private-lender participation had grown from an insignificant proportion to more than two-thirds of the total.

A set of factors converged at the end of the 1970s to create the Latin American debt crisis. Another round of oil price increases worsened terms of trade. Renewed global recession sharply depressed prices for commodity exports, and interest rates increased. All of these problems, which added to debt-service burdens, were initially perceived as temporary phenomena that could be bridged through short-term borrowing. But the situation discouraged domestic savings and investment and encouraged massive capital flight, and Latin American economic growth rates declined for the first time in four decades. Borrowers had increasingly undertaken risky, short-term, variable-rate loans, further adding to the debt-servicing load. Banks began to refuse new loans, denying access to capital markets when debt servicing was the most difficult.

The debt problem became a crisis when Mexico, at the time the world's second largest debtor, announced on August 12, 1982, that it could no longer meet its external debt-service obligations. Thereafter other governments indicated illiquidity and inability to meet their foreign debts.

With the advent of the debt predicament in 1982 and the accompanying decrease in borrowers' creditworthiness, Latin Americans increasingly requested debt rescheduling. Complex negotiations subsequently developed between the borrowing entities and private banks, multilateral financial institutions, and creditor governments. (The following discussion of actors and negotiations draws on Parkinson, 1987.)

At the time of the Mexican announcement in 1982, Latin American external debt totaled about $315 billion. The three largest economies (Brazil, Mexico, and Argentina) accounted for about two-thirds of the total. Brazil was the world's largest debtor, having reached a level of about $100 billion in 1982. Chile, Colombia, Peru, and Venezuela together held much of the remainder. All Latin American countries, however, had borrowed heavily in relation to the size of their economies. U.S. bank claims in Latin America totaled some $82.5 billion, about a quarter of their overseas lending. Two-thirds of that total was held by the nine largest U.S. banks. The exposure of European and Japanese banks was sizable but far smaller as a percentage of their total international claims. Many smaller banks participated in external credits through syndicates.

Two "clubs" represented creditor governments and private banks, respectively. Neither club had a fixed membership or an institutional structure. The Paris Club was composed of sovereign representatives engaged in government-to-government loans. Originally established in 1956 to deal with the serious financial situation in Argentina, it operated again in the general financial crisis after 1982. The London Club of commercial banks was organized in the mid-1970s to systematize the proliferation of banking syndicates (themselves formed to raise the vast sums involved in the 1970s lending). It operated informally, meeting only when negotiations with a particular borrower were in progress. Although the Paris Club was concerned with the interests of commercial banks, it did not allow them to participate in its proceedings.

The Cartagena Group emerged to represent most of the Latin American debtor governments. When the presidents of Mexico and Brazil met soon after the onset of the crisis, they considered but rejected the repudiation of debts in favor of rescheduling them. The United Nations Commission for Latin America and the Caribbean (ECLAC) and the Latin American Economic System (SELA) subsequently issued a joint report and sponsored several meetings to discuss collective action. The most important of these meetings took place in Quito in January 1984, attended by representatives (including presidents and prime ministers) from twenty-six Latin American regional governments. The final report postulated a program of reduced debt payments and interest rates, a lengthening of maturities, and elimination of trade barriers by developed countries. The indifferent response by creditors inspired eleven Latin American governments (Argentina, Bolivia, Brazil, Chile, Colombia, Dominican Republic, Ecuador, Mexico, Peru, Uruguay, and Venezuela) to meet at Cartagena, Colombia, in June 1984 to further consider a multilateral position. They issued a document establishing a formal consultative mechanism known as the Cartagena Group and agreed to meet regularly.

Almost all Latin American governments were involved in continuing negotiations with the International Monetary Fund (IMF), in which the United States played a major role, and with a consortium of private international banks led by New York–based Citibank. The IMF insisted that the governments adopt austerity programs aimed primarily at controlling inflation, reducing imports, and stimulating exports so as to generate foreign exchange for debt servicing and lessen the need to borrow from abroad in future years. The banks made refinancing of existing loans and negotiation of new ones contingent on such agreements. The IMF, in turn, made "bridging loans" to ease the shocks of austerity. The United States and the Bank for International Settlements (BIS) also provided some short-term bridging loans to help countries meet external liquidity requirements. When austerity and credit targets were not met, the IMF did not hesitate to withhold portions of loans and private creditors to interrupt loan disbursements. Debtor countries were reluctant to adopt the austerity measures because of internal political opposition and fear of social disruption, a consideration particularly important for the new delicately balanced democratic governments those in the midst of moving toward democracy.

The U.S. government concurred in the positions taken by the IMF and commercial banks. In 1985, however, a modest change in emphasis evolved with what came to be called the "Baker Initiative." U.S. Treasury Secretary James Baker unveiled his ideas at a combined meeting of the IMF and the World Bank Group in Seoul, South Korea, in October 1985. He proposed to build on the existing approach and seek growth in the debtor countries that would restore their creditworthiness. Baker called for a three-year term package of new commercial bank loans netting $20 billion to fifteen principal debtor countries, ten of whom were from Latin America. Those countries would be required to undertake long-term structural reform policies, strategy combined with a continued central role for the IMF, the opening of the economies to foreign trade and investment, and an expanded role for multilateral banking institutions. The initiative amended only marginally, not fundamentally, the original approach.

Some three and a half years later, on March 14, 1989, U.S. Treasury Secretary Nicholas Brady announced another Third World debt-relief proposal. The "Brady Plan" sought negotiations that encouraged debtor states to sell state-owned industries and reduce public spending, and for commercial banks to forgive part of the debt, accept lower interest payments, and even cancellations of existing bank loans and related charges. The plan was aimed at reviving economic growth and decreasing political and social tensions resulting from economic dislocations. Whereas the Baker Initiative was based on new commercial bank loans, the Brady Plan called for debt relief and service-cost reductions. Mexico was the initial and most important target of Brady's strategy, and after an eleven-month process of negotiating with the commercial banks, IMF, and World Bank, an agreement was reached. Similar agreements were concluded with nine other Latin American states, among them Venezuela, Costa Rica, Argentina, Uruguay, and, in mid-1992, Brazil, the last of the major targeted sovereign Latin American borrowers to agree to the Brady Plan.

On June 27, 1990, President George Bush announced the Enterprise for the Americas Initiative (EAI), which contemplated a western hemisphere free-trade area (FTA). The centerpiece of the proposal, the North American Free Trade Agreement among Canada, Mexico, and the United States, went into effect on January 1, 1994, creating the world's largest free-trade zone. In the meantime, the United States signed "framework agreements" on trade and investment with all other countries in the Latin American region except for Cuba and Haiti. (See Chapter 9 for details.) The EAI included a debt reduction element, which was in effect an extension of the Brady Plan. The United States proposed to ease some debt burden and to increase incentives for economic reform and environmental protection by agreeing, with conditions, to reduce bilateral government-to-government debt owed to the United States. A state's eligibility was determined by the degree of its movement toward an open investment regime. (As part of this approach, the United States would support natural resources management as an element of protecting the environment.) The program became operational on June 27, 1991, when the United States and Chile signed the first debt-reduction agreement. Subsequent arrangements were made with other Latin American borrowers. The EAI also contemplated the promotion of regional private investment with a Multilateral Investment Fund (MIF), which was established in the Inter-American Development Bank (IDB) on February 11, 1992 with an initial capital of about $1.3 billion, including a U.S. pledge of $500 million.

Before initiation of the Brady Plan, West Europeans had done little to ameliorate the debt crisis, looking to the United States for its resolution. The Brady Plan also failed to get the European's strong backing, since they were determined that commercial banks would not transfer their bad loans to the IMF and World Bank. The banks themselves expected those international institutions and creditor states to provide them guarantees. Nevertheless, agreements between creditors and the major debtors for debt and servicing reductions were finally worked out. Japan was more positively active. In 1987 it instituted the Nakasone Plan, which recycled $65 billion of Japan's balance-of-payments surpluses over a five-year period to assist Third World debtor countries, the largest of which were in Latin America. In 1988 Japan followed with the Miyazawa Plan, which proposed a voluntary reduction of the bank debt through a conversion into guaranteed bonds; a year later the scheme was incorporated into the Brady Plan. Japan helped finance the debt reduction efforts of individual Latin American states, such as Mexico and Venezuela (Purcell and Immerman, 1992). At the behest of the United States, Japan agreed to contribute $500 million to the IDB's Multilateral Investment Fund in support of Latin American private sector development. Canada, France, Portugal, and Spain also contributed in the combined amount of $257 million.

Debt, Trade, and Investment in the 1990s

By 1990 the debt problem was no longer considered to be in crisis. The situation remained serious and worrisome, however. Some obligations were not being serviced as agreed, any downturns in the global economy could easily regender the crisis, and poverty and social dislocations remained crucial domestic problems. But debt issues had become subsumed under larger considerations of international trade and investment. Official statements and studies issuing from the IDB, ECLAC, and SELA reflected the changed situation. They indicated that although the debt problem was a continuing reality, it had become more manageable and most Latin American states had recovered their credibility with outside investors. Debt reduction, lower interest rates, and varying degrees of economic recovery and opening had generally improved the financial outlook. The debt structure itself had improved, transformed into longer-term instruments (often converted into bond issues) that were traded on an active secondary market (Grosse, 1992a). Foreign direct investment, which had sharply declined during the 1980s, grew rapidly at the end of the decade and into the 1990s as new bank lending almost ceased. MNCs established new subsidiaries and expanded existing operations. Foreign investors purchased many of the formerly state-owned enterprises as they were privatized. Latin American governments also attracted a large return of flight capital that had earlier sought refuge in the United States and Europe.

U.S. Economic Policies and Aid Programs

An early source of U.S. assistance to Latin America was the Export-Import Bank of Washington (EXIM, later EIB), established in 1934 to help promote the recovery of U.S. foreign trade after its sharp decline during the world depression. According to the EXIM report of December 31, 1941, a total of $48.5 million in loans had been disbursed to the twenty Latin American states as of that date. The most significant single project consisted of assisting in the export of U.S. equipment and services for the construction of a steel plant at Volta Redonda, Brazil. After the fall of France in 1940 and throughout World War II, EXIM loans to

TABLE 10.1   U.S. Export-Import Bank Loans (U.S. fiscal years; millions of dollars)

Recipient	Postwar Period 1946– 1952	Mutual Security Act 1953– 1961	Foreign Assistance Act 1962– 1988	1989	1990	1991	1992	Total 1946– 1988
Argentina	101.7	304.2	1,205.8	–	–	–	2.0	2,148.3
Bahamas	–	–	63.8	–	–	–	–	58.8
Barbados	–	–	10.4	–	–	–	–	6.8
Belize	–	–	a	–	–	–	3.4	3.4
Bermuda	–	–	34.0	–	–	–	–	27.9
Bolivia	19.3	7.1	44.6	–	–	–	–	117.1
Brazil	158.5	996.8	2,281.5	26.0	22.5	–	–	5,044.0
Chile	104.2	169.1	384.4	–	24.1	–	–	1,073.3
Colombia	23.5	144.3	996.2	–	–	–	–	1,087.5
Costa Rica	–	19.4	42.7	–	–	–	–	99.4
Cuba	12.0	25.5	–	–	–	–	–	93.8
Dominican Republic	–	–	111.3	–	–	–	–	181.9
Ecuador	11.8	10.4	64.6	–	–	–	–	168.2
El Salvador	–	3.2	18.7	–	–	–	–	24.6
Grenada	–	–	–	–	–	–	–	–
Guatemala	–	13.4	100.3	–	–	–	–	46.2
Guyana	–	–	9.6	–	–	–	–	26.3
Haiti	14.0	11.0	3.1	–	–	–	–	38.8
Honduras	–	2.7	34.0	–	–	–	–	35.9
Jamaica	–	–	95.8	–	–	–	–	187.6
Mexico	180.1	301.9	3,242.6	10.3	11.1	–	23.7	4,534.8
Nicaragua	0.6	12.5	28.3	–	–	–	–	98.0
Panama	4.0	13.0	139.1	–	–	–	–	143.6
Paraguay	–	10.3	66.9	–	–	–	–	19.1
Peru	19.9	161.3	253.0	–	–	–	–	588.9
Suriname	–	–	5.8	–	–	–	–	5.9
Trinidad-Tobago	–	–	391.6	–	–	–	–	393.7
Uruguay	2.6	–	22.3	–	–	–	–	38.6
Venezuela	12.2	51.2	601.2	–	–	–	4.2	561.2
Other[b]	3.0	28.1	86.7	–	–	–	–	130.0
Total	667.4	2,285.4	10,338.2	36.3	57.8	–	33.3	16,983.6

[a]Less than $50,000

[b]Includes Latin American regional, Central American regional, and other West Indies–Eastern Caribbean programs

Note: Row totals include any capitalized interest, net deobligations, and repayments and may not add to sum of annual loans; column details may not add to totals due to rounding.

Source: Agency for International Development, U.S. Overseas Loans and Grants and Assistance from International Organizations; Obligations and Loan Authorizations, July 1, 1945–September 30, 1992 (1993).

TABLE 10.2   U.S. Economic Assistance: Loans and Grants (U.S. fiscal years; millions of dollars)

Recipient	Postwar Period 1946–1952	Mutual Security Act 1953–1961	Foreign Assistance Act 1962–1988	1989	1990	1991	1992	Total 1946–1992
Argentina	[a]	51.3	189.0	0.6	0.8	1.5	1.9	187.7
Bahamas	–	0.3	[a]	–	1.5	1.2	1.0	4.1
Barbados	–	–	3.8	0.3	[a]	[a]	[a]	4.1
Belize	–	1.4	97.8	10.4	8.4	9.0	6.2	130.4
Bermuda	–	–	–	–	–	–	–	–
Bolivia	4.1	192.5	1,152.8	80.4	109.0	155.2	182.8	1,352.9
Brazil	25.3	314.2	2,240.3	2.2	3.1	4.5	3.0	2,404.9
Chile	6.2	170.7	1,069.9	5.3	2.1	15.4	5.4	1,254.1
Colombia	3.3	106.5	1,441.3	11.1	21.0	20.7	24.0	1,468.8
Costa Rica	6.0	52.2	1,350.0	122.0	95.3	45.0	26.7	1,691.6
Cuba	0.5	3.8	–	–	–	–	–	4.0
Dominican Republic	0.8	2.1	1,325.2	81.2	25.7	22.0	22.2	1,420.2
Ecuador	5.1	49.3	567.5	40.6	23.9	24.5	27.6	793.7
El Salvador	2.4	11.1	2,534.8	307.0	246.7	227.8	268.8	3,617.2
Grenada	–	–	59.9	0.1	[a]	[a]	–	60.2
Guatemala	9.9	121.3	934.9	147.2	114.7	92.3	61.8	1468.7
Guyana	[a]	2.3	150.8	7.0	8.7	6.7	7.9	96.7
Haiti	2.7	61.0	664.9	63.0	58.9	81.3	51.0	917.1
Honduras	2.5	35.1	1,340.2	88.1	192.6	123.8	89.3	1,508.3
Jamaica	–	6.7	1,073.1	115.9	73.2	75.9	76.9	1,733.1
Mexico	93.9	40.2	303.3	69.8	41.5	57.6	40.3	631.1
Nicaragua	6.2	33.6	375.3	3.9	223.3	218.7	74.9	675.0
Panama	3.0	54.9	547.5	1.0	397.0	40.0	21.1	1,036.9
Paraguay	4.4	35.5	177.5	4.7	3.3	4.0	4.9	224.6
Peru	12.4	101.4	1,252.5	64.5	93.4	174.0	123.0	1762.2
Suriname	–	2.9	3.7	–	–	–	7.4	13.3
Trinidad-Tobago	–	7.9	35.9	2.2	0.1	[a]	[a]	43.2
Uruguay	2.8	34.0	166.7	0.1	2.6	1.6	3.0	173.0
Venezuela	1.6	16.3	186.6	0.7	1.1	1.0	1.6	207.2
Other[b]	1.8	43.7	2,229.9	197.3	161.5	158.2	187.5	2,889.1
Total	195.9	1,552.2	21,475.1	1,426.5	1,909.5	1,562.2	1,320.3	27,773.4

[a]Less than $50,000

[b]Includes Latin American regional, Central American regional, and other West Indies–Eastern Caribbean programs

Note: Row totals include any capitalized interest, net deobligations, and repayments and may not add to sum of annual loans; column details may not add to totals due to rounding.

Source: Agency for International Development, U.S. Overseas Loans and Grants and Assistance from International Organizations; Obligations and Loan Authorizations, July 1, 1945–September 30, 1992 (1993).

TABLE 10.3 Assistance from International Organizations, 1946–1992 (millions of dollars)

Recipient	IBRD	IFC	IDA	IDB	UNDP	Other UN	Total
Argentina	6,122.6	1,235.6	–	5,572.1	66.6	7.4	13,004.1
Bahamas	42.8	–	–	159.5	5.4	a	207.7
Barbados	95.4	1.6	–	139.4	7.2	0.2	268.1
Belize	–	33.3	–	–	1.0	4.8	44.9
Bermuda	–	–	–	–	0.5	–	0.5
Bolivia	296.0	97.9	790.1	1,827.9	65.2	17.1	3,094.2
Brazil	19,694.4	2,258.2	–	8,291.5	111.6	35.7	30,391.4
Chile	3,094.5	886.3	19.0	4,523.8	78.8	12.4	8,614.8
Colombia	7,511.8	425.2	19.5	4,931.4	73.0	39.9	13,000.8
Costa Rica	739.9	21.4	4.6	1421.7	17.5	7.2	2,213.3
Cuba	–	–	–	–	48.6	10.1	58.7
Dominica	–	0.6	–	–	–	–	0.6
Dominican Republic	556.9	55.9	22.0	1,028.0	34.6	13.9	1,721.3
Ecuador	1,714.1	74.8	36.5	2,435.0	56.4	16.0	4,332.8
El Salvador	392.1	1.0	25.6	1,130.4	33.2	14.8	1,597.1
Grenada	–	6.0	5.0	–	1.2	–	12.2
Guatemala	585.1	18.2	–	1,127.7	31.7	19.2	1,781.9
Guyana	79.4	3.7	171.0	426.6	32.0	5.9	718.6
Haiti	2.6	3.4	453.0	349.7	72.4	24.5	905.6
Honduras	717.0	13.0	214.9	1,310.3	39.1	11.4	2,305.5
Jamaica	1,000.2	59.4	–	895.9	30.0	5.1	2,030.6
Mexico	20,616.9	1996.9	–	7,876.5	66.5	31.9	30,588.7
Nicaragua	231.1	9.5	180.3	620.9	31.9	13.2	1,086.9
Panama	815.8	74.0	–	984.3	30.7	8.3	1,913.1
Paraguay	486.6	23.0	45.5	919.9	35.1	10.7	1,520.8
Peru	2,690.9	112.2	–	2,300.3	69.0	28.9	5,201.3
Suriname	–	–	–	22.3	12.2	0.7	83.0
Trinidad-Tobago	211.6	273.3	–	443.5	26.5	0.8	1,047.7
Uruguay	1,098.9	58.5	–	932.8	30.1	4.7	2,125.0
Venezuela	2,341.0	506.4	–	2,699.7	42.5	5.9	5,685.5
Other[b]	68.4	31.2	56.1	1,530.4	218.1	70.1	2,130.5
Total	71,339.3	8,247.7	2,043.1	53,901.5	1,371.4	420.8	137,689.2

[a]Less than $50,000.

[b]Includes Latin American regional programs, and other West Indies–Eastern Caribbean Programs, and Bermuda.

Abbreviations: IBRD=World Bank; IFC=International Finance Corp.; IDA=International Development Assoc.; IDB=Inter-American Development Bank; UNDP=United Nations Development Program

Source: Agency for International Development, *U.S. Overseas Loans and Grants and Assistance from International Organizations; Obligations and Loan Authorizations, July 1, 1945–September 30, 1992* (1993).

Latin America were aimed at developing sources of strategic raw materials and combatting Axis economic penetration, as well as building the Pan American highway and other projects. The EXIM report of July 1, 1945, listed more than $4 billion in authorizations to Latin America from 1940 to 1945.

The first publicly funded U.S. technical assistance programs in Latin America were instituted in 1939. The programs were not intended for major capital investments or to promote large-scale economic development, but to give limited assistance to specific projects jointly financed by the United States and the host government. In 1939 President Roosevelt established the Interdepartmental Committee on Scientific and Cultural Cooperation, which spent a total of $678,000 in Latin America through 1945. Most of the projects were in agriculture (notably a rubber development program), geology, civil aviation, child welfare, and statistical services. Another agency created in 1940, eventually called the Office of Inter-American Affairs, was devoted to U.S. technical assistance programs in Latin America; it was originally headed by Nelson A. Rockefeller. Viewed as a wartime agency only, it supervised a large number of cultural and commercial relations between the United States and Latin America. Technical assistance programs costing the United States $110 million through 1945 concentrated on the fields of health, agriculture, and education.

The Truman administration through 1952 attempted to explain to Latin America that problems in other parts of the world, first in Europe and then in Asia, were more pressing than those in Latin America and that Latin Americans should thus depend primarily for funds on the newly created international lending agencies (World Bank and IMF), and private investment capital, rather than on direct U.S. economic assistance. Technical assistance programs, however, were continued. U.S. policy was geared to the cold war, and the prospect of both Soviet expansion into Latin America and internal Communist revolution seemed remote.

Beginning in 1945 EXIM was authorized to finance some foreign development projects on the assumption that they would increase markets for U.S. exports. EXIM was the main source of U.S. postwar economic assistance to Latin America, but it gave Europe priority, and the sums authorized for Latin America were relatively small. EXIM projects in 1951, in response to the military needs of the Korean conflict, were aimed at facilitating Latin American strategic raw material production. The Interdepartmental Committee on Scientific and Cultural Cooperation (ICSCC) and the Institute of Inter-American Affairs (IIAA), a subagency of the Office of Inter-American Affairs that was transferred to the State Department when its parent was abolished, continued its technical assistance projects in the fields of agriculture, public health, elementary education, and vocational training. From 1946 through 1949 the ICSCC expended $10.4 million in Latin America, and the IIAA, $21.6 million.

The United States inaugurated a worldwide technical assistance program in 1950 under the Act for International Development. The program was informally called "Point Four" because it was the fourth point of President Truman's economic policy announced in his inaugural address of 1949. U.S. experience with technical assistance in Latin America largely provided the basis for global Point Four programs. Yet the region itself received less assistance than did Europe and Asia. Public administration and the improvement of industrial productivity were added as new fields of endeavor in 1951.

The Mutual Security Act (MSA) of 1951 emphasized the relevance of economic and technical aid to security concerns in the context of the cold war. The Communist threat in Latin America was not considered great, however, and the area was of low priority in MSA programs. The Truman and Eisenhower administrations continued to stress the "trade not aid" concept in Latin America and opposed large-scale development spending. Nevertheless, Latin Americans benefitted from several MSA programs, even if not to the extent they desired. In addition, the Agricultural Trade Development and Assistance Act of 1954 (PL480), an effort to reduce U.S. farm product surpluses in a constructive manner, provided for several programs, among them the overseas sale of surplus agricultural products followed by loans of "counterpart" funds that subsequently accumulated.

After Vice President Nixon's ill-fated Latin American trip in 1958, U.S. officials indicated a need to reexamine U.S. economic policy toward Latin America and showed a willingness to make changes. The Castro revolution in Cuba in 1959, and its association with the Soviet Union, further inspired U.S. attention to economic programs in the region. New developmental policies emerged toward the end of the Eisenhower administration. The Inter-American Development Bank was established in late 1959 with U.S. backing. In July 1960 the United States announced the $500 million Eisenhower Plan for Latin American economic development aimed at halting "the further spread of communism in the Western Hemisphere." At U.S. urging, the "Act of Bogotá" was adopted in September 1960 at an inter-American meeting to give multilateral support to the Eisenhower Plan.

The new program represented some fundamental changes in U.S. economic policies toward Latin America. The provision of long-term loans, repayable in soft currency, for social purpose projects such as low-cost housing, improved education, and land reform, revised the former policy of extending hard currency loans to be spent primarily on U.S. products. The United States continued to urge Latin Americans to provide an attractive climate for foreign investors in the economic development process, but it no longer insisted on private capital as the primary economic source.

The Alliance for Progress and After

Soon after his inauguration in 1961, President Kennedy proposed a ten-year Latin American economic and social development program to be known as the Alliance for Progress. Recipients of U.S. assistance were to agree to undertake measures seeking to assure maximum social progress. The Alliance for Progress built on programs initiated by President Eisenhower. It had originally been inspired by Brazilian President Kubitschek's proposal in 1958 for an "Operation Pan America" to raise dramatically Latin American living standards. A few months after Kennedy's proposal, an inter-American agreement, the Charter of Punta del Este, was signed to make the Alliance a multilateral program. In general, the United States promised to give long-term development assistance to Latin America in a "decade of progress." The program, to be administered by the IDB, promised significant financial contributions as well as assistance in development planning and social reform. U.S. economic and social aid was closely linked to the fear that the Castro revolution would spread to other parts of the region.

The developmentalist policy of the Alliance for Progress continued through the Kennedy and Johnson administrations, but the Nixon administration quickly shifted to a "low profile" in economic as well as other affairs concerning Latin America. In his first presidential address on hemispheric policy on April 14, 1969,

President Nixon referred to the Alliance as a "great concept" that had "done much good" in some countries. Although Nixon did not propose a formal end to the Alliance, he indicated that it would be downgraded on the grounds that it had not stimulated sufficient economic growth. He made no mention of its social purposes. Latin American economic aid expenditures declined after 1969, and policy rhetoric moved away from ideas and projects aimed at social change and economic development. The importance of trade over aid and of foreign investment capital for economic development was reemphasized. The Ford administration after 1974 made no basic changes in Nixon's economic policy toward Latin America. The Carter administration emphasized the human rights factor in its aid polices, which mainly affected military assistance programs, and economic assistance in general was not emphasized.

The Caribbean Basin Initiative

President Reagan announced the Caribbean Basin Initiative (CBI) at a meeting of the OAS in February 1982. Congress subsequently passed the Caribbean Basin Economic Recovery Act, which went into effect on January 1, 1984, with the purpose of stimulating the trade and growth of selected Circum-Caribbean beneficiary countries. It offered U.S. trade preferences by providing for duty-free access to the U.S. market over a period of twelve years, restricting certain products from such entry. In 1990 Congress enacted legislation at President Bush's request to make the CBI permanent. Most countries in the region were designated as beneficiaries, although their actual participation varied over the years. The twenty-four designated beneficiaries as of the beginning of 1994 were: Antigua and Barbuda, Aruba, Bahamas, Barbados, Belize, British Virgin Islands, Costa Rica, Dominica, Dominican Republic, El Salvador, Grenada, Guatemala, Guyana, Honduras, Jamaica, Montserrat, Netherlands Antilles, Panama, St. Kitts–Nevis, St. Lucia, St. Vincent and the Grenadines, Suriname, and Trinidad and Tobago. Cuba and Nicaragua were excluded from the program from the beginning. Grenada initially was proscribed but declared eligible after the U.S. military intervention in 1983. Aruba, formerly a part of the Netherlands Antilles, was individually designated in April 1986. Haiti was a beneficiary until November 5, 1991, when the United States imposed an economic embargo in accordance with multilateral sanctions imposed by the OAS. Three countries, Anguilla, Cayman Islands, and the Turks and Caicos Islands, are eligible but have not formally requested designation. The U.S. Virgin Islands and Puerto Rico, which have special U.S. constitutional statuses and statutory relationships, are also considered CBI beneficiaries for certain purposes.

The CBI as initially conceived closely tracked the Reagan administration's geopolitical views of the Caribbean Basin, which were sketched in terms of East-West conflict and reflected changing views of the causes of Central American conflict. The CBI blended opposition to Soviet expansionism with local developmentalism and the president's free-enterprise philosophy. Reagan's speech before the OAS and subsequent administration declarations all revealed this combination of concerns. He emphasized the strategic importance of the Caribbean to the United States, as well as U.S. economic interests and subregional economic problems, which he suggested threatened political and social stability and created conditions that could be exploited by the Soviet Union and Cuba. Economic problems also increased illegal immigration and facilitated the export of narcotics to the United States. In sum, a major border of the United States threatened to consist of hostile states, and the United States therefore had a vital interest in preventing economic collapse or the creation of Marxist-Leninist regimes in neighboring countries. By the time the 1990 measure was enacted, the cold war was over and the East-West aspects of the CBI were irrelevant.

The economic considerations of CBI programs were aimed at Caribbean export expansion and diversification and increased outside investment. The CBI "centerpiece" was the provision for duty-free access for most exports from designated Caribbean countries into U.S. markets. The exceptions included textiles and apparel, canned tuna, petroleum and petroleum products, most footwear, and certain leather and other goods. Sugar imports received limited duty-free treatment but were in effect subject to quota limits, in terms of the prior U.S. domestic sugar price support program. (Sugar remained subject to the tariff-rate quota system announced on September 13, 1990.) The 1986 law required ethanol imports to conform to special rules, allowed special access to the United States for apparel assembled in the Caribbean region from materials manufactured in the United States, and created a "safeguard mechanism" for U.S. industries injured by increased CBI imports. The CBI was supplemented by designated investment capital from Puerto Rico—low-cost funds derived from profits accumulated free of federal taxes by U.S. corporate subsidiaries in Puerto Rico under Section 936 of the U.S. tax code (thus called "936 funds"). Under this provision cooperative manufacturing ventures were promoted in which Caribbean countries supplied low-cost labor for the assembly of items manufactured in Puerto Rico and the United States.

The Andean Trade Initiative

On December 4, 1991, President Bush signed into law the Andean Trade Preference Act (ATPA). As the trade element of President Bush's "Andean Strategy" to deal with the narcotics traffic (see Chapter 11), the ATPA was a unilateral trade preference program aimed to promote economic development through private-sector initiative in the four Andean countries of Bolivia, Colombia, Ecuador, and Peru. It gave them duty-free entry into the U.S. market over a ten-year period (extending to December 4, 2001). The same categories of products were excluded from duty-free entry as under the CBI, in addition to rum and tafia. An official guidebook to the ATPA (U.S. Department of Commerce and U.S. Agency for International Development, July 1992) offered the following policy rationale: The ATPA offers programs to assist Bolivia, Colombia, Ecuador, and Peru with economic development and diversification, as well as to stimulate private sector initiative and offer new opportunities for U.S. entrepreneurs. If Andean coca growers and processors are to discontinue their activities, they must have viable alternatives to earn adequate income. Experience with the CBI, on which the ATPA is modeled (although the CBI is a permanent program that offers certain nontariff benefits the ATPA does not), promises increased trade, investment, and economic diversification.

Trade and Aid Policies of Other Actors

The United States stressed the multilateral nature of the CBI when it was conceived in 1982; consultation with other governments took place and they supplemented the U.S. programs. But it was agreed that each state would develop its own approach, with only a modicum of coordination in order to avoid duplication. Much of the effort on the part of these and other actors—Canada, Europe, Japan, and international financial institutions—in fact predated the CBI itself and, presumably, would have continued without it.

The United Kingdom, France, and the Netherlands for many years tended to concentrate their "Latin American" aid in their present and former dependencies. This practice left few resources for assistance to the vast majority of the region. Europeans generally tied aid closely to their exports, looking to improve their own balance of trade more than to promote Latin American economic development. Assistance was designed to improve commercial positions, and credits and loans usually were granted only to finance Latin American purchases of European products. Germany was the exception. Like the United States, Germany perceived that its interests were best served by a stable and prosperous world and linked its aid to anti-Communist ideology and the East-West conflict. Consequently, German economic aid to Latin America fit into its overall concern with the underdeveloped nations and centered on economic development programs initiated in the mid-1950s. Commercial goals were not lacking, and German aid credits were used to develop new export markets. However, in 1974 the German government reduced its development aid programs, stating, in effect, that easing its domestic tax burden took precedent over foreign assistance.

By the mid-1970s, members of the European Community (EC) had decided to direct their trade and aid policies toward Latin America through their own multilateral European institutions. More than 80 percent of the trade between the EC and Latin America was with the seven largest Latin American economies (Argentina, Brazil, Chile, Colombia, Mexico, Peru, and Venezuela). The EC was Latin America's largest trading partner after the United States, although the level of trade tended to decline from the 1970s into the 1990s. The relationship with Latin America was of much less significance to Europe than to the United States. Nevertheless, Latin America received a proportionally higher level of exports from the EC than did other less developed countries (LDCs), probably because it was the most economically advanced LDC region. Although Latin America represented a minor part of the EC's total trade, the area was a principal source of food and raw materials and an important market for manufactured surpluses.

The EC provided them special trade concessions (in the form of duty-free access to the EC market for most of their industrial and agricultural exports). The other regional states complained of further discrimination, saying that Lomé meant they were faced with unfair terms of trade not only in competition with the industrialized world but also with much of the rest of the Third World.

In 1971 the EC introduced the Generalized Preference Scheme (GPS) that gave concessional terms of trade for certain Third World exports, and later provided loans through the European Development Fund and the European Investment Bank and other forms of export assistance. These measures were aimed at helping developing economies to be more competitive with the First World in gaining access to European markets. But Latin Americans were highly critical of EC practices. EC officials acknowledged the Latin American complaint that the system was too restrictive and that preferences were given on few of the products in the first rank of Latin American exports.

The EC also established special trade preferences for former colonies of its member states in February 1975. After lengthy negotiations, the initial four-year Lomé Convention was signed between the EC and forty-six states in Africa, the Caribbean, and the Pacific (the ACP countries). The convention took effect on April 1, 1976. The number of eligible ACP countries and the benefits offered increased with subsequent treaty renegotiations and extensions. The fourth convention, which went into effect in 1990, is to expire in 1996. Until 1990 the only Latin American regional beneficiaries were the twelve Commonwealth Caribbean Countries and Suriname, as former colonies of the United Kingdom and the Netherlands, respectively. In that year the Dominican Republic, at Spain's urging, was allowed to adhere. The Lomé system provides for preferential markets in many products, special trade concessions (duty-free access to the EC market for most of their industrial and agricultural exports), a commodity export price stabilization agreement, cooperation in industrial and technical matters, increased aid disbursements and loans through the European Development Fund and the European Investment Bank, assistance in regional integration, and joint institutions. The large number of Latin American states not party to the convention expressed displeasure with the Lomé arrangements. They complained that Lomé meant they were faced with unfair terms of trade not only in competition with the industrialized world but also with much of the rest of the Third World. They reiterated pleas that the EC adopt a global policy toward LDCs and not favor the ACP countries to the detriment of others.

In the 1990s Europeans responded to Latin America's improved economic and political situation and the shift from highly protected to more open market economies. But they were unwilling to accept anything more than modest financial costs in trade and investment relationships. A new temporary element was the European Community Special Andean Trade Program, designed to support efforts by Andean countries to combat drug production. The EC adopted a plan to assist Colombia, Peru, Bolivia, and Ecuador with trade concessions on a range of their export goods over a four-year period, expiring in October 1994. The program excluded certain agricultural products and live animals. The EC also established a special program of financial aid to Colombia, which had initiated the request for EC support, over the same four-year period (U.S. Department of Commerce and U.S. Agency for International Development [July 1992].

Japan adopted an increasingly global foreign policy as it became the world's second largest market economy. Most of Japan's aid to Latin America was in the form of export credits rather than economic development grants, similar to the U.S. practice through EXIM. Japan actively traded with Cuba and it lent $10 million to Jamaica in 1981 for developmental purposes. In early 1986 Japan increased its trade credits and developmental assistance to the Circum-Caribbean countries.

Latin America was not an important part of Canada's foreign assistance program until 1964. Thereafter, bilateral aid and some Canadian contributions to the IDB were restricted to purchases of Canadian goods. Canadian assistance to Circum-Caribbean countries increased after the onset of Central American conflict in the late 1970s and the debt crisis of the early 1980s. Specifically, in early 1982 Canada announced an increase in developmental assistance to Central American countries, committing $105 million over a five-year period. In 1986 Canada announced a program to double its bilateral aid to the Commonwealth Caribbean—both the sovereign states and British dependencies—for the ensuing year, and simultaneously to implement a preferential free-trade arrangement with the same countries along the lines of the CBI (called CARIBCAN). In March 1990, Canada announced that certain items were no longer excluded and that Canada would write off C$182 million in CARIBCAN debts.

The Soviet Union's regional economic aid program outside of Cuba was small but its trade concessions were generous in nature if not in amount. Soviet economic aid to Cuba included balance-of-payments credits, technical assistance costs, project credits, and sugar subsidies. The Soviet Union normally did not provide aid in the form of either grants or outright loans. However, it gave trade transactions the character of economic assistance by allowing repayments in the form of commodities rather than currency (Goldhamer, 1972:184). This barter arrangement was automatically tied to Soviet products. Latin Americans complained about the inferior quality of Soviet goods and their overvaluation in account settlements. Except for Cuba, Latin American states enjoyed a trade surplus with the Soviet Union. Offers of economic aid and trade were often linked to the reestablishment of diplomatic relations with the Soviet Union.

Soviet foreign policy reorientations after 1985, and the subsequent dissolution of the Soviet Union, meant at least a temporary economic retirement from Latin America and only a residual relationship with Cuba. With the decline of the Soviet economy, subsidies and assistance to Cuba were drastically reduced. Castro, with a huge stake in the status quo, vehemently protested the changing relationship. In 1990 the Soviets discontinued subsidizing petroleum deliveries to Cuba and Cuban sugar exports to the Soviet Union, which were especially heavy blows to the Cuban economy. In fact, the Soviets put all trade on a commercial basis at world market prices. In 1990–1991 the Soviet Union sharply cut its Cuban grant and technical aid programs, including the number of technicians and advisers in Cuba. In July 1993, Russia agreed to grant Cuba a $380 million credit, only a fraction of the assistance issuing from Moscow in previous years, to facilitate trade and to complete projects initiated by the former Soviet Union (Blasier, 1993).

The Holy See sponsored a development assistance program in support of papal pronouncements concerning social and economic justice for the poor. Pope Paul VI in 1969 established a Vatican Development Fund for Latin America to be funneled through the IDB. Interest-free long-term loan projects were selected by the bank in consultation with the Vatican. According to a church communiqué, the fund would be used in "the fields of agrarian reform, over-all human well-being, workers' organizations and other areas of social and economic reform and general improvement in the developing countries which are members of the bank."

The stronger Latin American states sponsored assistance programs. Brazil, Mexico, Argentina, and Venezuela for a time provided economic aid and technical assistance to the poorer Latin American states. The most important programs were pursued by Venezuela, which used its oil wealth in the mid-1970s to enhance its emerging influence especially in the Circum-Caribbean as well as to avoid the inflationary consequences of investing more money in the domestic economy than it could absorb. In 1974 Venezuela contributed more than $500 million for loans to be made through the IDB and the World Bank. In December of that year Venezuela compensated six Central American states for holding back part of their coffee harvests in order to raise prices. It provided subsidies to those particularly hurt by rising oil prices and gave direct aid to the most underdeveloped of them.

Latin American assistance activities were reduced with the debt crisis in the 1980s, but certain efforts nevertheless continued. In 1980 Mexico and Venezuela established a joint oil facility for the energy-deficient countries in the Circum-Caribbean. The program financed almost a third of the petroleum requirements of nine countries (El Salvador, Guatemala, Honduras, Costa Rica, Nicaragua, Panama, Barbados, Jamaica, and the Dominican Republic), at a total value of about $300 million annually. The facility continued despite the debt problems in both countries. In addition, Mexico granted trade preferences to El Salvador, Guatemala, Costa Rica, Panama, and members of CARICOM and financed technical assistance programs around the area. Venezuela further assisted some of those economies in the 1980s by contributing direct Central Bank deposits (in Nicaragua, the Dominican Republic, Costa Rica, and Jamaica) and granting developmental project loans to Central American countries. Colombia offered substantial trade credits and modest technical assistance programs to several countries in the Circum-Caribbean.

MILITARY RELATIONS

Latin American Military Modernization

Toward the end of the nineteenth century, Latin American states began to develop their military establishments—most of which had been born during the earlier wars for independence—as a concomitant to the general thrust for national modernization. Thereafter, Latin American governments generally conceded that their continuous attempts to modernize and professionalize their military establishments required substantial foreign assistance. The Latin American armed forces underwent extensive development with active assistance from Europe and the United States, both in terms of professional training and in the acquisition of arms and equipment. As a result, levels of military modernization and foreign military influences in the region varied widely and complex patterns of international military competition emerged.

The motives of the extraregional states in giving military assistance were several. In general terms it was used as a way to gain political and economic as well as military influence in Latin America. Cooperative military instruments included sending military missions and instructors to other states, providing training and educational facilities for foreign personnel, pursuing diplomatic activities (such as exchanging armed service attachés, making visits, and awarding honors), and engaging in the arms trade.

Patterns of Relations to World War I

From the late nineteenth century until World War I, Latin American plans for military and naval reorganization and development led to sharp competition among the external states who vied to be entrusted with the task. Some foreign influence existed in the regional armies and navies dating from the wars for independence, but it was not until the Latin American states decided to develop their military establishments systematically that foreign training became an important part of Latin American international politics.

In the pre–World War I period, Germany and France were the most important military competitors, and Great Britain and the United States, both renowned commercial shipbuilders, retained the most influence in naval affairs. The German and French armies enjoyed high prestige and the support of their home governments in overseas activities. Their competition for military influence in Latin America and elsewhere was an extension of Franco-German antagonism in Europe. Germany was predominant in Chile's and Argentina's military affairs, and France prevailed in Peru, Uruguay, and Brazil. The two states competed with rough equality in Bolivia, Paraguay, and Guatemala. The United States exerted direct military influence on armies in those states in the Caribbean where it practiced post–1898 intervention. Influence was mixed in Ecuador, Venezuela, and Colombia, and was not significant in the other regional states.

External military assistance usually came in the form of armed forces missions and instructors sent to Latin America and offering the use of military facilities in the external state. German and French missions and instructors were invited to perform a variety of tasks in the major South American states. Chile, the first to begin military modernization, received its first German adviser in 1885. Thereafter the number of German officers increased, and they achieved positions far in excess of foreign officers elsewhere in Latin America. They reorganized the Chilean army, organized a general staff, established general conscription, reformed military education, and assumed direct command and training of troops. The German role became important in Argentina in 1899, when a military mission was engaged to organize and staff the new Army War College. It was later involved in other training schools and in writing Argentina's obligatory conscription law. Peru was the first Latin American state to establish close military collaboration with France and became a center of French military influence in Latin America. A French military mission arrived in 1896 and reorganized the Peruvian army along French lines. France also held a leading military position in Brazil. A French mission was engaged by the state of São Paulo in 1906 to train public forces and to establish a cadet school. Latin American military personnel were assigned overseas for professional training and education, regimental service, and observation at maneuvers. A few were sent to the United States, but most went to Europe, primarily to those states that sent missions to Latin America.

Latin American states also entered into armaments contracts with European munitions firms and U.S. and European shipbuilders, committing most regional armies and navies almost completely to foreign manufactures. Armaments orders were largely by-products of foreign service mission employment. The Latin American states, as a rule, were not weapons manufacturers and imported almost all of their armaments and equipment. The competition in military affairs affected the general competition in the export trade, as military orders could increase a country's volume of export trade considerably. In the industrial sphere, bitter rivalry developed among Krupp of Germany, Schneider-Creusot of France, and other arms manufacturers. Leading European armament firms made advances to Latin American governments until improved Latin American financial situations enabled them to make immediate payment. The French government, in granting general-purpose loans to Latin American governments, insisted on linking them to purchases from Schneider-Creusot. In spite of the French efforts, the German firms of Krupp and Mauser held the largest share of the Latin American military market prior to World War I.

The Interbellum Period

After World War I Latin American military leaders complained that their lack of war experience seriously handicapped service training. By then the last wars in which they had participated were more than a generation removed, and only a few Latin American officers had observed the recent war in Europe firsthand. They had been left behind by the revolutionary developments in military technology and tactics. Latin American military men thus felt that it was essential for them to learn from those who had recent experience and knowledge in modern war.

Outside of those small Caribbean states where the United States was directly intervening, at first it seemed that France would be free of military competition in Latin America. Not only was France's military reputation at its zenith as the leading European power, but the Versailles Treaty prohibited Germany from sending military missions and instructors abroad and abolished all German military educational institutions that might receive foreign officers. The treaty bound thirteen Latin American states and prohibited Germany from aiding the military forces of any other state in any way. French military circles confidently expected to inherit the prewar German position in South America in a period marked by severe legal restrictions on Germany. As it turned out, however, the Versailles Treaty proved to be ineffective and Germany soon returned to a position of influence.

The first years after the war witnessed a surge in French influence in Latin American armies, but the region soon received training missions not only from France, and eventually Germany, but also from Italy, Great Britain, the United States, and even Switzerland and Spain. The number of missions contracted by Latin American governments increased substantially in the 1920s and 1930s. Air and police missions were added to the traditional army and naval missions. Especially notable was the accelerated employment of air force training missions consequent to the rapid development of military aviation during the war. Italy entered the South American military scene in the 1920s and eventually gained extraordinary influence in Latin American military aviation. Britain and the United States initially followed their tradition of viewing military relations in essentially commercial terms, but in the 1930s they began to aim at counterinfluencing the presence of Germany and other Axis states for political reasons. Japan attempted to compete in the arms market but was relatively unimportant. A small number of

Russian officers of the old Tsarist army, several of high rank and reputation, came to Latin America for military employment after the Bolshevik Revolution of 1917, and some of them participated in the Chaco War between Bolivia and Paraguay in the 1930s.

As in the prewar period, the South American states were the most important arenas of competition during the years between the world wars. Chile reengaged German military instructors in 1924 over vigorous French protests based on the Versailles Treaty. German officers returned to Argentina in the 1920s and remained until 1940. Germany had a military monopoly in Bolivia between the wars until 1935 (the end of the Chaco War), after which an Italian military mission was engaged. Military relations remained intimate between France and Peru, with French officers assuming important army positions. France also sent air and naval missions to Peru, although the United States later sent a naval mission and replaced the French position in the Peruvian navy. France also resumed its work in Brazil in the 1920s in the state of São Paulo. It added missions to the Brazilian federal army and air force, including direction of the general staff school. A large and influential U.S. naval mission went to Brazil in 1922. Paraguay, Ecuador, Colombia, Venezuela, and Guatemala continued their eclectic ways, turning to more than one external military source.

Chile and Peru played surrogate roles for Germany and France, respectively. They sent their own training missions and instructors to other Latin American states and received other Latin American military personnel in their own military institutions, thus transmitting their mentors' systems to a broader audience. Chilean missions were sent to Colombia, Ecuador, El Salvador, Nicaragua, and Paraguay.

The external states continued to perceive the economic advantages inherent in dominant military influence, since the Latin American states required foreign armaments to continue their military modernization. They hoped that the partisan efforts of their officers would lead to extensive arms contracts. Furthermore, Latin American military establishments were expected to urge the adoption and imitation of foreign production practices and techniques within their own newly established armaments industries, which would lead to foreign industrial involvement in the region. The persuasive counsel of foreign military advisers gave the initial impetus for this development. Thus, the arms trade continued to be closely linked to military diplomatic activities. Foreign military officers were instrumental in establishing and promoting the new armaments industries because they were interested in seeing the Latin American units armed with implements with which the instructors were familiar. Military and diplomatic personnel cooperated closely with the representatives of their home commercial arms firms. Often the commercial representatives in Latin America were either retired or reserve officers. Thus, military instructors and missions stimulated the international arms trade.

Post–World War II

During the period surrounding World War II, the United States sought to displace European military influence in all of Latin America beyond most of the Caribbean area, where it was already predominant. As a result, military cooperation was established between the United States and almost all of Latin America, and the phase of European military influence in Latin America ended. With the rise of fascism and threat of war in Europe, and the consequent dangers perceived for the Americas, the United States urged the establishment of multilateral inter-American arrangements for hemispheric defense. During the war, an additional set of bilateral military relationships were established, which set precedents for postwar interaction. By the time war broke out in Europe in September 1939, the United States and other American governments had issued neutrality proclamations. However, most Latin American states were unable to patrol their own coastal waters effectively, so the United States secured permission for military bases and certain other rights and facilities from them. After the fall of France in 1940, U.S. negotiations with most Latin American states led to further base rights agreements, whereby U.S. requests were granted for airfields to be used as aircraft ferry relay points. The United States constructed or refurbished some Latin American naval bases, and agreements were signed permitting the United States to use Latin American airports, to fly over their territories, and to station maintenance personnel in the area.

In the late 1930s the United States began to substitute its military missions and instructors for those of the European states, continuing its efforts during the war and immediately after. By 1946 the United States was the only external state maintaining missions in Latin America, with seventeen of them in thirteen states. The Lend-Lease Act of March 11, 1941, ended legal restrictions on the supplying of arms to Latin America, allowing bilateral military assistance to be extended to certain Latin American states. Although Lend-Lease was designed to assist U.S. allies most directly involved in the European war, the president was empowered to transfer military articles to any state whose defense was deemed vital to the security of the United States. All Latin American states were declared eligible for aid except Argentina and Panama—Argentina had refused to cooperate with hemispheric defense plans, whereas Panama had other special military arrangements with the United States. Brazil received by far the largest portion of Lend-Lease arms furnished to Latin America, most of which were used to equip its expeditionary infantry force that saw action in Italy. Mexico (which sent an aircraft squadron to the Philippines), Chile, and Peru received most of the remainder.

After World War II the United States became Latin America's main source of military assistance, providing both standardized military equipment and training. In the first part of the postwar period the United States continued to rationalize military assistance in terms of the need for cooperative efforts toward a common hemispheric defense. The wartime principles of hemispheric defense were reaffirmed on a continuing basis in the Inter-American Treaty of Reciprocal Assistance (Rio Treaty) of 1947. Thereafter, U.S. officials claimed that the Rio Treaty was the "cornerstone" of U.S. military commitments to the region and the framework for regional and bilateral military programs.

From the end of World War II until 1952 the United States had no well-organized program of military assistance in Latin America. President Truman asked the U.S. Congress on two occasions, in 1946 and 1947, for authority to institute a program of inter-American military cooperation, but Congress refused the requests. The United States continued to supply some military equipment under the Lend-Lease Act, but only that which had previously been committed for delivery as of the end of the war. Under the Surplus Property Act of 1944, which authorized direct sales of U.S. military surpluses at reduced prices, Latin Americans purchased small arms, light naval vessels, and artillery pieces. The Mutual Defense Act of 1949 enabled Latin Americans, as signatories of the Rio Treaty, to purchase arms from the United States. However, no grant aid was available and requests for material far exceeded the amount available.

The most important basis for U.S.–Latin American military relations during most of the 1950s and until 1961 was the Mutual Security Act of 1951, passed in response to the Korean War. Portions of the legislation dealing with Latin America made military assistance contingent on the recipients' participation in "missions important to the defense of the Western Hemisphere." The act made it clear that it would be desirable to standardize the equipment, organization, and methods of the Latin American armed forces, and to orient them toward the United States and mutual security, in order to prevent Latin American arms purchases elsewhere, which might invite nonhemispheric military missions and advisers to the region. The United States also wanted to ensure the accessibility of strategic raw materials. Most of all, U.S. policy pronouncements claimed that the United States was not anxious to assume major responsibilities in Latin America in case of war. It desired to help the Latin American countries achieve a capability to protect their own territory, thus sparing the United States the necessity of assigning large numbers of troops to the region.

The assertion that the primary purpose of military aid was to strengthen Latin America's own capability to contribute to hemispheric defense cannot be accepted as the basis for U.S. policy. U.S. military planners seemed to recognize that an all-out Soviet attack on Latin America was a remote possibility, and that even if such an attack occurred the United States obviously would have to assume the burden of defense and retaliation. The military resources of Latin America in relation to the Soviet Union were so limited that massive aid would have been required to enable them to withstand a major attack. Even with such aid, the contribution they could make to self-defense against military aggression would inevitably be small. The United States at the time considered Latin America to be far behind the front lines of the cold war. The fact that military equipment assigned to Latin America was small in quantity and obsolete in quality indicated an assumption that U.S. armed forces would have been necessary to resist certain kinds of external attack. The conclusion to be made is that military aid was extended to preempt Latin American relations with other external actors and to promote internal stability in the Latin American states.

Under the provisions of the Mutual Security Act, Latin American states were able to make cash purchases of weapons and equipment. In addition, the act authorized direct grants of military equipment for selected states under bilateral agreements called Mutual Defense Assistance pacts. A total of sixteen such agreements were signed in the 1950s. Two kinds of U.S. military missions were authorized under the Mutual Security Act: (1) Military Assistance Advisory Groups (MAAG) to administer military transfers under the Mutual Defense Assistance agreements; and (2) Service Training Missions to help train Latin American armed forces in an advisory capacity. Every Latin American state received at least

TABLE 10.4 U.S. Military Assistance: Loans and Grants (U.S. fiscal years; millions of dollars)

Recipient	Postwar Period 1946–1952	Mutual Security Act 1953–1961	Foreign Assistance Act 1962–1988	1989	1990	1991	1992	Total 1946–1992
Argentina	–	4.2	261.6	0.1	0.1	4.0	1.3	269.2
Bahamas	–	–	0.2	a	0.1	0.1	0.1	0.5
Barbados	–	–	0.3	0.1	–	–	–	0.5
Belize	–	–	2.7	0.6	0.1	0.6	0.7	4.7
Bermuda	–	–	–	–	–	–	–	–
Bolivia	–	2.5	86.5	5.4	39.7	35.9	25.9	201.3
Brazil	26.9	206.7	414.0	0.1	0.1	0.1	0.1	640.5
Chile	6.7	64.3	146.0	0.1	0.1	3.3	0.4	220.7
Colombia	3.5	50.2	239.1	8.1	73.2	49.6	49.3	472.3
Costa Rica	–	0.1	38.6	0.2	0.2	0.3	0.2	39.7
Cuba	0.6	15.4	–	–	–	–	–	16.1
Dominican Republic	–	8.1	78.2	0.7	2.1	1.7	2.0	94.5
Ecuador	2.3	30.7	114.7	4.7	1.2	2.8	3.1	191.9
El Salvador	–	0.3	868.9	81.4	81.0	66.9	22.7	1,163.0
Grenada	–	–	0.1	0.1	–	–	–	0.2
Guatemala	–	1.7	60.8	9.4	3.3	0.4	0.2	75.5
Guyana	–	–	5.6	0.1	0.1	a	0.1	5.8
Haiti	–	3.9	9.1	0.1	0.6	1.8	–	15.3
Honduras	–	1.3	428.2	41.1	21.3	33.5	6.4	543.6
Jamaica	–	–	31.7	3.8	1.3	1.9	3.2	46.0
Mexico	–	3.9	12.4	0.2	0.2	0.6	0.6	17.9
Nicaragua	–	2.2	30.6	–	–	–	–	30.4
Panama	–	0.1	62.1	–	–	–	–	77.4
Paraguay	–	0.8	30.6	0.1	0.1	0.2	0.6	31.8
Peru	3.7	73.6	200.5	3.0	1.5	24.5	0.1	347.5
Suriname	–	–	0.2	a	a	–	–	0.2
Trinidad-Tobago	–	–	0.2	0.1	0.8	0.6	0.5	2.2
Uruguay	2.8	29.3	58.8	0.6	0.1	0.5	0.5	92.2
Venezuela	–	31.5	122.1	0.1	0.1	0.4	0.7	154.2
Other[b]	–	–	43.4	3.6	6.8	7.3	5.3	66.4
Total	46.5	530.8	3,347.0	164.0	234.1	237.1	123.8	4,821.3

[a]Less than $50,000

[b]Includes Latin American regional, Central American regional, and other West Indies–Eastern Caribbean programs

Note: Row totals include any capitalized interest, net deobligations, and repayments and may not add to sum of annual loans; column details may not add to totals due to rounding.

Source: Agency for International Development, U.S. Overseas Loans and Grants and Assistance from International Organizations; Obligations and Loan Authorizations, July 1, 1945–September 30, 1992 (1993).

one kind of mission and sometimes both. In addition, Latin American personnel were trained at U.S. military centers in the United States and Panama.

With the Alliance for Progress and an emphasis on economic and social development in Latin America, U.S. policy openly shifted from an emphasis on hemispheric defense to combatting internal subversion. The shift began near the end of the Eisenhower administration and was consummated in 1961 at the beginning of the Kennedy presidency. Economic and social development were assumed to occur best in a stable political environment. Military aid aimed at countering internal Communist subversion and insurgency was said to help promote that stability. A modicum of resources, such as small amounts for antisubmarine warfare, continued to be put into hemispheric defense, but internal stability clearly was the overriding goal.

Military assistance programs continued to consist of furnishing technical advisers, supplying grant material, and sponsoring formal training, as well as selling equipment for cash. The content of these programs, however, was changed to support Latin American counterinsurgency capabilities. Throughout the 1960s, U.S. officials, stressing the low probability of attack on Latin America from outside the hemisphere, attempted to discourage Latin American states from building up large conventional military forces and particularly discouraged arms purchases involving sophisticated aircraft and expensive naval vessels. Such expenditures were considered unwarranted diversions of resources from economic and social development projects; military replacement items should be of a kind and cost that would increase internal capabilities and enhance national development. In 1963 the International Police Academy was established in Washington, operated by the Agency for International Development. It was charged with assisting Latin American police forces to maintain civil security—specifically, to combat urban guerrilla activities.

Under the Alliance for Progress, Latin American armed forces placed a new emphasis on civic action, substantively supported by U.S. funds, equipment, and advisers. A number of enterprises fell under this rubric. By-products of military training transferred to civilian life ranged from literacy training of recruits to teaching technical skills enhancing civilian occupations. Other functions were directly aimed at assisting economic and social development, such as exploration of remote areas and opening new land, building schools and highways, improving sanitation and health facilities, and other projects useful to civilians, especially in rural areas.

A wide variety of objectives were pursued and variously stressed as functions of civic action. Emphasis was placed on economic and social development through nation-building and on strengthening the economy by modernizing basic facilities and improving the infrastructure. A related idea was that the armed forces should justify their expensive public maintenance by helping to develop their nations. Another goal was improving the image of the military and the central government in the eyes of a skeptical public. Special stress was placed on the relationship of civic action to counterinsurgency (the two doctrines were developed simultaneously in the 1960s). Here the intent was to rectify those conditions believed to inspire insurgency, such as poverty and unfulfilled expectations for a better life.

The United States sharply diminished its military presence in Latin America beginning in the late 1960s. Officials declared that not only was the hemispheric defense concept outdated, but that internal insurgency threats also were at a low level. Furthermore, Latin American counterinsurgency capabilities had improved. Consequently, personnel assigned to military groups were reduced and grant assistance funds were cut. A reduced training program and grant assistance fund were maintained.

An important debate in the U.S. Congress in 1967 revolved around the concern that scarce Latin American resources were being unduly devoted to military expenditures to the detriment of social and economic development. The Foreign Military Sales Act of that year imposed a limit of $75 million on direct arms sales to Latin America. Latin American states simply turned to other suppliers, especially European ones. In 1971 President Nixon exercised his discretionary authority and raised the ceiling to $150 million, a figure then agreed to by Congress in the legislation for fiscal year 1972. The rationale for the increased limit was that Latin Americans had a legitimate need to update their military equipment and that experience had shown that, if the United States was unresponsive to their requests, they would simply acquire what they wanted elsewhere at an increased cost. They would also view the U.S. position as indifferent and paternalistic. U.S. balance-of-payments problems gave further impetus to increased arms exports, and the sales ceiling was eliminated altogether in 1974.

Competitors in the Arms Trade

The United States was Latin America's chief, but not exclusive, source of military assistance for the first two decades after World War II. After the war, France, Britain, Italy, Spain, West Germany, and Belgium again received small numbers of Latin American officers in their educational and training institutions. However, other states had a primary concern with trade and lacked security interests in the region. With the exception of Soviet relations with Cuba after 1960, with Peru after 1968, and with Chile from 1970 to 1973, sales of military equipment by other states than the United States were essentially of economic significance, related to the balance of payments rather than to the balance of power. Great Britain and France pursued a policy of virtually unrestricted arms sales in the profitable Latin American market. Germany, beginning in the late 1960s, adopted a similar policy after lifting prior restrictions on arms transfers to developing nations.

When the United States deemphasized counterinsurgency and restricted arms sales to Latin America, the regional states turned to Europe as their chief suppliers. At the same time, the larger South American states competed vigorously to modernize their armed forces. Consequently, the volume and sophistication of arms transfers to Latin America increased dramatically. According to a study by the U.S. Department of State (1973) surveying arms sales to Latin America (excluding Cuba) from 1966 to 1973, Latin American states placed a total of $1.7 billion in orders during that period, 75 percent of them in Western Europe (mainly Britain, France, and West Germany). The United States received 13 percent of those orders, Canada 10 percent, and Australia 2 percent. Six South American states (Argentina, Brazil, Chile, Colombia, Peru, and Venezuela) placed 97 percent of the orders. Naval and air forces accounted for about 90 percent of arms expenditures by the six states, and ground forces the remaining 10 percent.

The Soviet-Peruvian military relationship that began in 1973 continued through the latter 1980s. Peru was the only South American nation receiving military transfers from the Soviet Union, primarily sales of helicopters and tanks. Soviet military advisers and technicians were resident in Peru, and Peruvian military personnel were trained in the Soviet Union. The Soviet fishing fleet that operated off the South American Pacific coast was granted access to Peruvian ports for support and maintenance.

The Human Rights Factor

Further dramatic reductions in U.S. military assistance to Latin America began in 1976 with congressional action and were extended by President Carter after 1977. The International Security Assistance and Arms Export Control Act of 1976 virtually eliminated several key elements of the aid program. It directed the elimination of U.S. military advisory groups around the world unless specifically authorized by Congress. Those in Latin America were reduced to three military personnel, with some specifically authorized exceptions.

President Carter introduced far-ranging executive restrictions on U.S. arms transfers. He stated that henceforth U.S. arms transfers would be viewed as exceptional rather than normal foreign policy instruments, that the United States as the world's largest arms exporter would take the initiative in reducing arms sales, and that human rights considerations in recipient countries would be an important factor in military assistance decisions. Congress approved the new presidential orientation. In 1976 Congress had required that reports be issued on those countries for which security was proposed and mandated an associated review process, and the extent of the "report cards" and the review process were expanded during the Carter administration. As a result, the United States ended its military assistance and prohibited arms transfers to Argentina, Chile (beginning in 1976), El Salvador, Guatemala, Nicaragua, Paraguay, and Uruguay. Brazil was not so prohibited but refused to accept further military aid in reaction to the publication of negative reports on the status of human rights there. All claimed unwarranted interference in their internal affairs.

Arms Transfers Revived

The Reagan administration revived transfers of weapons and equipment to Latin America, logically part of Reagan's policies based on opposition to Soviet-Cuban expansionism. Reagan's approach differed from Carter's in three main ways: (1) Arms transfers would have a central role in U.S. diplomacy for hemispheric security; (2) human rights concerns would be subordinate to security interests in decisions about military relations; and (3) commercial sales would be encouraged and would include making sophisticated weapons available to Latin American armed forces. U.S. officials said that the policy was designed to counter Soviet arms transfers that destabilized regions of strategic importance to the United States, and to establish the United States as a reliable supplier and thereby strengthen ties with allies. They said the Carter policy proved ineffective because the Soviet

Union and other major arms suppliers had not slackened their activities. Officials denied charges that commercial considerations were the driving force behind the new policy, which in practice amounted to a license for U.S. industry to sell anything anywhere.

While the Reagan administration sought to reelevate military assistance as an instrument of policy, legislative prohibitions and congressional controls in terms of human rights continued. Earlier decisions prohibiting arms transfers to Argentina, Chile, Paraguay, Uruguay, and Guatemala remained in effect, and questions were raised about human rights conditions in El Salvador. The administration itself chose to chastise Nicaragua, with whom it had hostile relations, about its human rights record. Reagan's effort to create an inter-American front against Communist penetration in the Southern Cone involved improving relations with military regimes in Argentina, Chile, Uruguay, and Paraguay. Cultivating their cooperation required, as a first step, reversing extant sanctions.

In April 1981, the administration introduced legislation to repeal the ban on arms sales to Argentina, followed by a similar request with respect to Chile. After considerable resistance, Congress agreed to lift sanctions on both countries, but only after the president had certified to Congress that they had made significant progress on human rights problems. The State Department decided to consider the Argentine and Chilean cases simultaneously because of their dispute over islands in the Beagle Channel, not wanting to appear to take sides. The case for Chile was difficult because Chile would not cooperate in resolving the murder case of Orlando Letelier, former Chilean ambassador to the United States, and an associate who had been assassinated in Washington. The Anglo-Argentine war of 1982 suspended certification considerations for a year and a half.

On December 10, 1983, inauguration day of the newly elected Argentine civilian President Raúl Alfonsín, President Reagan certified to Congress that Argentina had improved its human rights record and was eligible for the resumption of military transfers. A similar move was taken toward Uruguay in 1984 with the end of the military regime and return to democracy there. By then, General Augusto Pinochet of Chile and Alfredo Stroessner of Paraguay stood alone as military heads of state, and U.S. prohibitions on arms transfers remained in effect for both governments.

Human rights concerns in Central America posed special considerations. In Guatemala, General Roméo Lucas García presided over probably the most violently repressive regime in Latin America. The Reagan administration indicated its willingness to resume military aid to help combat Guatemala's insurgency problem, but the scale of state terrorism was so high that the administration could not convince Congress to resume military ties. Congress relented in the case of El Salvador, but by law required the executive to certify that El Salvador was making a "concerted and significant effort to comply with internationally recognized human rights," was "achieving substantial control over all elements of its armed forces," and was "committed to the holding of free elections at an early date." Certification was made in February 1981. With the subsequent holding of elections in El Salvador, the end of the Lucas García dictatorship in Guatemala and the holding of elections there, and resumption of the electoral process in Honduras, and the improved but still problematical human rights situations in all three countries, U.S. military transfers were unfettered. Arms transfers were again conducted, this time in the larger context of Central American conflict (see Chapter 11).

The administration was free to act independently when arms transfers did not involve questions of human rights. As a candidate, Reagan had pledged to promote weapons sales abroad and did so once in office. The State Department instructed U.S. diplomats, including armed services attachés, to assist U.S. manufacturers in marketing arms abroad. It canceled President Carter's order prohibiting such cooperation. Reagan approved sales of advanced aircraft to Third World states. Venezuela was a principal recipient, as the Reagan administration acceded to its request to purchase eighteen F-16 fighters on a cash basis. Concerns were expressed that the sale presaged unrestrained transfers of highly advanced weaponry in Latin America. As it turned out, other countries did not have the economic resources to buy extensive military arms.

DIPLOMATIC AND CULTURAL RELATIONS

Diplomatic Relations

Latin Americans were eager to have their sovereign existence recognized during their movements for independence, but such action by the external states was slow in coming. The United States was the first to recognize the new Latin American states, but it did not do so until 1821. U.S. leaders viewed the revolutions against Spain with sympathy, but they were engaged in difficult negotiations with Spain to secure the Floridas and felt that recognition would jeopardize those efforts. With the ratification of the Adams-Onís Treaty of 1821 providing for the cession of the Floridas, the United States began to recognize Latin American sovereignties in defiance of European governments. Great Britain soon followed, interested primarily in unrestricted trade with the Americas and in keeping Europe, especially France, from interfering in the revolutions. Britain granted recognition to the new states in 1825, and gave them some support to resist Spain's attempts of reconquest for the next half-century.

Spain, in its bitterness, sought to isolate Spanish America by refusing recognition. Only after the death of Ferdinand VII in 1833, which brought the liberals to power, did Spain temporarily abandon reconquest. Mexico was the first of the new states to be recognized by Spain, in 1836; delays in recognizing the others occurred because of intermittent hostility and pending negotiations over indemnification for Spanish losses in the revolutions and over the citizenship status of Spanish emigrés. Most of Spanish America had been recognized by 1864, but the process was not completed until the early 1890s (Víctor Alba in Davis, Wilson, and Others, 1975:88–89).

The position of the Soviet Union was a major factor in Latin American diplomacy in the twentieth century. After the Bolshevik Revolution of November 1917, Soviet diplomatic relations with Latin America were linked to Latin American Communist parties. Soviet policy focused first on developing the parties within the Comintern and secondarily on state-to-state diplomatic relations. The first Latin American Communist Parties were founded in Argentina (1918), Mexico (1919), and Uruguay (1920); the first diplomatic relations were not established until 1924 with Mexico, and then with Uruguay in 1926. Several other states recognized the Soviet Union and made diplomatic exchanges, but by 1939 all diplomatic relations had been severed because of subversive activities by local Communist parties.

During World War II, the Soviet Union, as a member of the Allies, resumed diplomatic ties in Latin America, beginning with Colombia in 1941; a total of fourteen countries were included by the end of the war. With the onset of the cold war in 1947, however, those ties were again restricted. By 1953 diplomatic relations were maintained only with Mexico, Argentina, and Uruguay, and further relations were not established until the 1960s. The special relationship with Cuba developed after the Castro revolution of 1959. To achieve its aims of strengthening its influence wherever possible in Latin America, the Soviet Union was willing to cooperate with virtually any type of Latin American regime, even militantly anti-Communist ones. The Soviet diplomatic offensive in Latin America resulted in numerous diplomatic ties established after the mid-1960s.

Throughout the Spanish Civil War (1936–1939) the incumbent Republican government maintained diplomatic relations with all but two Latin American states. In 1939 all of them except Mexico recognized the victorious Franco government and maintained relations throughout World War II. Mexico continued to refuse recognition despite Mexican adherence to the Estrada principle of universal recognition and continuity of diplomatic relations.

Culture and Propaganda

States commonly seem to assume that cultural exchange facilitates the realization of political goals. Although cultural exchange may be unnecessary when interests are complementary and cannot overcome wide divergences of interest, cultural relations may assist cooperation or mitigate conflict. Some states have emphasized the economic value of cultural exchange. French officials, for example, said that foreign students trained in French culture were the best promoters of French products, commercial methods, and technology (Goldhamer, 1972:131–132). Cultural relations have also been pursued in essentially ideological terms, such as the French "civilizing mission," the U.S. "democratizing mission," and the Spanish pursuit of "racial solidarity."

Although cultural relations in a broad sense existed throughout Latin American history, systematic governmental activity is a fairly recent phenomenon. For example, educated Latin Americans (especially South Americans), throughout the nineteenth century and well into the twentieth, were attracted to French culture. They adopted French philosophies, traveled to France, and sent their children to be educated there. Most of the interchange was by way of private rather than official means. French governments seemed unwilling to enter into official cultural exchange with Latin America even during the height of its cultural influence at the turn of the century and up to World War I.

Spanish cultural policies toward Latin America have been of special interest. A small precursor Pan Hispanic cultural movement began in the mid-nineteenth century, but the idea received little attention until the 1890s. This movement, known as *hispanismo* or, sometimes, *hispanoamericanismo*, was advocated by a group of Spanish luminaries that included Rafael Altamira, José Ortega y Gassett, José F. Gómez, Adolfo Gonzáles Posada, Miguel de Unamuno, and others. They attempted to persuade Spanish governments to establish official programs based on their ideas. The movement was later fostered by institutes for Spanish-American studies in Spanish universities, several journals on the subject, student and professorial exchanges, and Pan Hispanic political and commercial organizations.

Early advocates of hispanismo championed not only a cultural community among Spanish-speaking peoples, stressing kindred race and cultural solidarity, but also political rapprochement and increased economic interaction for the mutual benefit of Spain and America. Some writers called for some sort of confederation or league among Hispanic peoples, but this idea remained vague. Hostility toward the Pan American movement sponsored by the United States was a constant theme, and *hispanoamericanistas* viewed yankee imperialism and materialism as a major threat to hispanic values in Latin America. Antiyankeeism was stimulated by the war of 1898 and given further impetus by the long period of U.S. intervention in the Caribbean that followed. A Hispano-American cultural and economic congress was held in Madrid in 1900 with Spanish American attendance, signaling the official beginning of *hispanismo*. Further congresses assembled in different Spanish cities in 1908, 1910, 1912, and 1914. The Spanish government modestly supported the movement, sending representatives to Spanish American centenary celebrations (beginning with Argentina in 1910) and subsidizing several Pan Hispanic political and commercial organizations. It sponsored scholarships and fellowships for student and professor exchange (Rippy, 1958:205–209, 512–515). Latin American hostility toward Spain lessened somewhat and trade slightly increased.

Most students of the movement have viewed hispanismo basically as a cultural, partially economic, nonaggressive liberal movement stressing race, culture, and commerce, designed to promote Hispanic civilization and solidarity and to defend the culture against U.S. incursions. An important work by Frederick Pike (1971) confirms these features but also emphasizes that the Spanish adherents of the movement held antirevolutionary sentiments and represented the status quo. Pike believes that Spanish liberal and conservative supporters of hispanismo alike wished to prevent social revolution on both sides of the Atlantic. This sharing of social conservatism, in effect, left as the main difference between them the conservatives' rigid Roman Catholicism and the liberals' strong anticlericalism.

In the late 1930s, after falangist dictator General Francisco Franco came to power, hispanismo was converted to *hispanidad,* a concept fundamentally different from its predecessor. Hispanidad was widely popularized by Ramiro de Maeztu, an anarchist-turned-falangist, in his book *Defensa de la Hispanidad* published in 1934. He described the concept in mystical and reactionary terms, seeking revindication of Spanish world power. For inspiration, he turned to the sixteenth century, when Spanish imperial power had reached its zenith. According to the falangists, the bases for Spanish greatness had been devotion to the church, military and naval strength, and a hierarchical social order. That greatness had declined, and Spain had suffered three centuries of humiliation, the theory continued, because of the pagan Renaissance, the Protestant Reformation, and the consequent eroding effects of relativism in religion, egalitarian political ideals, and economic materialism. Falangists admired and felt a spiritual kinship with Italian fascism and German nazism. But they insisted that falangism was distinctly Spanish, rooted in the values of the Middle Ages when, it was claimed, Spain was already fascist. To promote Spanish regeneration in the 1930s, falangists called for reinstitution of religious intolerance and the Inquisition, the recovery of military strength and military values, and the resumption of empire in America (including large portions of the United States). England continued to be the eternal enemy, and France was vilified, but the United States and Pan Americanism received the most vociferous hostility. Falangism was also antimasonic, anti-Semitic, antidemocratic, antisocialist, and anti-Communist. The reestablishment of the American empire was absurd as a practical policy goal. Franco probably sought at most some degree of Spanish American sympathy for his regime.

Immediately after the Spanish Civil War and during World War II, organizations associated with the falangists engaged in a propaganda campaign in Latin America, sometimes in concert with German Nazi and Italian Fascist groups, even though Spain remained neutral throughout the war. Brazilian dictator Getulio Vargas initially sympathized with falangism and allowed Rio de Janeiro to serve as the Latin American center for Spanish propaganda activities, but Brazil nevertheless eventually sided with the Allies in World War II. (Actually, Vargas first sympathized with the Salazar brand of fascism in Portugal, which was older than the Franco regime.) Spain also cultivated relations with authoritarian governments in Argentina and Peru. It was active in Chile but eventually broke relations with that government. Spain financed the travel of sympathetic Latin American politicians, intellectuals, and students to Spain and established an Institute of Hispanic Studies in Madrid to give a scholarly veneer to hispanidad. Pan Hispanism was received enthusiastically in Latin America by right-wing elements. Its appeal was essentially restricted to those elements by the end of World War II and the defeat of the Axis powers.

During World War I and the following interbellum period, the leading external competitors disseminated propaganda in Latin America. During the war the regional states were courted by both sides of the conflict—by France, Great Britain, and then Italy and the United States on the one hand, and by Germany, supported by neutral Spain, on the other. Notable at the time was the work of the American Committee on Public Information (the Creel Committee), the first U.S. experiment in government-supported cultural exchange in Latin America. Created by President Wilson in 1917 and headed by journalist George Creel, the agency established a network of contacts around Latin America. These contacts, usually resident U.S. newspaper correspondents but sometimes government officials and Latin American nationals, distributed various kinds of communications media and advised on the content best received in their areas (Mock, 1942).

During the 1920s and especially the 1930s, as international frictions increased, external propagandizing in Latin America continued apace. Italy, Germany, and Spain actively sought to take advantage of their national communities in the region, but with mixed success. Those communities often were deeply divided among themselves over loyalty to European governments, even though they generally had affection for the former national homeland. After the United States announced its Good Neighbor Policy in 1933, European propaganda lost much of its appeal because it had a high antiyankee content. The United States signed multilateral cultural exchange conventions with Latin American states in 1936 at the Buenos Aires Conference, and in 1938 the State Department organized its Division of Cultural Relations to administer official activities and to assist private agencies in their cultural programs (Mecham, 1965:128–130).

Regularized cultural exchange programs have been prevalent since World War II. The most important ones have been maintained by France, the United States, West Germany, Great Britain, Spain, and the Soviet Union, although the People's Republic of China, East Germany, Italy, Iran, Korea, and the United Arab Republic also undertook some modest activities in the region. In addition, Argentina, Brazil, Mexico, Chile, and Cuba developed intraregional communications and educational exchange programs.

Several external states have maintained publicly funded cultural centers around the region. Most of them are private organizations receiving financial support from their home governments, including France's Alliance Francaise, Germany's Goethe Institute, the United Kingdom's British Council, Spain's Instituto de Cultura Hispanica, and the United States Information Agency. All of them engaged in a wide range of activities. They gave high priority to language classes (except for the Spanish-run centers), the operation of libraries, and various cultural programs. They provided scholarships for Latin Americans to study abroad, offered travel programs for the exchange of artists, intellectuals, and athletes, and distributed films, books, magazines, and newspapers. Most of the major external states sent government-supported teachers to staff schools originally intended to serve the children of their own resident nationals, but enrollments in these schools include large numbers of Latin American children as well. All major government broadcast services were aired to Latin America (Goldhamer, 1972:Ch. 9).

BIBLIOGRAPHIC COMMENT

Bernstein (1966), Grunwald (1978), and Hunter and Foley (1975) have analyzed Latin American international economic relations, and Bryan (1994) does so for the Caribbean. Sanderson (1992) addresses international trade. Some treatments of the debt problem are by Bianchi, Devlin, and Ramos (1985), Canak (1989), Cline (1993), Devlin (1989), Frieden (1992), Inter-American Development Bank (1985), Jorge and Salazar-Carillo (1992), Oliveri (1992), and Stallings and Kaufman (1989); Cole (1992) explains debt-for-equity and debt-for-nature swaps, Parkinson (1987) discusses the legal-institutional aspects, and Grosse (1992a, 1992b) analyzes the apparent end of the debt crisis. Marichal (1989) is a political-economic history of Latin American external debt. On certain U.S. economic programs, see U.S. Department of Commerce (1951), U.S. House Committee on Foreign Affairs (1981), and U.S. Department of Commerce and Agency for International Development (1992). Goldhamer (1972) gives information on numerous aspects of extrahemispheric states' interactions with Latin America. Mower (1982) discuss Latin American economic relations with the European Community, and Purcell and Immerman (1992) those of Japan. Barber and Ronning (1966) remains an insightful work on counterinsurgency, civic action, and U.S. assistance. Pike (1971) and Shapiro (1968) are on cultural relations. See Schoultz (1981) on questions of human rights.

CHAPTER ELEVEN

■

Violence and Accommodation

CERTAIN REALITIES AND NORMS of Latin American international politics have been violent in nature. This chapter deals with conflict involving the threat or use of force in the regional subsystem and efforts to resolve such conflicts. The analysis identifies the sources of contention, the principal actors and their calculations, conflict-resolution measures undertaken, and the outcomes or current status. Conflict analysis is facilitated by first identifying a number of general considerations about the phenomenon of violence in the Latin American subsystem. These considerations are then applied to a series of case studies in specific regional and subregional contexts.

SOME GENERAL CONSIDERATIONS

The Sources of Conflict

Violence in the Latin American subsystem has arisen essentially from five sets of sources or causes: (1) boundary and territorial disputes, (2) competition for resources, (3) imperial and power disputes, (4) ideological competition, and (5) migration of people and goods. Considerable overlap occurs among these sources, and specific cases may involve some combination of them. (The following commentary has been influenced by Child, 1985:Ch. 1, and Grabendorff, 1982.)

Border conflicts flow from disagreements over frontiers between contiguous sovereignties. They are related to territorial disputes in that they may lead to or be part of larger conflicts involving sovereign claims. Nationalist sentiments invariably accompany border and territorial conflict. Territorial conflicts usually stem from disputes over the possession of land terrain but may extend to oceanic rights. Strategic assertions entail important terrain and islands, transisthmian canal locations, or sea lanes. Resource conflicts have become increasingly important in furthering national development and economic well-being. Although the disputes themselves involve land or ocean territory, it is often the vital energy, strategic, or food resources that are at stake (such as petroleum, natural gas, minerals, hydroelectricity, and fish).

"Influence conflict" refers both to historic imperialism and to more recent competition to project national power. Both are closely associated with balance-of-power systems. This type of conflict usually includes questions of prestige or some other version of "national honor" and is often intertwined with ideological conflict. The ideological category goes beyond simple power considerations, however. Ideological conflicts deal with the struggle to impose, or resist the imposition of, political, economic, and social values. The principal rivalries have been between dictatorships and democracy, civilian and military regimes, and democratic capitalism versus various forms of Marxism. They have been pursued not only by the great powers but by certain regional states and nonstate actors as well.

Conflicts arising from the migration of people and goods are also multifaceted. A majority of the nineteenth-century European interventions were responses to problems arising from commerce, investments, and immigrants. Foreign investors and resident aliens appealed to their governments for redress when Latin Americans defaulted on their debts or mistreated foreign persons and property. Those governments demanded indemnity from Latin American states and at times threatened or used military force to gain compliance. Other migration conflicts deal with strains caused by the movement of people and goods across frontiers. Strife has often been caused by people migrating for essentially economic or political reasons from one polity to another. The flow of illicit drugs (the "narcotraffic") has become increasingly important, leading to considerable violence on the part of traffickers and to contentious interstate relations.

Regional and Subregional Patterns

Latin American regional and subregional patterns, especially those involving the distribution of power, are directly linked to conflict analysis. Boundary disputes have been prevalent within the region. Every Latin American state with a common land frontier with another has engaged in such conflict; only the Caribbean island states with no contiguous neighbors have avoided such quarrels. A series of European military interventions and other forms of power politics occurred in all parts of Latin America throughout the nineteenth century. Soviet attempts at subversion were widespread during the twentieth century interbellum period, as were U.S. covert paramilitary activities during the cold war. Guerrilla warfare from the late 1950s has been a common regional phenomenon, and the narcotraffic has more recently given rise to considerable transregional conflict.

Certain geographic and political factors have been significant in helping to determine subregional politics and the choice of policy instruments. During the nineteenth century Mexico was especially vulnerable to external intrusions, including military intervention, occupation, and great loss of territory, at the hands of the United States and Europeans. The last intervention in Mexico by the United States ended in 1914. The role of relatively weak Circum-Caribbean states in the great power competitions of the nineteenth century and as a sphere of U.S. influence in the twentieth have made it the most continuously susceptible of the Latin American regions to external force. The United States applied military force extensively during the first third of the century; the latest cases in the long history of such actions were the U.S. invasions of Grenada in 1983 and Panama in 1989. If one excludes the special case of the Anglo-Argentine war of 1982, no military interventions have occurred in the Southern Cone in the twentieth century, partly because of the region's remoteness from the mainstream of international politics.

In the Southern Cone, intraregional conflicts with little involvement from external powers have been especially important. The impetus for such conflict has been provided by the power calculations of the principal local states. Such calculations are not as relevant to the policy-making of other Latin American states. The legacy of conflict in the Southern Cone includes a long list of territorial and boundary disputes, power struggles that have led to war and threats of war, claims of sovereignty, and competition for resources. Southern Cone rivalry has been extended to the sea and seabed and to Antarctica, and nuclear questions were introduced and remain latent.

NINETEENTH-CENTURY PATTERNS AND CASES

Mexico and International Conflict

In the nineteenth century, Mexico was often of interest to one or another of the external powers. Spain sent an expedition to Mexico in 1829 in response to a Mexican law expelling Spanish citizens, but it was repelled by disease and the Mexican army. In 1838 France bombarded Vera Cruz and forced payment of claims to its nationals. The most important conflict, however, occurred in relations with the United States and France. The former took half of Mexico's territory as the result of war, and the latter occupied Mexico and temporarily made it a part of its empire.

Mexico's relations with the United States were dominated by boundary and territorial questions in the nineteenth century. The territorial limits between the United States and Mexico had not been fixed when the latter won its independence. An 1819 treaty, reaffirmed in 1828, agreed to the Sabine River as the frontier. The United States, however, was expanding westward across the continent to realize "manifest destiny," and U.S. leaders wanted to designate the Rio Grande (Rio Bravo) as the new boundary. They unsuccessfully employed diplomatic means to purchase the additional territory from Mexico, as well as more devious measures, such as bribing Mexican officials.

The area that now forms Texas was originally part of Mexico, but the Mexican government largely ignored it and allowed "Anglo" settlers to migrate there. U.S. citizens who began to settle in the sparsely inhabited territory in the 1820s eventually clashed with the central Mexican government. In 1836 Texas declared its independence and defeated a Mexican army sent to put it down. Texans wanted to be annexed as a U.S. state, but statehood was denied, largely because of the slavery issue. They thereupon established an independent republic, which the United States recognized in 1837. Despite the opposition of Britain and France, who wanted Texas to serve as a buffer between the United States and Mexico, the United States annexed Texas in 1845.

Continued disputes over the extent of the Texas territory after annexation resulted in the U.S.–Mexican war (1846–1848). Mexico said that Texas ended at the Nueces River; the United States claimed the Rio Grande. U.S. troops were sent to Texas, leading to full-scale warfare, with U.S. military invasion and occupation. The war was terminated by the Treaty of Guadalupe Hidalgo, signed on February 2, 1848. Under its terms, Mexico quit its claims to Texas, allowed the United States to fix the Texas boundary at the Rio Grande, and ceded the rest of its northern territory from Texas to the Pacific Ocean. The vastness of the new acquisition—almost half of Mexico's territory—did not satisfy some expansionists in the United States, however. An "all-Mexico" movement demanded total annexation, but their ambitions were frustrated by the slavery issue. The United States paid Mexico $15 million and U.S. troops withdrew in August 1848. Five years later, in 1853, the U.S. Minister to Mexico, James Gadsden, negotiated the purchase from Mexico of the Gila River valley in southern Arizona and New Mexico for $10 million.

Mexico was rocked by civil war beginning in 1857, and the liberal government of Benito Juárez in 1861 declared bankruptcy and repudiated all foreign debts. France, Britain, and Spain collaborated to coerce Mexico to honor their nationals' heavy claims, some of which were fraudulent. Their combined fleet appeared at Vera Cruz. The following year, in 1862, Britain and Spain reached agreements with Mexico and withdrew their troops. Napoleon III had much more in mind, however; he wanted to establish a French empire in Mexico. His motives seem to have been to enhance French commerce, to "contain" U.S. continental expansion, and to curry favor with the church in France by punishing Juárez and other anticlerical Mexican liberals.

After French troops occupied the capital, France formed the Empire of Mexico and named prince Archduke Maximilian of Austria, a Catholic, as chief of state. He and his wife, Princess Carlota, arrived at Mexico City in 1864. The following year, at the end of its own civil war, the United States, which had continued to recognize the Juárez government throughout the French occupation, demanded that French forces be withdrawn. Napoleon III removed French troops from Mexico, not only because of the U.S. position, but also because of Mexican forces that continued their resistance outside the capital city, opposition in France, and a tenuous political position in Europe. With French military support gone, Juárez's army deposed Maximilian; he was convicted by court martial and shot.

The 1848 peace treaty between Mexico and the United States did not end border friction. Numerous incidents continued to occur in the last half of the nineteenth century and into the twentieth. U.S. Marines landed in Mexico in 1913 as the Mexican revolution took an exceptionally violent turn. U.S. forces took Vera Cruz in 1914 and held it for almost seven months; General John J. Pershing led a U.S. military expedition into northern Mexico in an unsuccessful attempt to capture General Francisco (Pancho) Villa. This expedition was the last U.S. (or other foreign) military intervention in Mexico.

Southern Cone Conflicts

The nineteenth century witnessed a series of major South American wars or threats of war and power struggles. Involving in one way or another all of the subregional states, the wars were part of a larger expression of Southern Cone power politics and geopolitical thinking. The most intense leadership rivalry was among Argentina, Brazil, and Chile, the "ABC" states.

The rivalry between Argentina and Brazil for control of the Rio de la Plata region centered on Uruguay in the early national period. Portugal and Spain had contested the region for two centuries in the colonial era, it being the major point of contact between their empires. Argentina unsuccessfully tried to maintain the viceroyalty of La Plata under its control during the wars for independence, and afterward it actively meddled in the other La Plata states. Brazil, after gaining independence in 1822, pursued an aggressive policy of "manifest destiny," clashing with Argentine ambitions. Uruguayan patriots claimed independence from both Spain and Portugal and seceded from Buenos Aires, unrecognized by Argentina. In 1822 Brazil annexed Uruguay as the Cisplatine province of the independent Brazilian empire. In 1825 Uruguay declared its independence from Brazil, and Argentina entered the dispute on the side of the rebels; an indecisive three-year war ensued. Britain, its commercial interests in the area disrupted, intervened to force a settlement. It pressured Argentina and Brazil into signing the Treaty of Montevideo (1828), in which they both agreed to recognize Uruguayan independence, thus creating a buffer state between them.

Despite the 1828 treaty, attempts to control Uruguay continued throughout the nineteenth century. Intermittent civil war in Uruguay invited Argentine and Brazilian intervention and claims for territory. One of the most important developments was what Uruguayans called the Great War, beginning in 1836. An alliance between Argentine dictator Juan Manuel de Rosas and an Uruguayan political faction, the Blancos, conducted a siege of Montevideo from 1841 to 1851 against another faction, the Colorados, allied with anti-Rosas Argentines. From 1845 to 1850 French and British naval units blockaded Buenos Aires and simultaneously supported the Montevideans. After their withdrawal, Brazil joined the anti-Rosas alignment, partly because it was assured of a favorable settlement of its Uruguayan boundary, and was soon victorious. In 1851 Brazil forced a treaty upon Uruguay in which the latter renounced an earlier claim to almost half its territory along the northern frontier. Brazil thereafter expanded into the territories of each of the remaining seven contiguous states except Peru, but it did so through diplomatic negotiations.

From 1865 to 1870 the Uruguayan Colorados united with Argentina and Brazil to resist the expansionist moves of Paraguayan dictator Francisco Solano López. This union produced the Paraguayan War, known in Paraguay as the War of the Triple Alliance. A Blanco government, having poor relations with both Argentina and Brazil, had responded to Paraguayan overtures for a common policy in 1862. López had in mind a Paraguayan-led empire of central South American states, including Uruguay and Bolivia. Paraguay invaded Argentina and Brazil near their Uruguayan borders, and in May 1865 the triple alliance of those two states plus Uruguay was formed. A five-year war resulted, ending in March 1870 with Paraguay's complete defeat. Most of its male population was killed, and Argentina and Brazil took portions of its territory. Paraguay, no longer a power contender, was left as a buffer state between its neighbors.

The entire boundary between Argentina and Chile from north to south was disputed following the movements for independence. In 1881 a vague settlement provided for the frontier to run along the "highest peaks" of the Andes dividing the watershed. This provision was interpreted differently by each state. War was narrowly averted over a portion of the northern frontier known as the Puna de Atacama. After failing to reach agreement through direct diplomacy, Chile and Argentina agreed to arbitration by the United States, and in 1899 the U.S. arbiter divided the disputed territory. Objections were voiced in Chile, but the decision was accepted by both sides. Parts of the southern boundary remained in dispute, however. The 1881 treaty had divided Tierra del Fuego between the two states, giving Argentina sovereignty over Patagonia and Chile that over the Strait of Magellan (Chile agreed to neutralize the area). Disagreements then arose over the precise demarcation, and in 1896 the disputants turned to the British Crown for arbitration. King Edward VII handed down his award in 1902.

Important conflicts on the west coast of South America that developed in the early independence period continued in some respects into the late twentieth century. Chile, intent on dominating the Pacific coast, pursued aggressive policies toward Bolivia and Peru. In 1836 Bolivian President Andres Santa Cruz took advantage of political divisions in Peru to form a Peru-Bolivian Confederation. Chile immediately opposed it, perceiving a threat to its economic interests and strategic position, and went to war against the Confederation in 1836. Argentina did the same the following year but, feeling less threatened than Chile, it played a minor military role. Chile invaded Peru in 1838 and defeated the combined Peru-Bolivian army the following year, bringing an end to the Confederation. Chile built up its military and naval forces thereafter and in 1879 again went to war against the combined forces of Peru and Bolivia.

The War of the Pacific (1879–1883), along with the Paraguayan War, was the most serious nineteenth-century Latin American international conflict. The 800-mile Bolivian Pacific coastline was composed mostly of the barren Atacama Desert, where few Bolivians had settled. In 1866 Chileans discovered vast nitrate deposits near the site where the town of Antofagasta was built, and in 1874 Bolivia ceded a portion of its Atacama territory to Chile. The Chileans mined and exported the nitrates under an agreement with Bolivia until 1878, when a dispute over taxes led to military confrontation. Chile attacked the Bolivian desert regions in 1879, and Peru entered the war on the side of Bolivia. Some major actions were fought at sea, where Chile eventually achieved supremacy over Peru. Peru also bore the brunt of the Chilean land offensive, which involved a Chilean invasion of Peru and the sacking and occupation of Lima. U.S. and European governments, beginning in 1880, unsuccessfully attempted to terminate the war through mediation. Chile finally defeated the Peru-Bolivian alliance and made substantial gains through the peace settlements.

In the Ancón Treaty of October 20, 1883, Peru permanently ceded its province of Tarapacá to Chile. Chile was to occupy the Peruvian provinces of Tacna and Arica for a ten-year period, after which a plebiscite was to be held to determine their future status. Chile and Peru could not agree on the terms of the plebiscite, however, and its continuous postponement after 1893 embittered relations between the two states for the next thirty-five years. A compromise was finally reached through U.S. good offices in the Washington Protocol of 1929. Chile annexed Arica and returned Tacna to Peru.

A truce signed between Chile and Bolivia on April 4, 1884, provided for an indefinite armistice and for Chilean occupation of Atacama. In 1888 Chile unilaterally relabeled the territory of Atacama as the province of Antofagasta. A treaty formally ending the war was not signed until October 20, 1904. Under its provisions Bolivia gave up the territory, thereby confirming the loss of its coastline and access to the sea. In return, Chile indemnified Bolivia and agreed to build a railroad from La Paz to Arica for Bolivian use. Chile later allowed Bolivia to use Arica as a free port, but Bolivia never abandoned the idea of regaining its own Pacific port. In 1920 it appealed to the League of Nations for a seaport on the grounds that the 1904 treaty was null and void, but the League refused to intervene. Bolivia did not participate or receive concessions in the 1929 settlement between Chile and Peru. Bolivia then turned to the east for an outlet to the Atlantic—a concern that provided one of the bases for the Chaco War (discussed below).

Origins of the Falklands/Malvinas Dispute

The Falkland Islands, known in Argentina as the Islas Malvinas and located some 300 miles east of southern Argentina, had an ambiguous early history that complicated later claims to its ownership. The dispute dates from the discovery of the islands in 1592 and the subsequent contending colonial claims. France, Spain, and Britain at one time or another occupied and abandoned the islands between 1764 and 1811. In 1820, Argentina (then the United Provinces of La Plata) took possession based on rights of succession to Spanish territory. Britain later claimed ownership. At the same time, private U.S. sealing vessels were trespassing on the islands. The Argentine governor seized three of the vessels, which opened up a controversy between Argentina and the United States during which the *U.S.S. Lexington* destroyed the Argentine colony on the Malvinas. Britain took advantage of the situation by occupying the islands with military force in 1833. A British naval unit drove off an Argentine settlement and established effective British control for the next century and a half. Argentina never accepted British rule, and it regularly protested and asserted its own sovereign claims.

TWENTIETH-CENTURY PATTERNS
AND CASES TO WORLD WAR II

U.S. Imperialism in the Caribbean

During the first third of the twentieth century, the United States behaved as a great imperialist power. That behavior was especially based on geopolitical-strategic calculations about the Caribbean region combined with economic motives and, sometimes, democratic purposes. The beginnings of U.S. imperialism in the region date from the U.S. victory in its ten-week war with Spain. In addition to colonizing Puerto Rico, the United States intervened on numerous occasions and in various ways during this period in seven states—Cuba, Panama, Haiti, Dominican Republic, Nicaragua, Honduras, and Guatemala. Intervention assumed the forms of troop landings and military occupations (U.S. troops entered all seven states between 1898 and 1934), establishment of protectorates in Cuba and Panama, electoral supervision, and creation of customs receiverships. Most of the interventions were carried out with concern for the security of the Panama Canal, which was constructed during the early years of the century and started operating in 1914. In the initial stages of imperialism after 1898, the United States asserted its new world power with little hesitation in order to attain canal rights and to secure the Caribbean approaches to the Central American isthmus. A secondary motive later developed—intervention in the name of democracy and antidictatorship. Some interventions occurred to protect the lives and property of U.S. citizens. For a time, the focus was on the protection of capital investments ("dollar diplomacy").

U.S. imperialism increased after the conclusion of the last European military intervention in a sovereign Latin America state—in Venezuela in 1902/1903. Europeans residing in Venezuela had been heavily damaged in a civil war, but dictator Cipriano Castro excluded foreign claims. External states issued ultimatums and, when they were not met, Germany, Great Britain, and Italy blockaded Venezuela in concert. The United States had previously stressed that the Monroe Doctrine forbade territorial aggrandizement, but it did not protect any state against punishment for fiscal misconduct. After the blockade began, the United States successfully pressured the European states to accept arbitration of their grievances. Consequently, in 1904, President Theodore Roosevelt issued his corollary to the Monroe Doctrine, and the United States thereafter engaged in its own Caribbean intervention, largely in order to preempt that of the Europeans.

U.S. troops were continuously based in Panama from 1902 to 1914 during the construction of the canal. They intervened there during local disturbances from 1918 to 1920 and in 1925. The United States exercised its rights of intervention in Cuba by establishing a provisional military government from 1906 to 1909; it also briefly sent in troops in 1912 and again in 1916 (with some troops remaining until 1922) and threatened to do so again on numerous other occasions. U.S. forces intervened in the Dominican Republic in 1905 to restore order; another troop intervention in 1916 was followed by the establishment of a U.S. military government that lasted until 1924. U.S. Marines occupied Nicaragua from 1912 to 1925 and from 1926 until 1933. Marines were sent to Haiti in 1914. After a brief withdrawal they returned in 1915 and remained until 1934. U.S. troops were in and out of Honduras between 1903 and 1925. A brief military intervention occurred in Guatemala in 1920 to protect U.S. diplomats and private interests during political disturbances.

The Taft administration (1909–1913) began the U.S. practice of dollar diplomacy. Secretary of State Philander C. Knox manipulated U.S. investments and loans in the Caribbean region by encouraging financial groups and consortia to extend them in Santo Domingo, Haiti, and Nicaragua. This private capital involvement led to the landing of U.S. Marines to protect U.S. lives and property. The United States pursued arms control in Cuba, Nicaragua, and Mexico through supervision of sales and embargoes. U.S. "fiscal intervention" took place under U.S.-administered customs receiverships in the Dominican Republic beginning in 1905, in Nicaragua from 1911, and in Haiti starting in 1916. The receiverships involved U.S. fiscal control of the economies and were designed to bring about responsible management and to arrange for a restructuring of international debts.

U.S. armed forces carried out "civic action" projects during their occupations of Cuba, Panama, Nicaragua, Haiti, and the Dominican Republic. Under their aegis, internal order was restored, legal systems reformed, highways constructed, public education improved, and sanitation and public health programs instituted. Public schools were constructed, teachers trained, and public administration programs developed. Little political development took place, however.

The administration of Woodrow Wilson began intervention in the name of democracy and antidictatorship. A sharp distinction should be drawn between military action and the nonrecognition of governments as modes of intervention. Troop landings were not used to bring down dictatorships, nor were they immediately occasioned by constitutional-democratic motives, whereas nonrecognition or its threat was employed in such cases. Once military occupation was begun, however, local military and police forces in Nicaragua, Haiti, and the Dominican Republic were trained, organized, and led by U.S. Marines in the hope that they would be apolitical forces protecting future constitutional governments upon the withdrawal of U.S. forces (a hope totally unrealized). The United States also pursued "electoral intervention," with military supervision of elections prior to ending occupations. U.S.-supervised elections were held in Cuba, Panama, the Dominican Republic, Haiti, and Nicaragua. These practices developed by Wilson were continued by his successors, Presidents Harding, Coolidge, and for a time, Hoover.

U.S. conflict with Latin America was reduced considerably beginning in 1930 with the adoption of noninterventionist policies. President Hoover reduced the number of troops in the Caribbean, and President Franklin D. Roosevelt largely based his Good Neighbor Policy on nonintervention. The last troop contingents left Nicaragua in 1933 and Haiti in 1934, leaving no U.S. troops in Latin America for the first time since 1919. No further direct military interventions occurred until 1965, when forces were sent to the Dominican Republic. President Roosevelt resisted State Department pressures for armed intervention in Cuba in 1933 against the repressive Machado dictatorship, and the 1903 treaty with Cuba giving the United States interventionist rights was abrogated in 1934 (the United States retained the Guantánamo naval station). Likewise, the United States concluded a treaty with Panama in 1936 giving up rights to intervene in Panamanian affairs. The last customs receiverships, in Haiti and the Dominican Republic, were finally closed in 1941.

Soviet Subversion

After the Bolshevik Revolution of 1917, the Soviet Union attempted simultaneously to create loyal Communist parties in Latin America and to establish traditional diplomatic relations. These lines of policy proved to be contradictory. After Uruguay recognized the Soviet Union in 1926, the Soviet embassy in Montevideo served as Latin American headquarters for the Comintern and the dissemination point for its revolutionary propaganda. Soviet efforts to stimulate armed insurrections through local Communist parties were attempted in Mexico (1929), Argentina (1930), Chile (1931), El Salvador (1932), Chile again (1932), Cuba (1933), and Brazil (1935). All of the insurrections were suppressed, and they led to widespread outlawing of Communist parties and ruptures of relations with the Soviet Union—by 1939 all diplomatic relations between Latin American states and the Soviet Union had been severed. Soviet policy was much more cautious after 1935, with Moscow instructing local Communist parties to participate in popular front coalitions.

Inter–Latin American Conflict

Haiti and the Dominican Republic, both located on the island of Hispaniola, viewed each other with suspicion and enmity. After the Dominican Republic ejected Haitian occupation in 1844, border conflicts were frequent. According to Larman Wilson (in Davis, Wilson, and Others, 1975:202), the disputes had a racial dimension, with the border viewed as "a barrier against a Haitian black invasion or a Dominican mulatto invasion." In 1874 the two states agreed to a vague boundary, which was to be delineated by subsequent negotiations, but it remained undefined for the next six decades and frequent border clashes occurred. In 1934 and 1935 the presidents of the two states exchanged visits and announced that all border difficulties had been resolved. As it turned out, the difficulties were more excruciating than ever. In October 1937 Dominican military forces killed at least 12,000 and perhaps as many as 25,000 Haitian peasants near the border. Why the massacre took place has never been fully explained, although little doubt exists that the Dominican dictator, Rafael Trujillo, was responsible. A settlement was worked out using the peacekeeping machinery of the Inter-American System. The disputants signed an agreement on January 31, 1938, in which the Dominican Republic agreed to pay $750,000 as indemnity to Haiti and to fix responsibility for the "incident."

A South American war, especially violent and bloody, occurred between Bolivia and Paraguay from 1932 to 1935. The Chaco War originated in disputes over undetermined national frontiers. The area of the Chaco Boreal, a triangle of territory bound by the Pilcomayo, Paraguay, and Parapeti Rivers, was a void area until both Paraguay and Bolivia took increased interest in it. Paraguay desired to recover some of its lost national prestige after the War of the Triple Alliance; after the War of the Pacific, Bolivia wanted ports on the Paraguay River to give it access to the Atlantic through the Rio de la Plata system. Several frontier treaties were signed, but none went into effect. In 1906 Bolivia began building small forts (*fortines*) in the disputed region, and Paraguay soon followed suit. The controversy was intensified by rumors of the discovery of oil in the Chaco. Armed clashes occurred beginning in 1927, and full-scale war began in 1932. Attempts at mediation by the League of Nations and the Inter-American System failed. By 1935 Paraguay was in control of most of the Chaco and, with both sides exhausted, a truce was agreed to. Most of its provisions were included in a 1938 peace treaty signed through U.S. good offices. Paraguay, as the military victor, annexed most of the disputed area. The financial and human costs were huge for both sides. Some 50,000 Bolivians and 35,000 Paraguayans died in the war.

Peru and Ecuador had serious boundary disputes that dated from their earliest relations. Upon independence they both claimed the sparsely inhabited Amazon provinces of Jaen and Maynas lying to the north of the Marañón River (which eventually flows into the Amazon River). After 1910 Peru was in control of the most valuable portion of the disputed region. In that year the two states agreed to settle the question by direct negotiations or, if that method failed, to submit it for an arbitral award by the U.S. president. Nothing came of the agreement, however, and it was terminated in 1938.

Relatively large-scale military movements by both sides occurred in the area between July 1941 and January 1942, but no major fighting took place. The United States, which had entered World War II in December 1941, was unwilling to allow the destabilizing influences of fighting in South America and forced a settlement of the dispute. The relatively weaker Ecuador was prevailed upon to accept Peruvian sovereignty over the disputed territory, guaranteed by the United States, Argentina, Chile, and Brazil. An agreement was signed in Rio de Janeiro on January 29, 1942, after which a mixed Ecuadorian-Peruvian Boundary Commission was appointed to fix the agreed-upon boundary. After about 95 percent of the frontier had been marked, Ecuador protested that it did not conform to the Rio de Janeiro agreement and the commission's work was halted. In 1959 Ecuador declared the 1942 protocol void and renewed its claim to the disputed provinces. Lima rejected the claims and the dispute remained unresolved.

Colombia and Peru signed a treaty in Lima in 1922 fixing the boundary between them in the Amazon River Basin. In 1930 the demarcation was fixed by a bilateral commission. Under this plan, Colombia occupied a strip of territory called the "Leticia Trapezium," which included the Amazon River port town of Leticia. In September 1932, an armed irregular band of Peruvians seized the town and ejected the Colombian officials. The Peruvian government at first repudiated the act, but later it supported the seizure, sent regular troops into the area, and declared the 1922 treaty invalid. Colombia responded by sending military forces to the Leticia territory via the Panama Canal and the Amazon River, and in February 1933 the disputants severed diplomatic relations. Attempts at settlement by the Inter-American System and by Brazil failed because of Peru's uncompromising position. Finally, after a change of government in Peru, the disputants allowed the League of Nations Special Commission for Leticia to arrange a settlement. Colombia and Peru evacuated their troops from the area, and the commission took over its administration in June 1933, remaining for almost a year. Peru and Colombia continued their negotiations in Rio de Janeiro, with Brazilian mediation, from October 1933 until May 1934, when an agreement was reached. A protocol was signed in which Peru expressed regret for the incidents causing the dispute, reestablished diplomatic relations, and confirmed the Lima Treaty of 1922. Colombia then reoccupied Leticia.

POST–WORLD WAR II
PATTERNS AND CASES

U.S. Cold War Interventions

A new factor entered the Latin American subsystem after World War II with the creation of the U.S. Central Intelligence Agency (CIA). During the cold war period, CIA officials deliberately participated in the assassination of foreign leaders; trained private armies; bribed chiefs of state, labor union leaders, and other official and political figures; and engaged in other activities designed to discredit or remove what were considered to be leftist Latin American governments. The

CIA's covert interventions in Latin American politics became the subject of considerable controversy as a general picture of CIA activities in Latin America emerged from a variety of sources.

In 1974 and 1975 the U.S. intelligence community was investigated by a presidential commission and select committees in the House and Senate. Former directors of the CIA testified before Congress and stated their opposition to further assassinations as an instrument of U.S. foreign policy, a position reiterated by President Ford. After then, as John Prados (1986) observed, demands for intelligence reform gave way to equally strident ones to unleash the CIA. The reform movement proved abortive; Congress made do with the half-measure of "oversight" and CIA agencies interpreted their reporting requirements as narrowly as possible. The Reagan administration gave free rein to the CIA, resulting in the 1983–1984 mining of Nicaraguan harbors, which flouted the oversight prerogatives of the Senate Select Committee on Intelligence. As it turned out, questions about proper activities for an intelligence organization in a democratic nation and the legal basis for those activities still had not been resolved by the end of the cold war.

A new controversy in the 1980s, under the Reagan administration, involved the National Security Council staff's covert operations in Latin America in concert with private individuals and organizations. Congressional hearings in 1987 revealed that these operations were designed to circumvent congressional prohibitions on the covert use of the CIA as well as more direct U.S. armed force. More startling were the NSC staff's circumvention of U.S. Defense Department and CIA supervision and its privatization of covert actions.

The first important case of cold war conflict and U.S. covert intervention in Latin America occurred in Guatemala in 1954. The situation had its roots in 1944, when Dictator-General Jorge Ubico was overthrown after thirteen years in power. The following year an elected civilian president, Juan Arévalo, was inaugurated, who subsequently promoted fundamental social reform. He was succeeded in 1951 by President Jacobo Arbenz Guzmán, who initiated a number of radical economic and social changes. His efforts eventually brought opposition from the United States, which accused him of bringing Communists into his government and allowing them too much influence in Guatemalan politics. Arbenz attempted to integrate the Indian majority into the mainstream of Guatemalan national life through labor organization and agrarian reform, bringing strenuous opposition from the powerful landowning class. He also alienated influential foreign business interests, especially the United Fruit Company. Arbenz expropriated their properties, further straining Guatemalan-U.S. relations. He also employed Guatemalan and foreign leftists in his government (including the Argentine Che Guevara) and broadened diplomatic contacts with Communist states.

By early 1953 Guatemalan exiles were being trained in the neighboring states of Honduras and Nicaragua with CIA assistance and support. U.S. Secretary of State John Foster Dulles pushed an anti-Communist resolution through the Tenth Inter-American Conference at Caracas in 1954 that aimed at weakening Guatemala's position in the Inter-American System. The U.S.-sponsored exile force invaded Guatemala from Honduras on June 18, 1954. The Arbenz government appealed to the UN Security Council, which deferred the matter to the OAS over Soviet opposition. Before an OAS fact-finding team could arrive in Guatemala, the coup had succeeded and Arbenz had been sent into exile.

U.S. conflict with the Castro government in Cuba was the dominant focus of covert U.S. actions after 1959. Castro's 26th of July Movement, which took power on January 1, 1959, originally seemed dedicated to liberal democracy, and the United States recognized the Castro government on January 7, 1959. By the end of 1961, however, it was clear that Castro was running a dictatorship. On May 1, 1961, Castro formally announced that Cuba was "a socialist state," and the following December he stated that he would be a "Marxist-Leninist until the last day of my life." These developments were accompanied by an increasing orientation toward the Soviet Union. Castro defied the United States early in his regime. He confiscated U.S. and British oil refineries and confiscated other U.S. investments and property, abrogated the U.S.-Cuban mutual assistance pact, expelled U.S. military missions, and mounted a hostile propaganda campaign.

The Eisenhower administration canceled all imports of Cuban sugar on July 6, 1960. Three days later Soviet Premier Nikita Khrushchev proclaimed Cuba a protectorate and threatened to defend it with missiles against the United States. Cuban-U.S. diplomatic relations were ruptured on January 3, 1961. The United States attempted both to lead multilateral action (see Chapter 9) and to take unilateral measures against Cuba. The principal early unilateral effort consisted of U.S. support of a Cuban exile invasion to overthrow Castro in April 1961. The 1,500-man force, which included a large number of disillusioned former Castro revolutionaries, landed at the Bay of Pigs on Cuba's southern coast in hopes of catalyzing a popular uprising. The United States organized and financed the operation. Planned under President Eisenhower and carried out under President Kennedy, it was an utter failure. The Cuban armed forces easily subdued and imprisoned the invaders. Although the United States pledged to desist from any further invasions of Cuba as part of the settlement of the missile crisis with the Soviet Union in October 1962, it continued attempts to assassinate Castro. In 1975, Senate hearings revealed that eight efforts were made on Castro's life through various intermediaries from 1960 to 1965.

The United States sent troops to the Dominican Republic in 1965 in its first direct military intervention in Latin America since 1933. It took place in the aftermath of the thirty-one-year Trujillo dictatorship, which ended with his assassination on May 30, 1961, and in the context of U.S. experience with Castro's Cuba. Dominican individuals and groups with conflicting purposes had struggled with each other since Trujillo's death. None had been satisfied with the results and an unstable political situation existed. On April 24, 1965, a rebel army faction known as the "Constitutionalists," led by Colonel Francisco Caamaño, attempted a coup in support of civilian reformist politician Juan Bosch (who had been elected president and inaugurated in February 1963 but overthrown by a military coup seven months later). The opposing military "Loyalist" faction, led by General Antonio Imbert (who had participated in the assassination of Trujillo), was supported by most military units and the national police. The rebels were supported by a large number of civilians who had acquired arms by raiding a police arsenal. Military advantage fluctuated between the two sides during a civil war lasting more than four months and culminating with U.S. military intervention. The

United States landed 405 Marines in the capital city on April 28. The complement was increased thereafter, reaching a high of 23,000 troops (mostly from the U.S. Army) in the vicinity of Santo Domingo, with 10,000 more standing by offshore.

The United States justified the initial troop landing as protection for its nationals residing in the Dominican Republic. In an address to the nation on May 2, however, President Johnson asserted that Communists had joined the rebels and threatened to take control. After saying that "what began as a popular democratic revolution" had been "seized and placed into the hands of a band of Communist conspirators," he said that the U.S. goal had changed "to help prevent another Communist state in this hemisphere." The United States then received OAS endorsement of its intervention, but only after an exceptionally bitter debate, and the U.S. command was transformed into an international peacekeeping force. In fact, except for the Brazilian contribution, the Latin American presence was a token one. The external military peacekeeping units supported the Loyalist military faction in the Dominican Civil War. Finally, in late August, a settlement was signed by both sides. A year later, in September 1966, the peace force was withdrawn.

A broad set of clandestine operations was centered in Chile as the United States employed several tactics to disrupt the elected Marxist government of President Salvador Allende from 1970 to 1973. The Chilean election of 1970 was thrown into the congress when no candidate received a majority. ITT, the U.S. corporation, then offered $1 million to the Nixon administration for a bribery scheme to seek Allende's defeat in the Chilean congressional runoff. The offer was made through John A. McCone, former director of the CIA and then an ITT board member. The U.S. government, which had financed Allende's opposition in the campaign, declined the offer on the grounds that it would be unworkable, but thereafter it made several efforts to "destabilize" the Allende government and discredit his experiment of "socialism in democracy."

U.S. officials, including military personnel, encouraged Chilean military dissidents to make a coup prior to Allende's inauguration. As a prelude, certain Chilean officers attempted to kidnap General René Schneider, the commander in chief of the armed forces, who had refused to cooperate in a coup; but Schneider was accidentally killed in the clumsy kidnapping event on October 22, 1970. After Allende's inauguration, the United States encouraged and financed a wide spectrum of opposition groups, including other parties, certain trade and labor organizations, middle-class housewives, and right-wing terrorist groups; strikes and demonstrations were funded and coordinated through the CIA station in Santiago. In addition, the United States used its influence and voting power in the international lending agencies to put a "credit squeeze" on Chile. It did not stop grants and loans that had already been approved, but it blocked the approval of new ones. Finally, by mid-1973, Chile was in a desperate economic and social situation. The Chilean military overthrew Allende on September 11, 1973, in a brief but bloody coup in which Allende died.

The later disclosure that the CIA had financed the strikes that preceded the Chilean coup was confirmed by President Ford in a news conference in September 1974. Ford said that U.S. actions had been carried out in an attempt to help preserve opposition newspapers and parties in Chile. (In fact, the opposition press had continued to print during the Allende years, and opposition parties, including the most hostile, continued to function; only after the coup was the press suppressed and political parties banned.) Ford justified U.S. subversion in Chile as being "in the best interests of the Chilean people."

Guerrilla Warfare

Contemporary guerrilla warfare was introduced with Fidel Castro's successful exile invasion of Cuba and subsequent defeat of dictator Fulgencio Batista. Similar conflicts emanated from the Caribbean but extended into South America and, to an extent, Mexico. After about a year of consolidating his power after January 1, 1959, Castro openly encouraged violent revolution in the rest of the hemisphere through active assistance to guerrilla movements, especially in Venezuela, Peru, and Guatemala. Guerrilla activities in Latin America intensified in 1963 and 1964, and Cuban support continued until about 1968. During that time, Cuba added Colombia to its list of targets and Che Guevara led the insurgency in Bolivia.

Whereas Cuba urged and actively supported violent revolution in the rest of the region, the Soviet Union favored relations through "normal" diplomatic and economic channels. Soviet policy had continued to be generally unprovocative during World War II and through the 1950s, after the war vacillating in its covert activities and support for Latin American revolutionary groups. The Soviet Union urged caution in the early 1960s following Castro's success in Cuba and throughout the extended period of guerrilla warfare. Most orthodox (Moscow-oriented) Communist parties followed the Soviet lead and rejected armed insurgency in favor of more cautious tactics. China supported the militant Cuban posture for the violent overthrow of existing regimes, although it simultaneously attempted to increase its own diplomatic and trade contacts with Latin American states.

By late 1968 Castro had come to terms with the Soviet Union and tacitly accepted the Soviet doctrines of peaceful coexistence and evolutionary transition to socialism. Major guerrilla efforts had been liquidated in Peru and Bolivia and effectively controlled in Colombia, Venezuela, and Guatemala. Furthermore, economic problems forced Cuba to rely more on the Soviet Union. As the Cuban economy faltered, Soviet influence increased, and Cuban policy conformity may have been the price for continued Soviet assistance. Castro largely withdrew his support of insurgency movements, seeming to resign himself at least temporarily to the futility of exporting revolution. By 1970, after a year and a half of Cuban silence toward Latin American revolution, insurgent leaders began to criticize Castro for his withdrawal of support. The Soviet Union preferred cooperative state-to-state interaction after the mid-1960s, but it occasionally supported subversive activities that led to conflict with Latin American states—Colombia in 1967, Uruguay in 1968, Mexico and Ecuador in 1971, Bolivia in 1972, and Chile in 1973.

Soviet-Cuban support of guerrilla warfare revived with the successful Sandinista-led Nicaraguan Revolution of 1979 and increased insurgent activities in other Central American countries. In the new insurgent era, the Soviet Union and Cuba again disagreed over the appropriate approach. Their positions were reversed, however, with Cuba urging caution and the Soviets pressing an activist policy. (Their actions are illuminated below in the context of Central American conflict.)

Continuing British Boundary and Territorial Disputes

Great Britain and Venezuela had disputed a large portion of British Guiana from the beginning of Venezuelan independence. The problem continued after the British territory was granted independence in 1966 as Guyana. The dispute had seemed settled in 1899 when the decision of an international court of arbitration was accepted by both parties. However, in 1962 Venezuela reasserted its claims, declaring the 1899 agreement void. Venezuela had hired attorneys from the United States to represent its case in 1899; in 1962 it discovered that the will of one of those attorneys had stated that a secret "deal" had been made between the British representatives and a Russian arbiter.

Venezuela wanted the boundary to be moved some 150 miles to the east to the Essequibo River, which would give Venezuela about 53,000 square miles of territory constituting approximately three-fifths of Guyana. Venezuela protested Guyanese independence, asserting that the boundary question should have first been settled. In 1966, Great Britain, Guyana, and Venezuela signed an agreement establishing a mixed border commission and providing that, if the commission failed to solve the problem by May 1970, the dispute would be referred to the World Court or the UN secretary general. The mixed commission failed in its mission, but with direct negotiations the three states signed another agreement on June 18, 1970. The agreement suspended the 1966 protocol and provided for a twelve-year "cooling-off" period, to be extended automatically unless either Venezuela or Guyana decided otherwise. (The agreement was so extended in 1982.) In the meantime, Guyana was free to develop the disputed area and Venezuela was to press no further claims.

A long history of conflict existed over the ownership of Belize, formerly the colony of British Honduras. That conflict for many years complicated the process of its becoming an independent state. Spain had claimed the area in the sixteenth century but did not occupy it. Britain did not refer to British Honduras as a colony until about 1840. Guatemala and Great Britain signed a treaty in 1850 in which Guatemala recognized British sovereignty over Belize in return for certain concessions, one of which was the construction of a road connecting Guatemala City with the Atlantic coast. Since Britain never built the road, Guatemala declared the treaty void in 1939 and reasserted its claims to Belize on the grounds of territory inherited from Spain. Britain replied that Spain never effectively controlled the area, that it was not a part of the colonial Guatemalan jurisdiction, and that, anyway, Spain had ceded the area to Britain in 1670. Britain maintained control.

Guatemala reasserted its claims in the 1950s, when Britain began to consider granting independence to Belize. Belize did not join the short-lived West Indies Federation formed in 1958 and refused a Guatemalan proposal in 1960 that it become an internally self-governing "free associated state" under Guatemalan sovereignty. Guatemala broke diplomatic relations with Britain in 1963 when the latter allowed Belize internal self-government. Guatemala and Belize both rejected a U.S. proposal in 1971 that Belize be granted immediate independence after which it would "consult" with Guatemala on foreign and defense affairs. Belize desired independence but feared a Guatemalan military invasion once British protection was gone; Britain was willing to grant independence but not to guarantee the defense of the new state. Discussions between the United Kingdom and Guatemala broke down in 1981. Britain granted Belize independence on September 21 of that year, reluctantly relenting on the security issues and leaving a British force in Belize to guarantee its territorial integrity. Guatemala refused to recognized the new state.

Mexico also had claims to part of Belize based on succession rights to Spanish sovereignty, but it did not press them other than to assert its right to participate in any discussions on the status of the area. Mexico stated that it would not reactivate its claims if a solution was reached based on the wishes of the Belizan people.

On September 6, 1991, Guatemalan President Jorge Serrano recognized Belize as a sovereign state. Guatemala and Belize commenced diplomatic relations. Two years later, Guatemala and Belize pledged to refrain from using force against each other. On January 1, 1994, following earlier discussions between the British foreign minister and the prime minister of Belize, Britain withdrew most of its garrison and handed over defense responsibilities to Belize.

In 1965 the United Nations General Assembly, at Argentina's behest, approved a resolution urging Britain and Argentina to negotiate a peaceful resolution of the sovereignty question concerning the Falklands/Malvinas islands. The United Kingdom acquiesced, and in 1971 agreements were reached on matters of commerce, communications (including air service), educational and medical facilities, and cultural exchanges. The dispute was quiescent until 1975, when a British government study reported the possibility of oil in the surrounding continental shelf. This possibility reawakened interest in the islands on both sides (this section is taken from Atkins, 1984:22–33).

The United Kingdom subsequently proposed a "lease-back" scheme whereby Argentina would be granted formal sovereignty but Britain would continue administrative control in order to allow the Falklands inhabitants sufficient time to adjust to eventual Argentine governance. Settlers had eventually migrated to the Falklands after the assertion of British control in 1833. They numbered about 1,800 in 1980 and were engaged primarily in sheep raising. Most of the Falklanders were of British stock and strongly desired the status quo, wanting neither annexation to Argentina nor independence. The lease-back formula was defeated in the British Parliament in the face of vigorous opposition by the Falkland lobby in London.

Argentina then resorted to force. On April 2, 1982, Argentina invaded and took military control of the inhabited portions of the United Kingdom's Falkland Islands Colony, asserting that it was enforcing its rightful sovereignty over the Islas Malvinas. Costly naval, air, and land warfare ensued. The war effectively ended on June 14 with Argentina's defeat at the hands of British armed forces. The conflict seemed to begin as a series of events in a remote corner of the globe, but it ended with important consequences for international politics on several levels.

The British government, led by Prime Minister Margaret Thatcher, dispatched a naval force to the South Atlantic, 7,000 miles from southern English ports, and appealed for support from the United Nations and the European Community

(EC). The UN Security Council responded with Resolution 502, which condemned the Argentine action, demanded an immediate withdrawal of Argentine forces, and called on both governments to seek a diplomatic solution to their differences. The Soviet Union did not veto the resolution, apparently satisfied with the dilemma facing the United States. The EC also responded favorably to the British appeal, agreeing to condemn Argentina for the invasion and impose sanctions. In a resolution adopted on April 16, the EC Commission condemned the illegal Argentine aggression against a territory linked to the Community and urgently appealed to Argentina to implement UN Security Council Resolution 502. The EC banned arms sales to and embargoed imports from Argentina.

Soon after the Security Council action, the United States engaged in an intense mediation effort as a neutral third party. Hoping to commence negotiations and avoid open warfare, U.S. Secretary of State Alexander Haig pursued "shuttle diplomacy" from April 7–19 with visits to London and Buenos Aires and interim returns to Washington. The Thatcher government argued that democracies should not appease dictators and must resist aggression, and she insisted that Britain would not consider negotiations until Argentina unconditionally withdrew its troops in accordance with the Security Council resolution. A "paramount consideration" for the British was that the resident Falklanders be consulted and their wishes be respected. The Argentine government, in turn, said it would not remove its troops nor begin negotiations until the United Kingdom recognized Argentine sovereignty over the islands and recalled its naval task force. The U.S. effort effectively ended in impasse on April 19.

Argentina turned to the Inter-American System for support as a counter to UN Resolution 502 and EC sanctions. The initial response from other Latin American states was restrained. A meeting of the OAS Permanent Council from April 5–13 resulted in a "resolution of concern" that offered its "friendly cooperation in the search for a peaceful settlement." Argentina invoked the Rio Treaty just as the U.S. mediation effort ended, and the Twentieth Meeting of Consultation of Ministers of Foreign Affairs was convened April 26–28. By this time British forces had penetrated the hemispheric security zone as defined in the Rio Treaty. The foreign ministers adopted a resolution supporting Argentine claims to sovereignty but refused to invoke any sanctions, as Argentina had requested, against Britain.

The United States ended its neutrality on April 30, in favor of the United Kingdom and in strong opposition to Argentina. In announcing the change in policy, Secretary of State Haig said that "in light of Argentina's failure to accept a compromise, we must take concrete steps to underscore that the United States cannot and will not condone the use of unlawful force to resolve disputes." Consequently, among other measures, the United States suspended all military exports and Export-Import Bank credits to Argentina. It promised to respond positively to requests for material support for British forces short of direct U.S. military involvement. The United States then supported a short-lived Peruvian peace plan, presented on May 2, that strongly resembled earlier U.S. proposals. Argentina immediately rejected it.

The EC, UN, and Inter-American System continued their efforts as military action escalated. EC support for the British position had faltered, especially with the sinking of an Argentine cruiser on May 2 with heavy loss of life. It was widely perceived that the British had violated their own rules of engagement and that its moral advantage as the victim of aggression had eroded. Following relentless British bargaining, however, the majority overcame their objections and decided to extend the sanctions against Argentina indefinitely. In the UN Security Council, Secretary General Javier Pérez de Cuellar reported that his efforts had brought no agreement. The inter-American foreign ministers meeting was reconvened May 27–29. The final resolution, adopted after a particularly acrimonious debate expressing hostility toward both Britain and the United States, condemned British counterforce but again refused sanctions.

The military campaign came to an end on June 14, seventy-four days after the invasion, when Argentine units on the Falklands surrendered. The EC lifted its sanctions on June 20, warning that they would be reimposed if Argentina resumed warfare. On July 12 President Reagan announced that U.S. economic sanctions were no longer necessary. (The ban on military transfers, predating the conflict and requiring a human-rights certification to Congress, was not lifted until December 1983 when a new civilian government was inaugurated in Buenos Aires.) The United Kingdom continued its unilateral sanctions as well as the 200–nautical mile exclusion zone around the islands.

The United Kingdom remained in full control of the Falklands. It reintroduced British military power to the area ("Fortress Falklands") for an indefinite time, despite the expense to the British treasury and the depletion of its NATO forces. The disputants remained without diplomatic relations and technically were still at war, as Argentina had not formally declared an end to hostilities. The sovereignty issue remained alive but unresolved as Argentina continued to press its case in the United Nations. Nevertheless, some communication did occur, with Argentina and the United Kingdom speaking through their intermediaries—Brazil and Switzerland, respectively. Direct secret talks beginning in December 1983 broke down in acrimony. Friendlier and more formal talks were finally commenced, the last rounds at Madrid. As a result, in February 1990 the United Kingdom and Argentina reestablished diplomatic relations, almost eight years after the war had ended. Subsequent agreements were signed regarding investment promotion, military movements in the South Atlantic, and air and sea links between Britain and Argentina. Argentina continued to claim sovereignty and Britain continued to reject such claims. British unease was demonstrated in February 1994 when the United States agreed to sell Argentina thirty-six A4M Skyhawk attack aircraft. Britain strongly objected, arguing the aircraft endangered the security of the Falkland Islands. The United States noted that Argentina had been a peaceful democracy for a full decade and that the current government had renounced the use of force against the islands. Britain replied that a future Argentine government might use the planes to threaten the British territories.

Inter–Latin American Disputes

The dispute between Argentina and Chile over ownership of three islands in the Beagle Channel involved competing geopolitical and strategic calculations, access to possible petroleum and other resources, and the status of conflicting claims in the Antarctic. In 1971, Argentina and Chile agreed to submit their century-old dispute to binding arbitration as prescribed in existing bilateral treaties. Accordingly, the British Crown appointed a five-judge international court of arbitration (all of the judges were members of the International Court of Justice). After six years of hearings and studies, the court rendered a decision in 1977 finding that the three islands (Picton, Lennox, and Nueva) were "unquestionably Chilean," thus giving Chile control of the resource-rich sea area. From Argentina's point of view, Chilean possession of the islands negated the virtually absolute Argentine bioceanic principle that Chile was by nature a Pacific coast power and that Argentina must have hegemony in the Atlantic zone. Argentina also feared that Chilean rights in the Atlantic Ocean would threaten its Antarctic claims. The Argentine military government rejected the ruling in January 1978.

The disputants were on the verge of war in late 1978 when the Holy See observer to the OAS urgently proposed papal mediation. Both governments readily accepted this offer. The entire southern boundary zone, including the Beagle Channel and the contiguous oceanic triangle, was submitted for papal consideration. Two years later, on December 12, 1980, the pope presented his peace proposal. Chile was given sovereignty over the three islands plus a narrow fringe of territorial waters. Contiguous Atlantic waters were designated a condominium "sea of peace" reserved for common or concerted activities. Chile seemed ready to accept the papal decision, although it had resisted the sea-of-peace idea because the ocean resources were more important than the islands as such. Argentina did not reject the proposal outright, but it stalled on responding, reluctant to accept a Chilean presence in the Atlantic.

The process was interrupted by the Anglo-Argentine war of 1982. In the aftermath of that conflict, the negotiating climate for Argentina and Chile seemed unpropitious. Chile was convinced that Argentina had not negotiated in good faith since 1971 and had been too willing to consider the use of military force. Argentina strongly resented Chile's neutrality in the 1982 Anglo-Argentine war, which it saw as actually aiding the United Kingdom. The British Crown had been removed from its traditional role as intermediary between Argentina and Chile, and the United States was in no position to take initiatives. The United Nations lacked precedents in regional American disputes, and the disputants were not inclined to submit to the Inter-American System. Holy See mediation remained open, but Argentina's stalling tactics seemed to devalue that option. Yet the new civilian government in Argentina was determined to do something about the dispute and overcame the difficulties.

The papal role as third-party mediator was successfully revived. On January 23, 1984, the foreign ministers of Argentina and Chile signed a declaration in the Vatican pledging to solve the "southern question" in the framework of papal mediation. They returned to the Vatican to sign a treaty on November 29, 1984. It was ratified by both governments and went into effect in 1985. In the treaty, Chilean possession of the three islands was recognized, with sovereignty extending south to Cape Horn. Chile also gained maritime jurisdiction over a surrounding twelve-mile–wide zone, in which Argentina would be able to exercise free navigation. However, specific limitations on Chilean rights removed the possibility of maritime projection or claims of sovereignty that would normally accompany territorial possession. That is, Chile had physical access to the Atlantic Ocean but did not hold rights to juridical claims. Argentina was given maritime jurisdiction over the area outside the twelve-mile zone. The sea-of-peace idea from the 1980 proposal had been eliminated. The treaty specified that Argentine jurisdiction was not limited by requirements related either to sovereignty or joint economic exploitation. The bioceanic principle was recognized, and Cape Horn was established as the base for maritime boundaries. The signatories agreed to created a binational commission to facilitate the economic integration of the region, and to abstain from warfare in the area. Finally, the treaty provided for a five-year suspension of all disputes that might arise along the entire length of the common national boundary.

The agreement was a clear compromise aimed at satisfying the fundamental concerns of each side. Chile received the islands and access to surrounding resources. Argentina retained control of the Atlantic area near the islands, as well as jurisdiction over the eastern mouth of the Strait of Magellan to the north.

After World War II a number of ideological, boundary, and territorial clashes occurred in the Caribbean states. External actors joined in urging, opposing, or resolving the conflicts in various patterns. The conflicts initially entailed disaffected exiles invading their own national homelands and then extended to guerrilla warfare both in the Caribbean area and throughout much of the rest of Latin America.

Shortly after the war, exiles from a number of Caribbean states gathered in other nearby states to plan revolutionary attempts. Charges and countercharges of intervention among several nations ensued, along with a great deal of Caribbean conflict. An organization known as the Caribbean Legion, sponsored by "reform" governments in the Caribbean area (in Cuba, Guatemala, and Costa Rica), was composed of political exiles and adventurers representing a broad spectrum of political and other motivations. It was dedicated to the overthrow of dictatorships in the Caribbean. Charles Ameringer (1974:Ch. 2) concludes that the Caribbean Legion in fact never existed as a military organization with a permanent central command. Rather, he says, "the term was applied indiscriminately to a series of exile military operations and plots" with different leadership, sponsors, and objectives. The dictators (especially Rafael Trujillo of the Dominican Republic and Anastazio Somoza of Nicaragua) in turn encouraged activities against their at least nominally democratic neighbors. The government of Haiti, which was not so easily classifiable, was also involved in the dispute. Caribbean conflict seen only in terms of a confrontation between "democracies" and "dictatorships" distorts reality. Personal grudges and adventurism also motivated certain participants.

In 1950 an OAS investigating committee reported that exiles fighting against the government of their homelands tended to join with other nationalities who had similar purposes. The report said that many of those exiles were idealistic individuals who had been deprived of democratic guarantees in their own states and were seeking a return to political life. But others were "adventurers, professional revolutionaries, and mercenaries whose primary objective was the promotion of illegal traffic in arms and expeditions against countries with which they have no ties whatsoever." A U.S. State Department official wrote in 1950 that the dissident Caribbean Legion groups sought to bring about political changes by intimidation or armed invasion. He noted that revolutionary groups had been inspired by political exiles who aimed to return to active political life in their homelands, by force if necessary. Whatever their motives, their activities involved the use of territory by states in violation of international obligations.

The most recent "conventional war" in Latin America involving state forces occurred in 1967 between El Salvador and Honduras over boundary and migration issues. For most of the twentieth century, Salvadorans had left their densely populated homeland and migrated, legally and illegally, to lightly populated Honduras across an ill-defined border. Their search for work and land provoked Honduran resentment, and skirmishes frequently occurred between troops of the two states. The worst fighting in sixty years occurred in a week-long undeclared war in July 1969. Honduras instituted a land reform program affecting the Salvadoran land squatters just as an emotionally charged soccer championship series was being played by the two national teams. Following the rioting at the *fútbol* match, Honduran mobs attacked Salvadoran aliens. Diplomatic relations were suspended and troops were placed on alert. The conflict was dubbed the "soccer war," but the conflict was hardly a trivial one. The armed forces launched full-scale attacks. The OAS arranged a truce, which went into effect on July 18, and maintained a peacekeeping team on the frontier. An estimated 3,000 persons were killed during the conflict and 7,000 injured; extensive property damage also occurred. The dispute was set aside with the onset of sustained Central American violence after 1979.

CENTRAL AMERICAN CONFLICT

Complexities of the Confrontations

The Nicaraguan Revolution of 1979 triggered exceptionally complex, violent, and long-lasting strife in Central America. The conflict exacerbated confrontations in the subregion's international relations and created new ones and tapped into deep mutual suspicions among Central American neighbors. Regional developments, however, were overshadowed by the involvement of external actors. For the United States, Central America became a primary area of foreign policy concern and a significant source of domestic and international debate. The United States continued to play the leading role in the area, but other nations and groups were also prominent. Far from being an exclusive U.S. preserve, Central America became an internationalized arena. One of the most striking new conditions of Circum-Caribbean international politics was the concerted rise of assertiveness by local Latin American states in opposition to U.S. policy actions. The principal initiatives for conflict resolution, which the United States greeted with a distinct lack of enthusiasm, were undertaken by local states in concert. IGOs, both the OAS and the UN, played minor roles until late in the process.

After coming to office in 1977, President Carter imposed sanctions related to human rights abuses against the Somoza regime in Nicaragua, the military junta in El Salvador, and the Lucas García dictatorship in Guatemala. After the Sandinista-led revolution overthrew Somoza in 1979, President Carter accused the Soviet Union and Cuba of increased subversive activities in Central America. He was antagonistic toward the new Nicaraguan regime on the grounds that it was shipping Soviet-provided arms to leftist guerrillas in the emerging civil war in

El Salvador. U.S. military transfers were resumed to the Salvadoran government despite the lack of substantive reforms, and the distribution of aid to Nicaragua was suspended.

The Reagan administration, inaugurated in 1981, was determined to recapture U.S. control of Central American events. President Reagan stated that the United States had to act decisively to deter the Soviet-Cuban threat on the U.S. "southern flank." The administration charged Nicaragua with transshipping Soviet-bloc arms to Salvadoran insurgents and accused Cuba of providing arms and advisers to Central American guerrilla groups. The United States pursued a number of coercive and interventionist measures. It also broadened its policies to include persuasive and developmental strategies in response to domestic and international criticism and the growing recognition, on the part of at least some members of the administration, of the complexities involved. Nevertheless, the thrust of policy and rhetoric remained the same: The United States was unwilling to accept a Marxist government in Nicaragua and sought a military victory over leftist forces in El Salvador. In July 1983 President Reagan appointed the National Bipartisan Commission on Central America, headed by former Secretary of State Henry Kissinger, to recommend policies. The report, issued in January 1984, in substance, reinforced and justified as well as influenced government policy.

From 1981 to 1988, key U.S. policies included putting coercive pressures on Nicaragua and combining aid with various overtures to other Central American states, with El Salvador being the central concern. The United States armed, financed, and advised anti-Sandinista guerrillas (the contras); conducted military maneuvers in and with Honduras and naval exercises near Nicaragua; applied an economic boycott against Nicaragua; and even mined Nicaraguan harbors (an act of war). In the meantime, the U.S. invasion of Grenada in October 1983 led to speculation that it would be followed by military intervention in Nicaragua (in retrospect probably not a likely event after the end of 1981, although U.S. officials never ruled it out). In sum, the Reagan administration's actions toward Nicaragua were unprecedented. It justified its largely unilateral coercive measures (including support of insurgent forces, the mining of harbors, and economic boycott), in terms of collective defense and, in effect, carried out an undeclared war while continuing formal diplomatic ties.

Military arms and advisers and economic aid to El Salvador increased dramatically. Assistance was increasingly sent to Honduras, where a significant portion of the contra force operated and which allowed training of Salvadoran forces on its territory. Guatemala, ruled by a brutally repressive regime, received only marginal U.S. aid. The United States also prevailed upon the military government in Argentina, which had no traditional interests in Central America, to send military advisers to Guatemala and El Salvador and to advise Honduras on intelligence matters and train the contras along the Nicaraguan border. Argentina's war with the United Kingdom in 1982, and the accompanying hostility toward the United States, brought the withdrawal of the Argentine military presence in Central America.

The United States also bargained with friendly governments. The Caribbean Basin Initiative (CBI), proposed in 1981 and implemented in 1984, provided for trade preferences and economic aid to friendly governments. It was framed in terms of the Soviet-Cuban threat, but it also recognized poverty as a source of instability. Increasingly strong pressure was asserted on the Salvadoran government to follow a centrist course, institute an effective agrarian reform program, curtail right-wing death squads, and hold free and fair elections. The United States also sought to legitimize governments in Honduras and Guatemala with elections and to improve their human rights records.

Cuba made no secret of its strong support for the Nicaraguan government. Large numbers of Cuban teachers, medical and technical personnel, and military advisers were sent to Nicaragua, and Nicaraguans were trained in Cuba. Guerrilla forces in El Salvador received training and equipment from Cuba. The Soviets limited their direct involvement in the region, leaving much of the socialist bloc's activities in Nicaragua to East Germans, Czechs, and Bulgarians. Soviet military equipment was supplied, most notably tanks and helicopters, but not sophisticated aircraft.

Europeans exercised little influence on Central American events or on restraining U.S. actions. They drew back from supporting Nicaragua as it increasingly mistreated the opposition and moved away from pluralism and nonalignment. Most of all, the Grenada invasion in 1983 signaled that Central American conflict had entered a new and more serious phase. European governments wanted to avoid another alliance problem with the United States, but made it clear that they opposed U.S. military solutions in Central America. They also supported Latin American propositions for conflict resolution that directly challenged U.S. policies with formulas for negotiated settlements.

Conflict Resolution

The Central American conflict differed from previous situations mainly by virtue of the resistance of Central American states to simple U.S.-enforced settlement. Despite the strong and sustained assertion of U.S. power, it did not prevail. High U.S. officials from time to time negotiated directly with Nicaraguans. Central American issues were placed on the agenda of U.S.-Soviet negotiations. The several parties charged their opponents with intransigence and insincerity and little was accomplished toward ending the conflict. The Inter-American System was involved in various aspects of the conflict but its effectiveness had declined and mutual security provisions were not invoked. Its irrelevance to the conflict largely explains why certain Latin American states rallied around the Contadora Group as a substitute multilateral forum.

Latin American states comprising the Contadora Group (Colombia, Mexico, Panama, and Venezuela) organized themselves at a summit meeting held on the Panamanian island of Contadora in January 1983. The group proposed to serve as a mediator in seeking peaceful negotiated outcomes in Central America. It drew up a set of twenty-one principles designed to facilitate discussions between the United States and Nicaragua and, in El Salvador, between the government and insurgents. The principles included, among other things, limiting arms flows, prohibiting all foreign bases, withdrawing external advisers (including Cuban, East European, and U.S.), and ending support for insurgents (both Salvadoran guerrillas and Nicaraguan contras).

In time all five Central American states agreed to the list of Contadora principles. On July 28, 1985, in order to provide new impetus to what was then recognized as an ailing plan, four South American states—Argentina, Brazil, Peru, and Uruguay—joined in a Contadora Support Group. Ecuador had originally been a participant but dropped out after a conflict with Nicaragua led to a rupture of relations. In addition, European governments and political groups generally applauded the Contadora initiative, and their own policy preferences tended to follow the Contadora line. Europeans, despite their second thoughts and increasing ambivalence, remained concerned with Central America. An extraordinary meeting, held in September 1984 in Costa Rica, was attended by all EC foreign ministers, representatives of the four Contadora countries and five Central American countries, and observers from Spain and Portugal. Europeans committed little in the way of financial resources but joined in formally endorsing the Contadora proposals.

The United States gave no substantive encouragement to the Contadora Group. The Kissinger report proposed a "comprehensive regional settlement" but refused to accept any regime (that is, Nicaragua) that might serve as a "crucial stepping stone for Cuban and Soviet efforts to promote armed insurgency in Latin America." The report said: "The United States cannot use the Contadora process as a substitute for its own policy." The Contadora initiative lost momentum with time and events—and, its supporters argued, with U.S. intransigence.

In the wake of the impasse in the Contadora process, President Oscar Arias of Costa Rica proposed a peace plan (for which he won the Nobel Peace Prize) that became the basis for a significant and continuing conflict resolution effort. On August 17, 1987, the five Central American presidents of Costa Rica, Guatemala, El Salvador, Honduras, and Nicaragua met in Guatemala City to sign a document entitled "Procedure for the Establishment of a Firm and Lasting Peace in Central America." It became known informally as the "Esquipulas II Accords" after the town in Guatemala where in a June 1986 meeting the five presidents had discussed regional problems.

The plan had three interrelated purposes. It sought political reconciliation within each of the Central American states, the democratization of their domestic political processes, and the cessation of civil and international hostilities. It mandated a number of measures. In order to achieve national reconciliation, it called for the combination of a cease-fire in those countries where irregular or insurgent groups were active, amnesty policies to facilitate the cease-fire, and the beginning of dialogue between governments and all unarmed opposition groups as well as those who had accepted amnesty. In addition, governments committed themselves to promoting pluralist and participatory democracy, including restoration of individual freedoms and free and honest elections at an early date. Each state would create a broadly representative National Commission of Reconciliation to verify compliance and to monitor the democratization process. Urgent measures would be taken to attend to the problems of refugees and displaced persons.

The cessation of hostilities further and critically depended on certain international processes. Governments in and outside of the region were asked to cease aid of any kind, open or covert, to any irregular forces or insurgent movements and to prevent the use of their territory and the extension of logistical aid in support of aggression against other states. To ensure compliance, the plan provided for the creation of an International Commission for Verification and International Follow-up (*seguimiento*), to be composed of the secretaries general of the OAS and UN or their representatives and the foreign ministers of Central America, the Contadora Group, and the Support Group. This commission would undertake to verify and confirm compliance with the various commitments. A timetable was established with a series of preferred deadlines. Although those deadlines were seldom met, the process continued into the 1990s.

Luís G. Solís-Rivera (1987), chief of staff of the Costa Rican Ministry of Foreign Affairs and adviser to President Arias, articulated Costa Rican thinking and explained the assessments behind the Arias plan. He said that Central American agreement represented the region's determination to forge its own destiny. Until then all peace initiatives had come from outsiders. Even the Contadora process was an external effort from the point of view of Central Americans. The Esquipulus document acknowledged the Contadora efforts and the encouragement of the Support Group, the EC, and Pope John Paul II with appreciation. It also noted, however, that Central Americans must take the lead in solving their problems and that these external groups must work with Central Americans as partners rather than as tutors.

The plan emphasized the idea that Central American peace would not be lasting unless founded on effective democracy, which could not be achieved with the prevailing social injustice and impoverishment of the masses. Peace could not be perceived as a return to the pre-1979 status quo, which had caused many reformers to adopt radical positions in the first place. Symmetry was also an important principle; Costa Rica admitted that its prior view of Nicaragua as the central problem in Central America was an impediment to a realistic regional arrangement. Instead, it said, all Central American governments had to be measured by the same standards if the agreement was to be credible. Finally, simultaneity of measures was crucial to success. A vicious circle had plagued discussions about the conflict, with one side arguing that democracy had to come before suspension of armed force and the other side persuaded that no political concessions could be made until military actions had ceased. Esquipulus II sought to break this circle with the simultaneous application of security and political measures, thus giving guarantees to all. Simultaneity, Solís said, had allowed the signing of the plan.

The United Nations and the Organization of American States became increasingly involved in the Esquipulus II peace plan. UN Secretary-General Pérez de Cuéllar negotiated with Central American governments over the conditions and extent of possible UN diplomatic and military involvement in conflict resolution. In 1989 the Security Council approved the organization and deployment of the civilian-military UN Observer Group in Central America (ONUCA). ONUCA subsequently engaged in extensive peacekeeping and election-monitoring operations in Central America. The OAS, which historically had dealt with Central American conflict but had been shunned in favor of the Contadora and Esquipulus processes, eventually played a significant role. It formed a partnership with the UN with a specified division of labor for the two entities. The OAS was active in the peace verification process and assumed the major (and highly delicate and controversial) third-party function in the resettlement of the Contras in 1990–1991 (Child, 1992).

The Central American peace process was persistently prosecuted by several actors for several years and eventually achieved a number of the goals envisioned in the Esquipulus II Accords. The end of the cold war and events in the Central American states facilitated progress, although serious problems continued to characterize the changed situations. The process was particularly difficult in Nicaragua, El Salvador, and Guatemala, yet significant changes occurred in all three states.

In Nicaragua, where nine years of civil war had cost more than 30,000 lives, the contending parties undertook to carry out the requirements of the peace process. In March 1988 the Sandinista government and contra leaders negotiated a temporary cease-fire, which expired in November 1989. In August 1989 the five Central American presidents devised a general plan to disarm the contras by December 5 in anticipation of general elections set for February 25, 1990; although in fact the disarmament was not accomplished. The United States had urged postponing demobilization until after the elections to ensure Sandinista compliance, while reducing its support for the contras to encourage them to take part in the electoral process. They did so but not as a political party. Instead they supported, but did not join, the United Nicaraguan Opposition (UNO) and its presidential candidate, Violeta Barrios de Chamorro (Shugart, 1992:137–139). Chamorro and the UNO won the elections and the Sandinista government abided by the results. On March 17, 1990, the UN Security Council, supported by the United States, approved a plan to send armed peacekeeping troops to Central America, initially to separate Nicaraguan rebel and Sandinista forces and to disarm the contras in both Nicaragua and Honduras. (The United Nations already had about 240 unarmed peacekeepers in Nicaragua and elsewhere in Central America who were monitoring the cessation of external support for insurgent groups.) On April 19, the Sandinista government, the contras, and representatives of president-elect Chamorro reached agreement on an armistice and the disarming of the contras. Cardinal Obando y Bravo, head of the Salvadoran National Reconciliation Commission, also signed the accord and agreed to oversee their implementation, with UN and OAS assistance. The accord established a permanent immediate cease-fire; rebel leaders promised to start turning over their weapons to UN forces on April 25 (presidential inauguration day). About 600 UN troops went to El Salvador and Honduras on April 22, 1990, to verify the cease-fire and supervise the establishment of five rural security zones. The contras moved into the zones, where UN forces received their weapons and OAS representatives provided various kinds of material assistance. Under a separate program, the UN and OAS returned the contras and their families to Nicaragua or third countries. Most irregular forces were disarmed and the regular armed forces were reduced from about 80,000 to about 15,000. A separate agreement was signed with the Yatama, a Miskito Indian group. The Chamorro government also enacted three amnesty measures, the last on August 18, 1993.

Despite the end of civil war, the Nicaraguan political process remained in turmoil and stalemate. The UNO coalition collapsed, and elements of former contras and Sandinista soldiers persisted in rural violence. The government succeeded in disarming the various groups but not in satisfying them as to several issues. The economy remained stagnant and standards of living, badly deteriorated by years of civil war, did not improve.

Arduous negotiations were also held in El Salvador, aimed at ending the civil war there in terms of the peace plan that led to the settlement in Nicaragua. Yet in late 1989 El Salvador's internal war still raged. In 1990 and most of 1991 negotiations were conducted, but stalled over disagreement on the terms of a cease-fire. Finally, in late 1991, with the war at a standoff, the talks gained momentum. The United States pressured President Alfredo Cristiani, who strongly supported the peace plan even though it was opposed by party colleagues. The insurgents were isolated, with Cuba in crisis and the Sandinistas out of power in Nicaragua. With UN Secretary General Javier Pérez de Cuellar serving as mediator, the UN sponsored further talks in Venezuela, Mexico, and the United States. The two sides signed a cease-fire accord that took effect on February 1, 1992, ending the twelve-year civil war that had taken some 70,000 lives. Some 1,000 UN peacekeepers and observers arrived to support the process.

By mid-July 1993, not all elements of the cease-fire agreement had been realized, but highly significant ones had: the FMLN was disarmed, demobilized, and deactivated; the army's military strength was substantially reduced; the UN appointed a Truth Commission to investigate major human rights cases, which subsequently issued a hard-hitting report; officers considered the worst violators of human rights were dismissed (on July 1, 1993, the entire military high command retired); paramilitary police forces were disbanded; the Legislative Assembly passed an amnesty for participants in the civil war, excluding those involved in major human rights cases; and former guerrillas were reintegrated into the political system (in the general elections in 1994, presidential candidate Rubén Zamora, a political representative for the FMLN during the war, came in second, and numerous former insurgents were elected to the Legislative Assembly and as mayors of municipalities).

Thus the civil war in Guatemala stood as Central America's only remaining internal military conflict. Not until 1991 were the government and guerrillas willing to make concessions necessary for an agreement. In January President Jorge Serrano pledged to improve Guatemala's human rights record (one of the worst in Latin America) and to reach a "total" peace agreement with the guerrillas. The talks, which commenced in April 1991 in Mexico, were held in the name of the Central American peace process. The government was represented by army generals; leaders from the four main rebel groups organized as the Guatemalan United Revolutionary Front (URNG). The National Reconciliation Commission served as mediator, headed by Roman Catholic Bishop Rodolfo Quezada Toruno and with the active participation of the United Nations observer. In November 1991 the talks deadlocked over the issues of international human rights monitors, responsibility for the violence and government indemnization for the victims, and the future of militias accused of human rights abuses. The government rejected the guerrillas' demands and consequently rural violence increased.

In May 1992 the talks resumed in Mexico, but the army was disdainful of the insurgents' military capabilities and the guerrillas were unwilling to disarm without guarantees of safety. President Serrano soon expressed frustration at what he called the insurgents' "vague demands" and the talks broke down; the war continued. In January 1993 negotiations recommenced at the UN in New York. On March 30, Guatemala's military chiefs, at the urging of the United States, forced President Serrano to resign after he attempted to suspend the constitution and assume personal power. The Congress elected Ramiro de Leon Carpio, a well-known human rights activist and critic of the armed forces, to take office on June 6, 1993 and serve out Serrano's term of office (until January 1996). The new president sought to restart negotiations and end the thirty-two-year insurgency that had taken no less than 100,000 lives.

THE NARCOTICS TRAFFIC

In the early 1980s, the problem of the illicit narcotics traffic in the hemisphere (the "narcotraffic") entered inter-American relations as a high-priority issue. Although it had existed for many years, its expansion after the late 1970s made it an enormous business enterprise and created a major policy dilemma for all governments involved. The narcotraffic became one of the most compelling and acrimonious issues in U.S.–Latin American relations.

Market demand stemmed primarily from drug consumption in the United States, the world's largest consumer of illicit drugs. In the latter 1980s, U.S. consumers spent about $110 billion annually on illegal drugs, a figure corresponding to almost 3 percent of GNP. Those consumers numbered some 25 to 30 million marijuana smokers, 5 to 6 million cocaine users (including the cocaine derivative "crack"), and more than a half-million heroin addicts. With the growth of drug-related urban crime and violence (and its extension to the suburbs, small towns, and even rural areas), narcotics financing of organized crime, and the devastating social consequences of increasing numbers of youth involved with drugs, the narcotraffic became a major public-health and crime issue.

The supply of cocaine grew at an estimated annual rate of 10 percent throughout the 1980s. As the U.S. market became saturated, traffickers looked for new markets to absorb the surplus. By the end of 1986, Europe had begun to import significant amounts, and by mid-1987 it was evident that even Latin American societies were seeing increasing cocaine abuse.

Suppliers in other countries, especially in Latin America, responded to the U.S. demand. Latin America was the source of all the cocaine, four-fifths of the marijuana, and two-fifths of the heroin consumed in the United States. Nine countries accounted for most of the U.S. illegal drug imports, dominating cultivation, refining operations, transshipping, and money-laundering schemes. Mexico produced about 40 percent of the marijuana and heroin and transshipped about one-third of the cocaine imported into the United States. Mexico was Latin America's only heroin-producing country—the remainder came from non-Latin sources such as Pakistan and Burma. Colombia supplied about 25 percent of the marijuana destined for the United States and cultivated up to 10 percent of the cocaine. The Colombian Medellín Cartel was the largest cocaine syndicate in the world and came to control as much as 75 to 80 percent of the cocaine exported from the Andean region. Its wealth was so vast that it publicly and credibly offered in 1988 to pay off Colombia's $10 billion external debt in return for the cancellation of Colombia's extradition treaty with the United States. Peru, the world's largest cultivator of coca leaf (cocaine's raw material), produced 50 percent of the cocaine destined for the United States. Bolivia was the second largest, accounting for 40–45 percent. Jamaica produced up to 15 percent of the marijuana that entered the United States and was a major transshipment country for cocaine. Belize accounted for up to 10 percent of the marijuana and became an alternate trafficking route. The Bahamas was a favored site for laundering money and a major transshipment point for both cocaine and marijuana. Panama was a transit point for cocaine and a major center for money laundering. Antidrug programs aimed at the countries mentioned above led, after the mid-1980s, to trafficking activities elsewhere. Coca production was soon begun in Argentina, Brazil, Ecuador, Paraguay, and Venezuela. The Dominican Republic, islands in the Eastern Caribbean, Guyana, and Suriname became alternate trafficking routes.

Cooperative international drug eradication and interdiction programs, led by the United States, were undertaken. U.S. policymakers had determined that they could not modify consumer behavior very much and so decided to emphasize the attack on the source and flow of drugs, leading to several multilateral efforts. In April 1986 in Rio de Janeiro the OAS adopted a program for regional antinarcotics cooperation, and the following November an Inter-American Drug Abuse Control Commission was created. In October 1986 ministers of justice and attorneys general from thirteen Latin American countries and the United States met in Mexico to discuss narcotics problems, and in March 1987 a Caribbean Regional Conference on Drug Abuse was held in Belize (U.S. Department of State, 1987b).

The most important efforts, however, were U.S.-led bilateral actions. Interagency field efforts were undertaken with Mexico. Colombia agreed to extradite drug lords to the United States for trial. The United States entered into agreements with Peru in 1982 and Bolivia in 1983 designed to eradicate the supply of drugs and induce small farmers to switch to other crops. In 1986 the United States and Bolivia cooperated in an exercise called Operation Blast Furnace. U.S. Army helicopters airlifted Bolivian National Police on a series of raids aimed at destroying the laboratories that processed coca leaf and the coca fields themselves. In 1988 Operation Snowcap, headed by the U.S. Drug Enforcement Agency (DEA) assisted by U.S. Special Forces, the U.S. Border Patrol, and police in several Latin American countries, conducted anticocaine activities.

The U.S. Anti–Drug Abuse Act of 1986 was designed to strengthen the U.S. antinarcotics efforts at home and abroad. It sought to lower domestic demand with tougher law enforcement, educational programs, drug testing, treatment and rehabilitation programs, and increased penalties for traffickers. It increased resources for the interdiction of narcotraffic and for eradication, crop-substitution, and enforcement programs abroad. The law mandated the annual International Narcotics Control Strategy Report to assess the situation in drug-producing and drug-trafficking nations, nineteen of which were in Latin America. The president was required to certify whether those countries were cooperating fully with the United States in narcotics control before they could receive foreign aid; trade and economic sanctions were also provided for. Sanctions were imposed on Bolivia in 1986 and 1987 for not acting seriously to eradicate its coca crop. In

1988 Panama was "decertified" because of the activities of General Manuel Noriega. While cooperating with the CIA and DEA, Noriega had created a large narcotics-trafficking and money-laundering center. A U.S. federal court convicted him in absentia on drug-related charges.

Progress was made in eradicating the source of narcotics and interdicting flow. Nevertheless, production and supply far outstripped demand. With increasing resources devoted to antinarcotics programs, seizures in all categories of illicit drugs skyrocketed as did drug arrests. Even so, the U.S. government intercepted only 3 percent of the marijuana and 10 percent of the cocaine entering the United States. Antinarcotics programs soon faced immense problems, and international cooperation was hampered by a variety of factors. Markets in the United States were not diminished and even grew in Europe. U.S. drug policies were undermined by inadequate resources, lack of bureaucratic coordination, and their subordination to "national security" concerns (the longtime toleration of Noriega as a useful anti-Communist "asset" despite evidence he was a drug kingpin is an excellent example). In Bolivia the introduction of U.S. military forces was widely condemned and that instrument was rejected by other governments in the region. The Medellín Cartel, through threats and outright violence, eventually succeeded in forcing the Colombian government to suspend extradition of traffickers to the United States. Colombian officials had some success arresting or killing the Medellín leadership and interrupting trafficking operations, but they were soon replaced by the rival Cali Cartel. In Latin America official corruption, mismanagement, and rivalry made action difficult. Peasants resisted change; coca had been their mainstay for centuries and was considerably more profitable than any other crop.

The Reagan administration and bipartisan majorities in the U.S. Congress stayed the course on the "supply-side" approach to international drug control. They continued the focus on eradication of drug cultivation and processing in supplier countries and crop-substitution programs for the growers, interdiction of narcotics shipments, increased U.S. military roles in the efforts, and better law enforcement by police and courts in source states. On the domestic "demand-side," policy emphasized law enforcement over prevention and treatment. In late 1988, the Congress, disappointed with the results so far, enacted a second Anti-Drug Abuse Act. In effect the law mandated a shift in emphasis rather than fundamental change in strategy. More resources were put into demand-side efforts, particularly in law enforcement, and supply-side efforts were continued (Bagley, 1992b).

The Bush administration, which took office in January 1989, also pursued a supply-side strategy in the continuing war on drugs. It increased funding for demand control with an emphasis on law enforcement. In particular, it attempted to "militarize" the international war on drugs (Bagley, 1992b). In late 1989, the administration expanded the role of the U.S. armed forces in counterproduction and interdiction actions, despite opposition from military leaders. On December 20, 1989, the U.S. armed forces unilaterally intervened in Panama, removed General Noriega from power, and sent him to the United States for trial on drug-trafficking and money-laundering charges (he was subsequently convicted and imprisoned). Shortly after the intervention, on February 15, 1990, President Bush participated at the Andean Drug Summit in Cartagena with the presidents of Colombia, Peru, and Bolivia. It produced several bilateral agreements between the United States and the other states regarding intelligence gathering and sharing, extradition, the problem of money laundering, the illegal small-arms trade, and public awareness (Bagley, 1992a).

Soon after the Cartagena meeting the Bush administration announced its "Andean Strategy," which contained a number of elements. A $2.2 billion development aid package for Bolivia, Colombia, and Peru was conditioned on their acceptance of military aid. The Andean Trade Preference Act was enacted into law as the trade element of the Andean Strategy, offering a unilateral U.S. trade preference program for Bolivia, Colombia, Ecuador, and Peru (see Chapter 10). Thus both aid and trade aimed to help the Andean states move away from coca cultivation and trafficking to other crops and forms of livelihood. Military aid was designed to convince the Andean states to deploy their public forces into zones of narcotics production and transport. The U.S. Army drew up a plan envisioning coordinated attacks by the armed forces of Bolivia, Colombia, and Peru on drug cartel targets, to the dismay of many high-ranking U.S. military officials and government leaders in the three Andean states.

A second summit was held from February 26–27, 1992, in San Antonio, Texas, attended by the presidents of Bolivia, Colombia, Ecuador, Mexico, Peru, and the United States and the foreign minister of Venezuela. U.S. proposals contained no shifts in premises or priorities, and the Latin Americans continued to insist on less U.S. unilateralism and more economic aid. The participants signed an agreement pledging more cooperation in their antinarcotics actions, including the creation of regional police training centers, mutual legislation to control money laundering and chemical shipments, and improved means of sharing of intelligence and evidence. Neither development aid nor coordinated Andean military action were mentioned (Bagley, 1992a).

The Clinton administration, which took office in January 1993, shifted the operational focus of antinarcotics efforts. Experts in the field generally agreed that the narcotraffic had not been reduced despite years of expensive and intense efforts to restrict it. A National Security Council review concluded that U.S. military interdiction efforts had little effect in reducing the flow of cocaine into the United States. By the end of 1993 a revised U.S. approach had been decided upon. Congress reduced overall aid to the Andean states for drug control and cut military and police aid in particular. The administration decreased funding for the U.S. armed forces counternarcotics programs, reducing their roles in drug interdiction, but increased resources for cocaine eradication in the Andean states and law enforcement on the U.S.-Mexican border. On the demand side, the administration shifted the emphasis to treatment and prevention programs over law enforcement. On January 11, 1994, a State Department official said that, rather than focus on interdiction (which had proved a failure in the past) the United States would concentrate on drug-crop eradication and local police training, crop substitution, and programs to reduce the demand for drugs at home. Officials did not indicate why they expected the policies that had been tried in the past—and found wanting—to succeed.

BIBLIOGRAPHIC COMMENT

Grabendorff (1982) constructs a good model of Latin American interstate conflict, and Child (1985) authoritatively focuses on South America. The Paraguayan War is analyzed by Kolinski (1965), the War of the Pacific and the Tacna-Arica dispute by Bulnes (1955), and the Chaco War by Rout (1970) and Zook (1960). Wood (1966) addresses Latin American wars in the decade 1932–1942. Anderson (1981) and M. J. R. Martz (1978) provide analyses of the "soccer war" between El Salvador and Honduras. On the U.S.-Mexican War, see Price (1967) and Singletary (1960). The following list on specific territorial and boundary conflicts is highly selective: Zook (1964) analyzes the Ecuador-Peru dispute, and Barrera Valverde (1982) gives an account of the 1982 Ecuador-Peru border dispute from an Ecuadorian perspective. Area (1984) collects documents and chronologies regarding Venezuelan-Colombian territorial controversies; Vázquez Carrizosa (1983) articulates the Colombian point of view. Braveboy-Wagner (1984) analyzes the Venezuelan dispute with the United Kingdom over Guyana territory. Sabaté Lichtschein (1985) provides a legal analysis of the entire range of Argentine territorial and boundary problems, and Goñi Garrido (1984) analyzes the Beagle Channel controversy from Argentine perspectives. W.S. Smith (1991), P. Beck (1988), and Dillon (1989) evaluate the Falklands/Malvinas problem. Studies of various aspects of nineteenth-century European interventions in the region include Arnáiz y Freg and Balaillon (1965) on France in Mexico, Cady (1929) on foreign intervention in the Rio de la Plata, and W. C. Davis (1950) on Spain in Peru and Chile. A few general works on U.S. imperialism and interventions prior to the Good Neighbor Policy are by Foner (1972), Kane (1972), Munro (1964), W. T. Perkins (1981), and Ronning (1970). On post–World War II CIA activities in Latin America, see Prados (1986), U.S. Senate Select Committee to Study Governmental Operation with Respect to Intelligence Activities (1975a, 1975b, 1976), and U.S. House Committee on Foreign Affairs (1975). On covert activities under Reagan, see Marshall et al. (1987) and U.S. Senate Select Committee on Secret Military Assistance to Iran and the Nicaraguan Opposition and U.S. House Select Committee to Investigate Cover Arms Transactions with Iran (1987). Post–World War II Caribbean turmoil is handled by Ameringer (1974) and U.S. Department of State (1962). For works on guerrilla activities see the Bibliographic Comment following Chapter 6, and for those on Soviet subversion, that following Chapter 4. Among the large number of works that appeared on Central American conflict are Blakemore (1984), Blachman, Leogrande, and Sharpe (1986), Burns (1987), Calvert (1988), Child (1992), Erisman and Martz (1982), Etheredge (1985), Falcoff and Royal (1987), Leiken (1984), McNeil (1989), Newfarmer (1984), Pastor (1987), Ropp and Morris (1986), and Woodward (1988); see also *The Report of the President's Bipartisan Commission on Latin America* (1983). On the Contadora initiative, see Cepeda and Pardo (1985), and Bagley (1987). Solís-Rivera (1988) explains the Arias peace proposal. On the Grenada intervention of 1983, see Beck (1993), Lewis and Mathews (1984), and Seabury and McDougall (1984). On the Panama intervention of

1989, see Watson and Tsouras (1990) and Donnelly, Roth, and Baker (1992). On drug trafficking, see Bagley (1992a, 1992b), Bagley and Walker (1994), Craig, (1985), Mabry (1989), MacDonald (1988), McCoy and Block (1992), Scott and Marshall (1990), and W.S. Smith (1992); Walker (1989) is a historical study of inter-American drug control efforts.

PART FIVE

■

Conclusion

Intense debates have long taken place about the consequences of policies and interactions in the Latin American subsystem. Conflicting views have emerged concerning the effects of foreign policy instruments and international interactions concerning trade, investment, economic and military assistance programs, and diplomatic and cultural relations, as well as political and economic coercion, subversion, military and paramilitary intervention, and war. They have raised issues and questions over which serious analysts disagree, especially concerning the influence of strong external states on the policies and political systems of the regional Latin American states. Chapter 12 concludes the book with a presentation of general explanations and prescriptions and provides a critique of the major theories of Latin American international relations.

CHAPTER TWELVE

— ■ —

Explanations and Prescriptions

A NUMBER OF THEORIES have appeared in the study of international relations that are especially relevant to Latin America, and some have been formulated with particular reference to the region. The principal theories include the realist-idealist dichotomy, the Marxist critiques and alternatives, liberal developmentalism with its various shades of analysis, economic theories of modernism and neoliberalism, and the variants of dependency theory (especially structuralism and neo-Marxism). These theories of international relations purport to explain Latin America in the international political system and offer policy prescriptions for the various actors.

THE THEORETICAL ENTERPRISE

All of the theories mentioned above (and analyzed below) are heavily policy oriented. They are concerned both with explaining state behavior and the international system and with influencing state policies and the decisions of other actors. Prior to engaging in specific theoretical critiques, therefore, a brief review of the nature of theory and the relationship to policy is in order.

Most international relations (IR) specialists today agree on the importance of theoretical inquiry. A theory is a set of propositions designed to explain a class of phenomena, such as those analyzed in this book. Furthermore, IR specialists tend to be practical as well as scientific and philosophical, interested in policy prescriptions along with objective analysis and subjective understanding. Indeed, the latter two enterprises have often led to interest in policy problems.

"Theory" is often used colloquially or pejoratively to connote an untested idea or opinion in political discourse. For the purposes of this book, this meaning and practice are emphatically rejected. A mere subjective preference is not the equivalent of theoretical judgment in any critical sense. A cardinal rule for serious political analysts (including those who wish to influence policies) is to be self-conscious about their intellectual processes—to understand the nature of one's thoughts and those of others through theoretical analysis.

The various intellectual processes that people may engage in are represented by the different kinds of statements they make. In the case of international relations

and other social sciences, we should distinguish between five categories of assertions: (1) descriptive (factual), (2) explanatory, (3) predictive, (4) normative
(value), and (5) prescriptive. Explanatory statements give meaning to descriptive
statements, typically answering some form of the question "why?" Predictive
statements are usually derived by extrapolating trends and applying explanations
to presume future conditions. Political scientists are by and large modest about
their predictive claims, but prediction is particularly relevant when it considers
policy consequences before the fact of implementation. Normative statements express a preference in terms of right and wrong, desirable and undesirable, and
other value-based objectives. Prescriptive statements go beyond assessment or
contemplation to offer advice with the purpose of affecting events. Prescriptive
statements usually have normative and predictive elements; that is, they are normative in the sense that purposes proceed from some image or view of a desirable
state of affairs, and are predictive when stating what course of action will accom-
plish a given purpose.

These statements are reflected in three kinds of political theory: (1) empirical
(behavioral) theory, which analyzes politics by scientific methods; (2) normative
theory, which studies politics in philosophical, ethical (perhaps tied to legal), or
ideological terms; and (3) policy theory, which offers advice for policy action.
These theories are separate but not mutually exclusive; in fact, the theories examined here fall under the category of policy theory but include empirical and normative elements.

No matter what specific purposes one may bring to the study of IR, the beginning point is to strive to understand objectively the world in which we live. Thinking may then shift to normative evaluations. Both objective and subjective
understanding may be applied to policy prescription. Normative conclusions may
go beyond clarifying values about proper behavior by recommending what should
be done in matters of action. Empirical theory may tell policymakers the best way
to achieve a desired goal—what is possible or not—after what is desirable has already been determined. Thus, knowledge of politics may be applied to solving actual problems.

The expectation of theorists to "use" political knowledge in the policy arena
raises questions about scholarship. Should theorists go beyond objective and ethical analysis about political behavior to prescribe policy? Those who answer in the
affirmative (and I am among them) argue that, since all policy is ultimately based
on values, a detached approach may not be particularly desirable. As Charles
Lerche succinctly put it, "if the serious scholars suspend normative judgment on
events, the function of assigning value to policy choices falls to political leaders,
journalists, and other manipulators of the mass psyche."

Wahlke and Dragnich (1966:16–17) entered an important caveat about policy
prescribing. They pointed out that disagreements arise over the identification of
both problems and solutions. Political knowledge cannot tell us whose problem
definition or policy prescription is right, because it cannot tell us what political
ends we ought to seek or to what particular goals our factual knowledge ought to
be applied. Furthermore, since prescriptive statements almost always have norma-

tive overtones, political knowledge may be used for purposes of which one may thoroughly disapprove. They note the often-cited Book V of Aristotle's *Politics*, which offers knowledge about the causes of revolution. That knowledge may serve very different purposes—those of a tyrant protecting his power against rebellious subjects, a democratic leader working for stability in an open society, an ego-gratifying agitator manipulating the revolution, and a leader using revolution as a means to human progress.

REALISM, IDEALISM, AND MARXISM

Realist and Idealist Perspectives

Plano and Olton (1988:18ff) gave useful definitions of realism and idealism as alternative approaches for formulating and evaluating foreign policy. The realist perspective, the oldest concept in IR theory and practice, is fundamentally pragmatic. In general terms, realism is a view of the world as it is, as distinguished from abstract or speculative preferences. In international relations, realists emphasize national interest as the fundamental guide to policy-making in the sense of the state's most vital needs of self-preservation, independence, territorial integrity, military security, and economic well-being. When a state bases its foreign policy strictly on national interest and power politics, it can be described as pursuing a realist, as distinguished from an idealist, policy. The realist defines interest in terms of power and emphasizes the balance of power as the principal guide to policy-making and to understanding the structure of the international system. The realist school starts with the assumption that power is the key factor in all international relationships. The wise and efficient use of power by a state in pursuit of its national interest is, says the realist, the main ingredient of a successful foreign policy.

Idealism is the pursuit of high principles, purposes, or goals. It is a representation of things as they might or should be rather than as they are. The idealist approach to international relations is based on principles involving international norms, legal codes, and moral-ethical values. The idealist believes that foreign policies based on moral-legal principles are more effective than power politics because they are more durable and better promote unity and cooperation among states. Political idealism involves not force and coercion but winning over the minds and allegiances of people to accept principles that ought to govern state conduct. This view assumes that foreign policies should strive to create a better world order and emphasizes international law, organization, and other regimes that regulate the system by accommodating conflict and facilitating cooperation.

Practices associated with realism—balance-of-power, strategic, and geopolitical calculations, and conflict—have been important aspects of the Latin American subsystem from its beginnings to the present. The policy implications of conflict in Latin American international relations have been especially profound for the United States as the most powerful external actor and the most willing and able to use coercive diplomacy. Nevertheless, the United States was not the first, nor is it the only, state to engage in power politics in Latin America. Power politics have characterized much of Latin America's relations with many external states as well as inter–Latin American relations, particularly by military regimes when they were in power in certain South American states in the Southern Cone.

The Marxist Alternatives

Marxism and the Leninist interpretation were among the earliest theoretical dissents from realism and imperialism from the mid-nineteenth century through World War I. Marxist-Leninist ideas offered alternatives to what proponents considered ineffective liberalism and idealism. A set of economic and political doctrines were formulated, characterized by the theories of dialectical materialism, surplus value, and class struggle. As developed by Karl Marx and Friedrich Engels in the middle to late nineteenth century, Marxism viewed the state as a device for exploitation of the masses by a dominant bourgeois (capitalist) class. They argued that the functioning of the international political system was rooted in social and economic factors. Although Marx said little about Latin America beyond a brief tract on Mexico, some of today's theories about the region's international relations recall the earlier Marxist arguments. This has been especially true of neo-Marxist dependency theory (discussed below). Of more immediate importance, however, were Lenin's interpretations, which have also provided the basis for subsequent theorizing.

Lenin made the most influential extensions of Marx's concepts. His theory of imperialism was set forth most cogently in his 1912 essay, *Imperialism—the Highest Stage of Capitalism*. To Lenin, the capitalist economic system was the driving force behind both colonization and war. Economic factors dominated the capitalist states' policies, which were inevitably imperialist. Lenin's influence was even greater after his seizure of power in Russia in 1917 and creation of the Soviet Union.

Initial Soviet assessments of Latin American society were heavily dependent on Marxist ideas of class struggle, with the conclusion that both "objective" and "subjective" conditions necessary for a proletarian revolution were lacking. The region was too advanced industrially to fit the Marxist precapitalist idea, but it was not describable as a mature capitalist industrial economy either. Thus, Latin America was unique in Marxian terms; it stood midway between precapitalist and mature capitalist stages. In addition, the middle and upper classes were too strong for a successful revolution by the small working class, which itself seemed too interested in achieving middle-class status. Following World War II, Soviet writers tentatively explored the notion that the region shared some common characteristics with the newly independent, precapitalist, non-Communist, underdeveloped Third World in Asia and Africa. In particular, U.S. economic domination offered the possibility of an anti-imperialist revolution, even though Latin America continued to have unique social and economic characteristics. Beginning in the mid-1960s they emphasized the decline of U.S. influence in the region. At the same time, traditional Marxism-Leninism was challenged by Latin American guerrilla groups who advocated Trotskyism, Maoism, and especially, fidelismo. With the end of the cold war, the disappearance of the Soviet Union, and the general eclipse of communism and its associated intellectuals, Marxist-Leninist theory fell into decline.

The Era of European Imperialism

Imperialism and balance-of-power policies provided a principal thrust of classic *realpolitik*. European imperialism during the nineteenth century took on special characteristics in Latin America. The regional states had a low capability level in relation to the outside world, making them subject to pressures from the more dynamic European powers. From the Latin American point of view, the external powers were not effectively restrained by the balance-of-power system. Nevertheless, certain aspects of the global balance-of-power system helped protect the Latin American states.

The European states were not uninhibited and conceivably they might have been even more unheeding of Latin American sovereignty. The era of "new imperialism" in the latter half of the nineteenth century and up to World War I, involving highly competitive European great power activities in the Middle East, Africa, and Asia, also marked the height of European interest in Latin America. The region figured in no significant way in the worldwide imperialism-colonialism thrust, however, and the Latin American states managed to maintain a measure of independence in comparison with much of the rest of the non–North Atlantic world. This situation was a curious one on the surface, considering that imperialism was then viewed as a normal product of international competition, that it was characterized by the development of the alliance system in Europe to divide colonial spoils, and that its causation is generally ascribed to economic motives.

The United States and Power Politics

The realist-idealist dichotomy relates particularly to the debates over the preferred approach to foreign policy-making in the United States. Many realists regard the United States as being misled by popular attitudes and moral self-righteousness into adopting idealistic guidelines in the making of foreign policy decisions. The result, according to the realists, is the inability of the United States to compete effectively with other states that base their policies on the hard realities of national self-interest. Idealists tend to reject the power-centered realist approach as Machiavellianism producing only short-term gains. For the idealist, the most successful policies have been based on values that have won both domestic and overseas support. The realist-idealist dichotomy in today's world should not be overstated, however. Realism and idealism may converge, and poiicy debates and decisions often attempt to reconcile the two. In practice, policies often have combined some mixture of realism and idealism. In such cases, realism specifies the means for achieving goals and idealism justifies the policies adopted.

During the twentieth century the United States has responded to what it considered to be security risks with strong coercive power and seemingly little regard for the consequences beyond the immediate situation being addressed. This approach was demonstrated by extensive interventions in several Caribbean states in the first third of the twentieth century, and more recently by rebel invasions of Cuba in the early 1960s, military interventions in the Dominican Republic in 1965, Grenada in 1983, and Panama in 1989, and a mix of coercive instruments in Central America in the 1980s. At other times, however, the United States has been sensitive to Latin American and world opinion and to the effects its actions might have in other parts of the hemisphere and the world. This approach seems to have prevailed with the adoption of noninterventionist policies in the 1930s and restraint, off and on, in the postwar period, most clearly during the first half of the Carter presidency. Idealism has also been reflected in the vacillating efforts to promote democracy and human rights at times during the twentieth century, sometimes paralleling *realpolitik*. As noted in Chapter 5, even though U.S. policy-makers often couch their Latin American policies in moral rhetoric, they almost always formulate policies in terms of the perceived realities of national interest and security.

The Caribbean became the most important extracontinental area for the United States after the turn of the century. It was clearly considered in the U.S. sphere of influence, and policies there were understandable in terms of strategic geopolitical calculations. Alfred Thayer Mahan's seapower thesis, dating from the 1890s, was the initial important geopolitical expression of U.S. interests (see Chapter 5). It influenced the thinking of U.S. policymakers virtually to the present day. Ironically, however, almost as soon as Mahan's theories became accepted as the foundation for U.S. policy in Latin America, events began to make them irrelevant. In previous centuries, technological changes had been absorbed in warfare without fundamental systemic changes, and the bases for national power tended to be measured, almost crudely, in terms of military and economic factors and in territorial holdings. This continuity of international political culture was seriously disrupted, however, after 1914, and even more after 1939, by awesome technological developments—the submarine, aircraft, "instant" communications, and, most profoundly, nuclear weapons. Mahan's doctrines concerning the Caribbean area, as well as his broader principles of sea power, were outdated by events and lost their validity. Nevertheless, they were highly relevant to power politics for the first half of the twentieth century in the sense that, in some form, they were accepted by U.S. strategists as an article of faith. This widespread view was evidenced especially by the sacrosanctity of the Panama Canal in statements by military men and diplomats through World War II until the dawn of the nuclear age.

The Caribbean area, with its important strategic position for the United States, most often has been the testing ground for emerging U.S. policies toward Latin America at large. There the United States first pursued military and economic intervention, "taught" democracy, and intervened against communism. Yet even the Caribbean has provided illustrations of the limits of U.S. power, even in the imperialist period during the first third of this century. U.S. actions probably deterred European interventions for the decade prior to World War I; but afterward U.S. coercion continued even though the threat of European incursions was virtually nil. The political price for U.S. interventions was high. The United States was intimately involved in the substance of Caribbean politics; it determined the appropriateness of constitutions, the eligibility of persons for election to presidencies, and the legitimacy of political parties. Furthermore, the proximate objective of enforcing democracy through intervention in order to serve long-range goals of stability was absolutely unrealized. After the U.S. withdrawal from Cuba, the Dominican Republic, Haiti, Nicaragua, and Panama, dictators arose in all of those states, several coming from police forces trained by the United States to protect constitutional government. In sum, intervention failed to meet long-range U.S. interests, aroused bitter antagonisms in many quarters, entangled the United States in daily participation in Caribbean politics, and left dictatorships behind.

U.S. policy failures after the 1960s further illustrate the generally dysfunctional character of conflict and policies of coercion by which U.S. interests are ill-served. For example, Castro was not brought down either by unilateral or multilateral means. If anything, Cuba was moved to a closer relationship with the Soviet Union and eventually won considerable sympathy in Latin America and other parts of the world. Furthermore, inter-American cooperation was seriously eroded by the Cuban issue. In Guatemala, the Dominican Republic, and Chile, where interventions achieved short-term goals of helping to bring down regimes or groups ideologically opposed by the United States, coercion helped to interrupt social change and had a destabilizing impact on those societies. Furthermore, unilateral interventions violated inter-American law, created a general atmosphere of Latin American hostility toward the United States inimical to inter-American cooperation in general, and heightened frictions among political groups within individual Latin American states. These costs seemed out of proportion to the benefits gained.

Conflict in Central America, beginning in the late 1970s and accelerated in the 1980s, continued to focus attention on important questions about U.S. policies of coercion. When Ronald Reagan became president in 1981, he sought to reestablish the U.S. presence in the region. Despite considerable effort, the administration, like that of President Carter before, did not resolve the problems it set out to deal with. In fact, the problems seemed to become even more complex and intractable. Central American conflict again concentrated attention on the conceptual bases for U.S. policy. The dominant calculations for U.S. actions were, paradoxically, drawn from a combination of strategic perceptions of Central America dating from the early twentieth century and more recent experiences far removed from Central America. On the one hand, official policy rationales—as well as much of the criticism put forth by policy opponents—were taken from experiential sources outside the arena to which they were applied. For example, much of the public debate about Central American conflict revolved around the "another Vietnam" syndrome, with contending positions drawing different "lessons" from the Southeast Asian experience. Strategic thinking, as revealed in Reagan administration statements and expressed in the Kissinger Commission report, derived not only from Central American policies devised more than eight decades before, but also from nineteenth-century European balance-of-power theory as shaped by perceptions of the post–World War II cold war. The principal question for U.S. policy orientation at the end of the Reagan presidency and the end of the cold war was not one of isolationism or withdrawal—the United States as both global superpower and regional actor will be deeply involved in Latin America—but whether it would pursue its interests unilaterally or multilaterally. The new conditions of the Latin American subsystem (see Chapter 2) call for a new multilateralism, including, perhaps especially, in the Circum-Caribbean. An effective foreign policy in the contemporary world requires cooperation within alliances and associations.

Latin American Realism

Latin American leaders have also formulated policies in terms of national interests and security. They have been concerned about military threats to their territorial integrity and physical safety posed by foreign incursions, whether the European great powers, the United States, or other Latin American states. From the earliest days of statehood, Latin Americans tended to band together when outsiders intervened or exerted other pressures. Since World War II, however, in most Latin American countries for most of the time, national security has been synonymous with national development, with emphasis on internal unity and economic well-being. External threat perceptions have tended to be limited to border and territorial disputes and, in the Circum-Caribbean, great power intervention.

In Peru the reformist military regime in power from 1968–1975 led an attempt by certain Latin American states to make economic relations a security matter. This was a revolt against U.S. domination of the Inter-American System and its insistence on an anti-Communist alliance, with an effort to amend the Rio Treaty, which provided multilateral guarantees against various forms of aggression, and to adopt a treaty on Collective Economic Security, intended to place multilateral economic guarantees on the same par as military and political ones. Neither effort succeeded but they did reflect a strong current in Latin American security thinking.

In the Southern Cone important political elements, most notably in Brazil, Argentina, and Chile, have thought in power political terms. Military men and their civilian associates in particular, dating from the nineteenth century, adopted geopolitical strategic perspectives. These theories were based on the organic theory of the state, an extreme version of power politics that views conflict as natural, inevitable, and necessary if a nation is to survive and achieve its "destiny" (see Chapter 3). This kind of thinking was responsible not only for giving impetus to conflict and arms races in the Southern Cone subsystem but for justifying domestic repression as well, especially by military regimes in the 1960s to the 1980s. Most of this geopolitical thinking cannot be taken seriously in theoretical terms, but it must be recognized as a source of action that discredited military regimes in the subregion and (among other reasons) made democratic development an imperative for Latin Americans. Geopolitical bases for policy declined dramatically with the return to democratic civilian governments.

LIBERAL DEVELOPMENTALISM

Development Theory in Comparative Politics

Comparative political analysis has purported to place Latin America in a larger-than-regional mold in terms of development theory and the concept of modernization. Many Latin Americanists (including myself) have long concluded that development theory failed to explain convincingly Latin American national development or to use satisfactorily Latin American data to support general assertions. Nevertheless, the theory has been the basis for important state policies and has been prominent in debates over them to the present day; moreover, some process of developmental change takes place, even if it is inadequately understood.

Thus, a serious consideration of development theory in the Latin American context is in order.

With the emergence of formerly colonial peoples as new sovereign nations over much of the globe after World War II, certain scholars detected the seeming irrelevance of the West European and North American experiences to the analysis of the new "developing world." In this sense, development theory provided a necessary corrective to traditional modes of comparative analysis, which tended to be misleading when applied outside the North Atlantic area.

Development theory loosely grouped Latin America with the "emerging nations" of Asia and Africa under the rubrics of "underdeveloped" or "developing," as distinguished from the "developed" nations of Western Europe and North America. "Developed" states were equated with the notions of "modern," "industrial," and "Western"; conversely, the "underdeveloped world" was characterized as "traditional," "preindustrial," and "non-Western," with its members often referred to as "new nations." Development theory suggested further that underdeveloped states go through a "transitional" process, moving from traditional to modern societies. Some development theorists suggested that certain imperatives of change move societies inexorably through a transitional process toward modernity.

Although development theory properly alerted us to the fact that Latin America is fundamentally different from Western Europe and North America, this awareness does not justify an assumption that Latin America is to be equated with Asia and Africa. Much of the Latin American region shares with other regions the challenges of change: It goes through social, economic, and political transformations; experiences frustration associated with economic dependence on the major industrial states; and desires to refrain from involvement in great power rivalries. But crucial and fundamental differences exist between Latin America and the rest of the developing world, as well as between the region and developed nations and within Latin America itself.

The various classifications associated with developing states—new, non-Western, industrializing nations—were highly questionable in the Latin American context. In the first place, Latin America was not composed of "new nations." Most of the Latin American states gained their sovereign independence between 1804 and 1824, well over a century before most Asian and African nations "emerged" into nationhood. Developmental theorists eventually accommodated this obvious reality, but they still tended not to understand the importance of the established traditions of Latin American nationhood. The earlier and different colonial heritage from the rest of the developing world and longer history of independence, combined with a unique sociocultural base, produced a distinct Latin American developmental tradition.

The region is difficult to classify with certainty as either Western or non-Western. The Roman Catholic heritage, European languages, and some other cultural aspects are distinctly Western. But non-Western indigenous American Indian and imported African cultures are interwoven in important patterns. Inasmuch as Spain and Portugal imposed a large degree of their Iberian culture and politics on Latin America, then it can be described as Western. Yet Spain and Portugal have been on the periphery of what was usually studied as Western civilization. Furthermore, the Latin American colonial heritage was different from most of the rest of the developing world.

The level of industrialization varies widely in Latin America. Some states, such as Haiti, Ecuador, Bolivia, and Grenada, might be considered preindustrial. Others, such as Mexico and Argentina, have reached relatively high levels of industrialization, and, most notably, Brazil has constructed a well-diversified and heavily industrialized economy. Furthermore, it does not necessarily follow that every nation with a low industrial level is correspondingly low in social or political modernity, or that industrialized nations are modern in all other respects. Uruguay and Costa Rica, for example, reached modern levels of social organization within representative democratic frameworks while their traditional, agriculture-pastoral, nonindustrial economies persisted. Argentina, high in most indicators of modernity, was recently governed by military regimes that may arguably be characterized as primitive.

Some broader methodological problems are associated with development theory. Latin America fits erratically into any theory of unilinear, inexorable movement from traditionalism to modernism. The assumption that there is such a steady progression from the old to the new may be criticized as a form of historicism, the idea of inevitable deterministic "forces of history." It also implies ethnocentrism, the view that developing nations ought to become like the model equating modernism with old, Western, industrialized states. More specifically with regard to Latin America, the region's history reveals no inevitable progression along a traditional-modern continuum. Traditional Latin American political, economic, and social structures have proved remarkably resistant to change.

This view does not deny that political development is susceptible to systematic theoretical explanation, nor does it argue against inter-area comparisons of the developmental process. Rather, it suggests that extant theory is only partially useful. It is inappropriate to append uncritically Latin America onto a theory derived from other experiences. Latin America should be included in the broader perspective of the international political system, but its special place in that system must be recognized in political analysis. Latin America is an identifiable region and a coherent international subsystem. As a practical policy as well as a theoretical matter, the region deserves attention on its own terms.

Policy Applications

Development theory has provided the basis for a significant portion of U.S. policy in Latin America. U.S. policymakers after World War II assumed that economic growth led to stable democratic societies. Many held the view that democracy must be based on a free-enterprise economic system. During the Alliance for Progress period, economic planning combined with social reform was stressed. A further assumption, reflected in aid programs, was that Latin American political violence was linked to poverty and that economic development would deter such political "instability." Development came to be subordinated to "anticommunism." By 1968 and the adoption of the Nixon "low profile" policy, developmentalism was essentially abandoned. It was rediscovered (and amended) by the Reagan administration and provided the initial rationale behind the Caribbean Basin Initiative and some other actions in Central America. Developmentalism also continued to be the favored alternative to coercion in the U.S. debate over Latin American policy, as well as in the advice coming from Europe and Latin America.

A debate over the relationship between foreign economic assistance and political and social change in recipient states was carried on in the context of development theory. These problems have important implications for U.S. policies, as well as to those of other actors such as the European Community and the international lending institutions. Critics of developmentalism charged that economic aid, either purposely or unwittingly, supported the Latin American status quo rather than stimulated reform. Other analysts suggested that economic aid lead to violence by breaking down existing social structures. Either connection between economic development and political change seems tenuous. The United States attempted with little success to influence political forms with economic aid; the failure of social experimentation under the Alliance for Progress is primary evidence. A connection doubtless exists between economics and politics, and Latin American economic needs are susceptible to influence from external states, but economic development cannot substitute for political development or compensate for political underdevelopment. Whereas technology and investment capital can be exported to facilitate economic development, the institutions and traditions of representative or social democracy cannot. Political forms must evolve according to national configurations rather than by copying foreign models.

Military Cooperation and Developmentalism

International military cooperation forms a special area of consideration for development theory and policies, particularly in the Latin American context. All Latin American states and their military establishments have depended at some time and to some extent on foreign powers for their military modernization. As with international economic consequences, the effects of international military relations are difficult to determine. External states gain influence when Latin American states rely on them for arms acquisitions, military organizations, and tactics based on the external models. Other areas, however, such as military philosophy and ideology and civil-military relations, are more difficult to measure and to assign causality.

A major debate among decision makers in seller states (especially the United States) and an important domestic issue among certain political groups in Latin America is the question of allocating resources for military expenditures that could be better spent for economic development or applied to a reduction of national expenditures. A related assumption voiced by critics of the arms trade, at least throughout the twentieth century, was that it has stimulated arms races among the regional states. The result may be that domestic political conflict in Latin American politics will intensify and that efforts to reduce those expenditures by external pressures will be futile. That arms purchases are directly related to arms races and the possibilities of armed international conflict has also been debated. A state's purported fear of an external military threat may be an excuse to buy arms for purposes of national military prestige and to maintain a military establishment by professional military men acting in their own self-interest.

The political-developmental effects of both military and economic programs have been subject to much criticism. An analytical point of departure concerning foreign military influences in Latin America is the "traditionalist" versus "revisionist" debate. These positions have been equated with "idealism" and "realism," respectively, in the debate over developmentalism and military cooperation. Although most of that debate has referred to U.S. influences, similar positions may be assumed regarding the European states in Latin America prior to World War II, particularly those of Germany and France.

The traditional/idealist view links international military relations to the frequent role of the Latin American armed forces as the direct arbiters of domestic politics. It maintains that Latin American military establishments are essentially defenders of the status quo and thwart political, social, and economic development. Furthermore, a number of traditionalist critics of U.S. military assistance programs see a causal relationship between military aid and conservative or reactionary Latin American militarism impeding national development. As a result, these critics claim that there is a positive correlation between military assistance and the increase in or maintenance of Latin American militarism, holding the United States responsible.

The revisionist/realist school holds, contrarily, that the fact of political involvement by Latin American military establishments is an expression, rather than a cause, of underdevelopment and that the armed forces may be mobilized to perform useful nation-building functions. They claim that the military in Latin America is peculiarly suited to strike a balance between stability and change since they embody a combination of authority and reform-mindedness. A few military regimes themselves claimed to have abandoned their role as defenders of the status quo and as allies of the upper class against civilian governments who sought reform. Revisionists tend to deny causal relationships between external military assistance and domestic military behavior, stressing internal rather than foreign factors influencing Latin American affairs. Others argue that U.S. military aid has played a positive role in Latin American modernization. Revisionists do not accept the idea that there is a causal relationship between military assistance and militarism.

Revisionists correctly insist that military regimes be viewed as part of the total structure and function of society. Their stress on military regimes as effective instruments of modernization, however, is at least open to question and, in view of the Latin American experience with military regimes over the past two decades, essentially discredited. The "revisionist" U.S. policy adopted in 1963, essentially unchanged until 1976 and revived in Central American policy in the 1980s, especially tended to accept a simplistic faith in the modernizing possibilities of the Latin American military. In the first place, this undifferentiated view ignores that individual officers or groups may and do act in a predatory manner. Second, the recent experience of a number of military governments challenges the assumption that even reform-minded military rule can be an effective instrument for progress. The record so far shows some achievements but mostly only partial success or outright failure. Furthermore, the blatantly repressive nature of certain military regimes flies in the face of developmentalist tenets and supports the traditionalist-idealist view. Especially in Southern Cone politics, concepts of "security" have justified military rationales for domestic intervention and repression.

A shortcoming of both theoretical perspectives, and of state policies based on them, is that they assume the institutional nature of all Latin American armed forces. They see them as organized into a cohesive military establishment and acting as a disciplined corporate entity, either for good or evil. Theories of Latin American civil-military relations must be revised to allow for the reality of "noninstitutionality" in many cases as a continuing rather than transitory state. In these instances, theory must also take into account the consequences of personalities and interpersonal relationships—that is, relations revolving around personal interactions among a chief executive, important military officers, and their key associates, rather than processes involving a bureaucratically well-organized "presidency" and "military establishment."

MODERNISM, MONETARISM, AND NEOLIBERALISM

The traditional, or "classical," view of what came to be known as "economic development" dated from the middle to the late nineteenth century in most Latin American states. That was the period when Latin American elites began to lead a conscious thrust for economic modernization, usually in alliance with foreign entrepreneurs. Economic development was seen as requiring the attraction of foreign capital by means of cooperation. Modernization, in concert with foreign assistance, was actively encouraged by certain elites who sought increased wealth for themselves as well as a cultural milieu comparable to that of the world's most prestigious nations. This position, which relates to the "modernist" category of nationalism noted in Chapter 3, continued in recent years in modified form as a school of economic thought sometimes labeled the "neoclassical" model.

An important economic policy debate developed after World War II between "monetarists" and "structuralists." This debate was especially intense in the late 1950s and early 1960s, until structuralism (discussed below) carried the day. Monetarist thinking was later identified with the orthodox economics championed by the IMF and with MNCs and the governments of most industrialized nations. The monetarist theory essentially argued that price stability is the main prerequisite for economic growth. Therefore, the major task in Latin American economic development was to control the inflation that retards long-term investment, undermines wages, leads to labor strikes, and in general inspires social and political instability as well as economic chaos. The principal causes of inflation were expansive monetary and fiscal policies and the increased role of government as the promoter of development through public spending and deficit financing. The monetarist solution was to return to a free-market system by increasing the economic role of the private sector and reducing government intervention. Disciplined monetary policies reducing aggregate demands, such as rejecting large wage demands, restricting credit, raising taxes, and reducing government spending and employment, suffice to reduce inflation. Such austerity programs decrease the demand for consumer goods imports, which increases exports and relieves balance-of-payment pressures. Control of inflation attracts foreign investment, a crucial source of investment capital.

Neoliberalism, which caught hold in the 1980s and continues into the 1990s, is the progeny of modernism and monetarism. It became dominant among the current generation of democratic leaders and is a rejection of structuralism. The thinking is rooted in the economic liberalism of the nineteenth century, which was closely linked to the political liberalism of the times. In the political sphere the emphasis was on democracy, individual dignity and freedom (liberty), constitutionalism and republicanism, civil liberties, and limited government. In the economic arena the stress was on individual initiative, free enterprise, free trade, and opposition to state intervention in the economy (*laissez-faire*). In Latin America, this dominant ideology of the capitalist industrializing world was challenged by mercantilism, a theory carried over from the colonial era that emphasized state-centered and state-directed economies and high levels of international trade protectionism. Inasmuch as those structures continued after World War II, they were sometimes referred to as neomercantilist.

As the cold war faded and then ended in the 1980s, and trade and investment assumed primacy in the international system, most Latin American leaders embraced the new liberalism in their international economic relations. It is reflected in such actions as the privatization of state enterprises, assistance to private-sector development, lowering of barriers to trade, and embracing of intraregional free trade and trade with the outside world (especially the United States). These policies reflect a number of Latin American attitudinal changes, alluded to at several points in this book: They are generally less defensive toward and more willing to cooperate with the outside world; are eager to reintegrate with and be an integral part of whatever new global system finally emerges; are disillusioned with the old defensive nationalism and economic models (involving import-substitution industrialization and protectionism) that are seen as failed; and are willing to apply alternative models for economic reactivation. All of this has been facilitated by the return to democracy and civilian rule and their increasing, if tenuous, popular legitimacy.

Neoliberalism has its critics. Some fear that free trade with the United States will lead to another kind of economic dependency. Others stress inevitable domestic consequences: Even if neoliberalism has macroeconomic benefits and certain sectors prosper from it (usually those who already hold most of the wealth), too many other people remain poor and have only marginal opportunities for betterment (Smith, Acuña, and Gamarra, [1994]).

DEPENDENCY THEORIES

In the immediate aftermath of World War II, the Economic Commission for Latin America (ECLA) published a comprehensive analysis of economic development in the region. That analysis, inspired especially by the emerging theories of the Argentine economist Raúl Prebisch, marked the formal introduction of structuralist economic theory, which challenged orthodox approaches. The structuralists were the intellectual offspring of Latin American economists, led by Prebisch and including the Mexican Víctor Urquidi and the Brazilian Celso Furtado. Their theories gained increasing favor as the basis for Latin American economic policies until they, too, were challenged and fell out of favor. Nevertheless, the theory of structural economic dependency has often been at the center of an ongoing debate about the economic aspects of Latin American development and related policies.

Prebisch's structuralist theory visualizes the world economy in terms of a "center-periphery" structure, with industrialized states forming the center and underdeveloped ones the periphery. Underdevelopment, the theory goes, was perpetuated by this structure primarily because the center sold increasingly expensive manufactured goods to the periphery in return for raw materials at increasingly unfavorable terms for underdeveloped markets. The unfair terms of trade, Prebisch said, were a form of colonialism, a dependence escapable only through the industrialization and sustained growth of the peripheral economies. Prebisch advocated prescriptions for economic development on a regional and global scale, involving convergent domestic and international reforms and measures. Prebisch advocated that Latin American states reduce their external dependency through the integration of their economies. He also urged them to broaden the size of their markets for local industry and join with other producers of primary exports in commodity agreements to limit supply and increase prices for goods sold. He appealed to the center for help in the way of public economic assistance, private investment, and trade preferences; but he emphasized that poor nations must depend primarily on themselves and not rely on external aid. "External cooperation is important," he said, "but only as a means of supplementing and stimulating internal action, not as a substitute for it."

Structuralists argued that the causes of Latin American inflation were to be found in economic structural (institutional) rigidities and inelasticities. They concluded that monetary policy alone could not reduce inflation over the long run or stimulate economic growth. They advocated structural reform of traditional institutions that proved incapable of adjusting to change. While Latin American industrialization, population growth, and urbanization increased the demand for food, the archaic land tenure system (*latifundia*) had not been able to increase the food supply significantly, with inflationary results. Industrial institutions and foreign trade patterns were also structured so as to increase inflation and retard growth. When imports grew faster than the export of primary mineral and agricultural products, balance-of-payments problems surfaced.

Structuralists had little faith in monetary policies, saying that austerity retarded growth, and they looked to government to bring about basic reforms. They advocated agrarian reform and government-supplied credit to modernize agricultural methods; government policies to encourage export diversification, including industrial products; heavy taxes on imported luxury goods and inefficiently utilized landholdings; and more public investment in the capital goods industry. They recognized the need to import capital in money and kind but argued that Latin America should pursue import substitution industrialization so as to become less dependent on imports. They also were the strongest advocates of Latin American economic integration.

In the late 1980s and into the 1990s, Latin Americans largely abandoned structuralism and its attendant policies as redemocratization, accompanied by economic neoliberalism, took hold. Economic integration was revived but reformed in order to seek parallel free-trade arrangements with the United States.

Neo-Marxist Dependency

A major school of dependency theory employed a generally Marxist frame of reference. In an important sense it was the "radical school" that offered an array of theories and prescriptions for economic development over the years. The theory went far beyond economic parameters, however, to construct also a general sociopolitical theory of international relations. The *dependistas* tended to agree with structuralists that archaic institutions were at the root of underdevelopment, emphasizing that the existing "modern" social sectors exploit national productivity rather than generate it for development. They rejected the structuralists' "reform the system" approach, however, and advocated a socialist revolution. Radicals would have eliminated the existing private agricultural system, instituted state ownership of large industries, and either excluded foreign investment or allowed it to operate only under the strictest controls. In the 1980s they called for renunciation of the foreign debt or for greatly reduced service payments. These solutions were attempted by several Latin American regimes, including Castro in Cuba, the elected government of Salvador Allende in Chile, and the military-socialist juntas in Peru and Bolivia. The Sandinista government in Nicaragua and the radical nationalist APRA government in Peru also advocated and in some ways were able to pursue such policies. Some Liberation Theologians also subscribed to this dependency theory.

A basic premise of the dependistas was that Latin American economic development was determined by the interests and activities of external capitalist states and MNCs operating in the world capitalist market. Latin American economies were dependent because they were conditioned by external capitalist forces over which they had little control. Economic dependence was seen as an inevitable result of international capitalist politics, with foreign investment, a corollary to the expansionist tendencies of capitalist economies (especially in the United States), invariably detrimental to the recipient. The dependency relationship ultimately was conflictual, according to this dependency theory, and in this sense it largely restated the Leninist theory of imperialism. Conflict was said to be caused by the search by industrial capitalist societies for raw materials, insufficiently supplied at home, and for outlets for manufactured products and capital, which were in an overabundance at home.

Economic dependence was said to have had a profound effect on internal Latin American economies—stagnation, unemployment, income inequality, and disequilibrium were seen as directly related to the underdeveloped state's subordinate position under the dominant capitalist states and MNCs. These economic effects in turn helped shape social and political structures as well. International inequalities retarded domestic economic development, consequently weakening power bases for the establishment of egalitarian social policies. Some dependency theorists spoke of "internal colonialism" within Latin American nations, whereby resources were continuously transferred away from majority underdeveloped social sectors to the minority advanced sector. The latter was linked to foreign capitalists and the international capitalist economy, thus intensifying unequal internal distribution of income and social rewards. Dependistas further argued that external military relationships were responsible for Latin American militarism—the widening gap between classes led to national disintegration characterized by military regimes supporting oligarchic or bourgeois interests.

Many other Marxist theorists implicitly rejected the idea of *dependencia*. For example, studies by Marxist scholars at the Institute of Latin American Studies at the Academy of Sciences of the USSR (Moscow) emphasized the growing independence of many Latin American states from U.S. domination. This position was ideologically consistent with Leninism, as anti-imperialism had to assume that independence was possible. It was also consonant with conservative (cautious) Soviet policies when they emphasized diplomacy with Latin American states rather than subversion.

Critics (myself among them) challenged the assumptions of dependency theory. They may have acknowledged that the theory contained a large element of truth, but they argued that it had major logical and empirical fallacies. They challenged the assertions that economic dependence was a necessary consequence of capitalist economies and that private foreign investment in Latin America invariably was exploitive, pointing out that powerful states, whether capitalist or noncapitalist, had always imposed economic dependence on weaker ones. They further noted that dependency theorists ignored the possibility of Cuba's economic dependency on the Soviet Union and confined their observations to relationships dominated by capitalist powers (Ray, 1973). We can also point out the cleavages within Latin America, where relatively weaker states complained of domination by the stronger ones. For example, such claims were common among the majority of members of the Latin American Free Trade Association against their colleagues Mexico, Brazil, and Argentina. This position was also taken by small states in the Southern Cone subsystem, which had little to do with the world capitalist economy. The basis for dependency was not capitalism but a disparity of power in which weak actors were vulnerable to exploitation in whatever kind of markets they operated.

Dependency theory also addressed the consequences of international military cooperation. The arms trade did not necessarily involve a political function if it was viewed by the actors strictly as a commercial transaction. If Latin American industries were unable to produce equipment, arms, and munitions in sufficient quantity or to provide updated models and spare parts, the Latin American armed services may have become dependent on foreign manufacturers. The relative independence in military affairs on the part of major states, especially Brazil and significantly by Argentina and Chile, indicated that dependency might be broken by local policy efforts despite the wishes of outside suppliers.

The impact of one military establishment on the institutions of another was not necessarily the most important consequence of military interaction. The professional level achieved by the regional armed forces varied widely, as they first copied European military establishments, especially French and German ones, and later that of the United States. The various external styles were reflected in Latin American military organization, training and educational methods, strategy and tactics, and arms acquisitions. This observation is superficial, however, if the impact was not of political consequence. It is not enough to observe, for example, that one or another Latin American army adopted French, German, or U.S. training methods or organizational schemes and then conclude that an influential linkage exists. Imitation may have been manifested only in appearances, with actual military behavior taking place that was alien to the external model. For example, the Prussian General Staff system was emulated by most Latin American states between 1890 and World War II. Yet it was also almost universally adopted around the globe by Germany's friends and enemies alike and even by its major rivals for influence in Latin America (France and the United States). Logically, the adoption of the German staff system did not necessarily indicate direct German political influence. Likewise, after World War II, most Latin American states imitated the U.S. Department of Defense and armed forces organization, but differing relations existed with the United States, and there were varying patterns of civil-military relations within Latin America as well. The analyst must attempt to ascertain how far imitation of external military systems led to substantive attitudes by Latin American military men toward their civil-military relations.

Trends in external military aid and Latin American militarism—the decade-and-a-half rise in military dominance of Latin America despite a sharp decrease in U.S. assistance from the mid-1960s to the late 1970s—present an incongruity for dependency theory and the traditionalist critique. Irving Louis Horowitz (1977) concluded that if theories of dependency had been cited to explain Latin American militarism, we might well have anticipated a sharp reduction rather than a pronounced increase in militarization. He argued that Latin American militarism was not so much a function of either dependency or developmentalism as it was a response to the inner history and military dynamics of the hemisphere and specific national conditions. Although neither dependency nor developmental perspectives were entirely removed from the realities of hemispheric conditions, it was clear that Latin American militarism should not be perceived as a mechanical response to foreign pressures, especially when such pressures move counter to observable trends.

BIBLIOGRAPHIC COMMENT

Little has been written on the realist-idealist theoretical dichotomy with reference to Latin America. Varas (1989) analyzes how U.S. and Latin American security assumptions are changing, opening possibilities for convergence. Fishlow (1985) summarizes post–World War II Latin American political economic theory and practice, and Iglesias (1993) reflects on the new Latin American consensus. Mansilla (1985) tackles the problem of defining Latin America as part of the Third World. Wiarda (1985) contains essays on development and dependency theories with significant reference to Latin America. Essays by Martz (1966), Stepan (1966), and Douglas Chalmers and Philippe Schmitter in Chalmers (1972) are early critiques of political development theory by Latin American specialists. Wiarda (1992) analyzes the question of a distinct Latin American developmental tradition. The literature on the roles of Latin American armed forces is reviewed by Atkins (1974), Rankin (1974), Roett and Tierney (1971), and Zagorsky (1992). Fitch (1979), Heller (1978), and Remmer (1978) assess the impact of U.S. military aid. Campos (1963, 1967, 1976) and Krieger Vasena and Pasos (1973) represent monetarism and traditionalism. Prebisch (1964, 1970) and Urquidi (1962, 1964) are influential structuralists. W.C. Smith, Acuña, and

Gamarra (1994) are critical of neoliberalism, and Sunkel (1993) offers a neostructuralist alternative. Frank (1967, 1969, 1972) was the pioneer neo-Marxist dependency theorist, followed by Bodenheimer (1971), Cardoso and Faletto (1969/1979), Cockroft, Frank, and Johnson (1972), Santos (1970), Szymanski (1981), and Thomas (1984). Analyses of dependency theory are undertaken by Bonilla and Girling (1973), Chilcote and Edelstein (1974), Ocampo et al. (1976), Ray (1973), T. Smith (1979), and Packenham (1992).

References

Acheson, Dean (1966). "Dean Acheson's Version of Robert Kennedy's Version of the Cuban Missile Affair." *Esquire*, 71 (February): 76–77.

Adams, Jan (1993). *A Foreign Policy in Transition: Moscow's Retreat from Central America and the Caribbean, 1985–1992.* Durham: Duke University Press.

Adelman, Alan, and Reid R. Reiding (eds.) (1984). *Confrontation in the Caribbean Basin: International Perspectives on Security, Sovereignty and Survival.* Pittsburgh: Center for Latin American Studies, University of Pittsburgh.

ALADI [Asociación Latinoamericana de Integración] (1980). *La Asociación Latinoamericana de Integración: Un Análisis Comparativo.* Buenos Aires: Secretaría General de ALADI.

Alba, Victor (1968). *Politics and the Labor Movement in Latin America.* Stanford, Calif.: Stanford University Press.

Alexander, Robert J. (1963). *Communism in Latin America.* New Brunswick, N.J.: Rutgers University Press.

——— (1965). *Organized Labour in Latin America.* New York: The Free Press.

Alvarado Garaicoa, Teodora (1968). *El Dominio del Mar.* Guayaquil, Ecuador: Universidad de Guayaquil.

Alvarez, Alejandro (1922). *International Law and Related Subjects from the Point of View of the American Continent.* Washington: Carnegie Endowment for International Peace.

——— (1924). *The Monroe Doctrine: Its Importance in the International Life of the States of the New World.* New York: Oxford University Press.

Ameringer, Charles D. (1974). *The Democratic Left in Exile: The Anti-Dictatorial Struggle in the Caribbean, 1945–1959.* Coral Gables, Fla.: University of Miami Press.

Anderson, Thomas D. (1981). *The War of the Dispossessed: Honduras and El Salvador, 1969.* Lincoln: University of Nebraska Press.

——— (1984). *Geopolitics of the Caribbean: Ministates in a Wider World.* New York: Praeger.

Araim, Amer Salih (1990). *Intergovernmental Commodity Organizations and the New International Economic Order.* New York: Praeger.

Area, Leandro (1984). *El Golfo de Venezuela: Documentación y Cronología.* Caracas: Universidad de Venezuela.

Arnáiz y Freg, Arturo, and Claude Bataillon (eds.) (1965). *La Intervención Francesa y el Império de Maximiliano.* México: Asociación Mexicana de Historiadores.

Atkins, G. Pope (1974). "The Armed Forces in Latin American Politics," in Charles Cochran (ed.), *Civil-Military Relations.* New York: The Free Press.

———— (1984). "Diplomacy in the South Atlantic Crisis," in Jack W. Hopkins (ed.), *Latin America and Caribbean Contemporary Record*, vol. 2. New York: Holmes & Meier: 22–33.

———— (ed.) (1990). *South America into the 1990s: Evolving International Relationships in a New Era*. Boulder: Westview.

———— (1991). "The United States and the Caribbean Basin," in David J. Myers (ed.), *Regional Hegemons: Threat Perception and Strategic Response*. Boulder: Westview.

———— (ed.) (1992). *The United States and Latin America: Redefining U.S. Purposes in the Post–Cold War Era*. Austin: Lyndon B. Johnson School of Public Affairs, University of Texas at Austin.

———— (1993). "Institutional Arrangements for Hemispheric Free Trade," in Sidney Weintraub (ed.), *Free Trade in the Western Hemisphere*, entire issue of *Annals of the American Academy of Political and Social Science*, vol. 526 (March): 183–194.

Atkins, G. Pope, and Larman C. Wilson (1972). *The United States and the Trujillo Regime*. New Brunswick, N.J.: Rutgers University Press.

Axline, W. Andrew (1979). *Caribbean Integration: The Politics of Regionalism*. London: Francis Pinter.

Bagley, Bruce M. (ed.) (1987). *Contadora and the Diplomacy of Peace in Central America*. Boulder: Westview.

Bagley, Bruce M. (1992a). "After San Antonio," in *Journal of Interamerican Studies and World Affairs*. 34:3 Fall:1–12.

Bagley, Bruce M. (1992b). "Narcotics Traffic," in G. Pope Atkins (ed.), *The United States and Latin America: Redefining U.S. Purposes in the Post–Cold War Era*. Austin: Lyndon B. Johnson School of Public Affairs, University of Texas at Austin.

Bagley, Bruce M., and William O. Walker (eds.) (1994). *Drug Trafficking in the Americas*. New Brunswick: Transaction.

Bailey, Norman A. (1967). *Latin America in World Politics*. New York: Walker.

Baily, Samuel L. (ed.) (1971). *Nationalism in Latin America*. New York: Knopf.

———— (1976). *The United States and the Development of South America, 1945–1975*. New York: New Viewpoints.

Barber, Willard F., and C. Neale Ronning (1966). *Internal Security and Military Power: Counterinsurgency and Civic Action in Latin America*. Columbus: Ohio State University Press.

Barclay, Glen St. John (1971). *Struggle for a Continent: The Diplomatic History of South America, 1917–1945*. London: Whitefriars.

Barnet, Richard S., and Ronald E. Muller (1975). *Global Reach: The Power of the Multinational Corporations*. New York: Simon & Schuster.

Barrera Valverde, Alfonso (1982). *Hombres de Paz en Lucha*, 2 vols. Quito: Ediciones J.L.I.

Beck, Peter (1988). *The Falkland Islands as an International Problem*. London: Routledge.

Beck, Robert J. (1993). *The Grenada Invasion: Politics, Law, and Foreign Policy Decisionmaking*. Boulder: Westview.

Behrman, Jack N. (1972). *The Role of International Companies in Latin America*. Lexington, Mass.: Lexington Books.

Bemis, Samuel Flagg (1943). *The Latin American Policy of the United States*. New York: Harcourt Brace.

Bernstein, Marvin (ed.) (1966). *Foreign Investment in Latin America*. New York: Knopf.

Berrocal Luciano (1989). "Perspectiva 1992: El Mercado Unico Europeo. ¿Nuevo Desafío en las Relaciones Europa-América Latina?" *Pensamiento Iberoamericano*. 15 (enero/junio): 205–225.

Bianchi, Andres, Robert Devlin, and Joseph Ramos (1985). *External Debt in Latin America: Adjustment Policies and Renegotiation*. Boulder: Lynne Rienner.

Blachman, Morris J., William M. Leogrande, and Kenneth E. Sharpe (eds.) (1986). *Confronting Revolution: Security Through Diplomacy in Central America*. New York: Pantheon Books.

Blakemore, Harold (1984). *Central American Crisis: Challenge to U.S. Diplomacy*, monograph supplement to *Conflict Studies* (London).

Blasier, Cole (1985). *The Hovering Giant: U.S. Responses to Revolutionary Change in Latin America*, rev. ed. Pittsburgh: University of Pittsburgh Press.

——— (1988). *The Giant's Rival: The USSR and Latin America*, rev. ed. Pittsburgh: University of Pittsburgh Press.

——— (1991). "Moscow's Retreat from Cuba," *Problems of Communism*, XL (November–December).

——— (1993). "Latin America Without the USSR," *North-South Issues*, II:4.

Bodenheimer, Susanne (1971). *The Ideology of Developmentalism: The American Paradigm-Surrogate for Latin American Studies*. Beverly Hills, Calif.: Sage.

Boersner, Demetrio (1990). *Relaciones Internacionales de América Latina: Breve Historia*, 4th ed. Caracas: Nueva Sociedád.

Boff, Leonardo (1985). *Church Charisma and Power: Liberation Theology and the Institutional Church*. New York: Crossroad.

Bonachea, Ramon L., and Marta San Martin (1974). *The Cuban Insurrection, 1952–1959*. New Brunswick, N.J.: Transaction.

Bonachea, Rolando E., and Nelson P. Valdes (eds.) (1972). *Cuba in Revolution*. Garden City, N.Y.: Anchor.

Bonilla, Frank, and Robert Girling (eds.) (1973). *Structures of Dependency*. Stanford, Calif.: Stanford University Press.

Boyd, Gavin (ed.) (1984). *Regionalism and Global Security*. Lexington: Lexington Books.

Braunthal, Julius (1967–1980). *History of the International*. v. 1. 1864–1914; New York: Praeger. v. 2. 1914–1943; New York: Praeger. v. 3. 1943–1968; Boulder: Westview.

Braveboy-Wagner, Jacqueline Anne (1984). *The Venezuelan-Guyana Border Dispute: Britain's Colonial Legacy in Latin America*. Boulder: Westview.

——— (1989). *The Caribbean in World Affairs: The Foreign Policies of the English-Speaking States*. Boulder: Westview.

——— with W. Marvin Will, Dennis J. Gayle, and Ivelaw L. Griffith (1993). *The Caribbean in the Pacific Century: Prospects for Caribbean-Pacific Cooperation*. Boulder: Lynne Rienner.

Bryan, Anthony T. (ed.) (1986). *The Organization of American States and the Commonwealth Caribbean: Perspectives on Security, Crisis and Reform*. St. Augustine: University of the West Indies, Institute of International Relations.

——— (ed.) (1994). *The Caribbean: New Dynamics in Trade and Political Economy*. New Brunswick, N.J.: Transaction.

Bryan, Anthony T., and Andrés Serbín (eds.) (1994). *Distant Cousins: The Caribbean-Latin American Relationship*. New Brunswick, N.J.: Transaction.

Buergenthal, Thomas, Robert E. Norris, and Dinah Shelton (1983). *Protecting Human Rights in the Americas*. San José: Editorial Juricentro.

Bulnes, Gonzalo (1955). *Guerra del Pacifico*, 2d ed., 3 vols. Santiago de Chile: Editorial del Pacifico.

Burns, E. Bradford (1987). *At War in Nicaragua: The Reagan Doctrine and the Politics of Nostalgia*. New York: Harper & Row.

Burr, Robert N. (1967). *By Reason or Force: Chile and the Balancing of Power in Latin America, 1830–1905*. Berkeley: University of California Press.

Caballero, Manuel (1986). *Latin America and the Comintern 1919–1943*. New York: Cambridge University Press.

358 REFERENCES

Cady, John F. (1929). *Foreign Intervention in the Rio de la Plata, 1838–1850.* Philadelphia: University of Pennsylvania Press.

Caicedo Castilla, José Joaquin (1970). *El Derecho Internacional en el Sistema Interamericano.* Madrid: Ed. Cultura Hispanica.

Cale, Edward G. (1969). *Latin American Free Trade Association.* Washington, D.C.: Department of State.

Calvert, Peter (ed.) (1988). *The Central American Security System: North-South or East-West?* Cambridge: Cambridge University Press.

Campos, Roberto de Oliveira (1963). *Economia, Planejamento e Nacionalismo.* Rio de Janeiro: APEC Editora.

———— (1967). *Reflections on Latin American Development.* Austin: University of Texas Press.

———— (1976). *O Mundo que Vejo e Nao Desejo.* Rio de Janeiro: Livraria José Olympio Editora.

Canak, William L., ed. (1989). *Lost Promises: Debt, Austerity, and Development in Latin America.* Boulder: Westview.

Candelaria, Michael R. (1990). *Popular Religion and Liberation: The Dilemma of Liberation Theology.* Albany: State University of New York Press.

Cantori, Louis J., and Steven L. Spiegel (eds.) (1970). *The International Politics of Regions.* Englewood Cliffs, N.J.: Prentice-Hall.

Cardoso, F. H., and Enzo Faletto (1969). *Dependécia y Desarrollo en América Latina.* México: Siglo XXI Editores. English trans. (1979). *Dependency and Development in Latin America.* Berkeley: University of California Press.

Carnegie Endowment for International Peace (1931). *The International Conferences of American States, 1889–1928.* Ed. James Brown Scott. Washington, D.C.

———— (1940). *The International Conferences of American States: First Supplement, 1933–1940.* Washington.

———— (1943). *Conferencias Internacionales Americanas: Primer Suplemento, 1938–1942.* Washington.

Carothers, Thomas H. (1991). *In the Name of Democracy: U.S. Policy Toward Latin America in the Reagan Years.* Berkeley: University of California Press.

Castañeda, Jorge G. (1993). *Utopia Unarmed: The Latin American Left After the Cold War.* New York: Alfred A. Knopf. México: El Colégio de México.

Cepeda Ulloa, Fernando, y Rodrigo Pardo García-Peña (1985). *Contadora: Desafio a la Diplomácia Tradicional.* Lima: Centro de Estudios Internacionales de la Universidad de Los Andes.

Chalmers, Douglas A. (ed.) (1972). *Changing Latin America: New Interpretations of Its Politics and Society.* Philadelphia: Proceedings of the Academy of Political Science, vol. 30.

Chilcote, Ronald, and Joel Edelstein (eds.) (1974). *Latin America: The Struggle with Dependency and Beyond.* New York: Halsted.

Child, John (Jack) (1980). *Unequal Alliance: The Inter-American Military System 1938–1978.* Boulder: Westview.

Child, Jack (1985). *Geopolitics and Conflict in South America: Quarrels Among Neighbors.* New York: Praeger.

———— (1988). *Antarctica and South American Geopolitics: Frozen Lebensraum.* New York: Praeger.

———— (1990). "Geopolitical Thinking," chap. 9 in Louis W. Goodman, Johanna S.R. Mendelson, and Juan Rial (eds.), *The Military and Democracy: The Future of Civil-Military Relations in Latin America.* Lexington, Mass.: Lexington Books.

_____ (1992). *The Central American Peace Process, 1983–1991: Sheathing Swords, Building Confidence*. Boulder: Lynne Rienner.

Cirincione, Joseph (ed.) 1985. *Central America and the Western Alliance*. New York: Holmes and Meier for the Carnegie Endowment for International Peace and the International Institute for Strategic Studies.

Cleary, Edward L. and Hannah Stewart-Gambino (eds.) (1992). *Conflict and Competition: The Latin American Church in a Changing Environment*. Boulder: Lynne Rienner.

Cline, William R. (1993). *Third World Debt: A Reappraisal*. Washington, D.C.: Institute for International Economics.

Cochrane, James D. (1969). *The Politics of Regional Integration: The Central American Case*. New Orleans: Tulane University Press.

Cockcroft, James D., Andre Gunder Frank, and Dale L. Johnson (1972). *Dependence and Underdevelopment: Latin America's Political Economy*. Garden City, N.Y.: Anchor.

Cohen, Isaac (1992), "Economic Questions," in G. Pope Atkins (ed.), *The United States and Latin America: Redefining U.S. Purposes in the Post–Cold War Era*. Austin: Lyndon B. Johnson School of Public Affairs, University of Texas.

_____ (1993), "A New Latin American and Caribbean Nationalism," in Sidney Weintraub (ed.), *Free Trade in the Western Hemisphere*, entire issue of *Annals of the American Academy of Political and Social Science*, 526 (March).

Cohen Orantes, Isaac (1972). *Regional Integration in Central America*. Lexington, Mass.: Lexington Books.

Cole, Daniel H. (1992), "Debt-Equity Conversions, Debt-for-Nature Swaps, and the Continuing World Debt Crisis," *Columbia Journal for Transnational Law*, 30:1: 57–88.

Connell-Smith, Gordon (1966). *The Inter-American System*. London: Oxford University Press.

_____ (1974). *The United States and Latin America*. New York: Halsted.

Connelly, Marisela, and Romer Cornejo Bustamante (1992). *China–América Latina: Génesis y Desarollo de Sus Relaciones*. México, D.F.: El Colegio de México.

Corkran, Herbert (1972). *Patterns of International Cooperation in the Caribbean, 1942–1969*. Dallas: Southern Methodist University Press.

Corominas, Enrique V. (1954). *In the Caribbean Political Arenas*. Trans. L. C. Foresti. Cambridge: Cambridge University Press.

Craig, Richard B. (1985). "Illicit Drug Traffic and U.S.–Latin American Relations." *Washington Quarterly*, 8 (Fall): 105–124.

Cuevas Cancino, Francisco M. (1955). *Del Congreso de Panamá a la Conferencia de Caracas, 1826–1954*, 2 vols. Caracas: Ragon.

Davis, Harold E., Larman C. Wilson, and others (1975). *Latin American Foreign Policies*. Baltimore: Johns Hopkins University Press.

Davis, Harold Eugene, John J. Finan, and F. Taylor Peck (1977). *Latin American Diplomatic History: An Introduction*. Baton Rouge: Louisiana State University Press.

Davis, William C. (1950). *The Last Conquistadores: The Spanish Intervention in Peru and Chile, 1863–1866*. Athens: University of Georgia Press.

Debray, Regis (1967). *Revolution in the Revolution? Armed Struggle and Political Struggle in Latin America*. New York: Monthly Review.

_____ (1970). *Strategy for Revolution*. New York: Monthly Review.

_____ (1976). *Che's Guerrilla War*. Harmondsworth: Penguin.

Dell, Sidney (1972). *The Inter-American Bank*. New York: Praeger.

Dent, David W. (ed.) (1990). *Handbook of Political Science Research on Latin America: Trends from the 1960s to the 1990s*. Westport: Greenwood.

Desch, Michael C. (1993). *When the Third World Matters: Latin America and the United States Grand Strategy.* Baltimore: Johns Hopkins University Press.

Deutsch, Karl W. (1988). *The Analysis of International Relations,* 3d ed. Englewood Cliffs, N.J.: Prentice-Hall.

Devlin, Robert (1989). *Debt and Crisis in Latin America: The Supply Side of the Story.* Princeton: Princeton University Press.

Díaz Albonico, Rodrigo (ed.) (1977). *Antecedentes, Balance y Perspectivas del Sistema Interamericano.* Santiago: Editorial Universitaria.

Dillon, G.M. (1989). *The Falklands, Politics, and War.* New York: St. Martin's.

Donnelly, Thomas, Margaret Roth, and Caleb Baker (1992). *Operation Just Cause: The Storming of Panama.* Lexington, Mass.: Lexington Books.

Dosman, Edgar J. (1992). "Canada and Latin America: The New Look," *International Journal.* 47:3 (Summer): 529–554.

Drekonja Gerhard K., and Juan G. Tokatlian (eds.) (1983). *Teoría y Práctica de la Política Exterior Latinoamericana.* Bogotá: Universidad de los Andes.

Duncan, W. Raymond (1985). *The Soviet Union and Cuba: Interests and Influence.* New York: Praeger.

—— (1992). "Russian-American Cooperation in Latin America Since Gorbachev," in Melvin A. Goodman (ed.), *The End of Superpower Conflict in the Third World.* Boulder: Westview.

Duran, Esperanza (1985). *European Interests in Latin America.* London: Routledge and Kegan Paul for the Royal Institute of International Affairs.

Ealy, Lawrence O. (1971). *Yanqui Politics and the Isthmian Canal.* University Park: Pennsylvania State University Press.

Eaton, David J. (1987). *The State of the Rio Grande/Rio Bravo: A Study of Water Resource Issues Along the Texas/Mexico Border.* Tucson: University of Arizona Press.

Ebel, Roland H., Raymond Taras, and James D. Cochrane (1991). *Political Culture and Foreign Policy in Latin America: Case Studies from the Circum-Caribbean.* Albany: State University of New York Press.

Edwards, Augustín (1937). *La América Latina y la Liga de las Naciones.* Santiago de Chile: Editorial Universitaria.

Eells, Richard (1976). *Global Corporations: The Emerging System of World Economic Power,* rev. ed. New York: The Free Press.

Enríquez Coyro, Ernesto (1975/1976). *El Tratado entre México y los Estados Unidos de América sobre Ríos Internacionales,* 2 vols. México: Universidad Nacional Autónoma.

Erisman, H. Michael (1992). *Pursuing Postdependency Politics: South-South Relations in the Caribbean.* Boulder: Lynne Rienner.

Erisman, H. Michael, and John D. Martz (eds.) (1982). *Colossus Challenged: The Struggle for Caribbean Influence.* Boulder: Westview.

Etheredge, Lloyd S. (1985). *Can Governments Learn? American Foreign Policy and Central American Revolutions.* New York: Pergamon Press.

Falcoff, Mark, and Robert Royal (eds.) (1987). *The Continuing Crisis: U.S. Policy in Central America and the Caribbean.* Washington, D.C.: The Ethics and Public Policy Center.

Falk, Richard A., and Saul H. Mendlovitz (eds.) (1973). *Regional Politics and World Order.* San Francisco: W. H. Freeman.

Farer, Tom J. (1988). *The Grand Strategy of the United States in Latin America.* New Brunswick, N.J.: Transaction Books.

Feld, Werner, and Gavin Boyd (1980). *Comparative Regional Systems.* New York: Pergamon.

Fenwick, Charles G. (1963). *The Organization of American States: The Inter-American Regional System.* Washington, D.C.: Kaufman.

Fernandez, Damian (1990). *Central America and the Middle East.* Gainesville: University Presses of Florida.

Fernández-Shaw, Felix (1963). *La Organización de los Estados Americanos (O.E.A.)*, 2d ed. Madrid: Ediciones Cultura Hispánica.

Ferris, Elizabeth G. and Jennie K. Lincoln (eds.) (1981). *Latin American Foreign Policies: Global and Regional Dimensions.* Boulder: Westview.

Ffrench-Davis, Ricardo, and Ernesto Tironi (eds.) (1981). *Hacia un Nuevo Orden Económico Internacional: Temas Prioritários para América Latina.* México: Fondo de Cultura Economica.

Findling, John E. (1987). *Close Neighbors, Distant Friends: United States–Central American Relations.* New York: Greenwood Press.

Fishlow, Albert (1985). "The State of Latin American Economics," Ch. 5, Inter-American Development Bank, *Economic and Social Progress in Latin America, 1985 Report.* Washington, D.C.

Fitch, John Samuel (1979). "The Political Impact of U.S. Military Aid to Latin America: Institutional and Individual Effects." *Armed Forces and Society,* 5 (Spring): 360–386.

Foner, Philip S. (1972). *The Spanish–Cuban-American War and the Birth of American Imperialism.* New York: Monthly Review.

Franco Filho, Georgenor de Sousa (1979). *O Pacto Amazónico: Ideis e Conceitos.* Belém: Falangola.

Frank, Andre Gunder (1967). *Capitalism and Underdevelopment in Latin America: Historical Studies of Chile and Brazil.* New York: Monthly Review.

—— (1969). *Latin America: Underdevelopment or Revolution.* New York: Monthly Review.

—— (1972). *Lumpenbourgeoise-Lumpendevelopment: Dependence, Class, and Politics in Latin America.* New York: Monthly Review.

Freres, Christian L., Alberto van Klaveren, and Guadalupe Ruiz-Giménez (1992). "Europa y América Latina: La Busqueda de Nuevas Formas de Cooperación," *Sínteses,* 18 (septiembre/ diciembre): 91–178.

Frieden, Jeffrey A. (1992). *Debt, Development, and Democracy: Modern Political Economy and Latin America, 1965–1985.* Princeton: Princeton University Press.

Frohman, Alicia (1990). *Puentes sobre la Turbulencia: La Concertación Política Latinoamericana en los Ochenta.* Santiago: Facultad Latinoamericana de Ciencias Sociales.

García Robles, Alfonso (1967). *The Denuclearization of Latin America.* New York: Carnegie Endowment for International Peace.

—— (1979). *The Latin American Nuclear-Weapon–Free Zone.* Muscatine, Iowa: Stanley Foundation.

Gauhar, Altaf (ed.) (1985). *Regional Integration: The Latin American Experience.* Boulder: Westview.

Gerassi, John (ed.) (1968). *Venceremos! The Speeches and Writings of Che Guevara.* New York: Macmillan.

Glinkin, Anatoli N. (1990). *Inter-American Relations from Bolívar to the Present.* Trans. Barry Jones. Moscow: Progress Publishers.

Goldhamer, Herbert (1972). *The Foreign Powers in Latin America.* Princeton, N.J.: Princeton University Press.

Gómez Robledo, Antonio (1959). *La Seguridad Colectiva en el Continente Americano.* Mexico: Universidad Nacional Autonoma.

Goñi Garrido, Carlos M. (1984). *Cronica del Conflicto Chileno Argentino*. Buenos Aires: Ediar Editores.

Gott, Richard (1970). *Guerrilla Movements in Latin America*. London: Nelson.

Grabendorff, Wolf (1982). "Interstate Conflict Behavior and Regional Potential for Conflict in Latin America." *Journal of Inter-American Studies and World Affairs,* 24 (August): 267–294.

———— (1992). "European Integration: Implications for Latin America," in Colin I. Bradford, Jr. (ed.), *Strategic Options for Latin America in the 1990s.* Washington, D.C.: Inter-American Development Bank.

———— and Riordan Roett (eds.) (1985). *Latin America, Western Europe, and the U.S.: Reevaluating the Atlantic Triangle*. New York: Praeger.

Greño Velasco, José Enrique (1972). "Las Políticas Nacionales en el Marco del Tratado de la Cuenca del Plata," *Revista de Política Internacional* (Madrid), no. 121 (May–June), pp. 99–122.

Griffith, Ivelaw Lloyd (1993). *The Quest for Security in the Caribbean: Problems and Promises in Subordinate States*. Armonk, N.Y.: M.E. Sharpe.

Grinspun, Ricardo and Maxwell A Cameron (1993). *The Political Economy of North American Free Trade*. New York: St. Martin's Press.

Grosse, Robert (1989). *Multinationals in Latin America*. London: Routledge.

———— (1992a). "The End of the Latin American Debt Crisis?" *North-South Issues* (November).

———— (ed.) (1992b). *Private Debt Solutions to the Latin American Debt Problem*. New Brunswick: Transaction.

Grunwald, Joseph (ed.) (1978). *Latin America and World Economy: A Changing International Order*. Beverly Hills, Calif.: Sage.

Grunwald, Joseph, Miguel S. Wionczek, and Martin Carnoy (1972). *Latin American Economic Integration and U.S. Policy*. Washington: Brookings Institution.

Guevara, Ernesto (1961). *Guerrilla Warfare*. New York: Monthly Review.

———— (1973/1974). *Obras Completas*, 5 vols.; Buenos Aires: Ed. Cepe.

———— (1985). *Guerrilla Warfare*. Introduction and Case Studies by Brian Loveman and Thomas M. Davies, Jr. Lincoln: University of Nebraska Press.

Gustafson, Lowell S. (1988). *The Sovereignty Dispute over the Falkland (Malvinas) Islands*. New York: Oxford University Press.

Gutiérrez, Gustavo (1973). *Theology of Liberation: History, Politics, and Salvation*. Maryknoll, N.Y.: Orbis.

Haar, Jerry and Edgar Dosman (eds.) (1994). *A Dynamic Partnership: Canada's Changing Role in the Americas*. New Brunswick, N.J.: Transaction Press.

Hagen, Virginia M. (1969). *The Latin American–United States Fishing Rights Controversy with Specific Reference to Chile, Ecuador, and Peru*. Washington, D.C. Library of Congress.

Hartlyn, Jonathan, and Samuel A. Morley (eds.) (1986). *Latin American Political Economy: Financial Crisis and Political Change*. Boulder: Westview.

Hartlyn, Jonathan, Lars Schoultz, and Augusto Varas (eds.) (1992). *The United States and Latin America in the 1990s*. Chapel Hill: University of North Carolina Press.

Hayes, Margaret Daly (1984). *Latin America and the U.S. National Interest: A Basis for U.S. Foreign Policy*. Boulder: Westview.

Hebblethwaite, Peter (1985). *Pope John XXIII: Shepherds of the Modern World*. New York: Doubleday.

Hebron, John D. (1993). "Turning over a New Leaf in the Americas," *Hemisfile*. 4:1 (January/February): 8–9.

Heilman, John G. (1973). *Ideological Conflict and Institutional Differentiation in West German Relations with Latin America.* Ph.D. dissertation, New York University.

Heine, Jorge (1991), "¿Cooperación o Divergencia? Hacia una Nueva Agenda en las Relaciones Europeo-Latinoamericanas," *Estudios Interamericanas.* 23:93 (enero/marzo): 106–158.

Heine, Jorge, and Leslie F. Manigat (eds.) (1986). *The Caribbean and World Politics: Cross-Currents and Cleavages.* New York: Holmes & Meier.

Heller, Claude (1978). "La Asistencia Militar Norteamericano a América Latina: Una Perspectiva Política." *Estados Unidos: Perspectiva Latinoamericana* (México), 4 (no. 2): 137–166.

Herman, Donald L. (ed.) (1973). *The Communist Tide in Latin America.* Austin: University of Texas Press.

Hermann, Charles F., Charles W. Kegley, Jr., and James N. Rosenau (eds.) (1987). *New Directions in the Study of Foreign Policy.* Boston: Allen & Unwin.

Herrera, Felipe (1970). *Nacionalismo, Regionalismo, Internacionalismo: América Latina en el Contexto Internacional.* Buenos Aires: Banco Interamericano de Desarrollo.

——— (1986). *Desarrollo e Integración.* Santiago de Chile: Editorial Emision.

Holbrik, Karel, and Philip L. Swan (1972). *Trade and Industrialization in the Central American Common Market: The First Decade.* Austin: University of Texas Press.

Holsti, K. J. (1992). *International Politics,* 6th ed. Englewood Cliffs, N.J.: Prentice-Hall.

Horowitz, Irving Louis (1977). "From Dependency to Determinism: The New Structure of Latin American Militarism," *Journal of Political and Military Sociology,* 5 (Fall): 217–238.

Hundley, Norris (1966). *Dividing the Waters: A Century of Controversy Between the United States and Mexico.* Berkeley: University of California Press.

Hunter, John M., and James W. Foley (1975). *Economic Problems of Latin America.* Boston: Houghton Mifflin.

Huntington, Samuel P. (1974). "Civil Violence and the Process of Development," in *Civil Violence and the International System,* Part 2. London: International Institute for Strategic Studies.

Iglesias, Enrique V. (1993). *Reflections on Economic Development: Toward a New Latin American Consensus.* Baltimore: Johns Hopkins University Press and Inter-American Development Bank.

Ince, Basil A. (ed.) (1979). *Contemporary International Relations of the Caribbean.* St. Augustine: Institute of International Relations, University of the West Indies.

Institute for European–Latin American Relations (Madrid) (1989). "The Group of Eight: A New Regional Actor for Latin America?" (Dossier No. 17).

——— (1991). "A New Attempt at Regional Integration: The Southern Cone Common Market." (Dossier No. 30.)

Inter-American Development Bank (1966). *The Inter-American Development Bank and Economic Integration of Latin America.* Washington, D.C..

——— (1974). *Fifteen Years of Activities.* Washington, D.C.

——— (1985). *Economics and Social Progress in Latin America: External Debt, Crisis and Adjustment: 1985 Report.* Washington, D.C.

Inter-American Institute for International Legal Studies (1966). The Inter-American System. Dobbs Ferry, N.Y.: Oceana.

Irish, Donald P. (ed.) (1978). *Multinational Corporations in Latin America.* Athens: Ohio University.

Jacobini, H. B. (1954). *A Study of the Philosophy of International Law as Seen in Works of Latin American Writers.* The Hague: Martines Nijhoff.

Jaguaribe, Hélio (1985). *El Nuevo Escenario Internacional*. México: Fondo de Cultura Económica.

James, Daniel (ed.) (1968). *The Complete Bolivian Diaries of Che Guevara and Other Captured Documents*. New York: Stein & Day.

Jameson [sic], Edward A. (1950). "Keeping Peace in the Caribbean Area." Washington, D.C.: Department of State.

Johnson, Cecil (1970). *Communist China and Latin America, 1959–1967*. New York: Columbia University Press.

Johnson, John J. (1990). *A Hemisphere Apart: The Foundations of United States Policy toward Latin America*. Baltimore: Johns Hopkins University Press.

Jorge, Antonio (ed.) (1993). *Economic Development and Social Change: United States–Latin American Relations in the 1990s*. New Brunswick, N.J.: Transaction.

Jorge, Antonio and Jorge Salazar-Carrillo (eds.) (1992). *The Latin American Debt*. New York: St. Martin's Press.

Kane, William E. (1972). *Civil Strife in Latin America: A Legal History of U.S. Involvement*. Baltimore: Johns Hopkins University Press.

Karl, Terry Lynn (1989). "Hegemonistas y Empresarios Políticos: Dependencia, Democratización y Cooperación en las Américas." *Estudios Internacionales*, 23:89 (abril/junio):183–223.

Karnes, Thomas L. (1961). *The Failure of Union: Central America, 1824–1960*. Chapel Hill: University of North Carolina Press.

Karol, K. S. (1970). *Guerrillas in Power: The Course of the Cuban Revolution*. New York: Hill & Wang.

Kaufman, Edy, Yoram Shapira, and Joel Barromi (1979). *Israeli–Latin American Relations*. New Brunswick: Transaction Books.

Kegley, Charles W., and Eugene R. Wittkopf (1988). *The Global Agenda: Issues and Perspectives*, 2d ed. New York: Random House.

Kelchner, Warren H. (1929). *Latin American Relations with the League of Nations*. Boston: World Peace Foundation.

Keogh, Dermot (ed.) (1990). *Church and Politics in Latin America*. New York: St. Martin's.

Keohane, Robert, and Joseph Nye. (1977). *Power and Independence*. Boston: Little, Brown.

Klaveren, Alberto Van (1990). "Las Relaciones Internacionales de América Latina en la Década de 1980: Cambio y Continuidad." *Estudios Internacionales*, 23:89 (enero/marzo):82–118.

———— (1992). "Enteniendo las Políticas Exteriores Latinoamericanas: Modelo para Armar." *Estudios Internacionales*, 25:98 (abril/junio):169–216.

Kolinski, Charles J. (1965). *Independence or Death! The Story of the Paraguayan War*. Gainesville: University of Florida Press.

Krause, Walter, and F. John Mathis (1970). *Latin America and Economic Integration*. Iowa City: University of Iowa Press.

Krieger Vasena, Adalbert, and Javier Pazos (1973). *Latin America*. London: E. Benn.

Kryzanek, Michael J. (1990). *U.S.–Latin American Relations*, 2d ed. New York: Praeger.

———— (1992). *Leaders, Leadership, and U.S. Policy in Latin America*. Boulder: Westview.

LaFeber, Walter (1993). *Inevitable Revolutions: The United States in Central America*, 2d ed. New York: W.W. Norton.

Langley, Lester D. (1976). *Struggle for the American Mediterranean: United States–European Rivalry in the Gulf-Caribbean, 1776–1904*. Athens: University of Georgia Press.

———— (1989a). *America and the Americas: The United States in the Western Hemisphere.* Athens: University of Georgia Press.

———— (1989b). *The United States and the Caribbean in the Twentieth Century,* 4th ed. Athens: University of Georgia Press.

Latané, John H. (1920). *The United States and Latin America,* rev. and retitled ed. Garden City, N.J.: Doubleday, Page. Original ed.: (1900). *The Diplomatic Relations of the United States and Spanish America.* Baltimore: Johns Hopkins University Press.

Leiken, Robert S. (ed.) (1984). *Central America: Anatomy of a Conflict.* New York: Pergamon Press.

Leonard, Thomas M. (1991). *Central America and the United States: The Search for Stability.* Athens: University of Georgia Press.

Levenstein, Harvey A. (1971). *Labor Organizations in the United States and Mexico.* Westport: Greenwood.

Leventhal, Paul L. and Sharon Tanzer (eds.) (1992). *Averting a Latin American Nuclear Arms Race: New Prospects and Challenges for Argentina-Brazil Nuclear Cooperation.* New York: St. Martin's Press.

Levin, Peter J. (1972). "The Development Program of the Rio de la Plata Basin." *Journal of Developing Areas,* 6 (July): 493–522.

Levine, Barry B. (ed.) (1992). *El Desafío Neoliberal: El Fin del Tercermundismo en América Latina.* Bogotá: Grupo Editorial Norma.

Levine, Daniel H. (1986). *Religion and Political Conflict in Latin America.* Chapel Hill: University of North Carolina Press.

Lewis, Sybil Farrell, and Dale T. Mathews (comps.) (1984). *Documents on the Invasion of Grenada, October 1983.* Rio Piedras, P.R.: Institute of Caribbean Studies, University of Puerto Rico.

Li, He (1991). *Sino–Latin American Economic Relations.* New York: Praeger.

Lincoln, Jennie K., and Elizabeth G. Ferris (eds.) (1984). *The Dynamics of Latin American Foreign Policies.* Boulder: Westview.

Liss, Sheldon (1965). *A Century of Disagreement: The Chamizal Conflict, 1864–1964.* Washington, D.C.: University Press.

———— (1969). *The Canal: Aspects of United States–Panamanian Relations.* Notre Dame: University of Notre Dame Press.

Lockey, Joseph B. (1920). *Pan Americanism: Its Beginnings.* New York: Macmillan.

Logan, John A. (1961). *No Transfer: An American Security Principle.* New Haven: Yale University Press.

Lowenthal, Abraham F. (1990). *Partners in Conflict: The United States and Latin America.* Rev. ed. Baltimore: Johns Hopkins University Press.

———— (ed.) (1991). *Exporting Democracy: The United States and Latin America.* Baltimore: Johns Hopkins University Press.

Lowenthal, Abraham F. and Gregory F. Treverton (eds.) (1994). *Latin America and the United States in a New World.* Boulder: Westview.

Lowenthal, David (1961). *The West Indies Federation.* New York: Columbia University Press.

Lynch, Edward A. (1991). *Religion and Politics in Latin America.* New York: Praeger.

Mabry, Donald J. (ed.) (1989). *The Latin American Narcotics Trade and U.S. National Security.* New York: Greenwood.

MacDonald, Scott B. (1988). *Dancing on a Volcano: The Latin American Drug Trade.* New York: Praeger.

Maeztu, Ramiro de (1941). *Defensa de la Hispanidad.* 4th ed. Madrid: Cultura Española.

Mahan, Alfred Thayer (1918). *The Interest of America in Sea Power, Present and Future.* Boston: Little, Brown.

Manhattan, Avro (1946). *Latin America and the Vatican*. London: Watts.

Mansilla, H. C. F. (1985). "Latin America Within the Third World: The Search for a New Identity, the Acceptance of Old Contents." *Ibero-Amerikanisches Archiv*, 11 (no. 2): 171–191.

Manzetti, Luigi (1992). "Economic Integration in the Southern Cone," *North-South Focus* (December).

Marichal, Carlos (1989). *A Century of Debt Crisis in Latin America: From Independence to the Great Depression, 1820–1930*. Princeton: Princeton University Press.

Marighella, Carlos (1970). "Mini-Manual of the Urban Guerrilla," *Tricontinental* (Cuba) (January–February).

———— (1971). *For the Liberation of Brazil*. Harmondsworth: Penguin.

Maritano, Nino (1970). *A Latin American Economic Community*. South Bend, Ind.: University of Notre Dame Press.

Marshall, Jonathan et al. (1987). *The Iran-Contra Connection: Secret Teams and Covert Operations in the Reagan Era*. Boston: South End Press.

Martin, David (1990). *Tongues of Fire: The Explosion of Protestantism in Latin America*. Oxford: Basil Blackwell.

Martz, John D. (1966). "The Place of Latin America in the Study of Comparative Politics," *Journal of Politics*, 28 (February): 57–80.

———— (1970). "Guerrilla Warfare and Violence in Contemporary Latin America," *Annals of the Southeastern Conference on Latin American Studies*, 1 (March): 141–165.

———— (ed.) (1988). *United States Policy in Latin America: A Quarter Century of Crisis and Challenge, 1961–1986*. Lincoln: University of Nebraska Press.

Martz, John D., and Lars Schoultz (eds.) (1980). *Latin America, the United States, and the Inter-American System*. Boulder: Westview.

Martz, Mary Jeanne Reid (1978). *The Central American Soccer War: Historical Patterns and Internal Dynamics of OAS Settlement Procedures*. Athens: Ohio University.

———— (1979). "SELA: The Latin American Economic System: 'Ploughing the Seas?'" *Inter-American Economic Affairs*, 32 (Spring): 33–64.

May, Ernest R. (1975). *The Making of the Monroe Doctrine*. Cambridge: Harvard University Press.

McClelland, Donald H. (1972). *The Central American Common Market*. New York: Praeger.

McCoy, Alfred W. and Alan A. Block (eds.) (1992). *War on Drugs: Studies in the Failure of U.S. Narcotics Policy*. Boulder: Westview.

McNeil, Frank (1989). *War and Peace in Central America*. New York: Scribners.

Mecham, J. Lloyd (1961). *The United States and Inter-American Security, 1889–1960*. Austin: University of Texas Press.

———— (1965). *A Survey of United States–Latin American Relations*. Boston: Houghton Mifflin.

Mercier Vega, Luis (1969). *Guerrillas in Latin America*. New York: Praeger.

México. Secretaria de Relaciones Exteriores (1975). *La Salinidad del Río Colorado: Una Diferencia Internacional*. México: Col. del Archivo Histórico Diplomático Mexicana, Serie Documental 13.

Milenky, Edward S. (1973). *The Politics of Regional Organization in Latin America: The Latin American Free Trade Association*. New York: Praeger.

Miller, Nicola (1989). *Soviet Relations with Latin America, 1959–1987*. New York: Cambridge University Press.

Millet, Richard, and W. Marvin Will (eds.) (1979). *The Restless Caribbean: Changing Patterns in International Relations*. New York: Praeger.

Mock, James R. (1942). "The Creel Committee in Latin America," *Hispanic American Historical Review,* 22 (May): 262–279.

Molineu, Harold (1990). *U.S. Policy Toward Latin America: From Regionalism to Globalism,* 2d ed. Boulder: Westview.

Mordecai, John (1968). *Federation of the West Indies.* Evanston, Ill.: Northwestern University Press.

Morris, Michael (ed.) (1990). *Great Power Relations in Argentina, Chile and Antarctica.* New York: St. Martin's.

Moss, Ambler H., Jr. (ed.) (1994). *NAFTA: Assessments of the North American Free Trade Agreement.* New Brunswick, N.J.: Transaction.

Moss, Robert H. (1972). *Urban Guerrillas.* London: Temple Smith.

Mower, Alfred Glenn, Jr. (1982). *The European Community and Latin America: A Case Study in Global Role Expansion.* Westport: Greenwood.

Mujal-Leon, Eusebio M. (ed.) (1988). *The USSR and Latin America: A Developing Relationship.* Winchester: Unwin Hyman.

_____ (1989). *European Socialism and the Conflict in Central America.* New York: Praeger.

Muñoz, Heraldo, and Joseph S. Tulchin (eds.) (1984). *Latin American Nations in World Politics.* Boulder: Westview.

Munro, Dana G. (1964). *Intervention and Dollar Diplomacy in the Caribbean, 1900–1921.* Princeton, N.J.: Princeton University Press.

_____ (1974). *The United States and the Caribbean Republics, 1921–1933.* Princeton, N.J.: Princeton University Press.

Myrdal, Gunnar (1957). *Economic Theory and Underdeveloped Nations.* London: G. Duckworth.

Navarette, Jorge Eduardo et al. (1980). *Alcances y Perspectivas del Nuevo Orden Internacional: Mesas Redondas.* México: Universidad Autónoma.

Newfarmer, Richard (ed.) (1984). *From Gunboats to Diplomacy: New U.S. Policies for Latin America.* Baltimore: Johns Hopkins University Press.

Niksch, Larry A., and Mark P. Sullivan (1993). "Peru's Shining Path: Background on the Movement, Counterinsurgency Strategy, and U.S. Policy," *CRS Report to Congress.* Washington, D.C.: Congressional Research Service, Library of Congress (March 1).

Nuñez del Arco, José, Eduardo Margaín, and Rachells Cherol (eds.) (1984). *The Economic Integration Process of Latin America in the 1980s.* Washington, D.C.: Inter-American Development Bank.

Ocampo, Jose et al. (1976). *Dependency Theory.* Riverside, Calif.: Latin American Perspectives.

Ogelsby, J.C.M. (1976). *Gringos from the Far North: Essays in the History of Canadian–Latin American Relations, 1866–1968.* Toronto: Macmillan.

Oliveri, Ernest J. (1992). *Latin American Debt and the Politics of International Finance.* Westport: Praeger.

Orrego Vicuña, Francisco (1976). *Los Fondos Marinos y Oceánicos: Jurisdicción Nacional y Régimen Internacional.* Santiago de Chile: Editorial Andres Bello.

Packenham, Robert A. (1992). *The Dependency Movement: Scholarship and Politics in Development Studies.* Cambridge: Harvard University Press.

Pan American Union/General Secretariat of the Organization of American States (1968). *Study of the Diary of 'Che' Guevara in Bolivia.* Prepared by the OAS Special Consultative Committee on Security at its Eleventh Regular Meeting.

Papp, Daniel S. (1988). *Contemporary International Relations: Frameworks for Understanding,* 2d ed. New York: Macmillan.

Parkinson, F. (1974). *Latin America, the Cold War, and the World Powers, 1945–1973.* Beverly Hills, Calif.: Sage.

———— (1987). "Some Legal and Institutional Aspects of the Debt Crisis." *Coexistence* (Netherlands), 24: 155–168.

Pastor, Robert A. (1987). *Condemned to Repetition: The United States and Nicaragua.* Princeton: Princeton University Press.

———— (1992). *Whirlpool: U.S. Foreign Policy Toward Latin America and the Caribbean.* Princeton: Princeton University Press.

Pearson, Frederic S., and J. Martin Rochester (1992). *International Relations: The Global Condition in the Late Twentieth Century,* 3d ed. New York: McGraw-Hill.

Perkins, Dexter (1927). *The Monroe Doctrine, 1823–1826.* Cambridge: Harvard University Press.

———— (1933). *The Monroe Doctrine, 1826–1867.* Baltimore: Johns Hopkins University Press.

———— (1937). *The Monroe Doctrine, 1867–1907.* Baltimore: Johns Hopkins University Press.

———— (1963). *A History of the Monroe Doctrine.* Boston: Little, Brown.

———— (1966). *The United States and the Caribbean,* rev. ed. Cambridge: Harvard University Press.

Perkins, Whitney T. (1981). *Constraint of Empire: The United States and Caribbean Interventions.* Westport: Greenwood.

Perry, William, and Peter Wehner (eds.) (1985). *The Latin American Policies of U.S. Allies: Balancing Global Interests and Regional Concerns.* New York: Praeger.

Pike, Frederick B. (1971). *Hispanismo, 1898–1936: Spanish Conservatives and Liberals and Their Relations with Spanish America.* South Bend, Ind.: University of Notre Dame Press.

———— (1977). *The United States and the Andean Republics: Peru, Bolivia, and Ecuador.* Cambridge: Harvard University Press.

———— (1992). *The United States and Latin America: Myths and Stereotypes of Civilization and Nature.* Austin: University of Texas Press.

Pittman, Howard T. (1981). *Geopolitics in the ABC Countries: A Comparison,* 5 vols. Ph.D. dissertation, The American University.

Plano, Jack C., and Roy Olton (1988). *The International Relations Dictionary,* 4th ed. New York: Holt, Rinehart and Winston.

Poblete Troncoso, Moises, and Ben G. Burnett (1960). *The Rise of the Latin American Labor Movement.* New York: Bookman.

Poitras, Guy (1990). *The Ordeal of Hegemony: The United States and Latin America.* Boulder: Westview.

Pontecorvo, Giulio (ed.) (1986). *The New Order of the Oceans.* New York: Columbia University Press.

Poppino, Rollie E. (1964). *International Communism in Latin America.* New York: The Free Press.

Portales, Carlos (comp.) (1989). *El Mundo en Transición y América Latina.* Buenos Aires: Grupo Editor Latinoamericano.

Prados, John (1986). *Presidents' Secret Wars: CIA and Pentagon Covert Operations Since World War II.* New York: William Morrow.

Prebisch, Raúl (1964). *Nueva Política Comercial para el Desarrollo.* México: Fondo de Cultura Económica.

———— (1970). *Change and Development: Latin America's Great Task.* Washington, D.C.: Inter-American Development Bank.

Price, Glen (1967). *Origins of the War with Mexico.* Austin: University of Texas Press.

Programa de Seguimiento de las Políticas Exteriores Latinoamericanas (PROSPEL) (1985). *Frente a la Crisis: Anuario de Políticas Exteriores Latinoamericanas, 1984.* Heraldo Muñoz (compilador). Buenos Aires: Grupo Editor Latinoamericano.

———— (1986). *Políticas Exteriores para Sobrevivir: Anuario de Políticas Exteriores Latinoamericanas, 1985.* Heraldo Muñoz, (compilador). Buenos Aires: Grupo Editor Latinoamericano.

———— (1987). *Continuidad en la Crisis: Anuario de Políticas Exteriores Latinoamericanas, 1986.* Heraldo Muñoz, (compilador). Buenos Aires: Grupo Editor Latinoamericano.

———— (1988). *Un Balance de Esperanzas: Anuario de Políticas Exteriores Latinoamericanas, 1987.* Heraldo Muñoz, (compilador). Buenos Aires: Grupo Editor Latinoamericano.

———— (1989). *A la Espera de Una Nueva Etapa: Anuario de Políticas Exteriores Latinoamericanas, 1988–1989.* Heraldo Muñoz, (compilador). Caracas: Editorial Nueva Sociedad.

———— (1990). *Anuario de las Políticas Exteriores Latinoamericanas 1989–1990: Frente a la Crisis: Anuario de Políticas Exteriores Latinoamericanas, 1989–1990.* Heraldo Muñoz, (compilador). Caracas: Editorial Nueva Sociedad.

Puig, Juan Carlos (ed.) (1984). *América Latina: Políticas Exteriores Comparadas.* Buenos Aires: Grupo Editor Latinoamericano.

Purcell, Susan Kaufman and Robert M. Immerman (eds.) (1992). *Japan and Latin America in the New Global Order.* Boulder: Lynne Rienner.

Quesada, Vicente G. (1918–1920). *Historia Diplomática Hispanoamericana,* 3 vols. Buenos Aires: La Cultura Argentina.

Radu, Michael and Vladimir Tismaneanu (1986). *Revolutionary Organizations in Latin America.* Boulder: Westview.

Rankin, Richard C. (1974). "The Expanding Institutional Concerns of the Latin American Military Establishments." *Latin American Research Review,* 9 (Spring): 81–108.

Ray, David (1973). "The Dependency Model of Latin American Underdevelopment: Three Basic Fallacies." *Journal of Inter-American Studies,* 15 (February): 4–20.

Remmer, Karen L. (1978). "Evaluating the Policy Impact of Military Regimes in Latin America." *Latin American Research Review,* 13 (no. 2): 39–54.

Rens, Jef (1959). "América Latina y la Organización Internacional del Trabajo." *Revista Internacional del Trabajo,* 60 (July):1–29.

The Report of the President's National Bipartisan Commission on Central America [Kissinger Commission Report] (1983). New York: Macmillan.

Rippy, J. Fred (1938). *Latin America in World Politics.* 3d ed. New York: F. S. Crofts.

———— (1958). *Globe and Hemisphere.* Chicago: Henry Regnery.

Robertson, William Spence (1923). *Hispanic Relations with the United States.* New York: Oxford University Press.

Rochlin, James (1992). *Canada as a Hemisphere Actor.* Toronto: McGraw Hill-Ryerson.

Rodley, N. S., and C. Neale Ronning (eds.) (1974). *International Law in the Western Hemisphere.* The Hague: Nijhoff.

Rodríguez Larretta, A. (1938). *Orientación de la Política Internacional en América Latina,* 2 vols. Montevideo: Peña.

Roett, Riordan, and James F. Tierney (eds.) (1971). "The Military in Latin America." *International Journal of Politics,* vol. 1 (Summer–Fall), entire issue.

Romualdi, Serafino (1967). *Presidents and Peons: Recollections of a Labor Ambassador in Latin America.* New York: Funk & Wagnalls.

Ronning, C. Neale (ed.) (1970). *Intervention in Latin America.* New York: Knopf.

Ropp, Steve C., and James A. Morris (1986). *Central America: Crisis and Adaptation*. Albuquerque: University of New Mexico Press.

Rout, Leslie B. (1970). *Politics of the Chaco Peace Conference, 1935–1939*. Austin: University of Texas Press.

Russell, Roberto (ed.) (1990). *Nuevos Rumbos en la Relación Unión Soviética-América Latina*. Buenos Aires: Grupo Editor Latinoamericano.

―――― (ed.) (1990). *Política Exterior y Toma de Decisiones en América Latina*. Buenos Aires: Grupo Editor Latinoamericano; Emece Editores.

Sabaté Lichtschein, Domingo (1985). *Problemas Argentinos de Soberanía Territorial*, 3d ed. Buenos Aires: Abeledo-Perrot.

Saborio, Sylvia et al. (eds.) (1992). *The Premise and Promise: Free Trade in the Americas*. New Brunswick, N.J.: Transaction.

Sampson, Anthony (1973). *The Sovereign State of ITT*. New York: Stein & Day.

―――― (1975). *The Seven Sisters: The Great Oil Companies and the World They Made*. New York: Viking.

Sanders, Thomas G. (1970). "The Church in Latin America." *Foreign Affairs*, 48 (January): 285–299.

Sanderson, Steven E. (1992). *The Politics of Trade in Latin American Development*. Stanford, Calif.: Stanford University Press.

Sandifer, Durward V., and Ronald L. Scheman (1966). *The Foundations of Freedom: The Interrelationship Between Democracy and Human Rights*. New York: Praeger.

Santos, Theotonio dos (1970). *Dependencia Económica y Cambio Revolucionario en América Latina*. Caracas: Ed. Nueva Izquierda.

Scheer, Robert (ed.) (1968). *The Diary of Che Guevara–Bolivia: November 7, 1966–October 7, 1967*. New York: Bantam.

Scheman, Ronald L. (1988). *The Inter-American Dilemma: The Search for Inter-American Cooperation at the Centennial of the Inter-American System*. New York: Praeger.

Schloming, Gordon C. (1991). *Power and Principle in International Affairs*. New York: Harcourt Brace Jovanich.

Schmitt, Karl M. (ed.) (1972). *The Roman Catholic Church in Modern Latin America*. New York: Knopf.

Schmitter, Philippe C. (1972). *Autonomy or Dependence as Regional Integration Outcomes: Central America*. Berkeley: University of California Press.

Schoultz, Lars (1981). *Human Rights and United States Policy Toward Latin America*. Princeton, N.J.: Princeton University Press.

―――― (1987). *National Security and United States Policy Toward Latin America*. Princeton, N.J.: Princeton University Press.

Schump, Walter (1971). *Las Guerrillas en América Latina*. Buenos Aires: Punto Critico.

Schuyler, George W. (1991). "Perspectives on Canada and Latin America: Changing Context ... Changing Policy?" *Journal of Interamerican Studies and World Affairs*. 33:1 (Spring), 19–58.

Scott, James Brown (1909). *The Hague Peace Conferences of 1899 and 1907*, 2 vols. Baltimore: Johns Hopkins University Press.

Scott, Peter Dale and Jonathan Marshall (1990). *Cocaine Politics: Drugs, Armies, and the CIA in Central America*. Berkeley: University of California Press.

Seabury, Paul, and Walter A. McDougall (eds.) (1984). *The Grenada Papers*. San Francisco: Institute for Contemporary Studies.

Segal, Aaron (1968). *The Politics of Caribbean Economic Integration*. Rio Piedras: University of Puerto Rico Press.

SELA—Sistema Económico Latinoamericano, Secretaria Permanente (1991). "La Iniciativa Bush para las Américas: Análisis Preliminar," *Nueva Sociedad*, 111:63–79.

Sepúlveda, César (1973). *El Sistema Interamericano.* Valladolid: Universidad.

———— (1975). *Las Fuentes del Derecho Internacional Americano: una Encuesta sobre los Métodos de Creación de Reglas Internacionales en el Hemisferio Occidental,* 2d ed. México: Editorial Porrúa.

Serbin, Ken (1993). "Latin America's Catholic Church: Religious Rivalries and the North-South Divide," *North-South Issues.* II:1.

Shavit, David (1992). *The United States in Latin America: A Historical Dictionary.* Westport: Greenwood.

Shaw, Royce Q. (1979). *Central America: Regional Integration and National Political Development.* Boulder: Westview.

Shugart, Matthew Soberg (1992). "Guerrillas and Elections: An Institutionalist Perspective of the Costs of Conflicts and Competition," *International Studies Quarterly.* (June): 121–151.

Sigmund, Paul E. (1980). *Multinationals in Latin America: The Politics of Nationalization.* Madison: University of Wisconsin Press.

———— (1990) *Liberation Theology at the Crossroads: Democracy or Revolution?* New York: Oxford University Press.

Singletary, Otis A. (1960). *The Mexican War.* Chicago: University of Chicago Press.

Slater, Jerome (1967). *The OAS and United States Foreign Policy.* Columbus: Ohio State University Press.

Smetherman, Bobbie B., and Robert M. Smetherman (1974). *Territorial Seas and Inter-American Relations.* New York: Praeger.

Smith, Peter H. (ed.) (1992). *Drug Policy in the Americas.* Boulder: Westview.

———— (ed.) (1993). *The Challenge of Integration: Europe and the Americas.* New Brunswick, N.J.: Transaction.

Smith, Robert Freeman (ed.) (1981). *The Era of Caribbean Intervention, 1898–1930.* Malabar: Krieger Publishing.

Smith, Tony (1979). "The Underdevelopment of Development Literature: The Case of Dependency Theory." *World Politics,* 31 (January): 247–288.

Smith, Wayne S. (ed.) (1992). *The Russians Aren't Coming: New Soviet Policy in Latin America.* Boulder: Lynne Rienner.

———— (ed.) (1991). *Toward Resolution? The Falklands/Malvinas Dispute.* Boulder: Lynne Rienner.

Smith, William C., Carlos H. Acuña, and Eduardo A. Gamarra (eds.) (1994). *Latin American Political Economy in the Age of Neoliberal Reform: Theoretical and Comparative Perspectives for the 1990s.* New Brunswick, N.J.: Transaction Press.

Solís-Rivera, Luís G. (1987). "Peace and the Future of Central America: A Costa Rican Viewpoint." Washington, D.C.: Friedrich Ebert Stiftung, Washington Office.

Springer, Hugh W. (1962). *Reflections on the Failure of the First West Indian Federation.* Cambridge: Harvard University Press.

Stallings, Barbara and Robert Kaufman (1989). *Debt and Democracy in Latin America.* Boulder: Westview.

Stallings, Barbara and Gabriel Székely (eds.) (1993). *Japan, the United States, and Latin America: Toward a Trilateral Relationship in the Western Hemisphere.* Baltimore: Johns Hopkins University Press.

Stepan, Alfred (1966). "Political Development Theory: The Latin American Experience." *Journal of International Affairs,* 20 (no. 2): 63–74.

Stoetzer, O. Carlos (1993). *The Organization of American States,* 2d ed. Westport: Praeger.

Stoll, David (1990). *Is Latin America Turning Protestant? The Politics of Evangelical Growth.* Berkeley: University of California Press.

Stuart, Graham H., and James Tigner (1975). *Latin America and the United States*, 6th ed. Englewood Cliffs, N.J.: Prentice-Hall.

Sunkel, Osvaldo (ed.) (1993). *Development from Within: Toward a Neostructuralist Approach for Latin America*. Boulder: Lynne Rienner.

Sutton, P. (ed.) (1991). *Europe and the Caribbean*. London: Macmillan.

Syzmanski, A. (1981). *The Logic of Imperialism*. New York: Praeger.

Taylor, Philip B. (1963). *Law and Politics in Inter-American Diplomacy*. New York: John Wiley & Sons.

Thomas, Ann Van Wynen, and A. J. Thomas (1963). *The Organization of American States*. Dallas: Southern Methodist University Press.

Thomas, C. (1984). *The Rise of the Authoritarian State in Peripheral Societies*. New York: Monthly Review Press.

Thompson, William R. (1973). "The Regional Subsystem," *International Studies Quarterly*, 17 (March): 89–117.

Tomassini, Luciano (ed.) (1981). *Relaciones Internacionales de la América Latina*. México: Fondo de Cultura Economica.

——— (ed.) (1982). *El Dialogo Norte-Sur: Una Perspectiva Latinoamericana*. Buenos Aires: Editorial Belgrano.

——— (1988). "El Análisis de la Política Exterior," *Estudios Internacionales*, 21:84 (octubre/diciembre), 498–559.

Tomassini, Luciano, con colaboración de Carlos J. Moneta y Augusto Varas (1991). *El Sistema Internacional y América Latina: La Política Internacional en un mundo Postmoderno*. Buenos Aires: Grupo Editor Latinoamericano.

Tussie, Diana (1994). *The Inter-American Development Bank*. Boulder: Lynne Rienner.

United Kingdom, Foreign and Commonwealth Office (1990), "Twelfth World Trade Union Congress, November 1990," *Background Brief* (October).

United Nations (1972). *Recopilación de Documentos Básicos de la Comisión Especial de Coordinación Latinoamericana*. New York.

U.S. Arms Control and Disarmament Agency (1975). *Arms Control and Disarmament Agreements: Texts and History of Negotiations*.

U.S. Department of Commerce (1951). *Foreign Aid by the United States Government, 1940–1951*.

U.S. Department of Commerce and U.S. Agency for International Development (1992). *Andean Trade Preference Act*.

U.S. Department of State (1962). *Inter-American Efforts to Relieve International Tensions in the Western Hemisphere*.

——— (1973). *Arms Sales in Latin America*.

——— (1987a). "The Holy See," *Background Notes* (March).

——— (1987b). *International Narcotics Control Strategy Report* (March).

U.S. House of Representatives, Committee on Foreign Affairs (1946, 1947). *Inter-American Military Cooperation Act: Hearings*.

——— (1950). *Twenty-ninth Report to Congress on Lend-Lease Operations*.

——— (1975). *The United States and Chile During the Allende Years: Hearings*.

——— (1981). *The Caribbean Basin Policy: Hearings*.

U.S. Library of Congress, Congressional Research Service (1977). *Background Documents Relating to the Panama Canal. Prepared for the United States Senate Committee on Foreign Relations*.

U.S. Senate, Committee on Foreign Relations (1977/1978), 5 vols. *Hearings on the Panama Canal Treaty and the Treaty Concerning the Permanent Neutrality and Operation of the Panama Canal*.

_____ Committee on Foreign Relations and U.S. House of Representatives, Committee on Foreign Affairs (1988). *Inter-American Relations: A Collection of Documents, Legislation, Descriptions of Inter-American Organizations, and Other Material Pertaining to Inter-American Affairs.*

_____ Select Committee on Secret Military Assistance to Iran and the Nicaraguan Opposition and U.S. House of Representatives, Select Committee to Investigate Covert Arms Transactions with Iran (November 1987). *Report of the Congressional Committees Investigating the Iran-Contra Affair with Supplemental, Minority, and Additional Views.*

_____ Select Committee to Study Government Operations with Respect to Intelligence Activities (1975a). *Alleged Assassination Plots Involving Foreign Leaders: An Interim Report.*

_____ Select Committee to Study Government Operations with Respect to Intelligence Activities (1975b). *Covert Action in Chile, 1963–1973: Staff Report.*

_____ Select Committee to Study Government Operations with Respect to Intelligence Activities (1976). *Final Report.*

Urquidi, Víctor L. (1962). *Free Trade and Economic Integration in Latin America.* Berkeley: University of California Press.

_____ (1964). *The Challenge of Development in Latin America.* New York: Praeger.

Van Alstyne, Richard W. (1955). "Britain in Latin America After 1865." *Current History,* 28 (March): 148–153.

Varas, Augusto (ed.) (1987). *Soviet–Latin American Relations in the 1980s.* Boulder: Westview.

_____ (ed.) (1989). *Hemispheric Security and U.S. Policy in Latin America.* Boulder: Westview.

Vargas Silva, Jorge A. (1979). *Terminología sobre Derecho del Mar.* México: Centro de Estudios Económicos y Sociales del Tercer Mundo.

Vázquez Carrizosa, Alfredo (1983). *Las Relaciones de Colombia y Venezuela: La Historia Atormentada de dos Naciones.* Bogotá: Ediciones Tercer Mundo.

Vellinga, Menno (ed.) (1993). *Social Democracy in Latin America: Prospects for Change.* Boulder: Westview.

Vernon, Raymond (1971a). *Multinational Enterprise and National Security.* London: Institute for Strategic Studies.

_____ (1971b). *Sovereignty at Bay: The Multinational Spread of U.S. Enterprises.* New York: Basic Books.

Wahlke, John C., and Alex N. Dragnich (eds.) (1966). *Government and Politics.* New York: Random House.

Walker, William O. (1989). *Drug Control in the Americas.* Rev. ed. Albuquerque: University of New Mexico Press.

Ware, David (1980). "The Amazon Treaty: A Turning Point in Latin American Cooperation?" *Texas International Law Journal,* 15 (Winter): 117–137.

Watson, Bruce W., and Peter G. Tsouras (eds.) (1990). *Operation Just Cause: The U.S. Intervention in Panama.* Boulder: Westview.

Watson, Hilbourne A. (ed.) (1993). *The Caribbean in the Global Political Economy.* Boulder: Lynne Rienner.

Weinberg, Albert K. (1935). *Manifest Destiny.* Baltimore: Johns Hopkins University Press.

Weintraub, Sidney (ed.) (1993). *Free Trade in the Western Hemisphere.* Entire issue of *The Annals of the American Academy of Political and Social Science.* vol. 526 (March).

Wesson, Robert (ed.) (1982). *U.S. Influence in Latin America in the 1980s.* New York: Praeger.

Wesson, Robert, and Heraldo Muñoz (eds.) (1986). *Latin American Views of U.S. Policy.* New York: Praeger.

Whitaker, Arthur P. (1954). *The Western Hemisphere Idea*. Ithaca: Cornell University Press.

Whitaker, Arthur P., and David C. Jordan (1966). *Nationalism in Contemporary Latin America*. New York: The Free Press.

Wiarda, Howard J. (ed.) (1985). *New Directions in Comparative Politics*. Boulder: Westview.

_____ (ed.) (1992). *Politics and Social Change in Latin America: Still a Distinct Tradition?* 3d ed. Boulder: Westview.

Wickham-Crowley, Timothy P. (1992). *Guerrillas and Revolution in Latin America: A Comparative Study of Insurgents and Regimes since 1956*. Princeton, N.J.: Princeton University Press.

Wilkins, Mira (1970). *The Emergence of Multinational Enterprise*. Cambridge: Harvard University Press.

_____ (1974). *The Maturing of Multinational Enterprise*. Cambridge: Harvard University Press.

Williams, Felicity (1984). *La Internacional Socialista y América Latina: Una Visión Crítica*. México: Universidad Autónoma Metropolitana.

Wilson, Larman C. (1964). *The Principle of Non-Intervention in Recent Inter-American Relations: The Challenge of Anti-Democratic Regimes*. Ph.D. dissertation, University of Maryland.

_____ (1986). "The Contemporary Practice of International Law in Central America: Intervention and Non-Intervention." *Towson State Journal of International Affairs*, 20 (Spring): 85–105.

Winchester, Simon (1991). *Pacific Rising: The Emergence of a New World Culture*. New York: Prentice-Hall.

Wood, Bryce (1961). *The Making of the Good Neighbor Policy*. New York: Columbia University Press.

_____ (1966). *The United States and Latin American Wars, 1932–1942*. New York: Columbia University Press.

_____ (1985). *The Dismantling of the Good Neighbor Policy*. Austin: University of Texas Press.

Woodward, Ralph Lee, Jr. (ed.) (1988). *Central America: Historical Perspectives on the Contemporary Crises*. Westport: Greenwood.

Yalem, Ronald (1970). *Regional Subsystems and World Politics*. Tucson: University of Arizona Press.

Yopo H., Boris (1991). "The Rio Group: Decline or Consolidation of the Latin American Concertación Policy?" *Journal of Interamerican Studies and World Affairs*, 3:4 (Winter):27–44.

Zagorsky, Paul (1992). *Democracy vs. National Security: Civil- Military Relations in Latin America*. Boulder: Lynne Rienner.

Zook, David H. (1960). *The Conduct of the Chaco War*. New Haven: Bookman Associates.

Zook, David H. (1964). *Zarumilla-Marañon: The Ecuador-Peru Dispute*. New York: Bookman Associates.

Acronyms

AACC	Anglo-American Caribbean Commission
ACAT	Continental Association of American Workers
ACP	Africa, Caribbean, and Pacific
ADELA	Atlantic Community Development Group for Latin America
AFL-CIO	American Federation of Labor–Congress of Industrial Organizations
AG	Andean Group
AIFLD	American Institute for Free Labor Development
ALADI	Latin American Integration Association
ALN	National Liberation Action
ARENA	Republican Nationalist Alliance
ARDE	Democratic Revolutionary Alliance
ATLAS	Unionized Latin American Workers' Group
ATPA	Andean Trade Preference Act
BIS	Bank for International Settlements
CACM	Central American Common Market
CARIBANK	Caribbean Bank
CARICOM	Caribbean Common Market, Caribbean Community
CARIFTA	Caribbean Free Trade Association
CBI	Caribbean Basin Initiative
CCD	United Nations Conference of the Committee on Disarmament
CCE	Central American Economic Cooperating Committee
CDNU	Christian Democratic World Union
CECLA	Special Latin American Coordinating Committee
CECON	Special Negotiating and Consulting Commission
CELAM	Conference of Latin American Bishops
CET	Common External Tarriff
CIA	Central Intelligence Agency
CICYP	Inter-American Council for Commerce and Production
CIPIC	Intergovernmental Council of Copper Exporting Countries
CIS	Commonwealth of Independent States

CIT	Inter-American Federation of Labor
CLASC	Latin American Confederation of Christian Trade Unionists
COAS	Council of the Organization of American States
CODECA	Caribbean Economic Development Corporation
CROM	Regional Confederation of Mexican Labor
CSLA	Latin American Syndicalist Confederation
CTAL	Confederation of Latin American Workers
CUTAL	Single Central Association of Latin American Workers
EAI	Enterprise for the Americas Initiative
EC	European Community
ECLA	United Nations Economic Commission for Latin America
ECLAC	United Nations Economic Commission for Latin America and the Caribbean
ECOSOC	United Nations Economic and Social Council
EEC	European Economic Community
EIB	Export-Import Bank of Washington
ELN	National Liberation Army
ENDC	Eighteen Nation Disarmament Commission
EPL	Popular Liberation party
ERP	Revolutionary Army of the People
ESAPAC	Central American Advanced School of Public Administration
EU	European Union
EXIM	Export-Import Bank of Washington
FALN	Armed Forces of National Liberation
FAP	Peronist Armed Forces
FAR	Revolutionary Armed Forces
FARC	Armed Forces of Colombia
FARN	Armed Forces of National Resistance
FDN	National Democratic Front
FDR	Democratic Revolutionary Front
FEAC	Inter-American Financial and Economic Advisory Committee
FIR	Revolutionary Leftist Front
FLN	National Liberation Front
FMLN	Farabundo Martí National Liberation Front
FPL	Farabundo Martí Popular Forces of Liberation
FSLN	Sandinist National Liberation Front
FSO	Fund for Special Operations
FTA	Free-Trade Agreement
GATT	General Agreement on Tariffs and Trade
GRULAS	Latin American Groups
GSP	Generalized System of Preferences
IAEA	International Atomic Energy Agency
IAS	Inter-American System
IBEC	International Basic Economy Corporation
IBRD	International Bank for Reconstruction and Development
ICAITI	Central American Institute of Industrial Research
ICFTU	International Confederation of Free Trade Unions

ICJ	International Court of Justice
ICSCC	Inter-Departmental Committee on Scientific and Cultural Co-operation
IDA	International Development Agency
IDB	Inter-American Development Bank
IFC	International Finance Corporation
IGO	Inter-Governmental Organization
IIAA	Institute of Inter-American Affairs
ILPES	Latin American Institute of Economic and Social Planning
IMF	International Monetary Fund
INTAL	Institute for the Integration of Latin America
IOEC	Organization of Iron Ore Exporting Countries
IPEB	International Organization of Banana Exporters
IR	International Relations
IRELA	Institute for European–Latin American Relations
ITT	International Telephone and Telegraph
LAFTA	Latin American Free Trade Association
LAIA	Latin American Integration Association
LDC	Less Developed Country
M-19	19th of April Movement
MERCOSUR	Common Market of the South
MIF	Multilateral Investment Fund
MIR	Movement of the Revolutionary Left
MISURASATA	Sandinista Unity of Miskitos, Sumos, amd Ramas
MNC	Multinational corporation
MPM	Montoneros
MPSC	Popular Social Christian Movement
MR-13	13th of November Revolutionary Movement
MSA	Mutual Security Act
NAFTA	North American Free Trade Agreement
NATO	North Atlantic Treaty Organization
NGO	Non-Governmental Organization
NIEO	New International Economic Order
NPT	Non-Proliferation Treaty
NSC	National Security Council
OAS	Organization of American States
ODECA	Organization of Central American States
OECS	Organization of Eastern Caribbean States
OIR	Revolutionary Integration Organization
OLADE	Latin American Energy Organization
OLAS	Organization of Latin American Solidarity
ONUCA	United Nations Observer Group in Central America
OPANAL	Organization for the Prohibition of Nuclear Weapons in Latin America
OPEC	Organization of Petroleum Exporting Countries
ORIT	Inter-American Regional Organization of Workers
PAFL	Pan American Federation of Labor

PCOAS	Permanent Council of the Organization of American States
PRD	Democratic Revolutionary Party
PRTC	Central American Workers' Revolutionary party
SELA	Latin American Economic System
SEM	Single European Market
SI	Socialist International
SUNFED	Special United Nations Fund for Economic Development
UN	United Nations
UNCDF	United Nations Capital Development Fund
UNCLOS	United Nations Conference on Law of the Sea
UNCTAD	United Nations Conference on Trade and Development
UNDP	United Nations Development Program
UNO	United Nicaraguan Opposition
URNG	Guatemalan United Revolutionary Front
VPR	Popular Revolutionary Vanguard
WFTU	World Federation of Trade Unions

About the Book and Author

The third edition of this respected text has been thoroughly updated to reflect post–cold war developments that have had a dramatic impact on virtually every aspect of Latin America's international relations. East-West conflict, which was played out especially in Central America and the Caribbean, is no longer relevant. At the same time, Latin American states have undergone political and economic transformations. Consequently, other issues—such as trade and investment, democracy and human rights, immigrants and refugees, drug trafficking, and the physical environment—have risen in importance.

The original purpose of this text is unchanged: It continues to provide a topical, current, and analytically integrated survey of Latin America's role in international politics. Still organized around the idea of Latin America as a separate subsystem within the global international system, the discussions give special emphasis to further regional subsystems (especially Mexico, the Circum-Caribbean, and South America beyond the Caribbean). Within this framework, Atkins examines the complex political, military, economic, and social structures and processes of both state power and interdependence. Analyzing the foreign policies of the Latin American states themselves as well as those of the United States and other countries toward Latin America, Atkins looks closely at the nature and role of non–nation-state actors in the region, including multinational corporations, international labor, transnational political parties, the Holy See, and guerrilla organizations. He gives particular attention to Latin American participation in international institutions at all levels.

G. Pope Atkins is visiting scholar at the Institute of Latin American Studies, University of Texas at Austin, and professor emeritus of political science at the United States Naval Academy, where he was a member of the civilian faculty from 1966 to 1993. He has lived and worked in Argentina and Ecuador and has been visiting fellow at the Institute of Latin American Studies at the University of London, the Fondo para el Avance de las Ciencias Sociales in Santo Domingo, and the international relations department at the London School of Economics and Political Science. In 1990–1991 he held the Distinguished Visiting Tom Slick Professorship of World Peace at the Lyndon B. Johnson School of Public Affairs. Professor Atkins has written extensively on Latin American international and comparative politics.

Index

Economic Commission for Latin America
(ECLA). *See* Economic Commission
for Latin America and the Caribbean
Economic Commission for Latin America
and the Caribbean (ECLAC), 78, 227,
193, 238–239
Economic integration, 173–189
Economic relations, 225–228, 265–282
Ecuador
balance of power, 39
capability analysis of, 52, 57, 61
coffee agreement and, 252
economic relations, 269, 272, 273, 274,
278, 280
geography, 32, 34
Holy See and, 138
integration and association, 184, 185,
186, 190, 194
Inter-American System and, 216
law of the sea and, 245, 247
League of Nations and, 231
military relations, 283, 285, 288
narcotics traffic and, 327, 329
nonalignment, Nonaligned Movement
and, 78
Organization of Petroleum Exporting
Countries membership, 252
Peru and, 39, 307–308
Spanish American union, 171,172
United States and, 126, 245
Ecuadorian Democratic Left, 155
Egypt, 207
Eighteen Nation Disarmament Committee
(ENDC), 241
Eichman, Adolf, 102
Eisenhower, Dwight D., 121, 310
Eisenhower, Milton, 121
Eisenhower Plan, 122, 226, 276
Eisenhower-Remón Treaty (1955), 256
El Salvador, 26
capability analysis of, 54, 57
Contadora and, 321
Democratic Convergence, 165
economic relations, 272, 273, 274, 277,
282
guerrilla groups, 164–165
Honduras and, 60, 319
integration, 177–180
Inter-American System and, 216, 224,
225
Israel and, 102

law of the sea and, 247
military relations, 285, 288, 291, 292
Nicaragua and, 319–320
nonalignment, 78
Republican Nationalist Alliance
(ARENA), 165
Salvadoran Communist party, 165
Social Democratic party, 165
Soviet Union and, 306
Spanish American union, 171, 172
United States and, 69, 127, 128, 129,
321
Electronics industry, 142
Emergency Advisory Committee for
Political Defense, 214
Ends-means analysis, 10, 73–77
Engels, Friedrich, 338
England. *See* United Kingdom
Enterprise for the Americas Initiative
(EAI), 92, 151, 176, 228, 259–260,
270
Esquipulus II accords. *See* Procedure for
the Establishment of a Firm and
Lasting Peace in Central America
Estrada, Genaro, 221
Estrada Doctrine, 221, 290
Europe. *See individual countries*
European Community (EC), 91–97, 191,
218, 279–280, 315, 316, 322, 345
European Union, 92
Expansionists of 1898, 117
Export-Import Bank of Washington
(EXIM), 271, 274, 275, 315
External debt. *See* Debt

Falangism, 88, 295–296
Falkland/Malvinas islands, 82–83, 90, 91,
181, 218–219, 304, 314–316
Farabundo Martí National Liberation
Front (FMLN), 164–165
Farabundo Martí Popular Forces of
Liberation (FPL), 164
Febrerista Revolutionary party, 155
Ferdinand VII, 293
Fiat, 142, 146
Fidelismo, 157, 338
Finland, 207
First National City Bank, 145
First South American Congress on Private
International Law (1888–1889), 172
Fishermen's Protective Act (1954), 245